THE ILLUSTRATED ENCYCLOPEDIA OF

WILD FLOWERS
& FLORA OF THE WORLD

THE ILLUSTRATED ENCYCLOPEDIA OF
WILD FLOWERS
& FLORA OF THE WORLD

AN EXPERT REFERENCE AND IDENTIFICATION GUIDE TO OVER 1730 WILD FLOWERS AND PLANTS FROM EVERY CONTINENT

3800 BEAUTIFUL ILLUSTRATIONS, MAPS AND PHOTOGRAPHS

MARTIN WALTERS AND MICHAEL LAVELLE

LORENZ BOOKS

This edition is published by Lorenz Books
an imprint of Anness Publishing Ltd
Blaby Road, Wigston, Leicestershire, LE18 4SE
info@anness.com

www.lorenzbooks.com www.annesspublishing.com

If you like the images in this book and would like to investigate
using them for publishing, promotions or advertising, please visit
our website www.practicalpictures.com for more information.

Publisher: Joanna Lorenz
Editorial Director: Helen Sudell
Project Editor: Simona Hill
Photographer: Peter Anderson
Illustrators: Andrey Atuchin, Penny Brown, Peter Bull, Stuart
Jackson-Carter, Felicity Cole, Joanne Glover, Paul Jones, Jonathan
Latimer, Carol Mullin, Fiona Osbaldstone, Denys Ovenden
Book and Jacket design: Nigel Partridge
Editorial Reader: Lindsay Zamponi
Production Controller: Wendy Lawson

PICTURE CREDITS

The publishers would like to thank the following people and
picture libraries for permission to use their images: Alamy page 9,
60t, 84b, 100b, 112, 132t, 228, 249, 263, 273, 334, 342, 352.
Ardea page 28br, 29tc, 31. DW Stock Picture Library page 336,
374, 424, 452b, 462, 468b, 476. Garden Matters page 70, 188,
358, 422. Garden and Plant Picture Library page 56b, 58t, 60b, 66,
74 Natural Science Image Library page 453, 458, 468t, 473, 480.
OSF page 486. Peter Barrett page 25bc. Photolibrary page 84t.
Photos Horticultural page 28bl, 120, 225, 231, 287, 407, 354, 366,
446, 452t, 456. FLPA page 58b, 70b, 72, 73, 82b, 100t, 102, 103,
108, 110, 111, 116, 121, 122, 130, 132b, 134b, 138, 148, 150, 154,
204t, 230, 274.

ETHICAL TRADING POLICY

Because of our ongoing ecological investment programme,
you, as our customer, can have the pleasure and reassurance
of knowing that a tree is being cultivated on your behalf to
naturally replace the materials used to make the book you
are holding. For further information about this scheme,
go to www.annesspublishing.com/trees

A CIP catalogue record for this book is available from the
British Library.

This title has previously been published as *The World Encyclopedia
of Wild Flowers and Flora* and *The Illustrated Encyclopedia of Wild
Flowers and Flora of the Americas*.

AUTHOR'S ACKNOWLEDGEMENTS

Martin Walters would like to thank the following people for their
help with researching information: Andy Byfield, Eleanor Cohn,
Carmen Dominguez, Chris Donnelly, Paul Ssegawa, Stella Tranah.

PUBLISHER'S NOTE

Although the advice and information in this book are believed to
be accurate and true at the time of going to press, neither the
authors nor the publisher can accept any legal responsibility or
liability for any errors or omissions that may have been made.

CONTENTS

INTRODUCTION

Wild flowers are plant species that are at home in a particular place, whether their habitat is natural or the result of human intervention. Purists argue that a wild flower must be native to an area to be truly wild.

Flowers are generally considered to be 'wild' if they grow without someone having planned where they should be planted. Yet, often they grow unplanned in man-made environments, from tiny seeds carried on the wind or deposited by birds and other animals.

In any location, from high mountain pastures to great forests, some plants will prosper and others do less well. Each pretty wild flower is the result of countless generations of plants that have striven to exist against staggering odds to ensure that their evolutionary 'line' will survive into the future. Some flowers have become highly adapted in order to grow in these places. They may be dependent not only upon their surroundings, but upon other plants, for example by providing shelter from weather, or a stem on which to grow. They may even be dependent upon animals for their survival, for example to help spread seed or promote root growth by grazing. Many strange and wonderful plant species have been shaped by their homes, the weather and by other inhabitants of their habitat into the perfect form for survival.

It is the showiest flowers that we tend to spend the most time looking at – we often easily walk past myriad delicate wild flowers to gaze at one large bloom. Every time we walk across a grassy patch we may carelessly crush hundreds of flowering plants underfoot. They are everywhere and many deserve a closer look. A detailed inspection of even the commonest wayside flower reveals an intricacy and beauty that the work of human hands can rarely approach. Wild flowers are among nature's loveliest gifts: carefree and simple, abundant and serendipitous, they provide an ever-changing panorama of colours, shapes, sizes and textures. It is precisely the informal spontaneity of wild flowers – the random mingling of colours and species, and the way that they change through the seasons – that delights us.

The natural floral jewellery that adorns so much of the Earth's surface has enraptured scientists, artists and writers throughout our history, yet it is easy to forget the true depth of this bounty. Its richness is what this book is all about. All flowering plants – even the tiniest ones – deserve our attention, and to understand them fully we must look both closely and carefully. Describing the wonders of just one flower could fill a whole book; to attempt to include here all the flowering plants in the world would be impossible. This book aims to present a selection of the world's wild flowers: it could be described as a 'look through the keyhole' at a world more beautiful than can easily be comprehended. Hopefully, however, you will be inspired to go out and take a fresh look at wild flowers and marvel over these truly remarkable plants growing all around us.

Below: A wild flower environment such as this grass verge will be teaming with insect life.

Right: A bluebell wood in springtime is often an inviting and attractive sight. These flowers should never be collected from the wild.

HOW FLOWERS LIVE

Flowering plants are the most diverse and widely studied group in the plant kingdom. Their classification is constantly evolving. They are found all across the Earth's surface, wherever plants have learned to live. From mountaintops and the high Arctic to lush tropical forests, flowers are a familiar feature of every landscape. This wide range of habitats has led to flowers assuming a huge diversity of form. In some cases, the flowers have become so reduced as to be insignificant when compared to the plant as a whole. In others, however, the plant itself may hardly be noticed until it produces a huge flower that seems to arrive from nowhere. All plants, however, have the same characteristics, and learning about the parts of a plant and how to identify them can be rewarding.

Flowers have even driven the process of evolution, harnessing an army of helpers that includes almost every conceivable form of land- or air-living creature to help with every phase of their reproductive cycle. Many of the showiest flower types trade rich, nutritious, sugary nectar in return for the services of the 'diner' in cross-fertilization. Flowers are the courtship vessels of plants and are often highly adapted to receive the attention of just a few creatures, some of which exploit this food source very successfully. Others use a variety of tricks and even entrapments to fulfil this need and yet others have abandoned the need for animals, preferring the wind to do the job for them.

Even after the seed is fertilized, the relationship of many species with animals does not end. There is a whole range of ingenious methods by which they recruit animals into spreading their seed for them, and by doing this they not only guarantee the survival of future generations but may also spread the offspring far and wide from the parent plants.

Left: The vivid colours of wild flowers are designed to attract pollinators but have also long attracted the attention of humans.

HOW PLANTS ARE CLASSIFIED

In an attempt to understand the world, humans have become fascinated with the classification of every aspect of it. While such classifications are useful to us, they do not naturally occur in nature and are at best approximations of the true nature of diversity.

Classification helps us to recognize millions of individual species of plants. In pre-literate times plant recognition was a practical necessity, since eating the wrong plants could be fatal.

The earliest written record of a system of plant classification can be attributed to Theophrastus (*c.*372–287BC), a student of Plato and Aristotle, to whom even Alexander the Great sent plant material that he encountered on his expeditions. In his *Enquiry into Plants* and *On the Causes of Plants*, Theophrastus included the classification of species into trees, shrubs, subshrubs and herbs, listing about 500 different plants; he also made a distinction between flowering and non-flowering plants.

The binomial system

The shift toward modern systems of classification began at the time of the Renaissance in Europe (1300–1600). Improvements in navigation, which opened up the world and enabled plants to be collected from much further afield, coincided with the invention of the printing press, which meant information about the new

discoveries could be published widely. Interest in plants increased enormously, and by the 17th century the number of known species was becoming too high to manage without a classification system. The British naturalist John Ray is credited with revising the concept of naming and describing organisms. However, most were classified using a whole string of words that resembled a sentence rather than a name. During the 18th century, the Swedish botanist Carl von Linné (1707–78), who published his work under the Latinized form of his name, Carolus Linnaeus, created a referable system of nomenclature that became the foundation of the system used today. He is often cited as the 'father' of modern taxonomy, or hierarchical classification.

Linnaeus chose to use Latin, then the international language of learned scholars, which enabled scientists speaking and writing different native languages to communicate clearly. His system is now known as binomial

Below: Primula vulgaris, *the primrose gets its genus (first) name from the Latin* primus *referring to its early appearance in spring.*

Above: Ferns and mosses represent an ancient lineage of plants that do not produce flowers or seed and, as such, are classified as lower plants.

nomenclature (from *bi* meaning 'two', *nomen* meaning 'name' and *calatus* meaning 'called'). Each species is given a generic name – something like a surname – and a specific name, the equivalent of a personal or first name. We still use this system, which has been standardized over the years, for naming and classifying organisms.

The generic (genus) name comes first, and always starts with a capital letter. It is followed by the specific (species) name, which is always in lower case. This combination of genus and species gives a name that is unique to a particular organism. For example, although there are many types of rose in the genus *Rosa*, there is only one called *R. rubiginosa* – commonly known as the sweet briar. (These names are italicized in print.)

The names of plants sometimes change. Name changes usually indicate reclassification of plant species, often as a result of advances in molecular biology. For example, the

Chrysanthemum genus has recently been split into eight different genera, including *Dendranthema*, *Tanacetum* and *Leucanthemum*. It may take the botanical literature years to reflect such changes, and in the meantime inconsistencies in the printed names of plants can appear.

Plant families

Another useful way of classifying plants is by family. Many families are distinctive in terms of their growth characteristics and preferences, while others are very large and diverse, including numerous different genera. There are 380 families of flowering plants, containing all the species known to science that have already been classified. The largest family is the Asteraceae (aster family), which contains 1,317 genera and 21,000 species. In contrast, some plant families are very small: an example is the Cephalotaceae, or saxifragales family, of which a single species, *Cephalotus follicularis*, is found growing along a small stretch of coast in western Australia.

As our understanding increases, and more species are discovered and classified, there is sure to be intense debate over the placement of new and existing species within families.

Above: The rose has been highly bred, and many of the types now in cultivation bear little resemblance to wild types. The genus name Rosa, *is the original Latin name for the plant.*

Below: Geranium *(shown here) is often confused with the closely related genus* Pelargonium *due to Linnaeus (mistakenly) classifying both as* Geranium *in 1753.*

*Below: Salad burnet (*Sanguisorba minor*) is a small herbaceous plant in Rosaceae, yet at first glance it does not appear even remotely similar to the woody genus* Rosa.

THE FIRST FLOWERING PLANTS

The earliest flowering plants appeared on Earth around 350 million years ago in the ancient carboniferous forests, although they really began their 'takeover' of the planet 120 million years ago, when the dinosaurs ruled the world.

The first flowers were probably quite insignificant by current standards, but their appearance, coupled with their ability to produce a protective fruit around the seed, marked the beginning of a new era. Despite their rather low key entrance in the early Cretaceous period, by the time the dinosaurs met their end some 55 million years later, most of the major flowering plant groups had already appeared.

Two distinct ways of life emerged for flowering plants. Some continued to reproduce as they had always done – letting the wind control whether pollen from one flower met another flower of the same type. Others, however worked in harmony with insects and other animals, which they enticed with sweet nectar and large, colourful flowers. The relationship was very successful and led to the almost infinite variety of forms and colours that we see around us in plants today.

Below: 500 million years ago non-vascular plants such as hornworts, liverworts, lichens, and mosses grew on Earth.

The first living things

The Earth is around 4.5 billion years old, and life is estimated to have begun around 3.75 billion years ago: for around 750 million years the Earth was (as far as we know) lifeless. It was a hostile environment, with a surface hot enough to boil water and an atmosphere that would have been poisonous to us, yet life is likely to have begun as soon as the surface was cool enough for water to lie on its surface. It was not life as we know it – more a thick soup of chemicals than the miracle of creation – but it was life. This was the situation for 500 million years, until a strange twist of fate assured the rise of the plants.

Primitive single-celled bacteria, which we now know as cyanobacteria, evolved from the existing life forms. They probably appeared remarkably similar to their counterparts, but with one spectacular difference. These cells

Below: 425 million years ago seedless vascular plants such as club mosses, early ferns and horsetails became evident.

were able to take carbon dioxide (which was then very abundant in the Earth's atmosphere) and water and convert them into sugar (an energy-rich food) and oxygen. The effect would have been barely noticeable at first, but over a period of a few hundred million years it changed the atmosphere from one rich in carbon dioxide to one that was at one point almost one-third oxygen. Over this time many of the formerly dominant species died out, but the plant-like bacteria gained the ascendance.

Despite this, plants remained water-bound for another 2.5 billion years. It was not until 425–500 million years ago (a date that is still hotly contested) that they made their first tentative appearance on land. The earliest forms were very simple in comparison to modern plants, but their descendants still exist and probably look similar in many respects – mosses and liverworts

Below: 200 million years ago seeded vascular plants such as the gymnosperms, seed ferns, conifers, cycads and ginkgoes thrived.

are the best examples. The first advance that we know of was marked by the appearance of a plant called *Cooksonia*, 430 million years ago. Within 70 million years, species had diversified and evolved to form lush tropical forests; despite being relatively new to the land, plants had made up for lost time in spectacular style.

The fossil record

Evidence of early plants has been found in the fossil record. As mud and other sediments were deposited, forming rocks, pieces of living organisms were deposited with them. Surviving as fossils, these give us an extraordinary picture of what the Earth was like at any one time. In addition, the chemistry of the atmosphere and hydrosphere (the oceans, rivers, lakes and clouds) of the time can be determined by analysis of the rock. These signs allow us to piece together the story and understand how plants have changed over time.

Darwin's theory of evolution

In 1859, the British naturalist Charles Darwin published *On the Origin of Species*. The work caused a stir at the

Below: 120 million years ago recognizable species of seeded vascular plants, such as magnolias and water lilies evolved.

time as it opposed conventional Church doctrine. Darwin argued that the Earth had been created not tens of thousands of years ago (as the Church claimed) but billions of years ago. The idea was seen as revolutionary or even heretical, but in fact it reflected a growing school of thought that recognized that animal and plant species could change over time. Darwin's grandfather had written on the topic, and Darwin himself acknowledged 20 predecessors who had added to the subject. His original contribution, however, was to sift through this increasing body of evidence and combine it with his own observations during his travels around the world from 1831 to 1836.

Darwin determined that single species, through environmental influence, were able to change over time to suit their surroundings. These changes happened not within the lifetime of an individual organism but through the inheritance of characteristics that were valuable in aiding survival and competing with other organisms for the essentials of life. Though he did not then understand the mechanism by which this happened, Darwin concluded that all modern species have evolved through the process of natural

Above: Though it is a modern species, this Magnolia *flower is very similar to the earliest flower forms of 120 million years ago.*

selection, or 'survival of the fittest'. The theory revolutionized the study of biology and his work remains a cornerstone of evolutionary science.

Since Darwin's time, the body of evidence has grown. There is still much that we do not know, but many evolutionary scientists believe that there are more species on the planet today than at any time in its entire history. We now mostly understand how changes are passed on to offspring and have been able to piece together an evolutionary hierarchy, where we can see when plants first appeared and how they have changed over time.

Below: Today there are more species of flowering plants in the world than there ever have been at any other time.

THE PARTS OF A PLANT

While plants have undergone many individual changes over millions of years, most of them still have features in common. Flowering plants generally possess roots, stems, leaves and, of course, flowers, all of which may be useful in identifying them.

Learning to recognize species is essentially a question of simple observation combined with knowledge of plant structure. This is because all modern flowering plants have evolved from a common ancestry – just as most mammals, birds and reptiles possess one head, four limbs, up to five toes per leg and sometimes a tail, because they are all variants of a prior design. Even when plants have become highly specialized, the common features still persist, albeit in a modified form, and this often betrays a relationship between species that appear unrelated.

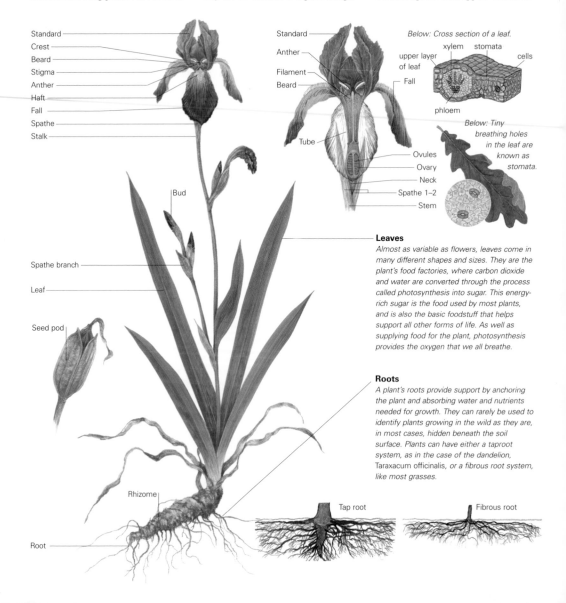

Standard
Crest
Beard
Stigma
Anther
Haft
Fall
Spathe
Stalk

Bud

Spathe branch
Leaf

Seed pod

Rhizome
Root

Standard
Anther
Filament
Beard

Tube

Fall

Ovules
Ovary
Neck
Spathe 1–2
Stem

Below: Cross section of a leaf.

upper layer of leaf
xylem   stomata
cells
Fall
phloem

Below: Tiny breathing holes in the leaf are known as stomata.

Leaves

Almost as variable as flowers, leaves come in many different shapes and sizes. They are the plant's food factories, where carbon dioxide and water are converted through the process called photosynthesis into sugar. This energy-rich sugar is the food used by most plants, and is also the basic foodstuff that helps support all other forms of life. As well as supplying food for the plant, photosynthesis provides the oxygen that we all breathe.

Roots

A plant's roots provide support by anchoring the plant and absorbing water and nutrients needed for growth. They can rarely be used to identify plants growing in the wild as they are, in most cases, hidden beneath the soil surface. Plants can have either a taproot system, as in the case of the dandelion, Taraxacum officinalis, or a fibrous root system, like most grasses.

Tap root

Fibrous root

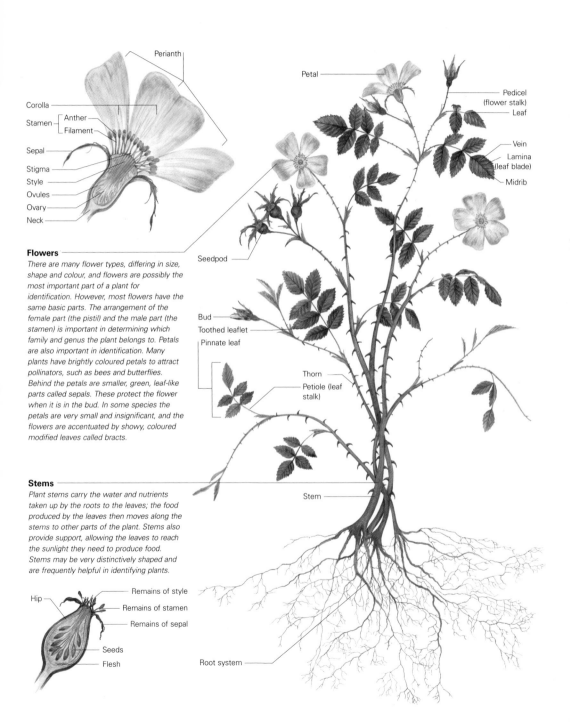

Perianth

Petal

Pedicel
(flower stalk)

Leaf

Corolla

Stamen — Anther
— Filament

Vein

Lamina
(leaf blade)

Sepal

Midrib

Stigma

Style

Ovules

Ovary

Neck

Seedpod

Flowers

There are many flower types, differing in size, shape and colour, and flowers are possibly the most important part of a plant for identification. However, most flowers have the same basic parts. The arrangement of the female part (the pistil) and the male part (the stamen) is important in determining which family and genus the plant belongs to. Petals are also important in identification. Many plants have brightly coloured petals to attract pollinators, such as bees and butterflies. Behind the petals are smaller, green, leaf-like parts called sepals. These protect the flower when it is in the bud. In some species the petals are very small and insignificant, and the flowers are accentuated by showy, coloured modified leaves called bracts.

Bud

Toothed leaflet

Pinnate leaf

Thorn

Petiole (leaf
stalk)

Stems

Plant stems carry the water and nutrients taken up by the roots to the leaves; the food produced by the leaves then moves along the stems to other parts of the plant. Stems also provide support, allowing the leaves to reach the sunlight they need to produce food. Stems may be very distinctively shaped and are frequently helpful in identifying plants.

Stem

Remains of style

Hip

Remains of stamen

Remains of sepal

Seeds

Flesh

Root system

LEAF FORMS AND SHAPES

While leaves vary considerably in appearance, all are basically similar in terms of their internal anatomy. Leaves are the factories within which plants produce their own food, although in some plants, they have become highly adapted and may fulfil a variety of other roles.

Leaves are able to breathe: air passes freely in and out through specialized pores known as stomata, which are usually found on the lower leaf surface, or epidermis. The stomata can be opened and closed by the plant to regulate water evaporation. This is crucial as it allows the plant to cool down, preventing damage through overheating, though the leaves of some plants (those in dry climates) have few stomata in order to conserve water. Leaves also contain vascular tissue, which is responsible for transporting water to the leaves and food from the leaf to other parts of the plant. The veins are easily visible on both the surface and the underside of most leaves. The same types of tissue are present in the plant's stems and collectively they form a continuous link from root tip to leaf tip.

Leaf fall

When leaves have finished their useful life the plant sheds them. Deciduous trees and shrubs shed all their leaves annually and enter a dormant phase, usually in the autumn in temperate areas or immediately preceding a dry season in warmer climates, to avoid seasonal stresses such as cold or excessive heat damage. Herbaceous

Above: Cacti live in very harsh dry conditions and have leaves that are reduced to small spiny pads.

plants (also known as herbs) and other non-woody plants normally lose all of their top growth, including the leaves, for similar reasons. Many plants of the arctic, temperate and dry regions fall into this category.

Plants that do not shed all their leaves at once are said to be evergreen. These plants ride out harsh conditions but may also enter a dormant phase where no new growth commences until conditions improve. Evergreen plants also shed leaves, but tend to do so all through the year, particularly during active growth periods. Many tropical plants fit into this category.

Leaf modifications

Leaves are arguably the most highly modified of all plant organs, and show a vast diversity of form and function. Flower petals are thought to have arisen from leaves. The adaptations in leaves often reflect ways in which

plants have changed in order to cope with specific environmental factors in their natural habitats.

Cactus spines are an example of an extreme leaf modification. The spines are part of a modified leaf called an areole. They are in fact modified leaf hairs, and the small furry base of the spine, or spine cluster, is all that remains of the leaf itself. Cacti and some other succulents have altered so that the stem is the main site of food production, and the leaves have adopted a defensive role.

Other leaf modifications include the development of tendrils to help plants climb, coloured bracts around flowers to attract potential pollinators, and – the most celebrated – traps that attract and ensnare insects to supplement the plant's mineral requirements.

Leaf shape

Leaves grow in a tremendous variety of sizes and shapes, which can be useful in helping to identify the plant.
• Leaf margins, or edges, occur in a variety of forms. The simplest is a smooth, continuous line, which is described as 'entire'. Often, however, the edge is broken up in a definite pattern, such as 'serrated' or 'lobed'.
• The apex, or leaf tip, may vary in shape, even between closely related species. This may reflect environmental factors. The base of the leaf is also variable and is considered along with the way the leaf is attached to the stem.
• Veination may form an identifiable trait. Monocotyledonous plants have parallel veins that run the length of the leaf. Dicotyledonous plants have a netted arrangement that is complex.
• Leaves can be categorized as simple or compound. A simple leaf is one single leaf blade on a stalk. Compound leaves are made up of a group of leaflets, with a single stalk, attaching the group to the stem.

Leaf arrangements

How leaves are attached or arranged on a stem can be a useful tool in plant identification.

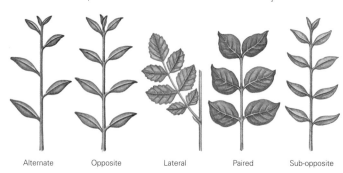

| Alternate | Opposite | Lateral | Paired | Sub-opposite |

Leaf shapes

Leaves are almost as varied as flowers in respect of their shapes, although they offer less of a clue as to the relationships between even quite closely related species. Similar shapes, sizes and colours of leaf may occur on quite unrelated species and it is thought that this is mainly due to the original environmental circumstances that a plant evolved within.

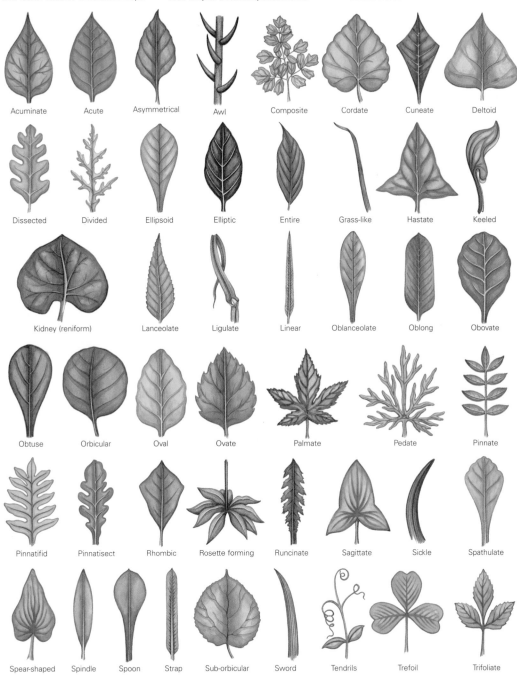

Acuminate

Acute

Asymmetrical

Awl

Composite

Cordate

Cuneate

Deltoid

Dissected

Divided

Ellipsoid

Elliptic

Entire

Grass-like

Hastate

Keeled

Kidney (reniform)

Lanceolate

Ligulate

Linear

Oblanceolate

Oblong

Obovate

Obtuse

Orbicular

Oval

Ovate

Palmate

Pedate

Pinnate

Pinnatifid

Pinnatisect

Rhombic

Rosette forming

Runcinate

Sagittate

Sickle

Spathulate

Spear-shaped

Spindle

Spoon

Strap

Sub-orbicular

Sword

Tendrils

Trefoil

Trifoliate

FLOWERS AND FLOWER FORMS

A flower is the reproductive organ of plants classified as angiosperms – plants that flower and form fruits containing seeds. The function of a flower is to produce seeds through sexual reproduction. The seeds produce the next generation of a species and are the means by which the species is able to spread.

It is generally thought that a flower is the product of a modified stem, with the petals being modified leaves. The flower stem, called a pedicel, bears on its end the part of the flower called the receptacle. The various other parts are arranged in whorls on the receptacle: four main whorls make up a flower.

• The outermost whorl, located nearest the base of the receptacle where it joins the pedicel, is the calyx. This is made up of sepals (modified leaves that typically enclose the closed flower bud), which are usually green but may appear very like petals in some flowers, such as narcissus.

• The next whorl is the corolla – more commonly known as the petals. These are usually thin, soft and coloured, and are used to attract pollinators such as insects.

• The androecium (from the Greek *andros* and *oikia*, meaning 'man's house') contains the male flower parts, consisting of one or two whorls of stamens. Each stamen consists of a filament topped by an anther, where pollen is produced.

• The last and innermost whorl is the gynoecium (from the Greek *gynaikos*

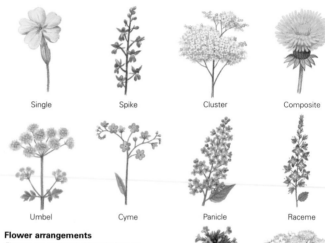

Single   Spike   Cluster   Composite

Umbel   Cyme   Panicle   Raceme

Whorled   Corymb

Flower arrangements
Flowers are arranged either singly or in groups that are known as inflorescences. These inflorescences form a variety of shapes which, although they vary quite widely from species to species, can be an extremely useful feature for identifying many flowering plants, and can easily be observed.

Flower shapes
Flowers display a wide variety of shapes that may be the result of individual flowers or the close arrangement into a flower-like compound inflorescence.

and *oikia*, meaning 'woman's house'), which consists of a pistil with one or more carpels. The carpel is the female reproductive organ, containing an ovary with ovules. The sticky tip of the pistil – the stigma – is where pollen must be deposited in order to fertilize the seed. The stalk that supports this is known as the style.

This floral structure is considered typical, though many plant species show a wide variety of modifications from it. However, despite the differences between genera, most flowers are simply variations on a theme and a basic knowledge of their arrangement is all you really need to get started with their identification.

Bell   Tulip-shaped   Cupped   Domed   Star-shaped   Funnel   Goblet

Pea-like   Saucer   Conical   Flattened   Tubular   Urn-shaped

Monoecious and dioecious plants

In most species, the individual flowers have both a pistil and several stamens, and are described by botanists as 'perfect' (bisexual or hermaphrodite). In some species, however, the flowers are 'imperfect' (unisexual) and possess either male or female parts only. If each individual plant has either only male or only female flowers, the species is described as dioecious (from the Greek *di* and *oikia*, meaning 'two houses'). If unisexual male and female flowers both appear on the same plant, the species is described as monoecious (from the Greek *mono* and *oikia*, meaning 'one house').

Attracting pollinators

Many flowers have evolved specifically to attract animals that will pollinate them and aid seed formation. These commonly have nectaries – specialized glands that produce sugary nectar – in order to attract such animals. As many

Different growing habits
Plants exhibit a variety of growing habits, often reflecting the type of habitat or niche they have specifically evolved to occupy. These are often important features to note when identifying a plant as the flowers may not be present all year round. The growing habits shown below describe all of the flowers that are featured in this directory.

Above: Flowers that attract bees will often have petals that form a wide surface for landing and copious amounts of nectar.

pollinators have colour vision, brightly coloured flowers have evolved to attract them. Flowers may also attract pollinators by scent, which is often attractive to humans – though not always: the flower of the tropical rafflesia, for example, which is pollinated by flies, produces a smell like that of rotting flesh.

There are certain flowers whose form is so breathtaking as to render them almost unnatural to our eyes. Flowering plants such as orchids have developed a stunning array of forms and many have developed intricate relationships with their pollinators. Flowers that are pollinated by wind have no need to attract animals and therefore tend not to be showy.

Above: Flowers whose petals form a protective cup or tube are especially attractive to butterflies or other insects with long mouthparts.

Types of inflorescence

Some plants bear only one flower per stem, called solitary flowers. Many other plants bear clusters of flowers, which are known as inflorescences. Most inflorescences may be classified into two groups, racemes and cymes.

In a raceme, the individual flowers making up the inflorescence bloom progressively from the bottom of the stem to the top. Racemose inflorescences include arrangements called spike, raceme, corymb, umbel and head. In the cyme group, the top floret opens first and the blooms continue to open downward along the peduncle, or inflorescence stalk. Cymes may be simple or compound.

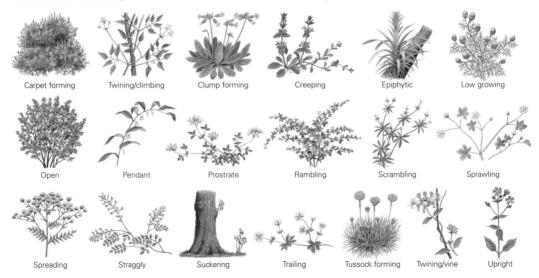

Carpet forming

Twining/climbing

Clump forming

Creeping

Epiphytic

Low growing

Open

Pendant

Prostrate

Rambling

Scrambling

Sprawling

Spreading

Straggly

Suckering

Trailing

Tussock forming

Twining/vine

Upright

THE LIFE CYCLE OF FLOWERING PLANTS

All flowering plants, from giant forest trees that live for thousands of years to the most ephemeral desert annuals that live for only a few weeks, follow the same pattern of life. Their lifespan, size, apparent durability and survival strategies vary considerably, but they have much in common.

Above: Field poppy, Papaver rhoeas, *is an annual that completes its life cycle in one season.*

Above: Wild carrot, Daucus carota, *is a biennial that grows one year and flowers the next.*

Above: Yellow flag, Iris pseudacorus, *is a perennial that lives and flowers for many years.*

All flowering plants begin life as seeds. These are in essence tiny, baby plants that have been left in a state of suspended animation with enough food to support them in the first few days of their new life. In order to grow, seed must be viable (alive). It is a misconception that seed is not living. It is and, like all living things, has a life-span. However, many types of seed can remain dormant for decades, waiting for the right opportunity to commence their cycle of growth and development.

Eventually, the seed will be triggered into germinating by the right combination of moisture, temperature and a suitable soil or growing medium.

Yearly life cycle of herbaceous plants
All flowering plants begin life as a seed. Some grow and flower within the first season, while others grow for several years before they flower. Herbaceous plants whether annual or perennial, grow and flower before dying back down at the end of the season.

Some seeds have specific needs; proteas and banksias must be exposed to smoke to prompt germination, and many berries, such as mistletoe, need to be exposed to the stomach acid of an animal. In most cases, the germinating plant is totally reliant on the energy stored in the seed until it pushes its growing tip above the soil.

The maturing plant

Once above ground the stem grows up toward the light and soon produces leaves that unfold and begin to harvest light energy. As the stems grow upward the plant also extends its roots down into the soil, providing

stability and allowing the plant to harvest both water and minerals that are vital to its growth.

Once the plant reaches its mature phase of growth, changes in its internal chemistry enable it to begin flowering. When this happens depends upon the species, but many plants – except those with the briefest life cycles – continue to grow while they produce flower buds. These buds develop into flowers, which are pollinated by the wind or by pollinators such as bees, moths or other animals.

Once a flower has been pollinated, it will usually fade quickly before turning into fruit, as the fertilized

ovary swells and the new seeds develop. The seeds will continue to develop within the fruit until the embryos are fully mature and the seeds are capable of growing into new plants. This may be very quick in the case of small herbs, but in some shrubs and trees it can take two or more seasons for the seeds to develop fully.

Plants may take just one season to reach flowering stage, or may live for many years before they flower. Once flowering begins, certain species flower repeatedly for many seasons, some lasting decades or even centuries. There is much variability between species, but most plants follow one of three main types of life cycle.

Annuals

Plants that live for a single growing season, or less, are called annuals. Their life cycle is completed within a year. In this time the plant will grow, flower, set fruit containing seeds, and die. Many common flowering plants adopt this strategy which has the advantage of allowing them to colonize areas quickly and make the best of the available growing conditions.

Biennials

Plants that need two growing seasons to complete their life cycle are known as biennials. Generally, biennials germinate and grow foliage in the first growing season before resting over the

winter. In the second growing season the plant enters a mature phase, in which it flowers, sets fruit and then dies. A biennial flowers only once before dying. A few plants may grow only foliage for several years before finally flowering and dying.

Perennials

All the remaining plant types live for three or more years, and may go on growing, flowering and producing fruit for many years. Some perennial species may take a number of years to grow to flowering size, but all of them are characterized by a more permanent existence than that of annuals and biennials.

Life cycle of a dandelion

Above: The flower begins life as a tight bud that opens from the tip to reveal the yellow petals of the tiny individual flowers.

Above: As the flower opens further, it widens and flattens in order to make a perch for the bumblebees, which are its pollinators.

Above: Once the flower has been pollinated, it closes up again and the plant commences the process of seed production.

Above: Once the seed is ripened, the flower bracts re-open, and the parachute-like seed appendages (achenes) spread to form a globe.

Above: As the ripened seed dries, it is easily dislodged and is carried away from the parent plant by even a light breeze.

Above: Once the seed has been dispersed, the flower stalk is redundant and quickly withers, leaving only the leafy rosette.

WHAT IS POLLINATION?

Before a flower can develop seeds for reproduction it must be pollinated: pollen must be moved from the male anthers to the female stigma. Some flowers self-pollinate – pollen from their own anthers is deposited on the stigma – but most need some outside help.

Wind moves the pollen for some plants, such as grasses, but others require the assistance of an animal pollinator. These move pollen from the anthers to the stigma of a flower, and also often carry it between different flowers or plants of the same species. Animals that commonly perform this task include butterflies, bees, hummingbirds, moths, some flies, some wasps and nectar-feeding bats.

The benefits of pollination

Plants benefit from pollinators because the movement of pollen allows them to set seed and begin a new generation. For the pollinators this action is an incidental by-product of their efforts to collect nectar and/or pollen from flowers for themselves. In evolutionary terms it is an example of two unrelated species adapting to mutual dependence, where both benefit. Some plants have become so dependent on a particular pollinator that their flowers have adapted to favour them.

Flower forms and pollinators

Wind-pollinated plants often have small, numerous and inconspicuous flowers. They produce huge amounts of pollen, which saturates the air to ensure that some reaches nearby plants.

Below: Pollinators, such as this swallowtail butterfly, feed upon the energy- and protein-rich nectar while pollinating the plant.

Plants pollinated by bees may have fragrant yellow or blue flowers that produce sweet nectar. Some plants are pollinated by beetles. Their flowers are usually white or dull in colour, mostly with yeasty, spicy or fruity odours. Flowers that rely on fly pollination are usually dull red or brown and have foul odours. Butterflies mainly pollinate flowers that are long and tubular – although this can vary – while moths typically pollinate flowers that are yellow or white and fragrant as they visit them at night.

Some plants are pollinated by birds, though they are far fewer than those visited by insects. Plants that attract hummingbirds, for example, have brightly coloured flowers but very little fragrance, since the birds have no sense of smell. All bird-pollinated flowers are similar in structure to those pollinated by butterflies, in that they have a long tubular shape.

Self and cross-pollination

While it is possible for some individual plants to pollinate their own flowers, this is not ideal. Many plants have developed some factor that promotes cross-pollination between different individuals of the same species.

Dioecious plants (those with separate male and female plants) easily achieve cross-pollination. Self-pollination is simply not possible.

Monoecious plants (those that produce both female and male flower parts on the same plant) avoid self-pollination by having their male or female parts mature at different times. In cases where the male and female structures mature at the same time, the physical separation of the stamens and stigma can help prevent self-pollination. However, self-pollination is the norm in some species and is advantageous in environments where there are few pollinators.

Fertilization

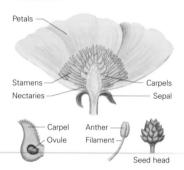

Above: In this buttercup the male flower parts (stamens, each comprised of an anther and a filament) are laden with pollen and surround ovule (egg) containing female parts (carpels).

Above and below: Bees tend to visit flowers whose petals form a wide enough surface for them to land upon. As they take the nectar the bees are dusted with pollen, which brushes on to the flowers they visit next.

Once a pollen grain has landed on the stigma, it must reach the ovaries of the flower in order to fuse with the female cell and begin to form a seed. It does this by germinating and growing a long thin tube that reaches down the style into the flower's ovaries. The pollen tube provides a pathway for the male chromosomes to reach the egg cell in the ovule. One pollen grain fertilizes one egg cell, and together they form the new seed.

SEEDS AND SEED DISPERSAL

For flowering plants, seed production is the main method of reproduction. Seeds have the advantage of providing the plants with a way to spread and grow in new places, which in some cases may be at a distance from the parent. Their ability to do this is extremely important.

If seeds were not dispersed the result would be many germinating seedlings growing very close to the parent plant, leading to a crowded mass of the same species. Each would be in competition with the others, and with the parent plant, for nutrients, light, space and water. Few of the offspring (or the parent) would prosper.

Seeds are dispersed using a number of strategies. The majority are carried by wind, water or animals, though some plants have adopted the strategy of shooting seeds out explosively.

Wind dispersal

Seeds that depend upon wind dispersal are usually very light. Orchid seeds, for example, are as fine as dust. In addition, composite flowers such as the dandelion, *Taraxacum officinalis*, have hairy appendages on each seed that act like parachutes, carrying the seeds over long distances.

The small size of wind-dispersed seeds is reflected in the amount of food reserves stored in them. Larger seeds contain greater food reserves, allowing the young seedlings more time to grow before they must begin manufacturing their own food. The longer a seedling

Below: In some species such as the opium poppy, Papaver somnifera, *the wind sways the ripe fruits, shaking out the seeds like pepper from a pepper pot. The wind then carries the seeds away from the parent plant.*

has before it must become self-sufficient, the greater its chance of becoming successfully established. However, large seeds are disadvantaged by the fact that they are more difficult to disperse effectively.

Explosions

Some plants have pods that explode when ripe, shooting out the seeds. Many members of the pea family, Papilionaceae, scatter their seeds in this way. Once the seeds are ripe and the pod has dried, it bursts open and the seeds are scattered. In some of these plants, such as common gorse, *Ulex europaeus*, seed dispersal is further enhanced because the seeds possess a waxy cuticle that encourages ants to carry them around, moving them further from the parent plant.

Water dispersal

The fruit and seeds of many aquatic or waterside plants are able to float. Water lily seeds, for example, are easily dispersed to new locations when carried by moving water, and coconuts can travel huge distances across seas and oceans, which is why coconut palms grow on so many Pacific islands.

Below: The Mediterranean squirting cucumber, Ecballium elaterium, *has a fleshy, almost liquid fruit that, when ripe, squirts its jelly-like contents – along with the seeds – some distance from the plant.*

Animal dispersal

The production of a nutritious, fleshy fruit that animals like to eat is another strategy that many plants have adopted. An animal eating the fruit digests only the fleshy outer part. The well-protected seeds – the stones or pips in the fruit – pass through the animal's digestive system and are excreted in droppings that provide a rich growing medium. The seeds are often deposited a long way from the parent plant by this means.

Many types of mistletoe have sticky fruits that are attractive to birds. The sticky berries create equally sticky droppings that the bird needs to 'rub off' on the branches of trees. The seeds are deposited, with the droppings, on the bark to grow into new plants.

A few plants, such as common burdock, *Arctium pubens*, produce seeds with hooks that catch on the fur of animals and are carried away. The animal eventually removes the burrs through grooming or moulting, and the seeds are then deposited.

Fire

Some plants living in fire-prone areas have evolved traits that allow them to use this to their advantage when reproducing or regenerating. For most of these species, the intensity of the fire is crucial: it must be hot, but not so hot that it cooks the seed. In addition, fires should not occur too frequently, as the plant must have time to mature so that new seed can be produced.

Many fire-tolerant species have cones that open only after a fire. Many plants that grow in the Australian bush or in the fynbos (the natural vegetation of the southern Cape) are reliant on fire. In many cases the heat triggers seed dispersal but it is the chemicals in the smoke that initiate seed germination.

HERBACEOUS PLANTS

Looking at plants in the wild, it quickly becomes apparent that there are two basic types. Those that have permanent woody stems, whose shoots do not die back, are generally referred to as trees and shrubs. The remainder lack permanent stems and are often described as herbaceous plants, or herbs.

Herbaceous plants are those that die to the ground each year and produce new stems in the following growing season. The word is used in a broader sense, however, to describe any plant with soft, non-woody tissues, whether it is an annual, perennial or bulb.

To understand how these plants live

Below: Grasslands are an ideal habitat for many herbaceous plants and provide a home for a rich diversity of species.

and grow, we can begin by looking at a seedling. In all seedlings and small plants it is the water content of the cells in the leaves and stems that holds the plants erect. All young plants are similar in this respect but as they grow, woody plants begin to build up the strengthening layers of their characteristic structure. Non-woody plants, on the other hand, always retain soft stems.

Above: The water hyacinth, Eichhornia crassipes, *is a non-woody plant that has become adapted to an aquatic lifestyle.*

Stem structure

Soft stems remain upright because their cells have rigid walls, and water in the cells helps retain their shape. This has the obvious disadvantage that during a dry period water can be drawn out of the cells; the cells become limp and the plant droops or wilts. Many species have stems with a soft inner part – commonly called the pith – that is used to store food. Others, however, have hollow cylindrical stems. In these, the vascular bundles (the veins that transport water, nutrients and sugars around the plant) are arranged near the outside of the stem. This cylindrical formation gives the stem a much greater strength than a solid structure of the same weight.

The relatively short lifespan of non-woody plants (compared with that of many woody plants) and the lack of a strong, rigid structure generally limit the height to which they can grow. Despite this, plants such as the giant hogweed, *Heracleum mantegazzianum*, can easily reach heights of 3–4m/10–13ft – larger than many shrubs. Such giants are rare, however, and most herbaceous plants are no more than 1–2m/3–6½ft in height.

Survival strategies

Non-woody plants usually produce completely new stems each year, because cold or other adverse weather (such as drought) causes the stems to die back to the ground. The climate in which the plant grows greatly affects the survival strategy it adopts. Some species survive periods of cold by forming underground bulbs or tubers for food storage, while others – the annuals – complete their life cycles within one growing season, after which the whole plant dies.

Herbaceous plants are generally divided into those with broad leaves (called forbs) and grass-like plants with very narrow leaves (called graminoids). Some species have become herbaceous vines, which climb on other plants. Epiphytes have gone one step further: they germinate and live their whole life on other plants, never coming in contact with the soil. Many orchids and bromeliads are epiphytes. Other species have adapted to life largely submerged in water, becoming aquatic plants. Many of these are rooted in the sediment at the bottom of the water, but a few have adapted to be completely free floating.

Below: Open woodland and forest clearings are often rich in herbaceous plants that enjoy the shelter and light shady conditions.

Right: Bulbs such as this petticoat daffodil, Narcissus bulbocodium, *flower in spring in alpine pasture before dying down to avoid the hot dry summer.*

A few species have adapted to use the efforts of other plants to their own ends. Some are semi-parasites – green plants that grow attached to other living, green plants. These unusual plants still photosynthesize but also supplement their nutrients by 'stealing' them directly from their unfortunate host plants. A few species, however, are wholly parasitic – totally dependent upon their host for nutrition. They do not possess any chlorophyll and are therefore classed as 'non-green' plants. Many remain hidden, either inside the host plant or underground, appearing to the outside world only when they produce flowers.

Subshrubs

Some plants, while they are woody in nature, resemble non-woody plants because of their small size coupled with their ability to shoot strongly from ground level or from below ground. They are known as 'subshrubs', a term borrowed from horticulture, where it is used to describe any plant that is treated as a herb in respect of its cultivation. In terms of wild plants it is used rarely to describe low-growing, woody or herbaceous evergreen perennials whose shoots die back periodically.

Small plants

The world's smallest plant species is water meal, *Wolffia globosa*, a floating aquatic herb which, when mature, is not much larger than the full stop at the end of this sentence. Despite its small size, it is a flowering plant. The flowers occur only rarely and would be hard to see without the aid of a microscope. It mainly reproduces vegetatively and quickly forms a large floating colony on the surface of slow-flowing or still water.

WOODY PLANTS

Any vascular plant with a perennial woody stem that supports continued growth above ground from year to year is described as a woody plant. A true woody stem, however, contains wood, which is mainly composed of structured cellulose and lignin.

Cellulose is the primary structural component of plants, and lignin is a chemical compound that is an integral part of the cell walls. Most of the tissue in the woody stem is non-living, and although it is capable of transporting water it is simply the remains of cells that have died. This is because most woody plants form new layers of tissue each year over the layer of the preceding year. They thus increase their stem diameter from year to year and, as each new layer forms, the underlying one dies. So big woody plants are merely a thin living skin stretched over a largely lifeless framework of branches. In effect, as a woody plant grows, the proportion of living material compared to the non-living parts steadily decreases.

Bamboos appear to be woody plants, and indeed do have permanent woody stems above the ground, but are more akin to the grasses, to which they are closely related, than to the commoner woody species. Essentially, they grow a dense stand of individual

Above: All woody plants can be defined by their permanent, often long-lived growth.

stems that emerge from underground stems called rhizomes. In many ways their biology is more like that of non-woody plants, despite their appearance.

Pros and cons of woody stems

There are more than 80,000 species of tree on earth and a considerably higher number of shrubby species. Although the exact number is not known, it is obvious even to a novice plant spotter that woody plants are an extremely successful group. This is because they are bigger than other plants, so they are able to gather more light and therefore produce more food. In areas where inclement weather induces plants to enter a seasonal dormant period, woody plants have the advantage of a head start when growth restarts. They do not have to compete with other emerging plants and can start producing a food from the moment they recommence growth.

Despite their obvious success, however, woody plants have not managed to dominate the entire

land surface. Only the largest trees are fully immune to the effects of large plant-eating mammals, and in some areas, such as the tundra, weather patterns are so extreme that only low-growing woody plants can survive, and they must compete with the surrounding herbage.

Support strategies

As well as trees and large shrubs, there are woody species that exploit other woody plants around them. Lianas, for instance, germinate on the ground and maintain soil contact, but use another plant for support. Many common climbers or vines are lianas.

Somewhat more unusual are the hemi-epiphytes, which also use other plants for support, at least during part of their life: some species germinate on other plants and then establish soil contact, while others germinate on the ground but later lose contact with the soil. The strangler figs, *Ficus* species, are interesting examples: they begin life as epiphytes,

Below: Bamboos are the only examples of the grass family to have evolved permanent stems above ground.

Below: Woody plants include the largest living plant species, the giant redwood Sequoiadendron giganteum, among their ranks.

Above: The permanent stems of woody plants are prone to disease, such as this canker, and older specimens contain much deadwood.

Above: Mistletoe is a shrubby plant that has adapted to be partially parasitic on other, larger woody plants such as trees.

Above: Cacti are highly specialized plants that are descended from woody ancestry and have highly specialized permanent stems.

growing on other trees, unlike other tree seedlings that have to start their struggle for survival on the forest floor. The young strangler fig grows slowly at first, as little water or food is available to it, but its leathery leaves reduce water loss. It then puts out long, cable-like roots that descend the trunk of the host tree and root into the soil at its foot. Now readily able to absorb nutrients and water, the young fig tree flourishes. The thin roots thicken and interlace tightly around the supporting tree trunk. The

Below: Evergreen shrubs, such as this Rhododendron ponticum, *produce food all year round and may form dense understory in deciduous woodland.*

expanding leafy crown of the strangler shades the crown of the support tree and its roots start to strangle its host. The host tree eventually dies and slowly rots away, leaving a totally independent strangler fig, which may live for several hundred years.

Other woody plants, such as the mistletoe, 'plug' themselves into a branch of a living tree and harvest nutrients directly from it. Apart from a free supply of food and water they gain the added advantage of being high above competing plants and trees, so that they receive enough light to photosynthesize. Mistletoe is a partial parasite that retains its woody stems and green leaves.

The largest plants
The identity of the world's largest plant is debatable, not only because woody plants are only partly living tissue, but also because it has still not been fully researched. In practice, it is extremely difficult to measure how much of a tree is actually living tissue, although the usual candidate is the giant redwood, *Sequoiadendron giganteum*. The banyan tree, *Ficus benghalensis*, can easily cover an area of 2 hectares/5 acres, and the related *Ficus religiosa* can allegedly cover even more. Whether any of these species are really the largest is a moot point, but it is certain that the title of largest flowering plant will always be held by a woody species.

The oldest plants
Among the oldest plants on Earth are the bristlecone pines, *Pinus longaeva*. Some individuals are known to be more than 4,000 years old and others are estimated to be 5,000 years old. Some creosote plants, *Larrea divaricata* ssp. *tridentata*, are even older. The creosote plant sends up woody stems directly from ground level, so that all the stems in a dense stand are clones of the original plant. An ancient stand in California's Mojave Desert, known as the King's Clone, is estimated to be 11,700 years old, although the individual stems live for much shorter periods.

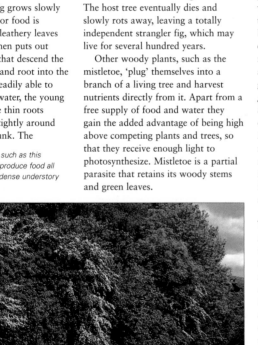

ECOLOGY AND HABITATS

The study of the ways in which plants, animals and their environment interact with one another is known as ecology. All evolutionary change takes place as a direct response to the ecological pressures that affect the plants and animals in a particular habitat.

Any given habitat will have a number of ecological pressures. Plants may be grazed by animals – or the plant species that thrive may be the result of changes in the wider environment, such as the changing seasons or the effect of flooding.

Interaction

To understand the complexities of even relatively small habitats, three basic principles must be remembered. First, living things do not exist as isolated individuals or groups of individuals. They are part of a continuum of life that stretches across the entire surface of the Earth. Second, all organisms interact with other members of their own species, with other species, and with their physical and chemical environments. Third, all organisms have an effect on each other and their surroundings, and as they interact with both they may actually change them over time: for example, trees gradually modify the soil they grow in by constantly dropping dead leaves that decompose and are incorporated into it.

Below: Plants such as the California poppy, Eschscholzia californica, are vulnerable to habitat loss.

Plant groups

The plants within an environment are grouped together in a number of ways.
• A 'species' is a natural group that interbreeds, or has the potential to do so, and will not normally interbreed with other related groups.
• A 'population' describes all the individuals of a given species in a defined area, such as all the dandelions in an area of grassland.
• A 'community' refers to the grouping of all the different populations that occur together in a particular area.
• An 'ecosystem' is the community, or series of communities, together with the surrounding environment. It includes the physical and chemical environment, such as the rocks, water and air.

In an ecosystem, all the organisms composing the populations and communities require energy for survival. In the case of the plants, that energy comes from the sun: plants use sunlight for photosynthesis, which converts the light energy into basic sugars, which the plant uses as its food and stores in the form of sugars, starches and other plant material. Any animals in the ecosystem derive their energy from this store, either by eating the plants or by eating other animals that feed on the plants.

Habitats

The location where a particular species is normally found is its 'habitat'. A single ecosystem may contain many different habitats in which organisms can live. Salt-marsh ecosystems, for example, include areas that are flooded twice daily by tides as well as areas that are inundated only by the highest tides of the month or the year. Different plants inhabit each of these areas, though there may be some overlap, but they are all considered inhabitants of the same ecosystem.

Above: Grazing animals may change or even destroy habitats where densities of animals become too high.

Some plants can thrive and reproduce in different habitats, as long as each provides the appropriate combination of environmental factors. The correct amount of light, water, the necessary temperature range, nutrients, and a substrate on which to grow – sand, clay, peat, water or even another plant may be appropriate. All these factors must be within the range of the plants' tolerance. Even a common plant will disappear from a habitat if an essential environmental factor shifts beyond its range of tolerance. For example, sun-loving plants, such as the common daisy, *Bellis perennis*, flourish in full sun but gradually disappear when surrounding trees and shrubs grow large enough to shade the area.

Common plants tend to be those that have adapted to withstand a range of conditions, whereas rare species survive where narrowly defined environmental conditions exist. It is due to their narrow range of tolerance that some plants become rare. Their lack of habitat may be due to gradual changes over thousands of years, such as climate change, that reduce suitable areas. Increasingly, loss of habitat is due to humans altering the landscape.

CONSERVING ENDANGERED SPECIES

Many plant species are now classified as endangered, because their long-term survival is under threat. There are many reasons for this, such as the erosion of a habitat, or the extinction of a key pollinator, and in some cases it is likely that the plant was never particularly numerous.

Extinction is a normal part of evolution, without it there would be no room for new species, but scientists are becoming increasingly concerned that the current rates of extinction are far above the rate at which species can easily be replaced. Attempts are now being made to prevent further loss of the world's rare plants.

Collecting wild plants

Though it may be tempting to pick wild plants, it is worth asking yourself why you want to do this. While it is true that some collections are undertaken as part of scientific research, some plants have been overpicked to the extent that they have become critically endangered. In the UK, for instance, the lady's slipper orchid, *Cyprepedium calceolus*, was so admired by enthusiasts and collectors that it was eventually reduced to a single wild specimen. The impact of collecting one plant may seem insignificant, but the small actions of many collectors can lead to extinction.

Introduced alien plants

Many plants have become endangered because of competition from a new arrival. When plants are taken from their native environments and introduced elsewhere, they can often become highly invasive, ultimately displacing the native plants. There are numerous instances worldwide of whole native plant communities being threatened by introduced plant species.

Climate change

It is likely that climate change will have a considerable impact on most or all ecosystems in the 21st century, and that changing weather patterns will alter the natural distribution ranges of many species or communities. If no physical barriers exist, it may be possible for species or communities to migrate. Habitats such as forest or grassland, for instance, may move to higher latitudes or higher altitudes if average temperatures increase. There is nothing new about this: at the end of the last ice age (12,000–10,000 years ago) many plant communities moved north or south in response to the rapid global warming that followed.

In most cases, the real danger to habitats arises where natural or constructed barriers prevent or limit the natural movement of species or communities. Many national parks, nature reserves and protected areas are surrounded by urban or agricultural landscapes, which will prevent the migration of species.

Protected areas

Every country in the world has defined areas that are managed for the conservation of animals, plants and other natural and cultural features. Only conservation *in situ* allows the natural processes of evolution to operate on whole plant and animal communities. It permits every link in the web of life, including invertebrates, soil microbes and mycorrhiza (fungi associated with plant roots), to

Below: Over collection of the edelweiss, Leontopodium alpinum, has resulted in it needing legal protection in Europe.

function and interact fully within the ecosystem and is essential to allow the continued development of resistance to fungal and other diseases.

Plant collections

Living collections of rare and endangered plants are a necessary inclusion in many botanic gardens. Their role is often indirect in relation to conservation; they serve to inform visitors of the danger of extinction that faces many species. However, the expertise developed in growing these plants can be useful when growing stocks for reintroduction to the wild and may improve our understanding of the needs of threatened plant species.

Seed banks ensure that plants that are threatened with extinction can be preserved. The seed is gathered by licensed collectors and, after treatment, is stored at sub-zero temperatures. The seed bank works out the best method to grow the seed so that, if the wild plants vanish, the species can be successfully re-introduced.

Re-introduction of wild plants

When plants have become rare, endangered or even extinct, it is occasionally possible to re-introduce them to areas or habitats where they formerly grew. This is rarely a simple matter, however. Its success depends on the removal of whatever pressure made the plant rare in the first place.

The café marron, *Ramosmania rodriguesii*, was thought to have been extinct for 40 years in Rodrigues in the Indian Ocean. However, in 1980 a teacher sent his pupils out on an exploratory trip to find interesting plants. One pupil unearthed a small shrub half-eaten by goats which the teacher identified as the café marron. Recent work has resulted in its producing seed for the first time, and it may yet be re-introduced to the wild.

WILD FLOWER HABITATS

Flowering plants live on every continent and can be found from the ocean shores to the mountains. They are the most successful group of plants on earth, but there are very few that can boast the ability to live anywhere. Even the most widespread species have their limits and, ultimately, their preferred habitats.

Wetlands

All plants need water to live, but many species are likely to suffer and die if they get too much. If there is excessive water in the soil it forces the air out, ultimately suffocating the roots. Some plants, however, are specially adapted to living in wetlands.

Wetland plants grow in seasonally waterlogged or permanently wet conditions. There are many types of wetlands, including swamps, bogs, salt marshes, estuaries, flood plains, lakeshores and riversides. Wetlands occasionally support trees: these areas, known as wet woodland or swamp forests, are filled with rare species that tolerate wet, shady conditions.

Wetlands are rich in flowers, demonstrating that where land and

water meet a rich habitat usually results. Until recently huge areas of wetland were being drained and turned into grassland or filled for development. While this continues apace in some places, wetlands are gaining a new stature in the 21st century. Many are now highly valued as natural sponges, in which water is retained on the land surface instead of flowing quickly to the sea, causing erosion and flooding as it goes.

Woodlands

Forest and woodland are extremely important habitats for many types of flowering plants, not least trees. Tree cover was once the natural vegetation over much of the Earth's surface and great forests stretched across vast tracts of every continent except Antarctica. Over the last 10,000 years

human activity has removed considerable amounts of this natural cover, particularly in Eurasia, and over the last century the trend has become a global one.

Despite the loss of forest, many areas remain and are very important havens for forest-dwelling flowers. Such flowers need to cope with low light levels for much (or even all) of the year, but trees provide a rich growing medium, through their decomposing fallen leaves, and may also provide homes for flowering climbers and epiphytes.

Exposed habitats

Where tree cover is not the dominant vegetation – whether due to human intervention or through natural

Below: A British hedgerow represents a complete ecosystem, mirroring a natural woodland edge.

1 Chaplock	19 Hawthorn
2 Grasses	20 Long-tailed tit
3 Buttercup	21 Orange tip
4 Red clover	22 Early purple
5 Bugle	orchid
6 Chaffinch	23 Tufted vetch
7 Bramble	24 White stitchwort
8 White-tailed	25 Honeysuckle
bumblebee	26 Red campion
9 Carrion crows	27 Brimstone
10 Nettles	28 Wren
11 Dandelion	29 Field rose
12 Germander	30 Beech
13 Bluebell	31 Robin
14 Lesser celandine	32 Cow parsley
15 Garlic mustard	33 Dog violet
16 Bullfinch	34 Hoverfly
17 Kestrel	35 Primrose
18 Blackthorn	

Above: Flowers and all kinds of flora can survive in many seemingly inhospitable places.

changes – conditions are much more favourable to those species that need a lot of light. Exposed areas are mainly either grassland or scrubland and many support a truly dazzling array of wild flowers.

In temperate zones, open spaces are among the most diverse wild flower habitats to be encountered. Even open areas

that are the result of human intervention, such as traditional hay meadows, are capable of supporting many flowering species. These rich habitats have become increasingly rare over the last 100 years, due mainly to agricultural improvement programmes, making those that remain precious.

Life in the extreme

In challenging locations from frozen mountain peaks to the hottest deserts, flowering plants have learned to eke out a living. Habitats of this kind are often referred to as fragile, and while the idea of a fragile desert or mountaintop may seem strange, it is entirely accurate. Extreme survival specialists are finely tuned to make the best of scarce resources. If the conditions change

even slightly, plants do not always possess the right adaptations and may face extinction. Alpine plants, for instance, are much beloved by gardeners, but need specialist care, and treatment that mimics, as closely as possible, the conditions they enjoy in the wild, if they are to survive in cultivation.

SCRUBLAND AND DESERT

Much of the Earth's surface is characterized by land that is dry for much of the year. The plants that live in dry areas are specifically adapted to deal with the harsh extremes of these environments and many have become highly distinctive in appearance.

Mediterranean scrubland

Regions described as Mediterranean scrubland tend to have hot, dry summers followed by cool, moist winters. These conditions occur in the middle latitudes near continental west coasts: the Mediterranean itself, south central and south-western Australia, the fynbos of southern Africa, the Chilean matorral, and the chaparral of California. Most rainfall occurs from late autumn to early spring, and for many plants this is the prime growing and flowering season.

Although rare, this habitat features an extraordinary diversity of uniquely adapted plants – around 20 per cent of the Earth's plant species live in these regions. Most plants that grow in these areas are fire-adapted, and actually depend on this disturbance for their survival.

Deserts

While they occur on every continent, deserts vary greatly in the amount of annual rainfall they receive and their average temperature. In general, evaporation exceeds rainfall. Many deserts, such as the Sahara, are hot all year round, but others, such as the Gobi Desert, become cold in winter.

Temperature extremes are a characteristic of most deserts. Searing daytime heat gives way to cold nights. Not surprisingly, the diversity of climatic conditions – though harsh – supports a rich array of habitats. Many are ephemeral in nature and often reflect the scarcity and

Above: Where vegetation is present, woody-stemmed shrubs and plants tend to be characteristic of desert regions.

seasonality of available water. Despite their harsh conditions, many deserts have extraordinarily rich floras that in some cases feature high numbers of species that are endemic.

Below: Australian mallee grows at the edge of desert regions and contains plants that are both fire- and drought-resistant.

1 Lehmann's mallee
2 *Melaleuca spicigera*
3 Clustered everlasting
4 Black kangaroo paw
5 Spiny cream spider flower
6 Cough bush
7 Azure daisy bush
8 Red kangaroo paw
9 Cactus pea
10 Hakea wattle

CONIFEROUS WOODLAND

Among the most ancient of flowering plants, conifers once dominated the whole of the Earth's surface. In modern times, however, they have become more restricted as broad-leaved flowering plants have become the dominant group.

Boreal forest

Also known as taiga or northern coniferous forest, boreal forest is located south of tundra and north of temperate deciduous forests or grass-lands. Vast tracts of this forest span northern North America, Europe and Asia. Boreal forests cover around 17 per cent of the Earth's surface. They are characterized by a cold, harsh climate, low rainfall or snowfall and a short growing season. They may be open woodlands with widely spaced trees or dense forests whose floor is in shade. The dominant ground cover is mosses and lichens, with a few specialized flowering plants.

Above: Coniferous woodland has a simple structure, a canopy layer and an understorey.

Tropical coniferous forest

Found predominantly in North and Central America, in tropical regions that experience low levels of rain and moderate variability in temperature, these forests feature a thick, closed canopy, which blocks light to the floor and allows little to grow beneath. The ground is covered with fungi and ferns and is usually relatively poor in flowering plants.

Temperate rainforest

In temperate regions, evergreen forests are found in areas with warm summers and cool winters. Conifers dominate some, while others are characterized by broadleaved evergreen trees.

Temperate evergreen forests are common in the coastal areas of regions that have mild winters and heavy rainfall, or in mountain areas. Temperate conifer forests sustain the highest levels of plant material in any land habitat and are notable for trees that often reach massive proportions.

Below: A conifer forest of north-western North America contains a wide variety of flowering plants.

1 Dogwood
2 Fireweed
3 Meadow goldenrod
4 Tiger lily
5 Calypso
6 Bunchberry
7 Yellow fawn lilies
8 Wood nymph
9 Rocky mountain lilies
10 Spring beauty
11 Dwarf waterleaf

HEDGEROWS

*Many agricultural landscapes are defined by hedgerows, which are important habitats for many plants.
A hedgerow is formed of a row of intermeshing shrubs and bushes and sometimes trees that form a
boundary to keep in live stock, and are home to a diverse range of creatures.*

Land clearance

Though a product of human activity,
not all hedgerows were planted. As
villagers and landowners cleared forest
areas for agricultural purposes,
especially in the UK, they would leave
the last narrow strip of woodland to
mark the boundaries of their land.

At the heart of an ancient
hedgerow is a dense shrub layer; at
intervals along it trees form a broken
canopy. At ground level a rich layer of
herbs grows along the base of the
hedge, at the field edge. The older the
hedgerow, the greater diversity of
animal and plant life it will support.
The easiest way to age a hedge is to
mark out a 30m/33yd stretch then
count the number of different species
of trees and shrubs it contains. It is
reckoned to take about 100 years for

each woody plant to establish itself, so
for each different species you find add
a century to the age of the hedge.
Hedgerows are effectively 'corridors'
for wildlife, allowing species to
disperse and move from one habitat
area to another. While it is difficult for
most plants to spread across open
fields, they can 'travel' along the base
of a hedge.

Vanishing hedgerows

The agricultural policies of recent
decades have led to concern about the
rate at which hedgerows are
disappearing. Between 1984 and 1993,
the length of managed hedgerows in
the UK alone decreased by nearly a
third. Hedgerow loss occurs not only

*Above: Hedgerows are often rich in species
that have been driven from much of the
surrounding landscape.*

when hedges are deliberately removed,
but also when they are left to become
derelict: if they are not regularly cut
and managed, they grow into open
lines of bushes and trees.

Pesticide or fertilizer damage can be
a particular problem on intensively
managed farmland, where weedkillers
have often been applied to hedge
bottoms to eliminate weeds. This has
proved to be damaging for the natural
wild flower population of hedgerows.
Almost as damaging is fertilizer 'drift'
(unintentional overspill) into the hedge
base, as it promotes the growth of
certain plant species at the expense
of others. Often, the species
that are favoured are of little
conservation value.

*Below: Hedgerows combine
attributes of merging
habitats.*

1 Dog rose
2 Honeysuckle
3 Lesser celandine
4 Red campion
5 Foxglove
6 Blackthorn

BROAD-LEAVED FOREST

Many types of forest can be classified as broad-leaved. The principal types are temperate lowland forests, tropical rainforests and cloud forests, and tropical and sub-tropical dry forests. All of these typically have large, broad-leaved trees as their dominant vegetation.

Forest flora

There are considerable variations between the species of wild flowers and flora that thrive in different types of forests and the location has a direct bearing.

Temperate deciduous forest

In cool, rainy areas forests are characterized by trees that lose their leaves in the autumn, in preparation for winter. By shedding its leaves, a tree conserves resources, avoiding the hardship of maintaining a mass of foliage through winter. Once on the forest floor the leaves decompose and provide a wonderfully rich soil.

Many low-growing plants that live in these areas take advantage of the winter and early spring when the trees are bare. During this time the absence of shade allows them to complete their life cycle in a few months while (for them) light levels are highest. The seed of some species wait in the soil until trees fall, or are felled, before they germinate and grow in the resulting clearing. These plants may make a dense, showy stand for a few years before the forest canopy closes once more and shades them out. Temperate deciduous forests are found around the globe in the middle latitudes: in the Northern Hemisphere they grow in North America, Europe and eastern Asia, and in the Southern Hemisphere there are smaller areas, in South America, southern Africa, Australia and New Zealand. They have four distinct seasons – spring, summer, autumn and winter – and the growing season for trees lasts about six months.

Tropical rainforest

Very dense, warm and wet, rainforests are located in the tropics – a wide band around the equator, mostly in the area between the Tropic of Cancer (23.5° N) and the Tropic of Capricorn (23.5° S). They grow in South America, West Africa, Australia, southern India and South-east Asia.

A fairly warm, consistent temperature, coupled with a high level of rainfall, characterizes tropical rainforests. They are dominated by semi-evergreen and evergreen trees. These number in the thousands and contribute to the highest levels of species diversity of any major terrestrial habitat type. Overall, rainforests are home to more species than any other forest habitat.

Dry forest

Tropical and subtropical dry forests are found in Central and South America, Africa and Madagascar, India, Indochina, New Caledonia and the Caribbean. Though they occur in climates that are warm all year round and may receive heavy rain for part of the year, they also have long dry seasons that last several months. Deciduous trees are the dominant vegetation in these forests, and during the drought a leafless period occurs, allowing the trees to conserve water. Throughout this period, sunlight is able to reach ground level and plants grow and flower beneath the trees.

Below: In the Northern Hemisphere, bluebells take advantage of the extra light in spring, when trees are bare, in order to grow and flower. They finish flowering just as the tree canopy above starts to fill in.

1 Bluebells

GRASSLAND

Windy and partly dry, grassland generally lacks woody vegetation, and the dominant plant type is, of course, grasses. Almost one quarter of the Earth's land surface is grassland, and in many areas grassland is the major habitat separating forests from deserts.

Grasslands, also known as savanna, pampas, campo, plain, steppe, prairie and veldt, can be divided into two types – temperate and tropical.

Temperate grassland

Located north of the Tropic of Cancer and south of the Tropic of Capricorn, temperate grasslands are common throughout these ranges. They experience a range of seasonal climatic variations typified by hot summers and cold winters. The combination of open, windy sites and dense stands of grasses mean that the evaporation rate is high, so little of the rain that falls reaches the rich soil.

The extraordinary floral communities of the Eurasian steppes and the North American plains have been largely destroyed due to the conversion of these lands to agriculture. In surviving areas of the North American tall-grass prairie, as many as 300 different plant species may grow in 1 hectare/2.5 acres.

Tropical grassland

The annual temperature regime in tropical grassland is quite different to that of temperate grassland: in tropical regions it is hot all year, with wet seasons that bring torrential rains interspersed with drier seasons. Tropical grasslands are located between the Tropic of Cancer and the Tropic of Capricorn and are sometimes collectively called savannas. Many savannas do have scattered trees, and often occur between grassland and forest. They are predominantly located in the dry tropics and the subtropics, often bordering a rainforest. The plant diversity of these regions is typically lower than that of other tropical habitats and of temperate grassland.

Montane grassland

At high elevations around the world montane grasslands occur. They are found in tropical, subtropical

Below: Characteristic plants of montane grasslands display features such as rosette structures, waxy leaf or stem surfaces.

and temperate regions, and the plants they contain often display striking adaptations to cool, wet conditions and intense sunlight, including features such as rosette structures or waxy surfaces on their leaves or stems. In the tropics these habitats are highly distinctive: examples include the heathlands and moorlands of Mount Kilimanjaro and Mount Kenya in East Africa, Mount Kinabalu in Borneo, and the Central Range of New Guinea, all of which support ranges of endemic plants.

Flooded grassland

Common to four of the continents, flooded grassland (as the name suggests) is a large expanse or complex of grassland flooded by either rain or river, usually as part of a seasonal cycle. These areas support numerous plants adapted to wet conditions. The Florida Everglades, for example, which contain the world's largest rain-fed flooded grassland, are home to some 11,000 species of flowering plants.

1 Iris
2 Feverfew
3 Anemone
4 Yellow asphodel

FIELDS

Farmland, fields or paddocks are essentially an environment constructed by humans, who have altered the natural landscape for the purposes of agriculture. The general term 'pasture' describes grassland, rough grazing land and traditionally managed hay meadows.

Rough pasture

There are two types of pasture – permanent and rough. Permanent pasture is closed in, fertilized and sown with commercial grass species. It is often treated with herbicides that allow only a few species of grass to grow, so that it does not support a wide range of wildlife species. Rough pasture is usually much older and is typically land that is very difficult to plough so is left undisturbed.

Pasturelands owe their existence to farm livestock, and are very sensitive habitats that can easily be over- or undergrazed. They generally contain a single early stage of native vegetation, which is prevented from developing further by grazing; if the animals are removed, shrubs quickly establish and woodland develops soon afterwards. This is because many livestock animals graze very close to the ground and, while this does not damage grasses (which regrow from just above their roots), many taller plants cannot tolerate it. Grazing animals also

Above: California poppies and lupines form colourful swathes in North American grasslands.

remove nutrients from the environment so many traditional grassland areas are fairly infertile.

The wildflowers of pasture are species that grow low and thus avoid being eaten by animals. They may creep or form low rosettes of leaves and, although diminutive in general, they often have large, showy flowers that readily attract pollinators.

Below: Pasture that has been left undisturbed and unmanaged is full of life, some of which may be readily found only in that habitat.

Meadows

A true meadow is a field in which the grasses and other plants are allowed to grow in the summer and are then cut to make hay. The plants are cut while still green and then left in the field to dry. In many countries this has been the traditional method of providing feed for cattle during the winter. Hay meadows support a huge range of wild flowers, some of which have become extremely rare as traditional haymaking has been superceded by modern farming methods.

Crop fields

Many fields are used to grow crops other than grass, such as grains or vegetables. In these situations, weed species often find the conditions to their liking and thrive there. Many of these are annual flowers and some – such as cornflowers, *Centaurea cyanus*, or poppies, *Papaver rhoeas*, are colourful additions to the agricultural landscape.

1 Poppy
2 Oxeye daisy
3 Hedge wound wart
4 Buttercup

HEATHS

Heaths are open landscapes that are usually treeless. Their vegetation consists largely of dwarf woody shrubs such as heathers. They are divided into two main types: upland heath (usually called moorland) and lowland heath.

Lowland heath

These habitats are under threat. They are restricted to the British Isles, northern Germany, southern Scandinavia and adjacent, mainly coastal, parts of western Europe, but equivalent vegetation types occur in cooler regions elsewhere in the world.

Lowland heath usually occurs where forest cover has been removed, usually as a result of human action, so to a large extent this is a habitat created by people. However, it can also occur on the drying surfaces of blanket bogs and fenland. In all cases, the soil under heathland is poor, with most of the nutrients having been leached from the topsoil by water. Heathland also occurs near the sea. Coastal heaths are more likely to be the result of natural factors such as the soil type and especially the exposure to high wind, which suppresses tree growth.

Above: Coastal heathlands are often exposed to high winds that cause a stunted growth.

Climate and soil

For lowland heath to occur, the climate must be 'oceanic', with relatively high annual rainfall (60cm–1.1m/24–43in) spread evenly throughout the year. The relative humidity remains moderately high even in the driest months. Winters are rarely very cold and summers rarely get very hot.

The continuous rain seeping into and through the soil promotes leaching (the loss of plant nutrients) and soils are poor as a result. If forest establishes in these areas it does not suffer from this nutrient loss – trees can maintain virtually all their nutrients within the living vegetation. It is possible that slow nutrient loss from a forest ecosystem will eventually lead to a patchwork of forest, scrub and heath. Under normal circumstances, either grazing or fires are necessary to prevent the re-invasion by scrub or colonizer tree species.

Plant adaptations

The term 'heath' is derived from the heather plant, and heathers, *Erica* species, form a major part of the vegetation. Heathlands are mostly species-poor. All the species that are present in a given area ultimately look remarkably similar. In open and often windswept conditions all the species present will possess minute leaves with adaptations such as sunken stomata to minimize water loss through transpiration.

Below: Heathland is often species-rich despite the poor soils.

1 Oak
2 Euphorbia
3 Lavender
4 Juniper
5 Broom
6 Strawberry tree
7 Thyme
8 Rosemary

MOUNTAINS AND MOORLAND

Collectively, mountains and upland areas make up around 20 per cent of the world's landscape, and about 80 per cent of our fresh water originates in them. Upland heath, or moorland, occurs at altitudes above 300m/980ft in most temperate zones but may be found at much higher altitudes in the tropics.

Mountains

All mountain ranges feature rapid changes in altitude, climate, soil, and vegetation over very short distances. The temperature can change from extremely hot to below freezing in a matter of a few hours. Mountain habitats harbour some of the world's most unusual plants, and collectively they are home to a huge range of species. This diversity is due to their range of altitude, which results in distinct belts, or zones, of differing climates, soils and plantlife.

Vegetation on a mountain typically forms belts. This is because as the altitude increases the temperature steadily decreases – by about 2°C per 300m/3.5°F per 980ft. This, coupled with the thinning of the atmosphere, leads to unusually high levels of

ultraviolet light and means that as plants grow higher on the mountainside they need special adaptations to survive. Typically as the altitude increases the plant species become increasingly distinct.

Below: Mountains are often isolated habitats and may contain a unique diversity of species.

Left: Mountain vegetation often forms distinct belts according to the altitude.

Moorland and upland heath

The vegetation in moorland regions is similar in character to that of lowland heath, but it grows on deep layers of peaty or other organic soil. Moorland characteristically occurs below the alpine belt and (usually) above the tree line. It is typically dominated by dwarf shrubs, such as heather, over an understorey of small herbs and mosses.

Natural moorlands (those which are largely unmanaged by people) are generally diverse habitats, containing stands of vegetation at different stages of growth. Animal grazing and burning may be the only factors preventing them from developing into scrub or woodland.

1 Gladiolus
2 Lobelia wollastonii
3 Protea
4 Giant groundsel
5 Saxifrage
6 Umbellifer
7 Mosses

TUNDRA AND ALPINE HABITATS

In the areas nearest the poles, and in the high mountainous places of the world, the conditions for plant growth become extreme. These cold, often frozen, environments present plants with a real challenge that only the hardiest species can withstand.

Cold places

The predominant habitat in the outer polar regions and on mountaintops is known as tundra. Although arctic and alpine (mountain) tundra display differences, they often support plants with similar adaptations.

Tundra is a cold, treeless area, with very low temperatures, little rain or snow, a short growing season, few nutrients and low species diversity. It is the coldest habitat to support plantlife.

Arctic tundra

The frozen, windy, desert-like plains of the arctic tundra are found in the far north of Greenland, Alaska, Canada, Europe and Russia, and also in some sub-Antarctic islands. The long, dry winters of the polar regions feature months of total darkness and extreme cold, with temperatures dipping as low as -51°C/-60°F. The average annual temperature is -12– -6°C/10–20°F.

The annual precipitation is very low, usually amounting to less than 25cm/10in. Most of this falls as snow during the winter and melts at the start of the brief summer growing season. However, a layer of permafrost (frozen subsoil), usually within 1m/39in of the surface, means that there is very little drainage, so bogs and ponds dot the surface and provide moisture for plants. The short growing season, when the sun gains enough strength to melt the ice, lasts for only 50–60 days. Ironically, the surface snow that marks the end of the growing season acts as an insulating blanket, ensuring that the plants do not freeze solid in winter.

The tundra supports communities of sedges and heaths as well as dwarf shrubs. Most of these plants are slow-growing and have a creeping habit, interweaving to form a low springy mass. This adaptation helps to avoid the icy winds and lessen the chances of being eaten by large grazing animals.

Above: Despite their harshness, tundra and alpine regions often support showy species.

Alpine tundra

Above the tree line and below the permanent snow line, alpine tundra is located high in mountains worldwide. In contrast to the arctic tundra, the soil of alpine tundra is very well drained and may become quite dry during the growing season, which lasts for about 180 days. Nighttime temperatures are usually below freezing.

Below: The tundra's short growing season often results in brief but dazzling displays of colour.

1 Cotton grass
2 Arctic poppy
3 Arctic forget-
  me-not
4 Cinquefoil

CLIFFS AND ROCKY SHORES

Rocky coasts and cliffs occur where the underlying rocks are relatively resistant to the constant pounding of the sea, rain and wind. They are found along coasts. Often the landscape is one of grandeur, characterized by steep cliffs, rocky outcrops and small bays with deep, usually clear, offshore waters.

Coastlines

Rocky coasts are often quite exposed and the constant exposure to salt-laden winds, coupled with a shortage of soil in which plant roots can anchor themselves, reduces the range of plants to a few specialist species.

Cliffs

Coastal cliffs, especially those in exposed locations, are often drenched in salt spray as the sea is driven on to the shore. Plants that grow above the spray line, out of reach of the waves and regular salt spray, are likely to be salt-tolerant, whereas those on the beach at the bottom of a cliff, or in rock crevices that are sometimes washed by salt spray, must be tolerant of salt to survive. Plants rarely grow near the base of cliffs that rise directly from the sea because the high wave energy prevents them from establishing.

Above: Many coastal plants, such as thrift, flower profusely despite their small size.

The exposure and lack of soil in all but the deeper rock crevices means that the plants that live on cliffs often face a similar challenge to those found in the higher rocky areas in mountain ranges. This is why they often show similar adaptations, such as deep roots, creeping or hummocky growth habit and the ability to withstand exposure and drought.

The rocky coast may include indentations known as fjords, formed by glaciers wearing away depressions that were subsequently flooded by the rising water following the end of the last ice age, 10,000 years ago. These fjords may have salt marshes at their head and may be surrounded by steep-sided wooded slopes, creating a rich and varied habitat.

Rocky shores

Bedrock outcrops and boulders dominate rocky shores. The lower zones of the rocks are flooded and exposed daily by the tides and support only marine plants, whereas the upper zones are flooded during unusually high tides or in strong storms. In spite of being frequently washed by seawater, salt-tolerant land plants survive here by being well rooted in crevices in the lower-lying rocks.

Below: The high winds of coastal regions mean that plants growing there are often short and ground hugging. Such plants usually have a strong root structure.

1 Sea lavender
2 Thrift
3 Cornish heath
4 Sea aster

BEACHES AND SAND DUNES

Coastlines are often areas of extreme biological diversity. Areas where one habitat meets another always offer an array of flora and fauna, as animals and plants from both habitats merge. Beaches may seem like the exception where plants are concerned, as they often have limited vegetation.

Beaches

Generally, beaches are made up of sand, gravel, cobbles (shingle) and fragments of seashells, corals or other sea creatures. The proportions of all of these vary from beach to beach. Level areas of sand that are exposed only during low tide are called sandflats. Although an amazing variety of animals thrive in this habitat, very few flowering plants survive, mainly because of wave action and the saltiness of seawater. Those that do grow on them usually occur near the high tide line.

Sand dunes

Usually occuring immediately inland from sandy beaches, sand dunes are found in many parts of the world but are less well developed in tropical and subtropical coastal zones, due to lower wind speeds and damper sand. There

Above: The salty conditions and unstable sandy soil can be challenging for plants.

Above: The showy flowerheads of sea holly, Eringium Maritinum, are common on dunes.

are exceptions, however, such as the vast desert dune expanses of the Namib Desert in south-western Africa.

Sand is blown from the beach and initially accumulates in a characteristic steep windward face and more gently sloping leeward face. A change to dune meadow or dune heath eventually happens as grasses establish and stabilize the dune system, usually some

way inland. These dune slacks become dominated by low scrub, which rarely exceeds 90cm/35in in height and is often much smaller. A few larger shrubby species are also capable of invading sand dunes to form scrub and can ultimately revert to woodland.

Below: Sand dunes are mobile, and may shift by several metres per year.

1 Sea rocket
2 Sea holly
3 Sea spurge
4 Sea bindweed
5 Yellow horned
   poppy
6 Burnet rose

RIVERSIDES AND WETLANDS

Wetlands are being lost at an alarming rate and many species that live in them are suffering. The habitats along rivers, waterholes and streams are critical landscapes: they help to maintain water quality and the shape and form of streams, as well as supporting species diversity in surrounding habitats.

Riversides

In their upper reaches, rivers are fast flowing with no vegetation in the water, although bankside vegetation is usually present. In the lower reaches, the water is calmer, and floating leaved and semi-aquatic plants can survive.

Riverside habitats are diverse. Grazed riverside pastures, flood meadows, marshes, reedbeds and riverine forest are common features beside many rivers, although the natural richness of the soil in the river flood plain has led people to cultivate and plant crops right to the edge of the

Below: Rivers are often home to a rich and varied selection of plant and animal life.

water in many regions. Rivers may also be altered, with their curves straightened and banks raised to create flood defences. All these factors mean that truly natural riverside habitats are scarce in areas of human occupation.

Wetlands

Marshes and flood meadows are low-lying wet areas that often flood on a seasonal basis. Reedbeds occur on land that is flooded for most of the year, often at the edges of lakes or in shallow lagoons, and often support a very diverse range of plants. Fens are areas where peat has been deposited over a long period and are often associated with extensive tracts of

Above: Reedbeds are often home to a rich diversity of plant and animal species.

marshes and reedbeds. They may contain large areas of open water and shallow, slow-flowing rivers, and are found on ground that is permanently, seasonally or periodically waterlogged.

1 Coral plant
2 Bromeliads
3 Vriesia
4 Flowering tree
5 Vridia
6 Bromeliad
7 Passion flower
8 Heliconia
9 Orchid
10 Strelitzia
11 Orchid
12 Rosy orchid

ESTUARIES, SWAMPS AND COASTAL MARSHES

Rivers eventually end by flowing out into the sea. As the river slows, the material that it has carried in the water is deposited, and sedimentary deltas, wetlands, lagoons, salt marshes and swamps may be formed.

River mouth habitats are usually extremely diverse and include abundant and rare species.

Deltas

A delta is formed where a river flows into a calm sea. As the river slows down it drops its sediment, which builds up over years to create a delta. Over time, the river splits into smaller channels called distributaries. Occasionally this can happen inland where a river flows into a low-lying basin. It forms an immense low-lying wetland, such as that of the Okavango Delta in Botswana, Africa.

Below: Tropical and sub-tropical marshlands are home to many beautiful plant species.

Above: Saltwater marshes are among the most productive habitats on earth.

Marshes and swamps

Salt marshes are made up of plant communities that are tolerant of being submerged for short periods by the tide. They can be 'transitional zones', which merge with nearby areas of reed swamp, sand dune, shingle, freshwater wetland or woodland, and are particularly rich in a wide variety of plants. They are often brackish (less salty than the sea but saltier than the river) and may contain a mixture of riverside and coastal vegetation types. The term 'swamp' is usually applied to warm, wet areas that are teeming with both animal and plant life. They are often (but by no means always) heavily forested, with trees that are highly adapted to waterlogged ground. Some of these areas may be very extensive and include both coastal and freshwater habitats, such as are found in the Florida Everglades.

Mangroves are marine tidal forests that are generally most luxuriant around the mouths of large rivers or sheltered bays, growing in both salt and freshwater. They are found in the tropics where annual rainfall is high.

1 Bald cypress
2 Floating hearts
3 Scarlet ladies tresses
4 *Thalia dealbata*
5 Sawgrass
6 Palmetto
7 Water spider orchid
8 Ghost flower orchid
9 Night fragrance orchid
10 Golden club
11 Water lettuce

OPEN WATER

Flowering plants face possibly their biggest challenge in open water. Plants living in this environment must be able to survive either submerged beneath or floating on the surface of a body of water, and all are specially adapted to allow them to do this.

Obtaining sufficient oxygen is the greatest problem facing plants that live in water. The muddy sediment at the water bottom has few air spaces, and therefore barely any oxygen present.

Lakes and ponds

A lake describes any large body of fresh water, ranging from small ponds to huge bodies of water. They can be an extremely variable habitat, ranging from almost lifeless, acidic mountain tarns to lowland lakes teeming with life. Lakes are closely associated with rivers, chiefly because some lakes are the source for rivers. Both are fresh

Below: Although certain plant species have evolved to live in the water, the richest diversity occurs where land and water meet.

Above: Open water is a challenging habitat for plants to survive in.

water and share similar characteristics, and many species are common to both habitats.

A pond is a body of water shallow enough to support rooted plants, which in time may grow all the way across it.

Slow-flowing rivers and streams

When rivers flow slowly they may support aquatic plants in a similar way to lakes. Plants that grow in slow-flowing rivers will be species that are able to root into the bottom sediment, to stop them being washed away.

As the river runs more slowly it warms up, favouring plant growth, though in areas where the banks are tree-lined this can reduce plant growth in the water. Some river plants are only semi-aquatic, growing out of the water on the bank when the stream dries up, before being re-flooded during rainy seasons.

1 Great willow herb
2 Flowering rush
3 Branched bur weed
4 Water crowfoot
5 White water lilies
6 Reed sweet grass
7 Yellow flag iris
8 Marsh marigold
9 Hemlock water
   dropwort
10 Marsh thistle
11 Bullrush

WILD FLOWERS OF THE WORLD

Learning to identify wild flowers can be a fascinating pastime. It is something that you can do practically anywhere and is a vital first step in helping you to understand more about the natural habitats in an area. Every flowering plant has specific characteristics that you can learn to recognize. It is simply a matter of practice and once the basics are learnt you can quickly become hooked.

It would be impossible to include every flowering plant in a single book of any size: more than 245,000 species of flowering plants are 'known' to science, and many of these are rare or inconspicuous. The plants included here are arranged first according to the region of the world in which they appear – Eurasia and Africa, the Americas, and Australasia and Oceania. Next, they are arranged according to plant family, so that all genera that have characteristics in common can be compared to each other. Plenty of the most common flowering plants from around the world are included in each region. Each of the represented species is accompanied by a description to help you identify the plant and better understand how and where it lives. As well as the common species, others have been included which, although they are less abundant, show some of the fascinating traits that have led to flowering plants becoming the most successful and diverse group of plants that have ever lived on Earth.

Left: Cyclamen are hardy plants with attractive leaves that are visible for much of the year in northern Europe. The flowers appear en masse from late winter into spring.

HOW TO USE THE DIRECTORY

The directory of flowers that follows the introduction includes a diverse selection of the most beautiful wild flowers. The information below shows you how to use the directory.

The plant kingdom can be divided into two major groups: flowering plants that produce seeds (known as 'higher plants') and those that do not flower, but instead produce spores (sometimes called 'lower plants'). The latter group includes the mosses, liverworts, ferns and their allies. Though many of these plants are important components of habitats worldwide, it has not been possible to feature this latter group here. Among the flowering plants, the gymnosperms (conifers and cycads) have been omitted. The choice made for this book concentrates on the

showy specimens that may be encountered in the wild, but also aims to illustrate the tremendous diversity of flower forms in the world.

The plants featured fall into two groups – the dicotyledonous plants are the large group, so-named because their seed has two distinct cotyledons, or embryonic leaves. The second group, the monocotyledons, contains plants that have only one seed leaf. The two groups differ evolutionarily, but both contain stunning examples of wild flower diversity.

Organizing the directory

The flowers are arranged according to their families, then genus and then species. Each family features four main plants, and up to four other flowers of note contained within a tinted box.

The introduction to each family describes common characteristics.

Each main entry discusses the primary characteristics of the plant. Wherever possible, this includes some helpful information about the type of habitat that the plant may be found in and may include other interesting facts about the species, how it interacts with wildlife and how people have used or exploited it over time. Any technical terms used in this description are supported by the glossary at the back of the book. It is followed by a detailed description to aid identification together with an accurate watercolour. A tinted box on the page describes other wild flowers of interest within the same family. Coloured maps show, at a glance, the natural distribution of the wild flowers.

Plant Family

Each wild flower belongs to a plant family. The directory of flowers is mostly arranged according to family. Each family shares a group of common characteristics, though visually the plants may seem quite different.

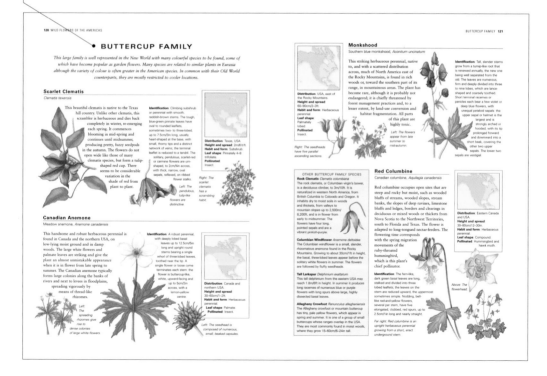

Other Common Name(s)
Some wild flowers have different common names in other regions and countries. These are listed underneath the primary common name.

Common Name
This is the most popular, non-scientific name for the wild flower entry.

Botanical Name
This is the internationally accepted botanical name for the wild flower entry. It is always in Latin.

Introduction
This provides a general introduction to the wild flower and may include information on usage, preferred conditions, and other information of general interest.

Identification
This description will enable the reader to properly identify the wild flower. It gives information on flower and leaf shape, size, colour and arrangement, and type of flower.

Canadian Anemone
Meadow anemone, *Anemone canadensis*

This handsome and robust herbaceous perennial is found in Canada and the northern USA, on low-lying moist ground and in damp woods. The large white flowers and palmate leaves are striking and give the plant an almost unmistakable appearance when it is in flower from late spring to summer. The Canadian anemone typically forms large colonies along the banks of rivers and next to levees in floodplains, spreading vigorously by means of thread-like rhizomes.

Left: The spreading rhizomes give rise to dense colonies of large white flowers.

Identification: A robust perennial, with deeply lobed basal leaves up to 12.5cm/5in long and upright round stems bearing a single whorl of three-lobed leaves, toothed near the tip. A single flower or loose cyme terminates each stem: the flower is buttercup-like, white, upward-facing and up to 5cm/2in across, with a lemon-yellow centre.

Distribution: Canada and northern USA.
Height and spread: 30–60cm/1–2ft.
Habit and form: Herbaceous perennial.
Leaf shape: Palmate.
Pollinated: Insect.

Left: The seedhead is composed of numerous, small, beaked capsules.

Habit
The habit is the way in which a plant grows. For example, it could have an upright, sprawling or rambling habit.

Profile
The profile is a botanically accurate illustration of the plant at its time of flowering.

Plant Detail
A small detail shows an important identifying feature of the plant.

Distribution: Canada and northern USA.
Height and spread: 30–60cm/12–24in.
Habit and form: Herbaceous perennial.
Leaf shape: Palmate.
Pollinated: Insect.

Map
The map shows the area of natural distribution of the featured plant. The relevant area is shaded in yellow. The natural distribution shows where in the world the plant originated. It does not mean that this is the only place where the plant now grows.

Distribution
This describes the plant's natural distribution throughout the world.

Height and spread
Describes the average dimensions the plant will grow to given optimal growing conditions.

Habit and form
Describes the plant type and shape.

Leaf shape
Describes the shape of the leaf.

Pollinated
Flora can be pollinated by many different animals and insects, as well as by the action of air.

Other family species of note
The flora featured in this tinted box are usually less well-known species of the family. They are included because they have some outstanding features worthy of note.

Species names
The name by which the plant is most commonly known is presented first, followed by the Latin name and any other common name by which the plant is known.

Entries
The information given for each entry describes the plant's main characteristics and the specific features it has that distinguish it from better known species.

OTHER BUTTERCUP FAMILY SPECIES
Rock Clematis *Clematis columbiana*
The rock clematis, or Columbian virgin's bower, is a deciduous climber, to 3m/10ft. It is naturalized in western North America, from British Columbia to Colorado and Oregon. It inhabits dry to moist soils in woods and thickets, from valleys to mountain slopes up to 2,500m/8,200ft, and is in flower from early to midsummer. The flowers have four long, pointed sepals and are a vibrant pinkish-purple.

Columbian Windflower *Anemone deltoidea*
The Columbian windflower is a small, slender, rhizomatous anemone found in the Rocky Mountains. Growing to about 30cm/1ft in height, the basal, three-lobed leaves appear before the solitary white flowers in summer. The flowers are followed by fluffy seedheads.

Tall Larkspur *Delphinium exaltatum*
This tall delphinium from the eastern USA may reach 1.8m/6ft in height. In summer it produces long racemes of numerous blue or purple flowers with long spurs above large, highly dissected basal leaves.

Allegheny Crowfoot *Ranunculus allegheniensis*
The Allegheny crowfoot or mountain buttercup has tiny, pale yellow flowers, which appear in spring and summer. It is one of a group of small buttercups whose ranges overlap in the USA. They are most commonly found in moist woods, where they grow 15–60cm/6–24in tall.

WILD FLOWERS OF EURASIA AND AFRICA

Europe, Africa and Asia, are collectively described as the 'Old World', to differentiate this region from the 'New World' – the name that was given to the newly discovered Americas. The botanical diversity of the Old World regions is huge, with some of the best-known and most spectacular flowers gracing their lands. Even so, vast tracts of the continents of Europe, Asia and Africa remain largely unexplored, and botanists still have much to discover about the plants that live in those areas. However, these continents are home to around two-thirds of the world's human population and the consequent pressure on natural habitats increases almost daily.

Above from left: Wild carrot (Daucus carrota), greater masterwort (Astrantia major) and snowdrops (Galanthus nivalis).

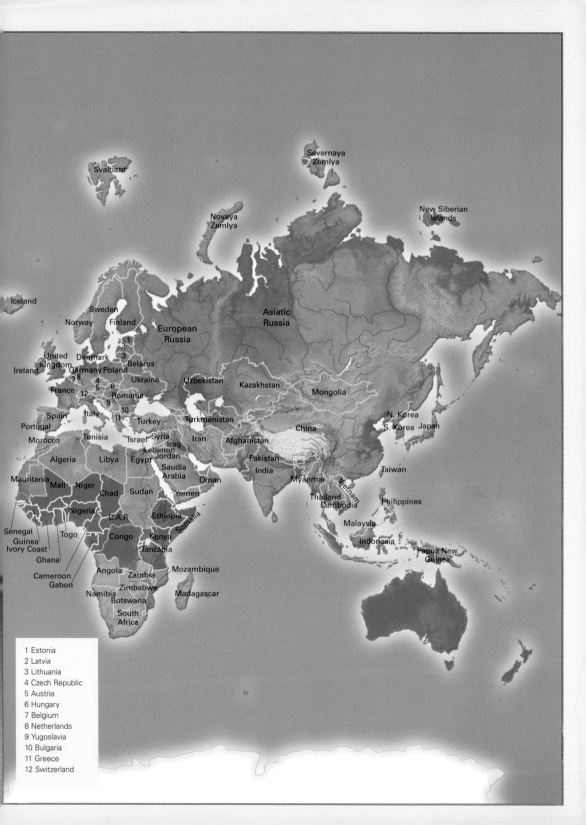

Svalbard

Severnaya
Zemlya

New Siberian
Islands

Novaya
Zemlya

Iceland

Sweden

Norway   Finland

European
Russia

Asiatic
Russia

United
Kingdom   Denmark
Ireland   Germany Poland
                1
                2
                3
            Belarus
France   7 8
         4
    12   5   6
             Romania
             9
Spain   Italy   10
              11
Portugal   Turkey
Morocco   Tunisia   Syria
                    Israel Lebanon
                         Iraq
Algeria   Libya   Egypt   Jordan

Ukraine

Uzbekistan   Kazakhstan   Mongolia

Turkmenistan

Iran

Afghanistan

China

N. Korea
S. Korea Japan

Taiwan

Mauritania   Mali   Niger   Chad
                  Saudia
                  Arabia   Oman
                         Sudan   Yemen
Nigeria
        C.A.R   Ethiopia
Senegal
Guinea   Kenya
Ivory Coast   Togo   Congo
Ghana   Tanzania

Pakistan
India

Myanmar
Thailand   Vietnam
Cambodia

Philippines

Malaysia
Indonesia
                  Papua New
                  Guinea

Somalia

Cameroon   Angola   Zambia   Mozambique
Gabon   Zimbabwe
        Namibia   Madagascar
        Botswana
        South
        Africa

1 Estonia
2 Latvia
3 Lithuania
4 Czech Republic
5 Austria
6 Hungary
7 Belgium
8 Netherlands
9 Yugoslavia
10 Bulgaria
11 Greece
12 Switzerland

BUTTERCUP FAMILY

There are around 1,800 species in the buttercup family, Ranunculaceae, and they are found mainly in the colder regions of the world. Many are well-known wild flowers, while some are more familiar as garden flowers. The group includes buttercups, anemones, delphiniums, aquilegias and clematis. Some genera are poisonous. Nearly all the buttercup family are herbaceous – clematis is the only woody genus.

Columbine

Culverwort, Granny's bonnet, *Aquilegia vulgaris*

A familiar plant because it is often seen as a garden escapee, columbine typically grows in light and medium soils and always prefers a moist situation. It is highly adaptable and can grow in full sun, the dappled shade of light woodland or in semi-shade.

Identification: A variable plant with stems branched in the upper parts to support numerous nodding, scented flowers, 25–40mm/1–1½in, usually blue, with spreading sepals, behind which are very short, strongly hooked spurs. It is in flower from mid-spring to midsummer. The leaves are mainly basal, dark green flushed blue, and much divided.

Far left: The distinctive flowerheads are held high above the mainly basal foliage.

Right: The seedhead splits at the top to disperse seeds when rocked by breezes.

Far right: Aquilegia self seeds and spreads quickly. It has a rangy habit.

Distribution: Europe.
Height and spread: 30–70 x 50cm/12–27½ x 20in.
Habit and form: Herbaceous perennial.
Leaf shape: Compound trifoliate.
Pollinated: Bee, particularly bumblebee.

Meadow buttercup

Tall crowfoot, *Ranunculus acris*

The golden-yellow spring flowers of the European buttercup are a common sight across its natural range, but it is also widely naturalized in eastern North America, through agricultural importation. It is common in damp grassland, on roadsides and in high pastures. Unlike the equally common creeping buttercup, *R. repens*, the meadow buttercup reproduces solely by seed rather than by runners (spreading overground stems that root at the leaf joints as they touch the ground) and so forms clumps.

Identification: A tall erect herb with smooth or slightly hairy flower stalks that are held high above the foliage. The lower leaves are strongly divided into three to seven lobes. They are toothed, hairy and occasionally marked with black, with none of the lobes stalked. The showy yellow flowers are to 20mm/¾in across, with five rounded, glossy petals, which are produced in great profusion from late spring to early autumn. The sepals are pressed flat against the flower, not downturned. The fruits are rounded, with short, hooked beaks.

Above left: The small distinctive spiky round fruits swell as soon as the petals drop.

Left: The foliage is mostly basal. The flowerheads are held above this on stout, sparsely leaved stems.

Right: The distinctive sunshine-yellow flowers of the buttercup are held aloft singly, on long thin stems.

Distribution: Europe; Asia.
Height and spread: 30–90cm/12–35in.
Habit and form: Herbaceous perennial.
Leaf shape: Palmate.
Pollinated: Insect.

Lenten rose

Hellebore, *Helleborus orientalis*

Distribution: Eastern Europe to western Asia.
Height and spread: 45cm/18in.
Habit and form: Evergreen perennial.
Leaf shape: Palmate.
Pollinated: Insect.

This highly variable plant grows in shade or semi-shade in deciduous woodland on lower mountain slopes. There is much uncertainty as to the number of subspecies. The fact that it is such a beautiful and reliable flower of winter and early spring has resulted in its widespread cultivation, with many cultivars and hybrids being grown in gardens. As a result, it commonly occurs as a garden escapee, often way beyond its original natural distribution.

Identification: Smooth or slightly hairy stems rise from a stout rhizome. The large, leathery, evergreen leaves are mainly basal, divided into seven or nine lance-shaped segments with highly serrated edges and purple stalks. The branched flower stalks bear one to four nodding or outward-facing, saucer-shaped, unscented flowers, each 60–70mm/2¼–2¾in across. The overlapping petals are cream tinged green flushed with purple, gradually changing to green following fertilization, with green nectaries and wide, funnel-shaped green anthers. The nodding, saucer-shaped blooms appear from late winter onward, before the new foliage.

Left: The flowerheads droop.

Above: Lenten roses flower in winter.

OTHER SPECIES OF NOTE

Pheasant's eye *Adonis annua*
This annual, also known as the flower of Adonis, grows to a height and spread of 15–30cm/6–12in. It forms clumps of green, fern-like foliage topped with deep red, anemone-like flowers in summer, chiefly on cultivated land.

Winter aconite *Eranthis hyemalis*
This clump-forming tuberous perennial from central Europe may form quite large colonies. In late winter or early spring it produces bright yellow flowers 20–30mm/¾–1¼in across, each borne above a ruff of dissected, bright green leaves.

Monkshood
Aconitum napellus

Monkshood is a variable, erect perennial, common across much of northern and central Europe. In mid- to late summer the tall, erect flowering stems bear dense racemes of indigo-blue flowers, held above the rounded, deeply lobed, dark green leaves.

Pasque flower *Pulsatilla vulgaris*
This clump-forming perennial is found chiefly on free-draining chalky or alkaline soils across much of Europe. The finely divided, feathery, light green leaves are very hairy when young and are topped in spring with upright or semi-pendent, silky, purple flowers.

Delphinium

Larkspur, *Delphinium elatum*

Delphiniums were so named by the ancient Greeks, who thought the shape of the flower bud resembled a dolphin. The flowers appear from early to late summer, and are mostly blue, occasionally pinkish or whitish, arranged loosely around almost the entire length of the flower spike, on robust upright stems. In Tudor England, some species in cultivation were called larkspur because the nectary looked similar to a lark's claw. The plant is encountered on roadsides and in fields, usually as a garden escapee.

Identification: The large rounded leaves are fairly deeply divided into five to seven or more coarsely toothed lobes. Each flower is 25–40mm/1–1½in long and up to 25mm/1in wide, with golden filaments in the centre and five petal-like sepals, the rear one elongated into a long, slender, curving spur; the two upper petals are united. The fruits are erect, smooth pods tipped with short beaks, open on one side.

Far right: The flower spikes are impressive, held above the foliage.

Distribution: Central and eastern Europe.
Height and spread: 90cm–1.2m x 30–60cm/35in–4ft x 12–24in.
Habit and form: Herbaceous perennial.
Leaf shape: Palmate, lobed.
Pollinated: Chiefly bee.

Below: Delphinium flower spikes are made of many florets.

Stinking hellebore

Helleborus foetidus

Stinking hellebore is a sombre, poisonous green plant found in lime-rich woodland and scrub. It sometimes occurs as a garden escapee. The flowers are green, edged with purple and appear from January to April. The leafy stems persist over the winter. The name comes from its odd, unpleasant smell.

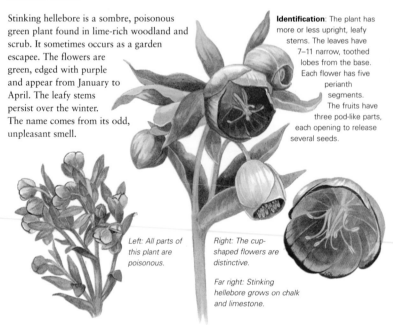

Identification: The plant has more or less upright, leafy stems. The leaves have 7–11 narrow, toothed lobes from the base. Each flower has five perianth segments. The fruits have three pod-like parts, each opening to release several seeds.

Distribution: South-western and western Europe, north to Great Britain and Germany.
Height and spread: 20–80cm/8–31in.
Habit and form: Herbaceous perennial.
Leaf shape: Narrow-lobed.
Pollinated: Bee.

Left: All parts of this plant are poisonous.

Right: The cup-shaped flowers are distinctive.

Far right: Stinking hellebore grows on chalk and limestone.

Green hellebore

Helleborus viridis

Thriving in woodland and scrub and rocky areas on lime-rich damp soil, green hellebore is much smaller than stinking hellebore. It has yellowish-green flowers appearing from February to April. This poisonous plant dies back to an underground stem in winter.

Distribution: Western and central Europe, extending east to Italy and Austria.
Height and spread: 10–15cm/4–6in.
Habit and form: Herbaceous perennial.
Leaf shape: Finely divided.
Pollinated: Bee.

Identification: Green hellebore usually has two basal leaves, each with 7–13 radiating toothed lobes. The bowl-shaped flowers grow in clusters of two to four and have oval perianth segments and numerous stamens. The fruit has three to eight pod-like parts, joined at the base, containing several seeds.

Far left: The stamens spread out from the centre of the flower.

Right: The flowers droop slightly and the leaves are toothed.

Love-in-a-mist

Nigella damascena

Love-in-a-mist is a delicate, blue-flowered annual from southern Europe. However, it is naturalized widely in cultivated fields and wasteland, flowering in August and September. It is a popular garden flower and is also sold by florists.

Identification: The short-stalked pale blue flowers are 20–30mm/¾–1¼in across with a ring of small, finely divided leaves beneath. There are normally five perianth segments and numerous blue stamens. The smooth, swollen, globular fruit contains many seeds.

Distribution: Southern Europe; western Asia.
Height and spread: 10–15cm/4–6in.
Habit and form: Annual.
Leaf shape: Finely divided.
Pollinated: Insect.

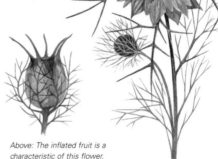

Right: Once established, the delicate flowers show well in a garden border.

Above: The inflated fruit is a characteristic of this flower.

OTHER SPECIES OF NOTE

Wolf's bane *Aconitum vulparia*
A tall, poisonous perennial with dark green, finely divided leaves and small, yellowish flowers. It is found in dry grassland and rocks up to 800m/2,600ft in France and the Netherlands and as far east as Russia and Poland.

Yellow anemone
Anemone ranunculoides
Similar to the wood anemone but with yellow flowers, yellow anemone flowers from March to May. It appears in woodland areas over most of Europe but rarely in the Mediterranean region. It has only one basal leaf.

Traveller's joy
Clematis vitalba
A vigorous climbing plant found in lime-rich woodlands, hedges and scrub throughout southern, western and central Europe. Traveller's joy can grow up to 30m/98ft, often covering large trees. It bears fragrant flowers from July to September and has feathery fruits.

Yellow pheasant's eye *Adonis vernalis*
This is a grassland perennial with divided leaves and large flowers with up to 20 petals. It flowers during April and May over eastern, central and southern Europe and as far north as Sweden.

Globeflower

Trollius europaeus

Globeflower is a long-stalked plant with globular, lemon-yellow flowers appearing from May to August. The flowers never open wide, but retain their globe-like shape. It grows in wet grassy areas, in woods and also around damp rocks, as well as in alpine pastures. Another popular garden plant, including a variety with orange flowers. Like many members of the family, it is poisonous.

Identification: A tall, hairless perennial with three-to-five-lobed basal leaves and more or less stalkless divided stem leaves. The flowers, with ten curved perianth segments, are each up to 50mm/2in across. The fruit is a cluster of wrinkled follicles.

Right: The flower is tightly packed and rounded in shape.

Distribution: The mountains of southern Europe.
Height and spread: Up to 70cm/27½in.
Habit and form: Herbaceous perennial.
Leaf shape: Divided.
Pollinated: Insect.

Below: The flowers grow aloft on tall stems.

Blue anemone

Anemone apennina

Growing widely in open woodland and scrubby areas, blue anemone is similar to wood anemone but has a downy-hairy underside to the leaves and blue, or (more rarely) white flowers appearing in March and April. It also grows naturalized locally in western Europe.

Below: The open, colourful flower is attractive to insects.

Above: These fleeting, woodland flowers will grow in shady parts of the garden.

Distribution: Southern Europe.
Height and spread: Up to 15cm/6in.
Habit and form: Creeping perennial.
Leaf shape: Palmate.
Pollinated: Insect.

Identification: The flowers are 25–35mm/1–1⅜in across with 8–14 perianth segments. The leaves are borne near the middle of the stem.

Right: This is a pretty flower of the woodland floor.

Forking larkspur

Consolida regalis

Forking larkspur is a downy plant found in arable fields, waste and disturbed land and waysides. From May to July it bears attractive violet to blue flowers, each with a backwardly-projecting spur. Larkspurs are often grown in gardens.

Identification: A medium, downy, widely branching plant with linear, lobed leaves. The flower is violet-blue to dark blue, 20–28mm/¾–1⅛in, with a 12–25mm/½–1in spur. The flowers are clustered in loosely branching panicles.

Right: The flowers carry a long, curving spur.

Far right: Larkspurs are often grown in garden borders.

Distribution: Mediterranean region; Central Asia.
Height and spread: Up to 1m/39in.
Habit and form: Annual.
Leaf shape: Very narrowly-lobed.
Pollinated: Insect.

Above left: All parts of forking larkspurs are poisonous.

Marsh marigold

Kingcup, *Caltha palustris*

Distribution: Europe, but rare in the Mediterranean region.
Height and spread: Up to 60cm/24in.
Habit and form: Creeping perennial.
Leaf shape: Heart-shaped.
Pollinated: Insect.

With its creeping habit, heart-shaped leaves and glossy yellow flowers, marsh marigold is an attractive wild flower. It thrives in wet places such as fenland, stream sides and damp woods, from lowlands to mountaintops, and flowers from March to August. It often forms clumps along the banks of streams. The unopened buds were once used instead of capers.

Left: This flower often grows in clumps.

Identification: A hairless perennial with hollow stems and long-stalked, dark green basal leaves. The stem leaves have shorter stalks and are smaller. The flowers are glossy yellow and are 12–50mm/½–2in across.

Below: The bright flowers liven up streamsides.

OTHER SPECIES OF NOTE

Creeping buttercup
Ranunculus repens
Found in damp areas throughout most of Europe, creeping buttercup is similar to bulbous buttercup, *R. bulbosus*, but lacks a bulb, having long, creeping runners instead. The flowers, with sepals not bent back, appear from May to September.

Goldilocks buttercup *Ranunculus auricomus*
Found in woods and hedges over most of Europe, goldilocks buttercup is a short, slightly hairy perennial with few yellow flowers, often with distorted petals of differing sizes.

Rocket larkspur *Consolida ambigua*
A medium-size stickily-hairy annual with branched stems, narrowly-lobed leaves and deep blue flowers with 12–18mm/½–¹¹⁄₁₆in spurs. Rocket larkspur inhabits arable fields and other cultivated ground, wasteland and waysides in Portugal, Spain, Greece and Turkey.

Field nigella *Nigella arvensis*
Distributed over much of Europe, except for the north, field nigella is an annual with finely divided leaves, pale blue, sometimes green-veined flowers, and fruits with five pod-like segments. It grows in cornfields and disturbed ground, flowering in June and July.

Wood anemone

Anemone nemorosa

Wood anemone is common in woodland and alpine meadows. The plant has a creeping habit and its pretty white flowers, which usually have pinkish or purple backs to the petals, appear from March to May. These flowers often occur in large numbers, carpeting the woodland floor before the trees are in leaf.

Distribution: Europe, but rare in the Mediterranean region.
Height and spread: Up to 30cm/12in.
Habit and form: Creeping perennial.
Leaf shape: Palmate, lobed.
Pollinated: Insect.

Identification: The plant is hairless and has upright flowering stems with a whorl of three leaves two-thirds up the stem. The large basal leaves appear after the flowers. The leaves are palmate, with toothed lobes.

Left and far right: Single flowers are up to 40mm/1½in across.

Variegated monkshood

Aconitum variegatum

A shrub of mainly meadows, woods and clearings, variegated monkshood is a medium tall plant. It produces a cluster of blue, helmeted flowers streaked with white, from July to September. The flower structure is specifically adapted for pollination by bees. Aconites are grown as garden flowers, but are poisonous.

Below: The flowers are highly distinctive.

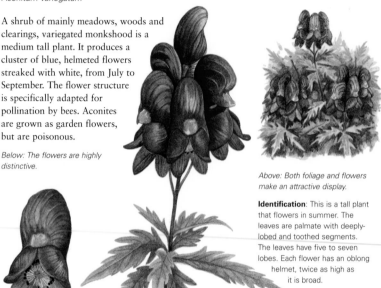

Above: Both foliage and flowers make an attractive display.

Distribution: Austria; Switzerland; southern Germany; Spain; southern and eastern France; Hungary; Italy; Poland.
Height and spread: Up to 1m/39in.
Habit and form: Herbaceous perennial.
Leaf shape: Palmate, deeply-lobed.
Pollinated: Bee.

Identification: This is a tall plant that flowers in summer. The leaves are palmate with deeply-lobed and toothed segments. The leaves have five to seven lobes. Each flower has an oblong helmet, twice as high as it is broad.

Right: Heavily hooded flowers give this species its common name.

Liverleaf

Hepatica nobilis

Liverleaf is a distinctive plant with evergreen leaves that are purplish on the underside. The pretty flowers, which can be blue-violet, purple, pink or white, appear in March and April. Liverleaf grows in lime-rich wooded and scrubby areas, and in mountains up to about 2,200m/7,200ft. Often grown in gardens, sometimes in a form with double flowers.

Identification: Flowers are solitary and 12–25mm/½–1in across. There are three sepal-like bracts below the six to nine perianth segments. The leaves are heart-shaped at the base and have three obvious lobes.

Right: The flower is star shaped.

Distribution: Europe, except the far north and south.
Height and spread: Up to 15cm/6in.
Habit and form: Perennial.
Leaf shape: Lobed.
Pollinated: Insect.

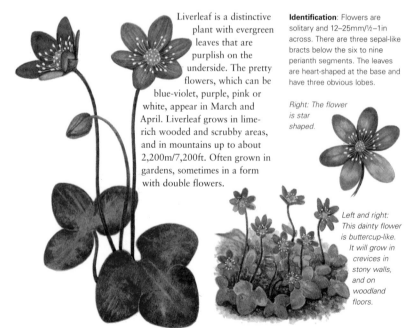

Left and right: This dainty flower is buttercup-like. It will grow in crevices in stony walls, and on woodland floors.

Alpine clematis

Clematis alpina

A scrambling, woody climber with twining stems and flower stalks, alpine clematis is found in wooded mountain areas and also on screes and scrub. It has delicate, pretty blue, violet or white flowers and feathery-tipped fruits.

Identification: The leaves are divided into three segments, each with three, toothed leaflets. The flowers are usually solitary and nodding, with four perianth segments. The fruits are tipped with a long-plumed style.

Left: The pretty flowers droop.

Distribution: Central Europe and southern mountain regions.
Height and spread: Up to 2m/6½ft.
Habit and form: Scrambling, herbaceous perennial.
Leaf shape: Divided.
Pollinated: Insect.

Left: The developing fruit looks like a bud.

Bulbous buttercup

Ranunculus bulbosus

Bulbous buttercup is a common downy-hairy plant found on dry, usually lime-rich soils, often in hay meadows and also as a 'weed' in gardens. The plant has divided leaves and bright yellow flowers from March to June. It takes its name from the bulbous base of its stem. Insects visit the bright flowers to seek the nectar secreted from the base of the petals.

Identification: The lower leaves are divided into three leaflets, the central one long-stalked. Each leaflet is further divided. The flowers are 20–30mm/¾–1¼in across with five sepals bent back. The stems are hairy and furrowed.

Distribution: Europe, except parts of the east.
Height and spread: Up to 50cm/20in.
Habit and form: Herbaceous perennial.
Leaf shape: Divided.
Pollinated: Insect.

Above: This flower is often found growing in weedy lawns and at roadsides in tufts.

Far left: This flower has distinct reflexed sepals.

ROSE FAMILY

The rose family, Rosaceae, includes trees, shrubs and herbs, and comprises about 100 genera and 3,000 species. Most members of the family have similar flowers, commonly with five petals and numerous stamens, but their fruiting arrangements vary considerably. The rose family includes some of our best-known wild flowers and has many showy flower species in its ranks.

Sweet briar

Eglantine, Rosa rubiginosa

This rose is noted for its flowers and also for the unique aroma of its leaves, which are particularly fragrant after rain. Strangely, while the leaves are so fragrant, the flowers are almost entirely without scent. It is most commonly found in open copses and old hedgerows, usually on limy soils, and will sometimes colonize chalk grassland. Because of its apple-scented foliage the sweet briar has held a cherished place in many old-fashioned gardens.

Left: Sweet briar forms an open, spreading shrub on chalky soils.

Right: Each bloom lasts a few days. New ones replace them over a period of weeks.

Identification: The sweet briar is a vigorous, arching, prickly-stemmed, deciduous shrub. The leaves are dark green, with five to nine oval leaflets 25–40mm/1–1½in long, with a finely-toothed margin. Cupped, single flowers up to 25mm/1in across, usually bright pink, appear in early to midsummer, and are followed by oval to spherical, orange-scarlet hips in late summer.

Distribution: Europe; northern Africa to western Asia.
Height and spread: 2.5m/8ft.
Habit and form: Deciduous shrub.
Leaf shape: Pinnate.
Pollinated: Bee, fly, moth and butterfly.

Right: The bright red hips often last well into the winter.

Japanese quince

Chaenomeles speciosa

The Japanese quince is noteworthy for the fact that it commences its flowering before the leaves emerge and can be in flower in late winter. It should not be confused with the related genus *Cydonia*, which is the source of the cultivated quince fruit. The plant tolerates a wide range of soils, although it prospers best in moist, well-drained soil.

Left: Japanese quince forms a loose sprawling shrub.

Identification: A vigorous, deciduous, spreading shrub with tangled, spiny branches and oval, glossy, dark green leaves 40–90mm/1½–3½in long. In spring the branches bear clusters of two to four scarlet to crimson, five-petalled, cupped flowers, up to 45mm/1¾in across. The flowers are borne on bare stems and may continue well into the spring, after the foliage has emerged, followed by aromatic, green-yellow fruit.

Distribution: Eastern Asia, including China.
Height and spread: 3 x 5m/10 x 16ft.
Habit and form: Deciduous shrub.
Leaf shape: Ovate.
Pollinated: Bee.

Left: Despite the name, this quince does not yield sweet fruit like the cultivated form of Cydonia oblongata.

Distribution: Europe.
Height and spread: 3m/10ft.
Habit and form: Deciduous shrub.
Leaf shape: Variable, palmate lobed or pinnate.
Pollinated: Insect; can self-pollinate.

Blackberry

Bramble, *Rubus fruticosa*

An extremely common plant, the fast-growing bramble is found in hedgerows, woodland, meadows and on waste ground. Its blossoms and fruits (both green and ripe) may be seen on the bush at the same time, which is an unusual feature. Blackberries have a tremendous range of site and soil tolerances and can grow in full shade (deep woodland), semi-shade (light woodland), or in sun. They can tolerate drought and strong winds but not maritime exposure.
Opinions differ as to whether there is one true blackberry with many aberrant forms, or many distinct types.

Identification: The leaves are borne on long, arching, tip-rooting stems. Brambles often form dense, impenetrable thickets along hedgerows or woodland margins. All blackberries have five-petalled, saucer-shaped, pink or white flowers, which appear in great profusion between late spring and early autumn, followed by tight clusters of black, spherical fruits.

Above: The stems carry thorns.

Far left: The blackberry forms an untidy, layered and spreading thicket.

Left: The berries ripen from midsummer onwards.

OTHER SPECIES OF NOTE

Dog rose *Rosa canina*
The dog rose flowers in early summer. Its general habit can be quite variable. The single flowers vary widely from almost white to a very deep pink, with a delicate but refreshing fragrance. The hips are produced in autumn.

Shrubby cinquefoil *Potentilla fruticosa*
This deciduous shrub, with a height and spread of about 1.2m/4ft, is in flower from early to midsummer. The yellow flowers are dioecious and are pollinated by bees and flies.

Scarlet geum *Geum coccineum* 'Borsii'
The moisture-loving scarlet avens originates in the Balkans and northern Turkey. A compact, clump-forming plant, it is noteworthy for its display of beautiful orange-scarlet flowers with prominent yellow stamens, on 30cm/12in stems, in late spring to late summer.

Mountain avens *Dryas octopetala*
The small mountain avens is distinguished from all other plants of the Rosaceae by its oblong, deeply cut leaves, which have white downy undersides, and by its large, handsome, anemone-like white flowers, which have eight petals. It blooms in midsummer.

Dropwort

Filipendula vulgaris

This tall, scented, vigorous perennial of dry soils is easily confused with meadowsweet, *F. ulmaris*, which prefers damp or seasonally waterlogged grassland. Dropwort prefers alkaline soil and cannot grow in the shade; for this reason it can sometimes be found growing at the base of an old wall. The plant is especially noted for attracting wildlife.

Identification: The abundant, fern-like dark green leaves are finely divided, toothed and hairless, with eight or more leaflets, each about 20mm/¾in long. In early and midsummer, slender, branching stems bear loose clusters, to 15cm/6in across, of white, sweetly scented, often red-tinged flowers. The seeds ripen from midsummer to early autumn.

Distribution: Northern Eurasia.
Height and spread: 75 x 40cm/29½ x 16in.
Habit and form: Herbaceous perennial.
Leaf shape: Pinnate.
Pollinated: Insect; can self-pollinate.

Below: Dropwort forms a tall and attractive clump of flowering stems above the fern-like foliage.

Above: Each flower gives rise to tiny fruits from midsummer onward.

Above right: The flower-heads are sweetly scented and noted for attracting wildlife.

Meadowsweet

Queen of the meadow, Bridewort, *Filipendula ulmaria*

Living up to its charming traditional English name, meadowsweet bears pretty, very sweetly-scented cream-coloured flowers from June to September. A tall, leafy-stemmed plant with pinnate leaves, it prefers damp grassland areas. The flowers contain salicylic acid, known for generations as 'nature's aspirin', and as a cordial it is used widely as an anti-inflammatory and to treat joint pain. The name 'aspirin' comes from *Spiraea*, the previous generic name for this species.

Above: This flower has long stamens that give the flower a fuzzy appearance.

Distribution: Europe, except for most of the Mediterranean region.
Height and spread: 50cm–2m/20in–6½ft.
Habit and form: Perennial.
Leaf shape: Pinnate.
Pollinated: Insect.

Identification: Pairs of large toothed leaflets are interspersed with pairs of much smaller ones. Basal leaves have up to five pairs of large leaflets, each 20–80mm/¾–3⅛in. The inflorescence can be up to 25cm/10in long with numerous flowers. It bears tiny, dry, spirally-twisted fruits.

Left: Meadowsweet grows in marshy ground.

Below: The flowerheads are feathery in appearance.

Agrimony

Church steeples, Sticklewort, *Agrimonia eupatoria*

Agrimony, an erect plant with a long spike of yellow flowers from June to August, is found in hedges, fields and grassy places. The flowers have a refreshing, spicy, apricot-like smell. It has toothed leaves which are dark green above and white-or grey-hairy beneath. For centuries all parts of the plant have been used to treat all manner of complaints from gout to healing wounds, easing coughs, curing colitis, cystitis, providing pain relief and aiding food allergies.

Above: The leaves have regular toothed margins.

Below: Each flower has four or five petals.

Distribution: Europe, except for the far north.
Height and spread: 15cm–1.5m/6in–5ft.
Habit and form: Perennial.
Leaf: Pinnate.
Pollinated: Insect.

Right: The flower spikes grow tall, making an imposing statement.

Identification: There are two to three pairs of small leaflets between each of three to six pairs of main leaflets. The flowers have four to five golden petals. The fruit has hooked bristles at the upper end.

Great burnet

Sanguisorba officinalis

Distribution: Most of Europe except the Mediterranean region.
Height and spread: Up to 1m/39in.
Habit and form: Perennial.
Leaf shape: Pinnate.
Pollinated: Insect.

Great burnet is a tall plant with toothed leaves and striking oblong, deep purple-brown flowerheads. It grows in damp grassland areas. Its name *Sanguisorba* means 'blood absorber' and it has been used to treat blood disorders for centuries. The word *officinalis*, from the Latin for 'workshop', 'herb store', 'pharmacy' (and also 'office') – describes any plant that is used for medicinal purposes.

Identification: Tall, with pinnate leaves on long stalks with 13 sharply-toothed leaflets. The oblong flowerheads have dull red sepals and only four stamens. The roots are black.

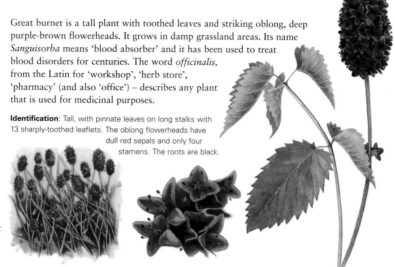

Right: The flowerheads are compact.

Centre: Each flower has four stamens.

OTHER SPECIES OF NOTE

Fragrant agrimony *Agrimonia procera*
This is a robust, aromatic plant with yellow flower spikes appearing from June to August. It is to be found mainly in western, central and southern Europe.

Salad burnet *Sanguisorba minor*
Growing in dry, rocky, typically limestone grassland areas, salad burnet is found in western, central and southern Europe. It has egg-shaped flowerheads with a mixture of male, female and hermaphrodite flowers. As its name suggests, the leaves have been used in salads for hundreds of years, and also as a dressing for wounds.

Creeping avens *Geum reptans*
Found in rocky and gravelly mountainous areas, creeping avens is a low-growing perennial with hairy, toothed pinnate leaves and bright yellow, round-petalled flowers that appear in July and August.

Water avens *Geum rivale*
The stems of water avens are erect and branched, rising from a base of pinnate leaves. From May to September the plant, which frequents damp meadows, woods and stream sides throughout Europe, except for the Mediterranean region, bears pretty and distinctive, bell-shaped, hanging flowers, each with a brownish-purple calyx and cream to pink petals.

Rosa webbiana

This is a common pink-flowered rose native to the Himalayas, growing wild from Pakistan to western Nepal. It typically grows on rocky slopes up to about 4,000m/13,100ft. It is also found in open forest, scrub and grassland, usually in fairly arid regions. The flowers, which appear in summer, grow in dense clusters, and the stems and leaves turn pink. It is often grown in gardens and produces slender, arching branches. In gardens it prefers well-drained soils and can tolerate semi-shade. The plant has medicinal properties.

Below: The deep pink flowers grow in dense clusters, and tend to get paler as they age.

Distribution: The Himalayas.
Height and Spread: To about 2m/6½ft.
Habit and form: Woody perennial.
Leaf shape: Compound.
Pollinated: Insect.

Right: The fruits are a good source of vitamins and flavonoids.

Identification: The shoots are slender and purplish-brown. The leaves are 30–40mm/1¼–1½in, with small, rounded, toothed, leaflets and prickly leaf-stalks. Each flower is 25–70mm/1–2¾in across. The stems and leaves also sometimes turn bright pink. The fruit is a flask-shaped hip, bright red with persistent sepals.

Wood avens

Herb bennet, Colewort, Dr Benedict's herb, *Geum urbanum*

Wood avens grows in shady places such as woodland edges and hedgerows. The flowers, upright and with small yellow petals, appear from June to August. In folklore, the plant was used to drive out evil spirits and to deter rabid dogs and poisonous snakes. Today the roots are sometimes used in flavouring ale and infusions are made to treat diarrhoea, heart disease, halitosis and mouth ulcers.

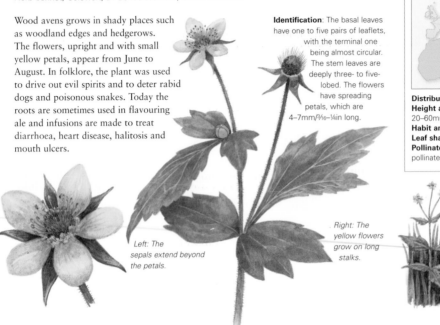

Identification: The basal leaves have one to five pairs of leaflets, with the terminal one being almost circular. The stem leaves are deeply three- to five-lobed. The flowers have spreading petals, which are 4–7mm/³⁄₁₆–¼in long.

Distribution: Europe.
Height and spread: 20–60mm/¾–2¼in.
Habit and form: Perennial.
Leaf shape: Pinnate.
Pollinated: Usually self-pollinated or bee.

Left: The sepals extend beyond the petals.

Right: The yellow flowers grow on long stalks.

Barren strawberry

Potentilla sterilis

This wild flower resembles a wild strawberry but does not produce any edible fruit, hence its common name. The white flowers, which appear early in February and March, have distinct gaps between the petals. This is one of the first flowers to open in the spring. It is a dull-looking, low-growing plant with blue-green leaves, which frequents grassy banks, open woodland and scrub.

Identification: The hairy leaves are trifoliate and serrated. The flowers, 10–15mm/³⁄₈–⁹⁄₁₆in, are borne one to three together on a relatively long stalk. The leaves have spreading hairs on the undersides.

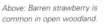

Above: Barren strawberry is common in open woodland.

Right: This flower has a spreading and creeping habit.

Distribution: Lowland and mountain regions of Europe.
Height and spread: Up to 15cm/6in.
Habit and form: Low-growing perennial.
Leaf shape: Trifoliate.
Pollinated: Insect.

Silverweed

Potentilla anserina

Distribution: Europe, except much of the south.
Height and spread: Up to 80cm/31in.
Habit and form: Perennial.
Leaf shape: Pinnate.
Pollinated: Insect.

Right: Silverweed has feathery leaves that have silvery hairs.

As its English name suggests, this is a silvery plant. It grows in damp grassy places and banks. It has a rosette of silkily-haired pinnate leaves with up to 25 leaflets. Its solitary yellow, five-petalled flowers appear from June to August. The French call it 'richette', a name thought to refer to the silver of the leaves and the gold of the flowers. The Latin name *anserina*, meaning 'of the goose' is said to have come from the shape of the leaves, which look like a goose footprint. A herbal tea can be infused from the roots and the leaves have been put into shoes to absorb sweat.

Identification: The leaflets, 7–25, are very sharply toothed and 10–14mm/⅜–⁹⁄₁₆in long. The flowers appear in the leaf axils, with petals of 7–10mm/¼–⅜in. The petals are considerably longer than the sepals. It produces long runners that creep along the surface of the ground, rooting at intervals.

OTHER SPECIES OF NOTE

Alpine cinquefoil *Potentilla crantzii*
The clusters of bright yellow, five-petalled flowers of alpine cinquefoil make a striking show in crevices and on rocky ledges in chalky regions of northern Europe, and on central and southern mountains.

Tormentil *Potentilla erecta*
Occurring widely on grassland, woodland and boggy areas in mountain regions, tormentil prefers an acid soil. The leaves have three to five leaflets and the flowers, appearing from June to September, are four-petalled and yellow.

Rock cinquefoil *Potentilla rupestris*
Growing on woodland slopes and in rocky areas in fissures and cracks, rock cinquefoil is very rare in the British Isles, probably having suffered at the hands of collectors and gardeners. In the rest of Europe it is more frequent. It has pretty, large, white flowers, borne in a branched cluster. The leaves are pinnate with five to seven oval, toothed or double-toothed leaflets.

Alpine lady's mantle *Alchemilla alpina*
Growing in rocky places in northern and western parts of central Europe, alpine lady's mantle is notable for its most beautiful leaves, made up of five to seven leaflets, which are silvery-silky on the underside. The small flowers are pale green or yellowish, appearing in dense clusters from June to August.

Creeping cinquefoil

Potentilla reptans

Sprawling, flowering stems growing from a rosette of leaves are an identifying feature of creeping cinquefoil. The name 'cinquefoil' means 'five leaves' and accurately describes the leaflets that are spread like the open fingers of a hand. The five-petalled yellow flowers appear from June to September. This pretty flower is often found on wasteland and at roadsides and beside footpaths.

Identification: Each leaf has five (sometimes to seven) toothed leaflets 5–70mm/³⁄₁₆–2¾in long. Flowers, with five, 8–12mm/⁵⁄₁₆–½in long petals are solitary and borne in the leaf axils. The flowers open atop tall stalks. The long creeping runner roots at the nodes.

Distribution: Europe except the far north.
Height and spread: 30cm–1m/12in–39in.
Habit and form: Creeping perennial.
Leaf shape: Palmate.
Pollinated: Insect.

Below: The runners root freely where the nodes touch the earth.

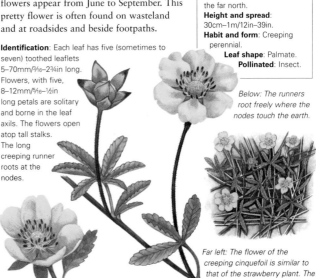

Far left: The flower of the creeping cinquefoil is similar to that of the strawberry plant. The flower is prominent in forests.

Rock's tree peony

Paeonia suffruticosa (rockii)

This fine peony is one of the larger woody species, belonging to a group known as tree peonies. It is named after Joseph Rock, a pioneer botanist and explorer who collected it in south-western China. It grows wild in the mountains of western China.

Tree peonies are often grown in gardens and thrive best in deep, rich soil with plenty of moisture. They also need protection from the wind. They are frost-hardy and resistant to most fungal diseases. Along with many other flowers they are used in traditional Chinese medicine.

Identification: The pink flowers are large and cup-shaped, to 30cm/12in across. However, many hybrids with different coloured flowers have been produced in cultivation, with flowers ranging from white to pink, red and yellow. The leaves are dark green, and bluish-green beneath.

Below: The fruit appears after the flower has faded.

Right: Rock's tree peony has shrub-like growth.

Distribution: Western China.
Height and spread: 2.2m/7ft.
Habit and form: Deciduous shrub.
Leaf shape: Alternate and lobed.
Pollinated: Insect.

Lady's mantle

Lion's foot, *Alchemilla vulgaris*

With its scalloped leaves and dainty lime green, star-shaped flowers, lady's mantle is a familiar grassland plant, well loved by gardeners and flower arrangers alike. After rain, droplets of water gather on the leaves and, in folklore, this gave rise to its use in alchemy (hence the generic name) as a source of 'celestial water'. The common name comes from the leaves, which were thought to resemble the cloak of the Virgin Mary and, even today, much of the plant is used to treat many specific female complaints, as well as for making teas and for cosmetic purposes.

Identification: The leaves are up to 60mm/2¼in wide with 7–11 lobes cut halfway to the leaf centre, each with 12 or more teeth. The flowers are pale green, 3–5mm/⅛–³⁄₁₆in, arranged in loose, branched clusters.

Distribution: Europe.
Height and spread: 10–50cm/4–20in.
Habit and form: Perennial.
Leaf shape: Lobed.
Pollinated: Insect.

Above: The individual flowers of lady's mantle are small and inconspicuous.

Left: Lady's mantle is a common garden plant suitable for the front of a border.

Right: The leaves of lady's mantle are distinctive in shape.

Wild strawberry

Woodland strawberry, *Fragaria vesca*

The familiar bright red, wild strawberry 'fruits' are not fruits or berries. They are formed from the swollen, fleshy bases of the white flowers, which appear from April to July, and the true fruits are actually the small, dry pips on the surface. The basal leaves of the plant form rosettes, and long stolons root to form new plants. Archeological evidence shows that wild strawberries have been consumed since the Stone Age. The leaves are still being used today as an astringent, tonic and laxative, and a slice of the fruit is said to relieve sunburnt skin.

Distribution: Europe.
Height and spread:
50mm–30cm/2–12in.
Habit and form: Perennial
Leaf shape: Trifoliate
Pollinated: Insect

Identification: The bright green trifoliate leaves, 10–60mm/⅜–2¼in long, have coarsely-toothed leaflets. Clusters of white flowers are carried on erect stems. The fruits are miniature strawberries, ripening to a bright red. They are edible, with a delicate flavour.

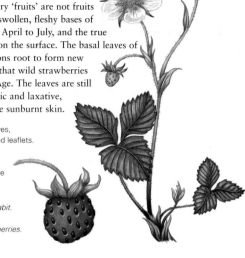

Left: Wild strawberry has a creeping habit.

Right: The fruits are tiny strawberries.

OTHER SPECIES OF NOTE

Snowy mespilus *Amelanchier ovalis*
A shrub or small tree, growing to about 3m/10ft tall, found in central Europe. It has dark bark and oval leaves with toothed margins and a covering of soft down beneath. The flowers have narrow, white, spreading petals and the rounded fruits ripen blue-black. It is typically found in open woodland and rocky mountain sites.

Sibbaldia *Sibbaldia procumbens*
Growing in rock crevices, on ledges and in mountain grassland, sibbaldia thrives in areas of prolonged snow cover. It is low-growing and stiffly-hairy with bluish-green trifoliate leaves and small, insignificant yellow flowers.

Burnet rose *Rosa pimpinellifolia*
This is a suckering shrub forming large, dense patches in coastal regions of western, central and southern Europe and north to Iceland and Norway. Unusually, the stems bear both straight thorns and stiff bristles. The flowers are white, sometimes pink, and it is remarkable for its purple-black hips (fruits).

African raspberry *Rubus pinnatus*
This tropical and subtropical species grows on forest edges and in gaps in forests. It flowers between April and June. It is an erect, hairless but prickly shrub, with trailing stems, having a blue-green waxy covering. The leaves have three pairs of leaflets plus a terminal leaflet.

Field rose

Rosa arvensis

Flowering bushes of field rose are an attractive sight in woods, and in hedges surrounding fields and meadows. The long trailing stems and branches are covered in scattered, hooked slender prickles and the white flowers appear in groups of up to three, in June and July.

Identification: This is a scrambling climber, growing to about 3m/10ft. The pinnate leaves have five to seven ovate, dull green leaflets. The sepals bend backwards once the flower has opened. The flowers of this species are always white and the fruits are familiar 'hips', which are smooth, oval and bright red.

Distribution: Western and central Europe.
Height and spread:
3m/10ft.
Habit and form:
Deciduous shrub.
Leaf shape: Pinnate.
Pollinated: Insect.

Below: The field rose produces trailing stems that form into dense mounds.

Far left: The fruits are oval red 'hips', that are attractive to birds.

PEA FAMILY

The pea family, Leguminosae, with about 18,000 species, is a very large cosmopolitan family containing herbs, shrubs and trees, many of which are useful to people, for example as food or timber. Some are grown as garden plants for their attractive flowers. They are also well known for fixing nitrogen in the soil, a feature exploited by farmers in crop rotation to enrich the soil.

Black medick

Medicago lupulina

This common roadside plant resembles clover until the yellow flowers appear, but is distinguishable when not in flower by the extra long stalk of the middle leaflet or by the black seeds that follow flowering. It tolerates a wide range of soils but prefers well-drained ground and is common in fields and dry downland. It is one of the plants identified as shamrock and is worn by the Irish to celebrate St Patrick's Day.

Identification: The leaves of this prostrate plant are three-lobed, light to mid-green with slightly serrated ends and occasional black markings. The small, pale yellow flowers emerge from the leaf axils and appear from mid-spring to late summer. They are self-fertile and are followed by small black, slightly coiled seedheads, which ripen from midsummer to early autumn.

Above: The dense flowerheads are a deep yellow colour.

Distribution: Europe.
Height and spread: 45cm/18in.
Habit and form: Creeping herbaceous perennial.
Leaf shape: Trifoliate.
Pollinated: Insect.

Right: The small, black, slightly coiled seedheads are the feature of this plant.

Spotted medick

Medicago arabica

Spotted medick, which grows in grassland and waste places, is easily recognizable by the black blotch on each of the three leaflets. Small insignificant yellow flowers appear from April to August and soon after the petals fall to reveal the pods, which are coiled spirally, and earn the plant its nickname, 'cogweed'.

Bottom left: The seed pods are highly visible.

Above and left: This plant is easy to recognize among grasses.

Distribution: Southern Europe; also southern Britain.
Height and spread: 50cm/20in.
Habit and form: Annual or short-lived perennial.
Leaf shape: Trifoliate.
Pollinated: Insect.

Identification: Spotted medick is the easiest of the yellow-flowered peas to identify because of the black blotch on the leaves. The leaflets are 5–7mm/³⁄₁₆–¼in long and the yellow pea-like flowers are 2–3mm/¹⁄₁₆–⅛in wide. They grow in stalked clusters. The stalks are hairy and the fruits are round and spiny, growing from a coiled stem. It is an annual that grows low to the ground.

Wood vetch

Vicia sylvatica

Distribution: Northern, central and eastern Europe.
Height and spread: 60cm–2m/24in–6½ft.
Habit and form: Clambering perennial.
Leaf shape: Pinnate.
Pollinated: Insect.

Wood vetch bears very pretty white, purple-veined flowers, often up to 20 in a cluster. It clambers over other plants in open woodland and often forms sprawling mounds on maritime cliffs and shingle. Vetch has been a familiar plant to humans throughout history, the most notable being *Vicia faba*, the broad bean, which was one of the earliest plants to be cultivated for food, according to evidence dating back to the Iron Age.

Identification: Leaflets in five to 12 pairs ending in a long, branching tendril. Flowers are 12–20mm/½–¾in and fruits 25–30mm/ 1–1¼in long, black and hairless.

Below: The pea-like seed pods are typical of this family.

Bottom: The whole plant has a trailing habit.

OTHER SPECIES OF NOTE

Common vetch *Vicia sativa*
Cultivated for fodder, common vetch also occurs widely throughout Europe in hedges, scrub and grassy wasteland areas. It has divided leaves and yellowish brown to black seedpods, which appear after the pretty purple flowers, singly or in pairs, from April to September.

Hairy tare *Vicia hirsuta*
A hairy, sprawling annual with pinnate leaves and purplish-white flowers, which appear in clusters from May to August. Hairy tare is notable for the fact that it only ever has two seeds in each black pod. It grows throughout Europe in grassy areas, wasteland and hedges.

Purple milk-vetch *Astragalus danicus*
From subarctic areas to the Alps, purple milk-vetch thrives in grassy and rocky places. It is a slender, sparsely-hairy perennial with purplish or bluish-violet flowers, which appear in dense clusters from May to July. It is thought to increase the milk yield of goats.

Sainfoin *Onobrychis viciifolia*
From June to September, sainfoin can be recognized by its spectacular long spikes of deep pink- or purple-striped flowers held above the leaves in lime-rich wasteland areas and on roadside verges in central, eastern and south-eastern Europe. Parts of the plant were once used to make a poultice to draw out boils.

Tufted vetch

Vicia cracca

A widespread and common climber, the tufted vetch favours grassy places, hedgerows, scrub, thickets and field boundaries. Its flower-laden stems festoon the hedgerows and long grasses of wayside places, attached by means of tendrils. It is quite variable across its range, especially in the shape and hairiness of the leaves, and is easily confused with similar species.

Identification: This scrambling perennial grows from a creeping rhizome, with angular, softly hairy stems. The pinnate leaves comprise up to 12 pairs of narrow, oblong leaflets, usually with hairy undersides, and end in a branched tendril. The flower spikes are up to 40mm/1½in long, and contain 10–40 bluish-purple flowers in dense clusters on one side of the stalk. They appear from early to late summer. They are followed by flattened, brown seedpods, 10–25mm/⅜–1in long, on short stalks.

Right: Each cluster has numerous purple flowers.

Far right: Tufted vetch has a scrambling habit.

Distribution: Europe.
Height and spread: Up to 2m/6½ft.
Habit and form: Climbing herbaceous perennial.
Leaf shape: Pinnate.
Pollinated: Insect.

White melilot

Melilotus alba

White melilot has creamy-white flower spikes and can grow up to 1.5m/5ft high. It is fairly common, typically seen in meadows throughout Europe; in the British Isles it is most common in southern and central regions, and rare in Scotland and Ireland. It is the only white-flowered melilot that grows wild in Europe. It is widely cultivated as a forage plant and is sometimes planted near beehives as it is an excellent source of nectar. Traditionally the plant has been used in herbal medicine as an anti-coagulant. It contains the chemical coumarin, giving dried plants the smell of new-mown hay.

Left: White melilot is a tall herbaceous plant made up of single branching stems. It grows on disturbed sites and wasteland and is highly invasive.

Right: The flowering stem.

Distribution: Most of Europe, except the north; Asia; introduced to North America.
Height: To 1.5m/5ft.
Habit and form: Erect annual or biennial.
Leaf shape: Trifoliate.
Pollinated: Insect.

Identification: The flower spikes grow to to 80mm/3⅛in long. The fruits are grey-brown, reticulately veined pods, 4–5mm/³⁄₁₆in long.

Meadow vetchling

Lady's slipper, *Lathyrus pratensis*

Farmers encourage this slender, scrambling plant to grow in their meadows as the nodules on its roots fix nitrogen from the air into the soil and so increase the richness of the earth. With its typical bright yellow flowers, it also contributes to the food value of hay and it is rich in protein, particularly the seeds. It frequents moist grassland, railway embankments, scrub and hedges.

Identification: The leaves are divided into a pair of leaflets measuring 10–30mm/³⁄₈–1¼in long and tipped with a tendril. The flowers are 20–26mm/¾–1in long and black pods 2–40mm/¹⁄₁₆–1½in long.

Distribution: Europe.
Height: 30cm–1.2m/12in–4ft.
Habit and form: Scrambling perennial.
Leaf shape: Divided.
Pollinated: Bee.

Above right: The seedpods are visible in late summer.

Far left: The flower can grow on stems that are up to 1.2m/4ft long, which scramble across damp grass, and can spread across a wide area.

Right: Meadow vetchling flowers from late spring to late summer.

Restharrow

Cammock, *Ononis repens*

Distribution: Western and central Europe
Height and spread: 40–70cm/16–27½in.
Habit and form: Shrubby perennial.
Leaf shape: Trifoliate.
Pollinated: Insect.

Restharrow acquired its English name from the plant's underground stems, which are creeping and tough and used to hold up the farmer's harrow when horse-drawn. This is a stickily-hairy, pink-purple flowering plant of dry grasslands and maritime sand and shingle with an unpleasant, fetid goat-like smell. Cattle that fed on the leaves produced tainted milk, butter and cheese. The folk-lore name 'cammock' comes from an old English word 'cammocky', which means 'tainted'. Historically, roots have been dug up to chew like liquorice root, and medicinal uses since the seventeenth century include treatment for kidney disorders, gallstones and ulcers.

Identification: Leaves are trifoliate, growing on hairy stems. The leafy shoots usually bear single flowers in the axil, from June to September. The fruits are small pods. The roots are dense and quite tough.

Right: Restharrow flourishes in an open sunny position.

Right: Restharrow is a common plant on chalk and limestone.

OTHER SPECIES OF NOTE
Sea pea *Lathyrus japonicus*
Patches of sea pea form large mats on seashore shingle on the coasts of northern and western Europe. It has bluish-green leaflets and clusters of showy, bright pinkish-purple flowers on short, stout stalks. The fat pods contain up to 11 seeds, which are edible but bitter-tasting.

Grass vetchling *Lathyrus nissolia*
This unusual legume has no leaflets or tendrils and, before flowering, resembles the grass in which it normally grows. It is found mainly in western, central and southern Europe. The typical crimson flowers appear from late spring to early summer and it has pale brown pods.

Everlasting pea *Lathyrus sylvestris*
This perennial climber is widespread and has stems up to 2m/6½ft long. Each leaf has one pair of leaflets and ends in a branching tendril. Large pink-and-red flowers appear on very long flower stems.

Spiny restharrow
Ononis campestris
The charming pink or purple flowers, often tinged with white appear throughout the summer. Spiny restharrow is a bee-pollinated, nitrogen-fixing, meadow perennial of poor soils. The whole plant is pleasantly-scented, especially when bruised. The roots can be chewed, liquorice-like and the plant has been used medicinally as a diuretic, and as a cough mixture.

Ribbed melilot

Melilotus officinalis

A native of scrub, disturbed ground and often clay and salty soils, ribbed melilot bears yellow flowers in long spiky clusters from June to September. The plant smells strongly of new-mown hay, particularly when drying, and was once much valued for making a plaster or poultice for dressing wounds.

Identification: The flower spikes are 40–70mm/1½–2¾in long. The fruits are hairless pods, 3–5mm/⅛–³⁄₁₆in long, ripening brown.

Below: This plant species is drought-tolerant.

Distribution: Europe, introduced in the north.
Height and spread: 40cm–2.5m/16in–8ft.
Habit and form: Branching biennial
Leaf shape: Trifoliate
Pollinated: Insect

Below: A prolific number of seeds are produced.

Far right: historically ribbed melilot was valued for its medicinal and homeopathic value.

White clover

Trifolium repens

This small creeping perennial is common in many grassland situations such as fields, pasture and lawns where it often forms extensive patches. It is most easily identified by the numerous erect white flowerheads that appear just above the grass. In many areas this very variable species is derived from cultivated stock rather than native plants, chiefly because of its inclusion in agricultural grass seed mixes. It is extremely common across much of Eurasia and has been spread further through agriculture. It is often mistaken for red clover, *T. pratense*, as its flowers can be tinged pink, but they lack leaves close below the flowerhead.

Identification: The prostrate stems creep extensively, rooting as they go, and white clover often forms large mats in grassy places. The leaves are trifoliate, with oval leaflets, generally about 15mm/⁹⁄₁₆in across, usually with a whitish band encircling the base. The flowerheads are held on erect, leafless stalks 20–50cm/8–20in tall; they are generally white, sometimes pink-tinted, and contain up to 100 florets. The flowers persist, turning brown, to enclose the brown pods of one to four seeds.

Distribution: Eurasia.
Height and spread: 20–50cm/8–20in; indefinite spread.
Habit and form: Creeping herbaceous perennial.
Leaf shape: Trifoliate.
Pollinated: Bee.

Above: The flowers droop and turn brown once fertilized and enclose the small seedpods.

Bird's-foot trefoil

Lotus corniculatus

This plant is variable in appearance and habit. It can be hairy or not, creeping or not. One sure way to recognize it, however, is from the leaves, which have five rather than three leaflets (even though it is named 'trefoil'), the lowest two being attached to the stem. It can also be identified when fruiting, by the seed pods, which are arranged from three to five and spread like the foot of a bird. The flowers are yellow with a reddish tinge and appear on stalked heads from April to September. Bird's-foot trefoil has more than 70 folk-names, including 'lady's shoes and stockings' (from the flower shape) and 'God Almighty's thumb and fingers'.

Below: The seed pods are the characteristic that give this plant its common name.

Identification: The leaflets are 4–18mm/³⁄₁₆–¹¹⁄₁₆in long and the flowerheads have two to seven flowers, each 10–16mm/³⁄₈–⁵⁄₈in. The plant has a sprawling habit and grows up through grassland. It also thrives on paths, rocky ground and roadsides, where it hugs the ground.

Distribution: Europe.
Height and spread: 50mm–35cm/2–14in.
Habit and form: Creeping or ascending perennial.
Leaf shape: Divided.
Pollinated: Wasp and bee.

Right: The flowers are large and bright yellow or orange.

Below: Bird's-foot trefoil can be found in grassland and is tough enough to survive grazing animals.

Kidney vetch

Anthyllis vulneraria

Distribution: Europe, except the far north.
Height and spread: 50mm–90cm/2–35in.
Habit or form: Annual, biennial or perennial.
Leaf shape: Pinnate.
Pollinated: Bumble bee.

The flowers of kidney vetch, which appear from April to September, are striking for their range of colours. They can be yellow, red, purple, orange, whitish or a combination of these hues, gracing grassy and rocky places from coastal areas up to 3,000m/9,840ft. The bluish, often hairy leaves are divided and the flowerheads have a kidney-like shape, giving rise to its common name and to its popular use as a cure for diseases of the kidney. The species name, *vulneraria* is from the Latin *vulnus* meaning 'a wound', and throughout the Middle Ages it was believed that this plant would speed up the healing process.

Identification: The leaves are pinnately divided, each with up to seven pairs of leaflets. The stems terminate in compact heads of numerous flowers, which enlarge to form persistent woolly heads enclosing the pods.

Above: The flowers are bunched together on long stalks.

Below: Each leaf has several leaflets.

OTHER SPECIES OF NOTE

Hare's foot clover *Trifolium arvense*
This upright species grows up to 20cm/8in tall, with spreading leaves. The trefoil leaves have stipules with long spiny points. The large, mostly pink, cylindrical flowerheads are covered in soft, creamy-white hairs.

Strawberry clover *Trifolium fragiferum*
Found almost throughout Europe, in grassland and often on heavy, damp soils, strawberry clover is a creeping perennial with pale pink flowers from April to September. It looks like white clover, *T. repens*, until the globular, pinkish and strawberry-like fruits appear. It is from these that the plant takes its name.

Greater bird's-foot trefoil *Lotus uliginosus*
Thriving in marshes, fens and wet grassland over most of Europe, greater bird's-foot trefoil forms new plants from underground stems and is a very hairy, erect perennial with divided leaves, slender pods and yellow or reddish-tinged flowers appearing from May to August.

Horseshoe vetch *Hippocrepis comosa*
This plant is easily recognized by its peculiar snake-like pods of many one-seeded joints, each curved in a horseshoe shape. The scientific name means 'horseshoe' in Greek. In late spring and summer. It has pretty bright yellow flowers, sometimes striped with red. It thrives on chalk and limestone soil in dry pastures and grassy cliffs in western, central and southern Europe.

Bladder senna

Colutea arborescens

Bladder senna is a many-branched shrub with pinnate leaves and bright yellow flowers from May to August. It has characteristic and interesting brown, papery pods that inflate, bladder-like, when ripe. A natural inhabitant of rocky and grassy slopes, open woodland and chalky soil, it is also widely cultivated as an ornamental shrub.

Identification: The pinnate leaves have four to six pairs of leaflets. The flowers are 16–20mm/⅝–¾in. The bladder-like pods are 50–70mm/2–2¾in.

Distribution: Central and southern Europe.
Height and spread: Up to 3m/10ft.
Habit and form: Deciduous shrub.
Leaf shape: Pinnate.
Pollinated: Insect.

Below: Bladder senna can grow into a pretty shrub.

Left: The pods are inflated.

Broom

Cytisus scoparius

Spineless, golden wands of flowering stems waving in the wind characterize this many-branched shrub. It frequents acid soil in open woodland, scrub, and heathland, preferring warm, sunny sites. It also grows in coastal areas where it takes on a prostrate form. The fragrant flowers, appearing from May to June, are typical of the pea family, having a big upper petal (often in the form of a tube), two at the sides and two at the base. The pods are black when ripe; they explode to release the seeds and curl up after splitting.

Identification: The trifoliate leaves have leaflets that are 6–20mm/¼–¾in long. Yellow flowers, 20mm/¾in, are borne on young twigs. The fruits are flattened pods 25–40mm/1–1½in, hairy and ripening black. The stems are slender and smooth.

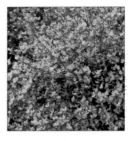

Above: The large yellow flowers are prominent.

Above: The fruit is a pea-like pod.

Right: The coastal form of the plant is low-growing.

Distribution: Europe.
Height: Up to 2m/6½ft.
Habit and form: Often prostrate shrub.
Leaf shape: Trifoliate.
Pollinated: Insect.

Crab's eye

Rosary pea, *Abrus precatorius*

Crab's eye is a hairy, woody climber, growing to more than 4m/13ft. The plant does well in sandy clay loams and loose sandy sediments but tolerates a wide range of soil types. It flowers between February and May. The leaves are picked and chewed as a snack, especially by children, since they taste sweet. The seeds are sometimes used in native jewellery for their bright coloration. However, they are poisonous and are sometimes crushed, and mixed with food to kill rats.

Identification: A woody climbing tropical vine. It is a legume with long, compound pinnately divided leaves, deciduous and alternate along the green stems. The flowers are small, yellow-white-pink and arranged in clusters. They grow densely on a thick stalk with a cluster of bracts at the base. The flower has a typical pea-like shape with the largest petal to 15mm/⁹⁄₁₆in. The fruit (a pod) is flat and about 30mm/1¼in long, covered with dense red-brown hairs, having a hooked tip. The base of the bean is black, while the rest is bright red and the beans remain attached to the edges of the pods for a long time. This seedpod curls back when it opens to reveal the seeds. The small, hard, brilliant red seeds with a black spot are very toxic; a single seed, if broken, can cause blindness or even death if ingested.

Right: The flat seedpod curls back to reveal the uniform-size seeds.

Right: Crab's eye has a clambering habit.

Distribution: Africa; Asia; India.
Height and spread: 4 x 1m/ 13 x 39in.
Habit and form: Woody climbing perennial.
Leaf shape: Compound.
Pollinated: Insect.

African indigo

Indigofera arrecta

Distribution: Africa.
Height and spread: 3m x 30cm/10ft x 12in.
Habit and form: Woody perennial.
Leaf shape: Simple.
Pollinated: Insect.

African indigo flowers mainly from November to May and grows well in grasslands, but is also a weed in gardens. It grows in secondary regrowth in abandoned fields. The plant is mainly used to make brooms, although the crushed leaves, mixed with cow ghee are used to treat boils through topical application. It is still used in some regions to make indigo dyes.

Identification: A stout shrubby perennial growing up to 3m/10ft, with ridged stems, which are densely covered with tiny white or brown hairs, which lie close to the surface. The leaves are alternate and pinnate with narrowly elliptic leaflets and a terminal leaflet, on stalks to about 50mm/2in. The flowers are borne in short, dense, axillary inflorescences, and are pale to deep pink in colour; the bracts and stalks are covered in dense dark hairs. The fruit is a straight, cylindrical pod, narrow and not flattened.

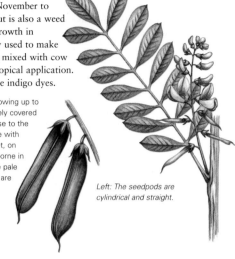

Left: The seedpods are cylindrical and straight.

OTHER SPECIES OF NOTE

Spanish broom *Spartium junceum*
Growing in open woodland, on dry slopes and waysides on chalky soil in the south and Mediterranean region, Spanish broom is a large spineless shrub made up of many cylindrical, bluish-green, rush-like stems with sparse leaves that quickly fall. The flowers, appearing from May to August, are large, bright yellow and sweetly scented.

Petty whin, Needle whin *Genista anglica*
This small, prickly perennial shrub with creeping smooth twigs, branching near the ground, thrives on the poor, acid soils of northern European heaths and moors. The yellow flowers appear in May and June at the top of short branches, and the pods have sharp points at both ends.

Gueldenstaedtia himalayica
This is a low-growing, mat-forming perennial found in the Himalayan region, notably in Bhutan and east into Tibet and China. It grows on dry, open slopes and has small pinnate leaves covered in silky hairs. The flowers are deep red or mauve with broad petals.

Pride of the Cape *Bauhinia galpinii*
This medium to large clambering shrub grows in the moister areas of the southern African veldt, climbing through other trees and shrubs in dense vegetation. It has evergreen foliage and brick-red, orchid-like flowers in summer.

Creeping bauhinia

Bauhinia fassoglensis (= *Tylosema fassoglensis*)

This is a large scrambling creeper, which often clambers over other vegetation. It is found wild from Sudan and Ethiopia south to Namibia, Mozambique and South Africa. Its radiating stems may reach up to 9m/29½ft long and grow up from a large underground tuber. It flowers between September and October and grows in disturbed sites, such as secondary regrowth. It has beautiful, showy yellow flowers. The seeds are eaten in many areas, usually cooked or roasted and the leaves and foliage are used as grazing. The tree also produces a fibre used for making cloth. The roots produce a brown dye.

Identification: A climbing shrub, with tendrils, up to 5m/16ft tall. The leaves are two-lobed and up to 17cm/6½in across. The flowers are yellow and borne in loose racemes; the calyx and young part of the stem have a covering of soft reddish hairs. The corolla has five petals, one of which is spurred. The fruit is a broad, flat pod.

Right: The plant's stem grows from a tuber.

Distribution: Africa.
Height and spread: 5m x 20cm/16ft x 8in.
Habit and form: Woody perennial.
Leaf shape: Bi-lobed.
Pollinated: Insect.

Right: Seed extracts have a range of medicinal uses.

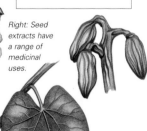

Cancer bush

Kankerbos, Balloon pea, *Sutherlandia frutescens*

A curious South African plant, the cancer bush is an attractive, small, soft-wooded shrublet that occurs naturally throughout the dry parts of southern Africa. The leaves, which have a very bitter taste, are made into tea to alleviate a variety of ailments, including stress, depression, anxiety and stomach problems. The lightweight, papery, inflated seedpods enable the seed to be dispersed easily by wind, giving rise to the common name 'balloon pea'.

Identification: The pinnate leaves, with leaflets 4–10mm/³⁄₁₆–³⁄₈in long, are grey-green, giving the plant a silvery appearance. The bright scarlet flowers, up to 30mm/1¼in long, are carried in short racemes at the ends of the branches from late spring to midsummer. The fruit is a large, bladder-like pod, which is almost transparent.

Right: The attractive, bright scarlet flowers are followed by the inflated papery seed pods that can be blown off and carried in the wind.

Distribution: South Africa.
Height and spread: 50cm x 1m/20in x 39in.
Habit and form: Shrub.
Leaf shape: Pinnate.
Pollinated: Sunbird.

Coral tree

Red-hot-poker tree, *Erythrina abyssinica*

This is a medium-size tree with a well-branched, rounded, spreading crown, found in tropical east Africa, in woodland and grassland. It closely resembles *E. latissima*. *Erythrina* comes from the Greek 'erythros' (red), alluding to the showy red flowers. The specific name means 'from Ethiopia'. It flowers mainly between July and November and grows in grassland and bush country. It is sometimes grown in gardens.

Below: The seeds are clearly visible within the fruit pod.

Identification: This is a deciduous tree, usually 5–15m/16–49ft in height. The bark is yellow-buff when fresh, otherwise grey-brown to creamy-brown, deeply grooved, thickly corky, and often spiny. When damaged, the tree exudes a brown, gummy sap. The leaves are compound, trifoliate and alternate; the leaflets are 55mm–15cm/2⅛ x 6in long x 60mm–14cm/2¼ x 5½in broad, with the terminal leaflet the largest, and smaller lateral leaflets. The flowers are spectacular, borne in strong, sturdy racemes. They are orange-red, up to 50mm/2in long with a tube-shaped calyx, split along the under surface almost to the base and separating into long, slender, distinctive lobes at the apex. The calyx and standard petal are a striking scarlet to brick red. The fruit is a cylindrical, woody pod, 40mm–16cm/1½ x 6¼in long, deeply constricted between the seeds, densely furry, light brown in colour. On ripening, it opens to reveal one to ten shiny, red seeds with a grey-black patch.

Distribution: Africa.
Height and spread: 15 x 6m/49 x 19¾ft.
Habit and form: Woody perennial.
Leaf shape: Compound.
Pollinated: Insect.

Below: The tree has a spreading crown.

Slenderleaf rattlebox

Showy rattlebox, *Crotalaria ochroleuca*

This spreading herb flowers in March and April and prefers sandy clay loams in secondary regrowth after cultivation among other weeds and in disturbed areas. It also grows in damp grassland, near rivers and at roadsides. The leaves and flowers are eaten as vegetables and the plant is often preserved in home gardens to provide such produce. Like many legumes it is sometimes grown in an intercropping regime to improve soil fertility.

Below: This plant has a spreading habit.

Distribution: Tropical Africa.
Height and spread: 3m x 50cm/10ft x 20in.
Habit and form: Annual/short-lived perennial herb.
Leaf shape: Compound.
Pollinated: Insect.

Right: The fruit pods hang from the stem.

Identification: Usually an erect annual or short-lived perennial herb with drooping branches. The leaves are compound, with three leaflets. The leaflets are linear to linear-lanceolate with appressed hairs on the under surface. The flowers are borne in loose racemes of large, pale yellow flowers, terminal or opposite the leaves, to 15cm/6in long, with the flowers growing closely together. The yellow petals have maroon veining and the keel has a long, projecting beak. The fruit is an inflated pod, broad and cylindrical with short hairs, almost stalkless, 50–70mm/2–2¾in long and 20mm/¾in wide, breaking open to set free many smooth orange-yellow seeds.

OTHER SPECIES OF NOTE

Wild cowpea *Vigna unguiculata*
An African herbaceous legume, growing to 1m/39in. This is an important crop, one variety of which produces 'black-eyed peas'. It flowers from October to December and thrives in well-drained, loose, sandy loams. It grows in disturbed areas, grassland and woodland. The leaves have three leaflets, with pointed tips. Two or more purple-blue pea-type flowers develop on long branched stalks. The fruit is a pod, cylindrical and narrow, ripening to eject white, red and black marked seeds.

Goat's-rue *Galega officinalis*
Long grown for fodder, the white or pale mauve flower spikes of goat's-rue make a showy display from June to September in damp wasteland areas of central, eastern and southern Europe. The plant has a leaflet at the leaf base and so is not able to clamber over other plants.

Crown vetch *Coronilla varia*
Cultivated for fodder and now established in rough grassland areas, crown vetch is a clover-like perennial with 10–12 prominent flowerheads in summer, varying in colour from white to pink to purple. The pods end in a long, curved 'beak'.

Jade vine

Strongylodon macrobotrys

The jade vine is one of the world's most impressive plants. This highly unusual species climbs up to 20m/65½ft high in the tropical evergreen lowland forests of the Philippines, notably on the island of Luzon. It was discovered in 1854, and has since become something of a speciality in greenhouse cultivation. It can be grown from seed or cuttings and needs warm conditions and a plentiful supply of water. In the wild it is threatened by the destruction of its forest habitat.

Distribution: Philippines.
Height and spread: To 20m/65½ft.
Habit and form: Clambering perennial.
Leaf shape: Ternate.
Pollinated: Bat.

Identification: The flowers are the most spectacular aspect of the jade vine. These dangle down in remarkable spikes (racemes), each consisting of up to 100 individual pea flowers. Each spike may be up to 1m/39in in length. The flowers are a strange luminous bluish-green, and in its native habitat it attracts bats.

Right: The dangling clusters of blue-green flowers are distinctive.

CABBAGE FAMILY

The Brassicaceae, or cabbage family, contain herbs or, rarely, subshrubs. The family includes familiar food plants such as cabbage, cauliflower, broccoli, Brussels sprouts, kohlrabi and kale, which have all been derived from a single wild plant through human selection. Members of the cabbage family are found throughout temperate parts of the world, with the greatest diversity in the Mediterranean region.

Honesty

Money plant, Silver dollar, *Lunaria annua*

Honesty can often be encountered in uncultivated fields across much of Europe, although most of the plants seen in the vicinity of human habitation are probably garden escapees. The eye-catching spring blooms are rich in nectar and therefore popular with butterflies. Later in the year the plant produces masses of attractive, translucent, silvery seedpods, which are used in floral arrangements.

Identification: The plant has stiff, hairy stems and heart-shaped to pointed leaves, coarsely toothed and up to 15cm/6in long. The cross-shaped flowers appear in mid- to late spring, borne in broad, leafy racemes up to 18cm/7in long. The green seedpods are 25–75mm/1–3in across, flat and circular and firmly attached to the stems. The large seeds are strongly compressed in two rows. A thin, translucent wall is formed between the two valves of the pod during the ripening process, creating the classic 'silver penny' when the seeds disperse.

Above: The flowers are pink-purple and occasionally white.

Right: The cross-shaped flowers are in loose clusters above the leaves.

Far right: The seedpods are flat and papery.

Distribution: South-eastern Europe; western Asia.
Height and spread: 60–90 x 30cm/24–35 x 12in.
Habit and form: Annual or biennial.
Leaf shape: Cordate-acuminate.
Pollinated: Insect.

Wallflower

Erysimum cheiri

The wallflower is very widely distributed, though it is actually a garden escapee across much of its range. It is thought to have been the result of a cross between two closely related species from Greece and the Aegean region, but this ancestry is obscure and the plant is now regarded as a species in its own right. It requires good drainage and can grow in nutritionally poor and very alkaline soil, so it is often seen colonizing old walls. It tolerates maritime exposure.

Identification: This shrubby, evergreen, short-lived perennial is in flower from mid-spring to early summer. It forms mounds of stalkless, narrow, spear-shaped, dark green leaves, to 23cm/9in long, the margins of which are smooth or have well-spaced teeth. Open, sweetly scented, bright yellow-orange flowers, up to 25mm/1in across, are produced in the spring.

Distribution: Southern Europe.
Height and spread: 25–75 x 30–40cm/10–29½ x 12–16in.
Habit and form: Partly woody subshrub.
Leaf shape: Lanceolate to obovate.
Pollinated: Bee and fly.

Far left: Wallflowers have an open habit.

Left: The flowers are cross-shaped.

Left: The short, dense inflorescence is very attractive when it appears in the spring.

Hoary stock

Matthiola incana

Distribution: Europe.
Height and spread: 60 x 30cm/24 x 12in.
Habit and form: Short-lived, slightly woody perennial.
Leaf shape: Lanceolate or linear lanceolate.
Pollinated: Insect, especially butterfly.

Hoary stock often resembles a wallflower growing on chalk cliffs and beside roads, where it could easily be mistaken for a garden escapee. It is the parent of the garden stocks. The flowers are highly fragrant and are said to smell of cloves. The plant prefers well-drained alkaline soils and can tolerate maritime exposure, actually prospering best in a cool, moist environment such as sea cliffs. This species is noted for its tendency to attract insects, especially butterflies and bees.

Right: The long, cylindrical seed pods ripen in late summer and split along their length to disperse the seeds.

Identification: A woody-based perennial or subshrub with narrow, grey-green to white hairy leaves, which are 50mm–10cm/2–4in long, and are mostly entire but occasionally deeply segmented or lobed. The upright racemes of sweetly scented flowers, mostly mauve or purple but also occasionally violet, pink or white, up to 25mm/1in across, are borne from late spring to midsummer, and the seeds ripen in 10cm/4in pods in late summer.

Right: The plant forms an attractive hummocky mass with showy flower-heads in early summer.

OTHER SPECIES OF NOTE

Candytuft
Iberis sempervirens
Perennial candytuft is a short, woody shrub that forms a dense mound of small, evergreen leaves, with heads of many tiny, white flowers in flat, terminal clusters at a height of 25cm/10in in spring. It is found throughout the mountains of Europe and Asia Minor.

Sweet alyssum *Lobularia maritima*
More usually known by its previous name of *Alyssum maritimum*, this short-lived perennial from the Mediterranean forms a dense mound of small green leaves, covered from late spring in compact heads of tiny, perfumed, white or occasionally pale purple-pink flowers.

Lady's smock *Cardamine pratensis*
Also known as cuckoo flower, this elegant plant grows in damp meadows, ditches, by ponds and streams and along woodland edges. It produces clusters of large, pale mauve to pink flowers in late spring.

Megacarpaea polyandra
This crucifer grows in the Himalayas, from Kashmir to central Nepal and Tibet, at 3,000–4,600m/9,840–15,100ft. Growing to 2m/6½ft, this perennial has large, deeply pinnately-lobed leaves. The flowers are creamy white or yellowish, growing in dense clusters. The young leaves are edible when cooked.

Aubretia

Wallcress, *Aubrieta deltoidea*

This carpet-forming perennial is found growing naturally among scree and on high moorland. It is very similar to rockcress, the *Arabis* species, but flowers a little later and blooms for a longer period. Its popularity in cultivation has led to its common appearance as a garden escapee, although many such plants are hybrids and the true species is generally restricted to mountains in southern Europe. The plant prefers moist, but well-drained soil, although it tolerates a wide range of soil types and can survive drought and periods of hot dry weather.

Identification: An evergreen, mat-forming, slightly woody perennial, it has small, mid-green, oval leaves, hairy and slightly toothed along the margin. The blue or purple, cross-shaped, four-petalled flowers, 15mm/⁹⁄₁₆in across, are produced in great profusion on small racemes, and cover the mat of leaves in late spring. The seeds ripen in early summer.

Above: The attractive, flowers appear prolifically in late spring.

Right: Aubretia forms a dense mat of stems.

Distribution: South-eastern Europe; Turkey.
Height and spread: 15 x 30cm/6 x 12in.
Habit and form: Slightly woody, creeping perennial.
Leaf shape: Ovate to obovate.
Pollinated: Bee.

Seakale

Crambe maritima

Seakale is a long-lived plant, characteristic of shingle (and also of sandy) beaches, its waxy, leaves helping it to tolerate salty conditions and its long, deep roots providing a secure anchor in this often dynamic habitat.

The young shoots and leaf stalks are edible and it has often been used as a vegetable in England. Other *Crambe* species grow in the Mediterranean, the Canary Islands and in the mountains of Africa, some being grown as attractive foliage plants, easily cultivated if they have good drainage. The flowers appear from June to August.

Identification: The leaves are grey and very fleshy. The small (10–16cm/4–6¼in across), white flowers are held on a branched inflorescence and have four petals forming a 'cross', typical for a member of the cabbage family (also known as the 'crucifers', 'cross-bearers'). There are four sepals, six stamens, a superior ovary and no style. The dry flower stems can often be seen blowing along the beach, and the corky fruits float away. In winter the leaves die back completely.

Distribution: Atlantic, Baltic and Black Sea coasts.
Height and spread: 60cm x 1m/24in x 39in.
Habit and form: Herbaceous perennial.
Leaf shape: Lobed with wavy margins.
Pollinated: Insect.

Above and top: Seakale grows in clumps.

Left: The fruit is a spherical, one-seeded pod.

Shepherd's purse

Capsella bursa-pastoris

This is a common plant found as a weed in fields, roadsides and wasteland throughout the world. It flowers most of the year, except at higher altitudes. It is grown in some countries as a salad or vegetable. It is variable in growth depending on the local conditions.

Left: The flowers are white and small.

Far right: The heart-shaped pods are a characteristic of this plant.

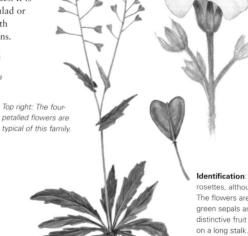

Top right: The four-petalled flowers are typical of this family.

Distribution: Worldwide.
Height and spread: 40 x 20cm/16 x 8in.
Habit and form: Herbaceous annual or biennial.
Leaf shape: Lance-shaped, most pinnately-lobed.
Pollinated: Insect.

Identification: The leaves mostly grow in basal rosettes, although some are clasping stem-leaves. The flowers are white, 2–5mm/1⁄16–3⁄16in across, have green sepals and are borne in loose racemes. The distinctive fruit is a flat, triangular, heart-shaped pod on a long stalk.

Red-fruited caper-bush

Capparis erythrocarpos

A scrambling shrub or climber, with grey branches (when young) and blunt leathery leaves, that is armed with sharp, paired, hooked thorns. It flowers between March and June. Red-fruited caper-bush grows well in wooded grasslands, often in thickets around termite mounds. The bright red fruits are edible and taste sweet. The plant is sometimes used as a hedge around homesteads.

Identification: A shrub or sometimes a climber, with pairs of short recurved spines. The leaves are alternate, simple, entire, oval and narrow to 85mm/3¼in, pointed or blunt, greyish-velvet when young, mostly hairless when older; the margin is often wavy. The flowers are solitary in the upper leaf axils, white, to 60mm/2¼in across. The fruit is an egg-shaped, ridged berry, ripening orange-red on a stalk to 20mm/¾in, not splitting when ripe.

Distribution: Tropical Africa.
Height and spread: 3 x 4m/ 10 x 13ft.
Habit and form: Woody perennial.
Leaf shape: Simple, oval and narrow.
Pollinated: Insect.

Right: The berry has ridges along its shape.

Right: This plant has simple leaves and large flowers with spreading stamens.

Sea rocket *Cakile maritima*
This plant grows on coastal sands near the tideline throughout Europe and around the Mediterranean. The grey-green leaves are slightly succulent and mostly pinnately lobed. The flowers, appearing from February to July, can be violet, pink or white and are borne in branched clusters. The flower stems elongate up to 60cm/24in and grow upright as the plant flowers and fruits. The fruit is adapted to dispersal by the sea as some of the seed capsules have the ability to float away.

Hoary cress *Cardaria (Lepidium) draba*
This is a variable, early-flowering perennial, common as a weed throughout Europe, but probably native to the south. It can be up to 90cm/35in tall and has branched, umbel-like dense clusters of small, white flowers. The greyish, oblong leaves are hairy and those at the base deeply toothed, while the pod is kidney-shaped. It often grows alongside roads in a compact form.

Horseradish *Armoracia rusticana*
Horseradish has been cultivated for more than 2000 years, its roots providing a hot flavouring and also medicinal value. Native to southern Russia and eastern Ukraine, it is now widespread elsewhere in Europe and North America. The small, white flowers grow on a branched inflorescence and the leaves are a shiny dark green.

Dame's violet, Sweet rocket *Hesperis matronalis*
This is a herbaceous plant with long spikes of white or violet flowers that produce a violet-like scent in the evening. Often grown in cottage gardens, it is native to southern Europe but is now naturalized in the UK, Canada and USA.

Kumkum

Maerua pseudopetalosa

A glabrous shrub of the dry savanna in flood-land. The foliage provides much-relished browsing for goats in Somalia. In parts of southern Sudan the plant is eaten but only as a famine-food after careful preparation to remove the toxic content. It flowers shortly before the onset of rainy seasons, in July to September, and grows in grasslands in drier areas.

Distribution: Tropical Africa.
Height and spread: 60 x 10cm/24 x 4in.
Habit and form: Woody perennial.
Leaf shape: Simple.
Pollinated: Insect.

Identification: A perennial shrub, 30–60cm/12–24in tall. The leaves are alternate, narrow-oval to 35mm/1⅜in, almost stalkless, with a pointed tip. The flowers are borne on stalks. Each flower, which has no petals, has four green, narrow sepals about 10mm/⅜in long. The fruit is a yellow capsule, round to oval, about 20mm/¾in across.

Watercress

Nasturtium officinale (previously *Rorippa nasturtium-aquaticum*)

This plant has important uses as a vegetable, particularly for its vitamins that in the past have provided protection against scurvy, and are now believed to have other major health benefits. Its method of cultivation reflects its natural habitat in shallow, running water, often calcareous springs or pure clear streams. A native to Europe, it is now naturalized in North America and New Zealand, where it can be a pest. Despite its name, this plant is not related to the *Tropaeolum* nasturtiums that belong to a different family and are native to South America.

Identification: A hairless perennial with dark green leaves and hollow, floating stems that creep and then turn upwards to produce a terminal cluster of small, 4–6mm/³⁄₁₆–¼in, white flowers from April to October.

Above right: The seed pods develop just below the flowers.

Distribution: Europe (except the far north) to Central Asia.
Height and spread: 60cm/24in.
Habit and form: Herbaceous perennial.
Leaf shape: Pinnately compound.
Pollinated: Insect.

Left: The seed pod is straight and contains two rows of seeds.

Garlic mustard

Jack-by-the-hedge, Poor man's mustard *Alliaria petiolata*

Although related to cabbages rather than onions, the leaves of this plant smell strongly of garlic when bruised, hence the names. 'Alliaria' echoes 'Allium' (the genus containing onions and garlics). The taste of the leaves is milder than garlic and may be used to add a subtle flavour in salads or cooking. The taproot has a scent like horseradish. It is found throughout most of Europe in habitats such as hedge banks and open woods, often on chalky ground and flowers from April to June. This herbaceous plant grows in western and Central Asia and northwest Africa.

Identification: The white flowers, 6mm/¼in across, grow in dense clusters on tall racemes above a basal rosette of hairless, glossy leaves.

Distribution: Europe, western and Central Asia, northwestern Africa; introduced and invasive in North America.
Height and spread: To 1.2m/4ft.
Habit and form: Biennial.
Leaf shape: Heart-shaped.
Pollinated: Insect.

Top left and left: This herbaceous plant grows prolifically.

Right: The pods curve upwards.

Wild spiderflower

Cat's whiskers, Spider wisp, *Cleome gynandra*

Distribution: Tropical Africa; Asia; Australia.
Height and spread: 5 x 3m/ 16 x 10ft
Habit and form: Herbaceous annual.
Leaf shape: Compound.
Pollinated: Insect.

Wild spiderflower is an erect, annual herb, much branched and sometimes becoming woody with age. It flowers between January and March and then again in July to September. It does well in abandoned fields, and along roadsides and in other places, especially where the soil has been disturbed. The leaves are eaten as a vegetable and a decoction of the roots is used to control fevers and also to induce labour in expectant women.

Identification: A much-branched erect annual herb to 1m/39in, the stout stem is usually thick, often purple and covered with sticky glandular hairs. The leaves are long-stalked, hairy, and palmately compound with three to seven leaflets like the fingers of a hand, each leaflet oval and hairy. The leaflets radiate from the tip of the leaf stalk, are smooth or with glands, and taper toward the base. The terminal flowering stalk reaches 30cm/12in and bears small leafy bracts. The petals are white, sometimes fading to pink, rounded at the apex, abruptly narrowed to a basal claw. The fruit is a capsule, 12cm/4¾in long, glandular and hairy. It splits when mature to release seeds.

Right: Each flower stalk is 10–20mm/ ⅜–¾in long with glandular hairs.

OTHER SPECIES OF NOTE

Wild mignonette *Reseda lutea*
This attractive plant is similar to *R. luteola* but not as tall and with yellow flowers, lobed leaves and oblong fruits. It typically grows on cultivated and waste ground, usually in calcareous areas. It is native to Mediterranean, southern and western Europe but naturalized throughout Europe except the far north. It flowers from June to September in northern Europe but from February onwards in the south.

Hedge mustard *Sisymbrium officinale*
This shrub has tall, erect, densely-flowered spikes and grows as an annual or biennial on hedgebanks, roadsides and wasteland in western Europe. Growing up to 90cm/35in tall, it has bristly, pinnate leaves that are deeply lobed, and tiny flowers, 3mm/⅛in across, which appear in June and July.

Wild candytuft *Iberis amara*
This charming plant grows on chalky soils, typically on grazed, rabbit-disturbed downland or embankments. Low-growing and much-branched, it reaches a height of about 30cm/12in. The lower leaves are spoon-shaped, the upper leaves lanceolate. It produces clusters of large fragrant white flowers, each up to 8mm/⅝in across, with the two outer petals twice as long as the inner petals. The fruit is a winged pod, notched at the top. It was once used to treat the medical conditions sciatica and gout. In Europe its distribution is mainly restricted to central and southern areas.

Weld

Dyer's weed, Dyer's rocket *Reseda luteola*

The tall, upright spikes of yellow-green flowers are common in chalk grasslands of southern England and other dry, stony and sandy habitats across Europe. This plant has been widely used to make a yellow dye that produces Lincoln Green, the dyed woollen cloth associated with Robin Hood, when combined with the blue dye of woad, *Isatis tinctoria*. It flowers from April to July in the Mediterranean area, and in September in the north.

Identification: Small flowers 4–5mm/³⁄₁₆in across with four petals and sepals, conspicuous stamens and a superior ovary. The plant is hairless, with alternate, simple leaves and its fruit is an open-topped, hollow capsule with many seeds.

Distribution: Europe (except the far north-west).
Height and spread: 1.3m/4¼ft.
Habit and form: Herbaceous biennial.
Leaf shape: Lanceolate, unlobed, wavy margin.
Pollinated: Insect, especially butterfly.

Below: Weld has an elegant appearance with its tall yellow flower spikes.

Left: The fruit capsule is oblong and held upright.

POPPY FAMILY

The Papaveraceae, or poppy family, contain herbs and rarely, shrubs or trees comprising 25 genera and 200 species that usually have milky or coloured sap. The largest genus in this group is the poppies, Papaver, with about 100 species, many of which are notable for their large, showy and fleeting flowers. Poppies grow on disturbed soil.

Field poppy

Common poppy, *Papaver rhoeas*

The field poppy is a species classically associated with heavily disturbed ground, hence its symbolic association with the battlefields of World War I. One of the reasons for this is that it has a particularly persistent seed bank. It is a common weed of cultivated land and waste places, in all but acid soils, although it is now becoming far less frequent due to modern agricultural practices.

Above: The fruiting capsule scatters tiny seeds when shaken by late summer winds.

Left: Although individual flowers are short lived, they are produced prolifically over the summer.

Identification: Erect or semi-erect branching stems, sparsely bristled, exude a white sap when cut. The oblong, light green, downy leaves, to 15cm/6in long, are deeply segmented with lance-shaped lobes. Solitary, bowl-shaped, brilliant red flowers, sometimes marked black at the petal bases, to 80mm/ 3⅛in across, are borne on short, downy stalks from early to late summer. The flowers are followed by hairless, spherical seed capsules, which release the seed from an upper ring of pores; they ripen from late summer to early autumn.

Distribution: Mediterranean Europe.
Height and spread: 60 x 15cm/24 x 6in.
Habit and form: Annual.
Leaf shape: Pinnatifid.
Pollinated: Insect.

Right: Field poppies form an erect, branching plant.

Himalayan blue poppy

Meconopsis betonicifolia

This is the classic blue poppy 'discovered' by Lt Col F. M. Bailey in southern Tibet in 1913, and brought into cultivation by Frank Kingdon-Ward in 1926. It is from the rocky mountain slopes of the Himalayas and grows there in moist acidic soils, in which the blue colour develops its greatest intensity. The plant is perennial but sometimes short-lived, and though much cultivated rarely naturalizes as a garden escapee outside its natural range.

Identification: Large basal rosettes of leaves are produced in spring; they are toothed, heart-shaped or flat at the base, 15–30cm/6–12in long and light blue-green, covered with rust-coloured hairs. In early summer the flower spike grows up to 90cm/35in. Drooping to horizontal, saucer-shaped, bright blue, sometimes purple-blue or white flowers, 75mm–10cm/3–4in across, with yellow stamens, are borne on bristly stalks up to 20cm/8in long, singly or sometimes clustered toward the top of the stem. It occasionally occurs as a pure white form var. *alba*, which is striking but is only rarely encountered outside cultivation.

Distribution: South-western China; Tibet; Burma.
Height and spread: 90 x 45cm/35 x 18in.
Habit and form: Herbaceous perennial.
Leaf shape: Oblong to ovate.
Pollinated: Insect.

Far left: The striking, erect and robust flower stems are held high over the leafy rosette.

Yellow horned-poppy

Glaucum flavum

The showy yellow horned-poppy is a familiar sight along much of the coastline of Europe, North Africa and western Asia, where it occurs on shingle or gravel beaches. The golden-yellow flowers of this short-lived perennial are followed in the latter part of the summer, by unusual, long, curling seedpods, which are often known as horns, hence the name. The plant exudes a yellow, foul-smelling latex when it is broken. All parts of it are poisonous.

Identification: A rosette-forming, slightly hairy plant with deeply lobed, hairless, rough, blue-green leaves, 15–30cm/6–12in long, the lobes incised or toothed. It produces branched grey stems of bright golden-yellow or orange, saucer-shaped flowers in summer; up to 50mm/2in across, they have golden anthers and a pale green pistil. The flowers are followed by the curling seedpods in late summer, which can be up to 30cm/12in long.

Distribution: Europe; West Africa; Canary Islands; western Asia.
Height and spread: 30–90 x 45cm/12–35 x 18in.
Habit and form: Herbaceous perennial.
Leaf shape: Pinnatifid.
Pollinated: Insect.

Above: The blooms are a striking yellow.

Right: The long, thin seedheads are the so-called horns that give the plant its name.

Oriental poppy

Papaver orientalis

Distribution: South-western Asia.
Height and spread: 90cm/35in.
Habit and form: Perennial.
Leaf shape: Pinnately lobed.
Pollinated: Insect.

Right: The flower forms clumps.

This magnificient perennial poppy is deservedly popular in gardens and makes a fine show in a border where its large flowers attract many insects, notably bees. It flowers mainly from May through July. In the wild its habitat is scrub and rough land, and it has become quite widely naturalized in Europe. While the wild type has deep red flowers, there are several cultivated forms with flower colours including orange, pink and white.

Identification: This tall poppy has notably bristly stems and leaves. The leaves are pinnately lobed. The lower leaves have long stalks and the upper leaves are mainly unstalked. the flower buds are hairy. The flowers are very large for a poppy – up to 18cm/7in across, bright crimson or orange-red. Each petal usually has a large dark patch at its base. The centre of the flower has a ring of dark violet anthers.

Right: The seedhead releases its seeds in the breeze.

FUMITORY FAMILY

The fumitory family, Fumariaceae, is closely related to the poppy family. However, its flowers look very different, being mostly small and usually having a pouch or a spur. There about 19 genera containing 530 species, which can mostly be found in northern temperate regions and in southern Africa. They are easy to recognize by their unusual flowers.

Climbing corydalis

Ceratocapnos (Corydalis) claviculata

A tall climber that is native in old woodland and scrub throughout much of Europe. It tends to occur on acid soils and often grows in rocky sites. Its distribution is patchy and local. It prefers a shady situation.

Identification: This is a scrambling climber. The leaves are pinnate and it also has branching tendrils that help it cling to other plants as it grows. Each flower is about 5mm/³⁄₁₆in long with a spur at the base. The creamy-yellow flowers grow in loose racemes of six to eight flowers. This annual plant has narrow stems that are also brittle. It tends to drape itself over other plants as it grows.

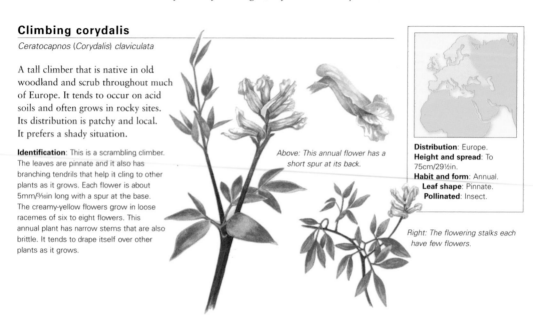

Above: This annual flower has a short spur at its back.

Right: The flowering stalks each have few flowers.

Distribution: Europe.
Height and spread: To 75cm/29½in.
Habit and form: Annual.
Leaf shape: Pinnate.
Pollinated: Insect.

Hollowroot

Bulbous corydalis, *Corydalis cava*

This pretty perennial has purple or white flowers and is often grown in gardens. It is quite widespread in Europe, but not very common in Britain, where it is an introduced species. It grows wild in woods and hedges in central Europe, north to southern Sweden.

Identification: Short and upright, with slightly grey-green foliage and a cluster of purple (or white) flowers. Each flower is about 25mm/1in long with a down-curved spur at the base. The plant grows from a hollow tuber.

Above: Note the short spur at the back of the flower.

Distribution: Central Europe.
Height and spread: 20cm/8in.
Habit and form: Perennial.
Leaf shape: Ternate.
Pollinated: Insect.

Left: Hollowroot is attractive in the garden when grouped close together. The natural habitat of this plant is the woodland floor.

Common fumitory

Fumaria officinalis

Distribution: Europe.
Height and spread:
40cm/16in.
Habit and form: Annual.
Leaf shape: Divided.
Pollinated: Insect.

This common fumitory prefers well-drained soils and is often found as a weed of gardens, wasteland and cultivated fields. It is a delicate, weak-stemmed annual with a clambering habit. When growing in profusion, the flowers, opening from May to October, can make an attractive sight.

Below: Common fumitory has a feathery growth form.

Identification: A scrambling annual with racemes of pink flowers and feathery foliage. Each flower is about 8mm/5⁄16in long with a dark tip. Each raceme may consist of more than 100 individual flowers. The fruit is about 25mm/1in long with a rough surface.

Below: The pink flowers have a dark purplish tip.

OTHER SPECIES OF NOTE

Yellow corydalis
Corydalis (Pseudofumaria) lutea
This annual likes to grow in rock crevices, or from the mortar of old walls. It produces clumps of pale green feathery foliage and flower stalks each with between 6–10 bright yellow flowers, each about 18mm/11⁄16in long. Native to southern Europe, it is a garden escapee.

Corydalis ochroleuca (= *Pseudofumaria alba*)
This native of south-eastern Europe has naturalized further north, to Germany, France, Holland, Belgium and Britain. Its flowers are cream, with a yellow tip, and its foliage greyer than that of yellow corydalis, *C. lutea*.

Common ramping-fumitory
Fumaria muralis
A plant of wasteland and hedgerows, found mainly in western Europe, north to south Norway. The flowers are pink with a reddish-black tip, each about 10mm/3⁄8in long and borne in racemes of up to 15.

White ramping-fumitory *Fumaria capreolata*
A scrambling annual with divided leaves that have pointed segments. The flowers are creamy-white with a reddish-black tip, each about 12mm/1⁄2in long. It grows mainly in hedgerows and on arable and wasteland. Native to Germany, France and Belgium, it has naturalized north to southern Norway.

Bleeding heart

Lyre flower, *Dicentra spectabilis*

The bleeding heart is named for its rosy heart-shaped flowers, with white inner petals, which dangle from arching stems. It grows in moist soils in light woodland cover, and is a particularly handsome plant, especially from mid-spring onwards, as the light green, deeply divided leaves emerge from the ground below the arching flower stems. It often dies down to ground level before the end of summer. All parts of the plant are mildly poisonous if ingested and can irritate the skin. An old English common name is 'lady in the bath', referring to the appearance of the flower when turned upside down.

Far right: The delicate, arching, stems are extremely striking.

Distribution: China; north-eastern Asia.
Height and spread: 80 x 45cm/31 x 18in.
Habit and form: Herbaceous.
Leaf shape: Two-ternate, fern-like.
Pollinated: Insect.

Identification: A clump-forming perennial with thick, fleshy roots and pale green, compound, almost fern-like leaves, 15–40cm/6–16in long, with oval, sometimes lobed leaflets. Arching, fleshy stems support arching racemes of pendent, heart-shaped flowers, 20–30mm/3⁄4–1¼in long, with mid-pink outer petals and white inner ones, in late spring or early summer. The stems rarely persist for long past midsummer, and by late summer the entire plant dies down to ground level until the following spring.

PINK FAMILY

The Caryophyllaceae, or pinks family, contain herbs or rarely subshrubs, mostly growing in temperate areas, with a few growing in tropical countries. The flowers typically feature a corolla of five distinct, frequently clawed petals. The common name 'pink' is derived from a word meaning scalloped, characterizing the petal edges of many in this family.

Clove pink

Carnation, *Dianthus caryophyllus*

This native of Eurasia has been cultivated since ancient times and there are classical Greek and Roman allusions to its use in garlands. The name *Dianthus* derives from the Greek *dios* (god) and *anthos* (flower), and literally means 'flower of the gods'. Despite its ancient history the wild form of this flower is rare and most wild populations are probably derived from cultivated stock.

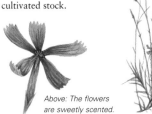

Above: The flowers are sweetly scented.

Identification: Slightly woody perennial with glabrous and glaucous stems and leaves. The leaves are linear, flat and soft in texture and entire along the margins, with conspicuous sheaths around swollen nodes. The conspicuous, fragrant, mostly solitary flowers have five broad petals with toothed edges, mostly flesh-coloured or pink, and are produced in loose cymes on stiff, ascending stems during the summer months. A variable plant that is often the result of escape from cultivation, from which many forms have been derived.

Left: The ragged petal edges appear zigzagged, hence the use of the word 'clove' meaning divided in the common name.

Distribution: Eurasia.
Height and spread: 30–60 x 25–30cm/12–24in x 10–12in.
Habit and form: Herbaceous perennial.
Leaf shape: Linear. .
Pollinated: Moth and butterfly.

Maiden pink

Dianthus deltoides

Some people say that maiden pink got its name from its delicate colour, reminiscent of a maiden's blushes, and because of its coy habit of closing its petals during overcast weather. Others think it is a corruption of 'mead pink', which means a pink growing in meadows. It is a delightful wild cousin of the cultivated pinks and carnations, flowering from June to September, with a most pleasing clove-like scent.

Right: The pink petals have whitish spots. The leaves are elongated.

Identification: A shortly-hairy plant with prostrate shoots bearing short leaves and usually single flowers on erect, rough, tufted, green or grey-green stems. The flowers are 12–20mm/½–¾in across with usually pink petals that are toothed and with whitish spots. Leaves are linear-lanceolate, blunt on non-flowering shoots, pointed and narrower on flowering shoots.

Right: Maiden pink has a tufted growth form.

Distribution: Europe, but rare in Mediterranean regions.
Height and spread: Up to 45cm/18in.
Habit and form: Perennial.
Leaf shape: Lanceolate.
Pollinated: Insect, notably butterfly and moth.

Large pink

Dianthus superbus

Distribution: Europe, except the far west and south.
Height and spread: Up to 90cm/35in.
Habit and form: Perennial.
Leaf shape: Lanceolate.
Pollinated: Insect.

Right: Large pink grows relatively tall for this family.

The striking, sweetly-scented flowers of the large pink, which are borne on grey-green stems from July to September, are noticeably bigger than those of other pinks and have attractive frilly edges. The plant is found in dry, often shady places. The leaves are edible when young or can be boiled to make an infusion which Chinese herbalists recommend for use as a contraceptive, a diuretic and an anti-infective.

Identification: Often prostrate at the base with erect flowering stems. The leaves are arranged opposite and are linear-lanceolate. The flowers are 30–50mm/1¼–2in across with purplish or pink, rarely white, petals, many times divided, giving deeply fringed edges.

Right: The petals of the large flowers are deeply dissected.

OTHER SPECIES OF NOTE

Cheddar pink *Dianthus gratianopolitanus*
This pretty flower is rare in Britain – only being found in the Cheddar Gorge. It is more widespread, though local in continental Europe. Low-growing, with greyish foliage, it has pure pink flowers each about 25mm/1in across. It prefers sunny rocks, mainly on limestone.

Carthusian pink *Dianthus carthusianorum*
Carthusian pink is found in mountain regions and dry grassy, stony places and open woods up to 2,500m/8,200ft. It is a hairless, tufted perennial with linear, pointed leaves and striking deep pink-purple flowers that appear in dense clusters from May to August.

Dianthus angulatus
This pink grows high in the Himalayas, from Pakistan to Himachal Pradesh, on dry, stony hillsides between about 2,500 and 4,000m/8,200 and 13,100ft. Its white flowers (fading to pink) have five spreading petals fringed with narrow teeth, borne on stems about 20cm/8in tall. Each flower is about 15mm/⅝in across. The leaves are linear and also finely toothed.

Ragged robin *Lychnis flos-cuculi*
With its apparently ragged, deeply lobed petals, ragged robin is one of the most attractive flowers of wet meadowland. Like other wetland plants, it has declined in recent years as a result of habitat destruction by modern agricultural practices.

Corncockle

Agrostemma githago

This attractive and once common weed of cornfields has become rare in the wild due to modern agricultural practices. The flower is at first male, the anthers shedding their pollen before the stigmas are mature; these are arranged at the mouth of the tube so that the visiting butterflies push their faces among them and pick up pollen. A day or two later the flower 'becomes' female and the stigmas occupy the mouth in the same way to receive pollen.

Identification: This annual herb has a tall, slender stem with a dense coat of white hairs. Narrow, lance-shaped leaves, 10–12.5cm/4–5in long, are produced in pairs and their stalkless bases meet around the stem. The large, solitary flowers, which appear from early to late summer, have very long stalks that issue from the leaf axils. The flowers are 40–50mm/1½–2in across, with purple, pale-streaked petals and a woolly calyx with five strong ridges and five long, green teeth that far exceed the length of the petals. The fruit is a sessile (stalkless) capsule, which opens with five teeth.

Distribution: Europe.
Height and spread: 60cm–1.5m/24in–5ft.
Habit and form: Annual.
Leaf shape: Lancoleate.
Pollinated: Insect.

Below: The long, green 'teeth' of the woolly calyx exceed the length of the petals and give this flower a distinctive appearance.

Tropical chickweed

Drymaria cordata

This chickweed species is quite a common annual herb in Africa and Asia. It is normally found growing in light sandy or loamy soils. It cannot tolerate deep shade and requires moist soil. The main flowering period is July and August. An infusion of the leaves is said to help stimulate the appetite. The plant is covered in sticky hairs, which may help in its dispersal.

Right: The small green flowers are sticky.

Identification: An annual herb with branched, sprawling stems and a long, slender taproot. The leaves are opposite or whorled, with or without stalks. The flowers are 2–5mm/¹⁄₁₆–³⁄₁₆in, with five oblong sepals, and three to five peals (petals sometimes absent). The fruit is a globular capsule opening two or three spreading valves. The seeds, numbering 3–25, are tan, reddish-brown, dark brown, black, or transparent.

Distribution: Africa; Asia.
Height and spread: 60 x 10cm/24 x 4in.
Habit and form: Annual herb.
Pollinated: Insect.
Leaf shape: Simple.

Left: Chickweed has a trailing growth habit.

Sea sandwort

Honkenya peploides

Sea sandwort grows on bare, salty sand and shifting dunes. With its low-growing stems and a strong root system that binds the sand, the plant helps form dunes by acting as a windbreak, with sand piling up on the windward side. If the wind changes and sands pile up on top of the plant, it adapts by sending up shoots from the buried stems, which root afresh, and a new surface carpet is laid down.

Identification: Fleshy, mat-forming dioecious creeping plant with glossy green ovate or oblong, fleshy stalkless leaves. The flowers are greenish-white, up to 10mm/³⁄₈in across, in axils, or one to six together at the end of a stem. Sepals and petals are equal in male plants, but the sepals are longer than the petals in female plants.

Distribution: Northern and western Europe; the Urals.
Height and spread: Up to 25cm/10in.
Habit and form: Creeping perennial.
Leaf shape: Ovate.
Pollinated: Insect.

Left: Sea sandwort may produce horizontal, low-growing stems.

Far right: The flowers are small and distinct. The seedpod appears after the flower.

Sea campion

Silene maritima (= S. uniflora)

Sea campion is an attractive plant with sprawling stems and large, simple flowers. It grows on cliffs, ledges, and rocky ground and also on shingle by the sea. A similar species, bladder campion, *S. vulgaris*, grows in grassy places such as roadside verges. Sea campion is mainly restricted to the coast. Hybrids between these close relatives are sometimes found.

Right: The prominent flowers attract insects.

Distribution: Western and north-western Europe.
Height and spread: 30cm/12in.
Habit and form: Sprawling perennial.
Leaf shape: Lanceolate.
Pollinated: Insect.

Right: The flower of sea campion has an inflated calyx.

Identification: This plant has sprawling, non-flowering stems. The flowers are held upright from a mat of grey-green, lanceolate leaves. The white, deeply notched petals overlap each other. Both sea and bladder campions have a bladder-like inflated calyx, persisting after flowering around the fruit capsule. Bladder campion is taller growing than sea campion and has several flowers to each flowering stem.

OTHER SPECIES OF NOTE
Red campion *Silene dioica*
A showy herbaceous perennial that is widespread and abundant, red campion is most often associated with woodland, shady places and hedgerows, although it can occur in open situations such as sea cliffs. It hybridizes freely with white campion, *S. latifolia*: the hybrids resemble red campion but are taller, with pale pink flowers.

Moss campion *Silene acaulis*
This most attractive mountain flower is found in arctic regions and the higher mountains of western Europe. It is very different from other campions with foliage forming bright green mats and short, upright stems bearing profuse rose-pink flowers from June to August.

Nottingham catchfly *Silene nutans*
This plant bears white, evening-scented flowers with deeply-lobed petals on sticky stalks. The Latin name refers to the 'nodding' one-sided inflorescences. Although called 'catchfly', it is actually pollinated by moths, which are attracted by the flowers, which open at dusk.

Silene moorcroftiana
Found from Afghanistan to Tibet, this pretty campion flowers from June to August on rocky slopes at altitude. It is a woody-rooted perennial that produces many flowering stems, each with a few white or pink flowers with deeply lobed petals. The fruit is a stalked capsule.

White campion

Silene alba (= S. latifolia)

A handsome familiar weed of arable land, roadside verges, and waste places on dry, especially chalky soils, white campion bears evening-scented white flowers from May to October. This plant is dioecious, which means that it has separate male and female plants. Campions have a characteristic thin inflated calyx and, in white campion, this calyx is much fatter in the female flowers.

Identification: The leaves are ovate or lanceolate-ovate, and those on the stem are stalkless. It is the leaves and the bladder-like flowers that are the main identifying features of this plant. The large, simple flowers each have five two-lobed petals that occur singly or in clusters on the stalk.

Below: The fruit is a capsule with 10 'teeth'.

Distribution: Europe.
Height: 30–80cm/12–31in.
Habit and form: Annual or perennial.
Leaf shape: Lanceolate.
Pollinated: Insect.

Below: White campion grows quite tall and its flowers remain open into dusk.

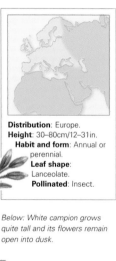

Chickweed

Stellaria media

The generic Latin name of this widespread and prolific weed means 'little star', referring to the arrangement of the ten petals and sepals of the flowers as seen from above. The plant is loathed by gardeners as it flowers throughout the year, producing countless seeds. A curious feature of chickweed is the line of hairs that run down the length of the stem. This collects drops of dew, which then run down the stem until checked by a pair of leaves. Some of the moisture is absorbed through the hairs and retained by the plant against times of drought.

Chickens and cage-birds all relish its greenery and seeds, and it can be eaten as a salad vegetable.

Top left: The flower petals of chickweed are deeply divided.

Identification: An untidy, much-branched annual, often overwintering. The lower leaves are ovate, pointed, and long-stalked. The upper leaves are more or less stalkless. The flowers are in few or many-flowered inflorescences. The sepals are 3–7mm/⅛–¼in, slightly longer than the deeply-divided white petals.

Distribution: Europe.
Height and spread: Up to 90cm/35in.
Habit and form: Annual.
Leaf shape: Ovate.
Pollinated: Insect.

Maiden's tears

Silene burchellii

A perennial herb found in a range of habitats, notably open woodland and grassland. It has large tuberous roots that are reputed to be edible. This species is also used medicinally to treat a variety of ailments. The pretty flowers are variable in colour, and appear mainly between November and December. They tend to open in the evening.

Identification: This perennial herb is usually covered with short hairs in all aerial parts. The stems are erect, up to 70cm/27½in tall and often branched lower down. The leaves are very variable in size and shape, narrowly linear to oblong-lanceolate and generally acute at the apex. The flowers are borne in simple, loose, one-sided racemes, each with two to seven flowers. The calyx is tubular, 1–25mm/½–1in. the petals are reddish-brown, purple, pink or mauve, sometimes white. the fruit is a stalked capsule 5–6mm/³⁄₁₆–¼in.

Above: The petals are deeply divided.

Distribution: Africa.
Height and spread: 70 x 10cm/27½ x 4in.
Habit and form: Perennial herb.
Pollinated: Insect.
Leaf shape: Simple.

Left: The flowers develop to one side of the stem.

Soapwort

Saponaria officinalis

Soapwort is a showy and pretty plant with pale pink flowers from August to October. When bruised and boiled in water, the green parts produce a lathery liquid that was once widely used for washing wool and woollen cloths. Hence, it was purposely cultivated in fields and gardens, especially close to woollen mills. Today it is to be found on roadsides, wasteland and in hedgerows and grassy places. Soapwort is often seen with double flowers, probably as a garden escapee. French herbalists still recommend extract of the plant as a shampoo for delicate hair. It is also used in the treatment of gout, rheumatism and skin diseases.

Distribution: From Belgium, northern Germany and central Russia southward.
Height and spread: Up to 90cm/35in.
Habit and form: Perennial.
Leaf shape: Ovate.
Pollinated: Moth.

Identification: A robust plant with thick, white, underground runners. The leaves are ovate with two parallel-sided veins almost as strong as the mid-vein. The flowers have five pale pink petals in a compact inflorescence. The calyx is cylindrical and often reddish.

Right: The leaves can measure up to 12cm/4¾in long.

Left: The flat flowers appear on upright growth.

OTHER SPECIES OF NOTE

Berry catchfly *Cucubalus baccifer*
This plant grows in grassy places over the south and east of Europe and north to the Netherlands and Russia. It has much-branching stems and drooping white flowers with the characteristic inflated calyx tube. Unusually, the fruits are black and berry-like.

Field mouse-ear *Cerastium arvense*
This genus of plants was given its English name, mouse-ear, in the 16th century, because of the short downy hairs on the mat-forming leaves. With its relatively large white flowers from April to August, it is a pretty sight in dry, chalky or slightly acid grassland and waysides.

Greater stitchwort
Stellaria holostea
Greater stitchwort is a familiar hedgerow wild flower with straggly, four-angled rough stems, large white flowers on long stalks and almost spherical ripe seed capsules. The common name refers to a preparation of the plant mixed with acorns and taken in wine as a remedy for easing 'stitches' in the side or similar pains.

Alpine gypsophila *Gypsophila repens*
This sprawling, hairless perennial of alpine regions has bluish-green, narrow lance-shaped leaves and white, pale pink or lilac flowers borne upright from prostrate stems from May to August.

Greater sea-spurrey

Spergularia media

With pink or white flowers from May to September, greater sea-spurrey frequents maritime sand and muddy salty areas inland. Interestingly, it often turns up on roadsides well inland in areas that have been contaminated with de-icing salt.

Identification: This plant is almost hairless with prostrate or ascending stems. The leaves are fleshy, opposite, and linear with short points. The flowers are 8–12mm/ ⁵⁄₁₆–½in in a loose inflorescence. The petals are pink or white, and are shorter than sepals.

Below: The pinkish-lilac flowers have five petals with white centres.

Distribution: European coastal and inland saline areas, except north-east.
Height and spread: Up to 40cm/16in.
Habit and form: Perennial.
Leaf shape: Linear.
Pollinated: Insect.

Below: This fleshy perennial grows to 40cm/16in tall on sand and shingle.

GERANIUM AND MALLOW FAMILIES

Geraniaceae, the geranium family, contain about 700 species of mostly temperate or subtropical annual or perennial herbs (and a few shrubs), typically with five-petalled flowers. It includes the familiar garden geraniums belonging to the genus Pelargonium. *Malvaceae, the mallow family, with about 1,800 species are mainly tropical and include hollyhocks, mallows, and the crop cotton.*

Bloody crane's-bill

Geranium sanguineum

This very pretty flower grows in a range of habitats, from grassy woodland to limestone pavement and on coastal sand dunes. The flowers appear in mid to late summer and are very attractive to insects.

Identification: A hairy perennial with a branching stem and deeply divided leaves with narrow lobes. The flowers are a bright deep reddish-purple, about 30mm/1¼in across and usually solitary. The flower stalks have a pair of short bracts about halfway up. Bloody crane's-bill often has a clumped, bushy habit and may be found on older coastal sand dunes as well as inland on limestone soils.

Above: Bloody crane's bill self seeds.

Left: The cup-shaped flowers form into a hummocky mass.

Distribution: Europe (except the north), east to Urals and Caucasus.
Height and spread: 30cm/12in.
Habit and form: Perennial.
Leaf shape: Pinnate.
Pollinated: Insect.

Meadow crane's-bill

Geranium pratense

This genus should not be confused with the showy geraniums grown in pots for greenhouse or home decoration, or for summer bedding, which are correctly known as pelargoniums. True geranium species, commonly known as cranesbills because of their beak-like seedpods, are a group of hardy perennials chiefly found in the temperate regions of Eurasia and North America. The meadow cranesbill is the most widespread and robust, with large, conspicuous blue flowers. The flowers are produced in abundance from early summer to mid-autumn.

Right: The large, blue flowers are followed by the long, pointed seedheads that give rise to the common name 'cranesbill'.

Identification: This hairy perennial, with a woody rootstock forming conspicuous clumps, has erect stems, which are sticky in the upper part, and long-stemmed, dark green leaves divided into seven to nine thin, toothed and divided segments. The 25–40mm/ 1–1½in saucer-shaped, pale violet-blue flowers are borne in clusters above the foliage. The flowers are followed by hairy, beak-like fruits, which curve down after flowering but become erect as they ripen. They have five segments that curl upwards to disperse the seeds explosively.

Right: The bright blue flowers are produced abundantly during the summer months.

Distribution: Europe.
Height and spread: 50cm/20n.
Habit and form: Herbaceous perennial.
Leaf shape: Palmate.
Pollinated: Bee or other insect.

Zonal pelargonium

Pelargonium zonale

Distribution: South Africa.
Height and spread:
90cm–3m/35in–10ft.
Habit and form: Subshrub.
Leaf shape: Circular.
Pollinated: Insect.

This plant, familiar in cultivation for growing in pots and bedding schemes, has its origins on the dry rocky hills, stony slopes and forest margins of South Africa, from the Southern Cape to Natal. The flowers of this strikingly beautiful species range from all shades of red to pink and pure white, and in its natural habitat it is an abundant and often conspicuous feature. *Pelargonium zonale* flowers throughout the year, with a peak in spring.

Left: The flowers are produced on conspicuous heads, ranging from red, through pink to pure white. The new growth of the characteristic 'horseshoe-marked' leaves are the perfect foil for the flowers.

Far right: The flowers are produced prolifically in spring.

Identification: This erect or scrambling, softly woody, evergreen shrub usually grows up to 90cm/35in but can reach heights up to 3m/10ft. The young branches are almost succulent and usually covered with hairs, but harden with age. The large leaves are often smooth and a characteristic dark horseshoe-shaped mark is often present. The distinctly irregular flowers are borne in a typically umbel-like inflorescence.

OTHER SPECIES OF NOTE

Wood crane's-bill *Geranium sylvaticum*
A pretty European flower of damp woods, hedges and meadows on limestone soils. It resembles bloody crane's-bill, *G. sanguinem*, but the leaves are less narrowly dissected and the flowers are usually pinkish-violet or even almost blue, but the colour is variable.

Dove's-foot crane's-bill *Geranium molle*
This is a short, hairy plant common in dry grassland, sand dunes and waste and cultivated land; often found in lawns. The leaves which have a rounded shape have five to nine lobes. The pink-purple, deeply lobed flowers are very small, often less than 10mm/⅜in across.

Geranium donianum
This alpine geranium from Nepal and Tibet is low-growing, reaching about 50mm–15cm/2–6in. It is found at altitudes of 3,300–4,500m/10,800–14,700ft on rocky mountain slopes. The flowers are pinkish-purple and each about 20mm/¾in across.

Musk storksbill *Erodium moschatum*
The purple flowers of this annual or biennial species from Europe are clustered in a flower-head at the top of the stems, from which develop long, pointed seedheads – hence the name. The fern-like leaves are hairy and slightly toothed.

Sun hibiscus

Lemon-yellow rosemallow, *Hibiscus calyphyllus*

Sun hibiscus is a fairly fast-growing perennial that flowers readily. It flowers mainly from January to April. It grows in thickets, along roadsides, in riverine forests, at forest edges and in disturbed areas. The leaves are edible and sometimes eaten as a vegetable. It is quite popular as a garden plant. It is native to South Africa, east Africa and Madagascar, and is also naturalized in Hawaii, as well as being widely cultivated.

Identification: This is a dense, perennial shrub with a rounded growth form. The leaves are large, light green, soft and velvety. The flowers are lemon-yellow, with a deep red to blackish centre, each about 10cm/4in across. The fruit is a papery capsule that splits open to reveal hairy or hairless seeds.

Distribution: Africa.
Height and spread: 3m x 30cm/10ft x 12in.
Habit and form: Woody perennial.
Leaf shape: Simple.
Pollinated: Insects, including butterflies.

Below: Sun hibiscus forms a dense, rounded shrub.

Left: The fruiting capsule is papery.

PRIMULA FAMIY

The Primulaceae, or primula family, occurs mainly in temperate and mountainous regions of the
Northern Hemisphere. Many species of Primula *are cultivated for their attractive flowers.*
The family contains about 20 genera and more than 1,000 species of perennials or herbs.
Cyclamen is a popular garden genus of the primula family.

Primrose

Primula vulgaris

Without doubt this plant is one of the most attractive and
best known of the primula family. It has long been
cultivated and its name derives from the Latin *prima rosa*
meaning 'first rose'. It frequently hybridizes with the related
cowslip, *P. veris*, although the flowers remain
pale yellow. Other colours arise through
hybridization with cultivated stock.

Identification: The rootstock becomes knotty with the
successive bases of fallen leaves and bears
cylindrical, branched rootlets on all sides. The leaves
are egg-shaped to oblong, about 12.5cm/5in long
and 40mm/1½in across in the middle, smooth
above with prominent, hairy veins and veinlets
beneath, the margins irregularly toothed, tapering into
a winged stalk. The fragrant flowers are pale yellow
with a darker centre and sepals forming a bell-shaped,
pleated tube. They appear from late winter to late spring,
each borne on a separate stalk and followed by an egg-
shaped capsule enclosed within a persistent calyx.

*Above: The primrose is a
woodland or
hedgerow plant.*

*Left: The
conspicuous
flowers are held
above a low rosette
of shiny green
leaves.*

Distribution: Europe.
Height and spread:
50mm–20cm/2–8in.
Habit and form: Herbaceous
perennial.
Leaf shape:
Obovate to
oblong.
Pollinated:
Insect.

*Right: Pink flowers,
growing wild are the
result of crosses with
cultivated plants.*

Giant cowslip

Primula florindae

The aptly named giant cowslip is native to
south-east Xizang in Tibet, where it grows in
marshes and along streams in the constantly
waterlogged soils. The species was named by the
renowned Himalayan plant explorer, Frank
Kingdon-Ward, in honour of his wife Florinda.
It was a true compliment as it is one of the most
imposing wild primroses to be seen and is
very fragrant. It requires a very moist,
acidic soil and flowers mainly from
early to late summer.

*Above and
left: The yellow
or rarely red
flowers have
a sweet
spicy scent.*

Identification:
Heart-shaped,
toothed, shiny
mid-green leaves
with rounded tips, on
stout winged stalks
40mm–20cm/
1½–8in long and often
tinged red, form large
herbaceous rosettes below
flowering stems that can reach
1m/3ft in height. Each
inflorescence consists of up to
40 pendent, funnel-shaped,
sulphur-yellow flowers,
smelling strongly of
nutmeg or cloves. Both the
stems and flowers are
farinose (dusted with a
mealy coating), and the overall habit
of the plant is
quite robust.

Distribution: South-eastern
Tibet.
Height and spread: Up
to 90cm/35in.
Habit and form:
Herbaceous perennial.
Leaf shape: Ovate
Pollinated: Insect.

*Left: The flowerheads
are held high above a
rosette of foliage.*

Oxlip

Primula elatior

Distribution: Europe.
Height and spread: To 30cm/12in.
Habit and form: Perennial.
Leaf shape: Rounded.
Pollinated: Insect.

The oxlip in Britain is mainly a woodland species with pale yellow flowers appearing in April and May. It is found in Europe north to southern England and southern Scandinavia. In continental Europe it also grows in damp meadows and sometimes by streams. It is a hairy perennial and its bright flowers attract pollinating insects. Oxlips sometimes hybridize with primroses and cowslips where the species grow close together.

Left: Primulas are short and grow with an upright habit.

Identification: The leaves are rounded towards the tip but narrow sharply towards the base. The pale yellow flowers grow several together, nodding on one side of the tall flower stalk. Each flower is about 15mm/⁹⁄₁₆in across.

Above: Oxlip has open, pale yellow flowers.

OTHER SPECIES OF NOTE

Cowslip *Primula veris*
This spring-flowering plant appears at the same time as the primrose, *P. vulgaris*, but is not as widespread (or as conspicuous) as that plant. It has a tight rosette of small, deep green, crinkled leaves and drooping clusters of small delicately scented yellow flowers on tall 25cm/10in stems.

Bird's-eye primrose *Primula farinosa*
This is a small primrose growing to about 15cm/6in, with obovate leaves growing at its base. The leaves have a characteristic mealy bloom, especially on the undersides. The pink flowers grow in an umbel at the top of the flower stem and each has a yellow 'eye' at its centre. It grows mainly in damp grassland.

Primula vialii
The pyramidal flowers of this highly unusual primula look like miniature red hot pokers. They are bicolored, with purple at the base and reddish fuchsia at the tip, borne on 40cm/16in stems during summer. It is native to China, but is now widely cultivated in gardens.

Yellow loosestrife *Lysimachia punctata*
This erect-growing perennial from south-eastern

and central Europe has lance- to elliptic-shaped, mid-green leaves that grow in whorls of three or four. The small, bright yellow flowers are borne in the leaf axils at the ends of the stems during the summer.

Ivy-leaved cyclamen

Sowbread, *Cyclamen hederifolium*

This pretty little cyclamen has a wide distribution stretching from south-eastern France, through central Europe, Greece (including Crete and many of the Aegean islands) and western Turkey. It inhabits woodland, scrub, and rocky hillsides from sea level to 1,300m/4,250ft, although its popularity in cultivation has led it to spread to other areas. The flowers are usually pink, but there is also a white-flowered form, though this is rare in the wild.

Identification: The pink flowers, with a purple-magenta, V-shaped blotch at the base of each petal, appear from mid- to late autumn. The leaves are very variable, and can be every shape from almost circular to lance-shaped. They vary from dull or bright plain green to plain silver with various forms of hastate (spear-shaped) pattern in between, with the pattern in silver, grey, cream or a different shade of green. The undersides can be green or purple-red.

Left: The flowers and foliage arise from a rounded tuber.

Distribution: Europe, chiefly the Mediterranean.
Height and spread: 15cm/6in.
Habit and form: Herbaceous perennial.
Leaf shape: Variable, chiefly ivy-shaped.
Pollinated: Insect.

Right: After flowering, the flower stalks coil down to the soil surface to deposit the seeds.

Below: The flowers mainly appear before the young leaves.

Yellow loosestrife

Lysimachia vulgaris

This perennial produces bright flowers in summer atop tall, softly hairy stems. It grows in damp ground such as in marshes, fens and alongside streams, rivers and lakes. It is found throughout Europe, but is absent from the north of the region. Yellow loosestrife is often grown as a garden plant and adds colour to water gardens and other damp sites.

Identification: Grows to about 1.5m/5ft tall, with erect stems and whorls of leaves. The long narrow inflorescences have many five-lobed yellow flowers. The plant spreads by sending out rhizomes.

Above: The tall erect stems of this plant, make it an imposing addition to the garden.

Distribution: Europe.
Height and spread: 1.5m/5ft.
Habit and form: Perennial.
Leaf shape: Lanceolate.
Pollinated: Insect.

Right: Yellow loosestrife is an abundant plant that can be invasive.

Left: The fruits of yellow loosestrife cluster at the top of the stems.

Sowbread

Cyclamen purpurascens

An evergreen perennial with shiny green leaves and pretty pink flowers. It grows mainly on rich moist soils in rocky woodland. Sowbread does well in the garden and thrives under shade, flowering from June to October. The seeds have a sweet covering that attracts ants, which then help to disperse the plant by carrying the seeds away to eat the sweet covering.

Above: The flowers rise up above the leaves on upright stems.

Distribution: Central and eastern Europe.
Height and spread: 20cm/8in.
Habit and form: Perennial.
Leaf shape: Round to heart-shaped.
Pollinated: Insect.

Identification: The foliage and flowers grow from a large underground corm. The plant has simple, rounded, heart-shaped basal leaves. Narrow flower stalks grow from the base, each producing a single fragrant pink flower with the lobes bent back upwards into a crown-like shape. The fruit capsules have tightly coiled stalks.

Right: The petals overlap tightly on the unopened flower.

Below: The leaves of cyclamen make this plant easy to identify even when not in flower.

Water violet

Hottonia palustris

Water violet is one of the prettiest of our waterplants with its whorls of delicate pale lilac flowers held aloft above the surface and opening in May to July. It is found in ponds and ditches across Europe, north to southern Sweden, and is also grown in garden ponds and water features. Water violet often goes unnoticed and looks like many 'water-weeds' below the water surface. However, when the flower stalks grow up they open into clusters of very pretty flowers.

Distribution: Europe.
Height and spread: 40cm/16in.
Habit and form: Perennial.
Leaf shape: Pinnate.
Pollinated: Insect.

Identification: The submerged parts of this species have whorls of pinnately dissected leaves. The flowering stalks grow straight up out of the water and bear whorls of pale flowers, each with a yellow central patch. Each flower is about 25mm/1in across.

Left: Flowering stalks appear above the water.

Far right: The seeds develop in small capsules.

OTHER SPECIES OF NOTE

Primula glomerata
A Himalayan species from western Nepal, which is also found as far as south-eastern Tibet. This primrose has pendent blue flowers in compact, rounded heads on stems to 30cm/12in tall. Each flower is funnel-shaped with notched petals, and the leaves have toothed margins. It grows on open slopes and flowers from August to November.

Primula involucrata
An Asian species, found from Pakistan to south-western China. The flowers are white, pink or blue, each with a yellow central 'eye', on slender stems about 30cm/12in tall. It grows mainly in wet ground and alongside streams, flowering from June to August.

Sikkim cowslip *Primula sikkimensis*
This pretty primula from Nepal and Tibet is common in damp sites and may appear in large numbers. It produces small clusters of yellow, scented flowers that droop. Each flower is up to 30mm/1¼in across with notched petals.

Primula aureata
A Himalayan species beloved of alpine gardeners and sadly over-collected in the wild. It is endemic to central Nepal where it grows on wet rocks at altitudes of 3,500–4,500m/ 11,500–14,700ft. The flowers are creamy-yellow with a golden patch in the centre.

Alpine snowbell

Soldanella alpina

One of the daintiest of alpine flowers, the alpine snowbell thrives in wet soil on mountain slopes, often around the melting margins of a snow patch. The small green leaves and bell-like nodding flowers are very attractive. It may also be grown as an alpine, usually under glass. It grows in the mountains of central Europe.

Identification: The rounded leaves are leathery in texture and dark green on long stalks. The flowers are in clusters of two to four on long stalks. The bell-shaped corolla is a delicate violet colour and has a deeply dissected fringe.

Right: The seeds contained in the seedhead are spread by the wind.

Distribution: Central Europe.
Height and spread: 50mm/2in.
Habit and form: Perennial.
Leaf shape: Rounded to kidney-shaped.
Pollinated: Insect.

Above: The flowers nod gently on flowering stalks that grow up from the low mat of leaves.

Auricula

Bear's-ear, *Primula auricula*

This primula species is native to central Europe, but has been introduced elsewhere. It is also a popular garden plant and many varieties have been produced in horticulture with flower colours varying widely. One of the common names is derived from the fanciful resemblance of the leaves to the ears of a bear.

Identification: A short perennial with fleshy, mealy leaves, usually toothed at the margins and arising from the base of the plant. The flower stalk bears a compact umbel of bright yellow flowers, each about 15mm/⁹⁄₁₆in across. Each flower has a pale ring at its centre.

Below and right and far right: The flowers are tubular at the base and open in a compact mass at the top of the flower stem.

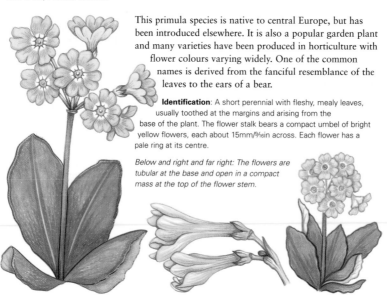

Distribution: Central Europe.
Height and spread: 15cm/6in.
Habit and form: Perennial.
Leaf shape: Rounded.
Pollinated: Insect.

Bog pimpernel

Anagallis tenella

Found mainly in damp grassland and bogs, this is a trailing plant with narrow stems that root at intervals from the nodes. The flowers appear from May to September.

Below: The seed rattles inside the capsule-like fruit.

Identification: The stems bear small, paired, almost circular leaves that are mostly arranged opposite. From these trailing stems arise slender flower stalks each bearing a single pale pink or whitish funnel-shaped flower with five deep lobes marked with narrow darker veins.

Distribution: Western Europe.
Height and spread: 30mm x 20cm/1¼ x 8in.
Habit and form: Perennial.
Leaf shape: Rounded.
Pollinated: Insect.

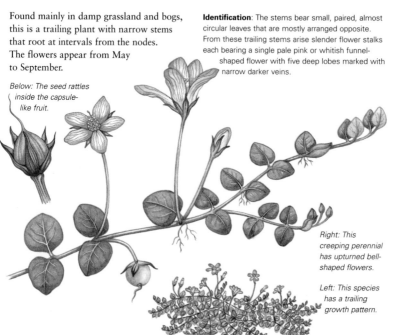

Right: This creeping perennial has upturned bell-shaped flowers.

Left: This species has a trailing growth pattern.

Sea milkwort
Glaux maritima

Distribution: Europe; North America.
Height and spread: 50mm x 30cm/2 x 12in.
Habit and form: Perennial.
Leaf shape: Elliptical.
Pollinated: Insect.

Right: The small pink flowers are stalkless, growing straight from the stem.

Sea milkwort is quite common on saline grassland and saltmarsh, as well as on and around coastal rocks and shingle, and occasionally on inland saline soils. It flowers from May to September. It has a wide distribution, especially around coasts. The flowers are inconspicuous and grow from the base of the leaves. They are five-lobed and the calyx is pink at the middle, with a paler edge. They are probably pollinated by small insects.

Below: Sea milkwort has mat-like growth.

Identification: A creeping perennial with fleshy, nearly opposite leaves. Each leaf is 4–12mm/³⁄₁₆–½in long. The flowers, about 4mm/³⁄₁₆in across, emerge from the leaf axils and each flower has a five-lobed pinkish or white calyx. Petals are absent. The fruit is a round capsule that splits into five to release the seeds.

Below: The fruit is a five-valved capsule.

OTHER SPECIES OF NOTE

Scottish primrose
Primula scotica
This is like a miniature bird's-eye primrose, *P. farinosa*, but the flowers are dark purple. This charming primrose is restricted to Orkney and northern Scotland, where it grows on coastal cliffs and dune grassland.

Creeping Jenny *Lysimachia nummularia*
With its cup-shaped deep yellow flowers, creeping Jenny is an attractive flower and one that is often grown in gardens. Its creeping habit makes it ideal for rock gardens. In the wild it is a plant of wet places, such as damp woodland and hedgerows, or stream banks. It is a hairless perennial with rounded leaves.

Yellow pimpernel *Lysimachia nemorum*
This is another low-growing species of damp places. Its leaves are more pointed than those of creeping Jenny and the flowers, which are a paler yellow each have a darker central 'eye'. Both species have a wide distribution in Europe, except for the far north.

Chickweed wintergreen *Trientalis europaea*
A charming little perennial flower of damp woods on acidic soils, especially associated with pine. Its leaves grow in a single whorl of five or six with a single flower on a slender stalk above. The flower is white usually with seven lobes.

Scarlet pimpernel
Anagallis arvensis

A widespread 'weed', easily identified by its bright red or pink flowers, though one form has blue flowers. The blue variety is often grown as a garden plant. It often grows in rough ground near crops and also on sand dunes. In the north of its range it tends to be coastal. The growth is trailing, and the weak stems often lie close to or along the ground. This species would be unobtrusive but for its startlingly bright red flowers, which stand out, held out on long, slender stalks.

Distribution: Europe.
Height and spread: 30cm/12in.
Habit and form: Annual.
Leaf shape: Oval.
Pollinated: Insect.

Right: If undisturbed scarlet pimpernel forms mats by rooting at the nodes.

Right: The red flowers are 10mm/³⁄₈in wide.

Identification: Scarlet pimpernel is a hairless annual 'weed' with weak square stems and opposite ovate leaves. The pretty flowers arise singly, and the pink or red corolla is five-lobed, opening wide in bright sunshine. The fruit is a rounded capsule that splits at its middle when ripe to release the seeds.

DOGBANE FAMILY

The genera and species of the Apocynaceae, or dogbane family, are distributed primarily in the tropics and subtropics and are poorly represented in temperate regions. Plants of the Apocynaceae are often poisonous, although some species provide medicinal drugs. They include trees, shrubs, herbs and lianas. There are about 2,100 species in the family.

White rubber vine

Landolphia owariensis

This is a liane climbing to 12m/39ft or more. It grows as a clambering climber up to the canopies in forests and at forest edges. In some undisturbed forests it can be abundant. It flowers mainly between March and July and thrives in sandy clay loams and sandy loams. The plant used to be tapped for its latex, which was used to make a kind of rubber. The flowers are important for honeybees in some areas and the fruits are used to make a sour but refreshing drink. The fruits are dispersed by birds and monkeys.

Identification: A climbing shrub or tree, but more often a woody liana. The young branches and tendrils have dense grey-brown hairs. Sticky white latex is found throughout the plant. The leaves are opposite, long oval, about 70mm–17cm/2¾–6½in long, rounded at the base and with a pointed tip. The flowers are white or cream-coloured, and sweet-scented. The fruit is edible, yellow or green, turning brown. It is rounded, usually 30–40mm/1¼–1½in across, smooth and yellow when ripe, with red markings and dotted with pale breathing pores (lenticels).

Right: The fruit is the size of a small orange with a woody shell.

Distribution: Tropical eastern and central Africa.
Height and spread: 12m x 50cm/39ft x 20in.
Habit and form: Woody perennial.
Pollinated: Insect.
Leaf shape: Simple.

Paste rubber

Saba comorensis

Another liane, climbing high on trees to 20m/65½ft. It flowers between August and November and is common in riverine forest and rainforest, at forest edges and in thickets. An infusion made from the leaves is used to treat backache and chest pain.

Above: The young fruit is pitted and green. It ripens to a red-orange colour.

Left: This liana can grow quite a distance along other trees in its habitat.

Distribution: Tropical Africa.
Height and spread: 20m x 60cm/65½ft x 24in.
Habit and form: Woody perennial.
Leaf shape: Simple.
Pollinated: Insect.

Identification: A climbing or scrambling creeper or shrub with hairless reddish stems dotted with white breathing pores. It clambers to about 20m/65½ft. The outer bark is dark brown and slightly rough. When cut it has a reddish appearance and exudes milky white latex. The leaves are large, oval to oblong, leathery and shiny. The sweet-scented flowers, white with a yellow throat, are borne in dense, many-flowered terminal bunches. The fruit, which is edible, is a large fleshy berry, rounded, 25–60mm/1–2¼in across, thick, green and lemon-like, becoming yellow or orange as it ripens.

Oleander

Rose bay, *Nerium oleander*

When oleander grows in the wild it occurs along watercourses, in gravel soils and damp ravines. It is widely cultivated, particularly in warm temperate and subtropical regions, where it grows in parks, gardens and along roadsides. It prefers dry, warm climates and may naturalize in such areas. The whole plant, including the sap, is toxic.

Distribution: Northern Africa; eastern Mediterranean; and South-east Asia.
Height and spread: 4m/13ft.
Habit and form: Evergreen shrub.
Leaf shape: Lanceolate.
Pollinated: Insect.

Right: Oleander forms a loose, attractive, evergreen shrub that is widely cultivated for its appearance.

Right: The individual flowers have five petals and may be pink or white. They are highly fragrant.

Identification: Oleander is a summer-flowering evergreen shrub with narrow, entire, short-stalked, leathery, dark or grey-green leaves, 10–23cm/4–9in long, with prominent midribs, usually arising from the stem in groups of three. The terminal flowerheads are usually pink or white; each five petal flower is about 50mm/2in in diameter and the throat is fringed with long, petal-like projections. The fruits are long, narrow capsules, 10–12.5cm/4–5in long and 6–8mm/¼–⁵⁄₁₆in in diameter, which open to disperse fluffy seeds.

OTHER SPECIES OF NOTE

Madagascar periwinkle *Catharanthus roseus*
An evergreen perennial, 45cm–1.2m/18in–4ft tall with flowers of white, pink and intermediate colours, above deep green, glossy, oval leaves. Originally a native of Madagascar, it is now widely naturalized in many tropical countries as a garden escapee.

Herald's trumpet, Easter lily vine
Beaumontia grandiflora
This evergreen, woody climber has large, white, funnel-shaped flowers with pointed lobes. It grows in the Himalayan region at 150–1,400m/492–4,593ft and flowers mainly in March and April. The flowers are about 10cm/4in across. The leaves are opposite and have a papery texture. It is often grown as a garden plant in tropical regions.

Indian oleander *Nerium indicum*
An evergreen shrub native to India, Afghanistan and central Nepal. It has long, pointed leaves and terminal clusters of red, pink or white fragrant flowers. Each flower is about 40mm/1½in across and five-lobed. Indian Oleander is used in Ayurvedic medicine to treat digestive problems and also skin complaints.

Elephant's trunk *Pachypodium namaquanum*
One of the oddest of plants, this tree-like plant grows in the Namib Desert of south-western Africa (northern Cape and southern Namibia). Its woody, spiny trunk reaches 2m/6½ft or more high and is topped by a mass of foliage. It is also known as 'halfmens' because of its fancied resemblance to a person (half plant, half human).

Simple-spined num-num

Carandus plum, Carrisse, *Carissa edulis*

A scrambling shrub or small tree with simple, opposite spines. The young leaves and twigs are often pubescent. This species grows well in savannah woodlands, thickets, forests, and in disturbed areas at medium altitudes (1,100–1,600m/3608–5,249ft,). It flowers mainly between July and October. The fruits are edible and eaten, especially by children. An infusion of the leaves is used to treat headaches, and the decoction of the roots is used to treat malaria.

Identification: The bark is dark grey with straight woody spines to 50mm/2in, often in pairs. Milky latex is characteristic to all members of this family. The leaves are opposite, leathery, shiny and dark green, to 50mm/2in, pointed at the tip and with a rounded base. The pink and white flowers are fragrant, and borne in terminal clusters. Each flower measures 20mm/¾in. The fruit is a rounded berry, about 10mm/⅜in, purple-black when ripe, sweet and edible, containing two to four seeds.

Distribution: Tropical Africa; tropical Asia; Indian Ocean islands; Australia.
Height and Spread: 5 x 3m/16 x 10ft.
Habit and form: Woody perennial.
Leaf shape: Simple, blade ovate, elliptic or almost orbicular.
Pollinated: Insect.

Left: This is a spiny shrub or small tree to 5m/16ft, sometimes seen growing as a climber.

GENTIAN FAMILY

Gentianaceae, the gentian family is well known for its brightly coloured flowers, which are popular as garden plants. Many plants of the family also have medicinal properties, and some are used as bitter flavourings, especially in Europe. There are about 1,225 species, mainly in temperate, subtropical or mountain regions.

Stemless gentian

Gentianella, *Gentiana acaulis*

In the wild this gentian grows in the Alps and Carpathian Mountains in dry acid grasslands, bogs, on rubble and scree slopes and occasionally in alpine woods, at elevations of 1,400–3,000m/4,593–9,840ft. Although it usually grows in acid soils it can sometimes also be found on chalky limestone or sandstone. Its intense blue, funnel-shaped flowers, which almost obscure the foliage, make it one of the showiest alpine plants that can be seen in Europe, when it appears in early summer.

Right: The low mat of foliage can be inconspicuous until the flowers appear in early summer.

Identification: The leaves in the basal rosette are 25–40mm/1–1½in long, lance- to egg-shaped and glossy dark green. On the short flower stems the leaves are smaller and broader. The solitary 50mm/2in trumpet-shaped, lobed flowers are vivid dark blue, spotted green within. They are produced terminally on short stalks in spring and early summer and are followed by stalked, ellipsoid seed capsules.

Distribution: Europe from Spain to the Balkans.
Height and spread: 10cm x 1m/4 x 39in.
Habit and form: Slow-growing perennial.
Leaf shape: Lanceolate.
Pollinated: Bee and butterfly.

Autumn-flowering gentian

Gentiana sino-ornata

This plant, discovered by the Scots plant hunter George Forrest in 1904 in south-west China, yields the richest tones of blue trumpets among the fallen leaves of late autumn. It is a native of north-west Yunnan and adjacent Tibet, and grows in wet ground. It prefers a rich acid soil, which drains well but will hold moisture, and is often found growing in well-oxygenated, moving water. The flowers exhibit a range of colour from royal blue to purple-blue, interspersed with greenish-yellow bands.

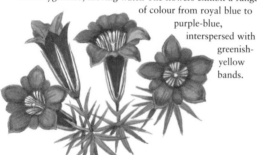

Identification: The stems of this prostrate perennial, 15–20cm/6–8in long, ascend at the tips and root at nodes. The basal leaves form loose rosettes; on the stems the dark green leaves are paired, narrowly lance-shaped, about 40mm/1½in long. The deep blue, tubular flowers, up to 50mm/2in across, are borne singly on the ends of the stems, with lobes twice the length of the tube. They have five bands of deep purple-blue, panelled green-white, on the outside and are paler within, sometimes with a streaked throat.

Right: The bright blue flowers appear at the end of the stems in damp acidic soils and give a stunning autumnal display.

Distribution: South-western China; Tibet.
Height and spread: 15–20cm/6–8in.
Habit and form: Prostrate herbaceous perennial.
Leaf shape: Lanceolate.
Pollinated: Insect.

Yellow wort

Blackstonia perfoliata

Distribution: Europe.
Height and spread:
45cm/18in.
Habit: Herbaceous perennial.
Leaf shape: Ovate, appearing perfoliate on flower stems.
Pollinated: Insect.

Yellow wort is an almost unmistakable plant that is able to grow in very alkaline soil. It is most commonly found growing on dry grassland over shallow chalk, limestone soils and occasionally on dunes. The eight-petalled, yellow flowers close in the afternoon and the waxy blue-green leaves are highly distinctive. The plant was given its botanical name in honour of an eighteenth-century London apothecary and botanist, John Blackstone.

Left: The basal rosette is inconspicuous when growing in grassland but the distinctive, blue-green, tall, upright stems with their encircling, slightly cup-shaped leaves are unmistakable.

Identification: The oval leaves, which are bluish-green and hairless, are stalkless and form a loose rosette at the base of the stem. The leaves on the stem are in pairs with their bases fused together, making it appear as if the stem passes through the middle of a single leaf. Between early summer and mid-autumn the yellow flowers appear on 45cm/18in stems. They have eight petals, joined at the base to form a short tube.

Below: The tight, green buds give rise to showy, yellow blooms.

OTHER SPECIES OF NOTE

Sea rose *Orphium frutescens*
The glossy pink stars of this bushy, evergreen perennial attract attention, especially when the surrounding vegetation goes brown and dormant. The sea rose is found in South Africa, along the south-western coast of the Cape, growing in clumps on sandy flats and marshes.

Feverwort *Centaurium erythraea*
The feverwort is a small, erect annual or biennial herb that is indigenous to Europe, western Asia and North Africa, and has become naturalized in North America. The stem grows up to 30cm/12in high and is topped with numerous pink or red flowers. It favours dry, shady banks, waysides and pastures.

Gentiana tubiflora
An Asian species, found at high altitude, 4,000–5,000m/13,100–16,400ft, from Himachal Pradesh to Tibet. It is a cushion plant with rosettes of tiny leaves and grows on open slopes and scree. When it flowers, the large blue flowers look most impressive.

Seaside centaury *Centaurium littorale*
A biennial that grows mainly on coastal sand dunes in western Europe, but also on inland sandy soils, especially in central Europe. It has narrow leaves and a flat-topped inflorescence made up of pink flowers, each about 12mm/½in across.

Great yellow gentian

Gentiana lutea

This large-flowered, tall species is found mainly in meadows, especially in alpine zones, up to about 2,500m/8,200ft in the Alps and other mountain ranges. Being poisonous, it is avoided by grazing cattle and sheep and stands out well in alpine pastures. A bitter extract is derived from the roots and used in a range of flavourings, medicines and alcoholic drinks.

Identification: A tall, erect gentian, reaching a height of about 60cm/24in. The sturdy stem is unbranched and has large oval leaves at intervals, the upper leaves clasping the stem. The yellow flowers appear in summer and grow in tight clusters from the bases of the upper leaves.

Below: Great yellow gentian has an upright growth habit.

Distribution: Central Europe.
Height and spread:
60cm/24in.
Habit and form: Perennial.
Leaf shape: Oval.
Pollinated: Insect.

Above: The flower has narrow, spreading petal lobes.

Spring gentian

Gentiana verna

Although small and less conspicuous than many, spring gentian is considered to be one of the most beautiful of all gentians. It also has the allure of rarity, at least in Great Britain, where it is only found in a few sites in northern England. It also occurs in the Burren in Ireland. In Europe in can be found scattered in the Alps and nearby mountain ranges. It typically grows on damp grassland, to an altitude of about 3,000m/9,840ft.

Below: The flower is prominent.

Above: The five lobes spread wide.

Identification: This is a compact, low-growing plant with small, oval leaves. The flowers open on erect narrow stalks from April to June and are bright blue, with a white centre. The tube is narrow and the five lobes spread out wide.

Right: The flowers are clear blue with a white centre.

Distribution: British Isles.
Height and spread: 50–75mm/2–3in.
Habit and form: Perennial.
Leaf shape: Oval.
Pollinated: Insect.

Field gentian

Gentianella campestris

This is a common European gentian of pastures and heaths, and is also seen in sand dunes. It is found throughout most of Europe, except for the far north. It has a wide flowering season from June through September. Species in the genus *Gentianella* differ from true gentians (genus *Gentiana*) in lacking the small extra corolla lobes between the main lobes, and also in having a fringe of hairs in the throat of the flower.

Identification: A fairly short gentian with simple or slightly branching stems bearing paired, lanceolate, pointed stem leaves. The narrow tube-shaped corolla opens into four lobes and is pale lilac or white in colour. The calyx has four unequal lobes.

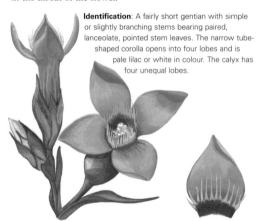

Distribution: Europe.
Height and spread: 20–30mm/¾–1¼in.
Habit and form: Biennial.
Leaf shape: Lanceolate.
Pollinated: Insect.

Above left: Field gentian's natural habitat, like its name suggests, is in grassland.

Left: The stems of field gentian have a branching habit.

Far left: The four petals are bluish-purple and open reluctantly unless bright sun is out.

Lesser centaury

Centaurium pulchellum

Centauries are related to gentians, but have smaller, pink flowers in clusters. Lesser centaury is found in damp ground, for example in woodland rides, and also close to the sea. It is local over much of Europe, especially in coastal sites, but is absent from the far north.

Distribution: Europe; and eastern, western and Central Asia.
Height and spread: to 20cm/8in.
Habit and form: Annual.
Leaf shape: Oval.
Pollinated: Insect.

Left: The stem is often branched.

Right: Lesser centaury has a bushy appearance, with its branched stems adding to the effect.

Identification: This plant lacks a basal rosette of leaves, and has a single or slightly branching stem. The stem has open clusters of small pink or white flowers, each flower with five (sometimes four) lobes. The leaves are oval and pointed with longitudinal veins.

OTHER SPECIES OF NOTE

Trumpet gentian *Gentiana clusii*
One of the most impressive of the gentians with large, deep blue trumpet-shaped flowers arising from a low tuft of basal leaves. A beautiful perennial flower of alpine meadows, notably in eastern France and southern Germany, usually on limestone, up to about 3,000m/9,840ft.

Fringed gentian *Gentianella ciliata*
This gentian is an erect biennial with lanceolate leaves. The blue flowers are large compared to the size of the plant, and measure up to about 50mm/2in across. A characteristic feature is the fringe of hairs around each of the corolla lobes.

Chiltern gentian *Gentianella germanica*
This bushy gentian takes its name from its British haunts – it is a local plant of the Chiltern Hills. In fact it has a wider distribution in Europe and is found in chalk grassland from the Netherlands southwards into central Europe. The bluish-purple flowers are about 30mm/1¼in across.

Gentiana tianshanica
This Asian gentian is about 25cm/10in tall and has dense clusters of flowers, each with a purple tube and blue triangular lobes. It grows mainly on alpine slopes of the Himalayas, from Pakistan to Uttar Pradesh, across to Central Asia. The species name refers to a Chinese mountain range.

Willow gentian

Gentiana asclepiadea

Willow gentian is quite a popular garden plant and grows well in shady borders, where its arching stems produce bright blue flowers. The wild species occasionally produces white flowers. The distribution stretches from central Europe to western Asia. It prefers damp sites such as shady woods, around rocky outcrops and mountain meadows.

Identification: A tufted perennial with slender stems and pointed leaves, each with between three and five obvious veins. The trumpet-shaped flowers have pointed lobes.

Distribution: Central and southern Europe to western Asia.
Height and spread: 60cm/24in.
Habit and form: Perennial.
Leaf shape: Lanceolate.
Pollinated: Insect.

Above: Willow gentian has long willow-like leaves.

Left: Willow gentian has an arching habit.

BELLFLOWER FAMILY

The bellflower family, Campanulaceae, contains 2,000 species, mainly in the northern temperate zone.
Most species are herbs, and many produce showy flowers, which are often blue in colour. A good
number are cultivated as garden plants. The corolla is usually lobed, often with a distinct tube, and
the flowers are attractive to insects.

Giant bellflower

Campanula latifolia

Bellflowers can be identified easily from their flowers, which have joined corollas, commonly bell-shaped with five equal lobes at the spreading mouth. Giant bellflower is a stout, hairy perennial of European woods and shady areas, typically on moist soil. It bears blue or pale blue (sometimes white) flowers during the summer. This decorative bellflower is sometimes grown as a garden plant.

Identification: A softly hairy plant with unbranched, angled leafy stems with regularly-toothed, ovate-lanceolate leaves. It has large blue bell-shaped, stalked flowers, 15–50mm/⁹⁄₁₆–2in, clustered in leafy racemes. The flowers are hairy on the inside, and this feature may help visiting bees to gain a secure foothold.

Distribution: Europe, but absent from north and south-west and most of the Mediterranean region.
Height and spread: Up to 1m/39in.
Habit and form: Perennial.
Leaf shape: Ovate.
Pollinated: Bee or self-pollinated.

Top left: The flower is deeply lobed.

Left: Showy flowers sit atop leafy stems.

Nettle-leaved bellflower

Campanula trachelium

Thriving in woodland and scrub areas, nettle-leaved bellflower bears pale blue or violet flowers from July to September. In the Middle Ages, plants that resembled parts of the body were used to treat specific bodily ailments; chopped roots of bellflowers were used in a gargle to relieve sore throats and tonsilitis because the shape of the flowers resembles a throat. Two popular names, 'throat-wort' and 'husk-wort' reflect this belief.

Identification: Nettle-leaved bellflower has hairy, unbranched, angled leafy stems. The leaves are ovate-lanceolate to heart-shaped. They are long stalked and bluntly toothed, resembling the leaves of nettles. The flowers appear singly or in twos or threes, have triangular, pointed petals and a white style in the centre.

Above: The flower colour varies from lilac-blue to almost white.

Far right: This campanula is also known as 'bats-in-the'belfry'.

Right: This tall plant self-seeds.

Distribution: Europe, north towards Sweden.
Height and spread: Up to 1m/39in.
Habit and form: Perennial.
Leaf shape: Ovate.
Pollinated: Insect.

Large Venus' looking-glass

Legousia speculum-veneris

Large Venus' looking-glass frequents cultivated and bare or wasteland, and produces violet flowers from May to July. The range of this interesting species has been much reduced by the use of modern herbicides.

Identification: This is a downy-haired, much branched annual with obovate leaves. The lower leaves are sometimes stalked. The flowers are up to 20mm/¾in across, often in loose clusters. It grows to about 40cm/16in tall. The upper leaves have wavy edges and are unstalked. The flower colour may vary from purple to lilac, or even, sometimes white. The narrow sepals are roughly the same length as the petals. The fruit is a capsule, up to about 15mm/⁹⁄₁₆in long.

Top: The flowers spread out wide in a star-like shape.

Right: Each petal narrows to a point at its tip.

Distribution: South-western and south-central Europe, north to the Netherlands.
Height and spread: Up to 40cm/16in.
Habit and form: Annual.
Leaf shape: Obovate.
Pollinated: Insect.

Right: The flowers have narrow sepals and lobed petals.

OTHER SPECIES OF NOTE

Bonnet bellflower *Codonopsis ovata*
This plant from the western Himalayas has small, oval, greyish and downy leaves, and two or more flowers on a stem. The drooping, bell-shaped flowers appear from early summer; they are pale greyish-blue with purple reticulations and inside have an orange-and-white base.

Harebell *Campanula rotundifolia*
This little wildflower is found beside streams, on heaths and moors, and in grassy places. It has a basal rosette of rounded or kidney-shaped leaves, with smaller, thin, pointed leaves up the stem, and large, pale blue bellflowers.

Clustered bellflower *Campanula glomerata*
The botanical name of this bee-pollinated plant exactly describes the shape and arrangement of its flowers. *Campanula* means 'little bell'. The pretty violet-blue flowers are gathered together or clustered at the tips of the stems. It is found on chalk and limestone grassland, scrub and open woodland, and cliffs and dunes by the sea.

Creeping bellflower *Campanula rapunculoides*
With its pretty clusters of violet-blue, bell-shaped flowers, creeping bellflower is a very invasive summer-flowering perennial, which was originally grown in gardens and is now naturalized in fields, woods and rough ground, spreading freely by root-suckers on roadsides and in hedges.

Peach-leaved bellflower

Campanula persicifolia

The peach-leaved bellflower is an extremely pretty wildflower noted for its tall, thin stems with a few scattered leaves, and large, open bellflowers, which are borne freely during the summer months. It was at one time grown as a culinary vegetable, but is now more commonly grown as an ornamental plant, this having led to its occurrence as a garden escapee in many areas. The plant prefers well-drained, alkaline soils and can grow in light woodland or open situations such as grassland.

Identification: The plant is a rosette-forming perennial with slender, white rhizomes and evergreen, narrow basal leaves, which are lance-shaped to oblong or oval, toothed, bright green and 10–15cm/4–6in long. Short terminal racemes of two or three, occasionally solitary, slightly pendent, cup-shaped flowers up to 50mm/2in across, varying from white to lilac-blue, are produced on slender stems or from the leaf axils, in early or midsummer. The seeds ripen from late summer to mid-autumn.

Distribution: Europe to western and northern Asia.
Height and spread: 1m x 45cm/39 x 18in.
Habit and form: Herbaceous perennial.
Leaf shape: Lanceolate.
Pollinated: Bee, fly, beetle, moth and butterfly.

Below: The tall, thin, showy flower stems support numerous open, slightly pendent, blue bellflowers.

Giant lobelia

Lobelia deckenii

The giant lobelia grows on Kilimanjaro in Kenya, between 3,700–4,300m/12,000–14,000ft, in an alpine region dominated by small shrubs. The plant is endemic to the area and exceptionally striking. In order to protect the sensitive leaf buds from the sub-zero night-time temperatures, it closes its leaves around the central core while the covered rosettes secrete a slimy solution that helps to insulate and preserve them. It is pollinated by birds, especially the brightly coloured sunbirds that inhabit the area. Several related subspecies exist on the mountains of East Africa, including *L. deckenii* ssp. *keniensis* on Mount Kenya. The plants are monocarpic – each rosette dying after flowering – but are characterized by extremely long lifespans.

Distribution: Restricted to a few east African mountains.
Height and spread: Up to 3m/10ft or more.
Habit and form: Rosette-forming evergreen perennial.
Leaf shape: Ovate to oblong.
Pollinated: Bird.

Right: Each flower is shaped for the bills of visiting sunbirds that feed on the rich nectar.

Identification: The thick, hollow flower stem, growing up to 3m/10ft, arises out of the centre of a tight rosette of leaves that are broadly oval to oblong, glaucous to shiny, strongly ridged down the midrib on the lower side, with clearly defined veination at almost right angles to the midrib. In immature specimens, the rosette of leaves is arranged in a tight spiral, with a cabbage-like central bud. The flower spike is covered with spiralling, triangular bracts that conceal blue flowers.

Ivy-leaved bellflower

Wahlenbergia hederacea

Ivy-leaved bellflower is a most charming, shyly-blooming plant of damp, shady places. It produces pale blue flowers from July to August. It likes acid, peaty soils such as in moorland, heaths and acid woodland. In Britain it is most common in south and south-western England and in Wales. It may be found growing in damp lawns.

Identification: Slender and creeping with weak stems and shallowly lobed, alternate ivy-like leaves. The bell-shaped lobed flowers measure 6–10mm/¼–⅜in, and arise individually on long stalks from the leaf axils.

Right: The flower is bell-shaped as its name suggests.

Right: The stems are weak.

Distribution: Western Europe, northward to Scotland.
Height and spread: Up to 30cm/12in.
Habit and form: Creeping perennial.
Leaf shape: Lobed.
Pollinated: Insect.

Below: This delicate flower can easily be damaged.

Water lobelia

Lobelia dortmanna

The nodding pale lilac flowers of water lobelia rise on leafless stems from rosettes of submerged leaves in late summer. It thrives in still or slow-moving, usually acid, water to a depth to 3m/10ft.

Identification: Aquatic plant with hollow stems and stalkless linear leaves arranged in a basal rosette. The flowers are 12–20mm/½–¾in with two upward-pointing and three downward-pointing petals and very reduced bracts.

Below and right: The delicate flowers droop from narrow stems above the water.

Distribution: Northern and north-central Europe, scattered to south-western France and Russia.
Height and spread: 60cm/24in.
Habit and form: Aquatic perennial.
Leaf shape: Linear.
Pollinated: Insect.

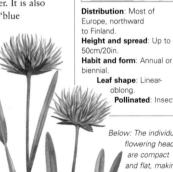

OTHER SPECIES OF NOTE

Spreading bellflower
Campanula patula
Spreading bellflower is a flower of open woods and scrubby grassland. It is found mainly in central and northern Europe, but is rare and local in Britain. It has pretty pale to purplish-blue flowers with deep, spreading lobes, opening in the summer months. It is grown in gardens, from which it sometimes escapes.

Round-headed rampion *Phyteuma orbiculare*
This is an upright, unbranched perennial of dry grassland and chalky soil. It has linear, stalked and toothed basal leaves and small flowers that are produced in dense, globular heads from June to August. The flowerheads appear green and open to clear blue with an unusual appearance. They fade to green at the end of summer.

Heath lobelia *Lobelia urens*
An erect perennial of acid heath and woodland, with solid leafy stems and oblong toothed leaves. Heath lobelia bears purple-blue flowers in loose spikes in August and September. It is found mainly in western and south-western Europe.

Codonopsis convolvulacea
This clambering perennial grows in Nepal, Burma and south-western China. It has attractive blue, bell-shaped flowers, often with a reddish ring on the inside, and with spreading lobes. Each flower is about 50mm/2in across. The leaves are smooth and shiny.

Sheep's-bit

Jasione montana

The English name of this bright-blue-flowering plant of lime-free soil, refers to the way it is cropped or 'bit' by sheep in the rough grass pastures, heath and shingle it frequents. The pretty blue flowering heads, appear from May to September. It is also known by the country names 'blue bonnets', 'blue cap' or 'blue buttons'. When the leaves or stems of the plant are bruised they emit a disagreeable smell.

Identification: Upright and slightly hairy, with wavy-edged linear oblong to lanceolate leaves. The florets are small, on globular heads, with a ruff of bracts beneath. Each floret produces a fruit capsule, which eventually opens to release seeds.

Below: The flowering heads are borne on narrow stems.

Distribution: Most of Europe, northward to Finland.
Height and spread: Up to 50cm/20in.
Habit and form: Annual or biennial.
Leaf shape: Linear-oblong.
Pollinated: Insect.

Below: The individual flowering heads are compact and flat, making them tolerant of wind.

EUPHORBIA FAMILY

The Euphorbiaceae, or euphorbia family, form one of the largest families of herbs, shrubs, and trees, generally characterized by the occurrence of milky, often toxic sap. The family contains mostly monoecious (bearing flowers of both sexes on one plant) and sometimes succulent and cactus-like. The flower structure is complex, with a female flower surrounded by several reduced male flowers.

Wood spurge

Robb's euphorbia, *Euphorbia amygdaloides* var. *robbiae*

The wood spurge is an attractive perennial plant of broadleaved woodland and shady banks. It spreads by underground runners until eventually the evergreen leaves form a low carpet over the ground, smothering smaller plants. Upright spikes of lime-green flowers emerge in spring and persist through early summer. The species is widespread across Europe, with this subspecies being restricted to north-western Turkey. The species has become popular in cultivation and can often be found outside its natural geographical range.

Identification: This bushy, softly hairy, evergreen perennial has reddish-green, biennial stems and spoon- to egg-shaped, leathery leaves, which are 25–75mm/1–3in long. The leaves are shiny dark green, becoming much darker in winter, and are closely set on the stems. From mid-spring to early summer it bears terminal flattened flower clusters, 18cm/7in tall, of greenish-yellow cyathia (groups of male and female flowers lacking petals and sepals) surrounded by cup-shaped bracts.

Distribution: North-western Turkey.
Height and spread: 60 x 30cm/24 x 12in.
Habit and form: Evergreen perennial.
Leaf shape: Obovate.
Pollinated: Insect.

Above left: The greenish-yellow flowers are cup-shaped.

Left: The flowers are held in spikes.

Castor oil plant

Ricinus communis

This fast-growing species, originally a native of north-eastern Africa to western Asia, has long been cultivated both for its ornamental value and also for the castor oil yielded by the seeds, which are highly toxic. As a result, the plant's range has been greatly extended and it is now a common wayside species in many tropical and subtropical locations worldwide.

Right: The flower-heads have male flowers at the base, and female flowers at the top.

Below: The leaves are 15–45cm/6–18in long, with six to 11 toothed lobes.

Identification: The succulent stem is 7.5–15cm/ 3–6in in diameter, and very variable in all aspects. The smooth leaves are alternately arranged, circular, palmately compound. The flowers are numerous in long inflorescences, with male flowers at the base and red female flowers at the tips; there are no petals in either sex, but three to five greenish sepals. The flower is followed by a round fruit capsule, 2.5cm/1in in diameter, on an elongated stalk that is usually spiny. The fruit is green at first, ripening to brown, and usually contains three attractively mottled seeds.

Distribution: Africa.
Height and spread: Up to 10–13m/33–42ft.
Habit and form: Shrubby perennial.
Leaf shape: Palmate.
Pollinated: Insect.

Sun spurge

Euphorbia helioscopia

Distribution: Europe.
Height and spread: Up to 50cm/20in.
Habit and form: Annual.
Leaf shape: Obovate.
Pollinated: Insect.

Right: Euphorbias take their name from Euphorbus, a Greek physician who used the plant medicinally.

The specific name of sun spurge comes from the Greek, meaning 'look up at the sun' and refers to the flat-topped flower-heads, which spread out to be fully exposed to the sunlight. Sun spurge can be heard as well as seen as, when fully ripe, the three-seeded capsule splits open with a crack, firing the seeds away from the plant. Ants are attracted by oil in the fleshy appendage of the seeds and gather them up to carry them further afield. The stems and leaves of spurges contain a poisonous milky juice.

Identification: Spurges are easily recognized from what looks like a single flower and is in fact a group of flowers with a female in the centre and several males, each represented by a stamen only. The structure is surrounded by four or five conspicuous glands. Sun spurge is upright and hairless with a single, reddish stem, and obovate, finely-toothed leaves, tapering to a narrow base.

Left: Small flowers with green oval glands form a broad umbel.

OTHER SPECIES OF NOTE

Basketball euphorbia *Euphorbia obesa*

This slow-growing, ball-shaped plant is a native of South Africa's Great Karoo. It consists of a single, smooth-bodied, spineless, olive-green, swollen stem, covered in mauve to pale green striped markings. As it matures it becomes slightly columnar, rather than globular. Flowers are produced in summer near the growing tip.

Indian acalypha *Acalypha indica*
Also known as the Indian copperleaf, this erect annual herb grows up to 75cm/29½in. It has numerous long, angular branches covered with soft hair and thin, smooth, egg-shaped leaves. The flowers are borne in long, erect spikes, and are followed by small, hairy fruits and minute, pale brown seeds.

Sea spurge *Euphorbia paralias*
Frequenting sandy and shingly coasts and flowering from April to August, sea spurge is a fleshy, grey-green perennial, branched from the base. The stem leaves are succulent, over-lapping and diamond-shaped below the flowers, which have small, horned glands on the rim.

Petty spurge *Euphorbia peplus*
Petty spurge is a common annual garden weed with oval, short-stalked leaves. It resembles sun spurge, *E. helioscopia*, but is smaller and usually more branched.

Caper spurge

Euphorbia lathyris

Caper spurge was formerly cultivated for its fruits, which were used, as true capers still are today, to flavour savoury dishes, especially in fish recipes. Oddly, this plant has also acquired a reputation for keeping moles at bay. It frequents shady, waste places and flowers in June and July. It grows as a casual weed over much of Britain and may be native locally in southern England.

Identification:
A stiffly erect, hairless plant with narrow, rigid blue-green leaves. The yellowish flowers, up to 20mm/¾in across, have two large, narrowly triangular bracts.

Distribution: Europe.
Height and spread: Up to 2m/6½ft.
Habit and form: Biennial.
Leaf shape: Linear to lanceolate.
Pollinated: Insect.

Right and below: Note the tall straight growth and the long triangular bracts.

Marsh spurge

Euphorbia palustris

Marsh spurge spreads by creeping stolons and grows in wet places such as marshes, along rivers, in coastal wetlands and also in wet woodland. It is found mainly in central and northern Europe, northern France, Belgium and southern Scandinavia. It flowers from April through July.

Identification: A stout-stemmed perennial with greyish leaves, growing to 1m/39in or more, with many non-flowering branches. The umbels have many rays, and the rounded floral bracts are yellow.

Above: The flowers open in bright yellow-green clusters at the tops of the stems.

Distribution: Europe.
Height and spread: To 1.5m/5ft.
Habit and form: Perennial.
Leaf shape: Lanceolate.
Pollinated: Insect.

Left: Marsh spurge is a clump-forming deciduous perennial.

Right: Often grown as a garden plant, marsh spurge is fast-growing but is poisonous, and touching it may cause irritation to the skin.

Portland spurge

Euphorbia portlandica

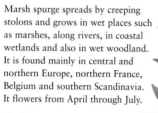

The early-summer flowering Portland spurge frequents sand dunes and occasionally limestone sea cliffs. Portland spurge has a local distribution around the coasts of north-western Europe, including the Channel Islands, Ireland, and southern and western Great Britain, north to Kintyre.

Identification: A stocky, hairless, blue-green plant, with thick stems from a central root and thick, stalkless, more or less obovate, slightly succulent leaves terminating in a sudden point. The older stems often turn reddish. The flowers appear in three- to six-rayed umbels. The glands have long 'horns'.

Below: Portland spurge has a sprawling habit.

Distribution: Western France; Ireland; Britain.
Height and spread: Up to 50cm/20in.
Habit and form: Biennial or perennial.
Leaf shape: Obovate.
Pollinated: Insect.

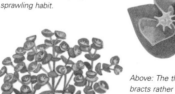

Above: The thick green 'flowers' are bracts rather than petals and sepals.

Right: The yellow-green flowers often have reddish stems and are surrounded by leathery leaves.

Candelabra tree

Euphorbia candelabrum

The candelabra tree is an African succulent species. Its name is derived from its shape, which, with its multiple-branched stem, resembles a candelabra. This unusual plant is widespread in the Horn of Africa and in eastern Africa along the Rift Valley. It is essentially a tree that is characteristic of dry Africa. It has medicinal properties, including the use of its sap, mixed with honey, to treat syphilis, and also as part of a treatment for leprosy.

Distribution: Africa.
Height and spread:
15 x 4m/49 x 13ft.
Habit and form:
Woody perennial.
Leaf shape: Simple.
Pollinated: Insect.

Identification: A tree up to 15m/49ft tall, with a thick trunk and erect branches with three to five spiny ribs or wings. Mature plants have no true leaves, but rather produce scales. The seedlings, however, do have leaves. The flowers are small green-yellow and fleshy, in groups of four to six next to paired spines.

Right: The tree is used for firewood, fencing and timber.

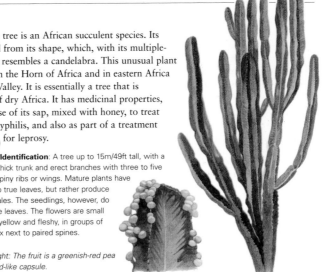

Right: The fruit is a greenish-red pea pod-like capsule.

OTHER SPECIES OF NOTE

Annual mercury
Mercurialis annua
A weed of cultivated ground occurring over most of Europe. Borne on separate plants and appearing from May to November, male flowers are carried on long erect spikes, while female flowers grow in few-flowered, stalkless clusters.

Sweet spurge *Euphorbia dulcis*
A perennial plant of shady places found mainly in central and southern Europe, sweet spurge flowers from May to July. It is naturalized in Denmark and Britain. Its stems are slightly hairy and it grows to about 50cm/20in tall. The leaves are oblong and untoothed. The young flowers are green at first, becoming purplish with age.

Euphorbia wallichii
This leafy-stemmed perennial ranges from Afghanistan to south-western China where its grows at 2,000–3,500m/6,500–11,500ft on open slopes and grazed land. It has sap that is unpalatable to animals and so can survive on grazed pastures. The yellow flowerheads are flat-topped.

Euphorbia cognata
This is another Himalayán species of open slopes to 3,600m/11,800ft altitude. This slender perennial produces inflorescences measuring about 15cm/6in across. The flowerheads have yellow-green bracts.

Dog's mercury

Mercurialis perennis

Named after Mercury, the Roman god of trade, who is supposed to have discovered it, dog's mercury is an extremely common hedgerow and woodland herb. Flowering from May to October, it has a fetid smell that attracts midges for pollination and is extremely poisonous. These hairy plants are either male or female and patches entirely of one sex are normal.

Identification: Hairy, unbranched plants form carpets of elliptical, flat, green leaves about 30cm/12in above the ground. Long spikes of male flowers have a mass of yellowish-green stamens. Female flowers are hidden among the upper leaves. The fruit has three rounded segments.

Right: The male flowers have long stamens.

Distribution: Europe.
Height and spread: Up to 40cm/16in.
Habit and form: Perennial.
Leaf shape: Elliptical.
Pollinated: Insect.

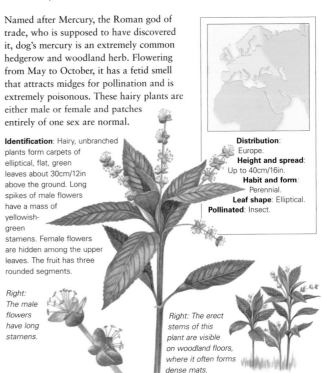

Right: The erect stems of this plant are visible on woodland floors, where it often forms dense mats.

STONE PLANTS AND CRASSULAS

The Aizoaceae, or stone plant family, are particularly strongly represented in southern Africa. Many of its species are decorative, so are widely cultivated and some have become naturalized outside their normal range. The Crassulaceae, or crassula family, contains mostly succulents, with flowers that are very similar to those of members of the rose and saxifrage families.

Houseleek

Hens and chicks, *Sempervivum tectorum*

This commonly cultivated perennial succulent plant is occasionally found as a persistent colonist of old walls. It was formerly also frequent on thatched roofs of houses, but is now rarely found in this habitat. The genus *Sempervivum* comprises a range of succulent, rosette-forming, evergreen perennials that originate in the mountainous areas of Europe, central Asia and northern Africa, often growing in crevices in the rocks. The plant requires well-drained soil and can tolerate drought. Each rosette is monocarpic (it blooms once and then dies).

Identification: An evergreen, mat-forming, succulent perennial, it has open rosettes up to 10cm/4in across of thick, oval to narrowly oblong, bristle-tipped leaves, to 40mm/1½in long, which are blue-green often suffused with red-purple. The leaves often show seasonal variations in colour. In early to midsummer, it

bears cymes, 50mm–10cm/ 2–4in across, of red-purple flowers on upright, hairy stems growing to 15cm/6in tall. The seeds ripen from mid- to late summer.

Left: The fleshy rosettes, form are tightly packed.

Left: Each red-purple flower has numerous petals.

Right: One flowerhead arises from the centre of the rosette.

Distribution: French and Italian Alps.
Height and spread: 10–30cm/4–12in.
Habit and form: Succulent, evergreen, rosette-forming perennial.
Leaf shape: Obovate to narrowly oblong.
Pollinated: Insect.

Silver jade tree

Crassula arborescens

Found on granite or in quartzite areas, this distinctive, large, shrubby succulent is perfectly at home growing between boulders or in crevices. The plants are mainly found in areas of winter rainfall and are very tolerant of drought. The species has a scattered distribution in South Africa, from the Little Karoo to the Hex River Valley.

Right: The flowers appear in autumn to winter.

Below: Though tree-like, the silver jade tree is actually a shrub.

Identification: Cylindrical branches bear grey-green leaves, tinged purple, to 75mm/3in long, with red margins that continue down both sides of the leaf. The leaves are oval, with rounded tips, tapering below, with entire margins. The leaf stalks are absent or very short. The old leaves gradually become deciduous. The succulent stems are up to 12.5cm/5in in diameter, frequently branched, and older specimens have peeling bark. The grey flowers are tinged pink at the tips, with five to seven petals, which are borne on long flower stalks.

Right: The pale grey-blue colour is partially due to the grey bloom that is naturally present.

Distribution: South Africa.
Height and spread: 4m/13ft.
Habit and form: Shrubby succulent.
Leaf shape: Ovate.
Pollinated: Insect.

OTHER SPECIES OF NOTE

Lithops terricolor
These so-called 'living stones' have evolved to survive dry conditions while also evading detection by browsing animal species. They are masters of deception, producing pairs of stone-shaped succulent leaves that resemble the pieces of quartz among which they grow.

Conophytum minutum
A species of succulent plants native to the winter-rainfall deserts of South Africa and Namibia. They are commonly known as stone plants because of their cryptically mineralesque appearance until the autumn, when the first rains stimulate the appearance of pink-lavender or white flowers.

Rosea ice plant *Drosanthemum floribundum*
This ground-hugging perennial, with small, stubby, light green, succulent leaves, produces dazzling metallic-purple flowers each spring. It is known to survive in very hot, dry conditions and easily colonizes large, flat, open spaces in South Africa's Little Karoo, with one plant covering an area as large as 2sq m/22sq ft.

Stonecrop *Sedum acre*
A loosely tufted, mat-forming, evergreen perennial, widespread through much of Europe, the Mediterranean region and Turkey and naturalized in the eastern USA. Its bright yellow flowers appear in small cymes from early to mid-summer. It thrives in dry gravel soils and is drought tolerant.

Hottentot fig

Ice plant, Pigface, *Carpobrotus edulis*

A vigorous, prostrate plant, rooting as it spreads, with flowers that open only in the afternoon, the so-called hottentot fig is an immensely showy plant when encountered *en masse* and is extremely tolerant of maritime exposure. Although it was originally restricted to coastal and exposed areas around the South African coast, human activities have resulted in it spreading over large parts of Australia, southern Europe and California, where conditions are similar to those in its original home.

Identification: The stems are spreading or prostrate, up to 2m/6½ft long, 8–12mm/⅜–½in thick, with two cleft angles; flowering shoots have two fleshy internodes. The three-sided leaves are 40–75mm/1½–3in long, 8–15mm/⅜–⅝in wide, bright green, often tinged red along the edges; the upper surfaces are distinctly concave, causing them to curl slightly inwards; the keel is minutely toothed. Daisy-like flowers, 70–90mm/2¾–3½in across, open after noon in sun in spring and summer; they are yellow at first, becoming flesh coloured to pink, usually densely streaked when dry. Fig-like, edible fruits follow the flowers.

Distribution: Cape Province, South Africa.
Height and spread: 10 x 90cm/4 x 35in.
Habit and form: Mat-forming succulent perennial.
Leaf shape: Triangular.
Pollinated: Insect.

Right: Tight, fleshy buds give rise to large, showy blooms.

Below: The long, trailing stems form a loose mat.

Tiger's jaws

Faucaria tigrina

This interesting little succulent, commonly known as tiger's jaws (the genus name *Faucaria* is derived from the Latin for 'jaws') due to the teeth-like structures on the leaves, is a native of South Africa. The triangular leaves with pointed fleshy parts, are concave on the upper part, making them look like open jaws.

Distribution: Eastern Cape Province, South Africa.
Height and spread: 10 x 50cm/4 x 20in.
Habit and form: Low shrubby succulent.
Leaf shape: Triangular to rhombic.
Pollinated: Insect.

Identification: The plant forms succulent rosettes of triangular to diamond-shaped or oval leaves, tapered on the upper surface with very rounded lower surfaces, with the tips pulled forward and chin-like. The leaves are grey-green with numerous white dots arranged in rows and 9–10 stout, recurved, hair-tipped teeth along each margin.

Above: The plant builds woody stems with age and tolerates very droughty conditions.

Far left and left: Large, stalkless, daisy-like, yellow flowers, 50mm/2in across, are produced in late summer and early autumn.

SAXIFRAGE FAMILY

The Saxifragaceae, or saxifrage family, include herbaceous perennials and deciduous shrubs.
It is found worldwide. In cultivation the family includes food and ornamental plants,
although in the wild the plants are typical of arctic and boreal regions. Many species are popular
as rock garden plants and thrive in stony conditions.

Purple mountain saxifrage

Saxifraga oppositifolia

The purple saxifrage is frequently found on damp mountain rocks. It also sometimes grows at the foot of a mountain, from seeds washed down by fast-flowing streams, but rarely persists here as it is easily out-competed by other vegetation. It is an extremely widespread species, stretching from the Arctic down into the mountains of Europe, western Asia and North America. It tends to be variable due to the environmental variance across its large range. The plant is well known for its ability to flower very early in the year, but may produce a few additional flowers later in the summer. The flower colour is unusual among wild saxifrages.

Identification: A flat, mat-forming, opposite-leaved saxifrage, it has rosettes of stiff, oblong or elliptic, dark green leaves, to 5mm/³⁄₁₆in long, on branching stems. The leaves are very densely packed and often secrete lime at the tips, giving the appearance of white flecks. In early summer, the plant bears solitary, almost stemless, cup-shaped, deep red-purple to pale pink, or rarely white flowers, to 20mm/¾in across.

Below right: This tiny plant flowers profilically in spring and early summer.

Distribution: Arctic; Eurasia; North America.
Height and spread: 25mm x 20cm/1 x 8in or more.
Habit and form: Mat-forming, evergreen perennial.
Leaf shape: Oblong to elliptic.
Pollinated: Insect.

Heartleaf saxifrage

Elephant's ears, *Bergenia cordifolia*

Found chiefly in damp, rocky woodland and meadows in northern Asia, heartleaf saxifrage forms clumps, which can become quite extensive, of large, evergreen leaves with a leathery texture. The clusters of small flowers, borne in late winter, are easily visible above the persistent, dark green, purple-tinged leaves. The flowers may persist for several weeks, gradually fading in colour. Although it grows in shade and moist ground, it is extremely drought tolerant, and its general appearance and dimensions may vary considerably, according to the particular habitat it is growing in.

Identification: This clump-forming perennial grows from tough, thick rhizomes in distinctive rosettes of circular to heart-shaped leaves, to 30cm/12in long, with rounded or serrated, toothed margins and hairless, sometimes puckered surfaces. The leaves are deep green, sometimes tinged red-purple in winter. Panicle-like cymes of pale red to dark pink flowers on red flower stems appear in late winter and early spring. The entire inflorescence may be 40cm/16in or more tall, sometimes much larger than the leaves.

Distribution: Siberia; Mongolia.
Height and spread: 40cm/16in or more.
Habit and form: Evergreen perennial.
Leaf shape: Rounded to heart-shaped.
Pollinated: Insect.

Rue-leaved saxifrage

Saxifraga tridactylites

This little annual saxifrage often grows on dry walls, in dry grassland, limestone rocks or on sandy soils. It is found throughout most of Europe except the far north. It is locally common in Britain and Ireland, but rare in Scotland.

Identification: This plant produces small white flowers in loose clusters. Each flower is about 4–6mm/³⁄₁₆–¼n across on a long stalk and with notched petals. A low-growing annual with sticky hairs. The leaves mostly have three to five lobes and often have a reddish tinge.

Distribution: Great Britain.
Height and spread: 10cm/4in.
Habit and form: Annual.
Leaf shape: Mostly lobed.
Pollinated: Insect.

Right: The leaves have three 'fingers', hence the botanical species name 'tridactylites'.

Below: This species lives at low ground.

Above: The seedhead.

OTHER SPECIES OF NOTE

Saxifraga fortunei
A deciduous perennial herb from Japan, with large panicles of white blossoms that rise in profusion on 50cm/20in red stems from rosettes of handsome, large, dark green, glossy, rounded leaves during the autumn.

Astilbe chinensis
This herbaceous perennial from China and Korea reaches 70cm/27½in and is at its most handsome when the short, white, flushed pink or magenta flower panicles arise above the coarse mid- to light green foliage during the summer months.

St Patrick's cabbage *Saxifraga spathularis*
The odd common name of this saxifrage comes from its large, fleshy leaves, which grow up in a rosette, fancifully resembling a cabbage, and from its distribution in the mountains of western Ireland. It is also found in Portugal and Spain. It grows on damp rocks and near streams, producing clusters of white, red-spotted flowers.

Golden saxifrage *Chrysosplenium oppositifolium*
From mid-spring until midsummer the tiny flowers of this low, slightly hairy, creeping perennial deck roadside ditches and other damp places. The flower petals are golden green and the young, stalked, wavy-edged, evergreen, opposite leaves are similar, so may not easily be seen.

Starry saxifrage

Saxifraga stellaris

Starry saxifrage is often quite common on wet, rocky mountain sites, and also alongside flushes and next to mountain streams. The flowering season is mainly June through August, and it mostly grows up to about 2,000m/6,500ft altitude.

Below: The white petals have two yellow dots, helping to distinguish them from others in the species.

Right: The flowers grow from a basal rosette of leaves.

Distribution: Europe, but absent from the low countries.
Height and spread: 20cm/8in.
Habit and form: Perennial.
Leaf shape: Obovate.
Pollinated: Insect.

Identification: This very pretty saxifrage has thin flower stalks growing from a basal rosette of leaves. The flowers are in loose panicles. Each flower is 10mm/³⁄₈in across, the petals opening into a star-like shape. Each petal has two yellow spots near to the base. The leaves are fleshy and toothed.

Yellow saxifrage

Saxifraga aizoides

Yellow saxifrage is a common upland and mountain flower, often found next to streams and on wet rocks to over 3,000m/9,840ft. It also grows close to glaciers. In the north it may grow down to sea level, but it is absent from most lowland in Europe. It flowers mainly from June to September.

Below: The five yellow petals are arranged alternately with the green sepals.

Identification: This low-growing creeping perennial with narrow, oblong, bright green leaves has clusters of yellow or orange flowers, each about 15mm/ 9⁄16in across. The petals sometimes have tiny red spots.

Above: Yellow saxifrage has cushion-like growth.

Right: The bright yellow flowers contrast with the green mat of foliage, and add colour to the rock garden.

Distribution: Europe; Canada; northern USA.
Height and spread: 10–15cm/4–6in.
Habit and form: Perennial.
Leaf shape: Oblong.
Pollinated: Insect.

Meadow saxifrage

Saxifraga granulata

This plant is locally common in rich grassland such as meadows and pastures, usually on neutral or calcareous soils. There is a garden form that has double flowers and this sometimes establishes itself as a garden escapee. It is often found among grasses. Each summer bulbils form in the axils of the basal leaves, and these persist over the winter to grow again the following spring.

Identification: The flowers are large and pure white, each about 30mm/1¼in across, in loose, branched clusters. The leaves grow in a rosette, are kidney-shaped and long-stalked and have coarse teeth.

Above: The flowering stems grow tall, making this plant suitable for naturalizing in meadows.

Left: The white flowers are delicately veined with green.

Right: Meadow saxifrage grows in unimproved grassland, growing from a basal rosette of leaves.

Distribution: Locally common in Europe but absent from the far north.
Height and spread: 50cm/20in.
Habit and form: Perennial.
Leaf shape: Lobed, rounded.
Pollinated: Insect.

Alpine saxifrage

Saxifraga nivalis

Mountain rocks and cliffs are the typical habitat of this saxifrage. It prefers shady ledges and also grows on scree and moraines, to an altitude of around 2,000m/6,500ft. This pretty alpine flower is sometimes grown in rock gardens. It is a local plant in the British Isles, mainly in Scotland, north-western Ireland and northern Wales.

Identification: A perennial saxifrage with a basal rosette of leaves, from which grows a tall, leafless flowering stem, up to about 15cm/6in tall. At its top is a dense panicle of small white or pink flowers, each about 6mm/¼ across. The oblong leaves are toothed, green above and purple-red beneath.

Distribution: Northern Europe.
Height and spread: 15cm/6in.
Habit and form: Perennial.
Leaf shape: Oblong.
Pollinated: Insect.

Left: The basal leaves form a rosette.

Above: The white flowers, which may be pink to purple beneath, appear in tight heads.

OTHER SPECIES OF NOTE

Ancient king *Saxifraga florulenta*
This spectacular saxifrage produces a large spike up to 45cm/18in tall with flesh-coloured flowers, from a basal rosette of leaves. It flowers once and then dies after setting seed. It is a rare species found in the Maritime Alps of southern France and northern Italy. It grows in cliffs and rocky crevices between 1,900–3,250m/ 6,230–10,660ft, flowering between July and September.

Saxifraga jacquemontana
This species is quite common from Pakistan and Kashmir to south-eastern Tibet up to about 5,200m/17,000ft. It has a dense mat of leaves and solitary yellow, nearly stalkless flowers.

Saxifraga saginoides
This plant grows moss-like, in large green cushions at about 4,300–5,200m/ 14,000–17,000ft in the Himalayas and south-eastern Tibet. The yellow flowers are tiny, each only about 5mm/³⁄₁₆in across, growing close to the cushion of leaves.

Kabschia saxifrage *Saxifraga burseriana*
Popular with alpine gardeners, this species from the Austrian and Julian Alps and Dolomites is quite rare in the wild. It has grey-green cushion foliage and large white flowers that appear in the spring. Many cultivated garden varieties of this attractive species are available.

Alternate-leaved golden-saxifrage

Chrysosplenium alternifolium

This unobtrusive plant is a perennial herb of damp habitats, including wet woods, streamsides and marshy places. It is local in distribution and absent from Ireland. Golden-saxifrages are sometimes grown in gardens.

Identification: The leaves are kidney-shaped, and arise alternately from the stems. The lower leaves have long stems. The flowers are small and yellow-green, each about 3mm/⅛in long and surrounded by yellowish bracts.

Distribution: Europe, except the far north.
Height and spread: 20cm/8in.
Habit and form: Perennial.
Leaf shape: Kidney-shaped.
Pollinated: Insect.

Above: The flowerheads sit neatly above leaves that are held flat and at a distinct angle to the stem.

Far right: The flowering stems are sturdy.

VIOLET FAMIIY

The violet family, Violaceae, is found all over the world (most typically in temperate regions) and contains 800 plant species. Many, such as pansies and violets, are familiar as garden flowers, and have colourful, scented flowers that are attractive to insects, often with a spur containing nectar. The fruit is a capsule containing large seeds.

Heath dog-violet

Viola canina

This variable plant flowers from April through July and grows wild in a range of soils, usually acid, such as sandy heaths, but also open woodland, and on dunes and sometimes in fens. It has a wide distribution but is local. In Great Britain it is uncommon.

Below: Heath dog-violet is low growing, like most species of violet.

Identification: The stems are upright and spreading, and the leaves are triangular, bluntly toothed and thick in texture. The flowers are usually a true blue colour and the spur is greenish-yellow. The lower petal (lip) has thin dark lines. This plant can produce extensive colonies when grown in appropriate conditions.

Distribution: Europe.
Height and spread: 20cm/8in.
Habit and form: Herbaceous perennial.
Leaf shape: Triangular.
Pollinated: Insect.

Below: Note the spur at the base of the flower for identification purposes.

Mountain pansy

Viola lutea

The mountain pansy is one of Europe's prettiest wild flowers. The feature that best distinguishes pansies from violets (both, however, are in the same genus) is that in pansies the two lateral petals are directed upwards. This pansy is locally common in upland areas, especially in hilly grassland, up to about 2,000m/6,500ft. It is mainly found in central and western Europe, but is absent from Ireland.

Identification: Bright yellow flowers are typical of this pansy, though the flowers are sometimes purple, or a mixture of purple and yellow. The stipules are large and leaf-like. The leaves are oval or lanceolate and have blunt teeth. The spur is short.

Left: Easy to identify by its face-like flowers, the mountain pansy grows in grassland and verges.

Below: The large flowers stand out well.

Distribution: Central and western Europe.
Height and spread: 10cm/4in.
Habit and form: Herbaceous perennial.
Leaf shape: Oval.
Pollinated: Insect.

Heartsease

Wild pansy, *Viola tricolor*

The heartsease is a variable species but it may always be readily distinguished from the other violets by the general form of its foliage, which is very deeply cut. The species is an annual or short-lived perennial, but crosses from it and other species have given rise to garden pansies. It is very widely distributed, and is found from the Arctic to North Africa and north-west India. Several varieties have been distinguished as subspecies.

Distribution: Eurasia from the Arctic to the southern Mediterranean.
Height and spread: 5–15 x 30cm/2–6 x 12in or more.
Habit and form: Annual or short-lived herbaceous perennial.
Leaf shape: Lanceolate to ovate.
Pollinated: Insect, especially bumblebee.

Identification: The stems are generally very angular, erect to ascending and free branching. The leaves are deeply cut into rounded lobes, the terminal one being largest, with blunt tips and round-toothed margins; the upper leaves are lance-shaped to oval. The flat-faced flowers, 6–30mm/¼–1¼in across, vary a great deal in size and colour: they are purple, yellow or white, and most commonly a combination of all three. The upper petals are generally the most showy and purple, with the lowest and broadest petal usually yellow. The base of the lowest petal is elongated into a spur, as in the violet.

Below: The small, usually tricoloured flowers vary in colour.

OTHER SPECIES OF NOTE

Marsh violet *Viola palustris*
This is a violet of acid bogs and marshes, often growing with bog-moss (*Sphagnum*). It is also found in wet heathland, and wet woods. It has a wide distribution, from Europe to Asia, North America and the mountains of northern Africa. The leaves are almost circular and the flowers are pale lilac.

Common dog-violet *Viola riviniana*
As its name suggests, this is one of the commonest of European wild violets, found from sea level to high mountains, in woodland, heath and grassland. The leaves are heart-shaped and the flowers bluish-violet, with a pale spur.

Viola biflora
This charming violet grows at about 2,500–4,500m/8,200–14,700ft from Pakistan to south-western China, on slopes and also in forests and scrub. The bright yellow flowers are marked with dark brown streaks and measure about 15mm/⅝in across. The leaves are kidney-shaped.

Viola cornuta
The strong purple flowers of this plant emerge from early to late summer. It originated in the Pyrenees, and is found in pastures and rocky grassland on calcareous soils at 700–2,300m/2,300–7,500ft. It was once used extensively in crosses with Victorian pansy stock to introduce its vigorous tufted growth and perennial habit to cultivars.

Sweet violet

Viola odorata

The classic florist's violet, the sweet violet was exported widely from Europe in colonial times as it was a popular cut flower in the late 19th and early 20th centuries. It is highly fragrant, and on a still day its scent can be detected before the flower is seen. It is the parent of many violet cultivars, and is still grown commercially.

Identification: Robust, prostrate stolons creep and spread this stemless, perennial plant. The leaves are heart-shaped, with scalloped or slightly serrated edges, dark green, smooth, sometimes downy underneath; they arise alternately from stolons, forming a basal rosette. Flower stalks arise from the leaf axils from early spring to early summer, each bearing a single deep purple, blue to pinkish or even yellow-white bloom. The flower is five-petalled, the lower petal lengthened into a hollow spur beneath and the lateral petals with a hairy centre line, with a pair of scaly bracts placed a little above the middle of the stalk. In autumn, small, insignificant flowers, without petals and scent, produce abundant seed.

Distribution: Europe.
Height and spread: 15cm/6in.
Habit and form: Herbaceous perennial.
Leaf shape: Heart-shaped.
Pollinated: Insect, especially bee.

Right: The seed capsule splits into three when ripe.

Below: The showy, fragrant, mostly blue flowers give this plant its name.

WOOD SORREL AND BALSAM FAMILIES

The wood sorrel family, Oxalidaceae, consists of about 800 species of mainly tropical and subtropical annual and perennial herbs, with a minority preferring temperate areas. The balsam family, Balsaminaceae, has about 850 species in temperate and tropical regions. They are annual or perennial herbs and have weak, translucent stems with watery sap, and unusual flowers.

Wood sorrel

Oxalis acetosella

This pretty plant has delicate flowers that brighten the dark woodland floor in spring and early summer. It also grows among shady rocks and in damp hedgerows. Its range extends from most of Europe, across to China and Japan. The sap is acidic, and wood sorrel has been used as a pot-herb and also medicinally to treat fevers and other ailments.

Identification: Wood sorrel spreads by thin rhizomes. The leaves are clover-like with three indented, heart-shaped leaflets. The flowers, which have five even-size petals, are white or pinkish and suffused with lilac veins, each flower about 10–15mm/⅜–⅝in across. The fruit capsule is oval and measures about 4mm/³⁄₁₆in.

Left: The petals are delicately veined.

Right: Wood sorrel can often be found in rich soil at the woodland edge.

Distribution: Europe; Asia.
Height and spread: 15cm/6in.
Habit and form: Herbaceous perennial.
Leaf shape: Compound, clover-like.
Pollinated: Insect.

Indian balsam

Himalayan balsam, Policeman's helmet, *Impatiens glandulifera*

Familiar as a weed of damp places such as riverbanks, this large balsam is native to the Himalayas. It thrives in wasteland, especially in cool, damp conditions. Its flowers exude a sickly-sweet odour and they are attractive to bees and other insects.

Identification: A tall, hairless annual with vigorous growth. The hooded flowers are pink-purple or sometimes white, each about 30–40mm/1¼–1½in, with an angled spur. The fruits are elongated capsules that spring open suddenly when ripe to fling out the seeds. The leaves grow in whorls and the stem is hollow and reddish.

Right: The seedpods are long and thick and explode when ripe.

Left: This plant can be a highly invasive weed in areas where it has not naturalized.

Distribution: Himalayan region; widely naturalized.
Height and spread: To 2m/6½ft.
Habit and form: Herbaceous perennial.
Leaf shape: Lanceolate, toothed.
Pollinated: Insect.

Creeping woodsorrel

Procumbent yellow-sorrel, *Oxalis corniculata*

Distribution: Tropical Africa; Europe.
Height and spread: 30cm x 50mm/12 x 2in.
Habit and form: Annual herb.
Leaf shape: Simple.
Pollinated: Insect.

Right: The yellow flowers are about 13mm/½in across.

Creeping woodsorrel is a delicate-looking, low-growing, herbaceous plant. It has a narrow, creeping stem that readily roots at the nodes. The trifoliate leaves are subdivided into three rounded leaflets and resemble a clover in shape. Some varieties have green leaves, while others have purple leaves. The leaves have inconspicuous stipules at the base of each petiole. It grows as a weed of cultivated and disturbed ground, and at roadsides, especially under shade. It is widely naturalized in Europe, including in Great Britain. The leaves are sometimes chewed fresh for their acidic taste.

Identification: An annual or perennial herb with many erect branching stems, 10–30cm/4–12in tall, creeping and rooting at the nodes. The leaves are alternate and compound on slender stalks to 80mm/3⅛in long, with three heart- or wedge-shaped greenish-purple leaflets. The fruit is a slightly hairy capsule to 25mm/1in long.

OTHER SPECIES OF NOTE

Bermuda buttercup *Oxalis pes-caprae*
Actually a native of South Africa, despite its common name, this species is also cultivated and is naturalized in warmer parts of Europe, notably in the Mediterranean region, and locally north to northern France and southern Great Britain. It has clusters of large yellow flowers, mainly from March to June.

Oxalis incarnata
A small, hairless perennial with delicate trifoliate leaves. Each leaflet is heart-shaped. The flowers are a pretty pale lilac with a network of darker veins. Native to South Africa, it is quite popular as a garden plant, and is also established in mild regions of Europe.

Small balsam *Impatiens parviflora*
Native to Central Asia, this balsam is now widely established as an introduction in Europe. It is like a smaller version of touch-me-not balsam, *I. noli-tangere*, and has small, pale yellow flowers. It, too, likes to grow in woodland and other shady sites. The flowers are unspotted with an almost straight spur and open mainly in late summer and autumn.

Balsam *Impatiens burtonii*
This balsam is a perennial herb with small white to pale pink flowers. It grows in disturbed areas in forests, along rivers, in swampy places as well as montane forests. The range includes Cameroon, Zaire, Tanzania, Kenya and Uganda. Balsams derive their generic name *Impatiens* ('impatient') from the plant's seedpods.

Touch-me-not-balsam

Yellow balsam, *Impatiens noli-tangere*

This species grows in damp woods and shady sites across much of Europe, including northern Great Britain. Though other balsams have been introduced to that region, this is the only one that is native. It is usually found growing in damp, nutrient-rich soils such as in wet woodland or along the banks of streams and is quite common in the Lake District. A pretty, rather delicate plant, it is sometimes grown in gardens, but is rather difficult to germinate from seed. Germination may be aided by allowing the plants to seed themselves, and disturbing the soil. As with other balsam species, the seeds ripen in pods that explode, ejecting the seeds some distance from the parent plant.

Identification: It is an annual plant growing to 50cm–1m/ 20 x 39in and has erect stems with swollen nodes. The leaves are alternate and have 10–15 coarse teeth on each side, and the spurred flowers are yellow with tiny brown speckles. The spur curves forwards underneath the flower.

Distribution: Europe; Asia; North America.
Height and spread: To 1m/39in.
Habit and form: Erect; annual.
Leaf shape: Ovate.
Pollinated: Insect.

Below: When the seedpods mature, they 'explode' when touched or moved suddenly, sending the seeds several metres away. This mechanism is also known as 'explosive dehiscence'.

CARROT FAMILY

The Apiaceae, or carrot family, contains mostly temperate herbs, with the highest diversity in the northern, world and tropical uplands. They are characterized by flowers in umbels, hollow stems and sheathing flower stalks. Many species are important as food crops, and for aromatic compounds that are used as spices, although this usage masks the fact that the majority of species in this family are highly toxic.

Sea holly

Eryngium alpinum

There are more than 200 species of *Eryngium* or sea holly as it is more commonly known, and while they do not all come from maritime locations, they do all share a tendency to grow on very well drained sites. This particular species looks like a teasel (*Dipsacus* spp.), although it is not related at all. Its tough, bright green, veined basal leaves become more and more pointed and divided as they go up the stem, and end in a ruff of spiky bracts that look like steely blue feathers, inside which is the matching domed flower-head.

Identification: A perennial with basal rosette of leaves, 75mm–15cm/3–6in long, that are persistent and ovate to triangular-cordate, spiny toothed and soft. The upper leaves are more rounded, palmately lobed and blue tinged. The cylindrical-ovoid disc of sessile flowers comprises 25 or more small steel-blue or white flowers held among spiny bracts. These are followed by small, scaly fruits.

Distribution: West and central Balkans.
Height and spread: 45cm/18in.
Habit and form: Herbaceous perennial.
Leaf shape: Rounded.
Pollinated: Bee.

Left and far left: The 'teasel-like' flowers are held high above the basal rosette of leaves.

Fennel

Foeniculum vulgare

Fennel is a well known culinary herb, often grown in gardens and as a consequence it has been spread far beyond its original range. It is found naturally in the Mediterranean areas of Europe where it grows in dry, stony calcareous soils near the sea, and while it is in leaf all year, it is chiefly noticed when the scented flowers appear from August to October. It often has a coastal distribution, though it cannot stand high wind so is usually found a little way inland.

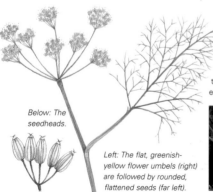

Below: The seedheads.

Left: The flat, greenish-yellow flower umbels (right) are followed by rounded, flattened seeds (far left).

Identification: A slender, glaucescent, aromatic perennial or biennial growing to 2m/6½ft with soft, hollow stems, ascending and branching alternately at flowering. The leaves, to 30cm/12in, are triangular in outline, three to four pinnate and extremely finely cut with segments. The flowers appear in the summer and are in compound umbels, 10–40 rayed, bisexual and yellow; followed by ovoid-oblong, ridged fruits.

Distribution: Europe.
Height and spread: 2m/6½ft.
Habit and form: Herbaceous perennial.
Leaf shape: Pinnate (filiform).
Pollinated: Insect, especially bee and fly.

Left: The tall flowering stems are very striking, although the plant often goes unnoticed when not in flower.

Ground elder

Goutweed, Bishop's weed, *Aegopodium podagraria*

Distribution: Europe, often spread further by cultivation.
Height and spread: 70cm/27½in.
Habit and form: Herbaceous perennial.
Leaf shape: Bipinnate.
Pollinated: Insect, especially bee.

Far right: The pretty white umbels of this flower are very noticeable, and appear around midsummer.

This small herbaceous plant is common in hedgerows and cultivated land and a common garden weed. Ground elder was once greatly valued as a pot herb, and for its medicinal qualities, leading to its being transported well outside its natural range, where it has since become a problem plant. The large, pretty, white flowers appear in early to midsummer and in warmer regions are followed by flattened seed vessels, which when ripe are detached and blown about by the wind.

Identification: A herbaceous plant with multiple stems arising from elongated rhizomes and fibrous roots, with a strong scent, glabrous, to 70cm/27½in tall. The basal leaves are long petiolate, bipinnately divided.The leaflets are mostly glabrous or with a few short stiff hairs on the main veins below, ovate to oblong, serrate to doubly serrate. The small, five-petalled, white flowers appear in terminal pedunculate compound umbels. The fruits are slightly compressed, ellipsoid, glabrous, with a conspicuous groove, although they are only viable in warmer regions.

Great masterwort
Astrantia major

This clump-forming perennial has rounded flower-heads, surrounded by papery, whitish, faintly pink bracts. It is found in moist woodlands and on the banks of streams in sub-alpine regions across central and eastern Europe.

Cow parsley *Anthriscus sylvestris*
This familiar plant of European temperate woodland edge, wayside and pasture looks very similar to some poisonous species so care must be taken when identifying it. Its large white umbels are extremely showy and often form a major constituent of unimproved grassland.

Carom *Trachyspermum ammi*
An important source of an aromatic spice, carom is very common to Indian and African cuisine. It closely resembles thyme in flavour. India is one of the most important sources of the plant, although it is probably of eastern Mediterranean origin, perhaps from Egypt.

Wild carrot *Daucus carota*
This flower occurs naturally on cultivated and wasteland, among grass, especially by the sea and on chalk, throughout Europe, parts of Asia and North Africa. It has long been domesticated for human use.

Parsley

Petroselinum crispum

Parsley was native to central and southern Europe although cultivation of the plant for use as a herb has led to its becoming widely naturalized elsewhere, especially within the temperate regions of the Northern Hemisphere. The plant naturally inhabits grassy places, walls, rocky outcrops and dry hedgerow banks. It is a biennial herb that is in flower from June to August, displaying tiny, star-shaped, green-yellow flowers in flat-topped umbels.

Distribution: South-eastern Europe; Sardinia.
Height and spread: 30–75cm/12–30in.
Habit and form: Biennial.
Leaf shape: Pinnate.
Pollinated: Insect, especially fly.

Identification: A stout, erect glabrous biennial, with a clean, pungent smell when crushed. The stems are solid and striate, with branches ascending. The three-pinnate leaves are bright green, with 4–12 pairs that are ovate in outline, cuneate at the base and toothed, with a long petiole. The upper cauline leaves are small. Yellowish flowers appear in flat-topped, compound umbels, to 50mm/2in across in summer, followed by small, rounded flattened seeds. Oblong, greyish-brown fruits 3mm/⅛in long, with spines on the curved surface, ripen from late summer to early autumn.

Above right and right: The small, greenish-yellow flowerheads can easily be overlooked in the wild among other vegetation.

Sweet cicely

Myrrhis odorata

This plant grows wild in grassy highland or cool grassy sites. In Great Britain it tends to replace cow parsley, *Anthriscus sylvestris*, at roadsides in northern hilly regions and in Scotland. This species has a long history of use as a herb and flavouring, and this probably explains why it often grows close to houses.

Identification: A tall perennial with attractive feathery foliage, smelling of aniseed when crushed. The leaves are twice or three times pinnate, sheathing the stem at the base. The white flowers, each about 4mm/³⁄₁₆in across, are in flat-topped umbels. The fruits are long and narrow and turn black when ripe.

Right: Sweet cicely is clump-forming. The feathery leaves can measure up to 50cm/20in.

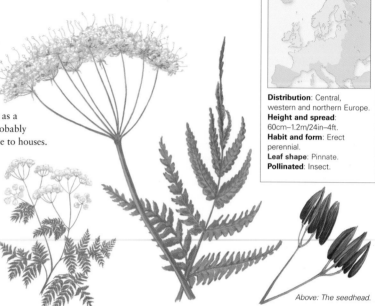

Distribution: Central, western and northern Europe.
Height and spread: 60cm–1.2m/24in–4ft.
Habit and form: Erect perennial.
Leaf shape: Pinnate.
Pollinated: Insect.

Above: The seedhead.

Alexanders

Smyrnium olusatrum

This tall, handsome umbellifer is usually found growing in hedgerows in coastal regions. It also grows on cliffs, wasteland and woodland edges. Its native range is mainly southern and western Europe. In former times it was used as a pot-herb and eaten like celery.

Identification: Dark green shiny and bright yellow-green umbels of flowers identify this stately umbellifer. The stems are broad, becoming hollow as they age. The flowers, each about 3mm/¹⁄₈in across, develop in rounded umbels, and have an unpleasant smell that attracts a range of insects, notably flies.

Below: Alexanders grows tall and has shiny leaves.

Below left: The fruit is rounded and ridged.

Distribution: Southern and western Europe.
Height and spread: 1.5m/5ft.
Habit and form: Biennial.
Leaf shape: Ternate.
Pollinated: Insect.

Below: Alexanders was used as a pot herb in Medieval times. It flowers very early in the year.

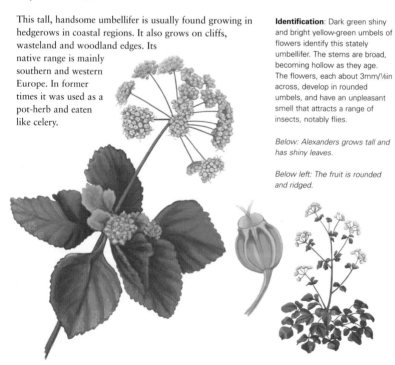

Sanicle
Sanicula europaea

Sanicle is a plant of shady woodland, especially oak, beech or ash woods. It often covers large areas of the woodland floor. The flowers appear between May and August. The name comes from the Latin word for 'cure', referring to its use in medicine. Extracts of sanicle have been used to treat many ailments, from coughs to diarrhoea.

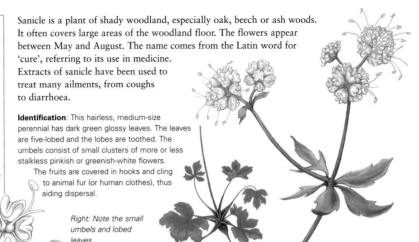

Distribution: Europe.
Height and spread: 60cm/24in.
Habit and form: Perennial.
Leaf shape: Lobed.
Pollinated: Insect.

Identification: This hairless, medium-size perennial has dark green glossy leaves. The leaves are five-lobed and the lobes are toothed. The umbels consist of small clusters of more or less stalkless pinkish or greenish-white flowers. The fruits are covered in hooks and cling to animal fur (or human clothes), thus aiding dispersal.

Right: The flowers can be white to pale pink.

Right: Note the small umbels and lobed leaves.

OTHER SPECIES OF NOTE

Lesser water parsnip *Berula erecta*
This is a common aquatic or semi-aquatic plant growing in or near shallow water and in marshes. It grows to about 1m/39in, but its hollow hairless stems often sprawl. Its submerged leaves are finely divided. It grows throughout Europe, except the far north.

Rock samphire
Crithmum maritimum
A compact plant of coastal cliffs and rocks (sometimes sand and shingle), this branching perennial has grey-green succulent leaves with narrow segments. It produces tight clusters of yellow-green flowers. It grows along the Atlantic coasts of Europe as far north as Holland. The leaves are edible and were once gathered for food.

Hemlock water-dropwort *Oenanthe crocata*
This is quite a common tall umbellifer of river banks, ditches and marshes. It is hairless and its hollow, grooved stems reach about 2m/6½ft. Although pleasantly scented, all parts of this plant are poisonous.

Garden angelica *Angelica archangelica*
The familiar preserved stems are from this species, which grows wild in marshes, ditches and riverbanks. It is often grown in gardens, and is a handsome tall plant with green or purplish stems and large yellow umbels. It has a long history of use as a medicinal and culinary herb.

Moon carrot
Seseli libanotis

The favoured habitat of moon carrot is dry, open scrub and rough grassland on calcareous soil. It is a rare and local species in Great Britain, in the south-east where it seems to be decreasing. Extracts of this species have been shown to have anti-bacterial properties and may have potential in protecting food from bacterial attack.

Identification: A fairly tall umbellifer with a ridged stem, and pinnate leaves with pointed leaflets. The stems have a fibrous base. The flowers are white or pale pink in rounded umbels.

Distribution: Europe except the far north; rare in Great Britain.
Height and spread: 1.2m/4ft.
Habit and form: Biennial or perennial.
Leaf shape: Pinnate.
Pollinated: Insect.

Above: The fruit is oval and ridged.

Right: The flowers are tiny and are clustered in tightly packed umbels.

Giant hogweed

Heracleum mantegazzianum

This is a notorious and quite invasive large umbellifer, native to south-western Asia, but which has become established as a weed over much of Europe, after being introduced as a garden plant. It is huge, producing stout towering stems to 5m/16ft or more. It should be treated with respect, as its juice can cause serious skin blisters, during sunny weather (a photo-sensitive reaction).

Identification: A huge, sturdy plant with ridged stems that have red spots. The stems can be up to 10cm/4in across. The leaves are pinnate, with toothed lobes and the lower leaves may be 2.5m/8ft long. The umbels are also large, up to 50cm/20in across, with 50–150 branches. The white flowers are each about 8–20mm/⁵⁄₁₆–¾in across.

Distribution: South-western Asia and the Caucasus; widely naturalized.
Height and spread: To 5m/16ft.
Habit and form: Biennial.
Leaf shape: Pinnate.
Pollinated: Insect.

Far left: The plant can produce thousands of seedheads.

Right and far right: Giant hogweed is invasive. It can form dense stands that threaten other types of flora.

Wild celery

Apium graveolens

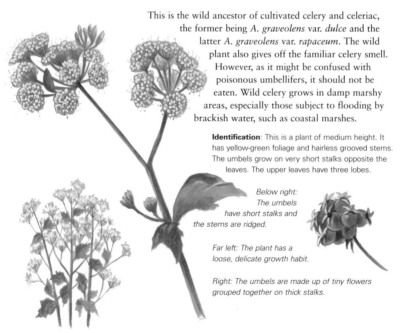

This is the wild ancestor of cultivated celery and celeriac, the former being *A. graveolens* var. *dulce* and the latter *A. graveolens* var. *rapaceum*. The wild plant also gives off the familiar celery smell. However, as it might be confused with poisonous umbellifers, it should not be eaten. Wild celery grows in damp marshy areas, especially those subject to flooding by brackish water, such as coastal marshes.

Identification: This is a plant of medium height. It has yellow-green foliage and hairless grooved stems. The umbels grow on very short stalks opposite the leaves. The upper leaves have three lobes.

Distribution: Europe north to southern and central Scandinavia.
Height and spread: 60cm/24in.
Habit and form: Biennial.
Leaf shape: Pinnate or ternate.
Pollinated: Insect.

Below right: The umbels have short stalks and the stems are ridged.

Far left: The plant has a loose, delicate growth habit.

Right: The umbels are made up of tiny flowers grouped together on thick stalks.

Scots lovage

Ligusticum scoticum

Scots lovage is a plant of exposed rocky coasts, typically growing on sea cliffs and rough coastal grassland. It is an edible plant, with a celery-like flavour. The stem is sweet and the root is aromatic. It is used in the preparation of herbal medicines and was once eaten by sailors.

Identification: The leaves are bright, shiny green and three-lobed, further divided into three. The umbels have greenish-white or pinkish flowers, each about 2mm/¹⁄₁₆in across. The fruits are narrow and egg-shaped, with narrow wings, and about 6mm/¼in long.

Right: Scots lovage has shrub-like growth.

Left: The plant is also known by the common name Scots licorice root, for the sweet flavour of the herb.

Distribution: North-western Europe, from Scandinavia to Iceland; around the coasts of Scotland and north and western Ireland.
Height and spread: 90cm/35in.
Habit and form: Perennial.
Leaf shape: Ternate.
Pollinated: Insect.

OTHER SPECIES OF NOTE

Angelica cyclocarpa
This striking plant is found in forest clearings and grazed areas in Nepal and southern Tibet. Its tough stems grow to more than 3m/10ft tall, and the upper leaves have inflated sheaths that enclose the developing umbels. The lower leaves may be 60cm/24in across. The mature umbels are flat-topped with yellowish flowers.

Milk-parsley
Peucedanum palustre
This plant grows in fenland and marshes through most of Europe except the far north. It is rare and local in Britain where it is the food plant of the rare swallowtail butterfly. It has purplish, tall, hollow stems and finely divided leaves. The flowers are greenish-white in spreading umbels.

Masterwort *Peucedanum ostruthium*
This plant has escaped from cultivation in many places, including Britain, although it is native to central and northern Europe. This hairy perennial has bright green, shiny leaves with oval, toothed lobes. The umbels of white or pinkish flowers have up to 60 rays.

Hogweed *Heracleum sphondylium*
A common umbellifer of hedgerows, roadsides, woodland edges and open woodland, hogweed grows throughout most of Europe. Its flat-topped umbels of white flowers are distinctive and may be 15cm/6in across. The fruits are rounded and flat, with broad wings.

Coriander

Coriandrum sativum

Like many members of this important family, coriander is a useful plant and has long been cultivated as a culinary herb. Oil is also extracted from its fruits and used for perfumes and pharmaceuticals. A native of northern Africa and western Asia, this short, hairless annual is naturalized in central Europe and also grown in gardens. It also grows on wasteland, sometimes from bird seed.

Distribution: Western Asia; north Africa; also widely naturalized.
Height and spread: 50cm/20in.
Habit and form: Annual.
Leaf shape: Lobed, ternate or pinnate.
Pollinated: Insect.

Identification: A hairless medium-size annual with lobed or pinnate leaves. The flowers are white, arranged in small umbels, with the outer petals being the largest. The fruits are aromatic and flavoursome.

Below: Coriander is a delicately branched annual.

Far left: The seeds are used in stews, curries and baking.

Lovage
Levisticum officinale

Introduced and naturalized over a wide area, lovage is a tall, strongly aromatic umbellifer, with medicinal, culinary and decorative uses. It is often grown in gardens and also turns up as a weed on rough ground, especially in hilly country and close to present or former habitations. The leaves give a pleasant flavour to salads and other dishes.

Identification: This is a tall, robust plant with yellow-green flowers, which appear in umbels to about 10mm/⅜in across. The individual flowers are about 2–3mm/¹⁄₁₆–⅛in, appearing from June to August. The fruits are 5–7mm/ ³⁄₁₆–¼in and winged.

Distribution: Midde East; widely naturalized.
Height and spread: To 2.5m/8ft.
Habit and form: Perennial.
Leaf shape: Pinnate or lobed.
Pollinated: Insect.

Above: Lovage is a tall herb.

Right: Hoverflies, wasps and bees are attracted to lovage.

Above: The fruits are oblong and winged.

Wild parsnip
Pastinaca sativa

Closely related to the cultivated parsnip, this plant is widespread across Europe, growing mainly in rough grassland, especially on chalky or limestone soils, often in coastal sites. Its leaves have a distinct parsnip smell when crushed, but the wild form lacks the swollen root of the cultivated form. The latter has long been grown as a vegetable and has sweet, swollen roots.

Distribution: Europe and Middle East.
Height and spread: 1.5m/5ft.
Habit and form: Biennial.
Leaf shape: Pinnate.
Pollinated: Insect.

Identification: A hairy plant with yellow flowers each about 1.5mm/¹⁄₁₆in across, in loose, spreading umbels, and yellow-green foliage. The stem is usually hollow. The fruit is oval and winged, about 5–7mm/³⁄₁₆–¼in.

Right: Each flowering stem produces umbels containing hundreds of individual flowers. The stem grows from a rosette of leaves at its base.

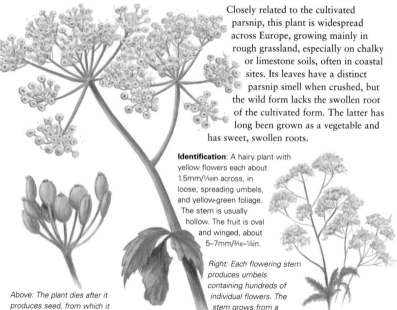

Above: The plant dies after it produces seed, from which it reproduces easily.

Wild angelica

Angelica sylvestris

Distribution: Europe to Central Asia.
Height and spread: 2.5m/8ft.
Habit and form: Perennial.
Leaf shape: Pinnate.
Pollinated: Insect.

Wild angelica is closely related to garden angelica (*A. officinalis*); the latter is used medicinally, as a confection and for flavour. It is a tall perennial with smooth stems usually found growing in fens and marshy areas or damp grassland or wet, open woods, from Europe (except the far north and south) east to central Asia. It is common in Great Britain and Ireland.

Identification: The lower leaves are pinnate, but the upper leaves are reduced to inflated stalks close to the stem. The stems are hairless with a purplish colour. The flowers are white or pinkish in umbels to about 15cm/6in across.

Far left: The stems are ridged and grow tall with pinnate lower leaves.

OTHER SPECIES OF NOTE

Upright hedge-parsley *Torilis japonica*
A medium-size plant with hairy stems, growing in rough grassland, hedges and roadsides throughout Europe, except the far north. Its fruits are densely covered in hooked spines. The umbels are long-stalked and the flowers white, pinkish or purplish.

Marsh pennywort *Hydrocotyle vulgaris*
An unusual umbellifer, marsh pennywort is well-named. Its rounded leaves are coin-shaped and it inhabits marshy ground. It grows low on the ground, spreading by creeping stems that root at the nodes. It is found from western Europe to central Asia and also in north Africa.

Thorow-wax *Bupleurum rotundifolium*
An erect annual growing to about 30cm/12in, found mainly in dry habitats in arable and wasteland. With its undivided leaves and small clusters of yellow-green flowers it is an unusual umbellifer. The common name probably refers to the stems that seem to grow (wax) through (thorow) the leaves.

Ferula jaeschkeana
A tall perennial growing to 2m/6½ft, native to the Himalayan region. It has large pinnate leaves with broad, toothed segments, and large umbels of yellow flowers, consisting of secondary rounded smaller umbels, each about 10mm/⅜in across. In fruit the umbels are up to 20cm/8in across with broad, flattened, winged fruits.

Large-flowered orlaya

Orlaya grandiflora

Although quite small, this annual umbellifer from southern Europe is very attractive, mainly because the outer flowers of the umbels have very large and conspicuous outer petals. It is mainly a lowland flower, found in dry grassland.

Identification: The stem is simple or branched and hairy at its base, but hairless elsewhere. The leaves are two to three times pinnate with oval segments; and the upper leaves are lobed. The flowers are white (or pink), the outer petals of the outer flowers are up to eight times longer than the others. The fruit is about 8mm/⅝in, oval, with hooked bristles.

Distribution: Mediterranean and south-eastern Europe.
Height and spread: 50cm/20in.
Habit and form: Annual.
Leaf shape: Pinnate.
Pollinated: Insect.

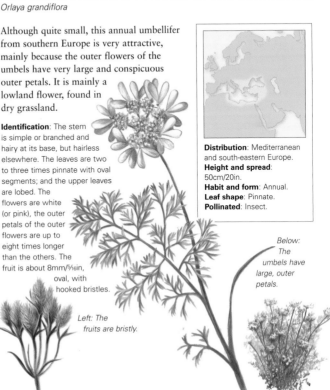

Below: The umbels have large, outer petals.

Left: The fruits are bristly.

BORAGE FAMILY

The borage family, Boraginaceae, contains about 2,300 species of shrubs, trees and herbs from temperate and subtropical areas; it is particularly well represented in the Mediterranean. Many of its members have medicinal or culinary uses. They typically have five-lobed, tube-shaped flowers and undivided, alternate leaves.

Green alkanet

Evergreen bugloss, Pentaglottis sempervirens

Green alkanet is a member of the forget-me-not family, but it is unusual in that the flowers do not grow in a curved spike as with most members of the family. The plant is native to south-west Europe, but is now naturalized in hedge banks and woodland edges in many areas outside this range. It is especially common close to towns and villages, probably due to its having been used at one time as the source of a red dye that was extracted from the roots. It can grow in deep woodland shade or open positions, although it usually requires moist soil and is common in damp, shady places, or by roads and in hedges, near the sea.

Identification: A coarsely hairy, taprooted perennial. It has strong, erect to ascending, fairly leafy stems, which arise from a basal rosette of pointed, oval to oblong, rough-hairy, mid-green leaves, which are 10–40cm/4–16in long. The stem leaves are smaller. From spring to early summer, it bears small leafy clusters of bright blue flowers, to 12mm/½in across, with stamens hidden inside the short, narrow flower-tube. The flower has five spreading lobes and a white eye.

Right: The small seedhead contains numerous seeds.

Left: Tall flower stems arise from the spreading leafy base.

Right: The flowers are eye-catching.

Distribution: Western Europe.
Height and spread: 30cm–1m/12–39in.
Habit and form: Herbaceous perennial.
Leaf shape: Ovate.
Pollinated: Insect.

Common borage

Borago officinalis

Borage is a hardy annual with obscure origins. It grows wild from central Europe to the western Mediterranean but has been used by people for so long that it is now naturalized in most parts of Europe; mostly near dwellings. It has been grown as a herb – the leaves taste like cucumber, despite their texture – and for its flowers, which yield excellent honey. The numerous bright blue flowers, held in loose, branching heads appear from late spring onward.

Below: Borage has a messy straggly habit.

Above and far right: The showy, star-shaped flowerheads sport numerous blue flowers, and are favoured by bees.

Identification: Borage is a robust, freely branching annual, with lance-shaped to oval, dull green leaves up to 15cm/6in long, covered with white, stiff, prickly hairs. The leaf margins are entire, but wavy. The round stems, 60cm/24in high, are branched, hollow and succulent, with alternate, stalkless, lance-shaped leaves, supporting branched clusters of five-petalled, star-shaped, bright blue flowers up to 25mm/1in across, over a long period in summer. The flowers are easily distinguished from those of every other plant in this order by their prominent black anthers, which form a cone in the centre. The fruit consists of four brownish-black nutlets.

Distribution: Central Europe.
Height and spread: 60cm/24in.
Habit and form: Annual.
Leaf shape: Ovate to lanceolate.
Pollinated: Bee.

Hound's tongue

Gypsyflower, *Cynoglossum officinale*

Distribution: Europe, except the far north, east to Asia.
Height and spread: 80 x 50cm/31 x 20in.
Habit and form: Herbaceous biennial.
Leaf shape: Root leaves elliptical, upper lanceolate.
Pollinated: Insect, particularly bee.

The erect, greyish spikes of this downy plant are often seen in sunny areas on dunes or other dry, sandy or calcareous soils, particularly in areas grazed by rabbits or near the coast, although it is not tolerant of maritime conditions. Most consider the smell unpleasant, similar to that of mice, and animals dislike the taste, usually avoiding it. The purple-red flowers appear from June to August. In many states of the USA it is considered a noxious weed. Although the leaves contain healing properties and it has often been used as a medicinal plant, it can also be poisonous.

Identification: The flowers are 10mm/⅜in across, the five petals and five sepals, characteristic of the borage family, forming a five-lobed funnel. The fruit is a large nutlet with hooked bristles.

Below: Hound's tongue often grows on disturbed ground.

OTHER SPECIES OF NOTE

Viper's bugloss
Echium vulgare
A European native, viper's bugloss is a bushy, upright biennial with narrowly lance-shaped to linear, toothed, white, bristly-hairy leaves. In early summer it produces short, dense spikes of bell-shaped flowers, blue in bud but ranging from purple or vibrant blue to pink or white.

Siberian bugloss *Brunnera macrophylla*
A native of woodlands in the Caucasus. Its leaves, up to 15cm/6in across, are roughly kidney shaped and provide an attractive foil for the sprays of starry, pale blue, forget-me-not-like flowers that appear shortly after the leaves.

Scrambling gromwell *Lithodora diffusa*
Native to France, Spain and Portugal, this plant is recognized by its sprawling habit. It has linear, deep green leaves and strikingly deep blue flowers, borne profusely from mid-spring to early summer. It prefers well-drained, moist, acid soil.

Omphalodes verna
This charming spreading perennial, a relative of the forget-me-nots, grows from the south-east Alps to Romania. Its dark green, grooved leaves cover the ground and in spring, small, white-centred, deep blue flowers appear on short, branched stems, each with two to four blooms.

Tower of jewels

Echium wildpretii

The tower of jewels is endemic to the Canary Islands. It produces a tall spike of crimson flowers with beautiful rosettes of silver leaves. Growing on mountains where it is mostly dry, cold and exposed to high ultraviolet radiation, this species shows similarities with other isolated alpine plant species, such as lobelias and groundsels, by attaining giant size to cope with alpine conditions instead of the more common miniature proportions usually associated with alpine plants. The plant is monocarpic: when the flowers fade, it dies, leaving behind a vast amount of seed.

Identification: A woody-stemmed, unbranched biennial or occasionally short-lived perennial, with a dense rosette of narrowly lance-shaped, silvery, hairy, light green leaves, to 20cm/8in long. In its first year it develops only leaves, but in the following year it produces a dense, column-like cyme, 2.5m/8ft tall or more, of funnel-shaped, red or pink flowers, which are often bird-pollinated.

Distribution: Canary Islands.
Height and spread: 2–3m x 75cm/6½–10ft x 29½in.
Habit and form: Biennial.
Leaf shape: Lanceolate.
Pollinated: Bird, bee.

Above: Each flower spike is made up of a multitude of tiny, pink flowers.

Alkanet

Common bugloss, *Anchusa officinalis*

This bristly, medium tall plant has bright purple-blue flowers, rarely white or yellowish, flowering from June to October. It is found in a range of well-drained but moist soils from sandy to heavier clay, from acid to alkaline, and can be found in meadows, hedge banks and wasteland, but not in shade. It has various medicinal properties and the roots produce a red dye.

Identification: The flowers have straight corolla tubes, up to 15mm/⅝in wide, with a white throat. They are borne on elongating, long, curved cymes on unbranched stems. The leaves are 10–20mm/⅜–¾in wide.

Below: The flowering stems coil at the top.

Left: The trumpet-shaped flowers are blue-violet.

Below: The fruiting head.

Distribution: Europe, particularly the Mediterranean, east to western Asia; introduced in to Great Britain and the USA.
Height and spread: 60cm/24in.
Habit and form: Herbaceous biennial or perennial.
Leaf shape: Oval-lanceolate.
Pollinated: Bee.

Wood forget-me-not

Myosotis sylvatica

This leafy, downy and much-branched plant is native to richer soils in woods and sometimes grasslands in Europe, but also grows as a garden escapee. It is a parent of many of the garden-grown hybrids. The flowers appear from April to August. The common name of this genus is possibly from a German legend in which a knight called these words as he was swept away after falling into a river while gathering these flowers for his lady. The delicate blue flowers appear in May and June.

Right: Wood forget-me-not is grown as a common garden plant for its pretty flowers.

Identification: Wood forget-me-not has pale blue flowers with yellow centres. The flat corollas are 6–10mm/¼–⅜in across. Unlike the similar water forget-me-not, *M. scorpioides*, it does not produce runners.

Below: The flowers are borne on slender stalks that curl downwards towards the tips.

Distribution: Europe; introduced in the USA.
Height and spread: 50cm/20in.
Habit and form: Herbaceous biennial or short-lived perennial.
Leaf shape: Ovate to elliptical.
Pollinated: Insect, usually bee.

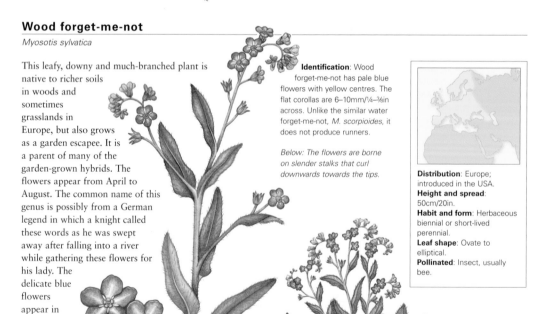

Common lungwort

Pulmonaria officinalis

A short, hairy plant that tolerates shade and grows in open, damp woods and hedge banks, usually on limestone. The distinctive, tongue-shaped leaves usually have white spots that caused herbalists to believe that they could cure spots on the lungs, hence the naming of the genus. The plant does, in fact, have a high mucilage content and has medicinal properties for chest conditions. The attractive flowers appear from March to May before most of the leaves, and turn from pink to blue or blue-violet.

Distribution: Europe, except the far north and west; naturalized in Great Britain.
Height and spread: 30 x 30cm/12 x 12in.
Habit and form: Herbaceous perennial.
Leaf shape: Oval-cordate.
Pollinated: Bee, and possibly other insects.

Left: The pink flowers turn blue as they age.

Far right: The leaves are distinctive, being covered in lighter spots.

Identification: The green, long-stalked leaves enlarge after flowering. The flowers have funnel-shaped corollas, 10mm/⅜in wide, growing in small clusters, and the fruit is an oval, rounded nutlet.

OTHER SPECIES OF NOTE

Heliotrope *Heliotropium europaeum*
A small, annual found in fields and wasteland in frost-free areas of the Mediterranean, western, central and southern Europe. It has small, yellow-centred white or lilac flowers borne on one-sided and coiled spikes. The stems are densely covered with soft hairs and the grey-green leaves have conspicuous veins.

White comfrey *Symphytum orientale*
Similar to but smaller than *S. officinale* with downy leaves and much-branched, unwinged stems, this plant has white flowers from April to May that produce a brown, warty nutlet. Native to Turkey, it has naturalized in damp, shady places such as woods, hedgebanks and grassy places in Europe, including Britain.

Field forget-me-not *Myosotis arvensis*
A very common annual in hedgebanks, fields, dry woods and on dunes. The pale blue flowers consist of a corolla up to 5mm/³⁄₁₆in wide, and the leaves are lanceolate and pointed. The flowers last from May to late autumn.

Oysterplant *Mertensia maritima*
This perennial grows on shingle and sandy coasts of northern Europe. It can be identified by its prostrate form and blue-grey, hairless, fleshy leaves, most of which grow in a basal rosette. From June to August the flowers appear on a terminal inflorescence, the bell-shaped corollas, 6mm/¼in wide, turning from pink to pale blue.

Common comfrey

Symphytum officinale

This is an erect plant with bristly leaves and drooping, terminal sprays of flowers that appear from May to June. It is found in marshes, fens, damp grassland and riversides. The boiled leaves were once used for flavouring in comfrey cakes, and some species of *Symphytum* are cultivated for use as fertilizers due to the ability of their long roots to access nutrients from deep in the soil. The plant also has a long and proven use as a medicinal herb, to treat various conditions.

Identification: The stems are distinctively winged while the corollas are tubular or narrow and bell-shaped, 12–18mm/½–¹¹⁄₁₆in long, with a long style. They range in colour from white, yellowish-white and pink to purple-violet. The fruit is a black, shiny nutlet.

Right: The flowers are bell-shaped.

Distribution: Europe, including Great Britain, and east to Siberia
Height and spread: 1.2m x 60cm/4ft x 24in.
Habit and form: Herbaceous perennial.
Leaf shape: Oval lanceolate, with the upper leaves narrower.
Pollinated: Insect, usually bee.

NETTLE AND HEMP FAMILIES

The nettle family, Urticaceae, is spread widely all over the world. Most are herbs, but a few are shrubs or small trees, several of which occur widely in temperate climates. Many of the species have stinging hairs on their stems and leaves. The hemp family, Cannabaceae, is a small family with just four species – three species of hops and a single species of hemp. They contain aromatic and useful compounds.

Stinging nettle

Urtica dioica

The common stinging nettle is an upright perennial that grows in damp forests or wherever land has been disturbed by humans. It has a much-branched yellow rhizome, which spreads over large areas, and from which grow numerous leafy shoots. The unisexual flowers are borne on separate plants, although monoecious specimens sometimes occur. All parts of the plant are covered in fine, stinging hairs: it is soon recognized, often through harsh experience!

Above: Tiny female flowers appear on separate plants to male ones (left).

Distribution: Northern Eurasia.
Height and spread: 1.2m/4ft.
Habit and form: Herbaceous perennial.
Leaf shape: Cordate or lanceolate.
Pollinated: Wind.

Identification: Numerous erect, quadrangular stems commonly grow to 1.2m/4ft tall, although they may far exceed this in favourable conditions. They are covered with long stinging hairs and short bristly hairs. The opposite, stalked, heart-shaped or lance-shaped leaves are serrated at the margin and covered on both sides with translucent stinging hairs. The flowers are arranged in drooping panicles, growing in groups from the upper leaf axils from late spring to early autumn.

Left and right: These robust plants spread to form extensive colonies.

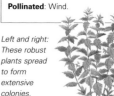

China grass

White ramie, *Boehmeria nivea*

This shrubby perennial from eastern Asia has the overall appearance of a stinging nettle, but lacks any stinging hairs. It can sometimes be encountered in the wild in rocky places up to a height of 1,200m/4,200ft. It is often found outside its original range due to its having been extensively cultivated for its fibres, which, when extracted from the stems, are the longest and strongest of any plant. It is sometimes found wild in India, Malaysia, China and Japan, and is probably a native of India and Malaysia.

Distribution: Eastern Asia.
Height and spread: 1–1.8m x 1m/39in–6ft x 39in.
Habit and form: Shrubby, herbaceous perennial.
Leaf shape: Ovate.
Pollinated: Wind.

Identification: A number of straight, coarse, bristly shoots are sent up from a perennial underground rootstock each season. The alternate leaves are broadly oval, 15cm/6in long or more, with pointed tips, wedge-shaped or rounded at the base, serrated along the margin, white-woolly underneath, giving a silvery appearance. The minute, greenish flowers are closely arranged along a slender axis, on densely branched panicles, mostly shorter than the flower stalk.

Hop *Humulus lupulus*
Fruits of cultivated varieties of hop are used to add a bitter flavour to beer and to help preserve it. The wild species is a climber with square bristly stems and palmately-lobed leaves. It grows throughout Europe in river valley woods, hedgerows and scrub. It is dioecious (male and female plants separate). Female plants produce the familiar clusters of hops – cone-like papery clusters with an aromatic scent.

Pellitory of the wall *Parietaria judaica*
This perennial, grows to 60cm/24in, in semi-shade or an open position. It is often found on hedge banks and dry walls, hence the name. It is reputed to be a medicinal plant, and is often found growing around ruined castles, churches and monasteries.

Roman nettle *Urtica pilulifera*
The Roman nettle bears its female flowers in little compact, globular heads, followed by ornamental seedpods, and was a medicinal plant of choice for the ancient Romans. It is also smooth, except for the stinging hairs, which contain a much more virulent venom than that of the common stinging nettle.

Hemp, cannabis *Cannabis sativa*
Notorious as the source of the drug, this plant also produces valuable fibres, oil and medicines. It is native to Asia and widely naturalized elsewhere, including across parts of Europe. The palmate leaves have narrow, toothed lobes.

Aluminium plant

Watermelon pilea, *Pilea cadierei*

This familiar plant is widely grown in gardens, or as a houseplant, although its origins are in the warm humid forests of Vietnam. It is instantly recognizable due to the variegated foliage that is unlike any other, with shiny silver, irregularly-shaped markings parallel to the lateral veins. These leaves are held opposite each other on square, green stems and they rapidly produce a thick ground cover in patches of open forest. Its small white flowers are produced at the ends of the stems in the summer but are mostly overshadowed by the conspicuous foliage.

Identification: A spreading, erect herb or sub-shrub, to 45cm/18in, with greenish or pink-tinged, soft, round stems, becoming rigid with age and woody at the base. The leaves are obovate to oblong-oblanceolate to 75mm/3in long, held in opposite pairs, simple, quilted, green with interrupted bands of silver centrally and on margins, with coppery-maroon veins. The flowers are minute, whitish becoming pinkish, perianth with four segments in male flowers, three in female.

Distribution: Vietnam.
Height and spread: 50cm/20in.
Habit and form: Spreading evergreen perennial.
Leaf shape: Oval.
Pollinated: Bee.

Below: The shiny, irregular markings on the leaves are instantly recognizable and give rise to this plant's common name.

Mind-your-own-business

Soleirolia soleirolii

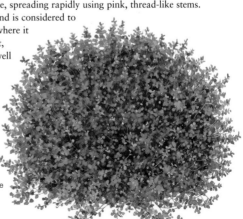

This semi-evergreen, creeping perennial, which forms a dense mat about 50mm/2in high, was originally introduced as an ornamental from Corsica across much of its modern range. It prefers moist soil and partial shade, spreading rapidly using pink, thread-like stems. It sometimes forms extensive mats and is considered to be an invasive weed in many areas where it has been introduced. It prefers moist, sheltered habitats and is especially well adapted for colonizing urban areas.

Distribution: Corsica, but now very widespread.
Height and spread: 50mm/2in, with indefinite spread.
Habit and form: Creeping herbaceous perennial.
Leaf shape: Rounded.
Pollinated: Wind.

Identification: The slender stems, which grow to 20cm/8in and root at the nodes, are delicate, intricately branching, translucent, pale green sometimes tinged pink. The leaves, 2–6mm/1⁄16–1⁄4in, are alternate and near-circular, short-stalked, minutely and sparsely hairy with a smooth margin. The solitary flowers, borne in the leaf axils, are minute, white, sometimes pink tinged, and followed by the glossy, one-seeded fruit, enclosed in a persistent calyx.

BIRTHWORT AND KNOTWEED FAMILIES

*The birthwort family, Aristolochiaceae, has about 500 species. The species are herbs or shrubs, mainly
found in tropical and warm temperate regions; several are climbing lianas. The knotweed family,
Polygonaceae, with 1,100 species is a cosmopolitan family of herbs, with some shrubs and a few trees.
It contains many familiar species such as docks, knotweeds, buckwheat and rhubarb.*

Asarabacca

Asarum europaeum

Asarabacca is an unusual
perennial found mainly in
woodland and scrub on
calcareous soils. It produces its
odd-looking flowers from
March through August and spreads by
means of rhizomes. In distribution it is
local, found scattered from central Europe
north to southern Scandinavia. In Britain it is
rare and declining with a patchy range in
England, Wales and south Scotland.

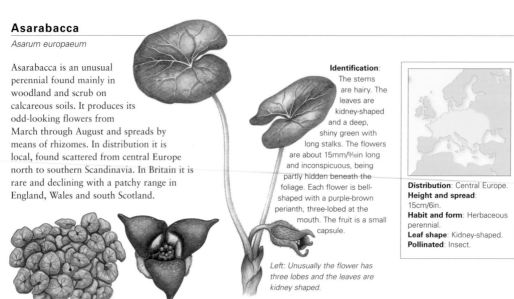

Identification:
The stems
are hairy. The
leaves are
kidney-shaped
and a deep,
shiny green with
long stalks. The flowers
are about 15mm/⁹⁄₁₆in long
and inconspicuous, being
partly hidden beneath the
foliage. Each flower is bell-
shaped with a purple-brown
perianth, three-lobed at the
mouth. The fruit is a small
capsule.

*Left: Unusually the flower has
three lobes and the leaves are
kidney shaped.*

Distribution: Central Europe.
Height and spread:
15cm/6in.
Habit and form: Herbaceous
perennial.
Leaf shape: Kidney-shaped.
Pollinated: Insect.

Birthwort

Dutchman's pipe, *Aristolochia clematitis*

Birthwort is a hairless perennial found in damp habitats. Native to
central and southern Europe, it is widely naturalized and was grown
as a source of medicine. However, like many medicinal species it is
poisonous, and has also been linked with kidney damage. The flowers have
a nasty smell that attracts flies. As its name suggests, the use of this species
was associated with birth, having been used to induce labour. The
alternative common name comes from the shape of the flower
resembling a traditional Dutch pipe.

*Below: The greenish flowers are
inconspicuous.*

Distribution: South and
central Europe.
Height and spread: 1m/39in.
Habit and form: Herbaceous
perennial.
Leaf shape: Oval.
Pollinated: Insect.

Identification: This species bears
oval leaves on long stalks, and
long yellow-green flowers. Each
flower is up to 35mm/1⅜in long,
with a narrow tube, opening with
a yellow-brown lip. The fruit is a
large capsule.

*Above: The fruit is a capsule
containing many seeds.*

Kindri

Bamba, *Oxygonum sinuatum*

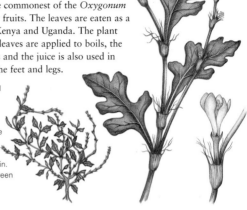

This is a decumbent or erect weedy annual with a wide distribution in eastern and southern Africa. It flowers from February to April and grows as a weed in secondary regrowth after cultivation. It is the commonest of the *Oxygonum* species and has unpleasant prickly fruits. The leaves are eaten as a vegetable, especially in Ethiopia, Kenya and Uganda. The plant also has medicinal properties: the leaves are applied to boils, the stems chewed for throat infections and the juice is also used in treatment of fungal infections of the feet and legs.

Distribution: Tropical Africa.
Height and spread: 90 x 10cm/35 x 4in.
Habit and form: Annual herb.
Leaf shape: Simple.
Pollinated: Insect.

Far right: Kindri is a many-branched annual herb.

Identification: An almost hairless annual weedy herb, bending over or erect to 90cm/35in. The leaves are alternate or oval to 60mm/2¼in long, the edge deeply cut into irregular rounded or acute lobes. The flowers are pink or white, 2–3mm/¹⁄₁₆–⅛in, inconspicuous, along terminal leaflets, in spikes up to 28cm/11in. The stems are glabrous to pubescent, green to reddish-brown.

OTHER SPECIES OF NOTE

Knotgrass *Polygonum aviculare*
This common annual weed is found throughout most of Europe. Hairless and sprawling, it has lanceolate leaves and clusters of small pink or greenish flowers. It grows on wasteland, roadsides, sea shores and other disturbed sites.

Noble rhubarb *Rheum nobile*
A most unusual looking plant in the same genus as rhubarb, this Himalayan species has an upright stem, shrouded in cream, drooping overlapping bracts, beneath which grow clusters of green flowers. It grows to a height of 2m/6½ft and is visible from a distance. The outer bracts are translucent, acting like a miniature greenhouse. The basal leaves are large, leathery and green, often with a red margin.

Japanese knotweed *Reynoutria japonica*
This tall perennial is notorious as a vigorous invasive weed in regions where it has been introduced or escaped from gardens, as in much of Europe. Native to China and Japan, it grows to 2m/6½ft tall with oval, pointed leaves and panicles of small white flowers.

Russian vine *Fallopia baldschuanica* (= *F. aubertii*)
This species is native to Central Asia and is now established, often as a garden escapee over much of Europe. It is a vigorous woody climber often planted to disguise unsightly fences or sheds. It can grow 4.5m/15ft in a year.

Abyssinian dock

Rumex abyssinicus

This dock species is a stout perennial herb growing to 4m/13ft tall with greenish-brown, tiny delicate flowers. It is widespread in central and eastern Africa, from Ethiopia south to South Africa and Madagascar. It flowers between November and January and thrives in volcanic soils in woodlands and bushland. The young stems and leaves are eaten fresh, mainly by herders, farmers and children. The leaves and roots are used in sauces as a flavouring and as extracts for making dyes and medicines. Tests have shown extracts to have both anti-microbial and anti-inflammatory properties.

Distribution: Tropical Africa.
Height and spread: 4m x 40cm/13ft x 16in.
Habit and form: Perennial herb.
Leaf shape: Simple, triangular.
Pollinated: Insect.

Identification: A large, erect perennial herb to 4m/13ft. The stem is greenish-red, to 30mm/1¼in wide at the base, with conspicuous sheathing stipules where the leaves emerge from the stem. The leaves are large and soft, to 30cm/12in long and 20cm/8in wide, triangular, with large, spreading basal lobes.

Above: The fruiting stem.

Right: This dock grows tall and erect.

MINT AND VERBENA FAMILIES

The mint family, Labiatae or Lamiaceae, contains the deadnettles and many well-known herbs such as mints and sage. They are found worldwide and number about 6,700 species.The verbena family, Verbenaceae, are related to the Labiatae, and is mostly tropical or subtropical, consisting of 950 species, ranging from herbs to trees such as teak, Tectona grandis.

Bugle

Ajuga reptans

Bugle is a handsome plant of damp woods, pastures and meadows. Its dense clusters of intensely coloured flowers are striking when viewed against the dark, sometimes blue- or bronze-green, foliage. Its species name means creeping, a characteristic that adds to its visual impact through the ability of its long stolons to cover large areas of ground. Bronze-leaved cultivars make attractive ground cover in gardens.

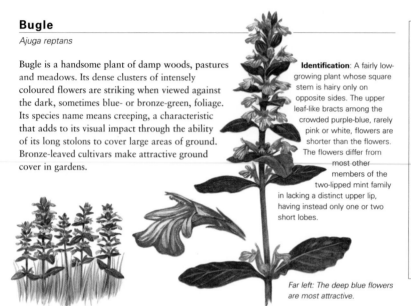

Identification: A fairly low-growing plant whose square stem is hairy only on opposite sides. The upper leaf-like bracts among the crowded purple-blue, rarely pink or white, flowers are shorter than the flowers. The flowers differ from most other members of the two-lipped mint family in lacking a distinct upper lip, having instead only one or two short lobes.

Far left: The deep blue flowers are most attractive.

Distribution: Europe to 61 degrees north, but scarce in the eastern Mediterranean and absent from most of the islands; south-western Asia; eastern Algeria; Tunisia.
Height and spread: 10–35cm/4–14in.
Habit and form: Herbaceous creeping, patch-forming perennial.
Leaf shape: Oval.
Pollinated: Bee and other insects.

Wood sage

Teucrium scorodonia

Wood sage has leaves with the dull green and crinkly texture of its edible namesake and even a hint of the characteristic scent, but otherwise bears little resemblance. It is an erect branching plant, but is too slow-growing to compete well with other plants. It therefore thrives in infertile and unstable habitats such as rocky slopes, screes, quarry and mine spoil, and on cliffs. Variations in the species allow it to exploit acidic and calcareous situations. Despite its name, it avoids shady habitats.

Identification: Flowers are 9mm/⅜in, hairy and pale greenish-yellow, rarely white or reddish, with protruding red-brown stamens. It has a five-lobed lower lip. The flowers are borne on upright spikes, which may or may not be branched.

Left: Wood sage has branching growth.

Above: The plant has pale yellow-green flowers.

Distribution: Southern, western and central Europe, from the Iberian Peninsula to Serbia and Montenegro and western Poland and northwards to Norway.
Height and spread: 15–50cm/6–20in.
Habit and form: Herbaceous perennial.
Leaf shape: Triangular-oval, heart-shaped at base.
Pollinated: Insect.

Ground-ivy

Glechoma hederacea

This plant is not related to common ivy, but it has the same habit. Its creeping stolons can be more than 1m/39in long, enabling it to cover large areas of ground quickly. Within the mint family, it belongs to the group that includes the culinary herbs, and although its scent is coarse, it is sometimes used in herbal teas. It has also been used, instead of hops, as a bittering agent in beer. It is found in shaded, often moist and fertile, marginal areas subject to disturbance, such as woodland rides, hedgerows and roadsides.

Below: The blue flowers.

Below: The plant spreads via underground creeping roots.

Distribution: Throughout most of Europe; western and northern Asia; New Zealand; USA.
Height and spread: 30cm/12in.
Habit and form: Flowering stems not entirely erect. Herbaceous perennial, patch-forming.
Leaf shape: Kidney-shaped to round/heart-shaped.
Pollinated: Insect, mainly bee.

Identification: The flowers are pale violet with purple spots on the lower lip and a flat upper lip. Bisexual flowers are about 15–22mm/⁹⁄₁₆–⁷⁄₈in, but smaller female-only flowers also occur. Clusters of flowers on the stem tend to be one-sided rather than in a whorl.

OTHER SPECIES OF NOTE
Yellow archangel *Lamiastrum galeobdolon*
This is a plant of old woodlands. Its whorls of beautiful golden-yellow flowers with red-brown markings are borne on erect stems whose leaves are narrower than those on its creeping stolons. Garden plants and escapees usually have silver blotches on the leaves.

Skullcap *Scutellaria galericulata*
This is widespread in Europe in damp grassy habitats by streams, rivers, marshes and water meadows. Its elegant violet-blue, rarely pink, flowers are whitish at the base and much longer than the fused 2-lipped sepal tube that surrounds them at the base. The resemblance of the sepal tube to a Roman helmet gives the plant its name.

Wild basil *Clinopodium vulgare*
A basil in neither scent nor appearance. It is an attractive softly hairy 30–80cm/12–31in tall perennial of usually calcareous dry grassy habitats and woodland edge, scrub, verges and embankments. Its flowers are pink-purple.

Balm *Melissa officinalis*
This tall perennial herb of southern Europe, western Asia and northern Africa has naturalized in southern England. It is widely grown for its calming properties. The flowers change from pale yellow to pink-white.

Cat-mint

Nepeta cataria

This strongly-scented plant is the one that many cats just cannot resist, but it also has a long history as a medicinal plant for humans and as a repellent for insects and some rodents. For this reason it has been widely planted, but it is not the same as the blue-flowered garden hybrid plant. Naturally, it grows in grasslands, waysides, and olive groves and on rough or rocky ground, on calcareous soils, in some places naturalized from cultivation.

Distribution: Spain eastwards to Turkey; widely naturalized from cultivation in northern and western central Europe.
Height and spread: 40cm–1m/16–39in.
Habit and form: Herbaceous perennial.
Leaf shape: Oval, heart-shaped at base.
Pollinated: Bee.

Identification: The leaves and stems are grey and woolly. The flowers are 7–12mm/¼–½in, and with their white colour and small purple spots and three-lobed lower lip, have a slightly 'frilly' appearance.

Below: Cat-mint has compact flowering spikes.

Above: The flower has a spotted lower lip.

White deadnettle

Lamium album

This is a common lowland evergreen species of roadsides, hedgerows, wasteland and arable land, where it spreads to consolidate its position by creeping rhizomes. It has a long flowering season and favours land with higher fertility and disturbed ground. It tolerates a little shade, but is generally absent from wet and shaded habitats.

Below: Whorls of white flowers grow amid nettle-like leaves.

Identification: With its four-angled square stem and nettle-like leaves, it is easy to see how this hairy plant could be confused with a stinging nettle. However, its white flowers clustered in an apparent whorl around the stem readily identify it as a member of the mint family. Each flower is about 20mm/¾in long and has five petals joined to form a tube with two lips, the upper hooded.

Below: The flowers have a hood and lower lip.

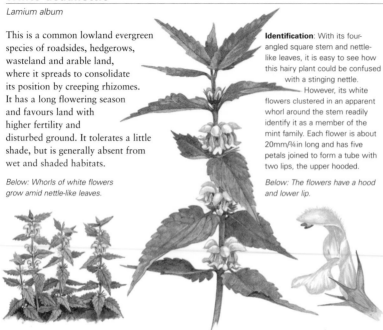

Distribution: Europe, but rare or absent in the south, Ireland and many islands; Himalayas and Japan.
Height and spread: 20–80cm/8–31in.
Habit and form: Herbaceous perennial.
Leaf shape: Ovate, pointed at the tip, heart-shaped at the base.
Pollinated: Insect, especially bumblebee.

Spotted deadnettle

Lamium maculatum

The large white blotch that occurs on the leaves gives this plant its common name. This feature also makes it a popular foliage plant for gardens. It spreads enthusiastically by creeping stems, above or below ground, which make it a good plant for ground cover, even in slightly shady situations. In the wild it is found in grassy and semi-shaded habitats, hedgerows, roadsides, rough ground, wasteland and olive groves.

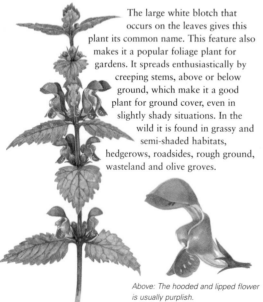

Above: The hooded and lipped flower is usually purplish.

Identification: Its leaves are generally smaller (20–50mm/ ¾–2in) than those of white deadnettle, *L. album*, but it is a very variable plant, particularly in the shape and tooth-pattern of the leaves and the colour of the flowers. The flowers are usually pinkish-purple but may also be white or brownish-purple, 20–35mm/¾–1⅜in long, the tube curved.

Below: The whorls of bright pink flowers are attractive to bees.

Distribution: Europe northwards, to around 54 degrees in Germany and around 59 degrees in north-central Russia. Found as a garden escapee in the UK.
Height and spread: 15–80cm/6–31in high, spreading up to three times the height.
Habit and form: Herbaceous perennial.
Leaf shape: Triangular-oval, coarsely and irregularly toothed.
Pollinated: Insect, especially bumblebee.

Hedge woundwort

Stachys sylvatica

The name of this plant refers to the medicinal use of its leaves to staunch bleeding. It is a fairly competitive plant of lightly shaded habitats, particularly those that are fairly moist and fertile, in woodland edges and scrub, hedgerows, road verges, river banks and flood plains. In these places it often keeps company with tall competitive plants such as stinging nettle and cow parsley.

Distribution: Europe, though rare in the Mediterranean region; Central Asia.
Height and spread: 30cm–1.2m/12in–4ft.
Habit and form: Rhizomatous herbaceous perennial.
Leaf shape: Oval-heart-shaped, pointed tip, edges roundly toothed.
Pollinated: Insect.

Identification: This is not a subtle plant. Everything about it shouts, rather than quietly suggests that it is a member of the mint family. The smell of its crushed leaves is strong and astringent. It is an erect, harshly hairy, square-stemmed plant capable of vigorous spread by underground rhizomes to form large stands. It is, nevertheless, handsome, with its whorls of dull reddish-purple flowers with white markings on the three-lobed lower lip borne on striking spikes. The flowers are 13–18mm/ ½–¹¹⁄₁₆in.

Left: The flowers are arranged in whorls.

Far left: The plant is invasive.

OTHER SPECIES OF NOTE
Red deadnettle
Lamium purpureum
A versatile softly hairy short-lived annual plant capable of flowering through most of the year in waste and disturbed land, including gardens. The purple-pink colour of its flowers is often suffused through the whole plant.

Betony *Stachys officinalis*
Betony graces species-rich grasslands and woodland margins with its elegant spikes of bright magenta coloured flowers. These are borne at the top of slightly hairy stems up to 75cm/29½in tall, which have only two to four pairs of oval crenate leaves.

Large self-heal *Prunella grandiflora*
Distinguished from self-heal by its larger 25–30mm/1–1¼in beautiful deep violet-blue flowers with a whitish tube and a much less leafy flower-head. It is found in woodlands and dry meadows across much of Europe, from the Iberian peninsula eastwards to Turkey, but is absent from the north and the islands.

Tibetan woundwort *Stachys tibetica*
This branching shrubby perennial grows on stony slopes at about 2,000–3,600m/6,500–11,800ft in Himalayan Pakistan and Kashmir. It has greyish foliage, stiff stems and narrow leaves. The flowers are pink, each about 25mm/1in, with a three-lobed lower lip.

Self-heal

Prunella vulgaris

This is a very aptly named plant having wide-ranging medicinal uses, from the treatment of wounds, ulcers and a variety of ailments to its use as an antibacterial and cure for worms. It is a versatile plant in other ways, too, able to survive in a wide range of habitats, but particularly in cut, grazed or trampled grasslands and in lawns where it keeps its head down, flowering on very short stems when necessary and sending runners into gaps to form new plants.

Identification: The flowers are violet, rarely pink or white, 10–14mm/ ³⁄₈–⁹⁄₁₆in. Both the bracts among the flowers, which are more like scales than leaves, and the sepals forming a two-lipped tube around the flowers, are tinged with a reddish-plum colour, and it is this coloration that gives the name to this plant's genus.

Distribution: Europe; temperate Asia; northern Africa; North America; Australia.
Height and spread: 50mm–30cm/2–12in
Habit and form: Creeping herbaceous perennial; patch-forming.
Leaf shape: Ovate.
Pollinated: Insect, mainly bee.

Below: Self-heal thrives in grassland and spreads quickly.

Wild marjoram

Origanum vulgare

This is the culinary herb oregano, so characteristic of Mediterranean dishes, and should not be confused with marjoram, its relative, pot marjoram, *Origanum majorana*, which is from north Africa and south-west Asia. Wild marjoram likes dry, sunny places, stony and rocky habitats, particularly limestone, dry grassland, scrub, hedgerows and roadsides, usually on calcareous soils. Like wild thyme, it has fairly deep roots that enable it to reach subsoil water.

Below: The tiny flowers appear in spikes on the plant throughout the summer and are very attractive to bees.

Identification: The bisexual flowers are longer than the two-lipped sepal tube. The flowers are violet-purple to pink or white, 6–8mm/¼–⁵⁄₁₆in. The stems and leaf-like bracts among the flowers can be quite variable, often appearing purplish. The leaves and stems are usually hairy.

Distribution: Europe except Crete, Balearics and a few other islands; western Asia and North America.
Height and spread: 30–80cm/12–31in.
Habit and form: Woody rhizomatous perennial.
Leaf shape: Ovate, sometimes shallowly toothed or crenate.
Pollinated: Insect.

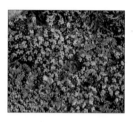

Left: Wild marjoram often shows bushy growth.

Wild thyme

Thymus praecox

With its massed purple-pink flowers at the tips of branches or along the length of the stem, and its fragrant leathery leaves, this plant is a frequent jewel of dry habitats such as scree, rock outcrops, lead-mine spoil, sand dunes and dry grasslands. Its creeping stems tolerate shallow burial, enabling it to display itself to its most photogenic advantage on anthills. It is usually associated with calcareous soils, but in northern and montane areas it can also occur in damp and acidic habitats.

Left: The lavender pink flowers bloom through the summer months and are very attractive to bees.

Above: Wild thyme has antiseptic properties.

Identification: A very variable species with respect to flower, leaf and stem characters. In north-western Europe, the stem hairs are mostly on two opposite sides only. The sepals are joined to form a bell-shaped tube with a distinct upper lip with three short teeth and a lower lip with two long teeth. The bisexual flowers are larger than female ones and have protruding stamens.

Right: Wild thyme often has creeping mat-like growth.

Distribution: Southern, western and central Europe.
Height and spread: Less than 10cm/4in.
Habit and form: Woody perennial, low mat-forming.
Leaf shape: Rounded oval
Pollinated: Insect.

Meadow clary

Salvia pratensis

Although often planted in gardens, this impressive plant is best seen in its native species-rich dry grasslands on chalk or limestone soils, for example in the wide valleys of European rivers, or locally in southern England, where it is now a rare plant. Though not uncommon in parts of Europe, it will always be vulnerable to changes in grassland management such as cessation of grazing or fertilization. It can also be found in sunny hedge banks and woodland margins. The name is a contraction of clear-eye, a reference to its medicinal use as an eye-wash.

Distribution: Europe; north-central Russia; Morocco.
Height and spread: 30cm–1m/12–39in.
Habit and form: Herbaceous perennial.
Leaf shape: Ovate, obtuse, heart-shaped at base.
Pollinated: Long-tongued bee.

Identification: The eye is drawn first to the beautiful, relatively large, 20–30mm/¾–1¼in violet-blue flowers with their strongly hooded upper lip and three-lobed lower lip. The sepal tube is two-lipped and like the much shorter leaf-like bract beneath it, is often tinged with violet-blue. The flowers are borne on striking spikes with four to six flowers in a whorl, distinguishing it from *Salvia verticillata* with 15–30 flowers.

Left: A single flower.

Left: The flowering stems are impressive.

OTHER SPECIES OF NOTE

Wild clary *Salvia verbenaca*
Wild clary has pale blue-violet flowers, which do not always open. They are much smaller, 6–10mm/¼–⅜in, than those of meadow clary, *S. pratensis*. It is found in dry, fallow places wasteland, roadsides, vineyards, olive groves, coastal garrigue, and dunes in southern and western Europe up to northern England.

Spearmint *Mentha spicata*
This is the strong, sweet-smelling mint grown as a pot-herb. It is a very variable plant but is usually more or less without hairs on its stem and long-oval toothed leaves. Although widely naturalized throughout Europe, its origin is unknown.

Round-leaved mint *Mentha suaveolens*
A sickly-smelling mint of damp places in southern and western Europe and naturalized elsewhere. It is recognizable by the white downy hairiness of both its stem and the underside of its almost stemless leaves.

Pennyroyal *Mentha pulegium*
Pennyroyal is variable, like many mints, but is one of the smallest and most prostrate. It is, sadly, a locally declining plant of damp grassy pool and stream edges. It has a pungent smell and lilac flowers in densely clustered whorls, but not at the stem tip. The stems are usually hairy and the leaves are small and short-stalked, and normally hairy beneath.

Corn mint

Mentha arvensis

Across Europe, the vegetative characteristics of this plant vary greatly. Its scent seems to be variable too, with descriptions ranging from 'mellow apples and gingerbread' to 'sickly' or like 'mouldy gorgonzola'. There is also disagreement over its value as a medicinal plant. Perhaps it is best left and simply enjoyed where it belongs, in wet or damp places in woodland clearings and rides, arable fields and edges of rivers and ponds.

Identification: Mints have their flowers in whorls around a square stem like other members of the family, but the flowers themselves are different. The flower still has five petals joined in a tube, but the tube has four more or less equal lobes, the upper being slightly notched. In corn mint, the sepals are joined around the lilac, white or pinkish flowers, in a bell-shaped hairy tube with five triangular teeth.

Distribution: Europe, but absent from most of the islands; northern Asia to the Himalayas.
Height and spread: 10–60cm/4–24in.
Habit and form: Herbaceous perennial or rarely annual.
Leaf shape: Broadly ovate or elongated, rounded at base.
Pollinated: Insect.

Below: Whorled flowers nestle on the stems.

Orange bird-berry

Hoslundia opposita

Orange bird-berry is a shrubby perennial herb growing to 2m/6½ft, regenerating and flowering after fire. It flowers from October to February and grows well in lowlands to highlands, in thickets, at forest edges and in secondary regrowth. The fruits are very sweet and eaten mainly by children. The decoction of the roots is used to treat stomach ache. The essential oil from this species has anti-microbial effects.

Identification: An erect herb or much-branched bushy shrub. The stems, hairy when young, and the branches are sharply four-angled. The branches are arranged opposite. The leaves are opposite or three-whorled, long oval to 12cm/4¾in. The small greenish-white flowers are borne in terminal inflorescences. Each flower is about 7mm/¼in across. The fruit is a rounded, ribbed berry, 6mm/¼ across, containing four roughened nutlets. The fruits are bright orange when ripe.

Right: The orange fruits are very attractive to birds.

Distribution: Africa.
Height and spread: 2m x 30cm/6½ft x 12in.
Habit and form: Herbaceous perennial.
Leaf shape: Simple.
Pollinated: Insect.

Left: Orange bird-berry is clump-forming with shrubby growth.

Lion's ear

Christmas candlestick, *Leonotis nepetifolia*

An erect, tropical annual, growing up to 2.4m/8ft tall. The stem is angled. The smooth leaves are toothed margins, and the orange flowers are borne in spiny clusters. It is a weed in fields and gardens. This plant is a favourite of sunbirds and butterflies. Smoking this dried herb gives a euphoria-like effect and exuberance due to one of the active components, the mildly psychoactive alkaloid leonurine (4-guanidino-n-butyl syringate) and other diterpenes (leosibiricine, leosiberine, isoleosiberine). The flowers are the most potent part and can also be used as a calming tea.

Identification: A tall woody annual herb, almost unbranched. The stiff stems are deeply ridged, with most parts being finely hairy. The leaves are arranged opposite, long, oval to 12cm/4¾in long. The flowers appear in dense rounded clusters at the upper nodes, bright orange tubular with a dense hairy upper lip. The fruit has four nutlets, long and thin.

Below: Lion's ear has stiff upright stems.

Distribution: Tropical Africa.
Height and spread: 2.4m x 50cm/8ft x 20in.
Habit and form: Annual herb.
Leaf shape: Simple, toothed.
Pollinated: Insect.

Below left: A flower cluster.

Right: The orange flowers grow in whorls on the stiff upright stems.

Kenyan tree basil

Ocimum suave

Distribution: Africa.
Height and spread: 1m x 20cm/39 x 8in.
Habit and form: Perennial shrub.
Leaf shape: Simple.
Pollinated: Insect.

This species is an ascending erect, branched perennial herb, growing to approximately 1m/39in high. It is quite common in upland forests in East Africa, and ranges from Guinea and Cameroon eastwards. It is also found in tropical Asia. It thrives in secondary shrub, in thickets and in the shade of large trees. It prefers well-drained, deep sandy loams. The leaves are used as a beverage, when steeped in hot or boiling water imparting an aromatic, cinnamon-like flavour to the infusion. It is also used in traditional medicine to treat coughs and influenza, and also as an insect repellent and perfume.

Identification: An erect herb or small woody shrub to 1m/39in, with a strong and pleasantly aromatic smell. The leaves are stalked but variable in shape, from long oval to nearly circular. The flowers are white-purple, about 7mm/¼in long, crowded along a simple or branched terminal head. The fruit contains four rough ovoid nutlets and lies within an enlarged calyx.

Left: This tall perennial grows mainly in shady forests.

OTHER SPECIES OF NOTE

Phlomis cashmeriana
This flower is locally common at 1,800–3,300m/ 5,900–10,800ft, from Afghanistan to Kashmir, growing on open slopes and wasteland. An upright perennial, it grows to about 90cm/35in, with toothed lanceolate leaves that have a covering of dense woolly hairs. It produces attractive whorled clusters of large purple or pink flowers, each with a hooded upper lip and a broad lower lip.

Large-flowered hemp-nettle
Galeopsis speciosa
This is a striking annual weed of cultivation and wasteland, often growing on damp peaty soils, up to 1m/39in. It has showy pale yellow flowers with a hooded upper lip and a purple-blotched lower lip and an equally distinctive sepal tube with five long spiny teeth.

Indian coleus *Plectranthus barbatus*
A robust, herbaceous shrub sometimes planted as a hedge in eastern Africa. Both green-leaved and variegated forms occur, sometimes on the same plant. It has ovate to ovate-elliptic leaves with bright blue flowers. It flowers mainly in June to July and grows in disturbed areas, secondary regrowth and rocky places to fairly high altitude. It is said that it is native to India and was probably introduced to East Africa.

Lantana

Shrub verbena, *Lantana trifolia*

Distribution: Tropical Africa; Central and South America.
Height and Spread: 3 x 1m/ 10ft x 39in.
Habit and form: Woody perennial.
Leaf shape: Simple, toothed.
Pollinated: Insect.

This attractive member of the verbena family flowers almost all year round and grows in natural grasslands and bushland. It is widely naturalized in Africa. Lantana's aromatic flower clusters (umbels) contain a mixture of blue and white florets. The flowers typically change colour as they mature, resulting in inflorescences that are two- or three-coloured. Some species are invasive, and are considered to be noxious weeds. Their spread is aided by their leaves, which are poisonous to most animals, while their fruit is a delicacy for many birds, which help to distribute the seeds.

Identification: A small scrambling shrub up to 3m/10ft. The stems have stiff hairs but no prickles. The leaves grow in threes, occasionally opposite, long, oval, the edge closely toothed, the upper surface wrinkled and sandpapery. The flowers arise on stalks, and are mauve, purple or pink. The fruit is a group of separate red-purple berry-like drupes, soft and edible only when ripe.

Left: Lantana has branching growth and pretty pink flowers.

FIGWORT FAMILY

The Scrophulariaceae, or figwort family, consist mostly of herbs but also a few small shrubs, with about 190 genera and 4,000 predominately temperate species. The species include many that are partial root parasites and a few that are without chlorophyll and are wholly parasitic. The family has a cosmopolitan distribution, with the majority of species found in temperate areas, including tropical mountains.

Cape fuchsia

Phygelius capensis

The common name of this plant reflects the flower shape, with long tubular flowers bearing a resemblance to those of the quite unrelated fuchsia. It has a very long flowering season, sometimes lasting four or five months. Originating from alongside streams in South Africa, this beautiful plant has long been cultivated for its racemes of brilliant scarlet flowers. Consequently, it is occasionally encountered as a garden escapee, usually near to habitations. It spreads extensively by root suckers and the top growth may die back to ground level if winter conditions become extremely cold.

Identification: A sprawling, stoloniferous, suckering, shrub or subshrub with lance-shaped to oval, dark green leaves up to 90mm/3½in long. They are mostly opposite in pairs, with the upper leaves sometimes alternate. In summer, it bears upright panicles, up to 60cm/24in long, of showy, yellow-throated, scarlet-orange tubular flowers, each 50mm/2in long, with five lobes, curved back toward the stems.

Distribution: South Africa.
Height and spread: 1.2 x 2.5m/4 x 8ft.
Habit and form: Suckering subshrub.
Leaf shape: Lanceolate to ovate.
Pollinated: Insect, bird.

Left and far left: The showy, yellow-throated flowers, shaped like the unrelated Fuchsia genus, appear in upright panicles during the summer and give rise to the plant's common name.

Foxglove

Digitalis purpurea

A common biennial or occasionally short-lived perennial of woodlands, hedge banks and wayside, wherever soil is disturbed, the foxglove provides a colourful display in midsummer. The flowers are most commonly purple but can be white and occasionally pale pink. It seeds profusely: a single plant can produce up to two million seeds. It does best in sandy, well-drained areas. It is distributed throughout Europe, though is absent from some calcareous districts.

Identification: Rosette-forming and very variable, the foxglove has oval to lance-shaped, usually toothed, sometimes white, woolly, dark green leaves, 10–25cm/4–10in long. Tall stems with alternate leaves support one-sided spikes of purple, pink or white, inflated, tubular, bell-shaped, two-lipped flowers, to 60mm/2¼in long, spotted maroon to purple inside, and produced in early summer. Oval fruits, longer than the tube formed by the sepals, ripen to brown.

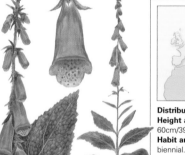

Distribution: Europe.
Height and spread: 1–2m x 60cm/39in–6½ft x 24in.
Habit and form: Herbaceous biennial.
Leaf shape: Ovate to lanceolate.
Pollinated: Insect, chiefly bumblebee.

Top: Each flowerhead is composed of single flowers.

Left: The whole plant, including the roots and flowers, is poisonous.

Chinese foxglove

Rehmannia glutinosa

This perennial plant from northern China is found in woodlands and stony sites and sports large, foxglove-like flowers. The species name *glutinosa* is derived from the word glutinous, referring to the sticky nature of the root. The plant received its generic name in honour of Joseph Rehmann, a 19th-century physician in the Russian city of St Petersburg. This possibly alludes to the fact that *Rehmannia*'s root is used medicinally in China, where it has been cultivated for more than 2,000 years.

Distribution: Northern China.
Height and spread:
15–30cm/6–12in.
Habit and form: Herbaceous perennial.
Leaf shape: Obovate.
Pollinated: Insect, especially bee.

Far right: Large, attractive, foxglove-like flowers emerge from the middle of the leaf rosette in the spring and summer.

Identification: This sticky, purple-hairy perennial has slender runners and rosettes of egg-shaped, scalloped, conspicuously veined, basal leaves, up to 10cm/4in long, which are mid-green above and often red tinted beneath. From mid-spring to summer, branched, leafy stems bear pendent, tubular, two-lipped flowers up to 50mm/2in long, in cyme-like racemes of a few flowers, or singly on long flower stalks, from the leaf axils. The flowers have reddish-brown tubes, marked with darker reddish-purple veins, and pale yellow-brown lips.

Snapdragon *Antirrhinum majus*
A south-western European native, snapdragon has naturalized across the world. It thrives on old walls and chalk cliffs. *Antirrhinum*, its botanical name, refers to the snout-like form of the flower.

Lancea tibetica
This small plant has a loose rosette of shiny, oval leaves and a cluster of mauve flowers, each with a narrow tube, a two-lobed upper lip and three-lobed lower lip. It spreads by underground runners. As its name suggests, it grows in south-western China and is also found in the Himalayas from Pakistan eastward. Its leaves, flowers and fruit are used in Tibetan medicine to treat lung disorders and to promote the healing of wounds.

Toadflax *Linaria vulgaris*
In most parts of Europe toadflax grows wild on dry banks, by the wayside, and at the borders of fields and meadows. It is abundant in gravelly soil and in limestone districts. It has grey-green, narrow leaves and yellow, snapdragon-like flowers on a spike up to 75cm/29½in tall from midsummer to mid-autumn.

Yellow figwort
Scrophularia vernalis
This perennial has the roughly square stems typical of figworts, and these are covered in soft hairs. It is a local flower of shady sites in central Europe, such as upland woods. Its leaves are heart-shaped at the base, and deeply toothed. The flowers are pale greenish-yellow and to about 8mm/⁵⁄₁₆iin long.

Knotted figwort

Common figwort, *Scrophularia nodosa*

The knotted figwort, common throughout western Europe, is similar in general habit to the water figwort, *S. auriculata*, though it is not distinctly an aquatic like that species. It is frequently found in woodland glades, hedge banks and in damp shady places with fairly rich soil, either in cultivated ground or wasteland. The 'fig' in its name is an old English word for haemorrhoids, which both the globular red flowers and the root protuberances were thought to resemble.

Identification: It is an upright perennial, hairless except for the glandular inflorescence. Short rhizomes, which are irregularly tuberous, give rise to sharply four-angled, non-winged stems, which support a panicle of flower clusters growing from the axils of the bracts. The lowest bracts are leaf-like, and the flowers are two-lipped, yellowish-green, up to 12mm/½in long, each with a brown upper lip. The leaves are oval, pointed and coarsely toothed, and often unequally decurrent down the leaf stalk.

Right: The tall flower stems emerge during late spring and early summer.

Left: The individual flowers are small and yellowish-green with a brown upper lip.

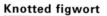

Distribution: Europe.
Height and spread:
40–80cm/16–31in.
Habit and form: Herbaceous perennial.
Leaf shape: Ovate.
Pollinated: Wasp (chiefly) and bee.

Common cow-wheat

Melampyrum pratense

The plant has blackish, wheat-like seeds, which can be made into a greyish bitter-tasting bread, known as 'poverty bread'. An old wives' tale claimed that pregnant women who ate the flour from the seeds of common cow-wheat would bear male children. In spite of the Latin name *pratense* meaning 'growing in meadows', the plant is rarely found in meadows, preferring woodland, hedgerows and moorland areas, where it flowers from May to September. The common name is said to come from the fact that it was much liked by cattle, and cows allowed to graze on the plants would produce the finest yellow butter. Like many plants in this family, common cow-wheat is hemiparasitic, which means that it has roots that attach to the roots of other plants to derive nourishment while, having green parts, it continues to feed in the normal w

Identification: Upright, with opposite, linear to ovate leaves. The two-lipped flowers are 10–18mm/⅜–¹¹⁄₁₆in, pale to bright yellow and arranged in a loose, one-sided spike, paired at the base. The bracts are green, ovate to linear-lanceolate toothed or entire. The calyx lobes are 4–5mm/³⁄₁₆in.

Distribution: Europe.
Height and spread: Up to 60cm/24in.
Habit and form: Annual.
Leaf shape: Linear to ovate.
Pollinated: Insect.

Right: An individual flowerhead.

Alpine bartsia

Bartsia alpina

The famous mourning flower of Swedish botanist Linnaeus, alpine bartsia is a mountain plant of cool wet places and snow beds, bearing dark purple flowers in July and August. Its range extends to North America and it is common in Iceland. The typical habitats are pastures, mountain slopes and also cliffs and ravines. It is rare in Great Britain. Like many members of the family, it is a hemi-parasite, which means that it gains nourishment partly from other plants. Its roots tap the roots of other species, such as heather, to steal nutrients.

Identification: This downy plant grows upright with solitary, glandular-hairy flowering stems. The leaves are ovate and toothed. The short, few-flowered inflorescences have purplish bracts, and the two-lipped flowers are 15–20mm/⁹⁄₁₆–¾in, dark purple with an open throat, and an upper lip longer than the lower one.

Above: The individual flowerheads are trumpet shaped and held in bracts at the tips of the stem.

Right and far left: Bartsia alpina grows on mountains and in ravines. It is a popular wild flower in Iceland.

Distribution: Northern Europe, southwards in mountain regions to the Pyrenees, southern Alps and Bulgaria.
Height and spread: 20cm/8in.
Habit and form: Herbaceous perennial.
Leaf shape: Ovate.
Pollinated: Insect, notably bumblebee.

Lousewort

Pedicularis sylvatica

Distribution: West and central Europe; Lithuania and Ukraine.
Height and spread: Up to 25cm/10in.
Habit and form: Biennial, often perennial.
Leaf shape: Linear.
Pollinated: Insect.

John Gerard, the sixteenth-century herbalist, supported the belief that Lousewort was so called because it infested sheep and other animals with lice. *Pedis* is Latin for louse. It is possible that the plant transmits liver-flukes, which are parasitic worms that rot the livers of sheep. Snails, carrying embryo liver-flukes, cling to its leaves and are grazed on by sheep. Sheep infested with liver-flukes almost always have lice too and these can spread rapidly through a flock. The plant thrives in wet places and is often submerged in winter. Lousewort has handsome pink or reddish flowers from April to July, and the fruits and seeds have an interesting net-like patterning.

Identification: A nearly hairless plant with many straggling branches growing from the base. The leaves, with a thick glossy look, are deeply and irregularly cut. The flowers are two-lipped, up to 25mm/1in long.

Above: The fruits develop in the leaf axils.

OTHER SPECIES OF NOTE

Crested cow-wheat *Melampyrum cristatum*
This is an exotic-looking plant of wood margins and dry places across most of Europe. Its yellow flowers, which have a purple tinge on the lower lip, grow in dense, four-angled spikes from June to September.

Yellow bartsia *Parentucellia viscosa*
This stickily-hairy, hemiparasitic, upright annual has pointed, roughly toothed leaves and yellow, two-lipped flowers from June to September. It thrives in damp, sandy, grassy places over southern and western Europe, north to Scotland.

Marsh lousewort *Pedicularis palustris*
Frequenting wet heaths and bogs, marsh lousewort was mentioned by Nicholas Culpeper, the 17th-century herbalist for use as a potion to influence the 'humours'. Like yellow rattle, *Rhinanthus minor*, its fruiting heads make a rattling noise when shaken, giving the plant the alternative name of red rattle.

Pedicularis bicornuta
This lousewort grows in the Himalayas, from Pakistan to Uttar Pradesh, at about 2,700–4,400m/8,800–14,400ft, on alpine slopes and high meadows, flowering in July and August. A very striking and handsome plant, growing to 60cm/24in, it has tall spikes of large yellow flowers, each to about 20mm/¾in across. The leaves are alternate and deeply lobed.

Yellow rattle

Rattle box, *Rhinanthus minor*

Yellow rattle, which grows in large patches in rough, grassy places, is so called because when the seeds are ripe, they rattle inside the capsules. Swedish farmers took this sound to mean that it was time for hay-making. The flowers, appearing from May to August, have a golden-yellow petal tube that resembles a hooked, pendulous nose and gave rise to the plant's generic name, from two Greek words meaning 'nose' and 'flower'.

Identification: Upright, short and hairy, occasionally branched. Stem usually black-spotted with long, narrow, oblong to linear, rough leaves, regularly toothed. The flowers, 13–15mm/½–⅜in, grow in spikes, each flower with a flattened and inflated calyx with four teeth. The upper lip of the corolla is flattened laterally and encloses the stamens.

Distribution: Most of Europe, but rare in the Mediterranean.
Height and spread: 10–60cm/4 x 24in.
Habit and form: Herbaceous perennial.
Leaf shape: Linear.
Pollinated: Insect.

Above: The fruit is a capsule.

Left: Yellow rattle proliferates in dry meadows.

Eyebright

Euphrasia nemorosa

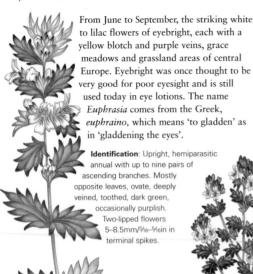

From June to September, the striking white to lilac flowers of eyebright, each with a yellow blotch and purple veins, grace meadows and grassland areas of central Europe. Eyebright was once thought to be very good for poor eyesight and is still used today in eye lotions. The name *Euphrasia* comes from the Greek, *euphraino*, which means 'to gladden' as in 'gladdening the eyes'.

Identification: Upright, hemiparasitic annual with up to nine pairs of ascending branches. Mostly opposite leaves, ovate, deeply veined, toothed, dark green, occasionally purplish. Two-lipped flowers 5–8.5mm/³⁄₁₆–⁵⁄₁₆in in terminal spikes.

Above: The flowers of this species have a yellow 'eye'.

Left: This medicinal plant prefers chalky soil and damp grassland for its habitat, where it will thrive and grow up to 40cm/16in.

Right: This plant has a history of herbal use for treating eye problems.

Distribution: North and central Europe, south to north-eastern Spain.
Height and spread: Up to 40cm/16in.
Habit and form: Annual.
Leaf shape: Ovate.
Pollinated: Insect.

Spiked speedwell

Veronica spicata

Spiked speedwell frequents rocky areas and dry grassland on usually lime-rich soil. It is an attractive plant with numerous blue flowers borne in dense spikes from July to September. Its habitats having been destroyed by ploughing, it is not now as common as it once was in many areas.

Identification: This is an upright, shortly-creeping, unbranched, hairy annual, which is woody at the base. The opposite leaves are 20–80mm/³⁄₄–3¹⁄₈in, linear to lanceolate-ovate, short-stalked and toothed. The flowers are 4–8mm/³⁄₁₆–⁵⁄₁₆in across, blue, long, leafless spikes.

Below: The tall flowering spikes are very attractive.

Above: The flower spikes rise over the foliage.

Right: The spikes are made up of individual flowerheads, which look attractive en masse, once the plant becomes clump-forming.

Distribution: Europe; rare in the west.
Height and spread: Up to 60cm/24in.
Habit and form: Annual.
Leaf shape: Linear.
Pollinated: Insect.

Great mullein

Candlewick plant, *Verbascum thapsus*

Great mullein frequents dry banks, open scrub and roadsides. Long before the introduction of cotton to Europe, fluffy layers of the hairs with which the plant is covered were scraped off to be made into candle wicks. The entire stem was also used as a flare, earning it the name 'high taper'. Although most parts of the plant are poisonous, the dried flowers were used to produce a pleasant-tasting cough medicine and a yellow hair dye, and the crushed leaves gave off an agreeably fruity scent when smoked with tobacco.

Distribution: Most of Europe, except the far north and much of the Balkans.
Height and spread: 2m/6½ft.
Habit and form: Biennial.
Leaf shape: Oblong.
Pollinated: Insect.

Right: The tall flowerheads taper with height.

Identification: A stately plant, covered with white or greyish woolly hairs. It has large, oblong basal leaves, up to 45cm/18in long. The tall, thick, leafy stem is finished in a dense, crowded, unbranched spike of yellow flowers, each 12–35mm/½–1⅜in with short corolla tubes and five spreading, almost equal lobes.

Above: Individual flowers are grouped densely, filling the flower spike.

OTHER SPECIES OF NOTE

Blue water speedwell
Veronica anagallis-aquatica
A hairless perennial with light green leaves and blue, violet-veined flowers borne on stalked spikes in the axils of the upper leaves from June to August. It frequents river and stream sides throughout Europe except for the far north.

Brooklime *Veronica beccabunga*
With a dense mass of thick, rounded, dark green leaves and dark blue, star-shaped flowers from late spring throughout the summer, brooklime thrives in wet and muddy riverside regions. It was used by 17th century herbalists as a cure for scurvy. It is still sometimes used in salads, although it tastes bitter.

Dark mullein *Verbascum nigrum*
The dark mullein is widely distributed all over Europe and in temperate Asia as far as the Himalayas. In eastern North America it is abundant as a naturalized weed. Its yellow flower spikes, up to 1.2m/4ft tall, rise from a basal rosette of soft, felted leaves in summer.

Germander speedwell *Veronica chamaedrys*
Commonly found on banks, in pastures and woods, germander speedwell flowers in spring and early summer. It has a creeping, branched rootstock, and strong stems that sport bright blue flowers streaked with darker lines and a white eye in the centre.

Ivy-leaved toadflax

Cymbalaria muralis

This delightful little plant with festoons of foliage and lilac-coloured, snap-dragon-like flowers from May to September was originally introduced as a garden plant in the 17th century and is now often found growing on old walls. Each flower has a yellow 'honey guide' on the lower lip to attract the bees that pollinate it. After the flowers are fertilized, the stalk gradually curves round until the capsules are firmly pushed into the cracks in the wall. When the seeds are released, some remain to germinate on the wall, wedged by means of ridges, while the developing root forces its way further into the crevice. The leaves of ivy-leaved toadflax are depressed in the middle like a cymbal, hence the generic name.

Distribution: Native among shady rocks and woods in the Southern Alps, Serbia and Montenegro, Italy and Sicily, but widely naturalized throughout much of Europe.
Height and spread: 50mm x 10–75cm/2 x 4–29½in.
Habit and form: Herbaceous perennial.
Leaf shape: Lobed.
Pollinated: Insect.

Identification: Hairless, sprawling plant with five to nine glossy, ivy-shaped, alternate, triangular-lobed leaves scattered along the stem. The flowers are pale lilac, with a two-lipped corolla and a curved spur with a yellow lip, solitary on stalks in leaf axils.

Far left: The plant has trailing growth and small, delicate flowers.

ACANTHUS FAMILY

The Acanthaceae, or acanthus family, contains mostly herbs or shrubs and comprises about 250 genera and 2,500 species. Only a few species are distributed in temperate regions. Typically, there is a colourful bract subtending each flower; in some species the bract is large and showy. The family is closely allied to the Scrophulariaceae (figwort family).

Bear's breeches

Acanthus mollis

This plant is a native of warmer parts of south-western Europe as far as the Balkans, and parts of North Africa. It is most commonly found in woodland scrub and on stony hillsides. In summer, creamy-white to slightly pink or purplish flowers appear on tall, erect stalks above the foliage. The generic name derives from the Greek *akantha*, meaning 'spine', referring to the toothed foliage of some species.

Identification: This large, clump-forming perennial has oval, deeply cut, smooth, bright green foliage. The basal leaves are 20–60cm/8–24in long on long leaf stalks; those on the upper stem are 10–30mm/ ⅜–1¼in long, more or less oval, toothed and stalkless. The leaves can be quite variable, being cut, lobed, or even deeply pinnately divided. The irregular and unusual flowers form on stiff, erect spikes, well above the foliage from early to late summer. The flower is tubular, with a large, three-lobed lower lip. It is suspended by spine-tipped bracts and a large calyx lobe; another forms a hood.

Left: The large, spiny leaves form a dense clump from which the flower spikes emerge.

Left: Each flower spike contains many small white flowers.

Distribution: Southern Europe, north-western Africa.
Height and spread: 1.2m x 60cm/4 x 2ft.
Habit and form: Herbaceous perennial.
Leaf shape: Ovate.
Pollinated: Bee.

Persian shield

Strobilanthes dyerianus

This soft-stemmed, evergreen shrub, native to Burma, is best known for its leaves, which are variegated, dark green and silvery purplish-pink on top but all purple underneath; the general effect is that the leaves are shimmering with iridescence. This quality has led to it becoming a popular foliage plant in the gardens of many warmer countries, where its use in cultivation has led to its occasional occurrence as a garden escapee. The flowers are pretty, if surprisingly low key given the spectacular foliage, being funnel-shaped, pale violet, and arranged on short spikes.

Identification: An evergreen subshrub with soft (not woody) stems, square in cross section. The unequal pairs of elliptic, toothed, dark green, opposite leaves, 10–18cm/4–7in long, have a puckered texture and are variegated dark green and silvery-metallic, purplish-pink on top and all purple underneath. It bears spikes of funnel-shaped, pale blue flowers, 30mm/1¼in long.

Left: The pretty, violet flowers appear on short spikes.

Right: Although the plant adopts a shrubby character, the stems remain quite soft and brittle.

Distribution: Burma.
Height and spread: 1.2m x 90cm/4ft x 35in.
Habit and form: Evergreen subshrub.
Leaf shape: Elliptic.
Pollinated: Insect.

Acanthus spinosus
Much like its relative *A. mollis*, this herbaceous plant from west Turkey grows about 1m/39in tall, but its leaves are more spiny and narrower. In summer, white flowers wrapped in pretty, spiny, mauve-purple bracts are borne on tall, erect stalks above the foliage.

Firecracker flower *Crossandra infundibuliformis*
The firecracker flower is a tropical shrub, native to southern India and Sri Lanka. Fan-shaped flowers appear in clusters on long stems, growing from the leaf axils. The flowers are yellow or salmon-orange in colour and can bloom continuously for weeks.

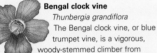

Bengal clock vine
Thunbergia grandiflora
The Bengal clock vine, or blue trumpet vine, is a vigorous, woody-stemmed climber from northern India, with broad-lobed leaves, bearing pendent racemes of large, showy violet or whitish flowers, with pale yellow tubes, which may reach 40mm/1½ in long and 75mm/3in across.

Acanthus hungaricus
A large, evergreen, clump-forming, herbaceous perennial from the Balkans, Romania and Greece, with long, handsome, shiny, deeply cut, thistle-like, basal leaves. Tall spikes of white or pink-flushed flowers with red-purple bracts emerge in early to midsummer.

Black-eyed Susan

Thunbergia alata

This familiar climbing plant, usually grown in cultivation as an annual, is actually an evergreen perennial in tropical climates. It is often found outside its natural range as a garden escapee. It is a fast-growing climber, native to tropical areas of east Africa, which twines around any convenient support, and bears bright orange flowers with black centres throughout summer. The genus name honours Carl Peter Thunberg, an 18th-century Swedish botanist.

Identification: This tropical evergreen twining vine, climbing or trailing, has triangular to egg-shaped leaves, sharply pointed, shaped like an arrowhead at the base, up to 75mm/3in long, entire or with a few coarse teeth; the leaf stalks are winged, about as long as the leaf. Solitary, flat, five-petalled, orange-yellow flowers, rarely white, to 50mm/2in wide, with black-purple flower tubes, are borne from the leaf axils on stalks longer than the leaf stalks. The flattened round seed capsule is about 12mm/½in wide, with a beak 12mm/½in long; the seeds are warty and ribbed.

Distribution: Tropical east Africa.
Height and spread: 6 x 1.8m/19¾ x 6ft.
Habit and form: Evergreen climbing perennial.
Leaf shape: Deltoid or ovate.
Pollinated: Insect.

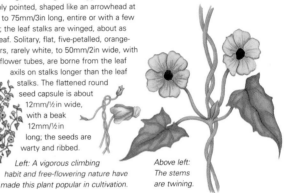

Left: A vigorous climbing habit and free-flowering nature have made this plant popular in cultivation.

Above left: The stems are twining.

Adhatoda

Malabar nut tree, Adulsa, Vasaka, *Justicia adhatoda*

Adhatoda is common in India, especially in the lower Himalayas (up to 1,300m/4,250ft above sea level) and to a slightly lesser extent in Sri Lanka. It favours open plains and is commonly found growing on wasteland. It is a small tree or large shrub that flowers in the cold season. Adhatoda leaves have been used extensively in Ayurvedic medicine for more than 2,000 years.

Identification: Adhatoda has smooth, ash-coloured bark, which is smoother on the branches. The opposite, broadly lance-shaped, taper-pointed, smooth or slightly downy leaves, which are 12.5–15cm/5–6in long, are borne on short leaf stalks. The solitary flower spikes emerge from the exterior axils on long stalks, the whole end of the branchlet forming a leafy panicle enveloped with large bracts. The white, tubular flowers are spotted with small rust-coloured dots; the lower part of both lips is streaked with purple. The fruit is a small, four-seeded capsule.

Distribution: Indian subcontinent.
Height and spread: 3 x 1.5m/10 x 5ft.
Habit and form: Evergreen shrub.
Leaf shape: Broadly lanceolate.
Pollinated: Insect.

Far right: Adhatoda is a usually erect and sparsely branched evergreen shrub, spreading with age.

Below: The rust-speckled white flowers are streaked with purple.

ACANTHUS, AFRICAN VIOLET AND SESAME FAMILIES

The acanthus family, Acanthaceae, and the African violet family, Gesneriaceae, are mainly tropical herbs and shrubs. Some are popular garden flowers. The sesame family, Pedaliaceae, is small (about 85 species) and consists mainly of tropical herbs and shrubs, several useful as a source of oil, and vegetables.

Spiny acanthus

Acanthus pubescens

This spiny shrub is native to eastern Africa, where it is typically found growing in open grassy sites, such as alongside tracks or roads and wasteland, and also at the edges of forests. It has long leaves, up to 30cm/12in long, with very prickly, deeply lobed margins. The flowers are pink-purple, occasionally white. It flowers mainly between July and September. In some parts of Africa, ash from the leaves is used for various medicinal purposes.

Identification: A shrub from 1.5 x 6m/5–19¾ft high. The leaves grow up to 30cm/12in long with prickly, lobed margins. The flowers are pink-purple occasionally white, up to 50mm/2in long in large terminal spikes. The calyx consists of four parts, with one lobe larger and prickly.

Distribution: Africa.
Height and spread: 6 x 1m/ 20m x 39in.
Habit and form: Perennial shrub.
Leaf shape: Simple.
Pollinated: Insect.

Centre left: The ripening buds.

Left: Spiny acanthus has large flower spikes and spiny foliage.

Sesamum calycinum ssp. angustifolium

This annual or perennial herb is fairly common in Africa, where it grows in cultivated and wasteland, abandoned gardens, at roadsides and in short grass, especially on sandy soils. It is easily identified by its large foxglove-like flowers, which are always white to pale pink. The leaves are greyish-green and densely covered in mucilage glands. The capsule is pale coloured with a short beak, bending upwards. It flowers mainly between September and November. The leaves are eaten as a vegetable and edible oil is extracted from the seeds.

Identification: An erect, sometimes spreading, herb, producing one or only a few branches from a woody base, 30cm–1.8m/12in–6ft, with more or less four-sided stems. The leaves are long and narrow, to 12cm/4¾in. The flowers are tubular, pink-red-mauve-purple, often spotted in the throat. The fruit is a narrow capsule, to 25cm/ 10in long, 4mm/³⁄₁₆in across, and straight.

Left: Each flower is tubular and bell-shaped.

Distribution: Africa.
Height and spread: 1.8m x 10cm/6ft x 4in.
Habit and form: Herbaceous perennial or annual.
Leaf shape: Simple.
Pollinated: Insect.

Left: Sesamum calycinum is an upright species with narrow leaves.

Pyrenean violet

Ramonda myconi

Distribution: The Pyrenees.
Height and spread:
12.5cm/5in.
Habit and form: Herbaceous perennial.
Leaf shape: Elliptic to rhomboidal.
Pollinated: Insect.

The Pyrenean violet is endemic to the Pyrenees and is found on shady rocks and in mixed woodland on rocky, limestone slopes. It has a scattered distribution through its range, with populations rarely staying constant in one area. The dark green, hairy rosette of leaves may easily be missed until the pretty, five-petalled, blue-violet flowers appear in late spring or early summer. The flowers are reminiscent of the related African violet, *Saintpaulia* species, to which this plant is distantly related.

Identification: A low-growing, stemless herb, with a basal rosette of wrinkled leaves up to 60mm/2¼in long, elliptic to diamond-shaped with rounded tips and marginal teeth, covered in red-brown hairs. Between one and six flowers are borne on glandular to hairy, red-tinged, leafless stalks, up to 12.5cm/5in tall, in early summer. Each five-lobed flower is 40mm/1½in across, violet to pink or white with a yellow, cone-shaped centre.

Left: The leaves are held in a tight basal rosette from which the flowers emerge.

OTHER SPECIES OF NOTE

Titanotrichum oldhamii
This pretty plant from Taiwan has a woody rootstock and produces several erect herbaceous stems with yellow, tubular flowers, which are red to maroon on the inside of the tube and borne in terminal racemes during the summer months.

Chirita lavandulacea
This upright annual, which is native to tropical Asia, has oval, prominently veined, translucent, hairy leaves that act as a perfect foil for the pretty, five-lobed, pale blue flowers. These are borne on short stalks, singly or in pairs and in groups of three to five, from the upper leaf axils.

Jancaea (Jankaea) heldreichii
This pretty mountain flower is the only species in its genus. It grows only in limestone crevices on Mount Olympus in Greece, at 1,000–2,400m/3,200–7,800ft. Long sought after by collectors, it is now rare and protected. It may be grown from seed. It has delicate pale lilac flowers and silvery foliage.

Haberlea rhodopensis
Another mountain plant, found in Greece and Bulgaria, this species grows as a rosette plant on rocks. From the base grow clusters of cylindrical bluish-violet, two-lipped flowers. The leaves are oblong and blunt, coarsely toothed and covered in soft hairs.

Cape primrose

Streptocarpus formosus

More than 100 widespread species of *Streptocarpus* are found, mostly in southern Africa. This species grows in subtropical forests where the summers are humid and wet, and the winters are warm and dry. It has a scattered distribution in forests and the sandstone gorges, where it grows in pockets of well-drained soil between the rocks. Surprisingly, each leaf of the clump is an individual plant with its own roots and flowering stems.

Distribution: Central Africa; South Africa; Madagascar.
Height and spread:
25cm/10in.
Habit and form: Rosette-forming, evergreen perennial.
Leaf shape: Oblong.
Pollinated: Insect.

Identification: A rosette-forming perennial with many hairy leaves, up to 45cm/18in long. Each inflorescence, up to 25cm/10in tall, bears one to four pale blue flowers up to 10cm/4in across. The flower tube is narrowly funnel-shaped, blue-mauve outside, the inside minutely spotted purple with a patch of bright yellow and purple streaks on the floor; the lobes are white or blue streaked white. The fruits, 18cm/7in long, unfold like a spiral when dry.

Below: The flowers appear from spring.

Right: The small perennial is clump-forming.

DAISY FAMILY

The Asteraceae, or daisy family, comprise herbaceous plants, shrubs and, less commonly, trees. This is arguably the largest family of flowering plants, containing about 1,100 genera and 20,000 species. The species are characterized by having the flowers reduced and organized into a composite arrangement of tiny individual flowers, called a capitulum – a tight cluster that superficially resembles a single bloom.

Daisy

Bellis perennis

Arguably the most widely recognized of all wild flowers, the daisy grows on roadsides, in gardens, and is often an unwanted weed. The plant is most commonly found growing in short grassland, particularly in cultivated lawns. It requires moist soil and the seeds usually germinate on worm casts left on the surface.

Identification: A stoloniferous, evergreen, rosette-forming perennial, with a flat basal rosette of spoon-shaped, bright green leaves, 12–60mm/½–2¼in long. From late winter to late summer, slightly hairy stems, 25mm–10cm/1–4in tall, carry single, large, white compound flowers, 12–30mm/½–1¼in across, with white ray florets, often tinged maroon or pink, and yellow disc florets, from pink buds.

Below: Daisy flowers open outright in full sun.

Distribution: Europe and Turkey.
Height and spread: 15cm/6in.
Habit and form: Evergreen perennial.
Leaf shape: Obovate.
Pollinated: Bee, fly and beetle.

Dandelion

Taraxacum officinalis

This familiar plant is probably native to all parts of the north temperate zone, in pastures, meadows and on wasteland, and is so plentiful that it is often considered a troublesome weed. Its flowers are more conspicuous in the earlier months of the summer, although it may be found in bloom almost throughout the year. It is not native to the Southern Hemisphere, although it has been widely introduced accidentally through agriculture and human activity.

Identification: The dandelion is a rosette-forming perennial with a thick taproot that is dark brown, almost black on the outside, white and milky within. Long, deeply cut, shiny, hairless leaves have margins cut into large jagged teeth, either upright or pointing backwards, with the teeth occasionally cut into smaller teeth. Shiny, purplish flower stalks, rising straight from the root, are leafless, smooth and hollow and bear single heads of composite, bright yellow flowers, made up of numerous strap-shaped florets, to 50mm/2in across. A bitter, milky juice is exuded when the stem is broken.

Right: Dandelion flowers and leaves are a familiar sight.

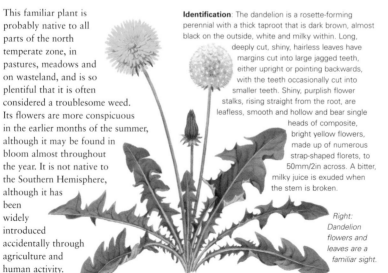

Distribution: Worldwide in temperate regions, often introduced elsewhere.
Height and spread: Up to 30cm/12in.
Habit and form: Herbaceous perennial.
Leaf shape: Runcinate.
Pollinated: Insect, especially bumblebee.

Sweet coltsfoot

Giant butterbur, Japanese butterbur, Fuki, *Petasites japonicus*

This species is a native of eastern Asia, naturally inhabiting damp, marshy areas, especially along riverbanks, although it is widely naturalized elsewhere as a garden escapee in moist woods and thickets. The plant is a master of metamorphosis, as it changes from an unimposing small flower stalk to a mound of large, kidney-shaped leaves on long, edible stalks. Individual plants are either male or female and both sexes must be present if seed is to be set. It can form very large colonies where conditions are favourable for its growth. The name 'butterbur' comes from a related European species reportedly used to wrap butter, despite the unpleasant smell.

Distribution: Eastern Asia: China, Japan and Korea.
Height and spread: 60cm x 1.5m/24in–5ft.
Habit and form: Herbaceous perennial.
Leaf shape: Reniform.
Pollinated: Insect.

Far right: The large leaves appearing in summer offer stark contrast to the small bracts of the flower stems.

Identification: Growing from a rhizome, the plant has kidney-shaped, irregularly toothed, basal leaves up to 80cm/31in across, hairy beneath, borne on stalks 90cm/35in long. Densely clustered corymbs of yellowish-white flower-heads, to 15mm/⅝in across, with oblong bracts below, are borne before the leaves in late winter and early spring.

OTHER SPECIES OF NOTE

Leopard plant *Ligularia przewalskii*
A native of northern China, this clump-forming perennial has huge, heart-shaped, leathery, deeply cut, toothed, dark green leaves that emerge purplish-red, but turn to brownish-green. Tall, narrow spikes of clear yellow, daisy-like flowers appear from mid- to late summer.

Globe thistle *Echinops ritro*
A native from central Europe to Central Asia, growing to 50cm/20in or more. The stiff, spiny leaves are dark green and 'cobwebby' above and white-downy below. In summer it bears spherical flowerheads, up to 50mm/2in across, which change from metallic blue to bright blue as the florets open.

Ox-eye daisy *Leucanthemum vulgare*

A familiar sight in fields throughout Europe and northern Asia. The generic name, derived from Greek means 'white flower'. The familiar yellow-centred, white flower-heads appear from late spring until midsummer.

Cornflower *Centaurea cyanus*
The cornflower, with its star-like blossoms of brilliant blue, is a most striking wildflower. It is fairly common in cultivated fields and by roadsides, though is in decline due to changing agricultural practices. The down-covered stems are tough and wiry.

Namaqualand daisy

Dimorphotheca sinuata

This showy annual grows naturally in the winter rainfall areas of south-western Africa, usually in sandy places in Namaqualand and Namibia. It creates sheets of brilliant orange when it flowers in early spring, drawing visitors from near and far. The genus name is derived from Greek *dis* (twice), *morphe* (shape) and *theka* (fruit), referring to the different kinds of seeds produced by the ray and disc flowers.

Identification: The aromatic leaves are slender, oblong to lance-shaped, or sometimes spoon-shaped, with coarsely toothed margins, light green, up to 10cm/4in long. The stems are reddish and covered by the masses of leaves around them. The orange, or occasionally white to yellow flowers, up to 80mm/3⅛in across, borne singly at the tip of each stem in winter, have orange centres (sometimes yellow). They need full sun to open and always face the sun. Around the centre at the bottom of the petals is a narrow, greenish-mauve ring.

Distribution: South-western Africa.
Height and spread: 30cm/12in.
Habit and form: Annual.
Leaf shape: Oblong to lanceolate or obovate.
Pollinated: Insect.

Left: The brilliant orange, tall-stemmed daisy-like flowers grow out of a mat of foliage.

Hemp agrimony

Eupatorium cannabinum

This tall striking plant can be seen in damp ground such as ditches, fens, wet meadows and marshes. The massed purple-pink tubular disc flowers, with their protruding white stigmas, seen at the top of the stems in late summer give it the appearance of candy-floss, an effect seen on a much smaller scale in the related small annual garden plant, flossflower, *Ageratum*. It has no relatives native to Europe, most *Eupatorium* species come from America.

Identification: Despite its names, the plant is not related to either hemp, *Cannabis sativa*, from which cannabis and marijuana are obtained, or the confusingly named agrimony, *Agrimonia eupatoria*, which is a member of the rose family. The divided, palm-like leaves do bear a superficial resemblance to the more elegant and more divided leaves of the cannabis plant.

Right: The seed head.

Distribution: Europe, fading out in Scotland and Finland; western and Central Asia; northern Africa.
Height and spread: 30cm–1.75m/12in–5¾ft.
Habit and form: Tall herbaceous perennial with woody rootstock.
Leaf shape: Sharply ovate and toothed leaflets.
Pollinated: Butterfly, moth, fly, bee.

Left: Hemp agrimony is tall and stately in appearance.

Edelweiss

Leontopodium alpinum

Edelweiss is an iconic plant, a symbolic representative of alpine plants and widely adopted as an organizational symbol or logo, particularly in Austria and Switzerland. Sadly, it is also symbolic of the devastating effects that thoughtless and indiscriminate collection of wild plants can have. Now desperately reduced in the dry alpine meadows that it once adorned with drifts of its white flower-heads, it is more likely to be found in less accessible sites such as high calcareous rocks and screes. Ironically, when transplanted to lower altitudes, it loses its most beautiful feature, the mantle of silvery-white hairs protecting it from the alpine sun.

Identification: As with the flowerheads of other members of the daisy family, the whole is so much more than the sum of its parts. Edelweiss has insignificant small yellow-white tubular flowers clustered into small heads which are themselves clustered into larger heads, all surrounded by a star of long silvery-white leaf-like bracts.

Right: The flowerheads are covered in hairs giving it a woolly appearance, an adaptation to the extreme climate of its mountain habitat.

Distribution: Mountains of Europe, from the Jura and Carpathians to the Pyrenees, central Apennines and south-western Bulgaria.
Height and spread: 50mm–20cm/2–8in.
Habit and form: Herbaceous perennial.
Leaf shape: Simple, long oval/linear.
Pollinated: Insect, mainly fly.

Guizotia scabra

An erect, usually perennial herb, flowering in March to May and growing typically in abandoned fields, disturbed areas and secondary regrowth, often growing profusely and gregariously. Also found along streams and in high rainfall grassland. The leaves are eaten as a vegetable and a decoction from the roots is used to prevent miscarriages and also in the treatment of peptic ulcers. This species is a weed that invades immediately after major crop harvests and can be regarded as a nuisance.

Identification: An erect, usually perennial herb to 2m/6½ft high, growing from a wiry rootstock, and rather variable in form. The leaves are opposite, without stalks, usually clasping in the stem towards the apex, narrowly oblong, with the edge often toothed, very rough to touch. The flowers are bright yellow, in loosely branched terminal heads, each flower with one row of outer ray florets. The ray florets are to about 20mm/¾in, with a three-toothed apex. The fruit is smooth, straight edged, three or four angled, with tiny black achenes, and no hairy pappus.

Above: The genus Guizotia *contains six tropical west African herbs.*

Far right: The flowerhead is daisy-like.

Distribution: Tropical Africa.
Height and spread: 2m x 20cm/6½ft x 8in
Habit and form: Perennial herb.
Leaf shape: Simple.
Pollinated: Insect.

Smooth sow thistle

Common sow thistle, Milk thistle, Annual sow thistle, *Sonchus oleraceus*

This widespread sow thistle is found in Europe, Asia and Africa, and is also widely naturalized as an introduction in America. It is an erect, soft annual herb with a smooth, pale bluish-green stem that exudes milky latex when cut. It flowers between July and September, and it is common in secondary regrowth and fallow fields. The leaves are edible and have a mild taste. They are also used as fodder for cattle.

Distribution: Europe; Africa.
Height and spread: 1.2m x 10cm/4ft x 4in.
Habit and form: Annual herb.
Leaf shape: Simple.
Pollinated: Insect.

Above: The seedhead is fluffy and white.

Identification: An erect unbranched annual herb to 1.2m/4ft, all parts with milky sap. The leaves are unstalked, as the leaf base clasps the stem. The leaf edge is sharply toothed and lobed, including pointed basal lobes, and it has a pointed tip. The pale yellow flowerheads are numerous and stalked, borne on a loosely-branched terminal inflorescence. The fruit is a small, roughened achene, strongly ribbed, with a tuft of thin silky white hairs and stiff straight bristles.

Thickhead

Redflower ragleaf, Fireweed, *Crassocephalum crepidioides*

This African composite is a common weed of farmland and disturbed ground, and often grows abundantly under tree crops. The seeds are usually dispersed by wind or water and can be found metres from where the parent plant was growing the previous season. Thickhead is used as food and medicine in many tropical and subtropical regions, notably in tropical Africa. Its fleshy leaves and stems are gathered and eaten as a vegetable, and the plant and its extracts also have a number of medicinal uses, including as a laxative and to treat indigestion.

Distribution: Tropical Africa, including Madagascar.
Height and spread: 1m x 10cm/39 x 4in.
Habit and form: Annual herb.
Leaf shape: Simple.
Pollinated: Insect.

Identification: This is an erect, slightly succulent, annual herb growing to 1m/39in, with pale green stems with white hairs. The leaves are alternately arranged along the stem. They are long and oval, simple or irregularly lobed or toothed to 20cm/8in long, dull green above, pale yellow beneath with white hairs. Leaf shape is variable – the smaller upper leaves are generally elliptical, while the larger lower leaves have two lobes at the base. All the leaves have toothed margins. The flowers are tiny and reddish-orange, in flowerheads 12mm/½in long, nodding in bud, in dense or loose clusters. Each head contains only tubular florets surrounded by one row of narrow outer bracts, often purple at the base. The flowerheads droop and are orange-pink. The fruit is an achene, brown-violet, topped by fine silky hairs, which are white and tinged reddish or mauve.

Far right: This is a tall plant with a stately appearance.

Blackjack

Farmer's friend, Cobbler's pegs, Beggar's ticks, Pitchforks, *Bidens pilosa*

This prolific annual herb is usually 1m/39in or less in height, with spreading branches. It flowers between May and October. It normally grows on cultivated land, and on paths and other disturbed areas, and also in forests and grassland. The shoot is sometimes used as a vegetable, especially during famine periods. The sap from the leaves is also used to speed up the clotting of blood in fresh wounds. It is considered a weed in tropical habitats.

Below: The seedhead contains burrs, which stick to animals.

Distribution: Tropical Africa; Australia; southern Asia; South America.
Height and spread: 1m x 30cm/39 x 12in.
Habit and form: Herbaceous annual.
Leaf shape: Compound and toothed.
Pollinated: Insect.

Identification: An annual herb, branching above, to 1m/39in tall, with a four-angled stem. The leaves are opposite, soft and hairy, mostly divided, to 85mm/3¼in long, variable in size and shape, with one to three ovate, toothed leaflets. The flowers are borne in heads about 12mm/½in across, the central disk florets yellow, the outer florets with white rays, sometimes absent. The 'flowers' are technically heads of tiny flowers. Each head has five or so white 'petals' (rays) around a dense cluster of yellow or orange florets. These rapidly mature to star-heads of the dry, pronged fruitlets. The fruits are black achenes, about 10mm/⅜in long, tipped with two to four barbed bristles, which catch on fur and clothing, aiding dispersal. The plant may fruit even when small.

Right: The plant is often eaten as a food source in times of scarcity.

Haemorrhage plant

Aspilia (Wedelia) africana

One of the commonest plants in African grasslands and abandoned farmland, the haemorrhage plant produces yellow flowerheads from April to June. Its leaves are used to treat wounds, to stem bleeding (hence the common name), to treat rheumatism and bee and scorpion stings. The leaves have been shown to help arrest bleeding and inhibit microbial growth, thus aiding the healing process. A decoction of the leaves is used as tonic and a diuretic, and an infusion is used in treating coughs and related ailments in children.

Identification: A woody, branching perennial herb, often spreading from the base, varying in height from 60cm/24in to about 1.5m/5ft, depending on rainfall and soil fertility. It reproduces from seeds. The leaves are opposite, ovate-lanceolate, 60mm–15cm/2¼–6in long and 30–70mm/1¼– 2¾in wide; they are rounded at the base with petioles about 10mm/⅜in long, hairy and with three prominent veins. The inflorescence consists of a solitary terminal flowerhead with a hairy stalk about 40mm–10cm/1½–4in long. The flowers have showy yellow heads with several florets. The fruits are four-angled achenes about 5mm/¼in long, bristly and minutely hairy.

Distribution: Africa.
Height and spread: 1.5m x 20cm/5ft x 8in.
Habit and form: Annual herb.
Pollinated: Insect.
Leaf shape: Simple, ovate-lanceolate.

Far right: The haemorrhage plant has branching growth.

OTHER SPECIES OF NOTE

Yarrow *Achillea millefolium*
A common and resilient plant of dry grasslands and waysides, with distinctive feathery leaves. Its far-creeping habit enables it to persist in lawns. A large number of flowerheads of white, or pink, ray and disc flowers are massed into a flattish larger head. It has a long association with healing and alleged magical properties.

Tansy *Tanacetum vulgare*
An eye-catching tall herb of waysides, wasteland and stream banks, often near settlements. Its regularly divided and toothed aromatic leaves, used to deter flies and vermin, provide a dark green backdrop to the flat clusters of bright yellow buttons formed by its disc flowers.

Corn marigold *Chrysanthemum segetum*
Once regarded as a troublesome cornfield weed, corn marigold has declined sharply with modern farming. It is native to the Mediterranean. Drifts of its solitary all-gold heads of disc and broad ray flowers with blue-green foliage are a treat to be found in fallow land, waysides and open garrigue.

Carline thistle *Carlina vulgaris*
A distinctive biennial of dry lime-rich grasslands and dunes across most of Europe. A ground rosette of cotton-downy grey-green spiny leaves comes first, followed the next year by an erect spiny stem bearing persistent heads of yellow-brown flowers surrounded by straw-coloured papery bracts, the outer ones spiny.

Ragwort

Senecio jacobaea

Beautiful they may be, but swathes of golden-yellow ragwort in pastures and paddocks can never be a welcome sight. The plant contains toxic alkaloids which, fresh or dry, are dangerously poisonous to stock, especially horses and cattle. Only the caterpillars of the cinnabar moths, which gorge themselves on the leaves using the accumulated toxins to deter predators, are likely to celebrate the effects of over-grazing or neglect that lead to a build up of ragwort in pastures. In some regions prevention of its spread is a legal requirement on agricultural land, but ragwort is a survivor and persists as one of the most common plants of artificial habitats, waste land and waysides.

Distribution: Europe, rare in the extreme south and north; western Asia; northern Africa; introduced into North and South America, New Zealand and Australia.
Height and spread: 30cm–1.5m/12in–5ft.
Habit and form: Herbaceous biennial or perennial; first year, leaves in basal rosette.
Leaf shape: Lyre-shaped, deeply pinnately lobed.
Pollinated: Insect.

Identification: Yellow flowers are in flat heads 15–25mm/⁹⁄₁₆–1in in diameter, with 12–15 ray flowers the same colour as the disc-flowers. It is generally taller and less branched than Oxford ragwort, *S. squalidus*, marsh ragwort, *S. aquaticus*, or the somewhat greyish hoary ragwort *S. erucifolius*.

Far left: The seedhead is fluffy.

Chamomile

Chamaemelum nobile

This is the plant used to make soothing chamomile tea. It has a long history of medicinal use as a sedative, digestive, anti-inflammatory and anti-spasmodic. The plant and its extracts have also been used as an insect repellent, and an anti-fungal plant tonic and a dye. This is also the plant of chamomile lawns. In the wild, these lawns occur in grasslands, commons and woodland clearings on damp sandy soils, where grazing keeps the sward short and chamomile can enjoy the advantage of its prostrate growth form. While its occurrence in such habitats has declined, the cultivated chamomile lawns popular since Elizabethan times have enjoyed a resurgence of interest, usually using a non-flowering variety.

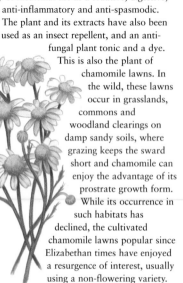

Above: The flowers are daisy-like.

Identification: Chamomile has the combination of yellow tubular disc flowers and white ray flowers of several of its relatives such as corn chamomile, stinking chamomile and scented mayweed. However chamomile can be distinguished from its other pleasantly aromatic relatives by its thread-like leaflets and its prostrate habit.

Distribution: Western Europe; northern Africa; Azores.
Height and spread: 10–30cm/4–12in.
Habit and form: Prostrate herbaceous perennial.
Leaf shape: Almost stemless, thread-like; two or three times divided, linear.
Pollinated: Bee, fly and beetle.

Below: Chamomile is an excellent groundcover plant.

Feverfew

Tanacetum parthenium

Feverfew is a strongly aromatic plant long cultivated for its medicinal properties, particularly for the treatment of fevers, headaches and migraine. It is a very frequent escapee from cultivation, now widely naturalized in waste places, walls, churchyards and waysides, never too far from habitation.

Identification: Its ridged stem, pale yellow-green leaves and button of bright yellow disc flowers surrounded by short white ray flowers give feverfew a distinctive appearance. Some garden varieties are 'doubles' having an excess of ray flowers.

Below: The seedheads dry on the flower stems.

Left: The flowerheads are bright yellow and white.

Distribution: Balkan mountains and south-western Asia; naturalized across Europe.
Height and spread: 25–60cm/10–24in.
Habit and form: Herbaceous perennial.
Leaf shape: Lower leaves pinnately divided with oval toothed lobes, upper leaves less divided and with shorter stalk.
Pollinated: Bee and fly.

Chicory

Cichorium intybus

The chicory flower is a remarkable clear bright blue. The plant has been used as a treatment for such everyday ailments as gallstones, intestinal worms and bruises. The leaves can be eaten green in salads but are paler, tender and less bitter when grown in darkness. *Cichorium intybus* var. *sativum* has been cultivated in Europe for its long stout taproot, which is roasted and ground as a coffee substitute or additive. It has often escaped from cultivation and naturalized into dry waysides and fields, often on calcareous soils. Introduced in eastern Asia, North and South America, Australia and New Zealand.

Distribution: Probably native in most of Europe, western Asia, northern Africa.
Height and spread: 30cm–1.2m/12in–4ft.
Habit and form: Herbaceous perennial.
Leaf shape: Basal leaves lobed; stem leaves lanceolate.
Pollinated: Insect.

Identification: The flowerheads, of all ray-flowers, are 25–40mm/1–1½in borne in leafy branched spikes. The basal leaves are lyre-shaped and divided, with a large heart-shaped terminal lobe. The stem leaves clasp the stem, and are often toothed. Although sometimes called endive, this name strictly belongs to the close relative *Cichorium endivia,* which is similar but with much thickened stalks to the terminal flowerheads.

Left: The flowers are blue, white or lavender.

OTHER SPECIES OF NOTE

Creeping thistle *Cirsium arvense*
A plant of waysides and wasteland and a very persistent weed of cultivation able to spread vigorously from root fragments. Its spine-free, separate heads of purple male and female flowers are valuable for insects and birds.

Cotton thistle, Scotch thistle
Onopordum acanthium
This tall thistle has purple flowers in solitary heads. It can grow to over 2m/6½ft and is easily recognised by the cloak of white-cottony hairs over its stem and leaves and the continuous, broad spiny wings on the stem. Paradoxically, it is rare in Scotland and its native range elsewhere in Europe is uncertain.

Goat's-beard, Jack-go-to-bed-at-noon
Tragopogon pratensis
A hairless, pale blue-green plant with a taproot. It has white-veined, grass-like leaves and large single heads of yellow ray flowers which, as its name suggests, close around midday. The spherical seedhead is beautiful, an architectural marvel of large interlocking feathery 'parasols'.

Greater knapweed *Centaurea scabiosa*
A tall handsome perennial of lime-rich dry grasslands, waysides and coastal dunes and cliffs. Its leaves are divided and its purple flowerheads showy with outer sterile, long-tongued tubular flowers beckoning insects to visit the inner fertile flowers.

Spanish oyster plant

Scolymus hispanicus

This is a handsome plant, its spreading habit and abundant golden-yellow flowerheads make it hard to miss along waysides and ditches and in uncultivated and waste land. It has been used as a herbal remedy, but mainly it has been widely collected, and occasionally cultivated, as a food plant; its stems and young basal leaves are used in salads, stews and omelettes. Also known as Spanish salsify, its roots, too, can be eaten. However, this plant does not give up its riches without a fight – its leaves and stem are very spiny!

Below: The plant is tall and spiny.

Distribution: Southern Europe up to north-western France.
Height and spread: 20–80cm/8–31in; spreading.
Habit and form: Herbaceous biennial or perennial.
Leaf shape: Lower leaves lobed; upper leaves narrow.
Pollinated: Insect.

Identification: The hairy stem has spiny toothed wings. The thistle-like flowerheads arise regularly along the stem. They are 20–30mm/¾–1¼in in diameter and consist of only ray flowers. The lower leaves are oblong, broadest above the middle, and divided. The upper leaves become more spiny and rigid.

Right: The flowers are bright yellow.

ERICACEOUS PLANTS

The Ericaceae comprise a large family, mostly shrubby in character, consisting of about 125 genera and 3,500 species of mostly calcifuge (lime-hating) plants, generally restricted to acid soils. The family is cosmopolitan in distribution, except in deserts, and includes numerous plants from temperate, boreal and montane tropical zones. The chief centre of diversity is in South Africa.

Scarlet heath

Erica coccinea

A variable species of heather, the scarlet heath is commonly found in the fynbos vegetation of the south-western Cape in South Africa, although it is most often noticed during its peak flowering season. This is mainly during the wetter, winter months, but it can be variable depending upon the form. As with many of the long-flowered heathers, this species is typically pollinated by small birds or more occasionally insects and has long tubular flowers that reflect this relationship.

Distribution: South Africa.
Height and spread: 1.2m/4ft.
Habit and form: Evergreen shrub.
Leaf shape: Linear.
Pollinated: Bird, occasionally insect.

Above left: The long tubular flowers of this species of heather are often pollinated by small birds.

Identification: An erect, much-branched evergreen shrub with numerous short, lateral, leafy branchlets, tightly clustered along the main branches. They are covered in small, needle-like leaves, 4–8mm/³⁄₁₆–⁵⁄₁₆in long, arranged in whorls of three. Both leafy and flowering growth is mainly hairless. Pendent, showy flowers, growing from just below the branch end are 6–15mm/¼–⁹⁄₁₆in long, in a range of colours from red, pink and orange, to yellow or green.

Cross-leaved heath

Erica tetralix

This small shrub grows throughout most of Europe, except the far north, typically in bogs, moorland and in wet heathland on acid soils, and sometimes in pine woods, from lowland to about 2,200m/7,200ft.

Identification: The foliage of cross-leaved heath has a green-grey appearance and is softly hairy. The leaves are narrowly lanceolate and grow in characteristic whorls of four (hence the name) at intervals up the stems. Each leaf has a rolled-back margin that hides the underside. The flowers are pale pink, each about 6–7mm/¼in long, inflated and oval, the anthers not protruding. They are borne in tight, nodding terminal clusters and open between June and October.

Above: The pink flowers are attractive at the ends of the stems.

Left: The dried seedheads.

Right: The flower stems form clumps in peaty soil.

Distribution: Europe.
Height and spread: 60cm/24in.
Habit and form: Herbaceous perennial.
Leaf shape: Lanceolate.
Pollinated: Insect.

Bearberry

Arctostaphylos uva-ursi

Distribution: Circumpolar.
Height and spread:
30cm/12in.
Habit and form: Trailing
evergreen shrub.
Leaf shape: Obovate.
Pollinated: Insect.

The bearberry is a small shrub, distributed over the greater part of the Northern Hemisphere, being found in the northern latitudes and high mountains of Europe, Asia and North America, throughout Canada and the United States. It is common on heaths and barren places in hilly districts.

Identification: A much-branched, evergreen shrub, it has irregular, short, woody stems covered with a pale brown bark, scaling off in patches, which trail along the ground forming thick masses, 30–60cm/ 12–24in in length. Evergreen, leathery leaves, 12–25mm/½–1in long, are spoon-shaped, tapering gradually towards the base to a very short stalk, with entire, slightly rolled-back margins. The upper leaf surface is shiny dark green with deeply impressed veins; the underside is paler, with prominent veins forming a coarse network. The young leaves are fringed with short hairs. Small, waxy-looking, urn-shaped flowers, reddish-white or white with a red lip, transparent at the base, contracted at the mouth, are arranged in small, crowded, drooping clusters, and appear at the ends of the branches in early summer, before the young leaves.

Top left: The leaves are simple.

Left: The small flowers appear on the branch tips in early summer.

OTHER SPECIES OF NOTE

Bilberry *Vaccinium myrtillus*
The bilberry, or whinberry, is a small, branched shrub of heaths and mountainous areas, with wiry angular branches, bearing globular waxy flowers and edible black berries, which are covered with a delicate grey bloom when ripe. The leathery leaves are at first rosy, then yellowish-green, turning red in autumn.

Heather *Calluna vulgaris*
Heather, or ling, is an abundant, sometimes dominant plant over large areas of heath and moorland, particularly along the Atlantic fringe of Europe. An evergreen shrub growing to 60cm/24in, it sports a profusion of small, bell-shaped, pink flowers in late summer.

Marsh andromeda
Andromeda polifolia
Known as bog rosemary, this subshrub chiefly occurs on raised bogs in northern Eurasia and the USA. The flowers are small, spherical, pink and produced in spring and early summer. The plant is threatened by the destruction of its habitat.

Bell heather *Erica cinerea*
Similar to cross-leaved heath, *E. tetralix*, but lacks hairs and its leaves number three to a whorl, not four. The flowers are bright pink-purple, each about 6mm/¼in long in an elongated inflorescence. It grows throughout Europe on heath and moorland on dry, acid soils.

Tree heath

Tree heather, *Erica arborea*

An evergreen shrub growing to about 9m/29½in in height. It is a common shrub of Mediterranean Europe, in maquis and similar habitats, and is naturalized further north to south-west Great Britain. It is also widely cultivated, and its old stems and roots are used to make traditional briar pipes; the wood is also used to make charcoal.

Distribution: Africa; Europe; Asia.
Height and spread: 9 x 1m/ 29½ft x 39in.
Habit and form: Woody perennial.
Leaf shape: Simple.
Pollinated: Insect.

Identification: A shrub or tree, 30cm–9m/12in–29½ft high, the trunk diameter to at least 50mm/2in; much-branched, with ascending branches. The leaves grow crowded together on the stem. They are narrow and glabrous, in whorls of three or four, appressed or ascending, needle-like, 2–6.5mm/¹⁄₁₆–¼in long, with minutely denticulate margins. The sweet-scented flowers are clustered towards the end of short lateral branches, where their density may give the impression of continuous flowers along the branches. The corolla is white or pinkish, campanulate, pendulous, 1.5–4mm/¹⁄₁₆–³⁄₁₆in long, widest at the mouth or almost so. The fruit is a glabrous capsule.

Rhododendron ponticum

A fast-growing, evergreen, small tree or large shrub, which occurs naturally in three main regions: around the Black Sea, in the Balkans and in the Iberian Peninsula. It can grow up to 6m/19¾ft in favoured conditions, which are, generally, acidic moorland and woodland. However, it is happy in almost any conditions, from open sunny spots to quite dense shade, and has become an invasive pest in Britain and other European countries. Fossil evidence in Irish peat deposits reveal that this plant once occurred as a native there, approximately 302,000–428,000 years ago, in a warm period that interrupted the most recent ice age, suggesting that it was once far more widespread than it is currently.

Identification: This vigorous, evergreen shrub has inverse lance-shaped to broadly elliptic, leathery leaves, 60mm–18cm/2¼–7in long, glossy, dark green above and paler beneath. In early summer it bears trusses of broadly funnel-shaped, reddish-purple, mauve or occasionally white flowers, up to 50mm/2in long, often spotted yellowish-green inside.

Left: The tightly arranged flowers appear in mid-spring.

Right: Rhododendron ponticum can form a large bush in time and often forms dense stands in light woodland cover.

Distribution: Europe; western Asia.
Height and spread: 6m/19¾ft.
Habit and form: Evergreen shrub.
Leaf shape: Broadly elliptic.
Pollinated: Insect, especially bee.

Labrador tea

Marsh tea, Wild rosemary, *Ledum palustre*

Labrador tea is an attractive evergreen shrub, native to central and northern Europe. Its range also includes Alaska, Canada and Greenland, and northern Asia. It grows mainly in tundra on peaty soils. The plant is poisonous, but has also been used medicinally, notably in homeopathic medicine in small doses to treat rheumatism and stings. The aromatic leaves are sometimes made into a tea-like drink – hence the name.

Identification: An evergreen shrub with rust-coloured twigs and dark green, tough, narrowly oblong leaves, hairy and rust-coloured on the undersides. The clusters of small creamy-white five-petalled flowers are fragrant and very attractive to bees. They develop in compact umbels. The fruit is a dry capsule.

Distribution: Northern Europe; circumpolar.
Height and spread: To 1.2m/4ft.
Habit and form: Herbaceous perennial.
Leaf shape: Oblong.
Pollinated: Insect.

Above: The individual flowers have spreading stamens.

Right: This plant has sturdy upright flowering stems.

Trailing azalea

Loiseleuria procumbens

Distribution: Central and northern Europe; circumpolar.
Height and spread: 50mm x 25cm/2 x 10in.
Habit and form: Herbaceous perennial.
Leaf shape: Elliptic.
Pollinated: Insect.

Right: The pink flowers are tiny.

This pretty little arctic-alpine mountain plant, related to rhododendrons and azaleas is a major element in arctic tundra habitats. It grows wild on mountain sites in rocky habitats and on upland peaty moorland, to about 3000m/9,840ft, from central Europe north to Scandinavia and Iceland. It is also found in northern North America, Greenland and northern Asia and in the mountains of southern Europe. It is sometimes grown as an alpine or rock garden plant and enjoys full sun, flowering in spring or early summer.

Right: This is a low-growing subshrub that hugs the ground.

Identification: A much-branched trailing shrub, growing to about 25cm/10in. The leaves are small, less than 10mm/⅜in, elliptic, with curved edges. The flowers are pink, each about 5mm/³⁄₁₆in across, in clusters of two to five flowers at the shoot tips. The corolla is bell-shaped with petals fused at the base. The fruit is a rounded capsule.

OTHER SPECIES OF NOTE

Tree rhododendron *Rhododendron arboreum*
This is the most widespread tree rhododendron of the Himalayan region, found from Pakistan through to south-eastern Tibet, in forests and scrub at about 1,500–3,600m/4,900–11,800ft. The leaves are to 20cm/8in long, glossy green above, with felty hairs beneath. The flowers are an impressive blood-red (sometimes pink or white) in clusters of 20. Each flower is bell-shaped, 50mm/2in long and five-lobed.

Himalayan pieris *Pieris formosa*
Found from Nepal to south-western China, this small evergreen tree had dark green lanceolate leaves and terminal spikes of globular white flowers that droop from their stems. Each flower is flask-shaped and narrowly lobed. The foliage is also attractive, the young leaves being bright red. The fruit is a globular capsule.

Fragrant wintergreen *Gaultheria fragrantissima*
This is a branching shrub growing to about 1.75m/5¾ft found in Nepal, Burma and south-eastern Tibet. It is fairly common in forests and shrubberies and flowers in April and May. As its name suggests, it bears fragrant flowers. These are small, white and pink and globular, developing in spike-like clusters. The leaves are smooth above and bristly beneath, and yield an antiseptic oil, which is used medicinally and also in perfumery. The fruit is dark, violet-blue and edible, about 6mm/¼in across.

Rhododendron ambiguum

Rhododendrons are a hugely diverse genus, with their centre of diversity occurring in Asia, especially in the east. This attractive, yellow-flowered rhododendron is native to near Mount Omei and Kangding in west Sichuan, China, where it grows in thickets on wooded hillsides and rocky, exposed slopes from 1,800–3,000m/5,900–9,840ft.

Identification: On this upright but compact, evergreen shrub, the bark of mature shoots is usually smooth, red-brown and peeling. The leaves are narrowly oval to elliptic, up to 75mm/3in long, shiny dark green above and blue-green beneath with a strong midrib. Loose trusses of between three and five widely funnel-shaped flowers, to 40mm/1½in, arise from terminal inflorescences in mid-spring. They are pale to greenish-yellow, often with greenish spots on the upper lobe, and with lobes as long as the tube.

Distribution: Sichuan and Guizhou, China.
Height and spread: 2m/6½ft or more.
Habit and form: Evergreen shrub.
Leaf shape: Ovate.
Pollinated: Bee.

Below: This rhododendron forms an upright, but relatively compact, bush.

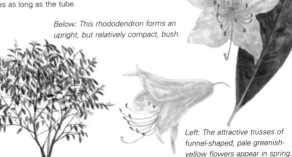

Left: The attractive trusses of funnel-shaped, pale greenish-yellow flowers appear in spring.

NIGHTSHADE FAMILY

The Solanaceae, or nightshade family, comprise herbaceous perennials, shrubs, or trees of about 85
genera and 2,800 species. The species are frequently vines or creepers, and while some are edible, others
are considered very poisonous, including henbane, deadly nightshade and many Solanum species.
The family includes many of our important food plants.

Henbane

Hyoscyamus niger

A widespread, but infrequent annual or biennial, henbane is found
throughout central and southern Europe to India and Siberia, often
occurring on wasteland, near buildings and in stony places from low-
lying ground near the sea to lower mountain slopes. As a weed of
cultivation it now also grows in North America and Brazil. It is
poisonous in all its parts, and is the source of the chemical
hyoscine, used medicinally as a sedative.

Distribution: Eurasia.
Height and spread:
90cm/35in.
Habit and form: Annual or
biennial.
Leaf shape: Ovate.
Pollinated: Insect.

Identification: A variable, coarse, leafy,
branched, strong-scented plant, henbane
is conspicuously sticky and hairy,
especially the stout stem. The stalkless
leaves are alternate and numerous, often
on one side of the branches. They are oval to broadly
lance-shaped, 50mm–20cm/2–8in long, rather
shallowly pinnately lobed, with up to ten unequal,
triangular, pointed segments. Numerous funnel-shaped
flowers appear between late spring and late summer, in
one-sided rows on long, downward-curving branches.
The flowers are 25–50mm/1–2in long and nearly or
quite as wide at the top, prominently purple-veined on a
pale, often greenish-yellow background, more distinctly
purple in the throat.

Below: The fruit capsules contain
up to 500 seeds.

Below: Henbane is
woody.

Right: The five rounded lobes of the
flowerheads are slightly unequal.

Chinese lantern

Winter cherry, Physalis alkekengi

Chinese lantern is a widespread species, found from Central
Europe to China. The name *Physalis* is from the Greek
phusa (bladder), referring to the bladder-like
calyx enclosing the fruit. The shape of
the calyx also accounts for the plant's
common name. The berries are edible and
very juicy, if acrid and bitter; all other
parts of the plant, except the ripe fruit,
are poisonous. The calyx and skin of
the fruit include a yellow colouring matter
that has been used for butter.

Identification: This vigorous,
spreading, rhizomatous
perennial has triangular-oval to
diamond-shaped leaves, up
to 12.5cm/5in long.
Nodding, bell-shaped, cream
flowers, 20mm/¾in long, with
star-shaped mouths, are
produced from the leaf
axils in midsummer. They
are followed by large, bright
orange-scarlet berries,
enclosed in five-sided,
papery, red calyces,
which greatly
increase in size
by the autumn to form
large, leafy
bladders up to
50mm/2in
across.

Distribution: Caucasus to
China.
Height and spread: 30 ×
60cm/12–24in.
Habit and form: Herbaceous
perennial.
Leaf shape: Triangular-ovate.
Pollinated: Bee.

Left: The tall stems
arise each season
from underground
rhizomes.

Far right: The creamy
flowers give rise to the
showy 'lanterns'.

Poison berry

Madagascar nightshade, *Solanum anguivi*

Distribution: Africa; India.
Height and spread: 2m x 50cm/6½ft x 20in.
Habit and form: Woody perennial.
Leaf shape: Simple.
Pollinated: Insect.

A woody shrub with alternate leaves and (usually) white or yellow flowers. The fruit is bright orange, becoming red when ripe, and is edible. The plant is common in secondary regrowth, thickets and at forest edges. It flowers mainly between April and July. This nightshade species has various medicinal uses, including in Ayurvedic medicine, being used, among other things, for treating skin diseases, fever and coughs. The fruit is used in the control of hypertension and also to increase the production of milk in lactating women.

Identification: An erect perennial woody herb or shrub to 2m/6½ft, hairy, with or without prickles on the stems and leaves. The leaves are alternate and simple, ovate, angular or lobed, with prickles on both surfaces. The flowers are white, yellow, pale blue or mauve. The fruit is a round berry, one to six berries on bent stalks, dark green and striped at first, turning orange, then red, blackening with age. It contains a large number of small, smooth seeds.

Right: Poison berry has shrubby growth.

Right: Despite the plant's common name the fruit is edible.

OTHER SPECIES OF NOTE

Mandrake *Mandragora officinarum*
The mandrake, the object of strange superstitions, is native to southern Europe. Its large brown, parsnip-like root runs deep into the ground. Dark green leaves spread open and lie upon the ground, among which primrose-like white, purplish or bluish flowers appear in summer or autumn, followed by yellow fruits.

Deadly nightshade *Atropa belladonna*
A famous plant, and the source of a potent poison, atropine, a compound that is also useful in medicine, used among other things, to dilate the pupil of the eye. This effect was also used to enhance female beauty – hence the specific name *belladonna* meaning beautiful woman. It is a bushy perennial with dull green leaves looking like those of potato. The flowers are bell-shaped and dull purple and the fruits are juicy, black and cherry-like, unfortunately attractive to children, but deadly (only a few can be fatal).

Bitterweet *Solanum dulcamara*
A scrambling poisonous woody perennial with pointed leaves and purple flowers with bright yellow anthers, each about 15mm/⅝in long and drooping, borne in loose clusters. The shiny, oval berries are yellow-green, ripening to red. It grows throughout Europe in a wide range of habitats including ditches, fenland, woods, hedges, rough ground and coastal shingle.

Black nightshade

Solanum nigrum

The black nightshade is an annual, one of the most common and cosmopolitan of wild plants, extending almost over the whole globe. It is frequently seen by the wayside and is often found on rubbish heaps, but also among growing crops and in damp and shady places. It is sometimes called the garden nightshade, because it so often occurs in cultivated ground. The berries contain the alkaloid solanine, which is toxic, and may be fatal if ingested in large quantities. The plant flowers and fruits freely, and in the autumn the masses of black berries are very noticeable.

Identification: A variable, hairy, much branched, annual herb. The stem is green and hollow, up to 30cm/12in in height. Oval to lance-shaped leaves have bluntly notched or waved margins, usually untoothed. The flowers are white, with yellow anthers, approximately 6mm/¼in, in clusters of about five at the ends of stalks. The berry-like fruits are green at first and dull black when ripe.

Distribution: Worldwide.
Height and spread: Up to 30cm/12in.
Habit and form: Annual.
Leaf shape: Ovate to lanceolate.
Pollinated: Insect.

Above: The berries turn from green to black from late summer onwards.

Far left: Vigorous and free branching, black nightshade becomes a bushy mass.

BINDWEED FAMILY

The bindweed family, Convolvulaceae, has a wide distribution, being found in both temperate and tropical regions. It contains about 1,600 species, many of which are clambering and twining herbs or shrubs. Many have heart-shaped leaves and funnel-shaped solitary or paired flowers. Species of morning glory, Ipomoea eriocarpa, are often grown in gardens.

Hairy bindweed

Calystegia pulchra

Named for its hairy stems and leaf-stalks, hairy bindweed is very pretty, with large pink flowers, striped white, opening between July and September. It is widely naturalized and thrives on waste land and rough ground and in hedgerows. It is possible that hairy bindweed arose as a garden hybrid, or it may perhaps be native to north-eastern Asia. It is often grown in gardens and frequently escapes into the wild, blurring its natural distribution.

Identification: Hairy bindweed resembles the giant bindweed, *C. silvatica*, but its stems are usually obviously hairy and the leaves more parallel-sided. In addition, its flowers are always mainly pink. Each flower is 50–75mm/2–3in across. The inflated sepal-like bracts almost hide the calyx.

Distribution: Europe; Asia.
Height and spread: 2m/6½ft.
Habit and form: Herbaceous perennial.
Leaf shape: Simple.
Pollinated: Insect.

Far left: The stems are thin and twist around and over other surfaces.

Left: The flower is trumpet-shaped.

Hewittia sublobata

(= *H. malabarica*)

This is a creeping vine that does well in grasslands, thickets and at forest edges and flowers between August and November. Its leaves are sometimes eaten as a vegetable, especially during famine periods. The leaves are also used for treating sores, and a root decoction is drunk in Tanzania to treat threadworm. The range is from The Gambia to west Cameroon, and throughout tropical Africa. Also in Asia and Polynesia.

Right: The white trumpet-like flowers are typical of the family.

Identification: A climbing or prostrate perennial herb with slender stems, occasionally rooting at the nodes. The leaves are variable, oblong or ovate, cordate or hastate at the base, hairy on both surfaces; margin entire or toothed, 30mm–16cm/1¼ x 6¼in long x 10–30mm/⅜–1¼in across. The fruit is a one-celled hairy capsule about 10mm/⅜in across, containing two to four seeds. The flowers are borne in one or three-flowered clusters. The corolla is pale yellow or whitish with a dark purple-red centre. The capsule is roughly spherical to almost square, hairy, crowned with the persistent style.

Distribution: Tropical Africa; tropical Asia.
Height and spread: 2m x 20cm/6½ft x 8in.
Habit and form: Herbaceous perennial.
Leaf shape: Simple.
Pollinated: Insect.

Left: This species typically thrives on trees.

Giant bindweed

Calystegia silvatica

Distribution: Eurasia; North America.
Height and spread: Up to 5m/16ft.
Habit and form: Herbaceous climber.
Leaf shape: Cordate or sagittate.
Pollinated: Insect.

Bindweeds are known as 'morning glories', referring to their habit of opening early in the day, with the bloom fading by mid-afternoon. Giant bindweed has alternate leaves, and is characterized by showy, white, funnel-shaped flowers, usually appearing in spring until early autumn. The plant is very widespread, with subspecies occurring across Eurasia and North America. The genus *Calystegia* can be distinguished from the closely related *Convolvulus* genus by its floral characteristics: *Calystegia* species have a pair of large bracts that overlap the calyx, whereas *Convolvulus* species have very small bracts that are distant from the calyx.

Identification: A strong, rampant, stoloniferous, perennial climber, with stems up to 5m/16ft and alternate, heart-shaped or arrowhead-shaped leaves, up to 15cm/6in long. White, rarely pink-striped, trumpet-shaped flowers are between 60–90mm/2¼–3½in across, rarely deeply five-lobed, with bracts strongly pouched and overlapping. It may be confused with the related *C. sepium*, although its has larger flowers than that species.

Above: The tightly wrapped buds unfurl in the morning, but each flower lasts just one day.

Left: Despite its showy flowers, its vigorous smothering habit has made this plant unpopular in cultivated areas.

OTHER SPECIES OF NOTE

Mallow-leaved bindweed
Convolvulus althaeoides
A low-growing, trailing perennial that produces rosy-pink or pink to purple, funnel-shaped flowers over silvery to grey-green leaves in early to midsummer. It is common on dry rocky soils in the Mediterranean and southern Europe.

Hedge bindweed *Calystegia sepium*
This is a common European flower of fenland, marshes, hedges and rough ground, where it clambers to about 3m/10ft. It often twines itself around fences. It has arrow-shaped bright green leaves and large, usually white (sometimes pale pink) funnel-shaped flowers, opening from June to September. Although pretty, it is vigorous in growth and can be an aggressive weed.

Porana grandiflora
The genus *Porana* resembles *Ipomoea*, and both are rampant climbers with attractive flowers. This species grows in Nepal and Bhutan where it clambers over shrubs and flowers from August to October. The funnel-shaped flowers are mauve with a narrow tube opening to 45mm/1¾in across. The leaves are heart-shaped and pointed, to about 12cm/4¾in long and with silvery hairs beneath.

Snow creeper *Porana racemosa*
Found from Kashmir and Bhutan to China, the snow creeper clambers on trees and shrubs and bears clusters of small white flowers, giving a fanciful impression of patches of snow when seen at a distance.

Morning glory

Ipomoea eriocarpa

Morning glory normally grows well along roads and paths and as a creeper in the bush and disturbed sites. Also found in dry, deciduous woodland and grassland, often on sandy soils, to about 1,530m/5,000ft altitude. It flowers mainly between November and February. In some regions a decoction of the leaves is drunk to relieve menstrual pain.

Identification: This variable annual herb grows either prostrate or as a climber or creeper. It has hairy slender stems with both long and short hairs. The leaves are small, oval to heart-shaped or long oblong and usually arrow-shaped at the base. The flowers are small, in few-flowered clusters, mauve, white or pink. The fruits are hairy ovoid-spherical capsules 5–6mm/³⁄₁₆–¼in in diameter, containing black seeds, splitting open when ripe.

Right: Morning glory has a twining habit, on a thin stem.

Distribution: Tropical Africa.
Height and spread: 1m x 10cm/39 x 4in.
Habit and form: Annual herb.
Leaf shape: Simple.
Pollinated: Insect.

DOGWOOD, BUCKTHORN AND VINE FAMILIES

The dogwood family, Cornaceae, is small and contains trees and shrubs, with a few herbs, mainly found in temperate regions. The buckthorn family, Rhamnaceae, contains tropical and temperate trees, shrubs and climbers. The vine family, Vitaceae, consists mainly of climbers, though some are shrubs.

Swedish cornel

Cornus suecica

Swedish cornel forms colourful patches among dwarf shrubs in heaths, open thickets and forests in northern regions. The flowerheads are extremely showy consisting of four large white bracts, surrounding small purple flowers, which appear mainly in early summer. These are followed later in the year by small bunches of bright red fruit. The plant is widely distributed in northen Europe to northern Japan, and in northern North America. The flowers are quite unusual in that they open 'explosively', possibly to help spread pollen if there are too few insects around.

Identification: Swedish cornel is a low-growing, rhizomatous perennial, with slender, freely branching creeping stems emanating from a woody underground rootstock. A few opposite pairs of stem leaves, and egg-shaped to lance-shaped, mid-green leaves in terminal whorls are borne on short stems. In early summer, inconspicuous, purple-red flowers are surrounded by four white, 12mm/½in long, elliptic bracts, in a cyme 25mm/1in across. They are followed by clusters of scarlet fruits. The foliage gradually changes to bright red in the autumn.

Distribution: Circumboreal.
Height and spread: 10–15 x 30cm/4–6 x 12in.
Habit and form: Creeping herbaceous perennial.
Leaf shape: Ovate to lanceolate.
Pollinated: Insect.

Left: The berries are bright red and appear in profusion on the shrub in the autumn.

Tatarian dogwood

Red-barked dogwood, *Cornus alba*

This suckering, deciduous, colonizing shrub, found throughout Siberia to Manchuria and northern Korea, forms clumps of stems reaching a height of up to 3m/10ft. The young twigs are an intense blood-red in the winter and the leaves turn many beautiful colours. The insignificant flower cymes are followed by white to very pale blue fruits.

Identification: Most stems of this upright shrub branch little, except near the tip. It has vivid blood-red bark in winter, which in spring reverts to nearly green. It is smooth, except for lenticels, or leaf scars, which encircle the stems. The leaves are opposite, simple, oval to elliptic, tapering to a point, 50mm–11.5cm/2–4½in long, with the major leaf veins parallel to the curving leaf margins. They emerge yellow-green, darkening with maturity to medium or dark green and often reddening in autumn. Small, yellowish-white flowers are held in flattened cymes, 40–50mm/1½–2in in diameter, in late spring to early summer. The fruits, white or tinged blue, ripen in midsummer.

Right: Cornus is often cultivated as a garden plant, or planted on banks at the side of busy roads, for its winter foliage. The stems of the shrub turn deep pink or orange and remain that colour throughout the autumn and winter.

Distribution: Northern Asia.
Height and spread: 3m/10ft.
Habit and form: Deciduous shrub.
Leaf shape: Ovate to elliptic.
Pollinated: Insect.

Left: The berries.

OTHER SPECIES OF NOTE

Cornelian cherry *Cornus mas*
Native to Europe and western
Asia, this vigorous deciduous
shrub grows to 4.5m/15ft.
The yellow flowers
appear in early spring
before the dark green
leaves. The
bright red fruits
are edible.

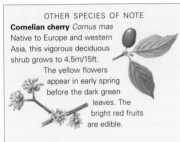

Dogwood *Cornus sanguinea*
A deciduous shrub found throughout Europe and
western Asia, except the far north, dogwood has
reddish twigs, opposite leaves and clusters of
dull white flowers that ripen into round black
fruits. It is planted in gardens, often as a hedge
and provides good autumn colours on both
stems and leaves.

Buckthorn *Rhamnus cathartica*
This deciduous European shrub or small tree
grows to about 6m/19¾ft tall. It is also found in
north-western African and western Asia. The
oval leaves are long-stalked and toothed, and the
flowers are small, greenish and inconspicuous.
The rounded berries are green at first, ripening
black, and are eaten by birds, though mildly
poisonous to people.

Grape vine *Vitis vinifera*
The best known member of its family, the grape
vine is grown for its edible fruits which are eaten
raw, dried, or made into drinks, including wine.
Native to western Asia, it is widely grown.

Mwengele

Cyphostemma adenocaule

The young leaves and shoots of this
perennial herb are eaten as a vegetable or in
soup, and the roots are also eaten after
boiling. It also has many medicinal uses: the
leaf sap is applied to cuts, or mixed with
honey to soothe a sore throat, and the root
is even used to treat malaria. It also has
insecticidal properties. It flowers between
March and June and does well
in sandy loams, although it is
adapted to a wide variety of
soil types. It grows in
moist savannah
woodlands, riverine
vegetation and thickets.

Identification: A common herb or
climber using coiled tendrils that arise
opposite the leaves. The
stems grow from a woody
rootstock with small
fibrous tubers. The leaves
are compound to
15cm/6in long on a twice-
branched stalk. The leaves
are alternate and the fruit is a
fleshy berry, red to purplish-
black. The flowers are white, less than
3mm/⅛in, tubular with four petals. The
slightly hairy berry is about 8mm/⅝in
across, with one or two seeds within.

Distribution: Tropical Africa.
Height and spread: 5m x
30cm/16 x 12in.
Habit and form: Perennial
climber.
Leaf shape:
Compound.
Pollinated: Insect.

*Right: The
fruit and
leaves are
eaten.*

*Below: The plant grows
from a very large tuber.*

Helinus mystacinus

Distribution: Tropical Africa.
Height and spread: 10 x
1m/33ft x 39in.
Habit and form:
Woody perennial.
Leaf shape: Simple.
Pollinated: Insect.

*Right: The plant is a woody
climber, attaining moderate
dimensions.*

This woody climber anchors itself using single curling tendrils.
It flowers from May to July and grows in a wide variety of
habitats, the commonest being secondary regrowth in forest
clearings, where it often forms a dense climbing tangle.
It thrives in fertile black humus. The leaves and stems are
crushed and the extract added to local brews to speed up
fermentation. Sometimes the infusion from the leaves is
used to treat jaundice.

Identification: This is a climber with hairy coiled tendrils and
reddish hairy branches. The flowers have a distinct
pentagonal disc. They are borne in axillary umbels, and
are greenish-white. The petals are obovate,
rolled around the stamens. The leaves
are alternate with hairs close to the
surface, broadly oval, 30–60mm/1¼–2¼in
long. The flowers occur in small groups on
stalks beside the leaves, in tiny, yellow-green hairy
cups. The fruit is a hairy oval or round capsule,
5–7mm/³⁄₁₆in long, hanging down, covered with pointed
bumps. It ripens from red to blue-black.

*Left: The
greenish-white
flowers are
pentagonal.*

PROTEA FAMILY

The Proteaceae, or proteas, include about 80 genera and 1,500 species, with representatives in South America, South Africa, India, Australia and New Zealand. The name is derived from the shape-shifting Greek god Proteus, in reference to the extreme variability of leaf form in the family. The genus Protea *is well known for its spectacular flowers.*

Marsh rose

Orothamnus zeyheri

The marsh rose is one of the finest of all the proteas and one of the star attractions of the famous "fynbos" communities of the southern Cape of South Africa. It grows mainly on south-facing slopes at 500–800m/1,600–2,600ft. Now rare and threatened by collection, it is protected in a couple of reserves. It is a difficult species to cultivate, so protection of its wild populations is all the more important. The flowers keep remarkably well (over a month) after cutting, which is partly why it is so sought after. It is adapted to survive occasional fires, and ants carry the seeds below ground, where they later germinate. The seeds can survive for 35 years or more, ready to germinate when conditions are right – often after a fire.

Identification: This shrub is usually single-stemmed growing to 4m/13ft. The leaves are leathery, about 60mm/2¼in long, with hairy edges. The flower-heads, each about 60mm/2¼in long, are very pretty, and consist of yellow flowers, surrounded by shiny red bracts. The fruits develop two months after flowering.

Below left: The flowers appear on the plant all year around.

Right: The plant attains a great height and lives for about 10 years.

Distribution: South Africa.
Height and spread: To 4m/13ft.
Habit and form: Perennial shrub.
Leaf shape: Elliptic.
Pollinated: Insect.

Tristemma mauritianum

This species is widespread in tropical Africa, including Madagascar and Mauritius. It flowers mainly between August and September. It grows in marshy clearings in rainforest, in swampy riverine forest and prefers permanently moist soils that are rich in humus. The fruits are edible and sweet but are slightly acidic. The young shoot is also edible.

Identification: An erect or scrambling perennial herb, to 2m/6½ft, with thick square stems and narrowly winged, short, stiff, purplish bristles. It is usually short lived. The broadly oval leaves, arranged opposite are to 12cm/4¾in long, with five to seven conspicuous parallel veins. The flowers are pale pink-mauve, crowded in a terminal head, and are almost stalkless. The fruit is a capsule surrounded by the persistent cup-shaped calyx.

Distribution: Africa.
Height and spread: 2m x 20cm/6½ft x 8in.
Habit and form: Perennial herb.
Leaf shape: Simple.
Pollinated: Insect.

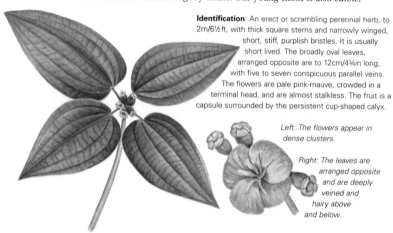

Left: The flowers appear in dense clusters.

Right: The leaves are arranged opposite and are deeply veined and hairy above and below.

OTHER SPECIES OF NOTE

Protea neriifolia
This is the first *Protea* ever to be mentioned in botanical literature. It is a very widespread species and occurs from sea-level to 1,300m/ 4,250ft in the southern coastal mountain ranges from just east of Cape Town to Port Elizabeth, South Africa. It is an ornamental shrub with huge flowers, from green to silvery-pink.

Leucadendron argenteum
This beautiful tree with its soft silver leaves is endemic to Table Mountain and the slopes above Kirstenbosch Botanical Gardens, South Africa, where it grows in dense stands. The grey-green leaves are covered with fine, silvery hairs, which reflect the light and give the leaves a soft, velvety feel. The leaves are sometimes used for making unusual mats or bookmarks.

Peninsula conebush *Leucadendron strobilinum*
This stout shrub is endemic to the Cape Penninsula, and is most abundant at higher altitudes and to the north, being especially common on Table Mountain. It has separate male and female plants, which grow in damp rocky situations.

Melastoma normale
This large, hairy shrub grows on slopes and scrubland from Nepal to China and South-east Asia, at about 1,000–2,000m/3,200–6,500ft. It produces terminal clusters of five-petalled pink flowers, each about 50mm/2in across and with a hairy calyx. Five of the ten stamens are long and curving. The leaves are lanceolate and stalked, with three to five veins and are hairy beneath. The fruit is berry-like.

King protea

Protea cynaroides

Probably the best-known protea, this plant is prized worldwide as a magnificent cut flower and in South Africa is honoured as the national flower. The king protea has one of the widest distribution ranges of the genus, occurring across the south-western coast of South Africa, except for the dry interior ranges, at all elevations from sea level to 1,500m/4,900ft. Large, vigorous plants produce six to ten flowerheads in one season, although some exceptional plants can produce up to 40 on one plant.

Identification: The king protea is a woody shrub with thick stems. Its height and spread may vary according to locality and habitat, but all plants have large, dark green, rounded to elliptic, glossy leaves. Goblet or bowl-shaped flowerheads, 12.5–30cm/ 5–12in in diameter, are surrounded by large, colourful bracts, from creamy-white to deep crimson, produced at various times of the year according to location.

Left: Each flowerhead, is 30cm/12in in diameter.

Right: King protea is a low-growing bush.

Distribution: South Africa.
Height and spread: 90cm–2m/35in–6½ft.
Habit and form: Evergreen shrub.
Leaf shape: Rounded to elliptic.
Pollinated: Bird.

Yellow pincushion

Leucospermum conocarpodendron

This species falls into the category of "tree pincushions" because it has a single, thick trunk. It is locally abundant throughout the granite and sandstone soils on dry slopes in the northern Cape Peninsula of South Africa. The flowers are bright golden-yellow and the bush is quite spectacular when it is covered in an abundance of flowers. Flowering usually commences as soon as the hot weather starts. The fruit is released two months after flowering and is dispersed by ants.

Distribution: Northern Cape Peninsula, South Africa.
Height and spread: 5 x 3m/16 x 10ft.
Habit and form: Rounded shrub.
Leaf shape: Lanceolate to elliptic.
Pollinated: Bird.

Identification: Though it is a large shrub it has a rounded, compact, neat appearance. Large lance-shaped to elliptic, stalked, grey-silver leaves, covered with a layer of minute hairs, toothed at the end and tipped with red dots, are crowded around the upright stems. The flowers, about 80mm/3⅛in in diameter, are like large pincushions, with numerous bright lemon-yellow, white-tipped segments.

Left: The shrub is laden with flowers in early summer, and is visited by pollinating birds.

MILKWEEDS

The Asclepiadaceae, or milkweeds, comprise mostly herbaceous perennials, lianas and twining shrubs with white (often poisonous) sap, comprising nearly 350 genera and 2,900 species, many of which are vines and some of which are cactus-like succulents with reduced leaves. Many species have medicinal properties.

Silk vine

Periploca graeca

The generic name for this vine comes from the Greek *peri* (around) and *ploke* (woven), and refers to its twining habit. The glossy leaves provide a perfect foil for the interesting, if unpleasantly scented, star-shaped flowers, which are followed by curious fruits. The silk vine is usually found in woods, thickets and riverbanks throughout this range. All parts of the plant emit a milky sap when broken or cut. The sap and fruit are poisonous.

Below: The flowerhead.

Identification: The silk vine is a vigorous, deciduous, woody, twining climber. The leaves are opposite, 25–50mm/1–2in, oval to lance-shaped, glossy, dark green, turning yellow in autumn. The flowers, up to 25mm/1in across with five downy, spreading lobes, are borne in long-stalked corymbs of eight to 10 from early to late summer; they have a yellow-green exterior and maroon to chocolate interior. They are followed by pairs of narrowly cylindrical seedpods, up to 12.5cm/5in long.

Distribution: South-eastern Europe to western Asia.
Height and spread: 10m/33ft.
Habit and form: Woody, twining climber.
Leaf shape: Ovate to lanceolate.
Pollinated: Insect.

Left: Silk vine climbs vigorously by twining around the stems of other plants.

Giant carrion flower

Stapelia nobilis

An interesting succulent, found intermittently from South Africa as far north as Tanzania, that has olive-green, erect branches, which give the plant a cactus-like appearance. It bears large, foul-smelling, starfish-shaped flowers that are pale yellow with reddish stripes, covered with white hairs. The flowers are said to look flesh-like and this, when combined with the rotting meat odour, attracts its main visitor, the fly, for pollinating.

Identification: The stems are four-sided, rigid, spineless, 15–20cm/6–8in tall and 30mm/1¼in in diameter. They are pale green and robust, and the angles are winged with small teeth. One or two flowers are borne from the base to midway up the stem, and are 25–35cm/10–14in across, flat to slightly bell-shaped, with a short dark red tube, which is densely wrinkled, and a dark purple-brown corona. The lobes are oval with elongated tapering points, pale ochre-yellow, with many tiny, wavy crimson stripes and fringed with hairs.

Distribution: South Africa to Tanzania.
Height and spread: 15–20cm/6–8in; indefinite spread.
Habit and form: Succulent.
Leaf shape: Absent.
Pollinated: Fly.

Left: The olive-green branches are robust, held erect and lined with small teeth, and give this plant a rather cactus-like appearance.

White's ginger

African viagra vine, *Mondia whytei*

Distribution: Tropical Africa.
Height and spread: 5m x 10cm/16ft x 4in.
Habit and form: Woody climber.
Pollinated: Insect.
Leaf shape: Simple.

Right: This is a creeping climber.

This species is a rare and threatened African vine. It is a robust, woody, evergreen climber bearing panicles of cream-yellow buds. When the buds open they display deep red inner petals. The leaves are large, attractive and heart-shaped. A root infusion is popularly used as an aphrodisiac and generally to improve blood circulation. It flowers mainly between April and July and grows in forests, thickets and savannah woodland. Threatened by over-collecting, it is also now cultivated in some places, such as in Kenya.

Right: The attractive mauve flowers open from cream-coloured buds.

Identification: A woody climbing shrub, growing to 5m/16ft, from a tuberous rootstock, the stems twining over bushes. It has conspicuously milky latex. It is easily recognized by a fringe of reflexed stipules at each node. The leaves are opposite, generally oval to almost circular, to about 20cm/8in in diameter. The flowers are small, borne in drooping clusters to 15cm/6in. The fruit is a pair of large diverging capsules about 12cm/4¾in long, containing many seeds bearing silky white hairs.

OTHER SPECIES OF NOTE

Hoya sussuela
This vigorous climbing vine from Indonesia has leathery, light green leaves, about 50mm–10cm/2–4in long, with a clear centre vein. The unusual waxy flowers are cup-shaped, dark maroon with pointed lobes arranged in a star fashion, with up to 10 flowers in an umbel. They have a strong musky odour.

Ceropegia ballyana
This robust, climbing, succulent-rooted vine from Kenya has unusual, green-white flowers with red-brown spots. The base appears triangular in profile, and with the twisted tips of the lobes the whole flower looks like a fairy light.

Swallow-wort *Vincetoxicum hirundinaria*
This tall perennial has erect stems and opposite, heart-shaped leaves. Clusters of small yellowish-green flowers arise from the bases of the upper leaves. A poisonous species, it grows in woods and rocky sites through much of Europe, though is absent from Britain and Ireland.

Hoya heuschkeliana
This hoya has a small range in the wild, being found only in forests in southern Luzon in the Philippines, where it grows as an epiphyte. Its unusual flowers are small and urn-shaped. Fortunately, it is easy to cultivate and is quite popular among specialists. It roots readily from cuttings and can be planted in a pot, hanging basket or grown on a moss pole. Its flowers are said to exude a smell like caramel.

Balloonplant

Balloon cotton-bush, *Gomphocarpus physocarpus* (= *Asclepias physocarpa*)

Balloonplant is a rather slender herb, native to Africa but naturalized elsewhere. It produces many insignificant flowers that develop into unusual yellowish-green translucent, soft, spiny balloons (hence the common name). The white to cream-coloured flowers appear in umbels and open in December through April. It prefers to grow in well-drained soils.

Identification: A herb growing up to 1.8m/6ft tall. The lower three or four leaves grow close together, while the upper leaves are opposite and rather crowded, narrowly lanceolate, and up to 20cm/8in long. The flowers are white or cream, borne in lateral, stalked umbels. The calyx is pink or greenish and five-lobed almost to the base. The unusually shaped fruit is yellowish-green, up to 75mm/3in, inflated, not pointed, and has a covering of stiff, slightly curved hairs.

Far right: Pretty flowers and unusual fruits make this a popular garden plant in southern Africa.

Distribution: Africa; invasive in Hawaii and New Caledonia
Height and spread: 1.8m x 60cm/6ft x 24in.
Habit and form: Herbaceous perennial.
Leaf shape: Lanceolate.
Pollinated: Insect.

CUCURBIT FAMILY

The Cucurbitaceae, or cucumber family, contains mostly prostrate or climbing herbaceous annuals. The family comprises 90 genera and 700 species, which are characterized by five-angled stems and coiled tendrils. It is one of the most important food plant families in the world, including squashes, gourds, melons and cucumbers. Most of the plants are annual vines with large, showy blossoms.

White bryony

Common bryony, *Bryonia dioica*

This vine-like plant is common in European woods and hedges. The stems climb by means of long tendrils springing from the side of the leaf stalks, and extend among trees and shrubs, often to the length of several metres during the summer. They die away after the fruit has ripened, although the large tuber survives in the soil and new stems grow the following year.

Right: The berries often persist until after the stems have withered.

Identification: A climbing herbaceous perennial, with tendrils arising from the leaf axils. The stems are angular and brittle, branched mostly at the base, very rough, with short, prickly hairs. The leaves are held on curved stalks, shorter than the blade, and are divided into five, slightly angular lobes, of which the middle lobe is the longest. Small, greenish-white flowers, generally in small bunches of three or four, spring from the axils of the leaves in late spring, with the sexes on separate plants. The plant produces red berries, which are most noticeable after the stems and leaves have withered. The berries are filled with juice with an unpleasant, foetid odour and contain three to six large seeds, which are greyish-yellow mottled with black.

Distribution: Europe.
Height and spread: Up to 5m/16ft.
Habit and form: Herbaceous vine.
Leaf shape: Palmately lobed.
Pollinated: Insect.

Left: Long stems clamber over other plants, attaching to them by means of tendrils.

Ivy gourd

Scarlet gourd, *Coccinia grandis*

Ivy gourd bears white or yellow flowers followed by scarlet fruits with white spots. It is a rapidly growing, climbing or trailing vine. In its native habitat it is a common, but not serious, weed that is kept in check by competing plants and natural enemies. In recent years, it has become an invasive weed in some tropical countries where it has been introduced.

Identification: An aggressive, fast-growing herbaceous perennial vine, with succulent, hairless stems produced annually from a tuberous rootstock, with occasional adventitious roots forming where they run along the ground. Long simple tendrils from the leaf axils wrap around the host plant. The leaves are alternate, smooth, broadly oval, five-lobed, 90mm/3½in long, with a short, pointed tip, heart-shaped base and minutely toothed margins. The white, bell-shaped flowers, 40mm/1½in long, usually solitary, are deeply divided into five oval lobes. The fruit is a smooth, egg-shaped gourd, bright red when ripe, 25–60mm/1–2¼in long.

Distribution: Africa; Asia; Fiji; and northern Australia.
Height and spread: Up to 30m/98ft.
Habit and form: Herbaceous vine.
Leaf shape: Broadly ovate to cordate.
Pollinated: Insect.

Left: The fast-growing stems quickly smother other plants.

Above left: Bright red fruits give this vine a very distinctive appearance.

Squirting cucumber

Touch-me-not, Exploding cucumber, *Ecballium elaterium*

This member of the cucurbit family is found in most of the Mediterranean region and Macronesia, growing in rich peat with some water and lots of sun. The vine has developed a unique strategy for the spreading of its seeds: while the fruit ripens, pressure develops inside. When the fruit separates from the stalk, for example if it is touched by an animal, the sticky seeds squirt out, hence the name.

Below right: The small, hairy seedpods explode when ripe.

Distribution: Mediterranean region and Atlantic islands.
Height and spread: 30 x 90cm/12 x 35in.
Habit and form: Trailing, slightly bushy herbaceous perennial.
Leaf shape: Palmately lobed.
Pollinated: Insect.

Identification: A trailing to slightly bushy herbaceous perennial with fleshy, triangular or heart-shaped leaves, palmately lobed, with a bristly upper surface and downy underside. It has yellow funnel- or bell-shaped flowers, about 25mm/1in across, sometimes with deeper yellow centres. Both male and female flowers appear on one plant, the male flowers in racemes, the female flowers solitary. The egg-shaped hairy seedpods, which are blue-green and 40–50mm/1½–2in long, enclose many seeds in a watery mucilage that is ejected explosively when the fruit is ripe.

Far left: The trailing stems spread to make a low mat of leafy growth.

OTHER SPECIES OF NOTE

Bryonia alba
This species is similar to white bryony, *B. dioica*. However, although the male and female flowers are separate, they grow on the same plant, unlike white bryony which is dioecious. The leaves differ too in that the central lobe is longer and has a more jagged margin. The ripe fruits are black. It is found in central Europe, in scrub and woodland. The inconspicuous flowers open from May to September.

Wax gourd *Benincasa hispida*
The wax gourd or winter melon is a trailing, fleshy vine, grown in many warm countries for its edible fruits. Its solitary yellow flowers are followed by melon- or cucumber-shaped fruit. It probably originated in China and now exists as a garden escapee across much of Asia.

Watermelon *Citrullus lanatus*
The watermelon grows widely in Africa and Asia, and in the Kalahari Desert the wild melons have been an important source of water and food to indigenous inhabitants, as well as explorers. The history of their domestication is obscure but a wide variety of watermelons have been cultivated in Africa since antiquity.

Cretan bryony
Bryonia cretica
The Cretan bryony has red berries and greenish-white five-petalled flowers. All parts are poisonous.

Tatior-pot

Ma kling, *Hodgsonia heteroclita*

This large, woody, climbing plant, from the tropical forests of South-east Asia, is cultivated as a food plant for its large fleshy fruits, which are similar to pumpkin, and its extremely oily seeds. It is rare in the wild, and many populations are considered endangered. Flowering starts at night and continues into the following day.

Identification: Up to 30m/98ft in height or spread, this climber has leaves that are deeply three or five-lobed, almost smooth with a few small glands. Climbing tendrils have two or three branches. The male and female inflorescences are separate: males are 15–35cm/6–14in long, on a 80mm–15cm/ 3⅛–6in stalk bearing 10–20 pale yellow, velvety, five-lobed flowers, each 30–50mm/1¼–2in long. The female flowers resemble the males but are solitary. The fruits are 15–20cm/6–8in in diameter, greenish-brown turning red-brown, smooth or shallowly grooved.

Above right: The oil-rich seeds can be eaten.

Distribution: Widely scattered in Sikkim, Bhutan, eastern India; southern China; Burma; Indochina; and Thailand.
Height and spread: Up to 30m/98ft.
Habit and form: Woody climbing plant.
Leaf shape: Palmately lobed.
Pollinated: Insect.

Below: Hodgsonia heteroclita is a vine.

Sponge luffa

Sponge gourd, Vegetable sponge, Wash sponge, *Luffa aegyptiaca* (= *L. cylindrica*)

Sponge luffa is a tropical, fast-growing vine with lobed leaves and yellow flowers. Both male and female flowers are on the same plant and are pollinated by bees. The fruits are smooth and cylindrical in shape and have white flesh. The young fruit is used as a cooked vegetable, although some gardeners grow it for the fibrous interior only. The young fruit can be eaten raw like cucumber or cooked like squash, while the young leaves, shoots, flower buds, as well as the flowers can be eaten after being lightly steamed. The seeds can be roasted as a snack, or pressed to produce oil. To prepare a sponge (loofah), the fruits are allowed to turn yellow, then harvested, the outer skin removed and the skeletons left to dry out. The dried fruit fibers are used as abrasive sponges in skin care, to remove dead skin and to stimulate the circulation. The vine is most commonly grown for the fibrous interior of the fruits. It flowers from March to July and thrives in fallow fields and secondary regrowth. It is frost-tender and requires full sun and plenty of water.

Identification: An annual or perennial herbaceous climber or trailing plant up to 15m/49ft. The leaves are five-lobed, up to 15cm/6in long, with trianglaur lobes. The flowers are yellow, up to 90mm/3½in across, male and female on the same plant. The fruit develops on a thick stalk, to 60cm/24in long, with a smooth surface.

Distribution: Tropical Africa.
Height and spread: 15m x 20cm/49ft x 8in.
Habit and form: Annual/perennial herbaceous climber.
Leaf shape: Simple, lobed.
Pollinated: Insect.

Left: The flowers are large and showy, and measure 50–75mm/ 2–3in across.

Below: Sponge luffa has trailing growth.

Momordica foetida

Some *Momordica* species are grown in cultivation for their fleshy fruits, which are oblong to cylindrical in shape, orange to red in colour. It flowers from December to March and grows in grasslands with black clay soils, although it is adapted to various soil types. It is also found at forest edges, wooded grassland and alongside rivers. The ripe yellow fruit is sweet and relished by children. The related bitter melon, *M. charantia*, is widely grown for its edible (though bitter) fruit, especially in China, and is often mixed with pork in a stir-fry. In Pakistan and elsewhere it is used as a constituent of curries.

Below: The fruit is bristly.

Identification: A hairy perennial climber or creeping herb from a stout perennial rootstock, with simple or forked tendrils opposite the leaves. The young stems are spotted dark green and the foliage smells unpleasant when crushed. The leaves are heart-shaped, alternate, often unlobed. The sexes are on separate plants; the female flowers are single, and appear on long axillary stalks, with five yellow petals. The fruit is pale yellow to brilliant orange, to 65mm/2½in long, and covered with soft orange bristles. They ripen and split open into three valves that contain seeds embedded in a red, jelly-like substance.

Distribution: Tropical Africa.
Height and spread: 5m x 10cm/16ft x 4in.
Habit and form: Perennial climber.
Leaf shape: Simple.
Pollinated: Insect.

Below: The trailing shoots have tendrils that cling to surfaces.

Cucumber tree

Dendrosicyos socotrana

Distribution: Socotra.
Height and spread: To 7m/23ft.
Habit and form: Tree-like.
Leaf shape: Rounded or heart-shaped.
Pollinated: Insect.

A botanical curiosity, the cucumber tree grows only on the South Yemen island of Socotra, which lies off the Horn of Africa. It is the only member of its genus and also the only tree in the cucumber family. Thick-trunked and with a flat crown, cucumber trees stand out in the rocky slopes. Although threatened by overgrazing, they are still fairly common. Sometimes the trees are felled and pulped for feeding livestock.

Identification: A swollen succulent trunk grows to a height of about 7m/23ft, spreading out at the top into a flat crown. The branches bear clumps of rounded leaves. The flowers grow in clusters directly from the stem.

Left: The tree has a remarkable thick, succulent trunk.

Right: All flowers are yellow.

OTHER SPECIES OF NOTE

Cucumber *Cucumis sativus*
This creeping vine, the ancestor of cultivated cucumbers, is probably native to India. It has been grown for 3,000 years. The cylindrical fruit has tapering ends and may be up to 60cm/24in.

Herpetospermum pedunculosum
A large herbaceous climber with heart-shaped pointed leaves and long, branching tendrils. It ranges from Himachal Pradesh to south-western China and grows supported by other shrubs. The flowers are large and bright yellow, each with a funnel-shaped tube opening to a diameter of 40–50mm/1½–2in. The leaves are long-stalked and roughly hairy. The fruit is also hairy and about 80mm/3⅛in long.

Trichosanthes tricuspidata
A climber, with a range from Nepal and India to China and South-east Asia. The leaves are deeply lobed (up to seven lobes) and the flowers are large and white, to 80mm/3⅛in across. The leaves are heart-shaped, about 20cm/8in, and the globular fruit (which has medicinal uses) is red with orange stripes, containing seeds in a green pulp.

Nara melon *Acanthosicyos horridus*
A leafless shrub native to the coastal region of the Namib Desert. It forms a densely tangled and spreading mass that can cover up to 1,500m²/1,790yd². Heavily armed with spines 25mm/1in long, it grows where underground water is available. Its oil-rich nuts are the staple diet of some of the indigenous Namib people.

Himalayan goldencreeper

Thladiantha cordifolia

Himalayan goldencreeper is a large climber native to the Himalayan highlands, at 600–2,500m/2,000–8,200ft, from Nepal and Bhutan. It is also found through Burma and China to South-east Asia. It clambers over other plants, clinging on with simple tendrils. It flowers mainly from April to June. The large shining yellow, bell-shaped flowers contrast well with the bright green foliage.

Distribution: India; Asia.
Height and spread: To about 2m/6½ft.
Habit and form: Perennial.
Leaf shape: Ovate.
Pollinated: Insect.

Identification: The leaves are stalked, ovate and pointed at the tip, with a rounded, heart-shaped base and narrow teeth along the margins; the blade about 10–15cm/4–6in. The surface of the leaves is rough and hairy. The flowers are bright golden yellow, each about 20mm/¾in, with the petals reflexed at the tips. The male flowers grow in the axils of broad bracts, in clusters. The fruit is oblong, about 35mm/1⅜in long.

Above left: The attractive bell-shaped flowers are golden yellow.

CARNIVOROUS PLANTS

Strictly, carnivorous plants are those that attract, capture, kill and digest animals and absorb the nutrients from them. They are by no means common, but several plant families have become specialists in this way of life. There are various ways in which plants have adapted to do this. Most carnivorous plants are small or medium-size herbaceous perennials; a few are woody climbers.

Round-leaved sundew

Drosera rotundifolia

This is an unmistakable plant with a widespread distribution. It is a small, short-lived, insectivorous herbaceous perennial, most often found in acidic bogs, but also in swamps, rotting logs, mossy crevices in rocks, or damp sand along streams, lakes, or pond margins. It is generally associated with sphagnum mosses, growing on floating sphagnum mats or hummocks. The plant compensates for the low level of nutrients available in its habitat by catching and digesting insects. The prey is caught on the sticky glandular leaf hairs, and the leaf then folds around it. The hairs secrete enzymes that digest the insect and enable the plant to absorb nutrients through its leaves.

Distribution: Europe; Asia; South Africa; North and South America.
Height and spread: 50mm–15cm/2–6in.
Habit and form: Herbaceous perennial.
Leaf shape: Orbicular.
Pollinated: Insect.

Identification: The leaves form a basal rosette, with their round, depressed blades lying flat on the ground; the upper surface of each blade, 6–10mm/¼–⅜in long, is covered with reddish, glandular hairs, each tipped with a sticky, glutinous secretion resembling a dewdrop, which traps insects. The leaf stalk is 20–50mm/¾–2in long and covered with sticky hairs. One-sided racemes, one to seven per rosette, consist of 2–15 small white flowers on 50mm–15cm/2–6in stalks, which straighten out as the flowers expand in summer.

Greater bladderwort

Utricularia vulgaris

Bladderworts are carnivorous aquatic plants with delicate, finely divided underwater leaves and emergent, snapdragon-like yellow flowers. Their most distinctive underwater features are small, bladder-like traps – oval balloons with a double-sealed airtight door on one end. When the door is closed, the bladder expels water through its walls, creating a partial vacuum inside, which sucks in small invertebrates or even tiny fish that trigger the trap doors. Enzymes are secreted to digest the prey and provide the plant with nutrients. Bladderworts are most commonly found floating freely in shallow water, or loosely attached to sediment, and are widely distributed throughout Europe, North Africa and the USA.

Left and far right: Flowering stems rise above the water, while the rest of the foliage remains under the surface.

Above right: The tiny bladders capture small aquatic invertebrates.

Identification: This water-living, herbaceous plant has no true leaves or roots. Instead, it has a green, finely divided, underwater leaf-like stem with small, seed-like bladders. The branched stem is up to 2m/6½ft long and can be floating, submerged, or partly creeping on sediment, sometimes anchored at the base by root-like structures. It overwinters above the sediment layer. Yellow, snapdragon-like flowers, up to 25mm/1in wide, have a prominent spur projecting below the lower lip and faint purple-brown stripes; they are held above the water on stout stalks in late summer. The globular brown seed capsules contain many seeds. The winter bud is ovoid to ellipsoid, to 20mm/¾in long.

Distribution: Europe; North Africa; and North America.
Height and spread: 15–45cm x 2m/6–18in x 6½ft.
Habit and form: Water plant.
Leaf shape: No true leaves.
Pollinated: Insect.

OTHER SPECIES OF NOTE

Great sundew *Drosera anglica*
The great sundew is similar to the round-leaved sundew but with taller and narrower leaves, about twice as long as they are wide. It is generally found in the same habitat and range as the round-leaved sundew but is much less common.

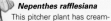

Nepenthes rafflesiana
This pitcher plant has cream-coloured traps nearly covered in dark red botches. It is distributed throughout Borneo and is an unusually variable plant, with various forms looking like completely different species. The pitchers are often visited by ants but the plant seems not to be specialized in its prey.

Drosera cistiflora
This very striking South African sundew has long, fine leaves and an erect habit, growing to 25cm/10in or more before producing several large, typically pink, flowers. There is also a giant form up to 50cm/20in tall and forms with different flower colours are known.

Roridula gorgonias
This perennial from South Africa, which grows to around 50cm/20in, is covered with sticky glands, which capture insects much as sundews do. The plants do not assimilate the nutrients from the dead insects they catch; instead, assassin bugs in the genus *Pameridea* eat the insects and their excrement is absorbed by the leaves.

Greater butterwort

Pinguicula grandiflora

Greater butterwort grows throughout much of the Northern Hemisphere. It is distinct in having one of the most striking flowers of the butterwort family (Lentibulariaceae) and superficially resembles a small African violet, *Saintpaulia* species, although they are unrelated. Greater butterwort is a small plant that grows in a rosette fashion, and has tiny transparent hairs that secrete sticky glue. There are also glands on the leaves, which are dry until an insect is captured. They then secrete acids and enzymes, which start to dissolve the insect before the same glands reabsorb the nutrient-rich fluid.

Distribution: Arctic Circle; Europe; Siberia; and North America.
Height and spread: 15cm/6in.
Habit and form: Herbaceous perennial.
Leaf shape: Obovate-oblong.
Pollinated: Insect.

Identification: The plant forms a rosette of oval to oblong, sticky, pale green leaves 30–50mm/ 1¼–2in long, with resting buds in the winter. In summer, solitary, trumpet-shaped, spurred, two-lipped, dark blue flowers, 25mm/1in across, with three widely spreading lobes and white throats, are borne on slender stems.

Pitcher plant

Nepenthes ampullaria

Distribution: Lowlands of South-east Asia.
Height and spread: Up to 20m/65½ft.
Habit and form: Woody liana.
Leaf shape: Lanceolate, sometimes ending in a pitcher.
Pollinated: Insect.

This carnivorous plant, native to swamps in the humid tropical lowlands of South-east Asia, is a woody vine that forms rosettes of trapping leaves. In its native habitat, the rosettes may arise anywhere along the vine, although in mature plants large clumps of pitchers form at the base of the climbing stem. These fill with rainwater and insects that fall into them, and drown; their decaying bodies yield nutrients absorbed by the plant.

Identification: A woody liana, with rounded, squat, deep red or green, sometimes mottled pitchers, up to 10cm/4in high, with round, horizontal mouths and narrow, reflexed lids that allow the broad pitchers to fill with rainwater. Wings on the front of the pitcher are broad, spreading and toothed. The basal traps are numerous and squat, with upper ones few and more cylindrical in shape, often with a dusty appearance due to a thick coating of fine hairs. Tiny, petal-less flowers with green-and-brown sepals are borne in spidery racemes. The shape and colour of the pitchers varies considerably according to location.

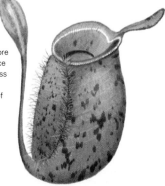

Left: Modified leaves form pitchers, which capture and digest unsuspecting insects.

PARASITIC PLANTS

When one organism 'steals' all of its food from another's body, it is called a parasite. The organism that is being robbed of its food supply is known as the host. The parasitic mode of existence can be found from bacteria and fungi to insects, mites and worms. Parasitism has also evolved in many families of flowering plants, and while many of them are quite unrelated, their lifestyle brings them together here.

Rafflesia

Rafflesia manillana

Dramatic and solitary rafflesia flowers are the largest single flowers in the world, with leathery petals that in some species can reach more than 90cm/35in across. A parasite that depends completely upon its host, the majority of the plant's tissues exist as thread-like strands entirely within vines of *Tetrastigma* species. The rafflesia plant is itself not visible until the flowers first bud through the woody vine, taking up to ten months to develop. The enormous flowers reportedly have a strong smell of rotting flesh and are believed to be pollinated by flies, although it is rarely encountered and its exact life cycle is obscure.

Identification: Only the flower ever emerges for the purposes of identification. It consists of five orange leathery petals, mottled with cream warts. There is a deep well in the centre of the flower containing a central raised disc, which supports many vertical spines. The sexual organs are located beneath the rim of the disc, and male and female flowers are separate. *R. manillana* has a flower 15–20cm/6–8in in diameter; it is the smallest of all rafflesia species.

Distribution: South-east Asia.
Height and spread: 15–20cm/6–8in (flower only).
Habit and form: Internal parasite.
Leaf shape: Absent.
Pollinated: Fly.

Cytinus hypocistis

This parasitic plant, found in Mediterranean forest and coastal scrub, lives on a shrub, the sage-leaved rock rose, *Cistus salviifolius*. Like many other parasites, it takes all its nourishment from the roots of its host and so has no need of leaves or other conventional green plant parts. It reveals itself only at flowering time, when its tight clusters of small very showy flowers erupt from the ground beneath the host plant.

Identification: Orange-and-yellow unisexual flowers are borne singly or in clusters of five to 10 at the apex of the flower spike in an umbellate pattern, appearing in spring to early summer. They are subtended by (usually) two bracts and have four bright yellow petaloid sepals, up to 12mm/½in long. The short flower stem is covered with yellow, orange or bright red, densely overlapping scales, resulting from vestigial leaves. Due to their low-growing nature, the flowers can often be hidden by leaf litter.

Distribution: Mediterranean; North Africa; Turkey.
Height and spread: 40–80mm/1½–3⅛in (flower only).
Habit and form: Internal parasite.
Leaf shape: Vestigial scales.
Pollinated: Insect.

Left: The tight clusters of showy flowers are the only part of this plant that may be seen above ground.

European mistletoe

Viscum album

*Far right: European mistletoe lives
on many deciduous tree species,
particularly fruit trees such as apple,
and lime, poplar and oak.*

Centuries of superstition and belief are attached to
mistletoe, and the tradition of "kissing under the
mistletoe" has persisted for many years. It is a partial or
hemi-parasite, relying on a host tree to provide it with a growing
platform and some nutrients, though it does have chlorophyll in
its leaves and can manufacture some food for itself through
photosynthesis. The generic name *Viscum* refers
to the stickiness of the seeds, a property
essential to the plant's propagation method,
as its seed must stick to the trunk of its
host long enough to germinate and
insert a root into the bark.

Identification: The leaves, borne on
repeatedly forked branches, are
evergreen and elliptical in shape. Male and female flowers are borne
on separate plants, with the flowers of both sexes produced in the
forks of the branches. Males flower between late winter and mid-spring,
producing small clusters of blooms with four petals; the female plants
produce sticky white berries in autumn.

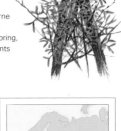

OTHER SPECIES OF NOTE

Red-berried mistletoe *Viscum cruciatum*
A native of the Mediterranean, the red-berried
mistletoe, although closely allied to *V. album*,
prefers a warmer and drier climate. It is very
similar in shape and form to *V. album* and grows
on a range of deciduous trees, especially olives.

Toothwort *Lathraea squamaria*
Also known as corpse flower, this
is a perennial parasitic plant, up to
20cm/8in tall, with a pinkish-cream
stem and scale-like, fleshy leaves,
said to resemble pointed teeth.
Flower spikes with cylindrical,
half-nodding, pink flowers on one
side appear in copses and shady
places in spring.

Common dodder *Cuscuta epithymum*
This small parasitic plant, containing no
chlorophyll, appears as a mass of tiny, red strings
all over gorse, *Ulex* species, *Thymus* species, or
other low-growing plants that act as its host.
Small spherical bunches of little pale pink
flowers appear in summer. Seeds sprout in the
soil, but wither once it attaches to its host.

Loxanthera speciosa
This unusual, large, woody shrub, with branches
to more than 3m/10ft, is an aerial hemi-parasite,
with large, red-and-white tubular flowers. It
grows in forests in Malaysia, Sumatra, Java and
Borneo, on host trees such as the tiup tiup,
Adinandra dumosa, and several *Ficus* species,
between sea level and 850m/2,800ft.

Purple toothwort

Lathraea clandestina

This spreading perennial, found in the damp
woods and streamside meadows of south-
western Europe, grows as a parasite on the
roots of willow, alder and poplar trees. The
plant does not produce true leaves but
vestigial leaves still occur in the form of
fleshy scales on the rhizomes. The purple
flowers, which appear in spring, are the only
parts visible above ground, but colonies of
the plant may have an indefinite spread. It is
found widely in temperate
regions, having been
imported with
garden trees.

Identification: A parasitic,
rhizomatous perennial,
with opposite, kidney-
shaped, stem-clasping,
scale-like white leaves,
5mm/³⁄₁₆in long. Dense
racemes of between
four and eight hooded,
tubular, two-lipped
mauve flowers, to
30mm/1¼in long, are
borne just above the
ground in early and
mid-spring.

*Right: The mauve flowers
are showy with an upper
lip that has a hooded
shape.*

*Below: The flowers that
appear in spring are the
only visible parts, but
colonies may be quite
extensive.*

DUCKWEED AND ARUM FAMILIES

The duckweed family, Lemnaceae, contains mostly perennial, aquatic, floating and submerged herbs that are reduced to small green bodies. The arum family, Araceae, consists of rhizomatous or tuberous herbaceous perennials. Its members are characterized by an inflorescence that is a fleshy spadix partially enveloped by a bract or spathe that is sometimes brightly coloured.

Lesser duckweed

Lemna minor

This tiny, floating, aquatic perennial, which often forms a seemingly solid cover on the water surface, is made up of many tiny individual plants. It is widespread throughout the temperate regions of the Northern Hemisphere, including North America and Eurasia. It is absent only from polar areas and the tropics. It occurs chiefly in freshwater ponds, marshes, lakes and quiet streams. It is able to spread most rapidly across quiet bodies of water that are rich in nutrients, such as nitrogen and phosphate. Flowering duckweeds are uncommon.

Below: Lesser duckweed seems to form a blanket over water.

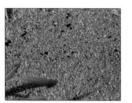

Identification: The tiny individual plants may be up to 15mm/⁹⁄₁₆in across, but are usually 2–4mm/¹⁄₁₆–³⁄₁₆in. Their leaves and stems are merged in a simple, three-lobed plant body, typically called a frond or 'thallus', though neither term is botanically precise. The frond consists of one to several layers of conspicuous air spaces and one to several veins. It is flattened, round to elliptic-oval in outline, generally symmetrical, with a smooth upper surface. A single root hangs down in the water.

Distribution: Temperate areas worldwide.
Height and spread: Unlimited spread over suitable water habitat.
Habit and form: Floating aquatic perennial.
Leaf shape: Rounded.
Pollinated: None.

Right: The flowers are microscopic.

Left: The small fronds form a dense floating mass.

Dragon arum

Voodoo lily, *Dracunculus vulgaris*

This bizarre plant, unique to the Mediterranean region, is reminiscent of an arum lily. It can be found growing in well-drained soils and full sun. It produces a spathe that, as it unfurls, reveals a slender, black central appendage, the spadix, which can reach 25cm–1.35m/ 10in–4½ft in length. The actual flowers, both male and female, are hidden deep inside the spathe, which features a bulbous chamber. It relies on flies and other insects for pollination and therefore emits a putrid smell, like dung and carrion, to attract them.

Identification: Unmistakable by sight or smell, this tuberous perennial with foot-shaped or spear-shaped, dark green basal leaves, 30cm/12in or more long, has a stem marked purple-brown. In spring or summer, foul-smelling, maroon-purple spathes, 60cm–1m/24–39in long, with erect, almost black spadices, are borne above the leaves, attracting large numbers of beetles and flies, which become trapped in the spathe chamber.

Left: The flowering stem is a dramatic sight once the bloom opens.

Distribution: Southern Europe to Turkey.
Height and spread: Up to 1.8m/6ft.
Habit and form: Herbaceous perennial.
Leaf shape: Pedate or hastate.
Pollinated: Insect.

Left: Clusters of fruit surround the remains of the flower spike.

White arum lily

Calla lily, *Zantedeschia aethiopica*

This plant is neither an arum (genus *Arum*) nor a lily (genus *Lilium*). It was introduced to Europe in the 17th century, and has naturalized in almost all parts of the world. The striking flower is made up of many tiny flowers arranged in a complex spiral pattern on the central spadix, the top 75mm/3in of which are male flowers with the lower 20mm/¾in being female. The whiteness of the spathe is caused by an optical effect produced by numerous airspaces beneath the epidermis. Its flowering season depends upon its location; plants in the Western Cape are dormant in summer, while in the eastern summer rainfall areas the species is dormant in winter, although it remains evergreen if growing in marshy conditions that are wet all year round.

Distribution: South Africa.
Height and spread: 90cm/35in.
Habit and form: Herbaceous perennial.
Leaf shape: Sagittate.
Pollinated: Insect.

Left: The foliage forms a clump in wet soil.

Identification: A clump-forming, rhizomatous, usually evergreen perennial, it has semi-erect, arrow-shaped, glossy bright green leaves up to 40cm/16in long. Flowers are borne in succession, and are large, pure white spathes, to 25cm/10in long, with creamy-yellow spadices. The spathe turns green after flowering and covers the ripening, succulent yellow berries.

Left: The white flowers are extremely striking.

Cobra lily

Arisaema candidissimum

This tuberous perennial from China is found on stony slopes and in open pine forests, in full sun, on dry, rocky, south-facing slopes. Cobra lilies emerge in late spring with stalks of pink pitcher flowers, which are striped with translucent, white, vertical veins. The central flower spike is male or female, with the tip slightly bent. Alongside the flower emerges a three-lobed leaf, which can reach up to 60cm/24in wide.

Identification: In summer the plant bears a conspicuous, sweetly scented, pink-striped white spathe, striped green on the outside, 75mm–15cm/3–6in long with a hooked, downward-curling tip. The inflorescence is up to 12.5cm/5in tall, depending upon habitat. A solitary, three-palmate, mid- to deep green leaf, very thick and leathery, with broadly oval leaflets, each 10–25cm/4–10in long and almost as broad, appears on a leaf stalk up to 35cm/14in tall, only after the spathe emerges.

Distribution: Chinese Himalayas.
Height and spread: 40cm/16in.
Habit and form: Herbaceous perennial.
Leaf shape: Palmate.
Pollinated: Insect.

Right: The greenish exterior of the flower belies the candy-striped interior.

Below: The single, large tri-lobed leaf appears only after the flower bud has emerged.

BANANA, STRELITZIA AND GINGER FAMILIES

The banana family, or Musaceae, contains large, often tree-like herbaceous perennials. Closely allied to this family are the Strelitziaceae, native to tropical south-eastern Africa and Madagascar. Zingiberaceae, or ginger, is a family of herbaceous perennials, mostly with creeping horizontal or tuberous rhizomes.

Abyssinian banana

Wild banana, Red banana, *Ensete ventricosum*

Often wrongly described as trees, bananas are, in fact, giant herbaceous plants. The "trunk" (technically a pseudostem) is made up of a series of tightly wrapped leaf sheaths. Each pseudostem grows from a bud on the true stem, which is an underground rhizome. Leaves emerge through the centre of the pseudostem and expand at the top to form large, glossy, oval blades, up to 4 x 1m/13ft x 39in in size. *E. ventricosum*, is a relative of the edible bananas, *Musa* species, and is a highly variable species with a large African range. The fruit is not eaten except in times of scarcity, but the young flowers are palatable when cooked.

Identification: The plant, though herbaceous, is tall and tree-like, with a pseudostem up to 5m/16ft, often variably stained purple, with whitish latex that reddens on exposure to air. The oblong- to lance-shaped leaves are borne on short stalks in a banana-like crown, erect or spreading, bright yellow-green or variably stained with red-brown, more or less glaucous beneath. The midribs are green, red or purple-brown. A drooping inflorescence bears a massive male bud. Mature fruits are banana-like but dry, bright yellow or yellow-orange with orange pulp. It seldom forms suckers from the base (as in other species) and is monocarpic.

Distribution: Africa.
Height and spread: 4–12m/13–39ft.
Habit and form: Tall herbaceous but tree-like plant.
Leaf shape: Oblong-lanceolate.
Pollinated: Insect.

Left: flowerheads appear when plants are about eight years old.

Bird of paradise

Crane flower, *Strelitzia reginae*

Possibly one of the best-known plants in the world, the strelitzia's fascinating blooms are sold as cut flowers by the million and this popularity has led them to be grown in gardens worldwide. *S. reginae* is, however, indigenous to South Africa, where it grows wild in the Eastern Cape, between other shrubs along the riverbanks and in clearings in the coastal bush. Mature plants can form large clumps in favourable conditions and are very floriferous, with flowers in autumn, winter and spring. When birds visit the flowers to help themselves to nectar, the petals open and cover their feet in pollen.

Identification: A large, clump-forming, nearly stemless evergreen perennial, with erect, oblong to lance-shaped stiff grey-green leaves with pointed or rounded tips, sometimes with a shallow notch at the end, to around 90cm/35in long. The flowers, borne on long, sheathed stalks, emerge from a glaucous, horizontal spathe about 12.5cm/5in long, green flushed purple and orange; the flowers are about 10cm/4in long, with orange sepals and blue, narrowly arrow-shaped petals, with rounded basal lobes.

Distribution: South Africa.
Height and spread: Up to 2m/6½ft.
Habit and form: Stemless evergreen perennial.
Leaf shape: Oblong-lanceoleate.
Pollinated: Bird.

Left: Large clumps of leafy growth appear from the underground stems.

Dwarf Savanna ginger lily

Costus spectabilis

Distribution: Tropical Africa.
Height and spread:
10cm/4in.
Habit and form:
Rhizomatous perennial.
Leaf shape: Ovate-lanceolate.
Pollinated: Insect.

Costus is a large genus with more than 100 species distributed in the tropical rainforests, mainly in Africa and South America. The dwarf savanna ginger lily, found in humid or semi-humid savannas all over tropical Africa, from Senegal to the eastern coastal zones, has one of the largest blooms of all, the showy yellow flowers being highly visible during the flowering period. The plant can easily be missed when not in flower, however, as it is a low, ground-hugging species. The plants remain naturally dormant and inconspicuous during the dry season, and flowering does not occur until after the traditional burning of grassland at the beginning of the rainy season.

Identification:
A rhizomatous perennial, largely stemless above the ground. The long snake-like rhizomes grow during the dry season and give rise to four-leaved spiral rosettes, that are flat on the ground. The leaves are pale green with red edges, obovate-cuneate, smooth above, downy below and cupped. Three to four bright yellow or bright orange flowers, located terminally, appear at the centre of the rosette. The fruit is a membranous capsule crowned by a persistent calyx.

OTHER SPECIES OF NOTE

Japanese banana *Musa basjoo*
Despite its name, the Japanese banana is a medium-size species from China, growing to about 2.5m/8ft tall before flowering, though it may become considerably taller with age. The leaves are bright, light green, sometimes with a reddish flush to the underside.

Aframomum sceptrum
Generally restricted to deep forest habitats in West Africa, the Congo and Angola, the 30cm/12in inflorescences of this species arise at the base of, or independently some distance away from, the tall and leafy shoots, clothed in 25cm/10in long sheathing leaves.

Ginger *Zingiber officinale*

Ginger is a herb indigenous to South-east Asia, although it is widely cultivated in the USA, India, China, West Indies and tropical regions. The plant is a creeping perennial on a thick tuberous rhizome, with narrow, deciduous lance-shaped leaves and a long, curved spike of white or yellow flowers.

Cardamom *Elettaria cardamomum*
Common in southern India and Sri Lanka, cardamom is a perennial plant. The simple, erect stems grow to 3m/10ft from a thumb-thick, creeping rootstock. The small, yellowish flowers, which grow on prostrate stems, are followed by the capsules, which are used as a culinary spice.

Green ripple peacock ginger

Kaempferia elegans

This plant is native to areas of Thailand, East Bengal, Burma and those parts of the Malay Peninsula with pronounced dry seasons, and is naturally deciduous. All *Kaempferia* species tend to be short, unlike many other plants in the Zingiberaceae. They are most notable for their foliage, which is often patterned and multicoloured, resulting in the common name of peacock ginger. The flowers, although usually inconspicuous, are a very pretty lilac. All the aerial parts die down in the dry season; the plant vegetates solely during the wet season.

Distribution: Southern Asia.
Height and spread: 15–20 x 30cm/6–8 x 12in.
Habit and form: Deciduous, rhizomatous herb.
Leaf shape: Oblong or elliptic.
Pollinated: Insect.

Identification: A low-growing, deciduous, rhizomatous herb. The smooth leaves are oblong or elliptic, broad and wavy, up to 15cm/6in long, with a pointed tip and rounded base, on short stalks. Lilac flowers with 50mm/2in green bracts appear almost daily amid the leaves during the summer months.

IRIS FAMILY

The iris family, Iridaceae, comprises herbaceous perennials growing from rhizomes, bulbs or corms and occurring in tropical and temperate regions, particularly around the Mediterranean, in South Africa and Central America. The flowers are single and almost stemless (as in Crocus), or occur as spikes at the top of branched or unbranched stems, each with six petals in two rings of three. Many are ornamental.

Yellow flag

Iris pseudacorus

A robust plant with beautiful, bright yellow flowers that occurs throughout much of Europe, North Africa, western Asia and the Caucasus. It has become widely naturalized outside its original range, as a garden escapee. It is common in wet habitats, including meadows, woods, fens, wet dune-slacks, and the edges of watercourses, lakes and ponds. In some areas it may also be found alongside coastal streams, on raised beaches, in saltmarsh and shingle.

Identification: An extremely vigorous, rhizomatous, beardless water iris. The 90cm/35in leaves are ribbed, with an especially prominent midrib, grey-green, broad, flat, sword-shaped and stalkless, with several bound together into a sheath at the base. In mid- and late summer, each branched, flattened stem bears four to seven showy flowers, 75mm–10cm/3–4in across, from very large pointed buds. The petals are yellow with brown or violet markings and a darker yellow zone on each fall. The roots are thick and fleshy, brownish on the outside, reddish and spongy within, pushing through moist ground parallel to the surface, with many rootlets passing downwards.

Distribution: Europe; northern Africa; western Asia; and the Caucasus.
Height and spread: 90cm/35in.
Habit and form: Rhizomatous perennial.
Leaf shape: Linear-lanceolate.
Pollinated: Bee.

Left: The tall flower spikes are often seen beside water among other vegetation.

Right: The seedpod.

Stinking iris

Roast beef plant, *Iris foetidissima*

Stinking iris is a medium tough plant that forms dense clumps of evergreen leaves that have a strong and unpleasant smell when crushed. It is widely cultivated because of its spectacular fruits in green capsules, turning brown during the winter to reveal bright red seeds, as much as for its flowers. The flowers open from May to July. This plant likes chalky soil and prefers open woodland, scrub and hedgerows and occasionally sand dunes.

Right: The fruit splits to release its bright red seeds.

Identification: An upright plant with an underground stem and long, shiny, dark green leaves with numerous parallel veins. Its flowers, 50–70mm/2–2¾in across, are dull violet tinged with yellow and with darker veins on the falls. Its purplish flowers have three petal-like segments (tepals) and also have three large yellowish styles.

Right: Like others of its genus, this iris forms a mass of sword-like leaves.

Distribution: Great Britain; France; Iberian Peninsula (not Balearic Islands); north-western Africa; Italy; and Sicily.
Height and spread: 50–60cm/20–24in.
Habit and form: Herbaceous (rhizomatous) perennial.
Leaf shape: Sword-shaped, pointed.
Pollinated: Insect.

Butterfly iris

Iris spuria

This medium to tall plant grows in damp places, usually in marshy areas or near the sea. Its attractive flowers blossom between May and July. The *spurias* are much used by garden designers because of their slender and elongated leaves, which look attractive in the garden all the year around. The species is widely cultivated and hybridized for use in the garden, with a number of varieties available.

Distribution: Europe; north-western Africa; and Asia.
Height and spread: 40–80cm/16–31in.
Habit and form: Rhizomatous perennial.
Leaf shape: Sword-shaped.
Pollinated: Insect.

Identification: The grey-green leaves are erect and tough, and the spathes are green, similar to the leaves but shorter. The flowers develop on tall stems in groups of two to four, are relatively small, grey-blue or lilac in colour, with darker veins and a yellow strip in the centre of the falls.

Left: Irises grow from rhizomes that sit just at soil level.

Iris lortetii
This extremely showy iris is found in Israel, Syria and northern Iraq, in areas where the rainy season is short and drought may occur for extended periods. It is 30–50cm/12–20in tall, with white flowers veined and dotted pink or maroon, deep maroon signals and mauve falls, speckled brownish-red.

Siberian iris *Iris sibirica*
This elegant non-bearded iris, forms clumps of narrow, grassy leaves, from which arise long, thin stems, with small groups of flowers, borne in late spring or early summer. The petals are bluish or whitish, with darker veins. This species is native to eastern and central Europe and northern Asia. It is widely grown in gardens, in the form of many hybrids, because of its attractive foliage and flowers.

Stool iris *Iris aphylla*
This is a short species, never taller than 30cm/12in. This bearded slender iris has stems branched below the middle, and curved lower leaves. It usually has three to five flowers of a beautiful dark purple colour, which blossom from April to May. Originating from eastern and central Europe, it is grown in gardens in cultivated forms. The genus *Iris* takes its name from the Greek word for a rainbow, referring to the wide variety of flower colours found among the many species.

Garden iris

Bearded iris, German iris, *Iris germanica*

This bearded iris is very robust with a branched stem arising from a thick rhizome. It grows in the wild in rocky, dry and grassy places. Although this species has become naturalized in many places, it is widely planted, with many cultivated varieties. It is a characteristic plant of cemeteries and also grows on wasteland and rubbish tips. One variety of this species yields 'orris root', used in the perfume industry.

Identification: The broad leaves are shorter than the flower stem; and the bracts, below each flower group, are green at the base and dry and rusty at the top. The fragrant flowers are large, 10cm/4in across, bluish-violet with a conspicuous yellow beard, and they appear in groups of two or three. They are typical iris flowers, with three outer tepals called 'falls', alternating with three inner petals, called 'standards'.

Distribution: Mainly western Europe and the Mediterranean region; widely naturalized.
Height and spread: 60cm–1m/24–39in.
Habit and form: Rhizomatous perennial.
Leaf shape: Sword-shaped.
Pollinated: Insect.

Below: Shoots emerge from the rhizome.

Left: This iris produces tall flowering stems.

Wild gladiolus

Gladiolus illyricus

The wild form of our garden gladiolus is a medium-size perennial plant with grass-like leaves, easily overlooked when it is not in flower. The commonly called 'glads' are cultivated in a wide range of colours, sizes and flower types, making them particularly useful for flower arrangements. The corm or bulb is a food-storage structure well adapted to the dry season of the Mediterranean area. It is similar to the field gladiolus, *Gladiolus italicus*, but is usually shorter and with fewer flowers per spike. It grows in stony pastures, maquis, and open woods. It flowers between April and June.

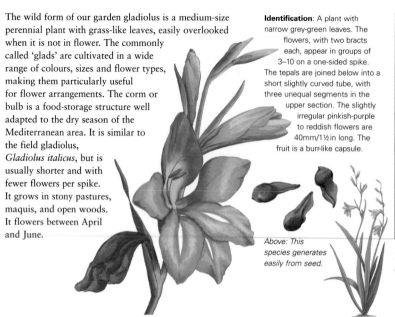

Identification: A plant with narrow grey-green leaves. The flowers, with two bracts each, appear in groups of 3–10 on a one-sided spike. The tepals are joined below into a short slightly curved tube, with three unequal segments in the upper section. The slightly irregular pinkish-purple to reddish flowers are 40mm/1½in long. The fruit is a burr-like capsule.

Above: This species generates easily from seed.

Distribution: Southern and western Europe to Asia; rare in south England.
Height and spread: 20–60cm/8–24in.
Habit and form: Herbaceous perennial.
Leaf shape: Narrow and lanceolate.
Pollinated: Insect.

Left: Tall flowering stems rise above the sword-like leaves

Field gladiolus

Gladiolus italicus

This is the common gladiolus in Mediterranean Europe, and it is also sold occasionally as cut flowers. It is a medium to tall plant arising from a globular corm covered in thick fibres. It frequents cultivated land (such as cereal fields), often in large numbers, and also grows in wasteland, on roadsides and hill slopes, and occasionally on garrigue. The attractive flowers appear from April to June.

Distribution: Southern Europe.
Height and spread: 40–80cm/16–31in
Habit and form: Herbaceous perennial.
Pollinated: Insect.
Leaf shape: Sword-shaped.

Identification: It is very similar to the wild gladiolus. *G. illyricus*, but its leaf bases are sometimes reddish-tinged, and often white-spotted. The reddish-purple flowers, 6–15 per spike, have upper tepals (perianth segments) broader and separated from the others, and the lowest bract is longer than the flowers. The seeds of its capsule fruit are not winged.

Right: The flowers appear on one side of the stem in a tall spike.

Waterfall gladiolus

New Year lily, *Gladiolus cardinalis*

Distribution: South Africa.
Height and spread:
40–90cm/16–35in.
Habit and form: Cormous
perennial.
Leaf shape: Linear-lanceolate.
Pollinated: Insect.

Right: The plant has strap-like leaves.

Far right: The tall flower stems are clothed in large flowers that are red.

The genus *Gladiolus* comprises about 180 species of cormous perennials that originate mainly in South Africa but also in western and central Europe, central Asia, north-west and east Africa. This species from South Africa, known as the waterfall gladiolus, is often found growing under waterfalls and, as its other common name suggests, is in bloom there in December to January, although it is now thought to be virtually extinct in the wild. The plant that is grown as a cultivated form is not the true species, but the result of cross-breeding.

Identification: A cormous perennial with flattened corms and narrow to broadly sword-shaped leaves produced in fan-like tufts. In summer, arching, one-sided spikes bear up to 12 widely funnel-shaped, bright red flowers, 50mm/2in across, with white patches in the lip tepals. Each flower has six tepals: usually one central upper tepal, three smaller lower or lip tepals and two side or wing tepals. Flowers open from the base of the spike, with the older flowers dying as new ones develop and open.

OTHER SPECIES OF NOTE

Table Mountain watsonia *Watsonia tabularis*
Native to the Western Cape, this plant bears striking stalks, 1.2–1.5m/4–5ft tall, of arching, goblet-shaped blooms, in a range of colours, from deep rose to salmon-orange, that appear between late spring and midsummer and are especially abundant the season after a fire.

Iris kumaonensis
Native to the western Himalayas, at altitudes of 2,400–5,500m/7,800–18,000ft, this iris has leaves 45cm/18in long and 12mm/½in wide, although at flowering time in the spring they are only 10–15cm/4–6in long around the large, pink-purple-veined flowers.

Iris lactea
This iris grows wild in central Asia and from Pakistan to Tibet, typically in cultivated areas such as around the edges of fields and alongside irrigation channels, normally at 1,500–3,300m/4,900–10,800ft. It flowers from April to June. The flowers are bluish-purple and the spathes are narrow and green, with a papery edge. The leaves are linear and grey-green.

Iris milesii
An iris of coniferous woodland and clearings, this Himalayan species has a branching inflorescence with large, showy mauve flowers marked with dark veins and spots. Each flower is up to 80mm/3⅛in across. The standards are large and spreading with a crinkly appearance.

River lily

Hesperantha coccinea

Once known as *Schizostylis coccinea*, this handsome plant from Transkei, South Africa, reaches 60–90cm/24–35in tall, with flowers borne in profusion in autumn. The name *Hesperantha* means 'evening flower', and the genus comprises 65 species, which are distributed through both the summer and winter rainfall areas of South Africa. The river lily is a species from the summer rainfall area and is widely distributed through the eastern provinces of the country, found chiefly along river edges and in water meadows, growing in full sun. The flowers are pollinated by butterflies and flies.

Identification: This vigorous, evergreen, clump-forming, rhizomatous perennial has erect, keeled, narrow sword-shaped leaves, up to 40cm/16in long, with distinct midribs. Spikes of 4–14 open, cup-shaped, scarlet flowers, 20mm/¾in across, on a one-sided, 60cm/24in spike, opening from the base upwards, are produced in late summer and autumn. There are also pink and white forms.

Distribution: Transkei, South Africa.
Height and spread: 60–90 x 60cm/24–35 x 24in.
Habit and form: Rhizomatous perennial.
Leaf shape: Linear-lanceolate.
Pollinated: *Aerpetes* butterfly and proboscid fly.

Below: The star-like, scarlet flowers are borne on tall spikes in late summer.

Peacock iris

Moraea tulbaghensis

The genus *Moraea* is native to South Africa, notably in grassland, savanna, fynbos and shrublands. This species (and several others) is threatened in its native range, as its habitat has been disturbed or destroyed. It grows on rich clay soils in the Western Cape, but only scattered fragments of the original vegetation remain. Peacock irises are valued as unusual and attractive garden flowers.

Far right: The flowers have attractive 'eyespots' and are either brick red or bright orange in colour.

Right: This iris is winter-flowering and is not often seen in the wild. However, it has been cultivated successfully.

Identification: It has three large spreading tepals, marked towards the base with bright patches, often with a shiny peacock-like eyespot, hence the common name. These markings presumably act as nectar guides for visiting insects. This species has bright orange-yellow tepals with large, blue spots at the base. Each flowering stem usually has two or three flowers.

Distribution: South Africa.
Height and spread: 45cm/18in.
Habit and form: Herbaceous perennial.
Leaf shape: Linear.
Pollinated: Insect.

Crocus vernus ssp. *albiflorus*

This form of *Crocus vernus* is the smaller, high mountain plant, often seen in spring to midsummer in the Alps and the Pyrenees, although the species may be found more widely in central and southern Europe. It is restricted to mountain turf in areas where there is a decidedly cold winter and a short alpine summer, with snow cover persisting until well into spring, and it can often be seen flowering as the snow melts in spring or summer. The flower is commonly white but can also be purple or striped. It rarely hybridizes with the other subspecies *C. vernus* ssp. *vernus*, even when populations overlap, as both occupy different habitats.

Identification: An herbaceous corm that, in time, forms extensive colonies. Dull, green, semi-erect to linear-lance-shaped leaves, with pale silvery-green central stripes, appearing in spring at the same time as the flowers, can be glabrous or pubescent; they elongate markedly as the flowers fade. The single white, goblet-shaped flowers, varying from pure white to being marked with purple, have a yellow style and anthers.

Distribution: Mediterranean, Balkans; south-western Asia.
Height and spread: 70mm–15cm/2¾–6in.
Habit and form: Herbaceous corm.
Leaf shape: Linear-lanceolate.
Pollinated: Insect.

Left and far left: The white flowers of this subspecies are borne singly at the same time as the leaves.

Right: Flowers may be white or can be marked with purple.

Montbretia

Crocosmia x crocosmiflora

This hybrid arose from two species native to South Africa – *Crocosmia aurea* and *C. pottsii*. It is a vigorous plant that is often grown in gardens, and it has become well established in western Europe, notably in western France, western England and western Ireland where it thrives locally especially in damp climates, often near the coast. Often seen alongside hedges or stone walls, and near rivers and on wasteland. It is a variable hybrid, and gardeners have selected many cultivars. It dies down in winter and regrows from its circular, flattened, corms in spring.

Distribution: Derived from South African species; widespread as a naturalized plant.
Height and spread: 80cm/31in.
Habit and form: Herbaceous perennial.
Leaf shape: Sword-shaped, narrow.
Pollinated: Insect.

Below:
The flowering
tips are long.

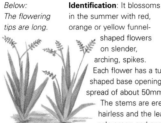

Identification: It blossoms in the summer with red, orange or yellow funnel-shaped flowers on slender, arching, spikes. Each flower has a tube-shaped base opening to a spread of about 50mm/2in. The stems are erect and hairless and the leaves pale green and narrow.

Above: The plants have arched flower spikes.

OTHER SPECIES OF NOTE

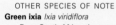

Green ixia *Ixia viridiflora*
From South Africa, the green ixia is one of the taller ixias, with upright, narrow, grass-like leaves, 40–55cm/16–22in long, surrounding a lax, many-flowered spike up to 90cm/35in tall. Each flower is a brilliant turquoise-green with a conspicuous purple-black, circular stain or 'eye' in the middle.

Ixia *Ixia paniculata*
A tall and slender plant, with a usually branched inflorescence of 5–18 flowers. The cream-coloured flowers have a very long, characteristic, often pale yellow tube. It flowers from September until December. It is native to the Cape region of South Africa and is widely cultivated.

Sand crocus *Romulea columnae*
Flowering in late winter and early spring, the tiny sand crocus has a rosette of deep green basal leaves. It is common in grassy and sandy habitats near the sea and on dry banks in western Europe and the Mediterranean. It is a rare species of south-western England and is common in the Channel Islands. Its crocus-like flowers are small, pale lilac or purplish with darker veins, and they are open only in full sunlight. It has a very short stem and in the ground a small corm. The flowers of this miniature crocus measure about 10mm/⅜in across, and because the flower stems are short, they are often overlooked, especially in cloudy weather when they do not open fully.

Autumn crocus

Crocus nudiflorus

The name 'crocus' is derived from the Greek, 'krokos', meaning saffron or saffron yellow, and the common name of the species, autumn crocus, is often also used for *Colchicum autumnale*, from the lily family. This crocus grows on meadows and pastures in northern and central Spain, up to about 2000m/6,500ft, but is naturalized elsewhere, including in Great Britain, especially in the north-west of England. The flowers appear from September to November. It grows in a wide range of habitats, including woodland, scrub and meadows, and spreads to form patches of purple flowers. The spice saffron is produced from the styles and stigmas of another crocus, *C. sativus*, a form unknown in the wild.

Below: Autumn crocus has a grassland habitat.

Distribution: South-western France; northern and eastern Spain; naturalized elsewhere.
Height and spread: 18cm/7in.
Habit and form: Herbaceous perennial.
Leaf shape: Linear.
Pollinated: Insect.

Left: The flowers are attractive.

Identification: This is a low to short cormous plant producing stolons, spreading to form patches. The green grass-like leaves, three to four from each corm, with a white central stripe, appear after flowering in the late winter. The flowers are deep purple to lilac, veined on the outside, with very long tepal-tubes and with a white to lilac throat. The stigmas have bright yellow anthers.

AMARYLLIS FAMILY

The Amaryllidaceae, or amaryllis family, comprise herbaceous perennials. It contains 50 genera and 870 species, which are found mainly in South Africa. Some also grow in South America and in the Mediterranean. The flower usually consists of six distinct or fused petaloid tepals, often with only a single flower on each stalk. Many species in this family have spectacular flowers.

Daffodil

Lenten lily, *Narcissus pseudonarcissus*

The wild daffodil is native to moist shady sites in western Europe at altitudes below 200m/650ft in light woodland. Its presence is generally considered to be a good indicator that the woodland is ancient. Cultivated daffodils are widespread in gardens and elsewhere but the distribution of wild populations is patchy, although where they do grow they tend to be abundant and make a fine display in spring.

Right: Plants produce seed but spread mainly through offsets.

Left: Older bulbs form clumps as they become established.

Identification: Thick, linear, mid-green, grass-like leaves, up to 20cm/8in high, appear at the same time as the flowers. The pale yellow flowers are usually solitary, held horizontally, and consist of six similar, yellow or white spreading perianth segments and a tubular golden-yellow corolla. Cultivated varieties of this species are widely planted and are naturalized in the wild, so distinguishing true wild populations can be difficult. The native plants always have a darker yellow flower tube and slightly twisted tepals, and the flowers are generally smaller and more nodding than in cultivated varieties.

Distribution: Western Europe.
Height and spread: 30cm/12in.
Habit and form: Deciduous bulbous perennial.
Leaf shape: Linear.
Pollinated: Insect.

Autumn narcissus

Small pheasant's-eye narcissus, *Narcissus serotinus*

This short and slender bulbous plant often grows in groups in dry habitats, such as on stony hillsides, and among rocks. It is native to the European Mediterranean region. It is an autumn-flowering species, from September to December, the flowers appearing before the leaves. The species name *serotinus* means 'late'. This species is quite popular as a garden plant, and does well in regions with mild winters. Otherwise, it does best in a cool greenhouse or alpine house.

Abovet: The fruit capsule contains quantities of tiny black seeds.

Identification: It produces one or two bluish-green linear leaves, which appear in the spring. The flowers have six white tepals and a golden-yellow, short, central lobed corona. The perianth tube is greenish. The flowers are either solitary, or sometimes paired, or with up to five on a stem, and they are strongly scented.

Distribution: Mainly western Europe (Mediterranean region); and North Africa.
Height and spread: 10–25cm/4–10in.
Habit and form: Bulbous perennial.
Leaf shape: Narrow.
Pollinated: Insect.

Left: When left to naturalize, autumn narcissus grows in clumps.

Poet's narcissus

Pheasant's-eye narcissus, *Narcissus poeticus*

In the wild this medium height daffodil grows in mountain meadows and deciduous woods, but it is frequently grown as an ornamental plant. It is a variable species that sometimes appears in large numbers covering fields in white. The bulbs flower in early summer, from April to June, and the flowers have a very sweet perfume.

Distribution: Southern Europe; naturalized in Britain; Belgium; and Germany.
Height and spread: 20–50cm/8–20in.
Habit and form: Bulbous perennial.
Leaf shape: Basal linear leaves.
Pollinated: Insect.

Below: Bulbs each produce several flowers and leaves and over time multiply to become clump-forming.

Identification: This daffodil has three to five bluish-green linear, flat leaves with a similar length to the stem. Its scented, nodding flowers are usually solitary with a small yellow corona with a red or brownish narrow curly rim. It has six white elliptic tepals, often slightly twisted.

Right: Seeds can be propagated but will take several years to flower.

OTHER SPECIES OF NOTE

Hoop-petticoat daffodil
Narcissus bulbocodium
This diminutive narcissus occurs naturally in Spain, Portugal, south-west France and Africa, and is commonly known as the hoop-petticoat daffodil because of the shape of its flowers. It is found on wet moors, meadows and marshes up to 1,000m/3,200ft, flowering in early to mid-spring.

Winter daffodil *Sternbergia lutea*
With flowers up to 50mm/2in long and often as wide, of bright clear yellow, this species has long been a garden favourite, a fact that has contributed to its depletion in the wild. It once grew wild in Mediterranean regions, from Spain to Iran and into Russia, but is now much reduced in number.

Bunch-flowered daffodil *Narcissus tazetta*
A medium-size hairless species with broad grey-green leaves. The flowers are bicolored, white with a deep yellow cup, and sweet-scented. It grows in the Mediterranean region in meadows, vineyards, garrigue and rock crevices. It is also widely cultivated as an indoor bulb or to provide cut flowers.

Green-flowered narcissus *Narcissus viridiflorus*
A short, slender plant with rush-like hollow leaves, generally one per bulb. The dull olive-green small flowers are borne in clusters and have a fetid scent. It grows in south-western Spain and Morocco at low altitudes, often near the coast.

Sea daffodil

Pancratium maritimum

An exotic member of the amaryllis family, the sea daffodil grows in coastal sand and dunes around the Mediterranean coastline and the Black Sea. Its sweetly and strongly scented, large white blooms are produced in summer and autumn, their six petals framing the corolla in the manner of a daffodil, *Narcissus* species, hence its common name. The plant reproduces vegetatively and through seeds, but despite the high number of seeds it produces, this method of reproduction is limited.

Identification: The fleshy, grey-green, strap-like leaves grow up to 50cm/20in long, and a long, partially flattened flower stem, to 40cm/16in, supports the inflorescence of 5–10 florets, embraced before blooming by two large, skinny sepals. Large, white, fragrant blooms, up to 16cm/6¼in across, with a slender, white perianth tube to 75mm/3in long, appear between late summer and mid-autumn. The fruit is a large, three-valved capsule.

Distribution: South-western Europe.
Height and spread: 40cm/16in.
Habit and form: Deciduous to semi-evergreen bulbous perennial.
Leaf shape: Linear.
Pollinated: Insect.

Right: The seed capsules still retain the remains of the flower.

Below: The clump-forming habit makes the flowers conspicuous among coastal dune grasses.

Spring snowflake

Leucojum vernum

This delicate bulbous plant grows in damp deciduous woods, copses and meadows. The two snowflake species described here are similar to snowdrops but with broader bright green leaves and a slightly different flower shape. Spring snowflake flowers from January to April and grows in damp places such as near streams and in wet woodland. It is widely cultivated and naturalized.

Below: The flowers have strap-like leaf blades and nodding white flowerheads, often with a green spot marking on them. They multiply when left undisturbed for several years.

Identification: The leaves are strap-shaped and deep green in colour. Leafless stems have a bract (spathe) towards the top. The flowers are solitary or paired, nodding and bell-shaped, 15–20mm/⁹⁄₁₆–¾in long, with six equal tepals, each with a green or yellow spot towards the tip.

Distribution: Southern and central Europe (mainly Belgium, France, and Germany, naturalized in Great Britain, Holland and Denmark.
Height and spread: 15–40cm/6–16in.
Habit and form: Bulbous perennial.
Leaf shape: Strap-shaped
Pollinated: Insect.

Above: Spring snowflake sets seed easily.

Right: Small and pretty, the bell-shaped flowers are appealing in late winter.

Snowdrop

Galanthus nivalis

This pretty little bulbous plant is native across much of Europe, although it is most plentiful in the eastern Mediterranean region. It is widely distributed from Spain to Russia, with several varieties and subspecies much planted in gardens outside its range and consequently found as garden escapees. Usually growing in large drifts on the banks of rivers and streams, in woodland and in damp grassland, it flowers during winter and early spring. The aptly named small flowers often push up through the snow and are white with pale green markings on their petals.

Right: The snowdrop is one of the earliest blooming bulbs, often appearing in midwinter in deciduous woodland.

Identification: The narrow, linear to strap-shaped, blue-green leaves appear at the same time as the flowers. The faintly honey-scented flowers are solitary, pendulous, to 20mm/¾in long, and appear in winter to early spring depending upon their location. The outer perianth segments are much larger than the inner ones, which do not spread on opening but form a cup containing the stamens; the inner perianth segments have a green patch towards their tip.

Distribution: Europe.
Height and spread: Up to 12.5cm/5in.
Habit and form: Deciduous bulbous perennial.
Leaf shape: Narrow linear.
Pollinated: Insect.

Left: The seedhead is a conspicuous green capsule.

Right: Snowdrops form dense clumps of foliage and flower in the late winter.

Cape flower

Guernsey lily, Japanese spider lily, *Nerine bowdenii*

This pretty bulbous plant from Cape Province is one of around 30 species in this genus, which is centred in South Africa. Its striking blossoms come in a wide spectrum of pink hues. The plant originates from mountain areas, where it thrives on rocky screes, mountain ledges and other well-drained areas where the soil is not too rich. The flowers appear early in the season, before the leaves, and form large, noticeable clumps over time.

Distribution: Western Cape, South Africa.
Height and spread: 45cm/18in.
Habit and form: Deciduous bulbous perennial.
Leaf shape: Linear.
Pollinated: Insect.

Identification: Narrow, strap-like, glossy, mid- to dark green leaves, to 30cm/12in, develop after the flowers appear from late summer to early winter. The distinctive, musk-scented flowers are formed of six strap-like petals, candy to deep pink, rarely white, darker at the midrib, with wavy margins and usually twisted at their ends. They are borne in heads of up to eight flowers, at the end of stiff stems up to 60cm/24in long.

Far left: The striking flowers occur in a variety of pink hues.

Right: Wild plants usually flower before the leaves appear. Those in cultivation may have both at the same time.

OTHER SPECIES OF NOTE

Blood lily *Haemanthus coccinea*
This is a very variable, summer-flowering bulbous perennial, occurring in widely varying habitats, mainly coastal scrub and rocky slopes, throughout the winter rainfall region of South Africa, from southern Namibia south. The flowerheads usually emerge before the leaves.

Amaryllis belladonna
Growing in the south-western Cape, *Amaryllis belladonna* has large clusters of up to 12 scented, trumpet-shaped, pink or white flowers, carried on a long purplish-red and green 50cm/20in stem in autumn. The strap-like leaves are deciduous and are produced after flowering.

Giant snowdrop *Galanthus elwesii*
Originally from south-eastern Europe, notably Turkey, this fine snowdrop has been widely naturalized elsewhere. It is taller and more vigorous than the common snowdrop *G. nivalis*, and reaches 25cm/10in. The distinctive feature is the green at the base and the top of the inner tepals of its flowers, which blossom in January or February.

Lapiedra *Lapiedra martinezii* is native to southern Spain and Morocco. It grows in rocky crevices or very stony soil near the sea or in very hot areas inland. In the autumn several pure white, fragrant, star-shaped, glistening flowers appear on a umbel inflorescence.

Summer snowflake

Lodden lily, *Leucojum aestivum*

This clump-forming medium-size plant flowers at the end of spring and beginning of summer. It is similar to spring snowflake, but larger and more robust. It grows in wet meadows and marshy ground, open woodland and stream margins, and it is also widely grown in gardens. The alternative common name comes from the tributary of the River Thames where it grows wild in willow thickets and wet meadows.

Distribution: Mainly central Europe, east to the Caucasus; widely naturalized.
Height and spread: up to 60cm/24in.
Habit and form: Bulbous perennial.
Leaf shape: Strap-shaped.
Pollinated: Insect.

Identification: The deep green strap-shaped leaves are well developed when flowering occurs. The hollow flattened stem ends in an umbel of two to five flowers, partly protected by a papery sheath. The attractive bell-shaped flowers have six white tepals, each tipped with a green spot.

Right: This plant forms attractive clumps of bell-shaped flowers.

WATER LILIES, CAPE PONDWEEDS AND CATTAILS

Nymphaeaceae, or water lilies, comprise aquatic plants with showy flowers that are often considered the most primitive flowering plants. The Aponogetonaceae (cape pondweeds) is also primitive, occurring in the Old World. The Typhaceae, or cattail family, is widespread in the Northern Hemisphere.

Water hawthorn

Cape pondweed, *Aponogeton distachyos*

Water hawthorn occurs naturally in the winter rainfall areas of the South African Cape region, where the edible flowers and buds, which have a strong vanilla scent, are a popular winter delicacy. It is adapted to growing in ponds and small lakes that dry up in summer. The plant flowers freely in the spring, then the tubers lie dormant in the sediment, sprouting and flowering again as soon as the pools fill in autumn. The long, oval leaves float on the water, but it is usually the sweetly scented white flowers, standing up out of the water above the leaves, which attract attention. There are several other species of *Aponogeton* in southern Africa, but *A. distachyos* is the best known.

Distribution: South Africa.
Height and spread: Variable spread.
Habit and form: Aquatic perennial.
Leaf shape: Oblong-lanceolate.
Pollinated: Bee.

Identification: Oblong to lance-shaped, bright green, sometimes brown, floating leaves, up to 20cm/8in long, on long stems, are evergreen except where water dries up seasonally. Small, scented, one-petalled white flowers, 30mm/1¼in across, with purplish-brown anthers, are enclosed in white spathes, to 20mm/¾in long, and borne in racemes with forked branches, 10cm/4in long, above the water surface.

Right: The floating leaves and sweetly scented showy white flowers make this a striking water plant.

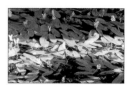

Reedmace

Bulrush, Common cattail, *Typha latifolia*

This stately water reed is well known, chiefly because of its huge distribution: it is found almost worldwide. The reedmace is instantly identifiable by its tall, sword-shaped leaves and distinctive fruiting spikes. It is mainly found in shallow water up to 15cm/6in deep in ponds, lakes, ditches and slow-flowing streams, and is equally tolerant of acid or alkaline conditions.

Identification: This tall, erect semi-aquatic plant grows from stout rhizomes up to 75cm/29½in long, just below the soil surface. The pale greyish-green leaves are basal, erect, linear, flat, D-shaped in cross section, 1–3m/39in–10ft tall; 12–16 leaves arise from each shoot. The flower stem is erect, 1.5–3m/5–10ft tall, tapering near the flower structure, which appears in midsummer. It is a dense, dark brown, cylindrical spike on the end of the stem, with the male part positioned above the female part, continuous or slightly separated.

Right: The tall flower spikes of reedmace are a familiar sight across much of the Northern Hemisphere.

Distribution: North and Central America; Eurasia; northern Africa; New Zealand; Australia; and Japan.
Height and spread: 1.5–3m/5–10ft; indefinite spread.
Habit and form: Semi-aquatic or aquatic rhizomatous perennial.
Leaf shape: Linear.
Pollinated: Wind.

Right: The tight brown seedheads separate into a woolly mass of seed in late winter.

Prickly water lily

Foxnut, *Euryale ferox*

The prickly water lily, the only species in the genus *Euryale*, is native to east Asia and China to northern India, where it may often be found in warm water ponds and lakes in lowland regions. It is quite closely related to the Amazonian giant water lily, *Victoria amazonica*: although it is not as large as that species, its leaves can be as much as 1.5m/5ft across, with bright purple undersides, laced with large veins and covered with spines. It is day-flowering, although the flower almost always opens underwater and self-pollinates before it opens.

Distribution: Eastern Asia.
Height and spread: Variable spread.
Habit and form: Aquatic perennial.
Leaf shape: Circular.
Pollinated: Insect.

Identification: A deep-water aquatic perennial with floating, rounded leaves, 60cm–1.5m/24in–5ft across, which are puckered, sparsely spiny, olive green above and purple beneath, with prominent, prickly veins. Shuttlecock-like flowers, up to 60mm/2¼in across, are produced in summer, with an inner row of white petals and an outer row of (usually) deep violet petals. Many-seeded, prickly berries, 50–75mm/2–3in across, follow the flowers. Nearly every part of the plant is covered with needle-sharp spines.

OTHER SPECIES OF NOTE

Yellow water lily *Nuphar lutea*
Known as brandy bottle, and widely distributed across Eurasia, north Africa, the eastern USA and the West Indies. It is often found in deeper, cooler bodies of water, where it forms dense mats on the surface. The globe-shaped, unpleasant smelling flowers are fly-pollinated and followed by decorative seedheads.

European white water lily *Nymphaea alba*
The white water lily is widely distributed across Eurasia and North Africa, mostly in water up to 1.2m/4ft deep, in marshes, ponds, slow-moving streams, lakes and canals. It is well known for the large, semi-double, white, faintly fragrant flowers it produces in mid- to late summer.

Dwarf reedmace *Typha minima*
This miniature bulrush is a slender aquatic perennial, relatively common across Europe and western Asia. It is smaller than its larger relatives, reaching just 75cm/29½in, and although the flower spikes are similar to those of the other species, the plant is much less robust and invasive.

Nymphaea candida
This large, white-flowered water lily, commonly found in ponds, lakes and slow-flowing streams in Europe and parts of north Asia, flowers from mid- to late summer. The flowers last a day, opening early and beginning to close by the afternoon; they are pollinated by flies.

Cape blue water lily

Nymphaea capensis

The Cape blue water lily's star-shaped, pale blue flowers are a common sight in freshwater lakes, ponds, ditches, canals, marshes and slow-moving streams across much of east and southern Africa, as well as Madagascar. This species is widely believed to be the same as the Egyptian blue lotus, *Nymphaea caerulea*, although it is in fact not a lotus but a tropical, day-blooming water lily. Wall paintings on ancient Egyptian monuments show that this flower was venerated as a symbol of life, and was used to induce euphoria and as an aphrodisiac.

Identification: An aquatic perennial with a thick rhizome. The mid-green leaves, arising from the rhizome, are alternate and spirally arranged, simple, rounded and toothed, with a wavy margin, 25–40cm/10–16in across, with slightly overlapping lobes, usually floating. The young leaves are purple-spotted beneath. Star-shaped, solitary flowers, 20–25cm/8–10in across, on long stalks, open during the day; they are highly fragrant, with four greenish sepals, numerous blue petals and yellow stamens. The flowers grow large when in deep water.

Distribution: Western Africa and Madagascar.
Height and spread: Variable.
Habit and form: Aquatic perennial.
Leaf shape: Rounded.
Pollinated: Insect.

Below: Striking blue flowers rise from beneath the water surface.

GRASSES, RUSHES AND SEDGES

The Poaceae, more commonly known as the grass family, form one of the largest families of flowering plants. The Juncaceae, or rush family, are a small monocot-flowering plant family. Many of these slow-growing plants superficially resemble grasses, but are herbs or woody shrubs. The Cyperaceae comprise grass-like, herbaceous plants, collectively called sedges, found in wet or saturated conditions.

Papyrus

Cyperus papyrus

Papyrus is native to wet swamps and lake margins throughout Africa, Madagascar and the Mediterranean region, and in particular Egypt and Sudan. The most conspicuous feature of the plant is its bright green, smooth, flowering stems, known as culms, each topped by an almost spherical cluster of thin, bright green, shiny stalks. Papyrus is famed as the fibre used by the ancient Egyptians to make paper.

Identification: The stems are stout, smooth, triangular in cross-section, 40mm/1½in thick at the base, surrounded at the base by large, leathery, tapering sheaths. They are topped by umbels of numerous, needle-like rays, 10–45cm/4–18in long, each surrounded at the base with a narrow, brown, cylindrical bract, up to 30mm/1¼in long. Greenish-brown clusters of 6–16 flowers appear at the end of the rays, followed by tiny dark brown fruits, borne in the axils of tiny scales.

Distribution: Africa; Madagascar.
Height and spread: 5m/16ft.
Habit and form: Aquatic perennial.
Leaf shape: Reduced to small bracts.
Pollinated: Wind.

Far left: Papyrus is a tall, robust, almost leafless aquatic perennial, growing from stout horizontal rhizomes that creep along the substrate under water and are anchored by numerous roots.

Giant reed

Arundo donax

This large perennial grass is native from the Mediterranean region to the lower Himalayas, although its popularity as a garden plant has led to it being introduced to many subtropical and warm temperate regions, where it often becomes naturalized as a garden escapee and can be invasive. Giant reed is found on sand dunes near seashores and does tolerate some salt, although it is most often encountered along riverbanks and in other wet places, usually on poor sandy soil and in sunny situations, where its tough, fibrous roots penetrate deeply into the soil. Reeds for musical instruments are made from its culms.

Identification: Culms up to 6m/20ft tall arise from thick, short, branched, fleshy rhizomes. The stems are 20–40mm/¾–1½in in diameter, smooth, hollow and reed-like, with many nodes and often with a white scurf. The numerous, smooth, flat leaves on the main stem are 30–70cm/12–27½in long, glaucous-green, drooping, rounded at the base and tapering to a fine point; they emerge from smooth sheaths, hairy tufted at the base. The flowers appear in mid- to late autumn in large, erect feathery panicles, 30–70cm/12–28in long, light brown or yellowish-brown, with lustrous silky hairs.

Distribution: Mediterranean to the lower Himalayas.
Height and spread: Up to 6m/19¾ft.
Habit and form: Perennial grass.
Leaf shape: Linear.
Pollinated: Wind.

Left: The architectural merits of this plant have led to its use as a garden plant.

Right: The tall stems are topped with a feathery flower panicle.

Common rush *Juncus effusus*
Common or soft rush is a long-lived perennial, wetland plant that grows in a tussock. It spreads by vigorous, underground rhizomes. It is found all over the temperate world, growing in acid or polluted soil in situations with plenty of water and sun. The bright green, hollow stems carry compact, brown or yellow flowers in summer.

Giant feather grass
Stipa gigantea
This grass from Spain and Portugal grows up to 1.8m/6ft tall and blooms early in summer. The flowering stems are strong and erect, and their alleged resemblance to oats, *Avena* species, gives the plant its other name of golden oats. The arching foliage is much shorter and forms a tidy clump.

Broadleaf bamboo
Sasa palmata
This bamboo is originally native to forests in eastern Asia, although it has become widely naturalized in woodlands and damp hollows elsewhere. It is evergreen

and fast growing, with large leaves arranged in a fan or palm-like shape, which eventually form a dense, spreading clump.

Greater woodrush

Luzula sylvatica

The genus name of the greater woodrush, *Luzula*, is derived from the Latin word meaning "glow worm". It probably alludes to the way that the soft, downy hairs covering the margins of each blade catch and hold dew, causing them to glisten in the morning light. It is these downy hairs that distinguish woodrushes from rushes, *Juncus* species. Woodrushes are common in temperate regions worldwide, and this Eurasian species is found in woods and shady places, as well as on open ground. The leaves remain green(ish) all winter, and in mountainous regions in western Europe they are used by most golden eagles to line their eyries. It is widely distributed in southern, western and central Europe, and south-western Asia.

Identification: Densely tufted, grass-like, tussock-forming, the greater woodrush has broadly linear, channelled, glossy, dark green leaves to 30cm/12in long, fringed with zigzagged white hairs along the margin. Groups of two to five small, chestnut-brown flowers are produced in open panicles to 75mm/3in long, from mid-spring to early summer.

Distribution: Europe and south-western Asia.
Height and spread: 70–80cm/27½–31in.
Habit and form: Evergreen rhizomatous perennial.
Leaf shape: Broadly linear.
Pollinated: Wind.

Right: The open, feathery flower-heads emerge from mid-spring onwards.

Metake

Arrow bamboo, *Pseudosasa japonica* syn. *Arundinaria japonica*

This woodland-dwelling bamboo from eastern Asia is frequently naturalized outside its range due to its popularity with gardeners. It is the most cold-tolerant bamboo, surviving temperatures as low as -24°C/-11°F. Plants often flower lightly for a number of years, although they can produce an abundance of flowers. Mass flowering severely weakens the plants, and they can take some years to recover.

Identification: An upright, spreading, bamboo up to 6m/20ft in height. The canes are erect, cylindrical, branched at each upper node, olive-green when young, maturing to pale beige. Lance-shaped or oblong, hairless, tessellated, dark green leaves, to 35cm/14in long, are silver-grey beneath and have yellow midribs. The plant usually forms a solid vertical mass of leaves, which cover and enclose it entirely from the ground to the top.

Distribution: Eastern Asia.
Height and spread: Up to 6m/19¾ft.
Habit and form: Rhizomatous evergreen bamboo.
Leaf shape: Lanceolate or oblong.
Pollinated: Wind.

Right: The tiny flowers are borne at the branch tips and only appear on mature plants.

LILY FAMILY

The lily family, or Liliaceae, is a large and complex group, mostly consisting of herbaceous perennials that grow from starchy rhizomes, corms or bulbs. The family includes a great number of ornamental flowers as well as several important agricultural crops. The plants have linear leaves, mostly with parallel veins, and flower parts in threes.

English bluebell

Hyacinthoides non-scriptus

This bulbous perennial is restricted to northern Europe and is chiefly found in the British Isles and along the sea coasts of Scandinavia and the Low Countries, where it thrives in the cool, moist, maritime conditions. It grows in deciduous woodland, where it carpets the ground, usually on slightly acid soils, and is also common in woodland clearings, on roadsides and occasionally in open ground. The distinct species is also threatened in many areas across its range because it hybridizes freely with the Spanish bluebell, *H. hispanica*, which is a more robust species.

Left: The flowers are distinct.

Identification: The plant is vigorous and clump-forming, with spreading, linear to lance-shaped, glossy, dark green leaves, 20–45cm/8–18in long. In spring, one-sided racemes that bend over at the top bear 6–12 pendent, narrowly bell-shaped, scented, mid-blue, sometimes white, flowers, up to 20mm/¾in long, with cream anthers. Blooms appear (according to local climate and conditions) from mid- to late spring.

Right: Bluebells seed easily.

Far right: Bluebells form dense blue carpets during spring in deciduous woodlands.

Distribution: Northern Europe.
Height and spread: 20–45cm/8–18in.
Habit and form: Bulbous perennial.
Leaf shape: Linear to lanceolate.
Pollinated: Insect.

Madonna lily

Lilium candidum

A large upright lily and one of the oldest plants recorded, being recognizable in paintings on Crete dating back 4,000 years. It has been cultivated for centuries and its original habitat (probably Turkey) is unknown, although it now occurs widely across that region. It is highly unusual in that it produces overwintering basal leaves. It grows in meadows and forests on sand and limestone, to elevations of 1,300m/4,250ft.

Identification: Broad, inversely lance-shaped, shiny, bright green basal leaves, 23cm/9in long, appear in autumn. In spring, the stiffly erect stems bear smaller, scattered or spirally arranged, often twisted, lance-shaped leaves to 75mm/3in long. From late spring until midsummer the plant produces a raceme of five to 20 sweetly fragrant, large, broadly trumpet-shaped, pure white flowers, 50–75mm/2–3in long, with yellowish bases and bright yellow anthers.

Left and right: The flower spikes sport 10–20 dazzling white, sweetly scented flowers in summer.

Distribution: Mediterranean.
Height and spread: 1–1.8m/39in–6ft.
Habit and form: Bulbous perennial.
Leaf shape: Inversely lanceolate.
Pollinated: Insect.

Turk's-cap lily

Lilium martagon

With its elegant stems of dusky red flowers and its ease of growth, the Turk's-cap lily or martagon has long been popular among gardeners. It was recorded in British gardens, for example, as long ago as the mid-16th century, possibly introduced by Crusaders or by monks. Dark blackish-red, white and double flowered forms have been grown in gardens, but some remain rare, perhaps debilitated over the centuries by viruses to which clonal lilies are often prey. In the wild, the species is widely distributed, and a number of local variants have been named

Distribution: Southern and central Europe, eastward to the Caucasus region and Siberia.
Height and spread: Erect to 1m/39in.
Habit and form: Bulbous perennial.
Leaf shape: Oblanceolate-obovate, to elliptic.
Pollinated: Moth and butterfly.

Identification: The plant arises from a bright yellow bulb, composed of many scales. The tall stem carries distinctive and widely-spaced whorls of leaves, and is typically topped by up to ten flowers. Each flower is 40–50mm/1½–2in across, purplish-red, with six strongly recurved perianth-segments, giving each bloom the appearance of a Turk's cap.

Left: The flowers are large on tall stems.

OTHER SPECIES OF NOTE

Snakeshead fritillary
Fritillaria meleagris
Native to north-western Europe, the snakeshead fritillary usually grows in damp meadows. The bloom, before the bud is fully opened, looks a little like a snake's head, hence the name. The nodding, tulip-shaped flowers are chequered in shades of purple.

Oriental lily *Lilium speciosum*
This tall Japanese lily can reach 1.5m/5ft and flowers late in the summer. The large, pendent, sweetly fragrant, white flowers are borne on long racemes of 12 or more, and are covered in carmine-red spots and stripes.

Lilium nepalense
This pretty lily grows wild at about 2,300–3,500m/7,500–11,500ft and on rocky slopes in the Himalayas. It produces attractive yellow drooping flowers, each about 15cm/6in long and sweet-scented, with spreading petals, curving backwards towards the tips. The stamens are protruding, with reddish anthers. The leaves are broadly lanceolate.

Pyrenean lily *Lilium pyrenaicum*
A handsome yellow 'Turk's-cap' lily endemic to the woods and meadows of the Pyrenees region of southern France and northern Spain. In spite of its local distribution in the wild, it is one of the easiest lilies to grow in gardens, where it can be naturalized in humid grasslands.

Orange lily

Fire lily, *Lilium bulbiferum*

The orange lily is a distinctive plant of sunny scrubland, grassy and rocky slopes and among bracken, and is endemic to the hills of central Europe. The species takes it specific epithet from its ability to produce bulbils along its stem, in common with many other *Lilium* species, but more noticeable than this feature are its brightly coloured flowers. While its bulbs are edible (sweet and mealy in flavour), it is mainly grown for ornamental purposes. It has long been cultivated, though the various garden forms rarely produce seed.

Distribution: Central and eastern Europe.
Height and spread: 40–60cm/16–24in, rarely reaching 1.5m/5ft.
Habit and form: Bulbous perennial.
Leaf shape: Lance shaped.
Pollinated: Bee.

Below: The fruit is a capsule.

Identification: Small scaly bulbs give rise to erect stems, clothed in numerous linear to lance-shaped leaves. Small bulbils are often produced in the upper axils of the leaves. Up to three large, upward-pointing and widely-campanulate flowers are produced on each stem. These are an intense flame-orange, and up to 17cm/6½in across.

Wild tulip

Tulipa sylvestris

The slender, scented clear-yellow flowers of the wild tulip are a characteristic, if declining, feature of meadows, grasslands and open woodlands across swathes of Europe into Russia and the western parts of Central Asia, yet the true boundary of its native distribution will probably never be known. In many countries it is undoubtedly an ancient introduction: in Great Britain, for example, it may well have been introduced by the Romans, though elsewhere it may have been introduced by accident, as a weed of cultivated orchards and vineyards. It has long been grown in gardens, though has declined in popularity, for while easy to grow, the plant is apt to produce numerous leaves and few flowers.

Identification: A slender hairless tulip, with two to four linear-lanceolate leaves, and usually with a single yellow flower, up to 40mm/1½in long. While erect in flower, the buds are distinctly nodding. The outer perianth segments are often reddish or greenish, while the inner segments lack the black basal blotch that characterizes many tulip species.

Distribution: Southern and south-eastern Europe, north to northern France, east to eastern Russia; widely naturalized elsewhere.
Height and spread: 10–50cm/4–20in.
Habit and form: Bulbous perennial.
Leaf shape: Linear-lanceolate, hairless, entire.
Pollinated: Beetle (possibly).

Left: The closed flowerhead.

Left: The wild tulip will grow freely in and around lawns and in cultivated areas

Star-of-Bethlehem

Ornithogalum angustifolium

Star-of-Bethlehem is a common and widespread plant of rocky and grassy places, scrub and open woodland through the southern parts of Europe. However, its native distribution is confused both by the occurrence of the closely-related *O. umbellatum* and of long-standing introductions across much of its range. In Great Britain, authors cannot agree on its status: its first wild record dates from 1650, though it was known to be growing in gardens for more than a century beforehand. Its ease of naturalization in wild situations reflects its persistence: it is popular among gardeners for its heads of starry white flowers, but it is often invasive.

Right: Star of Bethlehem forms colonies when left to its own devices.

Identification: Up to nine linear and often channelled leaves per bulb, each with a distinctive white stripe along the upper surface. The inflorescence is a short, umbel-like raceme. The lower flowers are borne on long ascending petioles. The flowers are white, star-shaped, to 45mm/1¾in across, with six perianth segments, each with a wide green stripe on the undersurface.

Distribution: Warmer parts of Europe, east to Syria and Israel; widely naturalized in the north.
Height and spread: 15–30cm/6–12in.
Habit and form: Bulbous perennial.
Leaf shape: Linear.
Pollinated: Insect.

Left: The flower is attractive with white petals that are green below, especially when still in bud.

Lily-of-the-valley

Convallaria majalis

Distribution: Europe, except the extreme north and south.
Height and spread: Stems to 35cm/14in.
Habit and form: Creeping, rhizomatous herbaceous perennial.
Leaf shape: Elliptic.
Pollinated: Beetle, fly and other insects.

Right: The red fruits contain seeds.

Far right: Lily of the valley forms extensive colonies.

This is a widespread species of open woodlands, scrub and upland pasture, both on acid and lime-rich soils. In the wild its flowering success is intimately linked to woodland management, providing great displays following coppicing or forest clearance, and flowering poorly in dark, neglected woodland. The Latin *majalis* translates literally as 'May': in France and Germany, the plant is a symbol of May Day. The plant is popular among gardeners, who grow a range of variegated, pink and double forms in addition to the typically white-flowered species. The plant is easy to grow, and where happy can be mildly invasive.

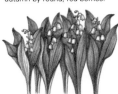

Identification: The leaves arise from a widely creeping rhizome, though their convolute petioles form a false stem, from which usually two (and up to four) leaves arise. Each leaf lamina is elliptic, untoothed and up to 20cm/8in long. Each 'stem' bears a single one-sided inflorescence of nodding flowers. Each flower is white, globose, 5–8mm/³⁄₁₆–⁵⁄₁₆in long and intensely fragrant; followed in autumn by round, red berries.

OTHER SPECIES OF NOTE

Spiked star-of-Bethlehem
Ornithogalum pyrenaicum
This species has a distinctive spike of greenish-yellow flowers. Largely confined to more southerly parts of Europe, it does occur as far north as southern England, where its young flowering shoots were formerly collected in large quantities to eat in the manner of asparagus.

Yellow star-of-Bethelehem *Gagea lutea*
The most widespread species of the genus *Gagea* in Europe, where it grows in damp woodland and scrub. However, its distinctive heads of starry greenish-yellow flowers are rarely seen, as many large populations only produce a handful of flowering spikes each year.

May-lily *Maianthemum bifolium*
A dainty species, widespread in ancient woodlands across much of Europe. The slender stem bears two heart-shaped leaved and is topped by a short, dense head of tiny white flowers. Its apparent fragility is some-times misleading: in gardens the plant can spread rapidly from underground rhizomes and is often difficult to eradicate.

St Bernard's lily *Anthericum liliago*
This lily grows in warm, dry meadows through southern and central Europe, though is rare and declining in Poland and Turkey. Its little-branched racemes of starry white flowers are attractive, and the plant is occasionally grown by gardeners.

Water Lily Tulip

Tulipa kaufmanniana

This relatively low-growing tulip, from rocky mountain slopes close to the snow edge in central Asia, has an average height of 15cm/6in, though it is a variable species in terms of height and bloom. The flower is long and white with a yellow tint on the inside and pink on the outside. The blooms, when they first open, are cup-shaped, though with pointed petals; eventually, on the sunniest days, they open flat into a characteristic hexagonal star shape from about a third of the way up the slender cup, so that when viewed from above they look almost like water lilies. The species has a scattered distribution across Kazakhstan, Uzbekistan, Tajikistan and Kyrgyzstan.

Identification: The plant has three to five lance-shaped, slightly wavy-margined, hairless, grey-green leaves, up to 25cm/10in long. Bowl-shaped flowers 30mm–12.5cm/1¼–5in across, are borne singly or in clusters of up to five, on slightly downy, often red-tinged stems in early and mid-spring. The flowers are cream or yellow, flushed pink or greyish-green on the outside, often with contrasting basal marks.

Distribution: Central Asia.
Height and spread: 15cm/6in.
Habit and form: Bulbous perennial.
Leaf shape: Lanceolate.
Pollinated: Insect.

Right: Tulips escape the extremes of summer heat and winter cold as an underground bulb.

Below: Bulbs may form dense clumps over time.

Glory-of-the-snow

Chionodoxa luciliae

This is one of approximately six to eight species of blue-flowered bulbs found locally in montane forests and open mountainsides of the eastern Mediterranean. Their bright blue flowers, opening early among the melting snow, have given rise to their generic name *Chionodoxa*, literally 'Glory-of-the-Snow'. The most handsome species are found in western Turkey, where three or four ill-defined species are found, including *C. luciliae*, which is apparently confined to the higher slopes of ancient Mt Tmolus, Turkey. *Chionodoxa luciliae* and the closely related *C. forbesii*, together with their pink and white colour variants, have long been popular in gardens, prized for their early colour and the ease with which they grow and naturalize.

Identification: Two narrow, channelled leaves give rise to one or two flowering scapes, each bearing up to four relatively large (16–20mm/⅝–¾in) flowers, of a rich lavender blue, fading to near white in the centre. The six perianth segments of members of the genus are fused at the base, a feature that distinguishes them from the closely related genus *Scilla*: indeed some botanists place *Chionodoxa* in the latter genus, a fact supported by the occurrence of fine, gardenworthy hybrids between the two.

Above and right: The star-shaped flowers are most attractive.

Distribution: Western Turkey.
Height and spread: 80mm–14cm/3⅛–5½in.
Habit and form: Bulbous perennial.
Leaf shape: Narrow, channelled and strap-shaped, hooded at the tip.
Pollinated: Insect.

Ramsons

Wild garlic, *Allium ursinum*

Ramsons is a common species of wild onion, found in damp, fertile woodlands across much of Europe, where it can form spectacular displays of gleaming white flowers in spring. In spite of its beauty, often its presence is first made known by its all-pervading and persistent smell of garlic. It is mildly flavoured and edible, and still occasionally used in soups, salads and stews. Though attractive, the plant is rarely grown intentionally by gardeners as it is highly invasive.

Identification: Each bulb produces two or three elliptic-oval, up to 20cm/8in long, leaves, and a single inflorescence with a terminal, more or less flat-topped head of starry white flowers. As with other members of the Liliaceae, individual flowers have six perianth segments. Each flower is up to 25mm/1in across. The whole plant smells strongly of garlic.

Above: The individual flowers are clustered together.

Left: Ranson's often grow in dense groups.

Distribution: Europe, though absent from some northern regions, and rare in the Mediterranean.
Height and spread: Up to 50cm/20in.
Habit and form: Bulbous perennial.
Leaf shape: Elliptic-oval.
Pollinated: Insect or self-pollinating.

Spring squill

Scilla verna

Distribution: Europe's Atlantic seaboard, from Portugal to Norway and the Faeroes.
Height and spread: 50mm–15cm/2–6in, rarely to 25cm/10in.
Habit and form: Bulbous perennial.
Leaf shape: Linear.
Pollinated: Bee and fly.

Spring squill is a an attractive bulbous plant with violet-blue flowers, endemic to the sea cliffs of western Oceanic Europe. The plant can be locally very abundant in coastal grasslands, creating a fine floral display in spring, along with species such as thrift, *Armeria maritima*, and sea campion, *Silene uniflora*. However, the plant has declined as cattle and sheep grazing has become increasingly uneconomic on coastal slopes, so that today the plant is often confined to the thinnest soils around rock outcrops, where summer droughts keeps the vegetation sufficiently open and short for this diminutive species. It is occasionally grown by specialist bulb growers.

Far right: This small plant has clusters of flowers on each stem.

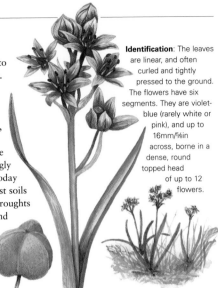

Identification: The leaves are linear, and often curled and tightly pressed to the ground. The flowers have six segments. They are violet-blue (rarely white or pink), and up to 16mm/⅝in across, borne in a dense, round topped head of up to 12 flowers.

OTHER SPECIES OF NOTE

Field garlic *Allium oleraceum*
A widespread species in Europe found in rough grassy places, on rocks and in scrub. It has lax heads of up to 40 dingy white to pinkish flowers, often supplemented by a cluster of bulbils, a common, vegetative means of reproduction in many *Allium* species. This ability to rapidly increase makes the species unsuitable for garden cultivation, where it can rapidly become a weed.

Wild leek *Allium ampeloprasum*
A tall bulbous plant found in scrub and open woodland, sea cliffs and rocky places in western Europe through to the Mediterranean region and eastward to Central Asia. Dense spherical heads of mauve flowers are borne on stems up to 1.8m/6ft. The species is notable as the probable parent of the cultivated Leek (*Allium porrum*), a distinct species known only from cultivation.

Autumn squill *Scilla autumnalis*
Although closely related to spring squill, autumn squill has quite a different appearance. It sends up flowering stems to about 25cm/10in, each stem with a tight raceme made up of 4–20 individual violet-blue small flowers, without bracts. The leaves do not appear until the autumn, after flowering has finished. It is rather a local species, typically growing in coastal sandy or rocky grassland. It is rather common around the Mediterranean. In Great Britain it is restricted to the extreme south.

Alpine squill

Scilla bifolia

Alpine squill is a variable species, common and widespread in grass, scrub and woodlands from sea level to the mountains, often up to the snowline. The plant is popular among gardeners for its show of rich blue flowers and ease of growth, lending itself to naturalizing in grass and under trees. In addition to the typical blue form, white and pink varieties have been selected.

Identification: The leaves typically appear in pairs (hence the plant's scientific name, *bifolia*), though occasionally there are up to six or seven per bulb. The flowers are rich to pale blue, occasionally paler in the centre, and up to 24mm/1in wide. They are borne in a loose inflorescence of 1–15 flowers.

Right: The fruit capsule is round and bulbous.

Distribution: Southern and central Europe, north to Belgium and Ukraine, east to central Russia, the Caucasus region and Syria.
Height and spread: Up to 20cm/8in.
Habit and form: Bulbous perennial.
Leaf shape: Broadly linear to lance-shaped.
Pollinated: Fly.

Below: Most Scilla species flower in spring, but a few flower in the autumn.

Meadow saffron

Autumn crocus, *Colchicum autumnale*

Meadow saffron is a widespread species through the agriculturally-unimproved meadows and open woodlands of Europe, where its pink, crocus-like flowers bloom in the autumn, weeks after the leaves have died down – giving rise to names such as naked ladies, naked nannies and star-naked boys (England) and *cul tout nu* (France). The genus *Colchicum* takes its name from Colchis on the Black Sea coast, made famous by the travels of Jason and the Argonauts, in search of the Golden Fleece: here, perhaps the most gardenworthy species of all, *C. speciosum*, is abundant. All parts of the plant are highly poisonous, and in many areas bulbs are systematically removed from meadows to prevent livestock casualties. But one toxic chemical – colchicine – is of considerable value, used for treating gout and for inducing ploidy (chromosome doubling) in living cells. The beautiful flowers, at a time of year when colour is declining in the garden, have ensured a popular following among gardeners, who grow the 'wild' single pink form, together with white and double varieties.

Identification: A clump-forming corm produces false stems of four or more glossy, broadly lance-shaped leaves up to 35cm/14in long. These die off during the summer – the end of the plant's growing cycle. The new season is 'kicked' off by the appearance of up to six large (up to 60mm/2¼in long) crocus-shaped flowers which appear without foliage.

Distribution: Western, central and southern Europe, eastward to western Russia.
Height and spread: Leaves up to 35cm/14in.
Habit and form: Clump-forming, cormous perennial.
Leaf shape: Broadly lance-shaped.
Pollinated: Bee and other insects.

Above: The fruit capsules.

Right: Autumn crocus is relatively large and rapidly spreads in grassland and under trees.

Grape hyacinth

Muscari neglectum

This species is one of the most variable species of grape hyacinth, growing in a wide range of stony and grassy places, typically with a mild winter climate (when the foliage is in growth), and dry and hot during the summer months (when drought initiates flower bud formation for the following year, while killing off competition from other plants). This species, and the closely-related *Muscari armeniacum*, are popular with gardeners and are very easy to grow and naturalize: but beware – once introduced, both species increase rapidly from bulb offsets and are virtually impossible to eliminate.

Identification: The leaves are linear and untoothed, to 40cm/16in. The inflorescence grows to 30cm/12in, and is topped by a dense spike of flowers, up to 40mm/1½in long. In common with other *Muscari* species, the lower flowers are fertile, urn-shaped and blackish-blue with a sharply-constricted, white-lobed orifice; the upper flowers are sterile, smaller and paler in colour. The flowers are distinctly starch-scented.

Distribution: Mediterranean; North Africa; Europe, north to eastern England, central Russia, Caucasus, Iran and Central Asia.
Height and spread: 50mm–30cm/2–12in.
Habit and form: Bulbous perennial.
Leaf shape: Linear and channelled.
Pollinated: Insect

Left: Grape hyacinths are a welcome sight in spring, with their unusual flowerheads of deep blue.

Solomon's-seal

Polygonatum multiflorum

Distribution: Temperate parts of Eurasia (rare in the Mediterranean); North America.
Height and spread: 30–90cm/12–35in.
Habit and form: Perennial rhizomatous herb.
Leaf shape: Perennial rhizomatous herbs.
Pollinated: Bumblebee.

Solomon's-seal is a plant of old woodland, scrub, forest margins and grassy glades, and is one of the most widespread species of *Polygonatum*. This elegant genus of 55 species is found widely across the temperate parts of the Northern Hemisphere. The popular name Solomon's-seal is thought to derive from the mark of the cut rhizomes, which bear a resemblance to Hebrew characters. These flowers have a quiet elegance and undemanding requirements.

Left Solomon's seal forms nodding heads.

Identification: The plant arises from a gently creeping, nobbly rhizome. Each stem initially grows vertical and erect (to minimize damage as it pushes up through soil and leaf litter), before gracefully arching at the tip. The leaves, each 50mm–15cm/2–6in long, arise alternately, in two rows along the middle and upper parts of the stem. Each leaf bears a dangling, stalked cluster of three to four (rarely six) tubular, greenish white flowers (17–18mm/⅝in long): collectively they form a row of udder-like flowers.

OTHER SPECIES OF NOTE

Angular Solomon's-seal
Polygonatum odoratum
A subtle beauty found in open, often rocky woods across Europe, where it often occurs with lily-of-the-valley, *Convallaria majalis*. The dangling, white-and-green flowers are scented, and the wild form – together with double and variegated selections – is easily, if rarely, grown in gardens.

Butcher's-broom
Ruscus aculeatus
This spiny-leaved low-growing shrub of woods is particularly abundant in heavily grazed woodland due to its unpalatable nature. In former times its stems were bundled together and used to scour butchers' blocks, hence its common name.

White asphodel *Asphodelus albus*
A handsome herb typically with an unbranched flowering spike that can reach more than 1m/39in in height. Its starry white flowers are borne in abundance, and contrast with the dark brown, papery bracts. In spite of its considerable beauty, it is rarely grown.

Small grape hyacinth *Muscari botryoides*
This plant resembles *M. neglectum*, but the flowers are slightly smaller and the leaves have prominent ridges. It grows in open woods and grassland to about 2,000m/6,500ft, notably in central Europe, flowering in early spring.

Summer asphodel

Asphodelus aestivus

A handsome, if coarse, perennial that produces impressive displays of tall, candelabra-like stems of white flowers in spring. The plant is common in scrub and woodland, grassland and stony ground in the eastern Mediterranean, often spreading into fallow land and field margins. Colonies can be very large, as the plant is unpalatable to grazing animals. It is rarely, if ever, cultivated.

Identification: The rootstock is a dense cluster of thick, finger-like tubers. The leaves are ribbon-like, grey-green in an untidy tuft. The flowering stems reach 1–2m/39in–6½ft, and are widely branched in their upper half, and bear abundant white flowers over an extended period. Each flower is up to 30mm/1¼in wide, bears six perianth segments, which are white with a central brownish-pink mid-vein.

Above: The fruit capsules.

Distribution: Portugal and the Mediterranean region east to Turkey and Israel.
Height and spread: 1–2m/39in–6½ft.
Habit and form: Tuberous rooted perennial.
Leaf shape: Ribbon or strap-shaped.
Pollinated: Solitary bee and other insects.

Below: Summer asphodel favours wasteland, rocky shores, garrigue and olive groves. It can grow in large stands.

Bog asphodel

Narthecium ossifragum

The erect, yolk-yellow flowering spikes of the bog asphodel are a distinctive feature of the acid bogs and wet heaths and moors of western Oceanic Europe, growing often in association with sundews, *Drosera* spp., and cotton grasses, *Eriophorum* spp. The scientific name *ossifragum*, meaning 'bone breaker', has arisen from the belief that sheeps' bones become brittle through grazing the plant. In reality, this particular plant was not to blame, but rather the general calcium-deficiency in the acid vegetation was the cause.

Identification: The flattened fans of short leaves are distinctive, and bear some resemblance to those of many iris species. Each fan bears a single, erect spike of up to 20 star-shaped flowers, each up to 18mm/¹¹⁄₁₆in across. In late summer, the whole plant takes on a rich orange hue, as the fruits mature.

Below: The flowerheads are made up of six narrow petals and six hairy stamens with bright orange anthers.

Below: Bog asphodel is a flower of acid heaths and moors.

Distribution: Atlantic Europe, south to northern Portugal, and east to Sweden.
Height and spread: 50mm–45cm/2–18in.
Habit and form: Rhizomatous perennial herb.
Leaf shape: Sword-shaped, held in a flattened fan.
Pollinated: Wind or insect, occasionally self-pollinating.

False helleborine

White hellebore, *Veratrum album*

This handsome, herbaceous perennial is a characteristic of humid grasslands and forest glades and margins, typically in the mountains of Europe and Asia. It favours both mown meadows and grazed pastures, reaching its greatest size and abundance under the latter conditions. This toxic plant is unpalatable to livestock and takes full advantage of the reduced competition following grazing. The root is also toxic and can have a paralyzing effect. It is occasionally mistaken for yellow gentian, the juices of which are used in bitter concoctions. Dilute extracts are sometimes used in homeopathic medicine, but the plant is dangerous.

Identification: A robust, erect clump-forming perennial to 1.5m/5ft or more, distinctive for its large, broadly elliptical and heavily pleated lower leaves, and its erect, much-branched panicle of flowers. Each flower measures up to 30mm/1¼in across, and is green to whitish-green.

Above: The flower is white above and green below, each petal marked with eight lines.

Distribution: Europe (except the north-west and Mediterranean regions); Turkey and the Caucasus; Central and eastern Asia; and Siberia.
Height and spread: 50cm–1.75m/20in–5¾ft.
Habit and form: Robust, rhizomatous herbaceous perennial.
Leaf shape: Broadly elliptical below, becoming shorter and narrower up the stem.
Pollinated: Insect.

Pineapple lily

Eucomis bicolor

These bulbous perennials, originating from wet mountain slopes and meadows in South Africa, are named pineapple lilies because of their unusual tight racemes of flowers topped by a small tuft of leafy bracts, similar to those of a pineapple, which are borne in late summer. These emerge amid a basal rosette of glossy green leaves and are borne on stout stems, giving the whole plant a highly distinctive look.

Far right: The individual flowerhead.

Left: The exotic-looking flowerheads resemble pineapples.

Identification: A large bulb, up to 75mm/3in in diameter, produces semi-erect to angular, strap-shaped, wavy-margined, light green leaves, growing up to 10cm/4in wide and 30–50cm/12–20in long. In late summer, maroon-flecked stems bear racemes, 15cm/6in long, of tightly packed, slightly pendent, pale green flowers up to 25mm/1in across, with purple-margined tepals. Each raceme is topped by a small tuft of leafy bracts, arranged in a loose rosette.

Right: The rosette of leaves gives rise to a single flower stem.

Distribution: South Africa.
Height and spread: 30–60cm/12–24in.
Habit and form: Bulbous perennial.
Leaf shape: Angular strap-shaped.
Pollinated: Insect.

OTHER SPECIES OF NOTE
Yellow asphodel *Asphodeline lutea*
A native of the eastern Mediterranean, yellow asphodel is a clump-forming evergreen perennial, with tightly wrapped, blade-like, narrowly triangular foliage. Tall flowering spikes, which become dense with fragrant, citron-yellow, star-shaped blooms, emerge in spring.

Scottish asphodel *Tofieldia pusilla*
A diminutive, creeping rhizomatous herb found in seeps and flushes in the mountainous areas of the Arctic, across much of the Northern Hemisphere. A true Arctic species (where it can be widespread and abundant), it is threatened in some of its most southerly locations, including England, Michigan and Minnesota.

Herb Paris *Paris quadrifolia*
Widespread across much of Europe, herb Paris is an indicator of species-rich woodlands, its favoured habitat. Many parts of the plant – the broad leaves, sepals and petals – typically occur in fours, hence its scientific name. The genus has a subtle beauty, and is gaining popularity with gardeners.

Snowdon lily *Lloydia serotina*
This is a graceful lily-like plant with relatively large (up to 30mm/1¼in across) pale pink flowers. It occurs widely in alpine and arctic regions of the Northern Hemisphere, including North America. In Europe, the plant is more localized, and isolated colonies on mountains in Wales are threatened by the changing climate.

Red hot poker

Kniphofia caulescens

Red hot pokers are more often orange than red but resemble the colour of glowing embers nonetheless. They are a distinctive group of plants, with their strong outlines making them instantly recognizable. They are frequented by nectar-feeding birds, such as sunbirds and sugarbirds, as well as certain insects. The genus *Kniphofia* is very closely related to the genus *Aloe*. As a result, the first *Kniphofia* to be described, *K. uvaria*, was initially named *Aloe uvaria*. *K. caulescens* is notable for its stems, which become woody, giving it the appearance of a small shrub. It is a widely cultivated plant that may occur as a garden escapee far outside its natural range.

Distribution: Eastern South Africa.
Height and spread: 90cm/35in or more.
Habit and form: Slightly woody herbaceous perennial.
Leaf shape: Linear.
Pollinated: Bird, sometimes insect.

Below: Red hot pokers are clump-forming.

Identification: The plant is an evergreen perennial with short, thick, woody-based stems and arching, linear, keeled, finely toothed, glaucous leaves, to 1m/39in long, which are purple at the base. Coral-red flowers fading to pale yellow, 25mm/1in long with protruding stamens, are borne in short, cylindrical racemes on 1.2m/4ft stems from summer to autumn.

Flame lily

Glory lily, *Gloriosa superba*

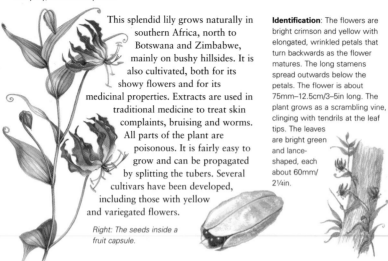

This splendid lily grows naturally in southern Africa, north to Botswana and Zimbabwe, mainly on bushy hillsides. It is also cultivated, both for its showy flowers and for its medicinal properties. Extracts are used in traditional medicine to treat skin complaints, bruising and worms. All parts of the plant are poisonous. It is fairly easy to grow and can be propagated by splitting the tubers. Several cultivars have been developed, including those with yellow and variegated flowers.

Right: The seeds inside a fruit capsule.

Identification: The flowers are bright crimson and yellow with elongated, wrinkled petals that turn backwards as the flower matures. The long stamens spread outwards below the petals. The flower is about 75mm–12.5cm/3–5in long. The plant grows as a scrambling vine, clinging with tendrils at the leaf tips. The leaves are bright green and lance-shaped, each about 60mm/2¼in.

Distribution: Southern and central Africa.
Height and spread: To 1.8m/6ft.
Habit and form: Perennial climber.
Leaf shape: Lanceolate.
Pollinated: Insect.

Left: Flame lily is a twining, scrambling plant with crimson and yellow flowers. It can be toxic and should be handled carefully.

Climbing asparagus

Asparagus africanus

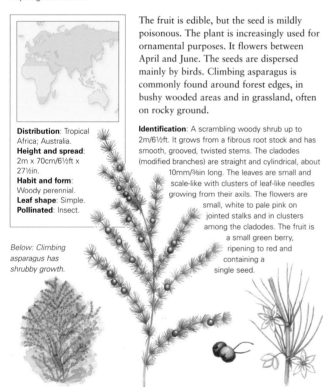

The fruit is edible, but the seed is mildly poisonous. The plant is increasingly used for ornamental purposes. It flowers between April and June. The seeds are dispersed mainly by birds. Climbing asparagus is commonly found around forest edges, in bushy wooded areas and in grassland, often on rocky ground.

Distribution: Tropical Africa; Australia.
Height and spread: 2m x 70cm/6½ft x 27½in.
Habit and form: Woody perennial.
Leaf shape: Simple.
Pollinated: Insect.

Below: Climbing asparagus has shrubby growth.

Identification: A scrambling woody shrub up to 2m/6½ft. It grows from a fibrous root stock and has smooth, grooved, twisted stems. The cladodes (modified branches) are straight and cylindrical, about 10mm/⅜in long. The leaves are small and scale-like with clusters of leaf-like needles growing from their axils. The flowers are small, white to pale pink on jointed stalks in clusters among the cladodes. The fruit is a small green berry, ripening to red and containing a single seed.

OTHER SPECIES OF NOTE

Toad lily *Tricyrtris stolonifera*
The toad lily is a stoloniferous perennial from moist woodland habitats in Taiwan. It has purple-spotted, deep green leaves, borne alternately on hairy stems that grow in a zigzag pattern. In late summer, it bears white or light pink, star-shaped flowers, heavily spotted with purple.

Foxtail lily *Eremurus spectabilis*
This is one of the most dramatic members of the lily family, with a dense cylindrical spike of white or greenish-yellow flowers up to 2m/6½ft in height. The genus *Eremurus* hails from the Middle East and Central Asia, and is becoming increasingly widely grown in gardens, for its dramatic architectural looks.

Asparagus *Asparagus officinalis*
This is a very variable fleshy-rooted herbaceous perennial, widespread through North Africa and much of Europe, east to Central Asia. It bears tall, graceful stems of fine foliage up to 2m/6½ft in height, and the young stems of selected cultivated forms provide the delicacy asparagus.

Aloe vera
This succulent aloe is almost stalkless. Its pea-green leaves, spotted with white when young, are 30–50cm/12–20in long and 10cm/4in broad at the base. Bright yellow, tubular flowers are arranged in a slender loose spike.

Krantz aloe

Aloe arborescens

The krantz aloe is a distinctive species that develops into a multi-headed shrub with striking grey-green leaves, armed with conspicuous pale teeth, arranged in attractive rosettes. It is most closely related to the smaller, and similar, *Aloe mutabilis*, which can be distinguished by its red-and-yellow flowers and broader leaves.

Below: The rosettes of bluish-green, spine-edged leaves are topped with attractive spikes formed from many heads of tubular flowers that have a rich supply of nectar.

Distribution: Southern Africa.
Height and spread: 2–3m/6½–10ft.
Habit and form: Shrubby succulent.
Leaf shape: Sickle-shaped and rounded.
Pollinated: Bird (particularly sunbird), bee.

Identification: The succulent, greyish-green to bright green, sickle-shaped leaves, borne in rosettes, vary considerably in length but average 50–60cm/20–24in. The leaf margins are commonly armed with firm teeth, which are white or the same colour as the leaves. There is also a form with smooth margins. Two or more flower spikes up to 90cm/35in long arise from each rosette in late winter and spring, usually simple but occasionally with up to two side branches. The scarlet, orange, pink or yellow flowers are borne in conical racemes and are rich in nectar.

Air potato

Potato yam, Bulbil yam, *Dioscorea bulbifera* var. *anthropophagorum*

Air potato is a perennial vine with broad leaves and two types of storage organs. The plant forms bulbils in the leaf axils of the twining stems, and tubers beneath the ground. These tubers are like small, oblong potatoes, and they are edible and cultivated as a food crop. The tubers often have a bitter taste, which can be removed by boiling. They can then be prepared in the same way as other yams, potatoes, and sweet potatoes. Air potato is one of the most widely-consumed yam species. It is important to note that uncultivated forms can be poisonous. These varieties contain the steroid, diosgenin, which is a principal material used in the manufacture of a number of synthetic steroidal hormones, such as those used in hormonal contraception. Air Potato has been used as a folk remedy to treat conjunctivitis, diarrhoea and dysentery, among other ailments. Air potato grows invasively in places such as in Florida. A fast-growing, large-leafed vine, it spreads tenaciously and shades out any plants growing beneath it. The bulbils on the vines sprout and become new vines, twisting around each other to form a thick mat. If the plant is cut to the ground, the tubers can survive for extended periods and send up new shoots later.

Distribution: Tropical Africa; Asia.
Height and spread: 12m x 20cm/39ft x 8in.
Habit and form: Perennial herb.
Leaf shape: Simple, heart shaped.
Pollinated: Insect.

Left: Air potato produces vine-like growth.

Identification: A perennial twining vine, sometimes spiny, with slender stems reaching up to 12m/39ft in trees and shrubs, arising from rounded or kidney-shaped brown underground tubers. The leaves are simple and heart-shaped, to 25cm/10in long and 20cm/8in across, the veins clearly parallel from the base, and with a pointed tip. Unusual aerial tubers or bulbils grow in leaf axils, rounded, becoming markedly angular. The flowers are greenish-yellow, tiny (2mm/¹⁄₁₆in), on long sprays opposite leaves. The fruit is a four-winged brown capsule, 20mm/¾in long, directed downwards, and opening by three valves to release winged seeds.

Above: The tuber has many medicinal uses.

TERRESTRIAL ORCHIDS

The Orchidaceae, or orchid family, comprises terrestrial, epiphytic or saprophytic herbs It is one of the largest families of flowering plants, with about 1,000 genera and 15–20,000 species. The terrestrial species often display ingenious relationships with their pollinators, and although the flowers are generally smaller than some of the epiphytic types they are equally intricate.

Lady's slipper

Cypripedium calceolus

This orchid, with large, solitary flowers with maroon-brown petals and a pouched, yellow lip, is found in open woodlands on calcareous soils, usually on north-facing slopes. It is widely distributed throughout Europe, and eastward across Asia to the Pacific coast and on into much of northern North America. There are several varieties across the range with different flower sizes to accommodate different pollinators. Despite this wide distribution, however, over-collection has made it rare and threatened over much of its range even though efforts have been made to protect it.

Identification: This terrestrial orchid has three to five oval to elliptic leaves, ascending, sheathing at the base, with pointed to tapered tips, sparsely hairy, 50mm–20cm/2–8in long. The stem is 40cm/16in tall, hairy, the hairs often glandular. Flowers are usually borne one per stem, less often two, in early to midsummer. The sepals and lateral petals are greenish-yellow to purplish-brown, 20–60mm/¾–2¼in long, the upper sepal lance-shaped to oval, the lateral sepals joined below the lip, the lateral petals narrowly lance-shaped and twisted. The lip is yellow, often purple-veined and dotted with purple around the orifice, and heavily pouched in the style of a slipper.

Distribution: Eurasia; North America.
Height and spread: 40cm/16in.
Habit and form: Herbaceous perennial.
Leaf shape: Ovate to elliptic.
Pollinated: Insect.

Bee orchid

Ophrys apifera

Bee orchids, although not particularly rare across their range, are unpredictable in their appearance, often varying hugely in numbers from year to year. This is probably due to the plant's habit of overwintering as a dormant tuber. Dry years reduce the size of the orchids, resulting in the plant not flowering for a year or more after. It is a frequently encountered species of limestone grasslands, old limestone quarries, maquis and sand dunes and is typically found in areas of short, grazed turf across Europe ranging eastward into northern Asia. The flower mimics the female of a Mediterranean bee species to attract potential 'suitors' who attempt to mate with it. When a male bee lands on the flower, pollen is dumped on its back and it flies off with this to cross-fertilize another flower. Despite this intricacy, many northern populations are self-pollinating as the bee is absent in their location.

Identification: An erect, perennial, terrestrial orchid, with small rosettes of oblong to egg-shaped leaves, 60mm/2¼in long, pointed at the tip, appearing early in the year. The erect racemes, up to 30cm/12in tall, have 2–11 flowers, each 25mm/1in across. The green or purplish-pink sepals and petals, and a brownish furry lip marked red-purple and yellow is supposed to resemble a bee. The flowers are borne in mid-spring and early summer.

Distribution: Europe; northern Asia.
Height and spread: 30cm/12in.
Habit and form: Herbaceous perennial.
Leaf shape: Oblong-ovate.
Pollinated: Bee.

Left: The bee orchid gets its name for its ability to attract male solitary bees to its flowers.

Greater butterfly orchid

Platanthera chlorantha

Distribution: Europe, extending south to northern Africa, and east to Turkey, the Caucasus and northern Iran.
Height and spread: 25–50cm/10–20in, occasionally reaching 65cm/26in.
Habit and form: Tuberous-rooted, herbaceous perennial.
Leaf shape: Oval to elliptical.
Pollinated: Night-flying moth.

The graceful, upright flowering spikes of the greater butterfly orchid are a distinctive feature of old, unimproved grasslands and woodland across much of Europe. Their distinctive flowers, superficially resembling a bird or insect in flight, are supremely well adapted to pollination by night-flying moths. They are sweetly scented, are apparently luminescent in poor light, and the long, nectar-rich spur directs the moths to the heart of the flower, where pollination can take place.

Right: The individual orchid flowers are greenish-yellowish-white.

Identification: The flowering spike of the greater-butterfly orchid arises from two large and broad leaves, and is composed of typically 10–30 relatively widely spaced, greenish-white flowers. Each flower is up to 25mm/1in across. The most distinctive feature is the long, slender spur, up to 40mm/1¾in long.

Below: The greater butterfly orchid is a native of unimproved grassland.

Himalayan lady's slipper
Cypripedium himalaicum
This pretty lady's slipper orchid grows from western Nepal to south-eastern Tibet, usually at 3,000–4,300m/9,800–14,000ft, either on slopes or in open forests and scrubland. It bears large flowers, each with an inflated bag-like lip, with streaky purple markings.

Fly orchid *Ophrys insectifera*
Fly orchid is an elusive orchid of open woodland, scrubland, and, more rarely, dry fen, over lime-rich soils. Like many species of the genus *Ophrys*, the flower mimics various insect species for pollination: in this case by the male digger wasp *Argogorytes mystaceus*, which is attracted to the flower by its resemblance to the female wasp, and also excited by pheromones produced by the flower.

Woodcock orchid
Ophrys scolopax
A handsome and widespread *Ophrys* species from the Mediterranean region. Today taxonomists recognize no fewer than 250 species of *Ophrys* (up from 60 during the 1980s), though to the untutored eye many seem remarkably similar. This suggests that the genus may be undergoing rapid evolution at the present time, perhaps reflecting the important role played by a wide variety of specialist pollinators. It grows in maquis, grassland and open woods.

Fragrant orchid

Gymnadenia conopsea

The fragrant orchid is an attractive orchid, distinctive for its sweet scent – likened to clove pinks and mock orange (*Philadelphus*) – and its rich pink colouration. Recently this species has been 'split' into three closely related species, *Gymnadenia conopsea*, *G. borealis* and *G. densiflora*, which can be found in grasslands, heaths and fens across much of Europe, at up to 3,000m/9,800ft in mountain regions. *G. borealis* and *G. densiflora* are threatened by gross habitat destruction, the lowering of water tables, and the cessation of traditional management practices.

Identification: A handsome, slender orchid, with a dense cylindrical spike in various shades of pink. Each flower is distinctive for its two lateral sepals, held horizontally, and for its long, slender spur. Three closely related, and recently defined, species make up the European fragrant orchid, and are distinguished on the basis of overall size, flower colour and morphology, and habitat preferences.

Distribution: Europe (though avoiding the Mediterranean lowlands); scattered through Asia (e.g. the Himalayas and China), eastward to Korea and Japan.
Height and spread: 15–40cm/6–16in, rarely reaching 60cm/24in
Habit and form: Tuberous-rooted herbaceous perennial.
Leaf shape: Narrow and strap-shaped.
Pollinated: Butterfly and moth.

Right: Each individual flower has a distinctive long spur.

Military orchid

Orchis militaris

The military orchid is one of Europe's more widespread species, often occurring in abundance in orchid-rich grasslands (including road verges) and open woodlands. In the southern part of its range it occurs in mountainous areas. Nevertheless, as one of the most attractive orchids in the region, the species has always been a target for orchid collectors, and it has been reduced to rarity in certain countries. In Great Britain, collecting, combined with habitat destruction and succession, rendered the species apparently extinct by 1914, and it was not until 1947 that the species was rediscovered as a native plant. Today the plant survives in just three locations, where it flourishes as the result of careful management and hand-pollination of the flowers.

Identification: A handsome and relatively large orchid, with a basal rosette of broad, glossy leaves, and a relatively dense, conical to cylindrical spike of up to 25 flowers. Each flower is anthropomorphic (i.e. human shaped), pale pink or lilac coloured, with deeper purple-pink spots and lobes.

Left: The military orchid has distinct 'arms' and 'legs' on the lower lobe.

Distribution: Europe, though rare or absent in the extreme south and north, extending eastward to the Altai Mountains and Lake Baikal in western and southern Siberia.
Height and spread: Typically 20–45cm/8–18in, rarely reaching 60cm/24in.
Habit and form: Tuberous-rooted, perennial herb.
Leaf shape: Broad, strap-shaped.
Pollinated: Bee and fly.

Left: Individual flower spikes appear among grassland.

Common spotted orchid

Dactylorhiza fuchsii

The common spotted orchid is a colourful and distinctive species of rough grassland across much of Europe, at its peak flowering in midsummer. Unlike many of Europe's orchids, this species is perhaps the least threatened, and today is as much a feature of roadside verges, spoil heaps, gravel pits and industrial sites, as more traditional, old grasslands. The genus *Dactylorhiza* (meaning 'finger-root') takes it name from its hand-shaped tubers, which distinguish it from its more widespread, ovoid-tubered relatives.

Right: The individual flowers vary from white to pale purple and are marked with purple spots.

Identification: An erect spike, with numerous spotted leaves, and a pink, pyramidal to cylindrical inflorescence typically 40mm/1½in or more in length. The lip of individual flowers is up to 12mm/½in wide, three-lobed and heavily streaked and spotted.

Below: Common spotted orchid often grows colonially, forming large swarms of cylindrical spikes of flowers.

Distribution: Europe, north to Finland, and east to Siberia, though rare in the Mediterranean region.
Height and spread: Stems to 50cm/20in, rarely 70cm/27½in.
Habit and form: Herbaceous, tuberous-rooted perennial.
Leaf shape: Strap shaped.
Pollinated: Bee, fly and other insect.

Violet limodore

Limodorum abortivum

Distribution: South and central Europe, extending east to Syria, Turkey, Iran and the Caucasus region.
Height and spread: Up to 80cm/31in.
Habit and form: A saprophytic, rhizomatous perennial.
Leaf shape: Reduced to dusky-violet coloured sheaths.
Pollinated: Insect.

The ghostly, purple-tinted violet limodore has one of the most unusual life cycles of any higher plant in Europe. This plant derives all its nutrition by parasitizing mycorrhizal fungi as opposed to generating sugars through photosynthesis of the sun's energy. As a result, leaves are superfluous, and thus reduced to purplish, sheathing scales, and the plant can also tolerate high levels of shade, often occurring alone in dense woodland. This unusual and attractive species has proved impossible to cultivate to date.

Right: The individual flowers are large with 'painted' lobes.

Identification: A robust plant, difficult to confuse with other species: their size, lack of leaves, and the overall dusky violet colour are diagnostic among European orchids. The large violet flowers are up to 50mm/2in across.

Below: The flower spikes have no leaves, and thrive near woodland.

Green-winged orchid *Orchis morio*
This orchid was once commonplace in well-drained dairy and sheep pastures across Europe, where its rich purple, and more rarely candy pink or white, flower spikes occurred in thousands, often in association with cowslips (*Primula veris*). Many western and northern European countries have lost their unimproved pastures and with them the green-winged orchid has vanished.

Burnt-tip orchid *Orchis (Neotinea) ustulata*
This species takes its English name from the rich red-brown of the unopened flower buds, resembling caramelized sugar. Wide-spread through much of Europe, the species has declined as its favoured short, species-rich grasslands are ploughed, fertilised or under-grazed.

Heath spotted orchid *Dactylorhiza maculata*
Closely related to the common spotted orchid, *D. fuchsii*, though typically daintier, this orchid has paler, more faintly spotted flowers. This species is easily obtained in cultivation.

Frog orchid *Coeloglossum (Dactylorhiza) viride*
One of Europe's most diminutive orchids, each green flower is superficially shaped like a leaping frog. This is a plant of short, nutrient-poor grasslands across a wide range of altitudes, and is declining rapidly in certain areas through reclamation of pastures, loss of traditional grazing and nutrient enrichment.

Early purple orchid

Orchis mascula

The early purple orchid is a widespread but local plant of woods, hedge banks, pasture and low coastal cliffs. It is very common on lime-rich or clay soils, particularly in warm, moist areas close to the coast. It is relatively common across Europe, in oak groves, undergrowth, meadows and on roadsides, up to a maximum elevation of 2,400m/7,800ft. The leaves are often marked with dark spots, and although purple is the most common colour, a white variant is occasionally encountered. The production of seed often heralds the death of the plant.

Identification: A terrestrial orchid with roots consisting of roundish tubers, from which arise erect, mid-green, often purple-spotted leaves 15cm/6in long. From spring to midsummer it bears light to dark purple flowers, 20mm/¾in long, in erect racemes to 30cm/12in tall. The lowest petal is three-lobed with a stout spur, wider than the bracts. The flowers have a mild vanilla-like aroma.

Distribution: Europe, except Iceland.
Height and spread: 30cm/12in.
Habit and form: Herbaceous perennial.
Leaf shape: Oblong-ovate.
Pollinated: Bee and moth.

Below: True to its name the early purple orchid flowers earlier than other orchids.

Marsh helleborine

Epipactis palustris

Marsh helleborine is a handsome orchid of wetlands, distinctive because of its large, gleaming white lip, which is hinged, a pollination adaptation that 'bounces' a departing bee into the overhanging stigma of the flower. This orchid is an indicator of species-rich open, mossy fen and dune slack habitats, but is declining across much of its range today as its favoured wet places are inexorably drained or polluted.

Below: Marsh helleborine spreads by a creeping rhizome system.

Identification: Perhaps the most attractive helleborine of the genus *Epipactis*, this species has a lax raceme that is distinctly one-sided, and comprises roughly 20 relatively large flowers, with three brownish-red sepals surrounding a prominent white lip and two pinkish-white petals.

Distribution: Europe though rare in the extreme south), extending east to Siberia, northern Iraq and western Iran.
Height and spread: Typically 20–50cm/8–20in.
Habit and form: A creeping, rhizomatous species, often forming extensive clonal patches.
Leaf shape: Pointed and broadly strap-shaped, with prominent veins.
Pollinated: Bee.

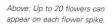

Above: Up to 20 flowers can appear on each flower spike.

Bird's-nest orchid

Neottia nidus-avis

The bird's-nest orchid is one of the strangest plants in Europe. It is one of a handful of species of orchids that have largely or wholly dispensed with the need to photosynthesize from the sun's rays, and is instead wholly reliant on fungi for nutrition. As a result, the plant is entirely brownish and chlorophyll-free, and typically grows in densely-shaded woodland, most commonly on well-drained chalk and limestone soils. This unusual life cycle allows this species to flower and fruit underground under exceptional circumstances (for example, if its growing inflorescence becomes trapped under a stone or branch), though how often this takes place is not known.

Left: The lower lip is two-lobed.

Above: This brown plant does not make chlorophyll, and gets its nutrients from tree roots.

Identification: With its upright spike of honey-brown flowers and leaves, the bird's-nest orchid is difficult to confuse with many other European plants. The flowers, each up to 12mm/½in wide, are largely crowded into a dense cylindrical spike, though a few of the lower flowers are characteristically widely spaced down the stem. The flowers are sweetly scented.

Distribution: Northern and central Europe, extending south to the Mediterranean, and east to Siberia and northern Iran; localized distribution in the Far East.
Height and spread: 20–40cm/8–16in.
Habit and form: A shortly rhizomatous, perennial herb.
Leaf shape: Leaves reduced to brownish, sheathing scales.
Pollinated: Fly and other insects.

Vanilla orchid

Nigritella nigra

Distribution: Central Europe, south to northern Spain, central Italy and Greece; with disjunctive populations in Norway and Sweden.
Height and spread: Up to 30cm/12in.
Habit and form: A slender, tuberous-rooted perennial herb.
Leaf shape: Narrowly lance-shaped.
Pollinated: Insect.

The vanilla orchid is one of Europe's best-loved orchids, prized by flower lovers for its dark coloration and rich scent. It is a characteristic plant of the lime-rich pastures and dry fens of the mountains of central Europe, dropping to lower altitudes towards the northern edge of its range in Scandinavia. In many parts of its range, the species is declining due to changes in traditional land use, particularly with the decline in hay making and rough grazing in mountain regions.

Left: The flower spikes are erect, growing in grassland and pastures.

Far right: The deep crimson flowers have pointed lobes.

Identification: An erect and relatively small growing orchid, distinct in Europe for its dense head of blackish-crimson flowers. The flowers have a distinctive and strong scent of vanilla. Red-coloured (subsp. *rubra*) and whitish-pink (subsp. *corneliana*) subspecies are treated by some botanists as separate species.

OTHER SPECIES OF NOTE

Violet helleborine *Epipactis purpurata*
This robust, clump-forming orchid, is often found in the densest woodland. Here it is clearly partially saprophytic, for occasionally pinkish, chlorophyll-free plants can be found. Violet helleborine takes it specific name from the purple suffusion across both flowers and leaves.

White helleborine *Cephalanthera damasonium*
A woodland orchid distinctive for its few, large egg-shaped white flowers. It is a characteristic of beech (*Fagus*) woodland. Scientific studies show that it acquires much of its nitrogen and carbon nutrition through an association with various fungal mycorrhizae, which, in turn, have a relationship with nearby trees.

Common twayblade *Listera* (*Neottia*) *ovata*
This species grows scattered through much of the Northern Hemisphere and is one of Europe's commonest orchids. A recent study of the plant's DNA has shown it to be closely related to the mycotrophic and chlorophyll-free bird's-nest orchid, *Neottia nidus-avis*.

Ghost orchid *Epipogium aphyllum*
One of Europe's most enigmatic orchids. Its ghostly pinkish-brown spikes occur sporadically in the deepest shade of broad-leaved woodlands. The plant is so difficult to find in Great Britain that some naturalists search for it in the dead of night, using powerful torches to highlight its ghostly spikes camouflaged against a background of brown beech leaves. There have been no official reports of sightings since 1986.

Red helleborine

Cephalanthera rubra

A handsome orchid of open woodland and scrubland red helleborine is typically found on lime-rich soils. The species is intolerant of competition from other plants, and many sites are kept open due to topography or light grazing. Research suggests that the colour and frilly lip of the species is similar to that of some bellflower (*Campanula*) species in the eyes of certain solitary bees, and pollination takes place as the bees are fooled into foraging for non-existent nectar. While widespread across much of Europe, this species is one of Great Britain's rarest, with fewer than 100 plants.

Identification: A slender orchid with rarely more than one lax flowering spike of typically 12 relatively large flowers in a beautiful shade of bright pink.

Distribution: Europe, extending north to southern Finland, east to the Urals, western Russia, northern Iran and Syria, and south to North Africa.
Height and spread: Slender stems to 45–60cm/18–24in.
Habit and form: Herbaceous, rhizomatous perennial.
Leaf shape: Spreading and lance-shaped.
Pollinated: Bee of the genus *Chelostoma*.

Below and left: The flower spikes produce bright pink flowers in early summer. The species is critically endangered in the UK.

Globe orchid

Traunsteinera globosa

The globe orchid is a beautiful and distinctive species of the hay meadows and pastures through the mountain ranges of central Europe, where it is commonly intermixed with red clover (*Trifolium pratense*). Research suggests that this association may be more than coincidental: the nectar-rich flowers of the clover may lure insects to colonies of the superficially-similar, yet nectar-free orchid, thus effecting pollination.

Identification: A slender orchid with a dense, globose head of sugar-pink flowers. Each flower measures up to 12mm/½in wide. The sepals are characteristically narrow to a spathulate, with a wispy tip, and the three-lobed lip is purple-spotted. In the wider Caucasus region, this species is replaced by the milky-white coloured related species *T. sphaerica*.

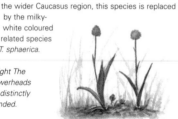

Right The flowerheads are distinctly rounded.

Above: The showy pink flowers are very attractive.

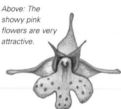

Above: Many individual flowers make up the flower spike.

Distribution: Central Europe, extending north to France, Germany and Poland, and east into western Russia; absent from much of the Mediterranean region.
Height and spread: Up to 65cm/26in.
Habit and form: Tuberous-rooted herbaceous perennial.
Leaf shape: Oblong to lance-shaped.
Pollinated: Insect.

Lizard orchid

Himantoglossum hircinum

Few European orchids can be more unmistakeable than the lizard orchid, a locally common species of rough lime-rich grasslands and scrubland across the warmer parts of Europe. Nevertheless, at the edge of its range, populations fluctuate, apparently reflecting subtle changes in climate: for example in Great Britain the plant was largely confined to Kent until the first few decades of the 20th century, when its distribution expanded rapidly. Yet, by 1935, populations were on the wane again, declining to approximately 10 well-established colonies. But with climate change, the species seems to be spreading again, perhaps due to changes in rainfall patterns, and today 20 colonies are known in Great Britain.

Left: The flower has a remarkably long lower lip.

Identification: A wintergreen rosette of up to 10 large, strap-shaped leaves gives rise to a robust spike of up to 80 large flowers, crowded in the upper half of the stem. The three sepals, plus two upper petals are greenish in colour and form a loose hood, but the long (to 60mm/2¼in), lizard-like lip (lower petal) is the most obvious feature of the flower. This comprises two short lateral lobes and one long central lobe, which uncoils like the spring of a watch.

Right: Although rare, local populations of the lizard orchid can be seen.

Distribution: Southern and western Europe, north to eastern England and the Netherlands, and extending into northern Africa.
Height and spread: 20–70cm/8–27½in, rarely to 90cm/35in.
Habit and form: A robust, erect tuberous-rooted perennial herb.
Leaf shape: Strap-shaped.
Pollinated: Bee and other insects.

Giant orchid

Barlia robertiana

Distribution: Mediterranean region and the Canary Islands.
Height and spread: 20–60cm/8–24in, occasionally to 80cm/31in.
Habit and form: Tuberous-rooted, herbaceous perennial.
Leaf shape: Broadly oblong.
Pollinated: Insect.

One of Europe's largest orchid species, the giant orchid is a familiar sight to early visitors to the Mediterranean region, where the species grows at low altitude in olive and citrus groves, open garrigue and in other grassy places. In spite of the fact that its dense inflorescence is sombre coloured, in some countries the species has fallen prey to collection, mainly for its roots, which are dried and ground up to produce 'salep', a principal ingredient in a hot milk drink and distinctive ice-cream.

Identification: A large orchid, with a cylindrical spike of tightly-packed flowers in sombre shades of purple, pink and green, giving the plant a somewhat damaged or dead look from a distance. Each flower bears a prominent 'anthropomorphic' lip, each with two 'arms' and 'legs', and the species is closely related to the lizard orchids (*Himantoglossum*).

Above and left: The giant orchid is insect-pollinated, though the flowers do not produce nectar, so visiting insects leave each flower unrewarded.

OTHER SPECIES OF NOTE

Man orchid *Aceras anthropophorum*
The man orchid has a patchy distribution, ranging from the Mediterranean region to Turkey, but is much reduced over its former range due to grassland disturbance. The yellowish flowers resemble small human figures, with the upper flower parts forming a 'helmet'.

Pyramidal orchid
Anacamptis pyramidalis
This orchid is so-called because of the obvious rounded-pyramid shape of the flowering spike, especially when young. The flowers are a beautiful deep pink, with a short spur; they have a faint fragrance and are moth-pollinated. The leaves are narrow and without any spots.

Autumn lady's-tresses *Spiranthes spiralis*
This orchid takes its English name from its row of delicate white flowers arranged in a spiral up the stem, like a lady's braided hair. Its small, flattened rosette of leaves makes it perfectly adapted to heavy grazing by stock – and this growth form also allows it to survive in tightly mown grass.

Creeping lady's-tresses *Goodyera repens*
This orchid has small white flowers borne in a slightly twisting spiral. It has net-veined leaves, and flowers with a narrow, spout-shaped outer lip. It spreads by means of long, creeping underground stems. It grows to 25cm/10in and typically in pine and birch woods.

Tongue orchid

Serapias lingua

The tongue orchid is a common species of open grassy places in the Mediterranean region, where it favours damp grassland in olive groves, garrigue and maquis communities at low altitude, often near the coast. Unlike most tuberous European orchids, members of this genus annually produce a number of new tubers on stolons, allowing the gentle spread of the species and the development of small, dense colonies. Under frost-free conditions, the species is relatively easy to cultivate in gardens, and can increase at a gratifying rate.

Identification: This species is characterized by dark reddish flowers, each comprising a dark-veined hood (consisting of the three sepals), and a distinctive, ploughshare-shaped lip. In *S. lingua*, up to nine flowers are borne thinly up each stem. The lip is 25–32mm/1–1¼in long, and has a single distinctive, shiny-red 'blob' in the throat.

Distribution: Western Mediterranean, east to Crete and Greece.
Height and spread: Up to 25cm/10in.
Habit and form: Tuberous-rooted herbaceous perennial.
Leaf shape: Narrow and strap-like.
Pollinated: Beetles, small wasps and other insects.

Above and left: The flower is quite distinctive, with a deeply protruding lower lip held on a tall stem.

Eulophia streptopetala

(= *Lissochilus streptopetalus*)

This orchid is fairly common, mainly in eastern Africa, for instance in Zimbabwe, where it grows at about 800–2,300m/2,600–7,500ft, normally flowering between October and December. There are about 200 species in this genus, mainly in Africa and Asia. The tubers of some are used to prepare the drink Indian salep. Various species and hybrids are now popular in cultivation as they are relatively easy to propagate and also produce impressive large spikes of flowers.

Identification: A tall species, growing to about 1.5m/5ft. It produces pseudobulbs, often about ground level. The leaves are large, lance-shaped and ribbed. The inflorescence, which appears before most of the leaves are fully developed, is many-flowered. Each flower has yellow-green sepals that are mainly purple on the inside and marked with purple spots on the outside. The petals are bright yellow on the outside and creamy yellow inside. Each flower has a yellow lip with purple side lobes and a purplish-red spur.

Far left: The flowers are mainly purple and yellow colour and droop downwards from the stem.

Right: The spikes grow very tall.

Distribution: Africa; Arabian Peninsula.
Height and spread: 1.5m x 20cm/5ft x 8in.
Habit and form: Herbaceous perennial.
Leaf shape: Lanceolate.
Pollinated: Insect.

Formosa windowsill orchid

Formosa pleione, *Pleione formosana*

The orchids of the genus *Pleione* are very popular in cultivation, mainly because of their beautiful wide flowers with narrow spreading sepals and petals and large, fringed lip. Another reason is that they are relatively easy to grow, being semi-hardy. They are ideal for borders, containers and in the conservatory, or as their common name suggests, windowsills. They can be propagated by division of the pseudobulbs. This species is from Taiwan and eastern China where it grows at 500–2,500m/1,600–8,200ft around the base of trees or on rocks. It has become rare mainly through over collection.

Identification: The leafless pseudobulb produces a spike of one or two flowers. Each flower is about 10cm/4in across, with (usually) pink spreading narrow perianth segments and a central large pale fringed lip with mottled markings on the inside. A single, deciduous, erect, elliptic, pointed leaf is produced.

Above: The central lip is fringed.

Below: This plant is cultivated as a houseplant as well as growing as a wild flower.

Distribution: Taiwan; eastern China.
Height and spread: 25cm/10in.
Habit and form: Half-hardy perennial.
Leaf shape: Elliptic.
Pollinated: Insect.

Below: This species basks in warm temperatures.

Pride of Table Mountain

Disa uniflora

Distribution: Western Cape, South Africa.
Height and spread: Up to 60cm/24in.
Habit and form: Herbaceous perennial.
Leaf shape: Lanceolate.
Pollinated: Butterfly (*Meneris tulbaghia*).

Far right: The bright red flowers are very prominent.

Disa is a large African genus and, although widespread, many species are endemic to small areas. The spectacular, brilliant red flowers of *D. uniflora*, which are the emblem of the Western Cape, are borne during summer and are found in fynbos, on rock flushes, in marshes and lakes, and in montane grassland. It is always associated with water, growing on the edges of permanent mountain streams or in wet moss near waterfalls, at altitudes varying from sea level to about 1,200m/4,000ft. The butterfly, *Meneris tulbaghia*, is the only known pollinator, although the plant readily multiplies by producing stolons that develop into new plants. After flowering, the plant and its tuber die back to provide food for the production of a fresh tuber.

Identification: A deciduous terrestrial orchid, with lance-shaped leaves up to 25cm/10in long, it produces short racemes of up to three, or rarely up to ten, brilliant scarlet flowers, each 75mm–12.5cm/3–5in across, with hooded upper perianth and spreading lower perianth segments. The hood is paler with darker red striations; the lower twin petals have a green stripe on the outer surface. The bud is tightly curled and upwards facing.

OTHER SPECIES OF NOTE

Slipper orchid *Paphiopedilum fairrieanum*
This slipper orchid has large curving sepals and petals, white with many maroon veins, and a glossy yellowish pouch. It is rare in its native habitat – open forest and rocky grassland in northern India and Bhutan – where it is threatened by collection, fires and overgrazing. It is highly prized by growers and collectors.

Moth orchid
Phalaenopsis stuartiana
The large spreading flowers with wing-like petals, often white or pale, tend to stand out at night, hence the common name. This species, native to the Philippines, grows in warm, lowland rainforests, sometimes as an epiphyte. Its fragrant flowers, each about 70mm/2¾in across, have broad, pure white petals and a lip marked gold and red-brown.

Satyrium princeps
This South African terrestrial orchid is a native of fynbos regions, especially in coastal districts. It has heads of scented white flowers that emerge from broad, flat basal foliage. It is extremely rare in the wild, with only scattered populations around the southern Cape.

Rothschild's slipper orchid

Sumazau slipper orchid, *Paphiopedilum rothschildianum*

This genus contains more than 60 species of tropical evergreen orchids found from India, through China and South-east Asia to New Guinea. Like the temperate slipper orchids (*Cypripedium*), they have a slipper-shaped inflated lip or pouch and wide spreading lateral petals. Many are grown by orchid enthusiasts and this trade threatens many species in the wild, though several are now propagated. Their typical habitat is damp mossy forest floor. This species is known from only a couple of sites at 600–1,200m/2,000–4,200ft on Mount Kinabalu in Borneo.

Right and below: This is a large and striking species.

Distribution: Borneo.
Height and spread: To 1m/39in.
Habit and form: Frost-tender perennial.
Leaf shape: Strap-shaped.
Pollinated: Insect (probably fly).

Identification: From the centre of the strap-like leathery leaves grow tall spikes bearing up to six large flowers. Each flower is up to 35cm/14in across, with boldly striped upper and lower sepals, a reddish, veined pouch and long, narrow, speckled petals spreading out horizontally on each side.

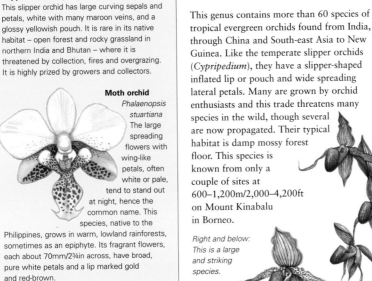

EPIPHYTIC AND LITHOPHYTIC ORCHIDS

These orchids depend upon the support of another plant, though they are not parasitic. They typically root into accumulations of plant debris in the forks of tree branches and manufacture their own food by photosynthesis. They are generally forest dwellers, many conducting their entire life cycles elevated in their host trees or on inaccessible rocky outcrops. They include some of the showiest of all flowers.

Dendrobium aphyllum

These deciduous, tropical, epiphytic orchids are widespread in South-east Asia, being found in low-altitude rainforests right up into montane forests. The large pale mauve and primrose yellow flowers have a strong violet fragrance and are borne from stem-like pseudobulbs before the new leaves appear. The foliage has a soft texture and is typically deciduous after a single season, though under some conditions leaves may last more than a year.

Identification: Pendent to semi-erect, long, slender pseudobulbs are slightly swollen at the nodes, with new growths appearing about flowering time. Oval, fleshy leaves, 12.5cm/5in long, often wavy along the margin, are often smaller near the tips of the canes. Pale mauve-pink flowers, 50mm/2in across, with primrose-yellow lips, are borne in pairs, emerging from nodes along the previous season's leafless growth, and are so numerous that the canes appear covered with blossoms.

Above: The leaves are fleshy.

Right: The flowerhead is spectacular.

Distribution: South-east Asia from southern and eastern India to south-western China, Thailand, Laos, Vietnam, Malaysia and South Andaman Island.
Height and spread: 60cm–1.8m/24in–6ft, trailing.
Habit and form: Deciduous epiphyte.
Leaf shape: Ovate to lanceolate.
Pollinated: Insect.

Four season orchid

Corsage orchid, *Cymbidium ensifolium*

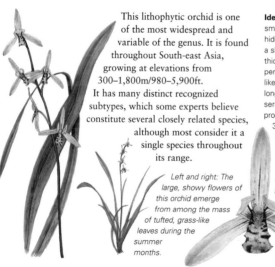

This lithophytic orchid is one of the most widespread and variable of the genus. It is found throughout South-east Asia, growing at elevations from 300–1,800m/980–5,900ft. It has many distinct recognized subtypes, which some experts believe constitute several closely related species, although most consider it a single species throughout its range.

Left and right: The large, showy flowers of this orchid emerge from among the mass of tufted, grass-like leaves during the summer months.

Identification: This plant has small, ovoid pseudobulbs, often hidden from view, clumped along a short rhizome that gives rise to thick, white, branching roots. The persistent, linear, tufted, grass-like leaves are up to 30cm/12in long, sometimes with minutely serrated tips. In summer, it produces upright racemes of 3–12 waxy, greenish-yellow flowers, each 25–50mm/1–2in across, with spreading sepals and petals streaked with red. Green or pale yellow, rarely white, lips, with wavy margins and callus ridges converging at the apex and forming a tube at mid-lobe base, are irregularly spotted red-brown.

Distribution: Indochina; China; Japan; Borneo; New Guinea; and the Philippines.
Height and spread: 30cm/12in.
Habit and form: Lithophytic orchid.
Leaf shape: Linear.
Pollinated: Insect.

Moth orchid

Phalaenopsis amabilis

Distribution: Philippines.
Height and spread: Up to 90cm/35in.
Habit and form: Epiphyte.
Leaf shape: Obovate-oblong.
Pollinated: Insect.

This robust epiphytic orchid from the Philippines is very variable, occurring at elevations up to 600m/2,000ft on the trunks and branches of rainforest trees, overhanging rivers, swamps and streams. The short, stem-like rhizome gives rise to long, shiny leaves, among which the spectacular, large, scented, white flowers are borne along pendent racemes and may persist for many weeks before dropping. This is one of the national flowers of Indonesia.

Identification: The short, robust stem is completely enclosed by overlapping leaf-sheaths. The long, fleshy, smooth, often branched, flexible roots are green at the end. The glossy leaves, seldom more than five, are fleshy or leathery, oval to oblong and blunt-tipped, up to 50cm/20in long. Pendent, simple or branched racemes, up to 90cm/35in long, ascending or arched, green dotted brown-purplish, bear numerous white, often fragrant flowers, with yellow-margined lips and red throat margins, 60mm–10cm/2¼–4in across.

Below: The large white flowers of the moth orchid are sweetly scented and often persist for months, high in the rainforest canopy.

OTHER SPECIES OF NOTE

Dendrobium densiflorum
This epiphytic orchid from India has bunches of showy, fragrant blooms on pendent, very densely flowered racemes that may reach 25cm/10in or more, arising from near the base of the stem. The lip of the flower is bright orange, with the rest of the flower paler yellow-orange.

Blue orchid *Vanda coerulea*
With its white or pale blue flowers dramatically marked with purple, this north Indian orchid's spectacular and unusual blooms are popular with orchid enthusiasts. As a consequence large numbers have been stripped from the wild. Today it is rare and its habitat is under threat.

Angel orchid *Coelogyne cristata*
This orchid is from the Himalayas, where it grows in cool mountain regions that experience dry cool winters and heavy rainfall during monsoon months. The pure crystalline-white flowers, up to 75mm/3in across, with a lip that has a deep yolk-yellow crest, grow in groups of three to 10 per stem.

Bulbophyllum medusae
This unusual South-east Asian orchid, found from Thailand to Borneo and the Philippines, is named after the snake-haired gorgon Medusa of Greek mythology because of its strange, fringed flowers, with lateral sepals that grow to 12.5cm/5in long. The arching umbels of flowers emerge from the base of the pseudobulbs.

Scorpion orchid

Air-flower arachnis, *Arachnis flos-aeris*

All *Arachnis* orchids are known as scorpion orchids, but the name is especially applied to this species. Mainly a lowland plant that inhabits more open areas in full sun, this is not strictly an epiphyte but a vining, monopodial orchid. It can be found scrambling over rocks and trees, usually at elevations up to 1,000m/3,200ft in wet tropical forests of South-east Asia. It is a large species, which will climb high into the treetops if given the opportunity.

Identification: It has a thick, robust stem that roots adventitiously on to supporting plants and thick, fleshy or leathery, dark green leaves, 18cm/7in long and notched at the tips. The fragrant flowers, up to 10cm/4in across with a fixed lip and four pollinia, are yellow-green horizontally striped or spotted maroon, or in shades of yellow to gold with red-brown markings. They are borne in arching, axillary panicles or racemes, pendent or ascending, up to 1.8m/6ft long, with many flowers that open over a long period.

Distribution: Thailand, western Malaysia and the Philippines.
Height and spread: 6m/19¾ft or more.
Habit and form: Climbing orchid.
Leaf shape: Obovate-oblong.
Pollinated: Insect.

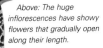

Above: The huge inflorescences have showy flowers that gradually open along their length.

WILD FLOWERS OF NORTH AND CENTRAL AMERICA

America was called the 'New World' by Europeans when they began settling there five centuries ago. The land is anything but new, however, and contains many plants with ancient lineages. North America was attached to Asia until recently, in geological terms, and many of the plants that grow there resemble species found across Eurasia. Throughout North and Central America an abundance of habitats produces a wealth of wild flowers; there is always something in bloom, in the deserts and chaparrals, on the coast, in woodlands, on rocky mountain slopes, in hedgerows or on the prairies. Although many habitats are changing or threatened, conservancy preserves across the region offer an opportunity to see the diversity of American wild flowers, which includes some of the world's rarest, most familiar and fascinating flora.

Above from left: Dark throat shooting star (Dodecatheon pulchellum); *Indian paintbrush* (Castillega angustifolium); *Whitestem sunflower* (Wyethia scabra).

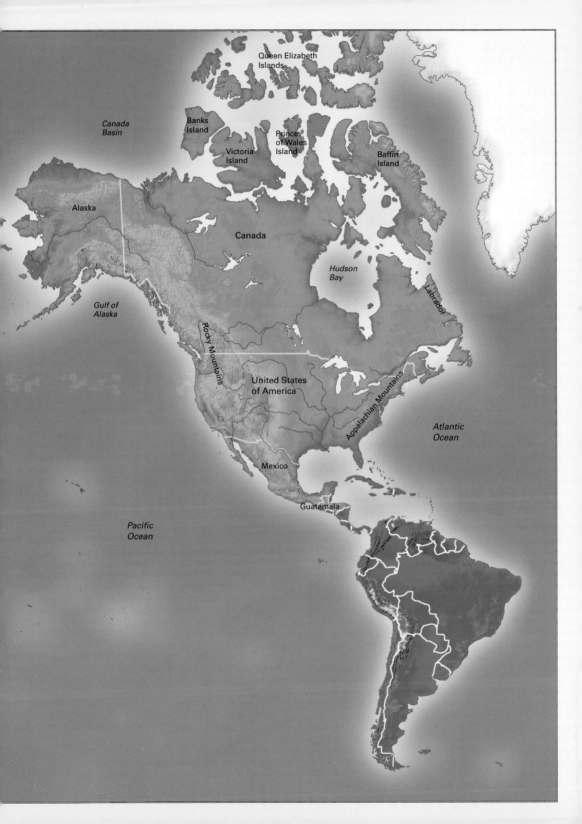

BIRTHWORT AND BARBERRY FAMILIES

The birthwort family, Aristolochiaceae, contains about 500 species of woody vines or herbs, often with heart-shaped leaves and quite large and showy flowers, frequently with a nasty aroma (like rotting flesh) to attract flies for pollination. The barberry family, Berberidaceae, consists of herbs and shrubs, typically with spiny stems, and mostly producing berry fruits. There are some 680 species.

Long-tailed wild ginger

Asarum caudatum

The flowers of this unusual plant are not easy to spot, as they grow very close to the ground and are shaded by the leaves. Like many other members of the family, the plant is aromatic. In fact, the stems and roots were used in earlier times as a substitute for ginger. There are several other species of wild ginger, found in similar moist, shady habitats.

Far left: The distinctive flowers tend to remain hidden beneath the large, heart-shaped leaves.

Identification: This creeping plant grows in moist woodland below about 1,500m/4,900ft, and produces purplish-brown or greenish-yellow flowers from April to July. The flower is partly hidden under the leaves and is up to 12cm/5in across, and has a bowl-shaped base, a slender tip and 12 stamens.

Below: The plant is commonly found in the woodlands of the north-western USA.

Distribution: British Columbia to north-eastern Oregon, south to central California.
Height and spread: To 15cm/6in.
Habit and form: Creeper.
Leaf shape: Heart-shaped.
Pollinated: Insect.

Northern inside-out flower

Vancouveria hexandra

This species takes its name from the unusual flowers, which look as though they are opening the wrong way round, facing back towards their stems. The plant is found in shaded sites in coniferous forests in the Pacific north-west. This and other species in the genus such as golden inside-out flower, *V. chrysantha*, which has yellow flowers, are useful in the garden because they provide good ground cover for shady areas.

Right: The plant has attractive flowers and leaves, and a ground-covering habit.

Identification: This flower grows in clusters and patches on the forest floor. The base leaves are pinnate and have a leathery texture. The flowers are most unusual, with the white sepals and petals bending backwards up the stems. The leaves are long and divided into lobes. The flowering period is May to July.

Distribution: Western Washington state to north-western California.
Height and spread: 15–50cm/6–20in.
Habit and form: Grows in patches.
Leaf shape: Lobed.
Pollinated: Insect.

Wild ginger

Asarum canadense

Despite its name, this plant is not related to the true gingers, but is so called because the rhizome has a strong spicy smell like ginger. Indeed, it is edible when cooked and can be used as a flavouring. It grows in woods with a rich soil and flowers in April and May. A similar species, with the lovely name 'little brown jugs', *A. arifolium*, has green-purple flowers and evergreen, triangular leaves.

Identification: The leaves are large and hairy, usually hiding the green-brown or red-brown flower which grows from between pairs of leaves. The flower is deep and cup-shaped with three sharply pointed lobes, and the fruit is a round capsule up to 30cm/12in across.

Left: The tiny flowers, with their three distinctive pointed lobes, nestle low to the ground beneath large, heart-shaped leaves. The flowers can be hard to spot.

Right: The white stems and fresh green leaves contrast pleasantly. These and the flowers are covered in fine 'hairs'.

Distribution: From Manitoba, North Dakota and New Brunswick, south to Florida.
Height and spread: 15–30cm/6–12in.
Habit and form: Low-growing.
Leaf shape: Heart-shaped.
Pollinated: Insect.

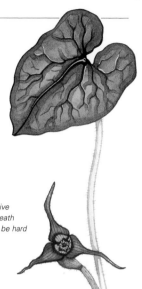

OTHER SPECIES OF NOTE

Common barberry *Berberis vulgaris*
A spiny shrub, native to Europe, but widely naturalized in North America. It is useful as a protective hedge around fields. The clusters of yellow flowers produce bright red berries that can be turned into drinks and preserves.

Blue cohosh
Caulophyllum thalictroides
This is a flower of damp woods, found mainly in the eastern states. The flowers are in loose clusters and are purplish-brown or yellow-green. The blue seeds are reported to have been used as a coffee substitute.

Twinleaf *Jeffersonia diphylla*
Each leaf is divided into two halves, hence the common name. The leaves are basal only. The plant loves rich, moist limestone woodland and the white flowers, with eight petals and four sepals appear in April and May. The genus name honours Thomas Jefferson who had an interest in botany.

Mayapple, Mandrake *Podophyllum peltatum*
The flower looks like that of an apple and opens in May, hence the common name, and the root resembles that of the (unrelated) true mandrake. The single white flower is fragrant, and the edible fruit is a large, yellow, fleshy berry. It grows commonly in oak-hickory forests.

Dutchman's pipe

Aristolochia macrophylla

The species name means 'large-leaved' and indeed, this plant has distinctive big leaves. The common name comes from the shape of the flower, which resembles the old-fashioned tobacco pipes once popular in the Netherlands. The usual habitat is damp woodland with rich soils, and the plant is also found alongside streams. The flowers open from April to June.

Identification: Tall-growing vine with striking brownish-purple S-shaped flowers. Each flower is 50mm/2in long, and the sepals open into three lobes. The long, untoothed leaves are bright green beneath. The fruit is a 10cm/4in long capsule, opening to reveal many winged seeds. The heart-shaped leaves are up to 25cm/10in long.

Distribution: From Michigan south to Alabama and Georgia.
Height and spread: To 20m/65½in.
Habit and form: Climbing vine.
Leaf shape: Heart-shaped.
Pollinated: Insect.

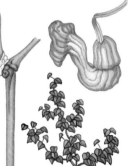

Far right: The plant grows as a vine, producing large dark flowers, then a long fruit.

BUTTERCUP FAMILY

*The buttercup family, Ranunculaceae, is well represented in the New World with many colourful species
to be found, some of which have become popular as garden flowers. Many species are related to similar
plants in Eurasia, although the variety of colour is often greater in the American species.
In common with their Old World counterparts, they are mostly restricted to cooler locations.*

Scarlet clematis

Clematis texensis

This beautiful clematis is native to the Texas
hill country. Unlike other clematis, this
scrambler is herbaceous and dies back
completely in winter, re-emerging
each spring. It commences
blooming in mid-spring and
continues until midsummer,
producing pretty, fuzzy seedpods in
the autumn. The flowers do not
open wide like those of many
clematis species, but form a tulip-
shaped red cup. There
seems to be considerable
variation in the shade
of red from plant
to plant.

Identification: Climbing subshrub
or perennial with smooth,
reddish-brown stems. The tough,
blue-green pinnate leaves have
oval to rounded leaflets,
sometimes two- to three-lobed,
up to 75mm/3in long, usually
heart-shaped at the base, with
small, thorny tips and a distinct
network of veins; the terminal
leaflet is reduced to a tendril. The
solitary, pendulous, scarlet-red
or carmine flowers are tulip-
shaped, to 20mm/¾in across,
with thick, narrow, oval
sepals, reflexed, on ribbed
flower stalks.

Distribution: Texas, USA.
Height and spread: 2m/6½ft.
Habit and form: Subshrub.
Leaf shape: Pinnately
four to eight trifoliate.
Pollinated: Insect.

*Right:
The scarlet
clematis
has a
scrambling
habit.*

*Left: The
pendulous
flowers are
tulip-like.*

Canadian anemone

Meadow anemone, *Anemone canadensis*

This handsome and robust herbaceous perennial
is found in Canada and the northern USA,
on low-lying moist ground and in damp
woods. The large white flowers and
palmate leaves are striking and give the
plant an almost unmistakable appearance
when it is in flower from late spring to
summer. The Canadian anemone typically
forms large colonies along the banks of
rivers and next to levees in floodplains,
spreading vigorously by
means of thread-like
rhizomes.

Identification: A robust perennial,
with deeply lobed basal leaves up
to 12.5cm/5in long and
upright round stems
bearing a single whorl of
three-lobed leaves, toothed
near the tip. A single flower
or loose cyme terminates
each stem: the flower is
buttercup-like, white,
upward-facing and up to
50mm/2in across,
with a lemon-yellow
centre.

Distribution: Canada and
northern USA.
Height and spread:
30–60cm/12–24in.
Habit and form: Herbaceous
perennial.
Leaf shape: Palmate.
Pollinated: Insect.

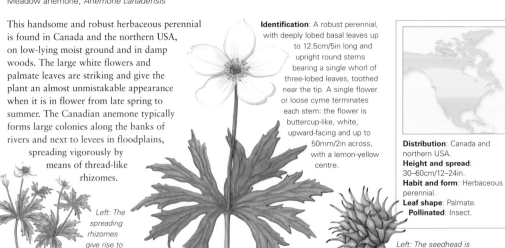

*Left: The
spreading
rhizomes
give rise to
dense colonies
of large white flowers.*

*Left: The seedhead is
composed of numerous,
small, beaked capsules.*

Monkshood

Southern blue monkshood, *Aconitum uncinatum*

Distribution: USA, east of the Rocky Mountains.
Height and spread: 60–90cm/24–35in.
Habit and form: Herbaceous perennial.
Leaf shape: Palmately lobed.
Pollinated: Insect.

Native to much of the USA, with a scattered distribution east of the Rocky Mountains, this striking herbaceous perennial is found in rich woods, or mountainous areas towards the southern part of its range. The plant has become rare, although it is probably not endangered. It is chiefly threatened by forest management practices and, to a lesser extent, by land-use conversion and habitat fragmentation. All parts of this plant are highly toxic.

Left: Flowers appear in late summer to mid-autumn from clumps of 60cm/24in tall plants with deeply lobed leaves.

Right: The seedheads have five parallel ascending sections.

Identification: Tall, slender stems grow from a turnip-like root that is renewed annually, the new one being well separated from the old. The leaves are numerous, firm and deeply divided into three to nine lobes, which are lance-shaped and coarsely toothed. Short terminal racemes or panicles each bear a few violet or deep blue flowers, with unequal petaloid sepals: the upper sepal or helmet is the largest and is strongly arched or hooded, with its tip prolonged forward and downward into a short beak, covering the other two upper sepals. The lower two sepals are vestigial.

Red columbine

Canadian columbine, *Aquilegia canadensis*

Red columbine occupies open sites that are steep and rocky but moist, such as wooded bluffs of streams, wooded slopes, stream banks, the slopes of deep ravines, limestone bluffs and ledges, borders and clearings in deciduous or mixed woods or thickets from Nova Scotia to the Northwest Territories, south to Florida and Texas. The flower is adapted to long-tongued nectar-feeders. Blooming time corresponds with the spring migration movements of the ruby-throated hummingbird, which is this plant's chief pollinator.

Distribution: Eastern Canada and USA.
Height and spread: 30–80cm/12–31in.
Habit and form: Herbaceous perennial.
Leaf shape: Compound.
Pollinated: Hummingbird and hawk moth.

Identification: The fern-like, dark green basal leaves are long, stalked and divided into three lobed leaflets; the leaves on the stem are reduced upward, the uppermost sometimes simple. The bell-like red-and-yellow flowers, several per stem, have five elongated, clubbed, red spurs, up to 25mm/1in long.

Above: The flowerhead.

Far right: Red columbine is an upright herbaceous perennial growing from a short, erect underground stem.

Western monkshood

Aconitum columbianum

A tall, attractive plant with blue, hood-shaped flowers growing mainly in damp woodland or subalpine meadows. Like many members of this genus, the plant is poisonous and has medicinal properties. The uppermost petal-like sepal forms the characteristic hood, arching over the rest of each flower and hiding the true petals.

Identification: The tall, leafy stems have lobed and toothed leaves and the flowering spikes develop their showy flowers in June to August. The sepals are dark purple to whitish-green, and the upper petals are pale blue or white. The hood is about 15–30mm/ ⁹⁄₁₆–1¼in. The plant is found in moist woodlands, subalpine meadows, and often thrives beside streams.

Above: The seeds in the pod are black, shiny and triangular.

Distribution: From New Mexico and Colorado, the southern Sierra Nevada, South Dakota and Montana, north to Alaska.
Height and spread: 30cm–2.1m/12in–6¾ft.
Habit and form: Herbaceous perennial.
Leaf shape: Palmately lobed.
Pollinated: Insect.

Left: All parts of the plant, which is also known as wolf bane, are poisonous.

Baneberry

Actaea rubra

This familiar plant of moist woodland often grows alongside streams, and has a very wide distribution in the USA, especially in northern and mountain sites. The plant grows rapidly to about 90cm/35in in height, then puts out long flower stems topped by clusters of small white flowers. The flowers have small petals and sepals, which fall early, revealing the many stamens. The flowers give way to berries in the autumn, which are often heavy enough to bend the stalk. The attractive berries look enticing, but are in fact poisonous, causing illness to humans and animals.

Above: Baneberry is one of the north's abundant woodland plants. The common name serves as a reminder to avoid the poisonous berries.

Below: The plant forms in clumps and is a common site in the USA.

Distribution: Through the west and north and north-east, and south to Nebraska.
Height and spread: 30–90cm/12–35in.
Habit and form: Herbaceous perennial.
Leaf shape: Pinnately divided.
Pollinated: Insect.

Identification: A branching plant with large, divided leaves and racemes of small white flowers, arising from the axils or terminally.

Round-lobed hepatica

Anemone americana

Distribution: From Manitoba to Nova Scotia, and south to Florida.
Height and spread: 10–15cm/4–6in.
Habit and form: Herbaceous perennial.
Leaf shape: Basal leaves have three rounded lobes.
Pollinated: Insect.

This is a pretty plant, with bright open flowers that can be white, lavender-blue or pink, with five to nine (often six) petal-like sepals, and many stamens. What seem to be sepals are in fact green sepal-like bracts. The flowers appear in early spring and the leaves persist throughout the following winter. The closely-related sharp-leaved hepatica, *A. acutiloba*, has more pointed leaf lobes. The main habitat of this flower is dry woodland.

Identification: Small herb with round-lobed leaves, and hairy flower-stalks.

Above and left: The delicate flowers of round-lobed hepatica balance on fine hairy stalks.

OTHER SPECIES OF NOTE

Blue anemone *Anemone oregana*
This anemone grows in woodland and scrubby hillsides from northern California to Washington State. Its flowers are usually lavender-blue, but can vary from white to pale pink, and appear from March to June. The flower stalks grow up from a whorl of basal leaves. The plant spreads by sending out underground stems.

Desert anemone *Anemone tuberosa*
This is mainly found in rocky deserts in Texas, New Mexico, Utah and California. In addition to the basal leaves there is a whorl midway up the tall stem. The pink-purple or white flowers are clustered around the flowering stems. The beaked seeds are in a woolly seed-head.

Wood anemone *Anemone quinquefolia*
This pretty, delicate woodland flower grows mainly in open woods and clearings across much of eastern North America. From the whorl of three divided leaves arises a central flower stalk. The flowers are white or pinkish, with four to nine petal-like sepals.

Thimbleweed *Anemone virginiana*
This tall, hairy anemone is a woodland flower, usually favouring rocky sites. It is mainly found from Alberta to Newfoundland, south to Georgia. The flowers are white or greenish-white and the name comes from the thimble-shaped pistils.

Scarlet larkspur

Cardinal larkspur, *Delphinium cardinale*

One of the USA's most attractive wild flowers, with brilliant red flowers on tall stalks. It is all the more impressive as it often grows in groups on sites such as scrub and rocky slopes, or woodland clearings. The similar red larkspur, *D. nudicaule*, has less showy, orange-red flowers, and is less tall and prominent.

Identification: The loose tall flower spikes open from May to July. The basal leaves are palmately lobed, and about 50mm–20cm/2–8in wide. Each individual flower is 20–30mm/¾–1¼in across, with five scarlet sepals, the upper sepal with a characteristic back-projecting spur. The four slim petals are yellow, often tipped scarlet.

Distribution: Mainly along the coastal ranges from central California, south to northern Baja California.
Height and spread: 30cm–2.5m/12in–8ft.
Habit and form: Herbaceous perennial.
Leaf shape: Broad, divided, with five to seven deeply toothed lobes.
Pollinated: Hummingbird, insect.

Below: Showy larkspur flowers brighten up chaparral and scrubby coastal areas.

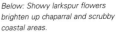

Right: Inside the scarlet sepals are four yellow petals with red tips.

Golden columbine

Aquilegia chrysantha

A beautiful wild flower growing mainly in moist habitats, across the south-west of the region. From a distance the flowers are daffodil-like. Not surprisingly this species is popular in gardens. It is easy to cultivate and is also the parent of many garden hybrids. In the wild it is thought to be retreating in the face of global warming. Columbines take their name from the Latin for dove, the flowers fancifully thought to resemble a group of doves. The similar yellow columbine, *A. flavescens*, is a mountain plant, with bent tips to the petal spurs.

Right: The plants form clumps, and reach a height of about 90cm/35in. The striking colour and spurs make the flowers distinctive and easy to identify in the wild.

Identification: A tall species, with large leaves repeatedly divided into leaflets, about 40mm/1½in long and with rounded tips. The showy flowers have many stamens and five protruding styles. The bushy plant has several stems bearing bright golden yellow flowers in July and August, each 40–75mm/1½–3in across. Each flower has five sepals and five petals, the latter with backward-projecting spurs.

Distribution: Western Texas, Colorado and New Mexico, west to Utah and Arizona.
Height and spread: 30–90cm/12–35in.
Habit and form: Herbaceous perennial.
Leaf shape: Large and divided.
Pollinated: Insect.

Centre left: Aquilegia comes from the Latin word for eagle, referring to the flower's spurs which supposedly resemble an eagle's talons.

Plains larkspur

Prairie larkspur, *Delphinium carolinianum*

This widespread species has several subspecies and related species, with varying flower colour (mostly white or blue), and the group is difficult to classify, especially as hybrids are common. Most blue-flowered species have white variants. The flowers open from May to July and the favoured habitats are open fields, prairies and hill slopes. When it first blooms, the flowers can carpet acres of prairie before the grasses take over. The stems are fuzzy, and usually simple, but on a vigorous plant will branch.

Identification: An erect and felty plant with a raceme of flowers that may be white, or pale (sometimes dark) blue. Each flower is about 25mm/1in across with five crinkled sepals, the upper sepal has a long backward-projecting spur. The four petals are in the centre of the flower.

Right: The plant is covered in tiny hairs. It forms clumps, and flowers appear in various shades, from white to blue.

Above: Larkspur growing among prairie grasses.

Distribution: Manitoba, North Dakota, Minnesota, Wisconsin, south to Texas, Missouri and Colorado.
Height and spread: 1.5m/5ft.
Habit and form: Herbaceous perennial.
Leaf shape: Large and pinnately divided.
Pollinated: Insect.

Right: Developing fruits eventually dry and split open.

Marsh marigold

Elk's lip, *Caltha leptosepala*

These bright, shining flowers appear in the eastern mountain range between May and August. Marsh marigolds, as their name suggests, grow in wet flushes and marshy sites high in the mountains. A typical habitat is around melting snowdrifts. The prominent flowers attract passing insects. The alternative name, elk's lip, comes from the shape of the leaves, which are curled. The related species, twin-flowered marsh marigold, *C. biflora*, nearly always has two flowers on each stalk.

Identification: A leafless stem grows up from a basal rosette of leaves and produces a cup-shaped white flower at its tip. Each flower is 15–30mm/⁹⁄₁₆–1¼in across, and comprises five to 10 petal-like sepals containing many stamens. The petals are absent.

Distribution: Mountains, from New Mexico and eastern Arizona north to Alaska.
Height and spread: 25mm–20cm/1–8in.
Habit and form: Herbaceous perennial.
Leaf shape: Long, oblong, with scalloped margins.
Pollinated: Insect.

Left: Flowers appear above the basal leaves on pink stalks.

Right: The seed pod.

OTHER SPECIES OF NOTE

White baneberry, Doll's eyes
Actaea pachypoda
Found in woods and thickets from Ontario and Nova Scotia south to Florida, the small white flowers appear in May and June. The names come from the white (sometimes red) poisonous berries that resemble the china eyes of old-fashioned dolls.

Nuttall's larkspur *Delphinium nuttallianum*
This is a low-growing species with blue or violet flowers, appearing from March to July. Mainly a western species, from British Columbia south to northern California, the plant is found on dry soils, sagebrush deserts and open pine woods.

Sagebrush buttercup *Ranunculus glaberrimus*
A small plant with fleshy stems, this is one of the first spring flowers to appear. It is another western species found in open pine woods. Sagebrush often appears next to juniper trees. It has shiny yellow flowers from March to June. The leaves sometimes have rounded teeth.

Marsh marigold, Cowslip *Caltha palustris*
A familiar, showy species, also known as the king cup, which inhabits marshes, swamps and stream sides. The large, bright and shiny yellow flowers are like those of a large buttercup and appear from April to June. The leaves are glossy, dark green and heart-shaped, with blunt, serrated edges. The stems are hollow.

White virgin's bower

Pipestems, Pepper vine, Traveller's joy, *Clematis ligusticifolia*

Like many members of this genus, this is a woody vine, clambering over other shrubs and trees, in a wide range of soils and habitats, from deserts to pine woods, though more typically in river valleys and gullys. The plant was used by Native Americans, who chewed the stems and leaves as a remedy against sore throats. This traditional use is reflected in the name pepper vine.

Identification:
From May to September it produces hundreds of small cream-coloured flowers, each about 20mm/¾in across, with five petal-like sepals. The fruit heads are also attractive, composed of feathery plumed seeds.

Right: A showy seed head.

Distribution: Western species, from British Columbia to southern California, Arizona and New Mexico; also introduced to Pennsylvania.
Height and spread: 3m/10ft.
Habit and form: Semi-woody perennial.
Leaf shape: Opposite, pinnately compound.
Pollinated: Insect.

Below: White virgin's bower has a clambering habit.

Blue columbine

Aquilegia caerulea

Blue columbine is a popular garden plant, in addition to being the state flower of Colorado. It has attractive large flowers, usually blue and white. In its various cultivated forms there are several colour variants ranging from pale blue to white, pale yellow and pinkish. Often the flowers are bicoloured and some forms have double flowers. It has been successfully hybridized with other aquilegias. In the wild it prefers mountain sites, such as montane aspen woods. The related alpine blue columbine, *A. saximontana*, is a much shorter plant found at higher altitudes only in Colorado.

Identification: A tall, bushy plant, growing to approximately 20–60cm/8–24in tall, with several stems, attractive divided leaves and beautiful flowers. The blooms are each up to 75mm/3in across, with five spreading blue sepals and five petals, and backward projecting spurs to 50mm/2in long. The sepals are often blue, but can be pale yellow or pink. The flowers open between June and August.

Distribution: New Mexico and Arizona, north to western Montana.
Height and spread: 90cm/35in.
Habit and form: Herbaceous perennial.
Leaf shape: Divided and lobed.
Pollinated: Insect.

Left: The sepals of most columbine forms are a different shade to the petals.

Crimson columbine

Red columbine, Sitka columbine, *Aquilegia formosa*

One of a number of red-flowered species that attract hummingbirds as pollinators, this is one of the most beautiful members of this genus. The spreading deep crimson and yellow flowers appear in May to August and are suspended from the branch tips. Crimson columbine readily adapts to many zones and conditions from rocky mountain slopes to sea level. Its sweet nectar attracts not only hummingbirds, but bees and butterflies and its flowers can be used as an edible salad garnish. Native Americans used the leaves and roots medicinally for a wide range of ailments.

Identification: The leaflets of the deeply divided leaves are about 40mm/1½in in length, and lobed and indented at the tips. The individual flowers are 50mm/2in across, each with five bright red petal-like sepals. The five yellow petals each have a backward-pointing spur.

Distribution: From Baja California north to southern Alaska, and east to Idaho, Utah and Wyoming.
Height and spread: 15–90cm/6–35in.
Habit and form: Herbaceous perennial.
Leaf shape: Divided and lobed.
Pollinated: Hummingbird and insect.

Left: The flowers are vibrant and showy.

Vase flower

Sugar bowls, Leather flower, Lion's beard, *Clematis hirsutissima*

Distribution: Mainly western, from British Columbia to northern Arizona and New Mexico, but east to Montana and Wyoming.
Height and spread: 20–60cm/8–24in.
Habit and form: Semi-woody perennial.
Leaf shape: Long, opposite, finely divided.
Pollinated: Insect.

Unusually for a clematis, this species is not a climbing vine, but grows as a clump producing several stems from a woody branched base. Each flowering stem has a single dull coloured red or purplish-brown flower, dangling down like an upside-down cup. The flowers open from April to July. It grows mainly in open pine forests, sagebrush and grassland. The rounded seedheads have long silvery plumes, giving this species its folk name lion's beard. The seed floss is traditionally used as tinder for starting fires.

Right: In contrast to their dull exterior, the flowers are richly coloured inside.

Identification: A hairy plant with carrot-like foliage. The flowers are 25mm/1in long, with four leathery sepals, hairy on the outer surface and joined towards the base, forming a cup shape.

OTHER SPECIES OF NOTE
Spring larkspur, Dwarf larkspur
Delphinium tricorne
This is a pretty woodland flower with an eastern distribution. It takes its species name from the horn-like fruit pods, three in number. The blue flowers are borne in a loose cluster. The plant is toxic, and it was apparently used by soldiers in the American Civil War to treat lice.

Pasque flower
Pulsatilla patens
A widespread grassland plant with blue, purple or white flowers. The common name comes from the Easter flowering time. The fruiting head is highly distinctive, being covered in silky hairs.

Common buttercup *Ranunculus acris*
This highly familiar flower of fields and meadows is found throughout North America, having spread vigorously after being introduced from Europe. Its bright yellow shiny flowers enliven meadows. There are five overlapping petals above five green sepals, which turn yellow as the flower matures.

Lesser celandine, Pilewort *Ranunculus ficaria*
A plant of shady and moist sites, forming an attractive carpet of dark foliage and deep yellow flowers. It has glossy, heart-shaped basal leaves and blooms from March to April atop slender stalks. It was once used as a treatment for piles.

Virgin's bower

Clematis virginiana

Virgin's bower is a common species, often seen clambering and trailing over shrubs, trees or fences, especially in moist riverside locations, and along woodland edges. It is sometimes grown in gardens as the female plant produces attractive displays of feathery plumed fruits in late summer and autumn.

Identification: The leaves have sharp-toothed lobes, with leaflets about 50mm/2in long. The flowers are white, in clusters from the leaf axils. Each flower is about 25mm/1in across with four or five white, petal-like sepals and no petals. Male and female flowers are borne on separate plants (the plant is dioecious). The female flowers have many pistils and the male flowers many stamens.

Distribution: Nova Scotia and Manitoba, south to Florida and west to Texas.
Height and spread: Stems to 3m/10ft.
Habit and form: Semi-woody perennial.
Leaf shape: Compound.
Pollinated: Insect.

Above: The female plant's feathery fruits.

POPPY FAMILY

The poppy family, Papaveraceae, consists of annuals, herbaceous perennials and low shrubs that are mainly restricted to the Northern Hemisphere, and the New World is not an exception to this. North America is especially rich in members of the poppy family, providing a concentration of species not found anywhere else in the world.

California poppy

Eschscholzia californica

California poppy is a well-known and highly variable plant: it exists as a long-lived prostrate perennial along the coast, an erect perennial in inland valleys, and an annual in the interior. As the name suggests, it is a native of California, extending from the Columbia River valley in south-western Washington into the Baja California peninsula and sporadically on to the Cape Region, west to the Pacific Ocean, and east to western Texas. It grows in grassy and open areas to 2,000m/6,500ft.

Identification: Erect or spreading, glaucous stems arise from a heavy taproot in the perennial forms. The blue-green leaves, basal and on the stem, are deeply dissected, with blunt or pointed tips. Large cup-shaped flowers, solitary or in small clusters, open from erect buds; the four petals, 25–50mm/1–2in long, are yellow, usually with an orange spot at the base, although the flower colour can range from a uniform orange to various orange spots and shadings at the base of deep yellow or golden petals.

Left: The large flowers often form extensive showy drifts.

Distribution: Western USA.
Height and spread: 50mm–60cm/2–24in.
Habit and form: Herbaceous perennial or annual.
Leaf shape: Deeply dissected.
Pollinated: Insect.

Celandine

Greater celandine, *Chelidonium majus*

This erect, leafy herb is confusingly named as it is a member of the poppy family and not a true celandine (the latter is in the buttercup family). It has pretty deep yellow flowers, and also bright yellow, poisonous sap, which can cause skin irritation, and was used at one time for treating warts. Greater celandine has a long history of medicinal use and is still employed in herbal medicine today for a wide variety of ailments.

Right: Inside the pods, the small black seeds have fleshy elaiosomes, which attract ants to disperse the seeds.

Identification: The flowers each have four yellow petals and are about 25mm/1in across, and borne in branching umbels. The long leaves are alternate, pale green and deeply divided.

Above: Greater celandine grows as a spreading weed in rough ground, around houses and at woodland edges.

Distribution: Europe and western Asia; introduced to eastern North America, where it is found from Newfoundland, south to Georgia, and west to Nebraska and Ontario.
Height and spread: 30–60cm/12–24in.
Habit and form: Biennial/perennial herb.
Leaf shape: Finely lobed.
Pollinated: Insect.

Matilija poppy

Tree poppy, *Romneya coulteri*

Distribution: Southern California and northern Mexico.
Height and spread: 90cm–2.5m/35in–8ft.
Habit and form: Shrubby perennial.
Leaf shape: Pinnately divided.
Pollinated: Insect.

This beautiful perennial has large, white, yellow-centred, solitary, scented flowers, which look like fried eggs and are the largest of any plant native to California. Found in southern California and northern Mexico, this suckering perennial is a fire-follower: it may occur in areas of sage scrub, or more typically in chaparral, or along rocky watercourses away from the immediate coast, up to 1,200m/4,200ft. Open or mildly disturbed terrain is usually favoured and mature chaparral or sage scrub limits its spread. It is popular in cultivation and can be found as a localised garden escapee.

Left: The strong upright growth and large, showy flowers make this a spectacular wild flower.

Identification: This tall, leaning, heavily branched, shrubby perennial is woody at the base. The leaves are 50mm–20cm/2–8in long, grey-green, pinnately divided into three or five main divisions, which may have a few teeth or again be divided. The leafy, branched stems grow in patches. Each bears five to eight large, fragrant, white flowers in late spring to midsummer. The flowers are 10–18cm/4–7in across, with six fan-shaped petals; the three sepals are smooth and differentiate this plant from other *Romneya* species. Its many stamens are yellow, forming a ball in the centre with a bristle-haired ovary.

Far left: The large, fragrant, white-petalled flower with its yellow centre has become a favourite of gardeners everywhere, leading to its widespread cultivation.

OTHER SPECIES OF NOTE

Cream cups *Platystemon californicus*
This annual native of California and the surrounding desert regions was once common in open fields, especially following fires, but in recent years it has become scarce across much of its range. The dainty, spreading, grey-green foliage is smothered with flowers of creamy-yellow to white in spring.

Wind poppy *Stylomecon heterophylla*
This beautiful and rare, red-flowered wild poppy is native to California. Along with their striking appearance, the flowers have a fragrance like lily-of-the-valley, which is quite a rarity for a poppy. Naturally found in grasslands and mountain foothills, the flowers appear off and on throughout spring and summer.

Bloodroot *Sanguinaria canadensis*
This herbaceous perennial is found throughout most of the eastern USA. It can reach 25cm/10in tall, but is only about half that height at the time of flowering. The flowers are up to 50mm/2in wide, with about 12 strap-like, satiny, white petals and yellow centres. The first blooms appear in late winter and continue into early spring.

White bearpoppy

Arctomecon merriamii

The white bearpoppy is a perennial found in flat desert scrub habitats such as the Mojave Desert. It prefers shallow, gravel, limestone soils, usually on rocky slopes between 900–1,400m/2,950–4,593ft; it is also, less frequently, encountered on valley bottoms. It is a distinctive plant, with blue-green basal leaves. From this, several long, blue-green stems arise, each bearing a single, showy white or pale yellow flower with a golden centre in the late spring.

Identification: The plant has glaucous, densely hairy stems and mainly basal leaves, which are egg- or wedge-shaped, 25–75cm/10–29½in long, with rounded teeth and dense shaggy white hairs. The white or yellow flowers are solitary, terminal, opening from nodding buds, with two or three long, hairy sepals. They have four or six free, oval petals, 25–40mm/1–1½in long, which generally persist after pollination. The fruits are oval to oblong, opening at the tip and containing a few oblong, wrinkled, black seeds.

Distribution: Mojave Desert and southern Nevada, south-western USA.
Height and spread: 35cm/14in.
Habit and form: Herbaceous perennial.
Leaf shape: Obovate or wedge-shaped.
Pollinated: Insect.

Above: The flowers are held high above the foliage.

FUMITORY FAMILY

The fumitory family, Fumariaceae, contains about 530 species, mainly in northern temperate regions, with a few in African mountains. Most of them are leafy herbs, with swollen underground parts. They tend to have succulent stems and the flowers are borne in racemes. The fruit is a single-chambered capsule. A number of species of Corydalis *and* Dicentra *are popular garden plants.*

Golden smoke

Scrambled eggs, *Corydalis aurea*

This weak-stemmed plant has clusters of bright yellow flowers, lending it its common name, scrambled eggs. The flowers appear from February to September and are pale to bright yellow, growing in groups of 4–12. It prefers light sandy soil and its favoured habitat is rough, rocky hillslopes and scrubland; it is also found under trees and along creek bottoms. It often invades disturbed sites such as roadsides, clearings and recently burned areas, although its survival in these locations appears to be short lived. Like many of its relatives, it is poisonous to livestock if consumed in large quantities. The Native American Navajo tribe are said to have used the plant for some medicinal treatments, but ingesting it should be avoided.

Identification: The dense leafy rosette produces weak stems with pinnate leaves and racemes of yellow, spurred flowers. Each flower is about 20mm/¾in long, and has tiny sepals, and four petals. The upper petal forms a hollow spur and a hood. The flower encloses six stamens. The leaves are a bluish-green, and divided.

Above: Corydalis *derives its name from the Greek for 'crested lark' after the shape of the flower, which resembles the bird's spur.*

Distribution: Widespread in the west, east of the Cascades and Sierra Nevada, and to Arkansas, Illinois and Pennsylvania.
Height and spread: 10–60cm/4–24in.
Habit and form: Annual or biennial.
Leaf shape: Twice-pinnate.
Pollinated: Insect.

Golden ear-drops

Dicentra chrysantha

This pretty flower often appears in abundance following scrub fires, the fire scarification causing the seeds to germinate. It also appears in disturbed wasteland. The flowering period is from April to September. The flowers have a strange, pungent aroma. This toxic plant is particularly dangerous to animals after a burn, when it is at its most prolific.

Identification: The dramatic flower spikes can grow up to 1.5m/5ft tall. The yellow flowers are an odd shape in that the outer petals extend out sideways. The blue-green foliage is feathery and fern-like, with pinnate leaves up to 30cm/12in long, with finely divided leaflets. The individual flower has four petals, the inner pair enclosing the six stamens.

Above: The plants are a common sight across California and the Sierra Nevada.

Left: The bright sulphur-yellow flowers bring vivid patches of colour to areas scorched by fire.

Distribution: Mainly southern California.
Height and spread: 45cm–1.5m/18in–5ft.
Habit and form: Annual/perennial.
Leaf shape: Pinnate.
Pollinated: Insect.

Tall corydalis

Roman wormwood, Rock harlequin, *Corydalis sempervirens*

Distribution: North-eastern USA and Canada.
Height and spread: 12.5–60cm/5–24in.
Habit and form: Annual/biennial.
Leaf shape: Pinnate.
Pollinated: Insect.

Tall corydalis is one of the most attractive of the genus, and often grown in gardens, in a number of cultivated forms. The wild form has pale pink or purple tubular flowers, tipped yellow, and there are garden forms with white or pink flowers. The multi-lobed leaves are a pale blue-green providing a pleasing contrast to the flowers. The main flowering time is May to September. It grows mainly in rocky clearings and disturbed areas, and does very well in full sunlight. Like others in its family, this plant thrives in fire-scorched zones and it is thought that the seeds require heat for germination.

Identification: Each flower is about 10cm/4in long and consists of four petals, the outer two with a rounded, upwardly projecting spur. The fruit is a slender and smooth capsule.

Above: The pale to dark pink and yellow blossoms dangle from slender branching stems through the summer months.

OTHER SPECIES OF NOTE

Case's fitweed *Corydalis caseana*
A tall, succulent species with hollow stems and fern-like foliage. The flowers are pale pink in dense racemes, each with a long, straight spur. It flowers in June to August in moist mountain soils from Oregon south to the central Sierra Nevada, and east to Colorado and Idaho.

Western bleeding heart
Dicentra formosa
The heart-shaped pink flowers over fern-like blue-green foliage are extremely striking. Its habitat is damp shady sites from southern British Columbia to central California. This is another popular garden plant.

Steer's head *Dicentra uniflora*
Although this is a common western species, it is often overlooked as it is so small, growing to about 10cm/4in. It prefers well-drained sites in open woodland or sagebrush. The pink or white flowers are a peculiar shape – like a cow's head, hence the common name. The plant blooms from early spring to late summer.

Wild bleeding heart *Dicentra eximia*
A pretty perennial, common in mountain woods in the eastern USA. It produces pink or red drooping, heart-shaped flowers, the inner petals resembling a drop of blood. It is also called staggerweed, and has been said to have an intoxicating effect on cattle. This is another popular garden species.

Dutchman's breeches

Dicentra cucullaria

This delicate nodding spring flower favours shade and is found on north-facing mountain slopes and in shady ravines, preferring long-undisturbed sites. It is pollinated mainly by bumblebees, which can reach the pollen with their long probosces. The short flowering season is April to May.

Identification: The flowers are white or pink, with a yellow tip, and are about 20mm/⅞in long. The flowers are sometimes damaged by bees biting through the sides of the petals to get at the nectar and pollen inside. The plant grows from a short root with many small bulblets. The basal leaves are finely divided.

Left: The seed pod contains shiny black seeds.

Distribution: Nova Scotia south to Georgia and west to Oklahoma and Mississippi; also in the Pacific north-west.
Height and spread: 10–30cm/4–12in.
Habit and form: Annual/perennial.
Leaf shape: Compound.
Pollinated: Insect.

WATER LILY FAMILY

The water lily family, Nymphaeaceae, contains aquatic plants of five genera and 50 species. The plants have showy flowers on long stalks, and are often considered primitive flowering plants. In the New World there are some remarkable examples of these plants: the family reaches its zenith in the huge plants of the tropical Victoria *genus, with their giant leaf pads and curious night-blooming flowers.*

Spatterdock

Yellow cow lily, Yellow pond lily, *Nuphar polysepala*

This perennial, water-lily-like plant from western North America can form extensive stands in the shallow waters of lakes, ponds, sluggish streams and canals. Mature plants have large 'elephant's ear' leaves and yellow flowers. Unlike the showy, many-petalled fragrant water lily flowers, spatterdock blossoms are simple yellow globes that partially open to reveal reddish poppy-like centres from early to late summer, standing just above the water surface. The leaves float on, or stand above, the water, on thick, fleshy stalks.

Identification: Fibrous roots anchor the scaly, log-like rhizomes to the sediment; the rhizomes are up to 20cm/8in in diameter and 5m/16ft long. The leaves are 10–45cm/4–18in long and 75mm–30cm/3–12in wide, green, heart-shaped, with a notched base, a blunt tip, a prominent mid-vein and a leathery surface; they rise directly from the rhizome, floating on or extending above the water. In early summer, large, delicate underwater leaves resembling lettuce precede the floating leaves. The flowers arise directly from the rhizome in summer. They are waxy, bright yellow, cup-shaped globes, 50mm–10cm/2–4in across, rising above the water; they usually have nine sepals, but can have up to 17; the stamens are reddish. The flowers are sweetly scented on the first day after opening, malodorous later.

Distribution: Western USA.
Height and spread: 5m/16ft or more.
Habit and form: Floating, aquatic perennial.
Leaf shape: Cordate.
Pollinated: Insect, especially fly.

Left: The fruits are urn-shaped. *Below: The leaves float.*

American lotus

Yellow lotus, Water chinquapin, *Nelumbo lutea* syn. *N. pentapetala*

This deciduous, perennial water plant occurs in quiet waters in ponds, lakes and the edges of slow-moving streams and rivers of eastern North America, the West Indies, Central America and south to Colombia. Its large, spongy rhizomes penetrate the mud beneath the water by as much as 2.5m/8ft, and the showy pale yellow flowers appear in late spring and summer. They are as magnificent as those of its Asian relative, *N. nucifera*, but it is less cultivated for ornament. It was probably originally confined to the floodplains of major rivers and their tributaries in the east-central United States, and was carried northward and eastward by Native Americans.

Identification: The stems arise directly from the rhizomes, reaching 2m/6½ft or more. The leaves may be 60cm/24in or more across, with the stalk attached to the underside of the leaf at its centre, without the cleft seen in *Nymphaea* species. The leaves float on the surface, flattened, in deep water, or stand above it in shallow pools; the margins tend to rise above the centre, creating a 'funnel' effect. The leaves are dull-satiny blue-green on top and pale green with prominent veins underneath. The large flowers, 25cm/10in across, have numerous pale yellow tepals, and anthers to 20mm/¾in long. Each bloom is borne singly on a long, stiff stalk, standing above the leaves. The woody rounded seedpods have a distinctive, flattened, pierced top like a showerhead.

Distribution: Eastern North America; West Indies; Central and South America.
Height and spread: Forms extensive colonies.
Habit and form: Aquatic perennial.
Leaf shape: Orbicular.
Pollinated: Insect.

Above left: Native Americans used the seeds and tubers for food.

Left: The blooms are held on long stems.

Indian pond lily

Spatterdock, Yellow water lily, *Nuphar lutea*

Distribution: Southern California, north to Alaska and east to Colorado.
Height and spread: Floating leaves and flowers, to 75mm/3in above surface.
Habit and form: Aquatic.
Leaf shape: Heart-shaped.
Pollinated: Insect.

Right: Floating leaves are attached at the stem, whereas submerged leaves are attached to the rhizome.

With its bright yellow flowers and shiny floating leaves, this aquatic plant adds welcome colour to slow rivers and ponds in the west of the region. The flowers open from April to September and float either just at the water surface, or raised slightly above the water. The plant is anchored in the mud and soil, and the shoots grow up through the water, producing the flat floating leaves and flowers at the surface. Native Americans used the seeds – either roasted, or ground into flour.

Identification: The submerged stalks may be 90cm/35in or more long, and the cup-shaped flowers each about 10cm/4in across. There are normally nine sepals, the outer ones greenish, and the inner ones forming the yellow flower. The petals are small and narrow, and about the same length as the stamens.

Right: The seed head.

OTHER SPECIES OF NOTE

Fragrant water lily *Nymphaea odorata*
These are exceptionally beautiful water plants native to the eastern USA, with floating leaves and large, many-petalled white, or less frequently pink, fragrant blossoms. The nearly circular floating leaves are deeply cleft, glossy green above, with red or purple undersides.

Yellow pond lily, Bullhead lily
Nuphar variegata
North America's commonest water lily is found in ponds and streams from much of Canada to Newfoundland and south to Pennsylvania. It has the typical yellow cup-shaped flowers, and the leaves have a V-shaped notch at the base.

Common spatterdock *Nuphar advena*
This species is very similar to yellow pond lily, *N. variegata,* and occurs mainly in the southern states, and north to New England, Ohio and Michigan. It is also found in Cuba, inhabiting slow-moving bodies of water. The heart-shaped leaves float just beneath the water's surface.

Pygmy water lily *Nymphaea tetragona*
Although this has a wide distribution across North America, it is rare in the west, in Washington State and Idaho. Its white flowers are small, about 60mm/2¼in across. It is popular in gardens because of its size and the beauty of the inflorescence. The blooming period is July to August.

Banana water lily

Yellow water lily, Mexican water lily, *Nymphaea mexicana*

This aquatic perennial was identified from specimens collected in Mexico, although it is also found in east and south Texas and in Florida. It grows in standing water, where its round floating foliage acts as a foil for the showy, fragrant, multi-petalled yellow flowers. It grows from a stout, tuberous rhizome and spreads by runners, typically inhabiting water 45cm/18in deep. It was abundant throughout Florida until the introduction of *Eichhornia crassipes*, which has crowded it out from former strongholds.

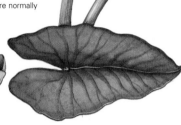

Distribution: South-eastern USA and Mexico.
Height and spread: Forms extensive colonies.
Habit and form: Deciduous or evergreen aquatic perennial.
Leaf shape: Ovate to orbicular.
Pollinated: Insect, probably beetle.

Right: The leaves and flowers can stand above the water.

Identification: Stems arising directly from the submerged rhizome bear oval to circular leaves, floating or emergent, with smooth to toothed or wavy margins; they are shiny deep green, blotched brown above, reddish-purple below, 10–20cm/4–8in across, split from one edge to the stalk, with pointed or rounded lobes, sometimes overlapping. The flowers appear from spring to autumn, with a musty fragrance.

Right: The flowers are fragrant.

CARNATION FAMILY

The carnation family, Caryophyllaceae, contains many familiar garden plants, such as sweet williams and pinks as well as carnations. There are about 2,300 species, mostly in the Northern Hemisphere, and many in the cooler regions. The herb members of the family often have characteristically swollen nodes. Many species have thrived in North America, since being introduced from Europe.

Moss pink

Moss campion, *Silene acaulis*

This attractive alpine is found throughout the Northern Hemisphere, and is a popular garden species. It is cushion-forming, creating mossy mats and pretty pink flowers on short stalks. A number of garden forms exist with white, double or golden flowers. The mat-growing habit is an adaptation to avoid excessive desiccation caused by strong winds in exposed habitats such as rocky cliffs and mountain slopes. This species thrives well in rock gardens which resemble the rocky crevices of its natural sites.

Left: The showy flowers make moss pink a popular choice for gardens.

Identification: The leaves are long and narrow, and the plant grows in the form of a moss-like mound. The deep pink flowers are each about 15mm/⁹⁄₁₆in across and the five petals are notched at the tips. The blooms open between June and August and nestle very low against the foliage, adding to the cushion-like appearance of the plant.

Distribution: From Alaska to Greenland, and on mountains further south.
Height and spread: To 65mm x 30cm/2½ x 12in.
Habit and form: Perennial.
Leaf shape: Opposite.
Pollinated: Insect.

Left: The plant grows low to avoid disturbance from bitter mountain winds.

Indian pink

Silene californica

Open, rocky woodland is the main habitat of the Indian pink, one of the prettiest wild flowers of the region. However, unfortunately it is not very common anywhere. The flowers open from May to July and are very striking, with a circle of bright crimson notched petals, clustered towards the tips of long, leafy stems. The stems are weak and sometimes collapse to trail on the ground.

Left: The ragged-looking flower attracts hummingbirds.

Right: The weak stems often collapse and trail on the ground.

Identification: The flowers are in a loose inflorescence. Each is about 40mm/1½in across, and has a long tubular calyx, with five teeth. The five petals are broad and notched towards the tip.

Distribution: Northern California and southern Oregon.
Height and spread: To 40cm/16in.
Habit and form: Perennial.
Leaf shape: Opposite.
Pollinated: Insect and hummingbird.

Stringflower *Silene hookeri*
The ragged looking flowers give the common name – each petal is divided and 'frayed'. Flowers may be white, pink or purple. The habitat is rocky ground in open coniferous forest or scrub, and it is found in southern Oregon and northern California.

White campion *Silene latifolia*
Another introduction from Europe that has spread through most of North America, in fields and wasteland. It is a branching plant, with white (or pink), sweet-scented flowers that open in the evening to attract moths.

Bladder campion *Silene vulgaris*
This pretty plant, with its clusters of white flowers and a bladder-like swollen calyx (the latter with obvious veins), is another European introduction, now a widespread weed.

Royal catchfly *Silene regia*
Perhaps the most splendid of the genus, with its heads of bright red, five-petalled flowers borne on tall herbaceous stalks, and leaves of a striking green, royal catchfly is endangered over much of its range, with a patchy distribution in the south-east of the USA. It blooms from May through October.

Fire pink

Silene virginica

This eastern species has sticky glandular hairs covering the stems. This feature is typical of many members of this genus, which are sometimes given the name 'catchfly' – the sticky hairs trapping small insects. The habitat is open woods, and also rocky slopes, often on sandy soils, as well as thickets. The common name is well chosen, as the flowers are a bright vivid red, in loose clusters on slender, often arching stems.

Identification: The sepals form a long sticky tube, above which the five, notched petals spread out impressively. The flowering period is from April to June. The fruit is a capsule containing many small seeds.

Above and rar right: Sticky hairs on the stem trap undesirable crawling insects to allow more welcome pollinators access to the flowers.

Distribution: New York west to Minnesota, Louisiana and Oklahoma.
Height and spread: 15–60cm/6–24in.
Habit and form: Perennial.
Leaf shape: Base leaves spoon-shaped; upper leaves opposite.
Pollinated: Insect.

Corn cockle

Agrostemma githago

Distribution: Introduced from Europe, but now found throughout most of the USA and southern Canada.
Height and spread: 30–90cm/12–35in.
Habit and form: Annual.
Leaf shape: Opposite.
Pollinated: Insect.

Far right: Corn cockle thrives in an open, sunny position.

The common name refers to one of the favoured habitats of this species – namely fields of cereal crops, notably wheat (often called corn in Europe). Formerly much commoner, it could cause problems as its seeds are poisonous and used to get into flour. It is a very pretty plant, with large pink-purple or white flowers. It grows in wasteland, such as fields and roadsides, and sometimes in grain crops. Some garden forms have deep red flowers. The corn cockle is one of many plants that have been successfully introduced to North America from across the Atlantic.

Identification: A tall plant covered in dense hairs, with single large flowers at the tips of long stalks. The flowers open between June and September, and each flower has five petals and five sepals, the latter extending beyond the petals. The flowers are large – to 50mm/2in across, and the fruit is a many-seeded capsule.

Above: Corn cockle is easy to grow in a sunny area of the garden.

Grass pink

Deptford pink, *Dianthus armeria*

The alternative name for this introduced flower refers to Deptford, in London, where this species was formerly abundant. It is a striking plant, with deep pink flowers in clusters atop stiff stalks. In many ways it resembles a miniature carnation. This is yet another introduced species that has thrived in dry fields and along roads, across many parts of North America.

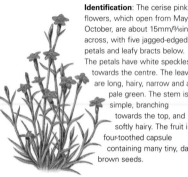

Identification: The cerise pink flowers, which open from May to October, are about 15mm/⁹⁄₁₆in across, with five jagged-edged petals and leafy bracts below. The petals have white speckles towards the centre. The leaves are long, hairy, narrow and a pale green. The stem is simple, branching towards the top, and softly hairy. The fruit is a four-toothed capsule containing many tiny, dark brown seeds.

Far left and above: The grass pink's cheerful blooms are a welcome sight in fairly open ground. The species' decline in Great Britain is due to urbanization or loss of pasture to arable land. An average plant will produce about 400 seeds, which leads to an abundance of carnation-like, attractive plants growing in swathes in North America, particularly in the east.

Distribution: Mainly eastern states, but also in parts of the west.
Height and spread: 15–60cm/6–24in.
Habit and form: Biennial or annual.
Leaf shape: Simple and narrow.
Pollinated: Insect.

Ragged robin

Lychnis flos-cuculi

Widely naturalized in the north-east of the United States, this introduced species is well-named for its scruffy looking flowers – the deeply divided petals give it a distinctly ragged appearance. It is found mainly in wasteland and in meadows, with a preference for moist soils.

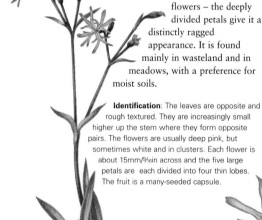

Identification: The leaves are opposite and rough textured. They are increasingly small higher up the stem where they form opposite pairs. The flowers are usually deep pink, but sometimes white and in clusters. Each flower is about 15mm/⁹⁄₁₆in across and the five large petals are each divided into four thin lobes. The fruit is a many-seeded capsule.

Above: The flower is often found with other meadow favourites, such as buttercups.

Distribution: From Newfoundland south to Maryland and west to Ontario and Ohio.
Height and spread: 30–90cm/12–35in.
Habit and form: Perennial.
Leaf shape: Lanceolate.
Pollinated: Insect.

Left: The flowers appear from May to August.

Soapwort

Bouncing bet, *Saponaria officinalis*

The strange common names reflect its use in earlier times as an aid in washing. The sap contains saponins that can create a soapy lather when the leaves are crushed. Bouncing bet is an old-fashioned term for a washerwoman. Soapwort spreads and forms colonies by means of underground stems. Double-flowered cultivars are widely available.

Identification: This robust species has smooth stems and clusters of white or pink scented flowers. Each flower is 25mm/1in across, and the fragrance attracts many insects, including moths. The leaves have three prominent veins. The fruit is the typical capsule, with many seeds.

Distribution: Throughout the region.
Height and spread: 30–75cm/12–29½in.
Habit and form: Perennial.
Leaf shape: Oval.
Pollinated: Insect.

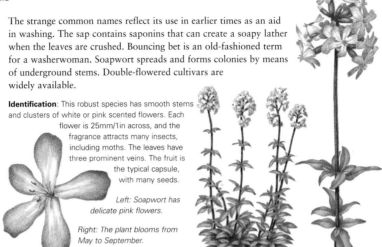

Left: Soapwort has delicate pink flowers.

Right: The plant blooms from May to September.

OTHER SPECIES OF NOTE

Beautiful sandwort *Arenaria capillaris*
This is a dainty little flower of sagebrush plains and mountain slopes, found from Alaska south to Oregon, Nevada and Montana. The small white, star-like flowers grow on long stalks from a leafy mat-like base.

Fendler's sandwort *Arenaria fendleri*
Common on rocky ledges in the southern Rocky Mountains, fendler's sandwort ranges south from Wyoming to Arizona, New Mexico and Texas. It has very narrow leaves that form a grass-like clump, up to 30cm/12in in diameter, and many small white flowers with prominent white stamens upon fairly long, brownish stalks.

Meadow chickweed
Cerastium arvense
A plant with a very wide distribution throughout the Northern Hemisphere. It has weak stems that often trail on the ground. The white petals of the bright flowers are deeply notched. It is often mistaken for mouse-ear chickweed, *C. vulgatum*, but that species has rounder, hairier leaves (hence the name).

Maltese cross *Lychnis chalcedonica*
A now-common garden plant that was introduced from Asia. The flowers are scarlet and the petal arrangement resembles a Maltese cross. Garden varieties with pink or white, and double flowers are available.

Star chickweed

Stellaria pubera

This chickweed is well-named as its pretty pure white flowers are indeed star-shaped. They stand out brightly against the dark green foliage of the woodland floor. It is found mainly in rich woods and also on rocky slopes, and the flowers open between March and May. The common name is supposedly due to chickens liking to eat the plant.

Identification: The very long petals are divided into narrow lobes. It resembles the European/Asian stitchwort, *Stellaria holostea*, which is naturalized in the USA, but has broader leaves. Each flower is 15mm/⁹⁄₁₆in across and the five petals are so deeply divided that there appear to be 10.

Distribution: New York, west to Illinois and Louisiana, south to Florida.
Height and spread: 15–40cm/6–16in.
Habit and form: Perennial.
Leaf shape: Elliptical, unstalked.
Pollinated: Insect.

Below: The plant has reportedly been used for soothing minor skin irritations.

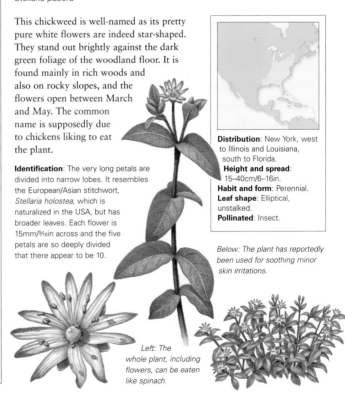

Left: The whole plant, including flowers, can be eaten like spinach.

CACTUS FAMILY

The Cactaceae contains mostly spiny succulents with photosynthetic stems, comprising about 130 genera and 1,650 species. The leaves are rarely well developed and fleshy, but generally reduced, absent altogether or associated with highly modified axillary buds called areoles, which bear spines. Most are native to the Americas, and are found as far north as Canada and south as Patagonia.

Plains prickly pear

Opuntia polyacantha

This is one of the more common prickly pear species of the west, and can become a serious nuisance on rangelands where cattle are ranched, as the pads full of spines break off easily and can get stuck in the noses of the cattle. As with all prickly pears, the flower is pretty, in this case usually bright yellow, opening from May to July. It grows in deserts and open plains, as well as among junipers. The egg-shaped fruits are brown when ripe.

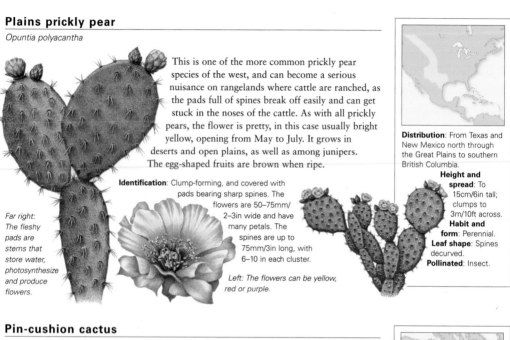

Far right: The fleshy pads are stems that store water, photosynthesize and produce flowers.

Identification: Clump-forming, and covered with pads bearing sharp spines. The flowers are 50–75mm/ 2–3in wide and have many petals. The spines are up to 75mm/3in long, with 6–10 in each cluster.

Left: The flowers can be yellow, red or purple.

Distribution: From Texas and New Mexico north through the Great Plains to southern British Columbia.
Height and spread: To 15cm/6in tall; clumps to 3m/10ft across.
Habit and form: Perennial.
Leaf shape: Spines decurved.
Pollinated: Insect.

Pin-cushion cactus

Coryphantha vivipara

This small, barrel-shaped cactus is sometimes found singly, but more often as a group. It has flowers varying in colour – yellow-green, pink, red or lavender. The fruit is green and smooth with brown seeds. It grows mainly in rocky deserts and on dry sandy soils in juniper, oak or pinewoods.

Identification: Each flower has many petals and is up to 50mm/2in across. The spines are in clusters of 3–10 and are long and straight, with a ring of shorter white spines surrounding them.

Distribution: From Mexico north to central Canada.
Height and spread: 40mm–15cm/1½–6in.
Habit and form: Perennial.
Leaf shape: Spines about 20mm/ ¾in long.
Pollinated: Insect.

Left: Once the flowers have finished, tasty berries develop.

Beavertail cactus

Opuntia basilaris

Distribution: Northern Mexico, to southern California, western Arizona and south-western Utah.
Height and spread: 15–30cm/6–12in; clumps to 1.8m/6ft across.
Habit and form: Perennial.
Leaf shape: Tiny bristles.
Pollinated: Insect.

The imaginative name refers to the flat, paddle-shaped stems of this well-known cactus. Although lacking long spines, it is protected by hundreds of sharp bristles. In the wild it is found in deserts and other dry rocky sites, and is also a popular garden species. It has attractive red or pink flowers on the edges of the joints, often almost covering the plant. Like other *Opuntia* species it can be easily propagated by breaking off a joint and planting it.

Identification: The individual flowers are 50–75mm/2–3in across, with many petals. The stem joints are up to about 30cm/12in long. The ripe fruit is egg-shaped and grey-brown and contains many seeds.

Left and above: The striking flowers are followed by a brown-grey oval fruit containing many seeds.

OTHER SPECIES OF NOTE

Plains prickly pear *Opuntia macrorhiza*
This low-growing cactus from the USA forms clumps up to 1.8m/6ft in diameter in mountainous, arid areas at 800–2,200m/2,600–7,200ft elevation. The bluish-green stems become wrinkled under very dry or cold conditions, and the large yellow flowers with their vivid red centres appear in early summer.

Saguaro *Carnegia gigantea*
This giant, fluted cactus, is slow-growing but can reach heights up to 12m/39ft and may live up to 200 years or more. It grows in mountains, desert slopes and rocky and flat areas of the south-western USA and in north-western Mexico. In May and June it bears creamy-white, bell-shaped flowers with yellow centres.

Rainbow cactus comb hedgehog
Echinocereus pectinatus
A low-growing cactus found in Arizona, Texas and Mexico, with bands of colourful spines, hence the name. The very large flowers, to 14cm/5½in across, may be pink, yellow or lavender.

Claret cup cactus, King's cup (strawberry) cactus
Echinocereus triglochidiatus
This is one of the most beautiful of all cacti, with deep, cup-shaped, bright scarlet flowers covering the plant during the spring.

Teddybear cholla

Opuntia bigelovii

Looking furry and cuddly from a distance (hence the common name), but actually covered with sharp, barbed spines, this cactus grows in hot deserts. It is a tall species, often the height of a small tree. The spines are not easily removed, so this is quite a dangerous species.

Identification: The joints are cylindrical and up to 25cm/10in long, covered in a fur-like mass of pale golden spines. The flowers are green or yellow, the petals often streaked lavender.

Distribution: North-western Mexico, central Arizona and south-eastern California.
Height and spread: 90cm–2.7m/35in–9ft.
Habit and form: Perennial.
Leaf shape: Spines, 25mm/1in long.
Pollinated: Insect.

Below: A dense covering of spines protects the stem from sunlight.

Above: The plant produces flowers but the fruits are usually sterile. It spreads when its branches fall and take root.

PURSLANE FAMILY

The Purslane family, Portulacaceae, consists of about 400 species, with the majority in warm or tropical regions, and from small trees and shrubs to herbs, many of which are succulent. A few, such as some Portulaca species, are edible, and many are grown as garden plants. The flowers are radially symmetrical, and they usually have four to six petals.

Western spring beauty

Claytonia lanceolata

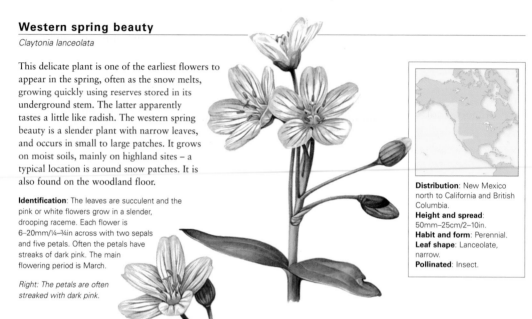

This delicate plant is one of the earliest flowers to appear in the spring, often as the snow melts, growing quickly using reserves stored in its underground stem. The latter apparently tastes a little like radish. The western spring beauty is a slender plant with narrow leaves, and occurs in small to large patches. It grows on moist soils, mainly on highland sites – a typical location is around snow patches. It is also found on the woodland floor.

Identification: The leaves are succulent and the pink or white flowers grow in a slender, drooping raceme. Each flower is 6–20mm/¼–¾in across with two sepals and five petals. Often the petals have streaks of dark pink. The main flowering period is March.

Right: The petals are often streaked with dark pink.

Distribution: New Mexico north to California and British Columbia.
Height and spread: 50mm–25cm/2–10in.
Habit and form: Perennial.
Leaf shape: Lanceolate, narrow.
Pollinated: Insect.

Red maids

Calandrinia ciliata

This is a large genus, with about 150 species. They are low-growing trailing herbs, and are mainly found in the tropics and subtropics. This species produces masses of very pretty bright red or pink flowers (rarely white). The flowers are borne on short stalks from the axils of the upper leaves. The habitat is open sites and wasteland, usually on moist soils.

Identification: Each flower is about 15mm/⁹⁄₁₆in across, with two sepals and five petals, and they open in April and May.

Distribution: Washington state south to California and New Mexico.
Height and spread: 50mm–40cm/2–16in.
Habit and form: Annual.
Leaf shape: Long, narrow.
Pollinated: Insect.

Right: The cheerful flowers open on sunny afternoons.

Far right: The plant is low-lying, and blooms among the grasses.

Flame flower

Talinum aurantiacum

This species is well-named for its orange or red flowers. It grows on rocky slopes and desert canyons in western Texas and southern Arizona. The swollen roots were cooked and eaten by Native Americans. It has an extended flowering season, from June through October. The flowers are sometimes strikingly streaked with red.

Identification: A single orange-red flower, about 25mm/1in across, grows in each upper axil. The stems are sturdy and the leaves are narrow and succulent.

Distribution: Western Texas and southern Arizona.
Height and spread: 15–35cm/6–14in.
Habit and form: Perennial.
Leaf shape: Long and narrow.
Pollinated: Insect.

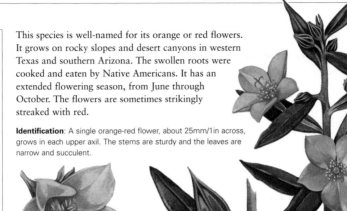

Left and right: One orange flower apppears on each leaf axil.

OTHER SPECIES OF NOTE

Pussy paws *Calyptridium umbellatum*
Pink flowers grow in dense clusters at the ends of the often trailing stems and resemble the soft pads on the underside of a cat's foot. Coniferous forests in the western states are the main habitat for this unusual plant, and the flowers appear from May to August.

Spring beauty *Claytonia virginica*
A low-growing plant with clusters of pink or white flowers, each with darker pink stripes, opening in March to May. As it often grows in large patches, it makes a pretty show in the spring in moist woodland, and also in lawns. Mainly in the east of the region.

Rose moss, Rose purslane *Portulaca pilosa*
Pink or purple flowers appear from June to October. Rose moss grows on sandy soils from North Carolina to Florida, and in parts of the south-west.

Tweedy's lewisia *Lewisia tweedyi*
A large-flowered alpine species found in certain mountains in Washington State – notably Mount Stuart, at 1,800–2,000m/5,900–6,500ft, and sometimes grown as a garden alpine. It is an evergreen perennial that favours sites with full sun, and produces beautiful blooms, white tinged with rose pink, with vivid yellow stamens.

Common purslane

Verdolaga, *Portulaca oleracea*

This is a common species, often encountered as a weed in disturbed ground, and also in gardens. However, it does have pretty yellow flowers, opening between June and September. An interesting feature of the species is that it is edible and has a long history of culinary and medicinal uses. The leaves and stems can be cooked and eaten. It is also known as little hogweed.

Distribution: Southern Canada and much of the USA.
Height and spread: To 15cm/6in.
Habit and form: Annual.
Leaf shape: Spoon-shaped, long.
Pollinated: Insect.

Below: Purslane leaves are quite commonly used in salads or for other culinary purposes.

Identification:
Often grows as a low creeper. The leaves are long and fleshy, and the five-petalled yellow flowers about 6mm/¼in across.

SORREL FAMILY

The sorrel family, Polygonaceae, is found mainly in the temperate regions. There are 50 genera and about 1,150 species, including trees, shrubs, lianas and herbs. They have small flowers, usually radially symmetrical, borne in racemes. The fruits are hard and seed-like. Sorrels include edible species such as rhubarb, Rheum rhabarbarum, *and some crops, such as buckwheat,* Fagopyrum esculentum.

Northern buckwheat

Eriogonum compositum

Several members of this genus are known as wild buckwheats. This species occurs on rocky open ground and flowers from May to July. It is a perennial that grows from a woody taproot. The seeds are eaten by many small animals, including ants, which may thus help in dispersal. The flowers are whitish or yellow and clustered tightly together in rounded heads.They provide an important source of food for butterflies.

Identification: The leaves are varied in shape – some being triangular, others heart-shaped or oval. The individual flowers are very small, about 3mm/⅛in across with six segments.

Above: The petals are creamy-white to lemon yellow.

Below: The flowering stem is stout and leafless.

Distribution: Northern California, north to Washington state and east to Idaho.
Height and spread: 10–50cm/4–20in.
Habit and form: Perennial.
Leaf shape: Heart-shaped or ovate.
Pollinated: Insect.

Sulfur flower

Eriogonum umbellatum

The creamy yellow clusters of tiny flowers give this wild buckwheat its common name. This flower grows wild on dry ridges, in sagebrush deserts and is tolerant to cold, dry mountain conditions. Wild buckwheats are a difficult group to distinguish and this species is also very variable, which adds to problems of identification. The plant's habit is low growing and carpet-forming.

Identification: The flowerheads are 50mm–10cm/2–4in across, and consist of many tiny cups, each with several tiny flowers, each just 6mm/¼in long, and with six segments. The leaves are hairy beneath and grow close together at the ends of the branches.

Above: A ball-like cluster of flowers.

Distribution: Eastern slopes of the Rockies from Colorado to Montana, from southern California to British Columbia.
Height and spread: 10–30cm/4–12in.
Habit and form: Perennial.
Leaf shape: Ovate.
Pollinated: Insect.

Left: Flowers fade in colour as the seeds form.

Water (swamp) smartweed

Water lady's thumb, *Polygonum amphibium*

This is a widespread species that also occurs in Europe and Asia. It grows quite happily in water or in mud around lakes and ponds, adapting to the prevailing conditions. The pink flowers are in dense clusters and produced from June to September. It grows quickly and can become a nuisance as an aggressive weed.

Distribution: North America.
Height and spread:
Terrestrial 60–90cm/24–35in;
aquatic stems to 2m/6½ft.
Habit and form: Perennial;
semi-aquatic.
Leaf shape:
Lanceolate-ovate.
Pollinated: Insect.

Identification: The flowers are very small – only about 4mm/³⁄₁₆in, and the tight flower clusters vary from 15mm–17.5cm/⁹⁄₁₆–7in. The seeds are dark brown to black and are an important source of nourishment for many water birds.

Above: This is the terrestrial form. In the water-based form, the leaves float.

Right: Flowers open from July to August.

OTHER SPECIES OF NOTE

Desert trumpet, Indianpipe weed, Bladder stem *Eriogonum inflatum*
This is a common desert species in Arizona, California and southern Utah. It has swollen grey-green stems that go red, then white with age; and tiny yellow flowers. These are only really noticeable after heavy rainfall. The dried stems were used by Native Americans as tobacco pipes.

Cushion buckwheat
Eriogonum ovalifolium
A variable species of sagebrush plains, woodland and rocky slopes, widespread in the west. It has distinctive, round, puff-ball-like heads of purple, reddish or cream flowers and the leaves are distinctive, a lovely sage green, and oval, as the name suggests.

Winged dock *Rumex venosus*
Sometimes known as wild begonia (though not related to true begonias), winged dock produces orange-red flowers in dense clusters and has reddish stems. It flowers from April to June on sandy grassland and in sagebrush deserts.

Sheep's sorrel *Rumex acetosella*
Originally from Europe, now well established throughout North America. The arrow-shaped leaves have a sharp flavour, and the clusters of tiny red or green flowers attract many insects.

Japanese knotweed

Polygonum cuspidatum (= *P. japonicum*)

This freely-suckering bushy plant has become notorious in recent years as a highly aggressive weed. It is an introduction from Asia and has spread rapidly. The young shoots can grow up even through asphalt and it is difficult to eradicate once established. The fresh young shoots are said to taste like asparagus, and the seeds are eaten by birds.

Distribution: Widespread.
Height and spread:
90cm–2.1m/35in–6¾ft.
Habit and form: Perennial.
Leaf shape: Rounded or ovate, tapering.
Pollinated: Insect.

Identification: The flowers, produced in the autumn, are greenish-white and borne in open clusters about 75mm/3in long, arising from the leaf axils. The stems are hollow and jointed and have a mottled surface pattern.

Above: The flowers are tiny and inconspicuous.

Left: The blooms are borne on panicles that tend to droop.

VIOLET AND PEONY FAMILIES

The violet family, Violaceae, comprises more than 800 species, widely distributed in temperate and tropical regions of the world: the northern species are herbaceous, while others, natives of tropical areas, are trees and shrubs. Members of the peony family, Paeoniaceae, contains mostly shrubby herbs with large, often showy, flowers. There are only two genera: Paeonia and Glaucidium.

Western pansy violet

Beckwith violet, Great basin violet, *Viola beckwithii*

This large-flowered violet is very attractive and has pansy-like reddish-purple flowers. It is native to open pinewoods and sagebrush habitats in the west, and flowers from March to May. The sagebrush violet (desert pansy) is very similar but has less divided leaves. This and many other violets are favourite garden plants with their cheerful, face-like colourful flowers.

Right: The leaves are mid-green and narrow.

Identification: The bi-laterally symmetrical flowers face outwards and are brightly coloured. The upper two petals are red-purple, the lower three mauve, with yellow patches and reddish lines, the central one pouched. The long-stalked leaves are grey-green and divided into three narrow segments. It is commonly found among sagebrush.

Right: Tiny clumps form, with flowerheads about thumbnail size.

Distribution: South-eastern California to north-eastern Oregon; east to Utah and Idaho.
Height and spread: 50mm–12.5cm/2–5in.
Habit and form: Perennial.
Leaf shape: Divided.
Pollinated: Insect.

Bog white violet

Long leaf violet, *Viola lanceolata*

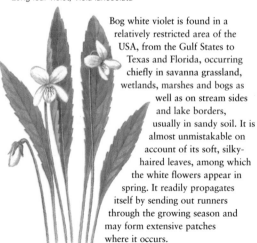

Bog white violet is found in a relatively restricted area of the USA, from the Gulf States to Texas and Florida, occurring chiefly in savanna grassland, wetlands, marshes and bogs as well as on stream sides and lake borders, usually in sandy soil. It is almost unmistakable on account of its soft, silky-haired leaves, among which the white flowers appear in spring. It readily propagates itself by sending out runners through the growing season and may form extensive patches where it occurs.

Identification: The leaves are basal, narrow or lance-shaped, 50mm–10cm/2–4in long, usually at least three times the width, irregularly toothed along the margin, tapering to the base, pinnately veined. The flowers are few, five-petalled, irregular in shape, white or light violet with purple markings on the three lower petals, beardless. They appear in late spring and continue into early summer. Self-pollinating flowers are also produced at the same time, lower in the leaf mass. The fruit that follows is a capsule. Sometimes confused with the similar and closely related *V. primulifolia*, which has more ovate leaves, although both species vary considerably.

Distribution: Gulf States to Texas and Florida, USA.
Height and spread: 15–20cm/6–8in.
Habit and form: Herbaceous perennial.
Leaf shape: Linear or lanceolate.
Pollinated: Insect.

Oregon violet *Viola hallii*
Sometimes called Hall's violet, this rare plant from the western USA favours open woodland at altitudes of 300–1,850m/980–6,000ft. The dissected leaves make a graceful foil for the tricoloured flowers, which have creamy-white lower petals and two deep violet upper petals.

Evergreen violet, Redwood violet
Viola sempervirens
Mats of thick leaves persist through the winter and the plant produces pretty yellow flowers from March to June. It is found from British Columbia south to southern Oregon (west of the Cascades) and to central California in redwood forests.

Woolly blue violet *Viola sororia*
A pretty plant with blue, purple or white flowers. It is found throughout the east of the region in damp woods, roadsides, meadows and also lawns. The flowering period is March to June. Garden forms with pure white and freckled flowers are available.

Canada violet, Tall white violet *Viola canadensis*
Widespread, mainly in southern Canada and northern USA, and in mountains elsewhere, this is a relatively tall plant with attractive flowers appearing from April to June. The petals have a yellow tint towards the base and a purplish tinge on the back. In some states, such as Connecticut, this violet is now listed as endangered.

Stream violet

Pioneer violet, *Viola glabella*

This violet occurs in woodland and near watercourses. Large colonies form bright green carpets, starred with yellow, under the trees in early spring. The plant occurs from Monterey County, California, northward into Alaska, at altitudes of up to 2,500m/8,200ft, with particularly fine stands around Portland and in Oregon. The species is also present in Japan. The heart-shaped leaves are often softly hairy all over and these emerge in spring, together with the bright yellow, neatly veined flowers.

Identification:
Knobbly green rhizomes range on, or just under, the surface, with true roots extending down into the soil. The leaves, on 50mm–10cm/2–4in stalks, are kidney- to heart-shaped and toothed. The flowers, up to 20mm/¾in across, are fresh yellow with purple veins, held above the leaves on leafy stems. They are followed by brownish capsules, which explode to disperse the seed.

Far right: The small yellow flowers have veined petals and resemble tiny faces.

Distribution: California north to Alaska; Japan.
Height and spread: 50mm–30cm/2–12in.
Habit and form: Herbaceous perennial.
Leaf shape: Reniform.
Pollinated: Insect.

Western peony

Paeonia brownii

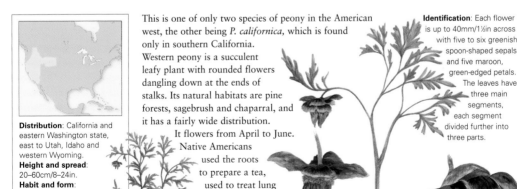

Distribution: California and eastern Washington state, east to Utah, Idaho and western Wyoming.
Height and spread: 20–60cm/8–24in.
Habit and form: Perennial.
Pollinated: Insect.
Leaf shape: Divided.

Right: The plant avoids drought damage by dropping its leaves.

This is one of only two species of peony in the American west, the other being *P. californica*, which is found only in southern California. Western peony is a succulent leafy plant with rounded flowers dangling down at the ends of stalks. Its natural habitats are pine forests, sagebrush and chaparral, and it has a fairly wide distribution. It flowers from April to June. Native Americans used the roots to prepare a tea, used to treat lung problems.

Above: The bowl-shaped flowers are green, gold and maroon.

Identification: Each flower is up to 40mm/1½in across with five to six greenish spoon-shaped sepals and five maroon, green-edged petals. The leaves have three main segments, each segment divided further into three parts.

MALLOW FAMILY

The mallow family, Malvaceae, consists of herbs, shrubs and trees of about 75 genera and perhaps as many as 1,500 species. It includes well-known plants such as hollyhock, Althea rosea, cotton, Gossypium, and the edible okra, Hibiscus esculentus. Other members of the family are used as sources of fibre. Most mallows have showy petals, which makes them popular as ornamental plants.

Scarlet globemallow

Red false mallow, *Sphaeralcea coccinea*

There are about 60 species of globemallows in the western mountains and many of these have orange-red flowers. This species, which is most commonly found in the Great Plains area, has bright brick-red flowers that are saucer-like in shape and arranged in clusters in the axils of the upper leaves. The globemallow grows in open sites such as dry grassland and pine and juniper open forests. Other common species include scaly globemallow, *S. leptophylla* and desert globemallow, *S. ambigua*.

Right: The flowering time is June to July. Each flower has leaf-like bracts underneath.

Identification: The plant has a woody base and arching foliage with short flower clusters. The individual flowers are about 30mm/1¼in across and have five petals. They open from April through August.

Right: The alternate leaves are deeply cut palmately and hairy underneath.

Distribution: Central Canada south to Montana, Idaho, Utah, to Arizona, Texas and New Mexico.
Height and spread: 50cm/20in.
Habit and form: Herbaceous perennial.
Leaf shape: Divided, toothed.
Pollinated: Insect.

Scarlet rose mallow

Scarlet hibiscus, Swamp hibiscus, *Hibiscus coccineus*

The scarlet rose mallow is a narrow, upright, herbaceous perennial with hemp-like leaves and extremely showy, deep red flowers that appear in mid- to late summer. Each flower lasts only a day, but new ones continue to open over a long period. It is attractive to many species of butterflies and hummingbirds.

It occurs naturally in swamps, marshes and ditches, from southern Georgia and Alabama to central Florida, and is frequently encountered along southern rivers and streams, where it towers above the other aquatic plants, hence its other common name of swamp hibiscus.

Identification: A tall, vigorous, sturdy, erect, woody-based, herbaceous perennial, with smooth, blue-green stems. The leaves are deep green, 75mm–12.5cm/3–5in across, palmately three-, five- or seven-parted, or compound, the divisions narrow and sparsely toothed. The flowers are solitary and hollyhock-like, five-petalled, with a prominent and showy staminal column, borne on long stalks from the upper leaf axils. The deep red petals are up to 80mm/3⅛in long, horizontally spreading.

Distribution: South-eastern USA.
Height and spread: Up to 3m/10ft.
Habit and form: Herbaceous perennial.
Leaf shape: Palmate.
Pollinated: Insect.

Left: The tall, rangy habit means that the deep red flowers are held well above the surrounding vegetation.

OTHER SPECIES OF NOTE

Mountain hollyhock *Iliamna rivularis*
Similar in appearance to *I. grandiflora*, mountain hollyhock grows to around 2m/6½ft, with a showy spike of large white or pink flowers in summer. It is widely distributed in mountains from British Columbia south to California.

Desert globemallow *Sphaeralcea ambigua*
Also known as the desert hollyhock, this is a loose, shrubby, herbaceous perennial of dry woodland, mountains and high desert regions in the south-western USA. Its orange, pink, white or red flowers are produced for much of the year.

Checkermallow *Sidalcea neomexicana*
Clusters of deep pink flowers appear from June to September. Checkermallow prefers moist soils near ponds and streams or in mountain sites. It is found from Oregon south to California, New Mexico and Mexico, and east to Wyoming.

Halberdleaf rose mallow *Hibiscus laevis*
The halberdleaf rose mallow is found in large colonies in marshy areas throughout the eastern USA, mainly from Minnesota to Pennsylvania and further south. It blooms from midsummer to early autumn. It often grows where mud has

deposited along the banks of rivers and in swamps. The pale pink to mauve to near-white flowers are showy and very attractive. The flowers are up to 15cm/6in in diameter.

Wild hollyhock

Iliamna grandiflora

This handsome plant bears large pink 'mallow' flowers on tall spikes in the summer. It is a plant of damp montane meadows and stream courses, and occurs through New Mexico, Arizona, Colorado, and Utah, at altitudes of 2,200–3,350m/7,200–11,000ft. Despite its wide distribution across these states, the plant occurs in sporadic locations and where it does grow it often has very low population numbers. The reason for its scarcity remains a mystery, although changes in land management practices could be partially responsible.

Identification: The tall stems and leaves are sparsely hairy; the leaves are palmate and deeply lobed, 50mm–10cm/2–4in long, and coarsely toothed. The coarsely hairy flower spike appears in summer. The bell-shaped flowers, intermittently distributed up the stem and opening from round buds, have petals 25mm/1in long, pink maturing to purplish or lavender, with densely hairy margins at the base. The staminal column is basally hairy and about 15mm/⅝in long. The fruits are flattened spheres.

Distribution: New Mexico, Arizona, Colorado, and Utah, USA.
Height and spread: 1–2m/39in–6½ft.
Habit and form: Herbaceous perennial.
Leaf shape: Palmate.
Pollinated: Insect.

Desert rosemallow

Hibiscus coulteri

This shrubby plant is covered in rough hairs and grows in hills and canyons in desert areas. It produces large pale yellow or whitish cup-shaped flowers, often with a red tinge. The closely related rock hibiscus, *H. denudatus*, has smaller pinkish-lavender or white flowers. Hibiscus species are commonly grown in gardens and many garden varieties have been bred from certain members of the genus, which contains 220 species.

Identification: The individual flowers are 25–50mm/1–2in across with five petals and many stamens, the latter joined at the base, forming a tube. The flowers open in succession from the bottom of the stem upwards. They open between April and August and can be white or creamy yellow in colour. The lower leaves are oval, but those further up the stems have three narrow lobes.

Far right: The plant is a shrubby perennial, herbaceous but with a woody base. It is highly tolerant of drought.

Distribution: Northern Mexico, western Texas, southern Arizona.
Height and spread: To 1.2m/4ft.
Habit and form: Herbaceous perennial.
Leaf shape: Divided, toothed.
Pollinated: Insect.

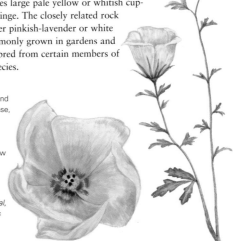

CUCUMBER FAMILY

The Cucurbitaceae is a medium-size plant family of 120 genera and 775 species, primarily found in the warmer regions of the world. It is a major family for edible fruits, representing some of the earliest cultivated plants in both the old and new worlds. It includes Cucumis *(melons, muskmelons and cucumbers),* Cucurbita *(squashes, marrows, and pumpkins) and* Citrullus *(watermelons).*

Buffalo gourd

Cucurbita foetidissima

This perennial, trailing vine occurs in dry, sandy areas, beside roads and railway tracks, predominantly in disturbed soils, throughout the south-west USA and into Mexico. It is often recognizable by its foetid odour before it is even seen, but despite this disagreeable characteristic various Native American and Mexican tribes used it for at least 9,000 years as a food, cosmetic, detergent, insecticide and ritualistic rattle. The deep yellow flowers appear during spring and early summer before the fruit.

Right: The melon-like fruits have a strong, disagreeable odour.

Identification: A prostrate or trailing vine with an extremely large taproot, which may attain a weight of more than 40kg/88lb in three or four years. The grey-green leaves are stiff, leathery and rough-textured, usually triangular in outline, tending to fold upward parallel to the midvein. The large, yellow flowers, 75mm–10cm/3–4in long and 25–50mm/1–2in wide, open in the mornings from late spring to early autumn; male and female flowers are borne on the same plant. The fruit is gourd-like but not as hard as other wild cucurbit species, spherical to elliptic, 50–75mm/2–3in in diameter, green with light green or yellow stripes, the whole fruit turning yellow or tan with age.

Distribution: South-western USA and Mexico.
Height and spread: 6m/19¾ft.
Habit and form: Perennial low-growing vine.
Leaf shape: Deltoid.
Pollinated: Insect.

Above: Buffalo gourd is a trailing vine.

Balsam-apple

Wild cucumber, *Echinocystis lobata*

This perennial, prostrate or climbing vine is found primarily in the north-eastern United States and Canada, although it is widespread elsewhere in forests, particularly those on floodplains or wetlands; it is occasionally found on agricultural land. It is strong-growing, with a large, tuberous root and long stems. The separate male and female blooms appear at the end of long flowering stems from early summer to mid-autumn. The spiny fruits split from the tip as they gradually dry out, revealing the seeds within.

Right: The spiny green fruit dries to a papery consistency when ripe.

Identification: This tuberous perennial herb climbs by means of double or triple corkscrew-like tendrils. The large leaves are alternate, circular to palmate, with three to five pointed lobes and serrated margins. The male flowers are borne in panicles from the leaf axils, the female flowers are solitary or paired, borne at the same axils. The calyx has six bristly lobes and the corolla is green-white with six slender petals up to 6mm/¼in long. The fruit is an oval or round, spiny pod, 50mm/2in in diameter, containing four seeds.

Right: The plant spreads quickly from an underground tuber.

Distribution: North-eastern North America.
Height and spread: 6m/19¾ft.
Habit and form: Climbing vine.
Leaf shape: Orbicular to palmate.
Pollinated: Insect.

Globe berry

Ibervillea lindheimeri

This native of North America is fairly limited in its range, which includes the south-west states of Texas, Oklahoma, New Mexico, Arizona and California. The small, elegant leaves can be unlobed or deeply three- or five-lobed and range from narrowly triangular to fan-shaped. The species is dioecious with flowers carried on slender branching stems, and the most ornamental aspect of this plant is the round fruit. The plants are usually found in open dry woodlands and open areas with rocky soil.

Distribution: South-western USA.
Height and spread: 2–4m/6½–13ft.
Habit and form: Climbing or trailing herbaceous perennial.
Leaf shape: Cuneate to rhombic-ovate.
Pollinated: Insect.

Right: The stems climb by means of long, corkscrew-like tendrils.

Identification: The leaves, up to 12.5cm/5in long on 40mm/1½in stalks, have three to five wedge- to diamond-shaped segments, with 12mm/½in teeth or lobes. The male flowers, borne five to eight per raceme, are yellow and tubular, with three stamens and five yellow or greenish-yellow petals that are not ornate. The solitary female flowers have three stigmas. The calyx is cylindrical and slightly downy. The globular fruits, 25–30mm/1–1¼in in diameter, are pale green, turning orange and then vibrant red, and containing around ten swollen, round seeds.

Below: The fruit turns vibrant red when ripe.

OTHER SPECIES OF NOTE

Star cucumber *Sicyos angulatus*
The star or burr cucumber is a vine that produces white flowers in summer, in small clusters at the end of long flowering stalks. It is found in thickets and along the banks of streams and rivers throughout eastern and central North America. The flowers are followed by clusters of small, red, spiny, oval fruits.

Cucamonga manroot *Marah macrocarpus*
This manroot is a common plant of dry areas of chaparral, washes, roadsides, coastal sage scrub and foothill woodland in south-west North America. It is most notable for its large, fleshy root, which may weigh as much as 45kg/100lb. The greenish-white flowers that appear in winter are quite insignificant, and the fruit that follows is egg-shaped and densely covered with stiff, flattened prickles.

Creeping cucumber *Melothria pendula*
This perennial vine has a very scattered distribution, from the southern United States down as far as Bolivia, being most commonly found in thin woods, thickets and at swamp edges, and often occurring in large numbers on disturbed ground. The yellow flowers appear in late spring and are followed by fruits that resemble tiny watermelons.

California manroot

Marah fabaceus

This perennial climbing or creeping vine can be found beside streams and washes, in shrubby and open areas up to around 1,600m/5,249ft. It is limited to California, principally the Mojave Desert and Baja California. Its common name refers to its surprisingly large tubers, which some claim look like a dead body when dug up, but which help it to survive the dry Californian summers. The prickly fruits look like cucumbers, although they are not edible. The plant dies to the ground after fruiting.

Distribution: California, USA.
Height and spread: 5–6m/16–19¾ft.
Habit and form: Trailing or climbing herbaceous perennial.
Leaf shape: Cordate.
Pollinated: Insect.

Identification: A large perennial with branched, coiling tendrils, the plant usually winds over and through other vegetation. The leaves are round or heart-shaped, with five to seven lobes. The male flowers appear in racemes or panicles, while the female flowers are solitary, usually borne in the same leaf axil; the flowers are cup-shaped, up to 15mm/⅝in across, yellowish green, cream or white, appearing in spring. The fruit is a spiny, round capsule containing four seeds.

Above: A quite variable, mounding, sprawling perennial.

Below right: The fruits appear from late spring.

GERANIUM FAMILY

The geranium family, Geraniaceae, comprises 11 genera and 700 species that usually feature five-petalled flowers and a beaked fruit that often disperses the seed explosively. Its members are primarily temperate annual and perennial herbs, frequently covered in glandular hairs. Most contain aromatic oils. The family contains both the true geraniums, Geranium, and gardeners' 'geraniums', Pelargonium.

Filaree storksbill

Clocks, *Erodium cicutarium*

This pretty little flower grows in many sites and has a wide distribution. It is a successful weed, colonizing wasteland and disturbed soils, especially on light, sandy substrates. It grows either as a small low-growing herb, or may be sprawling and many-branched. The leaves are fern-like, and up to 20cm/8in long. The name 'storksbill' refers to the fruit which is long, narrow and pointed.

Identification: The fern-like leaves (to 10cm/4in), are divided, with each segment further divided. The stems are often tinted red and the flowers are a pretty purple-pink, in loose clusters. Each flower is about 15mm/⅝in across with five petals, and the characteristic fruit is long and slender.

Distribution: Scattered throughout the region; introduced from Europe.
Height and spread: 25mm–30cm/1–12in.
Habit and form: Annual or biennial.
Leaf shape: Pinnately divided.
Pollinated: Insect.

Left: The flowers are among the first to appear in spring. Although pretty, it is considered a noxious weed that can damage crops and other native species.

Far left: Ripening seedpods twist into spirals.

Richardson's crane's-bill/Geranium

Geranium richardsonii

This attractive woodland flower is one of the commonest wild geraniums of the west of the region. It grows mainly under partial shade, for example in woods, at a range of altitudes from lowland to the mountains. The name 'crane's-bill' refers to the elongate pointed fruit.

Identification: Produces several stems with leaves about 15cm/6in across and with five to seven segments, and pointed lobes. The flowers are 25mm/1in across with five pale pink petals, veined purple. The fruit is about 25mm/1in long and pointed. In dry conditions the plant has few stems, flowers or leaves, but in moist soil it can become lush with many blooms.

Distribution: Western states, from New Mexico and California north to Oregon, Washington state and British Columbia; also in South Dakota and Saskatchewan.
Height and spread: 20–80cm/8–31in.
Habit and form: Perennial.
Leaf shape: Palmately lobed.
Pollinated: Insect.

Above: The petals are streaked.

Above left: The pointed fruit contains seeds with coiled 'tails', which help them penetrate the ground.

Wild crane's-bill

Geranium maculatum

This geranium flowers from April to June and grows in meadows, woods and scrub. The pink or white flowers grow in loose clusters, with between two and five flowers in each cluster.

Identification: Each flower has five sepals and five petals, measures about 40mm/1½in across, and contains 10 stamens. The palmately lobed leaves, measuring 10–12.5cm/4–5in, are grey-green and the lobes are deeply toothed. Like other geraniums, this species has the typical long, narrow fruit capsule that splits when ripe into five curved segments to release the seeds.

Distribution: Eastern distribution, from Georgia north to South Dakota, Minnesota, Ontario and Maine; west to Louisiana and Oklahoma.
Height and spread: 30–60cm/12–24in.
Habit and form: Perennial.
Leaf shape: Palmate.
Pollinated: Insect.

Above: The flowers have five petals and are pink to purple.

Far right: Leaves have five palmate lobes.

Woolly geranium

Northern geranium, *Geranium erianthum*

This herbaceous perennial from the Arctic is distributed across north-west North America and north-east Asia, and is most commonly found in woods and sub-alpine meadows and scrub, from low to fairly high elevations in the mountains, and also on grassy slopes near the sea. It is slender-stemmed and branched, with bright blue flowers and, although common, it is scattered in its distribution. It is easily seen when flowering in early summer, and often has later flushes of flowers, though the extent to which this happens varies considerably between locations.

Distribution: North-western North America and north-eastern Asia.
Height and spread: 50cm/20in.
Habit and form: Herbaceous perennial.
Pollinated: Insect.
Leaf shape: Palmate.

Identification: The basal leaves are 50mm–20cm/2–8in wide, with seven or nine deeply divided, acutely lobed and freely toothed divisions; the upper leaves are stalkless, with five or seven narrower divisions and hairy veins on the undersides. The leaves colour in autumn. Dense, umbel-like clusters of flowers appear in summer, occasionally with a later flush; the flowers are flat, not nodding, 25mm/1in across, with almost triangular petals, pale to dark blue-violet, with dark veins at the base and a dark centre. They are followed by explosive seedpods.

SPURGE FAMILY

The surge family, Euphorbiaceae, has more than 300 genera and 8,000 species, found mainly in warm regions. Most exude a white, noxious sap if broken. The name 'spurge' refers to the use of some species to purge the body as a laxative, although large doses can be poisonous. Some spurge are grown as ornamentals, although the family includes important economic crops.

Rattlesnake weed

Chamaesyce albomarginata

A low-growing spurge with small, bright flowers found in the west of the region, in deserts, dry grassland and also in pine/juniper woodland. It creeps close to the ground, sending out long stems with small, roundish opposite leaves. The common name comes from the fact that it was formerly thought to be useful in treating snakebites, but this quality has not been conclusively proven. The blooming period is from April to November.

Identification: The tiny white flowers are not quite what they seem – the four or five small white appendages give the impression of petals, each with a purple pad at the base. The fruit is a small triangular capsule that splits into three on ripening, each section with a single seed.

Above: The plant is low-growing with small flowers.

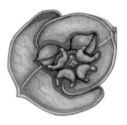

Above: The plant is also known as white-margined spurge, for its flowers.

Distribution: Mexico, south-eastern California, southern Utah, east to Oklahoma.
Height and spread: Stems 50mm–25cm/2–10in.
Habit and form: Perennial; creeping.
Leaf shape: Round or oblong.
Pollinated: Insect.

Leafy spurge

Euphorbia esula

This spurge was introduced to North America from Europe, and has, like many alien introductions, become a successful weed, spreading rapidly into open, disturbed habitats, partly as a result of its underground runners. It is toxic to livestock if they eat large quantities, on account of its poisonous, milky sap.

Identification: The plant has smooth stems and showy flower bracts. The flowers are tiny, associated in clusters with paired green bracts. The stem leaves are very narrow, while those near the flowerheads are heart-shaped and about 20mm/¾in long. The fruit is a round capsule.

Above: The leafy bracts appear before the tiny true flowers, which bloom in June. The seed capsules will eventually explode, dispersing the contents up to 4.5m/15ft from the parent plant.

Left: Due to the sap in the hollow stems, the plant is also known as wolf's milk.

Distribution: Northern USA and southern Canada.
Height and spread: 20–90cm/8–35in.
Habit and form: Perennial.
Leaf shape: Long, narrow.
Pollinated: Insect.

Flowering spurge

Tramp's spurge, *Euphorbia corollata*

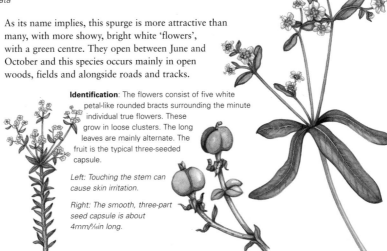

As its name implies, this spurge is more attractive than many, with more showy, bright white 'flowers', with a green centre. They open between June and October and this species occurs mainly in open woods, fields and alongside roads and tracks.

Identification: The flowers consist of five white petal-like rounded bracts surrounding the minute individual true flowers. These grow in loose clusters. The long leaves are mainly alternate. The fruit is the typical three-seeded capsule.

Left: Touching the stem can cause skin irritation.

Right: The smooth, three-part seed capsule is about 4mm/³⁄₁₆in long.

Distribution: Ontario and Maine, south to Minnesota, South Dakota and Florida; west to Texas.
Height and spread: 25–90cm/10–35in.
Habit and form: Perennial.
Leaf shape: Long, oblong.
Pollinated: Insect.

OTHER SPECIES OF NOTE

Wild poinsettia *Euphorbia cyathophora*
White, red or yellow leaves surround a cluster of tiny flowers. The plant flowers in August and September in open woodland and disturbed sites, often on sandy soils, and is found in Texas, Georgia and Florida, north to South Dakota and Minnesota. It looks a little like the true poinsettia, *Poinsettia pulcherrima*, popular at Christmas.

Cypress spurge *Euphorbia cyparissias*
This came from Europe and has spread throughout much of North America. It is found mainly on disturbed ground such as along roadsides and wasteland, and quickly forms large patches as it spreads rapidly from underground roots.

Toothed spurge *Euphorbia dentata*
Similar to wild poinsettia, but this has hairier stems and its leafy bracts are normally green or white at the base. It's a fairly indistinct plant as the flowers are small and greenish-white. It produces a milky sap that can cause irritation.

Snow-on-the-mountain, Ghost weed

Euphorbia marginata
This Midwest native is a softly hairy annual, growing to 1m/39in tall, with oblong, pale green leaves edged with white. A number of garden forms exist, notably 'White Top', an attractive, variegated cultivar.

Spurge nettle

Tread softly, *Cnidoscolus stimulosus*

There are about 75 species in this genus, found mainly in the tropical and subtropical USA. This species has large white, trumpet-shaped flowers. As if belonging to the generally poisonous spurge family were not enough to discourage browsers, spurge nettle is further protected by its covering of stinging hairs (like a true nettle). Contact often produces a painful rash like a nettle-sting.

Identification: Flowers in terminal clusters, each male flower about 25mm/1in across, with five spreading calyx lobes.

Below: The entire plant is covered in hairs or spines.

Distribution: Florida and Louisiana, north to Virginia and Kentucky.
Height and spread: 15–90cm/6–35in.
Habit and form: Perennial.
Leaf shape: Palmately lobed.
Pollinated: Insect.

Below: The flower is actually the calyx of the male plant.

PRIMROSE FAMILY

The primrose family, Primulaceae, includes 22 genera and around 825 species, occurring mainly in temperate and mountainous regions of the Northern Hemisphere. Only one species of Primula naturally occurs south of the equator in South America. The family also includes cyclamens and the aquatic water violet, Hottonia.

Dark-throat shooting star

Dodecatheon pulchellum

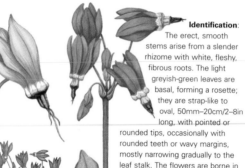

The dark-throat shooting star is commonly found in damp meadows and adjacent edges from Alaska to Mexico and eastward to the western edge of the Great Plains, mostly at elevations below 2,750m/9,000ft. It has intensely coloured flowers and a long flowering period from mid-spring to late summer, depending on location. The genus name *Dodecatheon* is translated from Greek and means 12 gods, and alludes to the usual number of flowers in the inflorescences of these plants.

Identification: The erect, smooth stems arise from a slender rhizome with white, fleshy, fibrous roots. The light greyish-green leaves are basal, forming a rosette; they are strap-like to oval, 50mm–20cm/2–8in long, with pointed or rounded tips, occasionally with rounded teeth or wavy margins, mostly narrowing gradually to the leaf stalk. The flowers are borne in terminal umbellate inflorescences of 2–12, on slender stalks. The sepals are green and persistent, and the petals are basally united with a short tube, a dilated throat and strongly reflexed lobes; the corolla tube is maroon, yellow above.

Distribution: Alaska south to Mexico.
Height and spread: 10–40cm/4–16in.
Habit and form: Herbaceous perennial.
Leaf shape: Oblanceolate.
Pollinated: Insect.

Far left: The nodding magenta or lavender flowers have strongly reflexed petals that give the plant its 'shooting-star' look.

White shooting star

Dodecatheon dentatum

This pretty primula relative, also known as Ellis' shooting star, has attractive flowers, which grow up in an umbel from its basal bed of leaves. It flowers from May to July and is the only shooting star to have consistently white flowers, although the petals do vary slightly in colour. It grows well near waterfalls and streams where there is plenty of shade and moist soil.

Above: From bud to full bloom the flowers seem to turn themselves inside out.

Identification: Small, dart-like flowers grow from a basal rosette of leaves. The stamens are maroon or yellow, forming the 'point' of the dart. The petals are usually white or cream, but sometimes pink or pale violet (for example, in Utah). The leaves are 30mm–10cm/1¼–4in long with toothed edges and a tapering base to a slender stalk. They are an attractive bright, fresh green.

Distribution: Southern British Columbia south to northern Oregon and east to central Idaho and northern Utah; Arizona and New Mexico.
Height and spread: 15–40cm/6–16in.
Habit and form: Perennial herb.
Leaf shape: Toothed.
Pollinated: Insect.

Left: The stalks and flowers are delicate.

Parry's primrose

Primula parryi

The bright colour of this primrose's attractive and soft-looking flowers makes it a favourite despite its unpleasant odour of rotting flesh. It is often found alongside streams and on wet ground. Genetic variation is ensured by the fact that it is heterostylous – some plants have long styles and short anthers, while others have the opposite arrangement, thus encouraging outbreeding.

Distribution: Idaho and Montana south to Nevada, northern Arizona, and northern New Mexico.
Height and spread: 75mm–40cm/3–16in.
Habit and form: Perennial herb.
Leaf shape: Oblong.
Pollinated: Insect.

Identification: The attractive flowers emerge from a bed of oblong leaves. The stalk is relatively stout and leafless; flowers are 15–30mm/⁹⁄₁₆–1¼in wide, and have five round petals, which spread out from a slender tube. The calyx and flower stalks are covered in tiny, glandular hairs. The leaves are 50mm–30cm/2–12in long, and fleshy.

Right: Just a light touch will bring out the plant's unpleasant smell.

Below: The flower has a deep, slender tube, ideal for insect pollinators to crawl into.

Sierra primrose

Primula suffrutescens

This unusual-looking primrose flowers from July-August. Its beautifully bright, slender flowers grow high above the leaves and flare outwards from a yellow tube with a yellow opening. The favoured habitat is rocky ground at high elevations. It grows in the treeless Arctic zone, 3,200m/ 10,500ft above sea level, so only determined hikers are likely to catch a glimpse of it. The colours are extremely vivid and distinctive.

Identification: The tall, leafless stalks rise above beds of basal rosettes of wedge-shaped leaves. They are topped with deep purple/pink flowers with five heart-shaped petals each, and vivid, orange-yellow centre tubes. The leaves are thick, with even teeth. In favourable conditions, swathes of the plant may form.

Far right top: Clusters of flowers form on a tall stem.

Far right bottom: The plant forms a low-growing mat.

Distribution: Mountains of northern California south to Sierra Nevada.
Height and spread: Flower stalks reach 75mm–15cm/3–6in.
Habit and form: Perennial herb.
Leaf shape: Wedge-shaped.
Pollinated: Insect.

Tufted loosestrife

Lysimachia thyrsiflora

The bright yellow, unusually formed flowers of this plant are characteristic: the erect stamens give a delicate, fuzzy appearance. Tufted loosestrife also occurs in Eurasia. It flowers from May to July, and the favoured habitats are ditches, swamps and lakes.

Below: The flowers form in compact, bottle-brush like clusters.

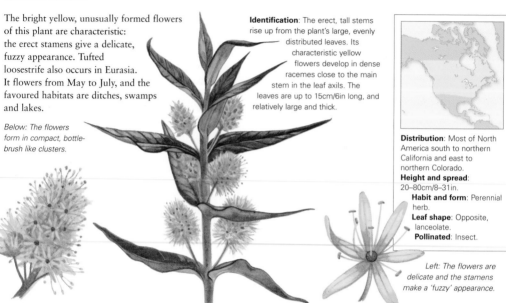

Identification: The erect, tall stems rise up from the plant's large, evenly distributed leaves. Its characteristic yellow flowers develop in dense racemes close to the main stem in the leaf axils. The leaves are up to 15cm/6in long, and relatively large and thick.

Distribution: Most of North America south to northern California and east to northern Colorado.
Height and spread: 20–80cm/8–31in.
Habit and form: Perennial herb.
Leaf shape: Opposite, lanceolate.
Pollinated: Insect.

Left: The flowers are delicate and the stamens make a 'fuzzy' appearance.

Western starflower

Indian potato, *Trientalis latifolia*

The beautiful, delicate pink flowers, which grow high above their leaves, are what characterise this plant. It flowers from April to June, and grows mainly in open woods and prairies. Native Americans are thought to have cooked and eaten the bulbs of the western starflower, but this is not advised. Despite its alternative name, modern sources do not mention edibility. Its specific name means 'wide-leaved'.

Identification: The pink petals of the flowers rest on their delicately thin stalks, which rise out of a patch of evenly arranged, large, ovate leaves each 30mm–10cm/1¼–4in long.

Far right: The plants grow from tubers and spread, via rhizomes, to form a carpet.

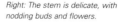

Right: The stem is delicate, with nodding buds and flowers.

Distribution: British Columbia south through the northern two-thirds of California and east to northern Idaho.
Height and spread: 10–25cm/4–10in.
Habit and form: Perennial herb.
Leaf shape: Oval.
Pollinated: Insect.

Bog loosestrife

Swamp candles, *Lysimachia terrestris*

This beautiful summer plant with its star-like, yellow flowers is in bloom from June to August. The alternative common name, swamp candles, comes from its tall clusters of flowers that stand out against the monotonous background of its boggy habitats. It was, in fact, inadvertently introduced into the north-west's cranberry bogs from eastern North America.

Identification: Erect stems adorned with clusters of bright yellow flowers with a circle of red spots. The petals may be marked with dark lines. The leaves are opposite and 50mm–15cm/2–6in long, lanceolate and spotted. The flowers open from the bottom of the spike to the top.

Distribution: Western Washington state and also widespread in the east.
Height and spread: 20–80cm/8–31in.
Habit and form: Perennial herb.
Leaf shape: Opposite.
Pollinated: Insect.

Above right: The flowers are bright yellow with an inner ring of red dots. The plant blooms from June to August.

Right: The branched cyme.

OTHER SPECIES OF NOTE

Starflower *Trientalis borealis*
Fragile-looking white flowers with golden anthers adorn an attractive spread of five to nine shiny leaves. It enjoys cool woodlands and peaty slopes ascending to subalpine regions.

Fringed loosestrife *Lysimachia ciliata*
This wetland plant has hairy leafstalks and an erect stem that bears yellow flowers, which rise on the stalks of opposite leaves. The beautiful flowers consist of five petals that are minutely toothed. The plant prefers damp woods or floodplains and ranges from Alberta east to Nova Scotia, south to Oklahoma, and north to North Dakota, also occurring in much of the West.

Whorled loosestrife *Lysimachia quadrifolia*
This plant has delicate, yellow flowers that rise on their stalks in star-like formation above a whorled bed of leaves. It enjoys dry or moist open woods and fields. The generic name *Lysimachia* is said to refer to an ancient Sicilian King (Lysimachus) who allegedly used the plant to pacify a bull. Colonists may also have fed the plant to cattle to calm them.

Snow dwarf-primrose *Douglasia nivalis*
This loosely-tufted perennial is native to the Pacific north-west. It has narrow hairy leaves and showy pink, lobed flowers and can be grown as an attractive alpine. One of only six species in this North American genus.

Featherfoil

Hottonia inflata

This floating aquatic plant flowers from April to June, appearing in abundance for a season before completely vanishing for sometimes up to seven or eight years, before reappearing as if by magic. It grows in pools, ditches, stagnant ponds and swamps, usually in water deeper than 30cm/12in.

Identification: Several thick, upright stalks, which emerge from the water, bear tiny greenish-white flowers which form in circles at the essentially leafless stalk joints. The leaves are 20–65mm/ ¾–2½in long, crowded at the base of the plant, and divided into narrow segments.

Distribution: Maine south to Georgia, west to Texas, and north to Missouri, Illinois, Indiana and Ohio.
Height and spread: Stems are 75mm–20cm/3–8in above water level.
Habit and form: Annual herb.
Leaf shape: Alternate, opposite or whorled.
Pollinated: Insect.

Above: The flower spikes rise above the water's surface.

Above: Individual flowers make up a flower spike.

HEATHER FAMILY

The heather family, Ericaceae, is large and mostly shrubby, comprising more than 100 genera and 3,400 species of mostly calcifuge (lime-hating) plants. The family includes shrubs, trees and herbs from mostly temperate, boreal and montane tropical zones. Some have edible fruits – for example blueberries and cranberries. Rhododendrons and azaleas have very showy flowers and are popular garden plants.

Dusty zenobia

Honeycup, *Zenobia pulverulenta*

This distinctive, extremely slow-growing, small deciduous shrub is a native of the coastal plain of the eastern USA, where it can be found in bogs and wet areas. It is the only species in its genus, and gets its common name from the dusty appearance of the bluish-green leaves. The small white flowers appear in the spring and are much more open than the pinched bells of *Vaccinium* and other related ericaceous species found in the same areas, adding to its distinctive appearance.

Identification: An open shrub with graceful, arching branches. The leaves are oval to oblong, pale green to grey-green with a waxy bloom and serrated margin, 25–50mm/1–2in long; they turn yellow-orange in autumn with a purplish-red tinge. Small bell-shaped, cream flowers with pale turquoise stems appear in early summer from the old wood. The pendent, white bells are plump and wide open and have a light citrus or anise scent.

Distribution: Eastern USA.
Height and spread: 60cm–1.8m/24in–6ft.
Habit and form: Deciduous shrub.
Leaf shape: Ovate to oblong.
Pollinated: Insect.

Far left: Although it eventually forms an open shrub, dusty zenobia is very slow growing.

Mountain laurel

Calico bush, Spoonwood, *Kalmia latifolia*

This large spreading shrub, native to eastern North America, is typically found around woodland edges, particularly by watersides or where light filters through the forest canopy. It is an evergreen with leaves clustered at the branch tips. Its star-shaped flowers range from red to pink or white, and occur in showy clusters. It is also known as spoonwood because native Americans used to make spoons from it.

Identification: This rounded, evergreen shrub may be dense and compact or open, depending on how much light it receives, with an irregular branching habit. The brown-tan bark is lightly ridged and furrowed, the trunks gnarled and twisted. The leaves are alternate, clustered toward the shoot tips, elliptic, 50mm–12.5cm/2–5in long, with pointed tips and smooth margins; they are dark green and glossy above, yellow-green in full sun. The lateral buds are hidden behind the bases of the leaf stalks. The flowers are pink, fading to white, up to 25mm/1in across; they appear in late spring in showy clusters at the branch tips, opening from star-shaped buds. The fruits are small, upright, dry, brown-tan capsules.

Distribution: Eastern North America.
Height and spread: 1.5–3.5m/5–12ft.
Habit and form: Evergreen shrub.
Leaf shape: Elliptic.
Pollinated: Insect.

Right: The star-shaped flowers can be pink or white and appear in showy clusters in late spring.

Mayflower

Trailing arbutus, *Epigaea repens*

Distribution: North America.
Height and spread: 10cm/4in or more.
Habit and form: Creeping evergreen shrub.
Pollinated: Insect.
Leaf shape: Ovate.

The delicate pink flowers of this small, evergreen, flowering shrub are among the first to appear on sandy soils across many parts of North America, mostly under the shade of trees in northern or mountainous areas. It is very low-growing and forms dense, slowly spreading mats, the creeping branches rooting along their length to form a shrubby thicket. It is widespread but by no means common: its growing sites are easily destroyed when disturbed by people or livestock and seldom recover.

Identification: The yellow-orange, trailing stems of this evergreen shrub root along their length at the nodes. The leaves, on hairy stalks, are alternate and broadly oval with a short point at the tip, 25–40mm/1–1½in long, rough and leathery with wavy margins and hairy undersides; they are often spotted with dead patches. The flowers, which are very fragrant, are produced at the end of the branches in dense clusters, sometimes in late winter but mainly in spring. They are white, to 15mm/⅝in across, with a reddish tinge, divided at the top into five segments that spread open in the form of a star. This low creeping, evergreen shrub has numerous trailing twiggy, yellow-orange stems, all of which have a tendency to root along their length at the nodes.

OTHER SPECIES OF NOTE

Ground pine heather *Cassiope lycopodioides*
This small, low-growing, evergreen shrub is found across the upper Pacific rim, from Japan through Alaska and British Columbia, down as far as Washington State, occurring at altitude in southern locations. The small white bells, with a red calyx, grow toward the top of the branches.

Large-fruited cranberry *Vaccinium macrocarpon*
This is the familiar cranberry grown commercially and used in cooking. It occurs naturally in eastern North America in acid boggy ground, forming a low-growing, creeping mat.

Alabama azalea *Rhododendron alabamense*
The flower of the Alabama azalea is typically white with a bright yellow blotch, but can sometimes be flushed with pink. Blooms appear in mid-spring, and their attractive lemon fragrance is most distinctive. It grows naturally in north-central Alabama, western to central Georgia and South Carolina, and is widely cultivated.

Flame azalea *Rhododendron calendulaceum*
This is found in dry open woods and also on treeless mountain slopes, for example in the southern Appalachians, and ranges from Georgia and Alabama north to New York and Ohio. It has beautiful large orange red or yellow flowers and is widely cultivated as an ornamental in gardens and parks.

Salal

Gaultheria shallon

This evergreen plant is one of the most common understorey shrubs in some coastal forests in Alaska, British Columbia, California, Oregon and Washington. In drier coniferous forests it can form an almost continuous shrub layer. It is also common in some wet or boggy coniferous forests, and in areas near the coast the shrub layer can be impenetrable. The small, white urn-shaped flowers appear at midsummer in clusters around the branch tips.

Identification: A creeping to erect shrub of variable height, it spreads by layering or suckering, with hairy, branched stems that arch and root at the nodes. The leaves are thick and leathery, shiny, oval, 50mm–10cm/2–4in are long and finely toothed. The flowers, white to pink, pendent bells, five-lobed, are borne singly along the axis of the stem tip, in groups of 5–15, the reddish flower stalks bending so that the flowers are oriented in one direction; they appear from late spring to midsummer. They are followed by berries that mature by late summer.

Distribution: North-western North America.
Height and spread: 20cm–5m/8in–16ft.
Habit and form: Evergreen shrub.
Leaf shape: Ovate.
Pollinated: Insect.

Left: Growth is largely upright.

Far right: The edible purple to black berries are often sweet.

CABBAGE FAMILY

The cabbage family, or Cruciferae (Brassicaceae), contains herbs or, rarely, subshrubs comprising about 365 genera and 3,250 species. The family includes familiar food plants such as cabbage, cauliflower, broccoli, Brussels sprouts, kohlrabi, and kale, which have all been derived from a single wild plant through human selection. The cabbage family is found throughout temperate parts of the world.

Pennsylvania bittercress

Cardamine pensylvanica

This perennial plant grows throughout much of North America. It is usually found in moist or wet soils, in wet woods, beside streams and along roadsides near woods. The flowering period varies according to its location, but is usually between early spring and midsummer. It can be confused with many similar species; the best way of identifying it is by its terminal leaflets, which are as large as, or larger than, the lateral leaflets.

Identification: The stems are erect, smooth or slightly hairy near the base, sometimes branched, up to 38cm/15in long, arising from a thickened rootstock. The leaves are alternate, pinnately compound with 5–13 smooth leaflets. The terminal leaflet is as large as, or larger than, the lateral leaflets, being up to 12mm/½in long and nearly as broad. All leaflets are oblong to oval, without teeth, toothed, or sometimes shallowly lobed. The tiny flowers, occurring in small groups on terminal racemes, are white, up to 6mm/¼in across, with four green, smooth sepals and four white petals, free from each other. The fruits are slender, cylindrical pods, ascending, up to 30mm/1¼in long, with a sterile beak. The seeds are pale brown.

Left: The fruit pods are long and slender.

Right: The plant is a biennial or herbaceous perennial.

Distribution: North America, from Newfoundland to Minnesota and Montana, south to Florida, Tennessee and Kansas.
Height and spread: 23–60cm/9–24in.
Habit and form: Herbaceous perennial.
Leaf shape: Pinnately compound.
Pollinated: Insect.

Waldo rock cress

Arabis aculeolata

Waldo rock cress is similar to the related McDonald's rock cress, *A. mcdonaldiana*, except that it is generally hairier and taller, with slightly smaller flowers. Its rosettes of glossy green, almost warty leaves send up short stems of bright pink flowers in summer. Restricted to the south-west USA, it occurs mainly on barren or shrub-covered shallow dry ridges, rocky outcrops and pine woodland at around 1,200m/4,000ft.

Right: The tall, thin flower stems are held high over the leaves.

Below: The showy flowers arise from reddish, tubular calyces.

Identification: The plant forms flattened rosettes of dark green oval-oblong to spoon-shaped leaves, with uneven to toothed margins. The basal leaves and lower parts of the stems are densely hairy, the upper parts are largely smooth. The flowers are almost 25mm/1in across, bright pink with spoon-shaped petals, borne in clusters at the top of 15–20cm/6–8in stems.

Distribution: South-western USA.
Height and spread: 10–20cm/4–8in.
Habit and form: Herbaceous perennial.
Leaf shape: Obovate-oblong.
Pollinated: Insect.

Beach wallflower

Coast wallflower, *Erysimum ammophilum*

The beach wallflower is a short-lived perennial with bright yellow flowers, native to sandy coastal bluffs and old, eroded, inner dunes. It will grow only in full sun, and is found principally in Californian sagebush habitat, with a very sandy substrate seemingly a prerequisite for this species. Where it occurs it provides bright patches of colour among the sagebushes. Its habitats are increasingly threatened by development, and the plant is less common than it was.

Distribution: California, USA.
Height and spread:
50mm–60cm/2–24in.
Habit and form: Biennial or short-lived perennial.
Leaf shape: Narrowly oblanceolate.
Pollinated: Insect.

Far right: The flowers appear from early spring to early summer on a raceme.

Identification: The plant usually has several stems 50mm–60cm/2–24in long. The basal leaves are narrowly lance-shaped, smooth or slightly toothed on the edge, 40mm–15cm/1½–6in long; the stem leaves are wider, especially near the flowers. The yellow flowers are four-petalled, with each petal 12–25mm/½–1in long. The fruits are spreading to ascending, 20mm–12.5cm/¾–5in long.

Below: The fruits are long and slender.

Heartleaf twistflower

Streptanthus cordatus

The twistflower's heart-shaped, blue-green leaves, with a white, powdery film, are commonly seen in early spring in the desert mountains of western USA. The plant is wide-ranging in rocky or sandy sagebrush scrub, pinyon/juniper woodland and ponderosa pine forest at 1,200–3,200m/4,000–10,500ft. Its long, slender, leaning stalk is topped by dark purple buds; as the flower stalk elongates, the lower buds open to yellow-and-purple twisted flowers. In moist springs the flower spikes may grow especially tall, with several dozen flowers arranged evenly up the stems.

Distribution: Western USA.
Height and spread:
20cm–1m/8–39in.
Habit and form:
Herbaceous perennial.
Leaf shape: Obovate.
Pollinated: Insect.

Identification: The stem, which has a woody base, may grow from 20cm–1m/8–39in tall, and is generally smooth. The basal leaves are widely oval, with teeth, often bristly, around the upper margins. The upper leaves are lance-shaped to oblong, pointed and wrapped around the stem. The flowers are yellowish-green in bud, becoming purple in flower. The tips are generally bristly, the petals projecting to 12mm/½in long, linear, purple. They are followed by upward-curving, flattened seedpods, 50mm–10cm/2–4in long.

Above: An unusual twisted flower gives this plant its name.

Right: The distinctive blue-grey leaves are covered in white powdery film.

OTHER SPECIES OF NOTE

Desert prince's plume
Stanleya pinnata var. *pinnata*
The desert prince's plume is a subshrub growing to 1.8m/6ft, with leathery blue-green leaves and yellow flowers. It is found in the high plains areas of the USA, from California to North Dakota, Kansas and Texas. The dense inflorescence appears in the autumn.

Smelowskia calycina
Close mats of silver fern-like foliage act as the perfect foil for the loose umbels of snowy flowers and tiny, upright, burgundy seedpods of this arctic plant. It is mostly found in high alpine or cold sites, typically those poor in nutrients such as scree and alluvial gravel, across Alaska and eastern Asia.

Gordon's bladderpod
Lesquerella gordonii
This pretty plant from the south-western USA and northern Mexico is a cool-season annual or short-lived perennial. It is more or less prostrate, and gives rise to a dense terminal raceme of yellow to orange flowers. The seedpods that follow are smooth and rounded, typically S-shaped, although sometimes may be straight.

Dame's violet

Sweet rocket, Dame's rocket, *Hesperis matronalis*

This plant has long been grown in European gardens, sometimes as a double-flowered form. The pink, purple or white flowers appear from April to August, and are fragrant, especially towards dusk, attracting moths. It has been successfully introduced to North America and can be found throughout the north in open woods, wasteland and roadsides. It is not widely cultivated in America.

Below: Hesperis is from the Greek for evening, which is when the fragrance of the flowers is at its best.

Distribution: Europe; now scattered throughout much of North America.
Height and spread: 30cm–1.2m/12in–4ft.
Habit and form: Herbaceous perennial/biennial.
Leaf shape: Lanceolate.
Pollinated: Insect.

Identification: A tall branching species, with terminal clusters of stalked flowers, each about 20mm/¾in long with four sepals and four petals. The leaves are 50mm–15cm/2–6in long and weakly toothed. The fruit develops as a long, slender pod about 50mm–10cm/ 2–4in long containing many seeds.

Right: The flowers are very symmetrical with four petals and four sepals. They are an attractive pink.

Spectacle pod

Dimorphocarpa wislizenii

The common name of this annual of weedy sites comes from the fruit pod, which has two, rounded lobes, looking like miniature spectacles. The genus *Dithyrea* is closely related and is referred to by the same common name. This particular species has greyish hairy foliage and produces pretty, four-petalled white flowers in thick clusters from February to May. The blooms are delicately fragrant. The plant's favoured habitats are dry grasslands and deserts, on sandy soils.

Above: The pods look like tiny pairs of spectacles, and make the plant easy to identify.

Distribution: Arizona and Utah east to Texas and Oklahoma, south to Mexico.
Height and spread: 60cm/24in.
Habit and form: Annual herb.
Leaf shape: Pinnately lobed.
Pollinated: Insect.

Identification: The stalks are usually branching, with pinnately lobed leaves to 15cm/6in long. The flowers are white, and each about 15mm/⁹⁄₁₆in long with four petals. The fruit is a flattened pod with two rounded lobes, often darker-coloured around the edges. Flowers will keep appearing on the plant as the seed pods come to maturity. The foliage, stems, buds and seeds are covered in fuzzy grey hairs.

Right: The spectacle pod has an open, weedy habit. It grows to 20–25cm/8–10in tall, and is often found along roadsides and in sandy areas from northern Chihuahua, south-western and western Texas, New Mexico, Utah and Nevada.

Western wallflower

Erysimum capitatum

This is a highly variable species with erect stems and dense clusters of attractive colourful flowers – orange-purple, orange or yellow, from March to July. It grows generally on dry soils, for example in sagebrush, but also (in the alpine form *E. capitatum* var. *purshii*) at high altitudes in mountain tundra. These alpine forms have short stems and are low-growing to protect them from cold, drying winds.

Identification: The four-petalled flowers are about 20mm/¾in across, ripening to produce very slender pods 50mm–10cm/2–4in long. The lower leaves are arranged in a basal rosette; the upper stem leaves are narrow with toothed margins.

Distribution: Mainly western, from British Columbia south to California and New Mexico.
Height and spread: 15–90cm/6–35in.
Habit and form: Biennial herb.
Leaf shape: Narrow and lanceolate (upper leaves).
Pollinated: Insect.

Left: The flowers have a sweet aroma with a hint of ammonia.

Right: The plants grow singly or in large patches.

OTHER SPECIES OF NOTE

Flatpod *Idahoa scapigera*
A tiny annual and uncommon plant of open grassland and sagebrush habitats, especially those that are damp early in the year, this is also found in some pine and fir forests, and sometimes on mossy rocks.

Shepherd's purse
Capsella bursa-pastoris
A very familiar sight in its native Europe, shepherd's purse has spread throughout the world as a successful weed. It grows throughout North America. The flat, triangular fruit pods resemble simple purses, and the plant produces tiny white flowers.

American sea rocket *Cakile edentula*
This fleshy and low-growing plant has pretty, four-petalled, pale lavender flowers. It is a common annual growing on unstable sands along the coast and around the Great Lakes. The leaves have a sharp flavour like horseradish.

Peppergrass *Lepidium virginicum*
A common weed whose seeds can be used as a flavouring and have a sharp taste like pepper. The leaves are also eaten as greens or in salads. Like many crucifers, it produces clusters of tiny white flowers. The little fruits are green, rounded and flat, and have a winged structure around them that helps with dispersal.

Double bladderpod

Rydberg twinpod, *Physaria acutifolia*

The most distinctive feature of this genus of downy perennial herbs is the bladder-like inflated fruit pod. This species has silvery foliage and grows up from a basal rosette of leaves. The flowering stems bear dense clusters of yellow flowers from June to August. Double bladderpod grows in coniferous forest, arid shrublands and gravelly or rocky dry soils.

Identification: The leaves are on long stalks and up to 10cm/4in long, with a rounded blade. The four-petalled flowers are each about 60mm/2¼in across, and the inflated fruit pod has two papery lobes, with a bristle-like style between them.

Below: The plant looks silvery due to the abundance of short hairs.

Distribution: Colorado, Utah and Wyoming.
Height and spread: 30mm–20cm/1¼–8in.
Habit and form: Perennial herb.
Leaf shape: Rounded, toothed.
Pollinated: Insect.

Below: The plants are usually less than 15cm/6in tall.

SAXIFRAGE FAMILY

Mainly found in northern temperate or cold climates, the saxifrage family, Saxifragaceae, has 35 genera and about 660 species, which are mostly perennial herbs with small flowers. It contains some popular garden genera such as Saxifraga, Bergenia *and* Astilbe. *The generic name means 'rock-breaker' and refers to the preferred habitat of many species, which is shattered rocks and screes.*

Diamondleaf saxifrage

Saxifraga rhomboidea

This pretty little saxifrage grows mainly in damp sites, at a range of altitudes, from sagebrush hills up to high in the mountains. Like many saxifrages, this one sends up a flowering stem from a light basal rosette of leaves.

Identification: As its common name suggests, the leaves are diamond-shaped or triangular. It produces tight clusters of tiny white flowers from May to August, opening right at the top of a tall hairy stem. Each flower cluster may be only about 20mm/¾in across, consisting of many tiny flowers, each with five petals, ten stamens and usually two prominent carpals. The stem is erect and tinged pink.

Right: The tiny flowers have white petals and red stamens.

Above: The leaves are thick in texture with blunt teeth. They are roughly diamond-shaped.

Distribution: Alberta and British Columbia south to Arizona and New Mexico.
Height and spread: 50mm–30cm/2–12in.
Habit and form: Perennial herb.
Leaf shape: Diamond.
Pollinated: Insect.

Purple saxifrage

Saxifraga oppositifolia

This saxifrage has a wide global distribution, in Europe and Asia as well as North America. While many saxifrages have white flowers, this one is unusual in having purplish or pinkish flowers, opening from June to August. Its leaves grow in a mat-like cushion at ground level and the flowers make a nice contrast with the dark green, often maroon-tinged foliage. The typical habitat is on rocks, screes, ledges and cliffs. Often grown as an alpine in gardens, for which several cultivars are available in various flower colours, including deep purple, pink and white.

Identification: Each flower has five spoon-shaped petals and is about 6mm/¼in across, with 10 stamens. The leaves are opposite and arranged in four overlapping rows along the stem.

Distribution: Northern North America.
Height and spread: 50mm x 20cm/2 x 8in.
Habit and form: Perennial herb.
Leaf shape: Oval.
Pollinated: Insect.

Left: The plant forms a low cushion over rocky ground.

Swamp saxifrage

Saxifraga pensylvanica

Well named, as its preferred habitat is swampy ground in bogs and wet meadows, this large saxifrage has a thick stalk, covered in sticky hairs, and produces clusters of small flowers, usually greenish-yellow in colour, from April through June. Interestingly, the young leaves are edible and may be added to salads or cooked as greens. It has been used to 'purify' the blood and to treat kidney and gallbladder stones. This species is endangered in Indiana and Kentucky and threatened in Maine.

Below: The flowers are usually yellow-green to whitish.

Distribution: North-eastern USA, from Ontario and Maine, south to North Carolina and west to Missouri.
Height and spread: 30–90cm/12–35in.
Habit and form: Perennial herb.
Leaf shape: Ovate to lanceolate.
Pollinated: Insect.

Identification: Each five-petalled flower is 4mm/³⁄₁₆in across, with 10 stamens, while the fruit develops as a capsule with two beaks. The lanceolate leaves have a toothed or wavy margin and tend to grow in a circular cluster.

Right: The flowering time of this plant is May to June.

OTHER SPECIES OF NOTE

Spotted saxifrage *Saxifraga bronchialis*
From the moss-like matted leaves narrow stalks bear open clusters of yellow-white flowers in June and August. It is common along mountain tracks and among rocks from Alaska and central Canada, and south to Oregon and the Rockies, to New Mexico.

Western saxifrage *Saxifraga occidentalis*
This is found from British Columbia south to Oregon, Nevada, Idaho and Wyoming. The preferred habitat is moist mountain slopes and rocky meadows. It has tiny white flowers borne on a reddish stem, from April to August.

Violet suksdorfia *Suksdorfia violacea*
This species takes its unusual name from the famous plant collector, W N Suksdorf, who was active in the Pacific North-west in the late 20th century. It is one of only three species in the genus. It is a slender plant with pink flowers with five long, slightly overlapping petals.

Foam flower *Tiarella cordifolia*
This plant takes its common name from the white flowers, which are tiny, with very fine stamens, and look indistinct and feathery or foamy from a distance. It grows in colonies in rich woodland, and also makes good ground cover in the garden. Cultivars may have pink and purple flowers.

Early saxifrage

Saxifraga virginiensis

This pretty saxifrage begins flowering in early spring (the season is mainly from April through June) on dry, rocky slopes and cliffs, mainly in eastern North America. Like many other species, the hairy flower stalk grows up from a basal rosette of leaves and carries a branching cluster of white flowers. The flowers of the early saxifrage are distinctly fragrant. It is another species that grows well in cool conditions in a rock garden.

Identification: The individual flowers, 6mm/¼in across, have five sepals and five petals, and a group of 10 yellow stamens. The fruit is a two-beaked capsule.

Left: The flowers form in loose, branched clusters.

Distribution: From Georgia, Louisiana and Oklahoma, north to Missouri, Illinois, Minnesota, Manitoba and New Brunswick.
Height and spread: 10–40cm/4–16in.
Habit and form: Perennial herb.
Leaf shape: Ovate to oblong.
Pollinated: Insect.

Above: The fragrant flowers can start to appear in March.

CURRANT FAMILY

The currant family, Grossulariaceae, consists of mainly shrubs, and has a fairly cosmopolitan range, although it is most common in the Northern Hemisphere. There are approximately 24 genera and 340 species. Their leaves are usually simple and spirally arranged, and the fruit is a capsule or berry. Some have edible berries, such as gooseberry and some currants, Ribes.

Flowering currant

Winter currant, *Ribes sanguineum*

The flowering currant is a deciduous woody bush from North America. It has pink flowers in pendent bunches, which are very attractive to bees and birds, appearing in spring, followed by inedible blue berries. It is most commonly encountered in open to wooded areas, moist to dry valleys and lower mountains, and ranges from British Columbia to northern California, from the coast to the east slope of the Cascades in Washington and northern Oregon, although it is widely naturalized elsewhere.

Right: The white-bloomed, blue-black berries appear in late summer.

Identification: The branches are softly downy, glandular, and red-brown. The leaves are 50mm–10cm/2–4in across, rounded with three to five lobes, heart-shaped at the base, dark green and slightly downy above, white felted beneath, irregularly toothed and finely serrated, pungently aromatic; the leaf stalk is glandular and downy. Dense, erect or pendent racemes, generally with 10–20 flowers per raceme, bear small tubular red or rosy pink flowers. They are followed by slightly hairy, blue-black fruits with a white bloom, which, unlike other species of this genus, are unpalatable.

Distribution: North America.
Height and spread: Up to 4m/13ft.
Habit and form: Deciduous shrub.
Pollinated: Insect.
Leaf shape: Rounded.

Left: The bush becomes laden with pendent bunches of pink flowers in the spring.

Fuchsia-flowered gooseberry

Californian fuchsia, *Ribes speciosum*

This is an attractive, normally evergreen shrub that produces red fuchsia-like flowers from January to May. These look impressive set against the glossy dark green foliage. In dry conditions it may lose its leaves during the summer. The native habitat is chaparral along the Californian coastal ranges. This is quite a popular garden shrub which is particularly useful as a hedge – its sharp spines providing a useful barrier.

Identification: The flowers droop from the branches and the very long stamens hang vertically downwards. The leaves are leathery and lobed and grow on short stalks close to the stems. The latter are covered in many sharp spines.

Distribution: California.
Height and spread: To 4m/13ft.
Habit and form: Evergreen shrub.
Leaf shape: Lobed.
Pollinated: Hummingbird and insect.

Left: The spiny shrub grows to 1.8m/6ft tall.

Far left: The foliage is lush and like that of a flowering currant.

False Mitrewort, Foam flower, Lace flower
Tiarella trifoliata
This species is usually found along streambanks and damp woods found from central California north to Alaska and east to Montana and Idaho. The leafy stems bear clusters of tiny white flowers, with a lacy appearance from a distance, which open between May and August.

Brookfoam
Boykinia aconitifolia
This pretty perennial with palmate leaves has delicate flower spikes with reddish stems and many small, white bells, each with a yellow centre. They appear in summer. A native of the Appalachian Mountains, it has mounds of bright green, leathery foliage produced in basal rosettes.

Island alum root *Heuchera maxima*
A perennial with a thick, fleshy rootstock and spikes of small, pinkish flowers in spring, held above rounded green leaves. It is rare, being found on canyon walls and cliffs, chaparral and coastal sage scrub below 450m/1,500ft, in only a few locations on the north Channel Islands, California.

Grass-of-Parnassus *Parnassia californica*
This is found in montane to subalpine stream banks and wet meadows from California to Oregon. It has solitary, conspicuous, cream flowers that look like pale buttercups. The leaves look very like those of the plantain.

Umbrella plant

Darmera peltata

The large, spreading leaves, held upright on their centrally inserted stalks, give this plant its common name. The small pink flowers grow in large, branched and rounded clusters, and open from April to June. Look for the umbrella plant alongside cold mountain streams where it grows in clumps among wet rocks, spreading by means of its thick, creeping rhizomes.

Identification: Each flower consists of five pink or white petals, each about 6mm/¼in long and there are 10 stamens. The leaves can grow up to 60cm/24in in diameter, the toothed leafblades are almost round and the leaf stalk is distinctly hairy.

Distribution: California and Oregon.
Height and spread: 60cm–1.8m/24in–6ft.
Habit and form: Perennial herb.
Leaf shape: Round, toothed.
Pollinated: Insect.

Below: The leaves turn red in autumn.

Left: It forms large, leafy clumps and is also known as Indian rhubarb.

False goatsbeard

Astilbe biternata

This woodland plant is the only species of *Astilbe* native to North America, found from Maryland southward to Georgia and Tennessee. Its large, bold foliage is quite distinctive, and the large, creamy-white, drooping, spike-like racemes of flowers are covered with tiny, cream-coloured blooms in midsummer. Unlike many in this genus, it is relatively rare in cultivation, and therefore hardly ever occurs outside its natural range.

Distribution: Maryland to Georgia and Tennessee.
Height and spread: 90cm/35in or more.
Habit and form: Herbaceous perennial.
Leaf shape: Pinnately compound.
Pollinated: Insect.

Far right: The distinctive glossy green leaves are topped with large, white, feathery flowerheads in midsummer.

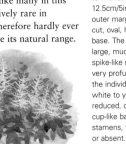

Identification: A clump-forming perennial with rhizomes branching below ground and leaves to 75cm/29½in long, conspicuously jointed at the base and junctions of the leaf stalks, glossy, red-green, sparsely hairy. The leaf blades are compound with three to five leaflets, each up to 12.5cm/5in long, with a toothed outer margin, sometimes partially cut, oval, heart-shaped at the base. The flowers are held on large, much-branched, feathery, spike-like racemes, appearing very profusely in early summer; the individual flowers are creamy-white to yellow, generally much reduced, consisting of a small, cup-like base with 10 elongated stamens, the petals minute or absent.

ROSE FAMILY

The rose family, Rosaceae, includes trees, shrubs and herbs and comprises about 100 genera and about 3,100 species. Most members of the family have flowers with five petals and numerous stamens, but fruiting arrangements vary. The rose family includes some of our best-known wild flowers, important fruits and garden plants. There are more than 2,000 cultivated varieties of apple and 5,000 of roses.

Swamp rose

Rosa palustris

The densely shrubby swamp rose grows in swamps and marshes, and along stream banks in eastern North America. Growing to a height of 1.8m/6ft, it blooms in early summer and is very fragrant. It is insect-pollinated, and birds that eat the fleshy hips help spread the seed.

Identification: A many-branched, deciduous shrub with stout, curved thorns, approximately 6mm/¼in long, with a flattened base. The leaves are pinnately compound, with narrow stipules at the base of the leaf stalk, barely extending out from the stalk until they flare at the end; the leaflets (usually seven) are oval to lance-shaped, with finely toothed edges. They are smooth on the upper surface and slightly hairy along the midrib underneath. The solitary flowers are pink and very fragrant. The hips are red, up to 12mm/½in thick, and may be either smooth or covered with minute hairs.

Right: The bright red hips appear from late summer onward.

Right: Swamp rose forms a small hummocky bush in wet areas. It has many arching branches.

Distribution: From Nova Scotia west to Minnesota, south to the Gulf of Mexico and east to Florida.
Height and spread: 1.8m/6ft.
Habit and form: Deciduous shrub.
Leaf shape: Pinnately compound.
Pollinated: Insect.

Dwarf serviceberry

Amelanchier alnifolia var. *pumila*

The dwarf serviceberry is a very variable and highly adaptable, fire-tolerant species, occurring throughout western and central North America. *Amelanchier alnifolia* is a multi-stemmed, deciduous shrub or small tree growing to 5.5m/18ft high. It is mainly found in thickets, at woodland edges and on the banks of streams in moist, well-drained soils, with the small bushy forms growing on fairly dry hillsides and the larger forms growing in more sheltered locations. The variety *pumila* is a naturally occurring dwarf alpine form native to mountainous areas of the West. The fruits are attractive to birds.

Identification: Five-petalled, white flowers, up to 20mm/¾in in diameter, appear in abundant, compact clusters in early spring before the leaves. The leaves are finely toothed, oval or rounded, pale to dark green, turning variable shades of yellow in autumn. In midsummer the flowers give way to small, round, edible berries, which ripen to dark purplish-black and are covered in a white bloom. They resemble blueberries in size, colour and taste.

Distribution: Western and central North America, from Saskatchewan south to Colorado and Idaho.
Height and spread: 90cm/35in.
Habit and form: Deciduous shrub.
Leaf shape: Oval.
Pollinated: Bee.

Left: White flowers appear in mid-spring, before the leaves, and are followed by edible fruits.

Indian plum

Oso berry, *Oemleria cerasiformis*

The Indian plum is a shrub or small tree with smooth, purplish-brown bark and is one of the first woody plants to bloom in the spring. The foliage emerges very early, and the fresh leaves taste of cucumber. The genus contains just this species, which has a native range along the Pacific coast in moist to moderately dry locations, especially in white oak woodlands and open forests of Douglas fir. It is most common at elevations below 250m/800ft but occurs up to 1,700m/5,700ft in the southern part of its range. The ripening fruits are highly attractive to many birds and mammals.

Identification: An erect, loosely branched, large, deciduous shrub or small tree, it has slender twigs, green turning to reddish-brown with conspicuous orange lenticels. The leaves are simple, alternate and generally elliptic or oblong to broadly lance-shaped, 50mm–12.5cm/2–5in long, light green and smooth above and paler below; the margins are entire to wavy. The bell-shaped, greenish to white flowers, 12mm/½in across, appear in early to mid-spring, in small clusters. The fruits are egg-shaped drupes up to 12mm/½in long, pink to blue-purple, borne on a red stem and edible but bitter.

Distribution: Pacific coast, USA.
Height and spread: 5m/16ft.
Habit and form: Deciduous shrub.
Leaf shape: Elliptic or oblong.
Pollinated: Insect.

Below: The berries attract wildlife.

Below: The bush is covered in white flowers in spring.

Arctic bramble

Arctic blackberry, Plumboy, *Rubus arcticus* subsp. *acaulis*

The arctic bramble (like many arctic species) has a circumpolar distribution, being native to northern parts of North America, Europe and Asia. Where it occurs in America it is fairly common in swamps and lakeside meadows, especially in peaty depressions rather than rocky limestone areas. The flowers appear in early summer, and are followed in late summer by sweet, shiny, red edible fruits like miniature raspberries. In full sun, the leaves often have a bronzy sheen.

Distribution: Circumboreal: northern North America, northern Europe and northern Asia.
Height and spread: 50mm–10cm/2–4in.
Habit and form: Dwarf shrub with herbaceous stems.
Leaf shape: Compound-trifoliate.
Pollinated: Insect.

Far right: The red berries often appear alongside the pink flowers from late summer onwards.

Right: The small red fruits resemble raspberries and are sweet tasting.

Identification: Alternate, leathery, trifoliate leaves have oval leaflets, 12–35mm/½–1⅜in long. The two lateral leaflets are stalkless and often deeply divided while the terminal leaflet has a short stalk; the tips are pointed to rounded, the margins smooth near the base, toothed near the tip. Solitary, bright pink to reddish-purple flowers, with five to eight petals 12–15mm/½–⅜in long and numerous stamens, appear in midsummer and are followed by deep red to dark purple, raspberry-like fruits, 12mm/½in across, in late summer.

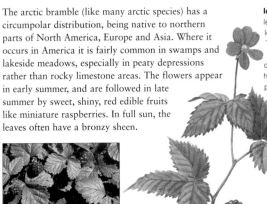

Cockspur thorn

Hog-apple, *Crataegus crus-galli*

This shrub or small tree has a short trunk and spreading, spiny branches and twigs. It is found on moist soils in valleys and low hill country across a wide range, up to about 600m/2,000ft altitude. It has also been commonly planted, both for ornament and as a protective hedge. The leaves turn bright orange and scarlet in the autumn. Clusters of white flowers are followed by red fruits that stay into the new year.

Identification: The leaves are leathery, shiny above, paler beneath and the twigs carry long, slender spines. The flowers have five white petals and are borne in large clusters in late spring and early summer. The fruits are small greenish or dull red haws in drooping clusters, and remain on the tree often through the winter.

Left: The leaves are spoon-shaped, dark and glossy.

Far left: The flowers have an unpleasant odour.

Right: The tree's height is about 7m/23ft when the tree reaches maturity, at about 25 years.

Distribution: Southern Ontario and Quebec to northern Florida, and west to eastern Texas
Height and spread: To 7m/23ft.
Habit and form: Shrub or small tree.
Leaf shape: Spoon-shaped, tapering at the base.
Pollinated: Insect.

Downy serviceberry

Shadbush, Juneberry, Shadblow, *Amelanchier arborea*

This plant's native habitat is moist soils in deciduous forests, but it is widely planted as an ornamental in parks and gardens, mainly for its attractive flower clusters. The strange names Shadbush and Shadblow apparently derive from the fact that the flowering coincides with the ascent of shad (fish) up the rivers to spawn in early spring.

Identification: A narrow-crowned tree or shrub with white, star-shaped flowers. Young leaves are fresh green, and downy on the underside. They have a rounded oval shape and are finely toothed at the edges. The berries turn an attractive shade of purple when they are ripe. The twigs are slender and reddish-brown, often with white hairs when young. The flowers have five narrow white petals, borne in terminal clusters, and open before the leaves in spring. The edible fruit resembles a small apple, and is purple when ripe.

Right: The attractive white blooms look like apple blossoms, and have a similar fragrance. They smother the plant in June and July. The plant is usually spotted alongside streams, in bogs, or other similarly wet habitats.

Distribution: Widespread in central and eastern North America, south to northern Florida.
Height and spread: To 12m/39ft.
Habit and form: Shrub or small tree.
Leaf shape: Ovate, elliptical, finely toothed.
Pollinated: Insect.

Left: The shrub or tree (here shown covered in blossom) is usually 5–12m/16–39ft tall with a trunk of about 15cm/6in diameter.

White mountain avens

Dryas octopetala

This pretty flower is found in exposed, windy locations where its prostrate growth habit and hairy leaves give it protection from the elements. Its usual habitat is rocky ground at medium to high elevations. The flowers appear from June through August, and the fruits contain silver-plumed seeds. It makes an attractive addition to the rockery, and is a popular alpine garden species.

Identification: A low-growing species, often forming extensive mats. The flower is 25mm/1in across and creamy white in colour, with 8–10 broad petals.

Distribution: Much of northern North America (also Europe and Asia).
Height and spread: 50mm–25cm/2–10in.
Habit and form: Shrublet.
Leaf shape: Lanceolate, with scalloped margins.
Pollinated: Insect.

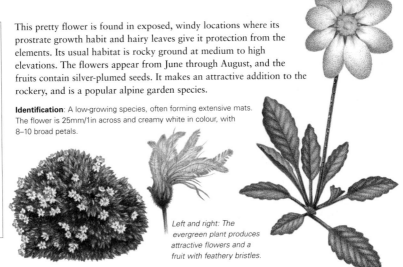

Left and right: The evergreen plant produces attractive flowers and a fruit with feathery bristles.

OTHER SPECIES OF NOTE

Beach strawberry *Fragaria chiloensis*
This a low-growing plant sending out runners, growing on dunes along the Pacific coast, from Alaska to mid California. The small white flowers produce strawberries about 20mm/¾in across.

Bigleaf avens, Large-leaved geum *Geum macrophyllum*
A widespread species of damp woods and meadows, with small yellow flowers appearing from April to August. The large leaves are pinnately compound and grow up to 30cm/12in in length.

False violet, Robin-run-away *Dalibarda repens*
This is a low-growing, creeping plant of damp woodland and boggy sites. It has a northern distribution and grows well in bog gardens. It superficially resembles a violet, though the flower has typical rose symmetry.

Purple-flowering raspberry *Rubus odoratus*
Unlike many of its genus, this lacks prickles. The rose-like flowers grow in loose clusters, and the fruits resemble raspberries. They have a pleasant flavour, but are full of seeds. The leaves are unusual in being shaped like those of a maple tree.

Agrimony

Agrimonia gryposepala

This is one of several similar members of this genus. The stem of this species has a characteristic strong spicy smell when crushed. The flowering stalk grows up tall between the leaves and carries a cluster of small yellow flowers.

Identification: The compound leaves are pinnately divided. The larger leaflets are 50mm–10cm/2–4in long, bright green and toothed, with many obvious veins on the surface. In between these large leaflets are much smaller leaflets. The individual flowers are only about 6mm/¼in across and have five petals. The fruit has hooked bristles at the tip.

Distribution: Mainly eastern North America.
Height and spread: To about 1.5m/5ft.
Habit and form: Herbaceous perennial.
Leaf shape: Pinnate.
Pollinated: Insect.

Below: The yellow cup-like flowers appear on a long stem.

Left: Blooms lower down the raceme open first.

Goatsbeard

Bride's feather, *Aruncus dioicus*

This tall plant has long arched or dangling clusters of tiny white flowers, and the diffuse appearance of these inspired the common name of 'goatsbeard' for this genus. It also has an unpleasant 'goaty' odour, attractive to flies. The main flowering season is May through July and this species favours damp sites in woodland.

Identification: The flowers are small, each about 3mm/⅛in across with five sepals and five white petals, the latter often dropping off early. The stalks rise well above the foliage. The leaves are large and divided, with toothed ovate leaflets each about 15cm/6in in length. The plant prefers partial shade and moist soil. It is popular in 'wild' gardens.

Above: Spikes of tiny cream flowers stick out horizontally from the main stalk. Male plants produce far more flowers than their female counterparts.

Distribution: Northern California to Alaska, and also in the east, and widespread also in Europe and Asia.
Height and spread: 90cm–2.1m/35in–6¾ft
Habit and form: Perennial herb.
  Leaf shape: Divided, toothed.
Pollinated: Insect.

Left: The plant forms large clumps in damp woodland sites. It is tall, reaching 1.2–1.8m/4–6ft in height.

Sierran mountain misery

Chamaebatia foliolosa

The fanciful common name of this species requires some explanation. It forms dense, impenetrable thickets, and because it has resinous leaves, walking through patches of this plant is a miserable experience indeed; the sticky leaves cling tightly to clothing and boots. The plants emit a heady odour, slightly medicinal and rather like tar, and the resin is actually very flammable. In hot weather patches burn easily, leaving nothing but parched black soil. But they then regenerate fast from the roots after all the competing species have perished. The favoured habitat is hillsides and open forests.

Identification: The attractive flowers are few in number and white, about 25mm/1in wide, with five petals, each one about 8mm/⅜in long. The foliage is fine and fern-like, with pinnately divided, feathery leaves. The fruit is egg-shaped and hard, with a single seed.

Right: The fern-like plant often forms a dense carpet of shrub in pine and conifer woods. It is also known as bear clover.

Distribution: Cascade Range and Sierra Nevada in California.
Height and spread: 20–60cm/8–24in.
Habit and form: Evergreen shrub.
  Leaf shape: Pinnate.
Pollinated: Insect.

Indian strawberry

Duchesnea indica

Distribution: Ontario, Michigan, Nebraska and Connecticut, south to Florida and west to Texas.
Height and spread: Stalks to 75mm/3in.
Habit and form: Creeping perennial herb.
Leaf shape: Ovate.
Pollinated: Insect.

As suggested by both the common and scientific specific name, this species is actually native to India, but is now widely naturalized in North America. The genus name is in honour of Antoine Nicolas Duchesne, a famous 17th and 18th century botanist. It resembles the true strawberry in its trailing stems and strawberry-like (though tasteless) fruits, and its creeping vines spread rampantly. It grows mainly as a weed, on disturbed ground and lawns.

Left: The fruits do not taste like true strawberries.

Identification: The yellow flowers are each 20mm/¾in across with five sepals, petals and leafy bracts, and open between April and June. The leaflets are long, ovate and toothed.

Left: The flowers can last through the autumn but are at their best from April to June.

OTHER SPECIES OF NOTE

Apache plume
Fallugia paradoxa
This white-flowered shrub has fluffy silvery fruit heads atop slender branches. It is these fruiting heads that give it its name. It grows on rocky slopes, deserts and open pinewoods, mainly from Mexico and in western Texas north to California.

Gordon's ivesia *Ivesia gordonii*
Densely clustered yellow flowerheads are a main feature of this species. These are borne on tall stalks arising from pinnately divided basal leaves. Look for it in the west, on riverbanks and rocky sites.

Rocky mountain rockmat
Petrophyton caespitosum
A remarkable species growing in the Rockies. It has pink or brownish-white flowers in dense clusters on stalks growing out of dense matted leaves. The roots anchor it into rock crevices.

Bowman's root Indian physic
Porteranthus trifoliatus
This woodland plant is mainly found in the east of the region. The star-shaped white or pinkish flowers have five narrow petals and open from May to July. Powdered root was used medicinally by Native Americans, hence the common names.

Queen-of-the-prairie

Filipendula rubra

The majestically named flower produces large fragrant clusters of small pink flowers that look feathery from a distance. It belongs to the same genus as the European meadowsweet. The favoured habitats are meadows, prairies and grassy thickets. It grows well in gardens and makes a colourful addition to borders. The flowering season is June through August.

Identification: The individual flowers are very small at 13mm/½in across, with many stamens. The compound pinnate leaves are divided and deeply lobed.

Distribution: Ontario, Iowa and Wisconsin, east to Newfoundland, south to West Virginia and North Carolina, and west to Missouri.
Height and spread: 2.3 × 1.2m/7½ × 3¾m.
Habit and form: Perennial herb.
Leaf shape: Pinnate.
Pollinated: Insect.

Right: The stems are 90cm–2.1m/35in–6¾ft tall. Tiny pale pink flowers appear through the summer months.

Common silverweed

Potentilla anserina

This species has a wide distribution, being found also in Europe and Asia. It grows low, forming patches, and has characteristically silvery leaves and yellow flowers through the summer. It prefers moist soils such as meadows and stream banks. It was once used in medicine and the cooked roots were eaten, and a root extract was used to tan leather. An infusion of the leaves is said to make a good skin cleanser, while a sprig left in a shoe will reportedly help prevent blisters.

Below: Flowers are hermaphroditic and pollinated by flying insects.

Identification: Each flower is about 20mm/¾in across, with five sepals and five petals, and many stamens. Flowers appear from May to August. The compound leaves have many rounded toothed leaflets.

Distribution: Western North America, across Canada and north-eastern USA.
Height and spread: Stalks to 30cm/12in; runners 90cm–1.8m/35in–6ft.
Habit and form: Creeping perennial herb.
Leaf shape: Pinnate.
Pollinated: Insect.

Below: The stems rise from clumps or tufts.

Shrubby cinquefoil

Potentilla fruticosa

This species is also found in Europe and Asia. It is an attractive shrub growing in a range of habitats, from mountain slopes, open forests, and plains. It grows well in cultivation, and there are several garden varieties available, some with larger, more colourful, flowers. The wild form flowers mainly between June and August.

Centre: Each leaf has three to eight leaflets. Leaf colour is medium to dark green, sometimes with a bluish tinge.

Above: Bright yellow flowers bloom through the summer.

Identification: The leaves are divided, usually with five leaflets, hairy beneath. Each flower is about 25mm/1in across with five sepals, five petals and many stamens.

Right: The shrub has upright branches and a rounded habit.

Distribution: Found right across northern North America.
Height and spread: 15–90cm/6–35in.
Habit and form: Perennial shrub.
Leaf shape: Pinnate.
Pollinated: Insect.

Sticky cinquefoil

Potentilla glandulosa

This cinquefoil is common in the west of the region, where it grows mainly in open exposed sites. It has bushy growth with several leafy, reddish, slightly sticky stems. The yellow flowers grow in loose branching clusters and open from May to July. The name 'cinquefoil' refers to the fact that the leaves of this and other species often have five leaflets, though in this species there can be more.

Distribution: Alberta and British Columbia south to California; east to South Dakota and Wyoming.
Height and spread: To 50cm/20in.
Habit and form: Perennial herb.
Leaf shape: Pinnate.
Pollinated: Insect.

Identification: Each flower is 15–20mm/ ⁹⁄₁₆–¾in across with five pointed sepals and five broad petals; the stamens number 25–40. The pinnate leaves have from five to nine ovate toothed leaflets.

Right: Petals vary from yellow-white to deep yellow.

OTHER SPECIES OF NOTE

Red cinquefoil *Potentilla thurberi*
This species has pretty, intense, raspberry-red flowers with deeper red centres, opening from July to October. It grows in damp meadows and also in coniferous forests, from north Mexico to New Mexico and Arizona.

Canadian dwarf cinquefoil
Potentilla canadenis
Found from Canada, south to Texas and Georgia, in rocky, open woodland and sandstone soils, this is low-growing and spreading in growth. It has pretty silvery stems and yellow flowers that appear in the early spring.

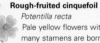

Rough-fruited cinquefoil
Potentilla recta
Pale yellow flowers with many stamens are borne in flat clusters from May to August. The stems are up to 50cm/20in tall and hairy. Introduced from Europe, it is now found in dry fields, roadsides and wasteland in North America.

Dwarf cinquefoil, Robbins' potentilla
Potentilla robbinsiana
An extremely small, hairy alpine plant growing at high altitudes in the White Mountains of New Hampshire. It is a rare species (and found in no other states), but coming back now that it has been protected from trampling by hikers and over-collection. It has pretty yellow flowers – up to 50 on any one plant – that bloom soon after the snow melts in May.

Canadian burnet

Sanguisorba canadensis

This is a plant of swampy and boggy habitats. The many stamens give the flower clusters a distinctly hazy appearance. Each flowerhead consists of many tiny individual flowers all tightly packed together in a cylindrical structure. The genus name comes from the Latin words for blood and drink – the sap was once believed to stem bleeding.

Distribution: Newfoundland west to Quebec and Manitoba, south to Michigan, Illinois and Georgia; also in parts of the north-west.
Height and spread: 30cm–1.5m/12in–5ft.
Habit and form: Perennial herb or shrub.
Leaf shape: Pinnate.
Pollinated: Insect.

Identification: The tiny flowers are about 6mm/¼in across, and the long stamens extend beyond the four small sepals (petals are absent). The pinnate basal leaves each have 7–15 stalked leaflets with toothed edges. The flowering period lasts from August to September.

Left: The stalks are up to 1.5m/5ft in height. The plant is known in some areas as caribou feed, Indian tobacco or marsh lily.

Multiflora rose

Rosa multiflora

This is an introduced species of rose, native to eastern Asia. It has small flowers, opening in May and June. It is very invasive and has become something of a nuisance weed in some parts of North America. It is however a useful garden plant as it forms dense spiny hedges and provides cover for birds and other wildlife.

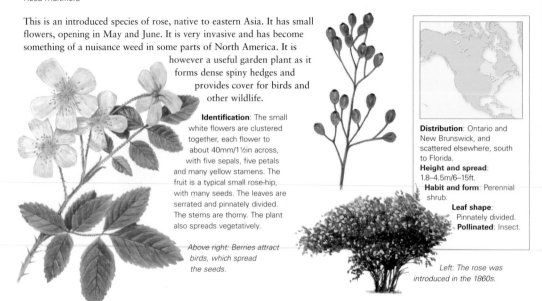

Identification: The small white flowers are clustered together, each flower to about 40mm/1½in across, with five sepals, five petals and many yellow stamens. The fruit is a typical small rose-hip, with many seeds. The leaves are serrated and pinnately divided. The stems are thorny. The plant also spreads vegetatively.

Above right: Berries attract birds, which spread the seeds.

Distribution: Ontario and New Brunswick, and scattered elsewhere, south to Florida.
Height and spread: 1.8–4.5m/6–15ft.
Habit and form: Perennial shrub.
Leaf shape: Pinnately divided.
Pollinated: Insect.

Left: The rose was introduced in the 1860s.

Rugosa rose

Wrinkled rose, *Rosa rugosa*

Another introduced rose, native to east Asia, this species has large pale pink or white flowers, and very prickly stems. The attractive flowers open mainly from June-September. In North America it is quite often planted on unstable sand, such as on coastal dunes, as it helps to bind the soil.

Identification: Each flower is 50–75mm/2–3in across, with five sepals and five petals, and many stamens. The leaves have dark green oblong leaflets, with a furrowed or wrinkled texture.

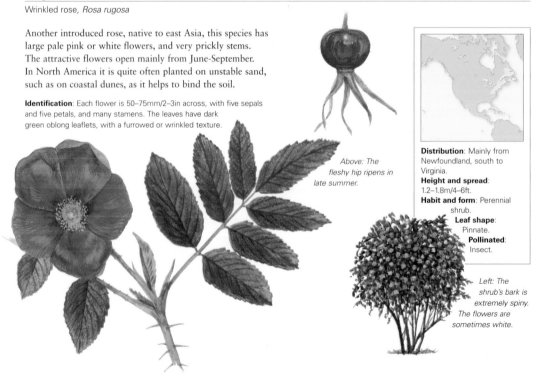

Above: The fleshy hip ripens in late summer.

Distribution: Mainly from Newfoundland, south to Virginia.
Height and spread: 1.2–1.8m/4–6ft.
Habit and form: Perennial shrub.
Leaf shape: Pinnate.
Pollinated: Insect.

Left: The shrub's bark is extremely spiny. The flowers are sometimes white.

Virginia rose

Rosa virginiana

As indicated by its name, this is a native species. It grows mainly in woodland clearings and also on the coast. It forms a dense shrub and has pink flowers from June to August. There are many rose species found in the region, several introduced from Europe, and they are often hard to identify. Many can be grown in gardens. The plant is thought to have some medicinal uses. However, its hairs are known to cause irritation in some people.

Distribution: From Newfoundland south to Georgia and Alabama.
Height and spread: 30cm–1.8m/12in–6ft.
Habit and form: Perennial shrub.
Leaf shape: Divided.
Pollinated: Insect.

Identification: The flowers are 50–75mm/2–3in across and the leaves have shiny toothed leaflets. The fruit is the typical bright red rose hip.

Left: The plant can form dense thickets.

Far right: The vibrant hip.

OTHER SPECIES OF NOTE

Prairie rose
Rosa arkansana
An attractive native rose with clusters of pink or white flowers and very prickly stems. Its leaves are softly hairy beneath, the buds pink and the fruit a bright red hip. It is usually found on dry ground; on prairies or in thickets.

Nootka rose *Rosa nutkana*
A thorny rose. It is an arching shrub with pale to bright pink flattish flowers from May to July and grows in wooded areas, mainly in upland and mountain sites from Alaska south to California.

Dwarf bramble *Rubus lasiococcus*
This trailing shrub produces flowering shoots with one or two white flowers from June to August. Another western species, found from British Columbia to California, it grows mainly in woods. The name *lasiococcus* roughly translates as 'woolly-fruited'.

Red chokeberry *Pyrus arbutifolia*
This is a native shrub related to pear. It produces clusters of attractive white or pink flowers from April to July. The fruit is more like a berry than a pear, and is dull red in colour. It grows wild in woods and clearings, but has also been adapted successfully to the garden.

Swamp dewberry

Bristly dewberry, *Rubus hispidus*

The dewberries are closely related to brambles (blackberry) and are placed in the same genus. This species likes swampy or moist soils and is typically found in damp clearings and open woodland. The flowering stalks grow up from trailing stems and carry loose clusters of white flowers. The edible fruits are enjoyed by many wild animals, including small mammals and birds.

Identification: Flowers are about 20mm/¾in across, and there are five sepals and five petals. The leaves have mainly three large toothed leaflets, and the fruit is like a blackberry, ripening red or blackish.

Right: The fruit resembles a blackberry.

Distribution: From Nova Scotia south to South Carolina.
Height and spread: 10–30cm/4–12in.
Habit and form: Creeping perennial shrub.
Leaf shape: Three leaflets.
Pollinated: Insect.

PEA FAMILY

In the Americas, the pea family, Fabaceae or Leguminosae, has many similar forms to those encountered in Eurasia. Several American species are extremely important economic plants, such as the groundnut (peanut) and the lupines, which are widely used in horticulture. The group includes plants that are trees and herbaceous or annual shrubs.

Groundnut

Bog potato, *Apios americana*

Groundnut is a North American species, found mainly in moist areas near streams or bodies of water where it can get full sunlight at least for part of the day. The very aromatic, pink or brownish-red flowers appear in early summer, but this varies according to the location. It is a nitrogen-fixing, perennial vine, which climbs by twining up shrubs and other herbs in an anti-clockwise fashion. It is herbaceous in the north of its range, but the brown-skinned, white-fleshed tubers, on underground rhizomes, survive the winter.

Below: The nut is a long green bean.

Identification: A twining vine with alternate leaves, pinnately compound, usually with five to seven broadly pointed leaflets. The flowers, usually pink, maroon or brownish-red, have a typical pea-like structure, with a relatively large concave standard with a small hood at its apex into which the narrow, sickle-shaped keel is hooked; they are about 12mm/½in long, occurring in compact racemes 75mm–12.5cm/3–5in long. The fruits are pods 50mm–12.5cm/2–5in long, containing 6–13 wrinkled, brown seeds.

Distribution: North America, from Ontario and Quebec in the north to the Gulf of Mexico, and from the prairies to the Atlantic coast.
Height and spread: 90cm–6m/35in–19¾ft.
Habit and form: Vine.
Leaf shape: Pinnately compound.
Pollinated: Insect.

Lady lupine

Hairy lupine, *Lupinus villosus*

The lady lupine is a hairy plant whose lavender-blue flowers have a red-purple spot on the standard, or upper petal. The plant gets its common and botanical names from the Latin *lupus*, meaning 'wolf', as it was once thought to deplete or 'wolf' the mineral content of the soil. It is native to the USA and occurs in dry sandy habitats of the south-eastern states.

Below: The spreading stems and long, hairy leaves form a dense, slightly shrubby mass through which the flower spikes emerge. Striking spikes of purple flowers are seen from spring to early summer, mainly in dry, open woodland.

Identification: The plant has a soft-woody base and a shrubby appearance, with silvery, upright or spreading stems up to 90cm/35in tall. The leaves, 25–75mm/1–3in long, are simple and lance-shaped, the lower ones clustered, the upper leaves alternate. They have a rounded base and pointed tip, and are covered with short, silver, densely shaggy hairs. The bracts at the base of each leaf are conspicuous. The flowers, which vary in colour from white, through rose to purple, are pea-like with a maroon-red spot on the upper petal and a two-lipped, silky calyx. They grow in erect clusters and are followed by woolly seedpods.

Distribution: North Carolina to Florida and west to Louisiana, USA.
Height and spread: 90cm/35in.
Habit and form: Herbaceous perennial.
Leaf shape: Lanceolate.
Pollinated: Insect.

American hog peanut

Amphicarpaea bracteata

Distribution: Eastern and central North America.
Height and spread: Up to 90cm/35in.
Habit and form: Annual vine.
Leaf shape: Trifoliate.
Pollinated: Insect.

There is only one species of *Amphicarpaea* in the Americas, although others exist in Asia and North Africa. The hog peanut is found in wet woods and thickets throughout eastern and central North America and is a twining annual, or occasionally perennial, vine. The flowers appear in late summer and early autumn and are unusual in occurring in two types. The visible flowers are violet and pea-like; flowers of the second type, which are cleistogamous (self-pollinating without opening) and without petals, are located near the base of the plant; they produce fleshy pods containing a single seed.

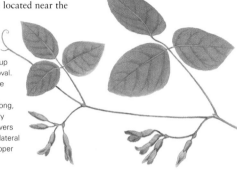

Identification: Thin, slightly hairy stems bear alternate leaves, each divided into three leaflets up to 75mm/3in long, but often much smaller, and oval. The lateral leaves are asymmetrical, tending to be slightly diamond-shaped on the outer edge. The flowers are irregular in shape, up to 20mm/¾in long, tinged purple to completely creamy-white, closely spaced in drooping racemes. Cleistogamous flowers with only vestigial petals are located low on the lateral branches, resting on or under the ground. The upper flowers form flat pods with several seeds.

OTHER SPECIES OF NOTE

Scarlet milk vetch *Astragalus coccineus*
This low-growing perennial bears racemes of vibrant red, pea-like flowers in late spring. Scarlet milk vetch is endemic to the canyons and ridges of the desert mountains of south-western USA, being widespread and locally abundant from Colorado to California.

Blunt lobe *Lupinus ornatus*
The blunt lobe or silvery lupine is so named because of its silvery, flattened leaves. It grows at elevations of 1,200–3,200m/4,000–10,500ft on dry flats and slopes in Washington, Idaho and California. It blooms from late spring to autumn, bearing spikes of flowers that are blue with a lilac spot at the base of the upper petal.

Campo pea, Pride of California
Lathyrus splendens
This is a 60cm–1.2m/24in–4ft, deciduous, vine or shrub with large crimson-red flowers. It climbs over chaparral shrubs and thrives in partial sun and the protection of other shrubs. The showy flowers attract hummingbirds and butterflies.

Goldenbanner *Thermopsis gracilis*
The slender, tall, erect spikes of bright yellow flowers are carried on loosely branched stems above the foliage, which is silky when young, becoming smooth with age. It is chiefly distributed in the west and north-west of North America in open, grassy places.

Canadian milk vetch

Astragalus canadensis

Canadian milk vetch is fairly common throughout most of eastern North America, at least as far south as Georgia. It prefers rich to moist soil and the creamy-white flowers appear in the summer. It is an important food source for birds, as it retains its seed late into the autumn and early winter. The plant is easy to identify while in flower, but vegetatively it can be mistaken for many other plants.

Distribution: Eastern North America.
Height and spread: 90cm/35in.
Habit and form: Herbaceous perennial.
Leaf shape: Pinnate.
Pollinated: Insect.

Identification: The multiple stems are erect, branching, reddish in strong sun. The leaves are alternate and pinnate, each with 13–20 pairs of leaflets, elliptic to oblong, abruptly pointed, with smooth margins. Axillary racemes up to 15cm/6in long, bearing 30–70 flowers, appear from late spring to late summer. The flowers are pea-like but elongated, up to 20mm/¾in long, creamy-white to greenish-white or with a tinge of lilac. The fruits are inflated, to 12mm/½in long, smooth, beaked with a persistent style, containing around 10 seeds.

Above: The strong, upright flowering stems arise from underground rhizomes and are divided near their bases.

Rose acacia

Moss locust, Bristly locust, *Robinia hispida*

This attractive shrub is native to the south and east of the USA, and is grown extensively also in gardens mainly for its attractive pink pea-flowers, which appear in late spring on short racemes of 3–12 blooms. A number of cultivated forms have been produced, including a more compact cultivar, 'Monument' with larger, lilac-pink flowers, and 'Macrophylla' with less bristly branches. North America has about 20 species of *Robinia*, mainly in the east, south to Mexico.

Identification: The bristly branches have pinnate leaves divided into 7–15 ovate leaflets. The flowers are in short dangling racemes, each with usually three to five pink or pale purple flowers. The fruits are bristly pods, 75mm/3in long. The leaves are divided into ovate leaflets.

Above: Each flower is 20–25mm/¾–1in across. The drooping racemes have about 10 light blooms a piece. They appear in late spring.

Distribution: South-eastern USA.
Height and spread: 2.25m/7¼ft.
Habit and form: Shrub.
Leaf shape: Pinnate.
Pollinated: Insect.

Left: The shrub is deciduous, with bristly branches.

Fairy duster

Mock mesquite, *Calliandra eriophylla*

Identification: The fluffy appearance of the flowers is caused by the numerous long pink stamens. Each flower also has five pink petals and a bright red style.

For most of the year this plant is easily overlooked, being low-growing for a shrub, and modest in appearance. However, that all changes in early spring when the remarkable flower clusters open. In some sandy and desert habitats swarms of fairy duster plants transform the landscape into a haze of pink, from February to May. Though the individual flowers are small, the densely clustered flowerheads look like pink fluffy dusters – hence the common name for this charming plant. The favoured habitats are sandy desert slopes and arid grasslands. The genus has 200 species, mainly in the tropics.

Below: Fairy duster blooms in spring, then again in the autumn. The leaves are alternate and pinnately divided.

Left: The flattened pods explode, or unzip, from the tip to the base, ejecting seeds several feet.

Distribution: Mexico and New Mexico north to southern California.
Height and spread: 20–50cm/8–20in.
Habit and form: Shrub.
Leaf shape: Twice pinnate.
Pollinated: Insect, wind.

Western sweetvetch

Hedysarum occidentale

This pretty vetch brightens meadows and open woodland with its conical spikes of pink-purple pea flowers, clustered in dense racemes. It is found mainly at fairly high altitudes, and most other species in this genus have a northern distribution.
The pods are unusual in opening crosswise rather than lengthwise like those of other pea family members.

Distribution: From Washington state south to Colorado and east to Montana.
Height and spread: 40–80cm/16–31in.
Habit and form: Herbaceous perennial.
Leaf shape: Pinnate.
Pollinated: Insect.

Identification: The compound leaves have between nine and twenty one ovate leaflets, each about 30mm/1¼in long with a characteristic covering of tiny brown dots on the upper surface. Each pea flower is 20mm/¾in long. The fruit is the typical flattened pod, with between one and four oval segments.

Right: The fruit has one to four chambers and sharp margins.

Below: Each flower stalk bears many pink-purple flowers.

OTHER SPECIES OF NOTE

Indigobush *Amorpha fruticosa*
This widespread shrub of riverbanks and islands forms thickets on moist and wet soils. Its most striking features are the long, erect racemes of purple flowers opening in May and June. The individual flowers are about 8mm/⅝in long with a single petal surrounding ten orange stamens.

Silk beach pea *Lathyrus littoralis*
This plant grows on coastal sand dunes along the Pacific coast from Washington State to central California. It has beautiful rose-pink and white flowers in racemes and pinnate leaves. Part of the natural gardens of this coast, often with Beach Morning Glory *(Calystegia soldanella)*.

White locoweed *Oxytropis sericea*
A hairy plant with grey foliage and racemes of creamy white flowers. Its favoured habitats are mountain meadows and slopes and it ranges from western Canada through Montana to south Idaho and Utah south to north Texas. This toxic species has been blamed for poisoning domestic livestock.

Harlequin lupine
Lupinus stiversii
The common name is for its striking and unmistakable tri-coloured flowers, which are yellow, pink and white.
Sandy or gravelly soils in oak and pine woods are its favoured habitat, and it ranges from the western slopes of the Sierra Nevada south to the mountains of southern California.

Blue alpine lupin

Lupinus lepidus

Arguably the prettiest of the alpine lupins, this species is at home on the thin, high altitude soils in the screes and rocky moorland of the Rocky Mountains, Cascades and Olympic Mountains of Washington State. It is well adapted to growing on volcanic soils and was the first species to colonise the slopes of Mount St Helens after the eruption of 1980. Its long roots penetrate deep into cracks and soils and the hairy leaves trap moisture from mountain mists, helping it to withstand dry periods.

Identification: The small palmate leaves are covered with silvery hairs. The scented flowers are a beautiful bright blue, usually with a prominent white patch, in dense racemes to 15cm/6in tall.

Distribution: Mountains of the Pacific north-west.
Height and spread: 30cm/12in.
Habit and form: Herbaceous perennial.
Leaf shape: Compound, palmate.
Pollinated: Insect.

Below: It is also known as dwarf lupine and is smaller than many other lupines, and is mat-forming.

Left: The flowers are blue to purple and occasionally white.

Butterfly pea

Clitoria mariana

This striking plant displays its dramatic, butterfly-like flowers from June to August. These are inverted, with the keel upwards and the standard petal pointing towards the ground. It enjoys dry soil, thickets and open woodland. The upside-down flowers mean that it is easily confused with the spurred butterfly pea, *Centrosema virginianum*. It has a shorter calyx tube than its calyx lobes, however, of which the opposite is true in the spurred butterfly pea.

Identification: A beautiful vine with large, showy lavender to pink pea flowers, which are usually solitary in axils of compound leaves, although they occasionally appear in groups of twos or threes. The leaves divide into groups of three ovate little leaves, each 25–65mm/1–2½in long.

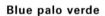

Above: The plant trails but rarely climbs.

Distribution: Minnesota east to New York, south to Florida, west to Texas, and north to Nebraska.
Height and spread: 30–90cm/12–35in.
Habit and form: Perennial climber.
Leaf shape: Three leaflets.
Pollinated: Insect.

Left: The flower has a large, rounded standard with a small notch at the tip.

Blue palo verde

Cercidium floridum (=Parkinsonia florida)

The Spanish name meaning 'green tree' is appropriate for this tree whose bark is a blue/green colour all year round. This is largely due to photosynthesis, which occurs primarily within the bark rather than in the leaves (the tree is leafless for most of the year), therefore conserving water through a reduction in surface area. Its bright yellow flowers appear in loose clusters from March to May. They are an important source of nectar and pollen for insects in the dry habitat. The plant's favoured habitat is a low sandy site.

Identification: A round tree covered loosely with yellow flowers (when in bloom) and with an unusual green/blue coloured bark. Each flower is about 20mm/¾in across, with five petals. There are few leaves, each about 15–20mm/⁹⁄₁₆–¾in long, with a pair of ovate leaflets. In mature specimens blooms cover the canopy, creating an outstanding display.

Right: Flowers are bright yellow with five petals.

Distribution: Southern California, southern Arizona, and north-western Mexico.
Height and spread: Up to 10m/33ft tall.
Habit and form: Shrub or tree.
Leaf shape: Paired leaflets.
Pollinated: Insect.

Right: The mounding habit reduces water evaporation from under the tree.

Western redbud

Cercis occidentalis

Western redbud is one of the most attractive shrubs of the western foothills. Native Americans used extracts from the bark for medicinal purposes and its shredded bark was also used for baskets. It thrives on dry slopes. The rosy pink flowers appear in all their glory from February to April.

Identification: This shrub is leafless when in bloom, with many erect stems and covered with rosy-pink bilaterally symmetrical flowers, forming in clusters along branches. The leaves are rounded and kidney-shaped, smooth and glossy, 30–90mm/ 1¼–3½in wide.

Distribution: Most of California east to southern Utah and central Arizona.
Height and spread: 1.8–5.1m/6–16¾ft.
Habit and form: Shrub or small tree.
Leaf shape: Round.
Pollinated: Insect.

Above and right: The pink flowers and pods are edible.

OTHER SPECIES OF NOTE
White priarie clover *Dalea candida*
A clover that thrives on plains and at roadsides, flowering from May to September. The bilaterally symmetrical flowers consist of dense, white spikes. It has bright green leaves and several branched stems.

Feather peabush, Feather plume
Dalea formosa
The feather peabush is a low, scraggy shrub with tiny leaves, dark bark and attractive bright yellow and purple flowers. It ranges from Central Arizona east to western Oklahoma and south to northern Mexico, living in high plains and deserts among other vegetation.

Purple prairie clover *Dalea purpurea*
This slender plant prefers the dry or moist soil of meadows and forest openings. The leaves have five narrow leaflets. Its thick flowers have dense, crimson-purple hairy spikes, which appear in all their splendour from May to August.

Wild indigo *Baptisia tinctoria*
A plant that prefers dry fields, this is widely distributed from Ontario and Maine south to Georgia and north-west to Tennessee, Indiana, Wisconsin, and Minnesota. It has numerous clusters of bright yellow pea-like flowers. Some species are used to produce an indigo dye.

Hog potato

Camote de raton, Pig nut, *Hoffmannseggia glauca*

This plant's Spanish name means 'mouse's sweet potato'; all the names refer to the many animals that get their nourishment from the plant's edible swellings on its roots. It is common along roadsides and as an agricultural weed, enjoying alkaline areas and growing in patches.

Identification: A low plant with yellow/orange flowers and pinnately compound leaves. The leaves have 5–11 pairs of oblong leaflets (3–9mm/ ⅛–⁵⁄₁₆in long), which are further divided.

Below: The plant has green, fern-like leaves and erect flower stalks.

Distribution: Southern California east to southern Colorado and Texas, and south to Mexico.
Height and spread: 10–30cm/4–12in.
Habit and form: Perennial herb or small shrub.
Leaf shape: Pinnate.
Pollinated: Insect.

Right: The flowers are orange-red with spread-out petals.

Smoke tree

Psorothamnus spinosus

From a distance, this remarkable tree appears grey and fluffy, like a puff of smoke. It is host to the flowering parasite Thurber's Pilostyles (*Pilostyles thurberi*), which produces tiny yellowish flowers that protrude through the bark in early summer. Its own flowers are blue-purple, produced in many short spikes. When in bloom, the tender blue flowers and silver-grey woody spikes make an unusual contrast, especially against the dry landscape.

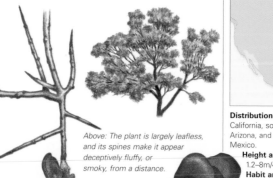

Above: The plant is largely leafless, and its spines make it appear deceptively fluffy, or smoky, from a distance.

Above: The indigo flowers appear in late spring and early summer.

Distribution: South-eastern California, south-western Arizona, and north-western Mexico.
Height and spread: 1.2–8m/4–26¼ft.
Habit and form: Perennial tree or shrub.
Leaf shape: Oblong.
Pollinated: Insect.

Identification: Intricately branched, ashy tree, with striking deep blue-purple flowers, each 15mm/⁹⁄₁₆in long. The leaves are notched at the tips, and 15–20mm/⁹⁄₁₆–¾in long.

Yellow pea

Golden pea, Buck bean, Buffalo bean, *Thermopsis rhombifolia*

This attractive plant is suspected of being poisonous. It looks like a lupin, and has beautiful yellow flowers appearing from May to August. It is usually found in patchy woodland or grassland areas, often on slopes. There are several varieties of yellow pea in the western USA, extending into western Washington, southern central Canada, and the western Dakotas.

Identification: The plant has slightly hairy hollow stems and yellow pea flowers in long racemes in the upper leaf axils. Three leaflets are each 50mm–10cm/2–4in long with a pair of broadly ovate stipules where the leafstalk joins them.

Above: The vibrant flowers were used by Native Americans for dyeing skin bags or arrows yellow, and reportedly boiled to make a very weak tea for stomach pains in humans and horses.

Distribution: Western Montana south-west to north-eastern Oregon and south through Nevada, Utah, Wyoming and Colorado to eastern Arizona and western New Mexico.
Height and spread: 60cm–1.2m/24in–4ft.
Habit and form: Perennial herb.
Leaf shape: Compound.
Pollinated: Insect.

Right: Up to six stems grow from each tap root. Large patches of the plant may form. It grows up to 30cm/12in in height.

Showy rattlebox

Crotalaria spectabilis

The name stems from the plant's dry rattling seeds in the pods. There are at least four species of *Crotalaria* in the region. The showy rattlebox displays its vibrant, yellow flowers from August to October. It grows mainly on waste ground and alongside fields and roads.

Distribution: Virginia and Tennessee south to Florida, west to Texas and Oklahoma, and north-east to Illinois.
Height and spread: 60–90cm/24–35in.
Habit and form: Annual herb.
Leaf shape: Simple, ovate.
Pollinated: Insect.

Identification: This erect plant has dark purple stems that lead up to its beautiful, elongated clusters of bright yellow flowers. Each flower is about 25mm/1in long. The fruit is an inflated pod with loose, rattling seeds when ripe. The leaves measure 50mm–20cm/ 2–8in long.

Above: The flowers appear from late summer to autumn.

Left: At maturity the plant can reach 1.5m/5ft in height.

OTHER SPECIES OF NOTE

Creeping bush clover *Lespedeza repens*
A clover-like, trailing plant that is useful for increasing the fertility of dry sites. Its seeds provide an important food for bobwhite quail. It enjoys open woodland and displays pink pea-like flowers from May to September.

Slender bush clover *Lespedeza virginica*
This attractive plant enjoys woodland, thickets and clearings. It has an upright stem, compound leaves and small clusters of pinkish-lavender flowers that appear between July and September.

Wild senna *Senna hebecarpa*
A native perennial that ranges from Ontario, Maine and south to Georgia and north-west to Tennessee and Wisconsin. It enjoys moist, open woodland and displays beautiful yellow to orange flowers from July until August. Leaves are even pinnate with up to 20 dark green and glossy leaflets.

Goat's rue,
Devil's shoestrings
Tephrosia virginiana
This was once fed to goats in order to increase their milk production. Its other name refers to the long stringy roots. The plant has a silvery appearance over all. The unusual but stunning flowers are yellow with pink wings atop a hairy stem, up to 50cm/20in in height.

Coral bean

Erythrina herbacea

This showy plant with its characteristic bold red, flame-like flowers is a member of a large tropical genus, which has more than 100 species. Its poisonous, showy red seeds are often used as beads. It flowers in all its glory from March to July. Interestingly, the species is a woody shrub in Florida and a herb in most other states.

Identification: Erect and prickly, this plant has leafy stems and separate flowering stems with bright red pea flowers, the long standard petal projecting well beyond the other petals. Each compound leaf has three leaflets, each 40–75mm/ 1½–3in long.

Above: Coral bean is a low flowering shrub.

Distribution: North Carolina south to Florida and west to Texas and Oklahoma.
Height and spread: 60cm–1.5m/24in–5ft.
Habit and form: Perennial herb.
Leaf shape: Compound.
Pollinated: Hummingbird.

Right: The drooping pods are constricted between the seeds.

Deer weed

California broom, *Lotus scoparius*

Like most other members of the pea family, this species can enrich soil with nitrogen, via its root nodules. Like many other flowering plants, it thrives after fire has ravaged chaparral-covered slopes. Its flowering season is between March and August. It grows quickly and is therefore very useful for stabilizing eroded slopes, securing the soil and preventing slippage.

*Right:
Blooms are
clustered.
The yellow petals
turn reddish with
maturity.*

Identification: The plant has tough, erect green stems with compound leaves and red-yellow flowers, which appear in the upper leaf axils and go red with age. Each flower is about 9mm/⁵⁄₁₆in long, with five petals. The fruit is a curved, slender, beaked pod containing two seeds. The leaflets are 6–13mm/¼–½in long.

Distribution: Most of California south to northern Baja California.
Height and spread: 30–90cm/12–35in.
Habit and form: Perennial herb.
Leaf shape: Three oblong leaflets.
Pollinated: Insect.

Left: The bushy shrub provides food for deer as well as birds and insects.

American vetch

Vicia americana

This slender climbing plant clings to other vegetation and structures by means of its coiling tendrils. Its showy pink-purple or reddish-lavender flowers are unusually big for the genus, looking more like those of a species of *Lathyrus*. They are clustered in loose racemes of 3–10 flowers, and open from May through July. Look for this flower in woodland clearings, banks and hedgerows.

Identification: On stalks from leaf axils, the deep pink flowers are 15–30mm/ ⁹⁄₁₆–1¼in long and tubular. The petals become bluer with age. Each leaf consists of 8–12 leaflets.

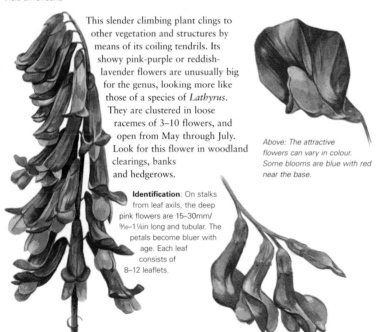

Above: The attractive flowers can vary in colour. Some blooms are blue with red near the base.

Distribution: Throughout the West; also in eastern Canada and the north-eastern United States.
Height and spread: 60cm–1.2m/24in–4ft.
Habit and form: Perennial herb/climber.
Leaf shape: Pinnately compound.
Pollinated: Insect.

Left: After producing its many blooms, the plant bears pods, about 30mm/1¼in long with five to seven seeds each. These tender seeds have been eaten by Native American Indians.

Spurred butterfly pea

Centrosema virginianum

The flowers of this showy but delicate vine are characterized by their upside-down position, and the spreading petals have a distinctly butterfly-like appearance. Vines reach up to 1.2m/4ft long and flower from July until August. This species prefers acid soils, as for example in sandy woods or fields.

Identification: A trailing or twining vine with violet pea flowers that are solitary or in groups of two to four and in axils of compound leaves. The flowers are 20–40mm/¾–1½in long and the keel has a small spur at its base. Three ovate lanceolate leaflets are each (26–65mm/ 1–2½in long).

Distribution: Maryland south to Florida, west to Texas and Oklahoma, and north-east to Missouri, Illinois and Kentucky.
Height and spread: 60cm–1.2m/24in–4ft.
Habit and form: Perennial herb.
Leaf shape: Divided, lanceolate.
Pollinated: Insect.

Left: Blooms are thumbnail-size and violet or blue.

Showy tick trefoil

Desmodium canadense

An erect, bushy plant with elongated clusters of pink or purple pea flowers. This is the showiest of the tick trefoils, distinguished by its leaf and fruit shape: the jointed fruits facilitate seed dispersal by breaking into segments that stick to clothes and animal fur. It thrives in moist open woods and at the edges of fields. Stalks bearing flowers grow horizontally from the tall upright stem, above the leaves.

Identification: The flowers are stalked and about 15mm/⅝in long. The fruit is a hairy, jointed pod with three to five segments. The compound leaves have three oblong, un-toothed leaflets with stipules at the base of the stalk.

Distribution: Manitoba east to Nova Scotia, south to Virginia, west to Missouri and Texas, and north to North Dakota.
Height and spread: 60cm–1.8m/24in–6ft.
Habit and form: Perennial herb.
Leaf shape: Pinnately compound.
Pollinated: Insect.

Left: The stems are pubescent, as are the leaves.

LOOSESTRIFE AND FUCHSIA FAMILIES

The loosestrife family, Lythraceae, contains 27 genera and about 600 species, mainly tropical, with a few in temperate regions, mostly herbs although some are shrubs or trees. The fuchsia family, Onagraceae, has about 18 genera and 650 species, mostly herbs and shrubs with many from the Americas.

Fireweed

Chamae(ne)rion (Epilobium) angustifolium

This attractive flower rapidly colonises burnt soil, hence its common name. It is found in many regions, including Europe and Asia. In Britain it is usually called rosebay willowherb. It often forms dense stands on disturbed land when its massed tall flower spikes create a colourful show. It prefers cool conditions, such as upland and mountain areas and also grows along roads and railways. It can be useful in the garden, but can spread rapidly, especially in damp soil. The plants spread by seed and by underground roots, forming large swathes of colour.

Identification: The flowers are a deep pink (sometimes white), opening from June to September, and the fruit is a slender pod containing many minute seeds.

Distribution: Scattered throughout.
Height and spread: 60cm–2.1m/24–6¾ft.
Habit and form: Perennial herb.
Leaf shape: Long, alternate.
Pollinated: Insect.

Left: The leaves are lanceolate and pinnately veined. The simple stems are reddish.

Showy evening primrose

Oenothera speciosa

This pretty evening primrose has large flowers under good conditions, but these may be quite small when the plant is stressed by drought. It can withstand arid sites and neglect which makes it very easy to grow as an undemanding garden plant. The pink or white flowers stand out well against the foliage and stay open late to attract moths. The flowering season is May to July. In the wild the favoured habitats are plains, prairies, and also wasteland such as roadsides.

Identification: The buds droop before opening into flowers that are usually to 75mm/3in across, with broad white petals with pink stripes. The long leaves have wavy margins and the fruit is a capsule with many seeds.

Distribution: Mainly in the east, but west to Texas.
Height and spread: 20–60cm/8–24in.
Habit and form: Perennial herb.
Leaf shape: Long, lanceolate.
Pollinated: Insect, especially moth.

Left: Tough stems support the leaves, which tend to have cut margins, especially near the base.

Swamp loosestrife

Water willow, *Decodon verticillatus*

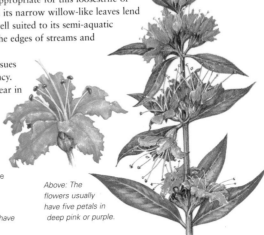

The first common name is more appropriate for this loosestrife of marshy and swampy habitats, and its narrow willow-like leaves lend it the other common name. It is well suited to its semi-aquatic habitat, forming large clumps at the edges of streams and lakes, and in waterlogged soils. Underwater stems have spongy tissues containing air as an aid to buoyancy. The pretty, dark pink flowers appear in July and August.

Distribution: From Nova Scotia south to Florida and west to Texas.
Height and spread: Stems to 2.4m/8ft long.
Habit and form: Perennial small shrub.
Leaf shape: Lanceolate.
Pollinated: Insect.

Identification: The flowers are about 15mm/⁹⁄₁₆in across, bell-shaped with five petals and stamens that extend beyond the flower. The fruit is a round capsule.

Above: The flowers usually have five petals in deep pink or purple.

Left: Tall, arching stems have woody bases.

OTHER SPECIES OF NOTE
Tansy-leaved evening primrose
Camissonia tanacetifolia
This is a low-growing species found mainly in the west. Its bright yellow flowers grow up from a basal rosette of deeply cut leaves, and open from June to August.

California fuchsia, California fire chalice, Hummingbird's trumpet *Epilobium canum*
The bright red, trumpet-shaped flowers are rich in nectar and attract hummingbirds. This is found in California, Oregon and parts of New Mexico.

Birdcage evening primrose, Devil's lantern, Lion-in-a-cage *Oenothera deltoides*
This plant of dry, sandy deserts is found from Oregon to southern California, Arizona and Utah. Its large white flimsy flowers open at night and drop in the morning. Dead plants resemble birdcages or baskets.

Evening primrose
Oenothera biennis
The large yellow flowers have a faint lemony scent and open at night to attract moths. Evening primrose is mainly found on wasteland, in weedy fields and roadsides.

Purple loosestrife

Lythrum salicaria

A familiar plant in Europe, introduced to North America where it has spread rapidly to become common throughout much of the region, in swampy ground, riverbanks and damp ditches. Its tall dense spikes of purple flowers are very prominent, especially where it forms large colonies. It is also a useful plant for the margins of garden ponds.

Identification: Individual flowers are 40mm–10cm/1½–4in across with four to six wrinkled petals. The flowering season is June to September. The stalkless leaves are heart-shaped at the base with a long narrow blade.

Below: The magenta flowers open from June to September, and can go on through October.

Distribution: Throughout most of the region.
Height and spread: 60cm–1.2m/24in–4ft.
Habit and form: Perennial herb or small shrub.
Leaf shape: Lanceolate to linear.
Pollinated: Insect.

Below: Purple loosestrife displaces native plants and threatens ecosystems.

DOGWOOD AND GARRYACEAE FAMILIES

The dogwood family, or Cornaceae, comprises about 15 genera, widespread in North America but largely absent from South America. They are mainly woody shrubs and treees. The Garryaceae family has two genera; Garrya, which is found in North America, contains only 16–18 species. Garrya are small evergreen shrubs or trees.

Pacific dogwood

Western dogwood, *Cornus nuttallii*

This variable, long-lived tree is found at low elevations in moist, open woods, extending from southern British Columbia to southern California, where it prefers the shade and humidity found under a canopy of conifers. The large white bracts stand out brilliantly and are often mistaken for flowers, although the true flowers are tiny and clustered in a centrally positioned head between the bracts.

Identification: The crown is rounded when growing in the open, irregular in the understorey. The bark is thin, grey, smooth when young, breaking into rectangular scales and blocks with age. The leaf buds are small and pointed; the flower buds are larger. The leaves are opposite, undivided, oval to elliptic, 75mm–12.5cm/3–5in long, with smooth to wavy margins, with distinctively curved veins, turning brilliant red in autumn. The tiny, greenish-white flowers, without petals, are borne in a dense, rounded head, surrounded by four or six large, showy, white to creamy-white bracts. The fruits are flattened, red drupes, borne in a tight cluster.

Above: The berry-like fruit.

Right: The tree has a straight main trunk and many branches.

Distribution: Pacific north-west.
Height and spread: 6–19¾m/20–65½ft.
Habit and form: Deciduous flowering tree.
Leaf shape: Ovate to obovate.
Pollinated: Insect.

Bunchberry

Cornus canadensis

The bunchberry is widely distributed, stretching from southern Greenland to Alaska and Maryland to South Dakota, occurring across boreal forests in a broad range of stand types and soil/site conditions. It has a distinctive, four-petalled flower-like bract and six-leaf combination that makes it easy to distinguish from other low-growing forest plants. The white bracts attract flying insects, which pollinate the minuscule true flowers. When an insect alights, its touch induces the flowers to catapult pollen at it.

Identification: Stems 10–15cm/4–6in tall and woody at the base arise from a spreading rhizome, often forming large colonies. The evergreen leaves are opposite, with four to six leaves in a whorl at the top of the stem, often with one or two pairs of smaller, leaf-like scales on the stem below; they are elliptic or oval, 25–50mm/1–2in long, with margins tapering to a point at both ends and curving veins parallel to the margins. In early summer, dense clusters of small, greenish-white to purplish flowers appear above the leaf whorl, surrounded by four showy, white to purple-tinged, petal-like bracts, 15mm/⅝in long. The fruits are bright red, fleshy and berry-like in a terminal cluster, ripening by midsummer.

Above: The bright red berries appear in the branch tips by midsummer.

Right: The short upright stems arise from a spreading rhizome.

Distribution: Southern Greenland to Alaska, and Maryland to South Dakota.
Height and spread: 10–15 x 30cm/4–6 x 12in.
Habit and form: Herbaceous perennial.
Leaf shape: Elliptic or ovate.
Pollinated: Insect.

Silk tassel bush

Garrya elliptica

This popular garden plant grows wild on dry soils, mainly in Oregon and California. It is named in honour of Nicholas Garry of the Hudson's Bay Trading Company. Its main feature is the long (male) and shorter (female) catkins, produced in winter and spring. These hang down in a most decorative manner. It is frost hardy, but does best in a sheltered sunny position. The shrub can develop into a tree of about 9m/29½ft in height. It is evergreen.

Distribution: Oregon and California.
Height and spread: To 4m/13ft.
Habit and form: Large shrub.
Leaf shape: Wavy, rounded.
Pollinated: Wind.

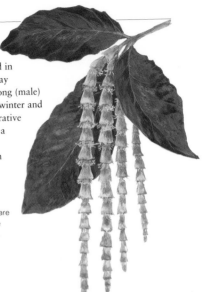

Identification: A large evergreen shrub, with rounded leaves that are grey and woolly underneath. The individual flowers are tiny and are clustered together in the dangling catkins. The fruits are purple-green with deep purple juice.

Left: The catkins are an atttractive feature in the winter months. The male catkins are showier, and about 30cm/12in in length, while the female catkins are followed by berries.

OTHER SPECIES OF NOTE

Flowering dogwood *Cornus florida*
This large shrub or small tree from the eastern USA has a short trunk and a full, rounded crown, spreading wider than its height. It blooms in the spring, as its new leaves are unfolding, with four showy, petal-like bracts, usually snow-white or pink, surrounding a cluster of tiny, inconspicuous, yellowish flowers.

American dogwood *Cornus stolonifera*
The American or red-stem dogwood is an elegant open shrub producing creamy-white flower clusters in spring and very attractive red stems in winter. It can be found in moist areas, in sun or shade, often along the banks of streams or slow-running water. The fruit of this dogwood is very attractive to woodland birds.

Roughleaf dogwood *Cornus drummondii*
This tough, thicket-forming deciduous shrub has soft, furry leaves and blooms in mid-spring, with white clusters of "true" flowers. In early autumn, the white fruit attracts forest birds, with the leaves turning to red, orange and purple.

Silky dogwood, Swamp dogwood
Cornus amomum
This is a medium-size shrub with clusters of white flowers, found mainly along streams and in wet soils, in the east of North America. It has slightly hairy red twigs and clusters of blue, berry-like fruit, maturing in late summer.

Pagoda dogwood

Cornus alternifolia

The species is shade-tolerant and is the dominant understorey shrub in aspen forests. It is often found along forest margins, on stream and swamp borders and near deep canyon bottoms. It is widely distributed from Newfoundland through New England to the Florida Panhandle, and west to Arkansas and Mississippi, where it often occurs alongside the commoner flowering dogwood, *C. florida*. It has tiered, horizontal branches. The light green summer foliage turns rich red and orange in autumn.

Distribution: Eastern North America.
Height and spread: Up to 9m/29½ft.
Habit and form: Large shrub or small tree.
Leaf shape: Elliptic to ovate-lanceolate.
Pollinated: Insect.

Identification: The slender branches of this large shrub or small tree are often horizontal and it develops a flat-topped crown. The smooth bark is dark green, streaky, eventually developing shallow fissures. The leaves are alternate, elliptic to ovate-lanceolate, with wavy margins, and often crowded at the end of the twig, appearing before the white, flat-topped or hemispheric, open flower cymes. Blue fruits ripen in late summer.

Below: Pagoda dogwood is a small tree.

Above right: Blue-black berries appear in August.

FLAX, MILKWORT AND WOOD SORREL FAMILIES

The flax family, Linaceae, consists of 250 species in 14 genera, including trees, lianes, shrubs or herbs.
Milkwort, or Polygalaceae, are herbs, shrubs or small trees, with 17 genera and 950 species. Wood
sorrel, Oxalidaceae, has about eight genera and about 800 species; some are trees, many are herbs.

Wild blue flax

Western blue flax, *Linum lewisii*

Sometimes considered a subspecies of *Linum perenne*, this pretty plant has delicate blue flowers atop slender stalks, opening from March to September. It is a plant of prairie, well-drained meadows and mountain slopes. It can thrive in cold, high and dry positions up to 3,000m/9,840ft. Many Native American tribes used its fibres to fashion rope.

Left: The plant spreads aggressively.

Identification: The blue flowers have five petals, and each flower is about 40mm/1½in across. Leaves are long and narrow with a single vein.

Below centre: The seed pods are urn-shaped.

Below: The flowers are pale blue to lavender and 10–20mm/ ⅜–¾in long.

Distribution: Mainly western, from Alaska and Canada to California and New Mexico; also in the western Great Plains.
Height and spread: 15–80cm/6–30in.
Habit and form: Perennial herb.
Leaf shape: Long, narrow.
Pollinated: Insect.

White milkwort

Polygala alba

This delicate flower has tiny white flowers in conical clusters. The name 'milkwort' refers to the fact that some species were thought to stimulate milk flow in cattle. The flowers open from March to October. White milkwort grows mainly on rocky hills and sandy soils. The spear of white flowers tapers towards the tip. Each flower has three petals and the crest is sometimes purple. There are five sepals; two are white and resemble petals and three are small and green.

Identification: Milkwort flowers are pea-like, and bilaterally symmetrical. There are five sepals; in this species the inner two are white and wing-like, and the three white petals have greenish bases.

Left and below: Until the flowers bloom, the grass-like stems are low-lying and hard to spot among other plants.

Distribution: Montana, Colorado, Arizona, Texas and New Mexico.
Height and spread: 20–35cm/8–14in.
Habit and form: Perennial herb.
Leaf shape: Long and very narrow.
Pollinated: Insect.

Redwood sorrel

Oxalis oregana

Distribution: Washington and coastal central California.
Height and spread: 50mm–17.5cm/2–7in.
Habit and form: Perennial herb.
Leaf shape: Trifoliate.
Pollinated: Insect.

Right: The pink flowers brighten up the forest floor from April to September. The petals are veined with dark pink-purple.

This dainty flower is characteristic of the ground flora in redwood forests of the Pacific north-west. It grows in colonies, covering large patches of the cool shady moist forest floor where it flowers from April to September. Both the leaves and flowers are attractive. The three leaflets are heart-shaped and the flowers are white or pink and funnel-shaped. The leaves contain oxalic acid so should not be ingested in large quantities. The evergreen form is slow spreading via rhizomes. The deciduous form is more aggressive.

Identification: Each flower is 15–20mm/⁹⁄₁₆–¾in across, with five petals, veined purple. The clover-like leaves have three leaflets, often with a pale patch at the centre. The heart-shaped leaves fold at night and in direct sunlight.

Below: The plant forms tightly-packed ground cover.

OTHER SPECIES OF NOTE

Chihuahua flax *Linum vernale*
This plant takes its name from the Chihuahua Desert where it is quite common in places. Its range is southern New Mexico, northern Mexico and western Texas. Its orange-yellow flowers have a reddish-purple centre.

Field milkwort, Purple milkwort
Polygala sanguinea
The very small pink or greenish flowers appear from May to October, and are tightly clustered into a dense flowerhead, and the purplish sepals are actually more noticeable. As indicated by its name, this milkwort grows in meadows and fields, as well as open woods. It has a scattered, easterly distribution.

Common wood sorrel
Oxalis montana
This decorative mountain flower is common from New England to the Great Lakes. It has clover-like leaves and showy, five-petalled white or pink flowers with darker pink veining from May to July.

Yellow wood, Sorrel sour grass *Oxalis stricta*
A widespread, vigorous weed of wasteland, roadsides and fields, this also often turns up in gardens. It has bright yellow flowers and trefoil leaves. The small seed pod explodes to disperse seeds up to 4m/13ft from the parent plant.

Violet wood sorrel

Oxalis violacea

Another pretty woodland species with clover-like leaves. The delicate pink flowers are often veined green towards the centre and borne in small groups of between two and eight. Open woods are the favoured habitat and the flowers open between March and October. In some states, such as Connecticut, it is endangered, possibly due to over-collection.

Identification: Each leaflet has an orange spot in the notch. The leaves have heart-shaped lobes and are purple underneath. The stems are leafless, about 10–15cm/4–6in long, and bear 5–13 flowers. The five petals form a flared tube, 25mm/1in across. The plant can reach a height of 20cm/8in.

Below: Blooms start to appear in early spring.

Distribution: Arizona, New Mexico and scattered further east.
Height and spread: 75mm–15cm/3–6in.
Habit and form: Perennial herb.
Pollinated: Insect.
Leaf shape: Trifoliate.

Below: There are three heart-shaped lobes per leaf.

CARROT FAMILY

A large family with about 450 genera and 3,500 species, the carrot family, Umbelliferae, consists mostly of aromatic herbs with hollow stems and flat- or round-topped clusters (umbels) of small flowers. Many have finely divided fern-like leaves. They generally grow in northern regions. Many species yield food or seasonings: for example carrot, parsnip, celery, coriander, caraway, parsley and dill.

Cow parsnip
Heracleum lanatum

The largest native member of the carrot family, cow parsnip is found over much of North America. The plant gives a show of many small white flowers from February to September. The family contains both edible and poisonous species. This one was used by Native Americans who ate the young stalks. Beware, however, as it can cause skin rashes. Typical of the family, the flowers appear in flattened umbels.

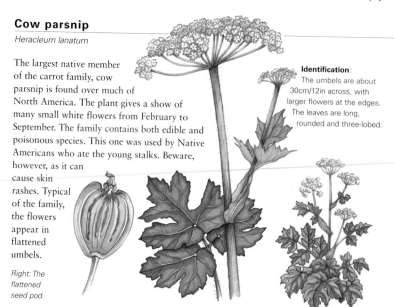

Identification: The umbels are about 30cm/12in across, with larger flowers at the edges. The leaves are long, rounded and three-lobed.

Right: The flattened seed pod.

Distribution: Most of the USA and Canada, but absent from Florida.
Height and spread: To 3m/10ft.
Habit and form: Perennial herb.
Leaf shape: Lobed, toothed.
Pollinated: Insect.

Left: The habit is tall and spreading.

Mexican thistle
Wright's coyote thistle, *Eryngium heterophyllum*

Although definitely thistle-like and spiny, this is not a true thistle, although both of this plant's common names – Mexican thistle and Wright's coyote thistle – would lead to that assumption. It has the typical carrot family umbels of flowers. In this species the umbels are domed and surrounded by prickly bracts. It flowers from July to October and grows mainly on sandy soils in grassland, open woods and along streams.

Identification: The tiny flowers that make up the umbels are a delicate pale blue. The umbels are about 15mm/⅝in tall, and 10mm/⅜in across and nestle within the protective spiny bracts.

Right: The flowerheads rise from spiny whorls.

Right: The flowers perch on leafy branched stems.

Distribution: Mexico, north to western Texas and Arizona.
Height and spread: 20–60cm/8–24in.
Habit and form: Perennial herb.
Leaf shape: Divided and spiny.
Pollinated: Insect.

Poison hemlock

Conium maculatum

This species is one of the most notorious of all the poisonous members of this family, and all the parts of the plant contain the toxic alkaloid coniine. Its effects were known to the ancient Greeks, who used it to kill people, possibly including the philosopher Socrates. It is native to Europe but has spread to many other countries, and is scattered throughout North America. It typically grows in colonies, for instance alongside roads and on wasteland.

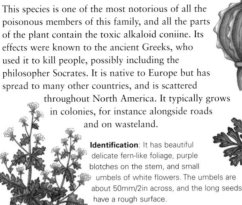

Distribution: Scattered throughout, except the far north.
Height and spread: To 3m/10ft.
Habit and form: Biennial herb.
Leaf shape: Divided with lobed leaflets.
Pollinated: Insect.

Identification: It has beautiful delicate fern-like foliage, purple blotches on the stem, and small umbels of white flowers. The umbels are about 50mm/2in across, and the long seeds have a rough surface.

Left: The plant grows from an inedible parsnip-like root.

Top: The seedhead.

OTHER SPECIES OF NOTE

Wild carrot *Daucus carota*
The ancestor of cultivated carrots. Originally from Europe it has spread over most of North America. The umbels of white or pink flowers bend inwards to form a basket-like structure when mature. The root of the wild carrot is much smaller than the cultivated forms.

Water hemlock *Cicuta douglasii*
This is another example of a deadly poisonous species, and proves the need for accurate identification in this family. It has swollen stem bases that help aerate the tissues in its wetland habitat, mainly in the Pacific coastal regions. The toxins are concentrated in the root stock, but also present in the stem and leaves. One bite ingested is enough to kill a human.

Spotted water hemlock *Cicuta maculata*
Another member of the family that looks very similar and is equally deadly. It is distinguished from water hemlock by its purple-streaked stems, but is otherwise very similar. It is highly poisonous to people and livestock alike.

Rattlesnake master *Eryngium yuccifolium*
Native Americans used the plant as an antidote to rattlesnake bites – hence the common name. It grows on prairie, and in open woods, and has greenish-white (later bluish), thistle-like flowerheads, and very spiny foliage. The leaves resemble those of the yucca.

Sweet fennel

Foeniculum vulgare

This is another introduction from Europe, where it is widely used as a flavouring in cooking. The young shoots are edible, and the leaves and seeds are used to add a mild aniseed flavour to salads and other dishes.

Distribution: Mainly Cascade Range and Sierra Nevada.
Height and spread: 90cm–2.1m/35in–6¾ft.
Habit and form: Biennial or perennial herb.
Leaf shape: Pinnate, triangular.
Pollinated: Insect.

Above: The capsule contains the seed-like fruits.

Identification: Tall, with feathery leaves and umbels of yellow flowers. The umbels are about 15cm/6in across, and the pinnately divided leaves are 30–40cm/12–16in long and roughly triangular in outline.

Far right: The foliage is fine and feathery. To be sure it is fennel and not the similar-looking poison hemlock, crush the foliage and check for an aniseed smell.

Ranger's buttons

Swamp white head, *Sphenosciadium capitellatum*

The common names of this plant refer to the compact white button-like umbels that develop separately on the end of the hairy branches. Ranger's button grows alongside streams, in marshy ground and in wet meadows, mainly in the west. It is found at 900–3,000m/ 2,950–9,840ft above sea level in subalpine forest, especially on the slopes of the Sierra Nevada mountain range.

Identification: The whitish, tight umbels are to 10cm/4in across and the long pinnate leaves are broad, with toothed leaflets up to 75mm/3in long. The plant is poisonous.

Distribution: Idaho and Oregon south to the mountains of southern California.
Height and spread: to about 2.1m/6¾ft.
Habit and form: Perennial herb.
Leaf shape: Pinnate.
Pollinated: Insect.

Right:
The flowerheads are in compact umbels, which look ball-like and fluffy. The plant blooms from July to August.

Left: The stems are usually stout, and generally reach about 1.5m/5ft in height.

Spring gold

Lomatium utriculatum

There are 80 species in this genus, all found in the western part of North America, and many are used in traditional medicine or as food. The flowers are tiny and bright golden yellow, arranged in umbels. The umbels each have about 15 compact flowerheads. They start to appear as early as February and continue through until June. This species prefers grassy woodland and meadows, and may also thrive in areas where cattle have grazed all the competing plants. Native Americans once ate the new leaves in spring and the taproot, which grows much like a carrot, can be roasted as a vegetable.

Identification: The umbels measure about 10cm/4in across, ripening in fruit to 25cm/10in across. The fruit is highly characteristic – flat and oblong, with winged edges. The leaves are mostly basal, pinnately compound, dissected into small, narrow segments. After flowering, umbels of seed cases form. The cases are attractive, with darker, ridged centres and surrounding wings.

Top right: The seeds smell of dill as they become ripe. The mature seed develops dark ribs, and has tiny 'wings' that catch the wind and aid dispersal. This happens in June.

Distribution: British Columbia south to California.
Height and spread: 10–50cm/4–20in.
Habit and form: Perennial herb.
Leaf shape: Divided.
Pollinated: Insect.

Left: The golden flowers look pretty against the feathery foliage. The plants can grow up to 50cm/20in tall.

Water parsnip

Sium suave

This wetland plant grows in shallow water and in swampy waterlogged ground. It has umbels of tiny white flowers and ridged stems. It is edible, and the roots may be boiled as a vegetable. However, this is not recommended as it resembles the deadly water hemlocks and mistakes can be made. The flowering period is July to September. Umbels hold clusters of 25–35 flowers each. The stem is thick and hollow with a fennel fragrance.

Identification: Umbels are 50–75mm/2–3in across and the pinnate leaves have toothed leaflets measuring up to 12.5cm/5in long and 50mm/2in across.

Left: The alternate leaves are divided into opposite leaflets.

Right: The fruit is oval or spherical and about 3mm/¹⁄₈in long.

Distribution: Scattered throughout the region, except the Arctic.
Height and spread: 60cm–1.8m/24in–6ft.
Habit and form: Perennial herb.
Leaf shape: Pinnate.
Pollinated: Insect.

OTHER SPECIES OF NOTE

Golden alexanders *Zizia aptera*
This shares its common name with *Zizia aurea*, but is distinguished from it by its heart-shaped basal leaves. It is mainly a western species. Its umbels of bright yellow flowers are about 65mm/2½in across. It is generally found along woodland borders or shores, and flowers from May to August.

Sweet cicely *Osmorhiza claytonii*
This hairy plant of the woods has small umbels of white flowers opening in May and June. The seeds have barbs that cling to fur or clothing, which helps dispersal. The leaves are fern-like, and the roots smell of aniseed when bruised. The plant is also known as sweetroot.

Black snakeroot *Sanicula canadensis*
From Ontario and Quebec, south to Florida, black snakeroot is found in dry woodland. It has greenish flowers in umbels and palmate leaves. It is a traditional medicinal herb. The fruits are bur-like, covered in barbs, containing two seeds.

Water pennywort
Hydrocotyle americana
The round, coin-like leaves give this plant its common name. It is a creeping plant of marshy habitats and damp woods, with a mainly eastern distribution. The flowers are tiny and greenish-white. The blooming period is February to September.

Golden alexanders

Zizia aurea

Bright golden yellow flowers stand out well against the rich green foliage. They grow in flat-topped umbels, with an unstalked flower at the centre of each umbel. The flowering season is April to June and the favoured habitats are damp woods, shores and meadows. This is a good garden plant, growing well in shady sites and in moist soils. It is attractive to butterflies.

Identification: The umbels are about 50mm/2in. The leaves are doubly divided, with up to 13 toothed, pointed leaflets, about 50mm/2in long.

Left: The fruits are about 4mm/³⁄₁₆in long.

Far right: Patches of Zizia aurea are found in moist soils.

Distribution: Nova Scotia and Manitoba to Florida, Texas and North Dakota.
Height and spread: 30–90cm/12–35in.
Habit and form: Perennial herb.
Leaf shape: Divided, toothed.
Pollinated: Insect.

GENTIAN FAMILY

Worldwide, the gentian family, Gentianaceae, comprises around 75 genera and 1,225 species, mainly herbs but also including a few shrubs or small trees. They are particularly well represented in mountain areas. Many have showy, bell-shaped flowers and are justly popular as garden plants. Some yield bitter compounds, which are used medicinally and for flavouring drinks.

Explorer's gentian

Gentiana calycosa

This leafy gentian species has pretty, funnel-shaped blue flowers that open mainly between July and October. The plant looks delicate but thrives in mountain conditions, tolerating cold winters and long summer days. It grows along streams and in meadows in the mountains and is one of the most attractive North American alpine flowers. Like many gentians it is suitable for growing in rock gardens.

Identification: The leaves are long, to about 30mm/1¼in. They are a soft green, smooth, ovate and opposite. The bell-shaped calyx has five lobes, as has the corolla, and the latter is bright blue, although sometimes can be tinged yellow or green.

Below left: The flower's corolla measures about 25–40mm/1–1½in length.

Distribution: The Sierra Nevada and the Rocky Mountains.
Height and spread: 50mm–30cm/2–12in.
Habit and form: Perennial herb.
Leaf shape: Ovate, oppposite.
Pollinated: Insect.

Left: The plants form tufts of colour. The habit is sometimes sprawling.

Closed gentian

Bottle gentian, *Gentiana andrewsii*

The common names reflect the flower shape of this attractive gentian. The flowers are shaped a little like a bottle and are almost closed at the tip. They grow in compact groups in the axils of the upper leaves, from August to October. This is one of the most common gentians in the east of the region and also one of the easiest to grow in gardens, where it prefers damp soil. In the wild its habitats are moist scrub and meadows. The flowers are different shades of blue depending on their stage of maturity.

Identification: The flowers are up to 40mm/1½in long and the five-lobed corolla has a whitish base. The leaves are up to 10cm/4in long, and grow in whorls below the flowers.

Distribution: Quebec and North Dakota, south to Virginia.
Height and spread: 30–60cm/12–24in.
Habit and form: Perennial herb.
Leaf shape: Ovate or lanceolate.
Pollinated: Insect.

Above centre: The closed flowers appear from late summer to early autumn.

Left: Multiple stems without branches grow from the taproot.

Prairie gentian

Tulip gentian, Bluebell, *Eustoma grandiflorum*

One of the finest flowers of the prairie, the prairie gentian has large, prominent bluish or purple flowers (sometimes pink or whitish), opening from June to September. It grows up tall among the prairie grasses, and the bell-shaped flowers open in small clusters at the top of the plants where they are obvious to passing insects. The plant tends to grow in damp sites in prairie, fields and meadows.

Distribution: Texas and New Mexico north to Nebraska and Colorado.
Height and spread: 25–70cm/10–27½in.
Habit and form: Annual or perennial herb.
Leaf shape: Ovate, opposite.
Pollinated: Insect.

Identification: The long ovate leaves have three prominent veins. Each flower is 80mm/3¼in across with five broad corolla lobes.

Above right: The bluish-green leaves are succulent.

OTHER SPECIES OF NOTE

Northern gentian *Gentiana affinis*
This decumbent or occasionally erect gentian from the western USA blooms in late summer, with sky-blue, tubular flowers, 20–30mm/¾–1¼in long, near the ends of the stems. The top edges of the flower petals have white spots on them. It is found in moist meadows and on the edges of aspen groves. It grows to 20–30cm/8–12in in height.

Centaury rosita
Centaurium calycosum
This has clusters of pink trumpet-shaped flowers from April to June. It grows in damp meadows and streamsides in the west, from northern Mexico to Texas, Utah and California.

Northern gentian *Gentianella amarella*
This familiar European biennial is also widespread in damp mountain meadows from Alaska south as far as New Mexico, but listed as endangered or threatened in Maine and Vermont. It is also known as the autumn dwarf gentian. The trumpet-shaped flowers are purple, blue or pinkish.

Stiff gentian *Gentianella quinquefolia*
Also called small agueweed, this is a pretty annual gentian with blue or lilac flowers and a rectangular stem. It has a mainly eastern distribution, but is endangered, partly due to over-collection, in many eastern states, and feared exterminated in Maine.

Catchfly gentian

Seaside gentian, *Eustoma exaltatum*

This is a close relative of the prairie gentian, with a more southerly and western distribution. It grows on the sandy coasts of California, as well as on inland salt and freshwater marshes of the Great Plains. It has very pretty, purple or white, crocus-like flowers, borne singly or in clusters, usually from May to October. The plant sometimes blooms nearly all year round.

Identification: The petals are fused at the base, and open out into five lobes, about 40mm/1½in across. The leaves are opposite, about 75mm/3in long and covered in a whitish bloom.

Distribution: California, Montana, and South Dakota, to Florida.
Height and spread: 30–90cm/12–35in.
Habit and form: Annual or short-lived perennial herb.
Leaf shape: Oblong, opposite.
Pollinated: Insect.

Below: Blooms are solitary or in few-flowered clusters.

Left: The plant grows to about 90cm/35in tall.

Felwort

Star swertia, *Swertia perennis*

This pretty mountain species has pale blue or purplish star-shaped flowers, spotted green or white, opening from July to September. The stem is thick and glabrous. Sometimes the flowers are very dark – almost black. Felwort grows mainly in damp meadows at high altitudes in the mountains and the north. It is also found in Europe, especially in northern European fens. It prefers moist ground.

Identification: Each flower is about 20mm/¾in across, with four or five petals and sepals, each with a star-like form. They are various shades of blue, with darker veins and light-coloured spots. The flowering period is July to August. The basal leaves are spoon-shaped or oblong, with rounded tips. The higher leaves are elliptic.

Above: The leaves are narrow and fairly fleshy.

Distribution: Alaska south to the Sierra Nevada; north to Canada through the Rockies.
Height and spread: 50mm–50cm/2–20in.
Habit and form: Perennial herb.
Leaf shape: Lanceolate.
Pollinated: Insect.

Left: Plants grow to 10–13cm/ 4–5¼in tall on thick stems. There may be one or more rosettes of basal leaves. These are spoon-shaped and may have a blunt or pointed tip.

Monument plant

Deer's ears, *Swertia radiata* (= *Frasera speciosa*)

This extremely tall, stately and conical plant has flowers clustered tightly to the stem. It may live for several years, but flower only once, after which it dies. The flowering season is May to August, and the plants are generally found in mixed conifer forests. The genus name *Swertia* is in honour of the Dutch botanist Emanual Sweert (1552–1612), while *Frasera* is named after the Scottish nurseryman John Fraser (1750–1811).
The plant's root has been used to make poisons as well as medicines.

Identification: The leaves of the huge basal rosette are long, narrow, smooth and a pale green. The flowering period is May to August. Leaves and flowers whorl evenly around the stem. The flowers are yellow-green, spotted purple.

Above right: The flower has four purple speckled petals, each with a line of stiff hairs down the centre. Narrow green sepals add to the spectacular effect. The blooms are 25–40mm/1–1½in wide with four stamens.

Distribution: Washington state south to central California, Texas, Montana and northern Mexico.
Height and spread: 1–2m/39in–6½ft.
Habit and form: Biennial or perennial herb.
Leaf shape: Lanceolate.
Pollinated: Insect.

Left: he flower spike is only seen once before the plant dies.

Fringed gentian

Gentianopsis crinita

The pretty blue trumpet-shaped flowers of this gentian develop at the top of separate stems. The name refers to the fact that the open edge of each petal has a distinct ragged fringe. It is a late-flowering species – August to November – and grows in damp meadows and wet thickets. One of the most beautiful of all gentians, it is also endangered.

Distribution: Manitoba east to Quebec, south to Georgia.
Height and spread: 30–90cm/12–35in.
Habit and form: Biennial herb.
Leaf shape: Ovate to lanceolate, opposite.
Pollinated: Insect.

Identification: Each flower is about 50mm/2in long and tubular. The calyx has four, unequal pointed lobes topped by the intense blue corolla. Fruits develop from November to January.

Left: One plant can yield up to 175 startling blue flowers in its two-year lifetime. In the first year there are no flowers and the plant remains very small.

Above: The fringed flowers remain closed on cloudy days.

OTHER SPECIES OF NOTE

Pennywort *Obolaria virginica*
This low-growing fleshy plant has purplish or white flowers and whorls of dark, thick stem leaves that seem to support them. It is found in damp woods and thickets from New Jersey and Pennsylvania south to Florida and Texas. The flowers open from March to May.

Large marsh pink *Sabatia dodecandra*
Similar to saltmarsh pink, but with larger flowers and reaching 60cm/24in, this is found from Florida and Louisiana north to Connecticut, although it is considered a threatened species in some parts. It is commonly known as the marsh rose gentian. The blooms are deep pink with a yellow centre, and have an attractive fragrance.

Slender marsh pink *Sabatia campanulata*
Another close relative to the above, growing on damp peat or sand along the coasts, from Massachusetts south to Florida, and also in the southern Appalachians. It is another plant that is decreasing in numbers, largely due to habitat loss or disturbance.

Lesser fringed gentian
Gentianopsis procera
(= *G. virgata*)
This is yet another endangered gentian, found on the prairie and in lowland forests in the mid-west. It flowers mainly from August to October. It looks very similar to the fringed gentian (*G. crinita*).

Saltmarsh pink

Sea pink, *Sabatia stellaris*

This gentian relative, also known as the rose of Plymouth, inhabits brackish coastal marshes and salty meadows. It likes open sandy soils, for example at the upper edges of saltmarshes and among sand dunes. Pink flowers appear from July to October, each with a bright yellow, star-shaped centre. Some plants produce white flowers. The plant is widespread along the Atlantic and Gulf coasts, becoming commoner in the south. In New York and New England this plant is rare.

Identification: The flowers are about 40mm/1½in across, and the red-edged sepals are shorter than the petals. The leaves are long and light green.

Left: White flowers are sometimes seen on this plant, but the blooms are usually pale pink.

Distribution: Coastal, from Massachusetts and New York south to Florida and Louisiana.
Height and spread: 15–45cm/6–18in.
Habit and form: Annual or biennial herb.
Leaf shape: Linear to lanceolate.
Pollinated: Insect.

Below: Each plant has one stem with branches. The stem and leaves are delicate.

NETTLE AND DOGBANE FAMILIES

The nettle family, Urticaceae, contains about 48 genera and 1,050 species. Most are herbs, but a few are shrubs or small trees, mainly tropical, though several occur widely in temperate climates. The 200 genera and 2,000 species of the dogbane family, Apocynaceae, are primarily found in the tropics, subtropics and neotropics. They are rich in alkaloids or glycosides and are often poisonous.

Blue dogbane
Amsonia tabernaemontana

A pretty flower of damp or wet woodland and streamsides, blue dogbane has light blue, star-shaped flowers borne in branching clusters, opening from April to July. Several plants have this specific name, which is in honour of the 16th century German herbalist Jakobus Tabernaemontanus. As its common name suggests, it is poisonous, and not just to dogs. It is usually found in clumps with numerous stems and few branches.

Right: Leaves are alternate and lanceolate. The stems are about 4–5mm/³⁄₁₆in thick and slightly hairy, rising from woody roots.

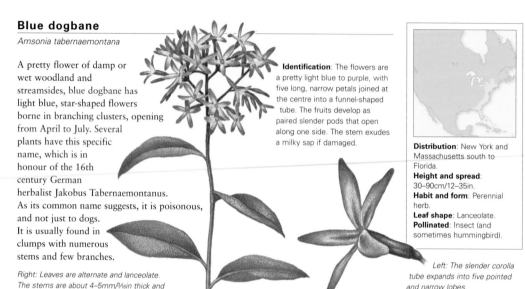

Identification: The flowers are a pretty light blue to purple, with five long, narrow petals joined at the centre into a funnel-shaped tube. The fruits develop as paired slender pods that open along one side. The stem exudes a milky sap if damaged.

Left: The slender corolla tube expands into five pointed and narrow lobes.

Distribution: New York and Massachusetts south to Florida.
Height and spread: 30–90cm/12–35in.
Habit and form: Perennial herb.
Leaf shape: Lanceolate.
Pollinated: Insect (and sometimes hummingbird).

Spreading dogbane
Apocynum androsaemifolium

This widespread flower grows in fields, roadsides and woodland margins. It forms a bushy plant with small pink flowers that droop. Opening from June to August, they are pink with darker pink stripes inside, and fragrant. They attract a huge number of butterflies. The plant is toxic and exudes a milky sap when broken. In some places it is a serious weed.

Identification: The bell-shaped, sweetly scented flowers are in clusters at stem tips and leaf axils. The sepals are tinged pink at the tips. The fruit develops in August and September, is cylindrical and contains many cottony seeds. The leaves are smooth on top and slightly hairy underneath. They are arranged opposite. The pods are 10–15cm/4–6in in length, and slender. The plant is reported to cause serious poisoning to livestock. Also, when entered by insects, scales in the throats of the flowers spring inwards, trapping intruders.

Distribution: Scattered throughout, except the Arctic; more common in the east.
Height and spread: 30cm–1.2m/12in–4ft.
Habit and form: Perennial herb.
Leaf shape: Ovate, opposite.
Pollinated: Insect.

Left: The plant is large and bushy. It prefers sunny hillsides, where the soil is well drained.

Clearweed
Pilea pumila

This nettle relative is an annual with translucent stems and small greenish-yellow flowers in the leaf axils. It grows in moist, rich soil, in shady sites, often forming large colonies. The leaves are nettle-like but lack stinging hairs. They are dark green above, whitish below. The plant is an important food plant for the larvae of several kinds of butterfly. Small flowers cluster on racemes in August.

Distribution: Throughout much of the east.
Height and spread: 10–50cm/4–20in.
Habit and form: Annual.
Leaf shape: Ovate, opposite, toothed.
Pollinated: Insect.

Identification: The small flowers develop in narrow, slightly curved racemes. The flowers lack petals and are about 4mm/³⁄₁₆in long. The tiny seed-like fruits are green, and are dispersed by the wind. In young plants, the stem looks translucent.

Right: Petal-less flowers on a raceme. The plant blooms in August, but the glossy leaves are its most attractive feature.

OTHER SPECIES OF NOTE
Periwinkle *Vinca minor*
Once introduced this became widespread, especially in the east. It is also commonly grown in gardens. An evergreen trailing plant, it has blue or purple (sometimes white) flowers that contrast well with its dark green foliage.

Lesser clearweed *Pilea fontana*
This plant is very similar to clearweed but has dull black seed-like fruits. It is found from Quebec south to Florida, in shady habitats on moist soil.

Bog hemp
Boehmeria cylindrica
Bog hemp or false nettle grows in swampy meadows, along streams and spring branches and in low wet woods in the eastern USA. The plant resembles a stinging nettle but has opposite leaves and no stinging hairs and is therefore harmless. Small greenish flowers cluster around the stem in mid- to late summer.

Wood nettle *Laportea canadensis*
The Canada nettle or wood nettle has sharp hairs along the stem which, when touched, can give a painful sting to exposed skin. It is found infrequently in wet woods in much of the eastern USA. Tiny feathery clusters of flowers appear from midsummer to early autumn.

Stinging nettle
Urtica dioica

This familiar widespread plant grows in damp rich forest soils and on waste ground. It deserves respect as the stems and leaf veins have tiny hollow hairs that release formic acid when brushed against. This causes 'nettle-rash' (urticaria) on the skin and can be quite painful. This probably evolved as a deterrent to grazing animals. Young shoots can be eaten like spinach and a tea made from an infusion of dried leaves.

Distribution: Throughout the region; also in Europe and Asia.
Height and spread: 60cm–1.2m/24in–4ft.
Habit and form: Perennial.
Leaf shape: Ovate, opposite, toothed.
Pollinated: Insect.

Identification: The individual flowers are inconspicuous, very small and greenish, each about 2mm/¹⁄₁₆in long. The leaves are coarsely toothed.

Above: Nettles form in familiar 'beds' or clumps.

MILKWEED FAMILY

There are about 350 genera and 2,800 species of the milkweed family, Asclepiadaceae, mainly from tropical and subtropical regions. The genus is named after Asclepius, the Greek god of healing, but some species are known to be toxic. These herbs, vines or shrubs mostly have opposite leaves, umbel-like flowerheads and milky sap. A number of house plants belong to the milkweed family.

Showy milkweed

Asclepias speciosa

This plant has grey-green leafy stems, topped by umbels of pinkish flowers, with some clusters also in the upper leaf axils. Like other members of this family, it has thick, milky sap, and this has reportedly been use for medicinal purposes. The flowering season is from May through August. Look for it in open forests, alongside streams and on dry sandy or gravel soils.

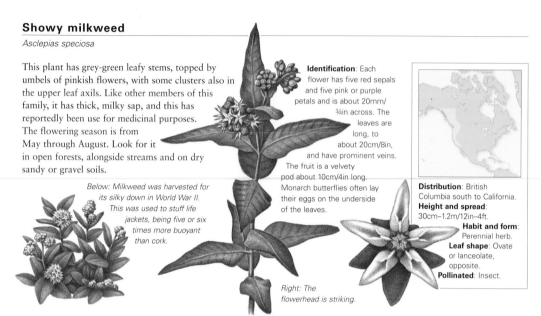

Below: Milkweed was harvested for its silky down in World War II. This was used to stuff life jackets, being five or six times more buoyant than cork.

Identification: Each flower has five red sepals and five pink or purple petals and is about 20mm/¾in across. The leaves are long, to about 20cm/8in, and have prominent veins. The fruit is a velvety pod about 10cm/4in long. Monarch butterflies often lay their eggs on the underside of the leaves.

Right: The flowerhead is striking.

Distribution: British Columbia south to California. **Height and spread**: 30cm–1.2m/12in–4ft. **Habit and form**: Perennial herb. **Leaf shape**: Ovate or lanceolate, opposite. **Pollinated**: Insect.

Butterfly weed

Orange milkweed, Chiggerflower, *Asclepias tuberosa*

An unusual milkweed in that it does not have milky sap, this species grows in dry places, such as prairies, open woods and rocky canyons. It produces umbels of orange, red or yellow flowers from April to September. These open at the top of the leafy and hairy stems. The flowers produce a large quantity of nectar that is particularly attractive to butterflies. The plant is also known as pleurisy root, hinting at medicinal or poisonous properties it has been thought to hold.

Identification: The umbels, which measure about 75mm/3in across consist of individual flowers about 15mm/⁹⁄₁₆in wide.

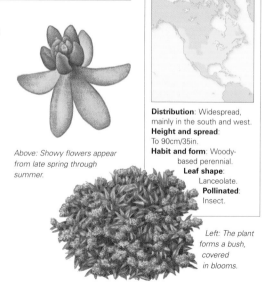

Above: Showy flowers appear from late spring through summer.

Distribution: Widespread, mainly in the south and west. **Height and spread**: To 90cm/35in. **Habit and form**: Woody-based perennial. **Leaf shape**: Lanceolate. **Pollinated**: Insect.

Left: The plant forms a bush, covered in blooms.

Swamp milkweed

Asclepias incarnata

As its name suggests, this is a milkweed of wetland habitats – swamps, shores and damp scrub. Its sap is less milky than most milkweeds. The flowers are borne in the typical milkweed cluster, at the top of tall leafy stems, and open from June to August.

Identification: Individual flowers are 6mm/¼in across, with five deep pink (or white) petals and a raised central crown. The fruit is an elongated pod to 10cm/4in long.

Distribution: Nova Scotia and Manitoba south to Florida and Texas; also in the Rocky Mountains.
Height and spread: 30cm–1.2m/12in–4ft.
Habit and form: Perennial herb.
Leaf shape: Long, opposite.
Pollinated: Insect.

Left: After the flowers come seeds that are both air and water-borne.

Above top: Each pink-tinged flower has two ovaries, five petals and a central crown.

OTHER SPECIES OF NOTE

White-stemmed milkweed, Wax milkweed
Asclepias albicans
As its name suggests, this has waxy, white stems. The flowers are a dull greenish-white and woolly, clustered in slightly drooping umbels. It grows in dry, rocky desert sites in California, Arizona and Mexico.

Poison milkweed, Horsetail milkweed
Asclepias subverticillata
The horsetail is another milkweed of western dry and desert sites. Like most milkweeds it is poisonous, but this one is especially dangerous to livestock. The small white and purple, five-petalled flowers open from May to September. The stems are tinged purple.

White milkweed
Asclepias variegata
With its rounded clusters of white, purple-centred flowers, this can be found in woodland in the north-east, from New York south to Florida.

Climbing milkweed
Sarcostemma cynanchoides
This unusual milkweed is a clambering vine with stems to 3m/10ft in length. It has clusters of white, green-tinged or purple-tinged, star-shaped flowers from June to September. The habitats are sandy soils on dry plains and deserts, from California to Texas.

Common milkweed

Asclepias syriaca

This tall, softly hairy plant has tight clusters of pink-purple flowers and long light green leaves that are downy on the underside. It grows mainly on wasteland, in abandoned fields and alongside roads. This poisonous plant is the food of the larvae of the monarch (or milkweed) butterfly which is poisonous to birds and other predators. The plant also has medicinal uses as it contains cardiac glycosides.

Identification: The flowers open from June to August, and each is about 15mm/⅝in across. The leaves exude poisonous milky sap when crushed or bruised. The fruit is a rough, many-seeded pod.

Distribution: Nova Scotia and Saskatchewan, south to Georgia and west to Texas.
Height and spread: 60cm–1.8m/24in–6ft.
Habit and form: Perennial herb.
Leaf shape: Long, opposite.
Pollinated: Insect.

Below: The fruit, or follicle, contains the fluffy seeds.

Left: The plants thrive and spread, partly because they are distasteful to livestock.

BINDWEED FAMILY

The bindweed family, Convolvulaceae, comprises mostly twining herbs or shrubs, sometimes with milky sap, comprising about 58 genera and 1,650 species. Many have heart-shaped leaves and funnel-shaped solitary or paired flowers. They are found in temperate and tropical regions. The genus Ipomoea contains morning glories with their showy flowers and also the sweet potato (I. batatas).

Field bindweed

Possession vine, *Convolvulus arvensis*

This European native grows from rootstock and seed, and spreads rapidly as an aggressive weed, therefore it is not always welcome in the garden. Yet it has beautiful flowers and often brightens up wasteland and roadsides. The large, funnel-shaped flowers are prettily patterned in white and pink, with yellow centres. The flowering period is long – from May to October. The flowers open each morning and close into a narrow twist in the evening.

Above: The flowers are trumpet-shaped and attractive.

Identification: Each flower opens to about 25mm/1in across and is a beacon to passing insects. Two long bracts sit below the calyx. Leaves that grow from seed are square with a notch at the tip. Plants from rhizomes lack these and have the more familiar heart-shaped leaves.

Distribution: Throughout, mainly in the west.
Height and spread: 30–90cm/12–35in.
Habit and form: Perennial herb.
Leaf shape: Triangular, arrow-shaped or ovate.
Pollinated: Insect.

Arizona blue-eyes

False flax, *Evolvulus arizonicus*

The imaginative common name refers to the bright blue or purplish flowers that open from April to October. The colour varies from region to region, those in the drier desert habitats being a less pure blue; in other regions the flowers are as clear blue as those of the true flax (*Linum*), hence the alternative common name. It grows in dry pinyon pine and juniper woodland, and in deserts.

Left: The stems are slender and sprawling.

Identification: The five-lobed corolla is to 20mm/¾in across and the flowers grow on narrow stalks. The upright stems have a covering of grey hairs. The leaves are green-grey and lanceolate.

Below: The spread is usually to just 30cm/12in. The plant is also known as the wild dwarf morning glory.

Distribution: Northern Mexico, New Mexico and southern Arizona.
Height and spread: To 30cm/12in.
Habit and form: Perennial herb.
Leaf shape: Lanceolate.
Pollinated: Insect.

Common morning glory

Ipomoea purpurea

Native to tropical North and Central America, this pretty climber is a popular garden plant, and also grows as a weed on waste ground. It grows quickly, clambering and attaching itself by tendrils, and produces large numbers of showy, funnel-shaped flowers, usually purple, but red and white forms are also found. Each flower opens in the morning but wilts by evening – hence the common name.

Identification: Each flower is up to 65mm/2½in across, with a trumpet-shaped corolla. The five sepals are fused at the base, and hairy. The leaves are usually heart-shaped.

Distribution: Widespread, especially in warmer regions.
Height and spread: Stems to 3m/10ft.
Habit and form: Annual climber.
Leaf shape: Heart-shaped or three-lobed.
Pollinated: Insect (and sometimes hummingbird).

Left: The vines extend to 1.2–3m/4–10ft in length.

Right: Attractive, round flowers appear from July to October.

OTHER SPECIES OF NOTE

Railroad vine *Ipomoea pes-caprae*
Despite its name, this native to the West Indies is now found typically on coastal sand dunes and beaches (rather then railways), mainly from South Carolina to Florida and Texas. Its purple or pink flowers open throughout the year.

Scarlet creeper, Star glory *Ipomoea cristulata*
This climber found mainly in Arizona and Texas, in dry brushland, has scarlet flowers with pointed lobes, opening from May to October.

Bush morning glory *Ipomoea leptophylla*
As its name implies, this is not a clambering vine like most of the other species, but grows as a leafy bush. It has dark-centred pinkish-purple flowers from May to July, and grows on sandy soils, mainly in the west.

Beach morning glory *Calystegia soldanella*
This is a bindweed rather than a true morning glory. It grows worldwide on sandy beaches and has pretty streaked pink flowers and thick kidney-shaped leaves.

Small red morning glory

Ipomoea coccinea

Another native of tropical North America, this is also grown commonly in gardens and has escaped into the wild, where it turns up on wasteland such as roadsides. The flowers are small and bright red, funnel-shaped and distinctly five-lobed. They open from July to October. The plant is also known as red star, possibly because each flower has five regular parts.

Identification: The flowers are small, only about 20mm/¾in across, red, with a yellow centre and with protruding stamens and stigma.

Distribution: Michigan and Massachusetts, south to Florida and Texas.
Height and spread: Vine, to 2.7m/9ft long.
Habit and form: Annual climber.
Leaf shape: Long, heart-shaped.
Pollinated: Hummingbird and insect.

Right: Flowers are up to 25mm/1in long.

Far right: This attractive vine likes to clamber through undisturbed field borders.

BORAGE AND POTATO FAMILIES

The borage family, Boraginaceae, contains herbs, shrubs and trees. There are 130 genera and 2,300 species, found worldwide, with some interesting representatives in the Americas. The potato family, Solanaceae, contains herbs, shrubs and trees of 94 genera and 2,950 species. They are often vines or creepers. Some are edible, and others are poisonous. Many have showy flowers.

Jimsonweed

Thornapple, *Datura stramonium*

Identification: A smooth plant with a green or purplish stem. The flowers, opening from July to October, are up to 10cm/4in across and have five lobes. The fruit is a prickly rounded or egg-shaped capsule.

This highly poisonous plant is native to the American tropics, but has now spread to many places in North America; it is also an occasional weed in Europe. The first common name comes from 'Jamestown', where it grew; the second from the spiny, rounded fruit. The fruit is highly toxic, as is the whole plant, and cattle and sheep are sometimes killed by eating it. The trumpet-shaped white or pale violet flowers are large and attractive. It grows mostly on wasteland as a weed.

Distribution: Widespread.
Height and spread: 30cm–1.5m/12in–5ft.
Habit and form: Annual herb.
Leaf shape: Ovate, lobed.
Pollinated: Insect.

Far left: The fruits are covered in prickles. They contain a few kidney-shaped, foul-smelling seeds.

Left: The plant grows 30cm–1.5m/12in–5ft tall. It contains hallucinogenic tropane alkaloids that produce an unpleasant 'high' and can be very dangerous.

Virginia bluebells

Virginia cowslip, *Mertensia virginica*

This eye-catching, early flowering perennial, with striking blue flowers opening from pink buds, is native to eastern North America. It is found in moist, rich woods and floodplain forests where it grows abundantly, usually on higher, dry areas, flowering in mid-spring. The plant enters a dormant phase in summer, the foliage dying to the ground until the following spring.

Identification: Erect to ascending stems, green with some purple at the base, emerge from a woody base, branching near the tips. The smooth leaves, up to 20cm/8in long, are arranged alternately, the lower leaves on winged stalks, oval, with margins smooth or slightly toothed at the tips, dull green above and silvery-green below. The upper leaves are reduced, becoming bracts at the base of the flower stalks near the top of the stem. Bell-shaped flowers, 30mm/1¼in long, are borne in lateral cymes.

Distribution: Eastern North America, from Ontario to Alabama.
Height and spread: 60cm/24in.
Habit and form: Herbaceous perennial.
Leaf shape: Ovate.
Pollinated: Insect.

Left: The striking blue flowers open from pink buds.

Right: The abundant growth of this plant disappears during the drier summer months until the following spring.

True forget-me-not

Water forget-me-not, *Myosotis scorpioides*

Distribution: Originated in Europe but widely naturalized across North America.
Height and spread: 90cm/35in.
Habit and form: Herbaceous perennial.
Pollinated: Insect.
Leaf shape: Oblong to lanceolate.

Above right: The tiny blue flowers have a yellow eye in their centre.

Right: The arching sprays of flowers appear from spring.

While this plant is a doubtful native of the USA, it has been adopted as the state flower of Alaska, and is frequently found in marshy places or beside rivers, in the shallow waters of ponds and lakes, and generally in lowland habitats the further north it grows. It is occasionally invasive in woodland. The stems are weak, often bent at the base, with alternately arranged willow-like leaves. Tiny blue flowers are located along the upper end of the stem, which unfurls in a 'fiddleneck' fashion. It is in leaf all year, and in flower from late spring to autumn, with the seeds ripening from midsummer.

Identification: A rhizomatous, spreading perennial, the plant has erect to ascending, angled, smooth stems, hairy near the base, and lance-shaped to oblong leaves up to 10cm/4in long. The flowers are bright light blue, with a yellow eye, 8mm/5⁄16in across, tubular, with five round, flat petals slightly notched at the tip. The calyx teeth are less than half the length of the calyx when flowering, each tooth forming a more or less equilateral triangle. The ripe fruit has stalks as long or twice as long as the calyx, with ovoid nutlets, which are rimmed.

OTHER SPECIES OF NOTE

James' cryptantha
Cryptantha cinerea jamesii
This variable and complex perennial species occurs in most dry habitats, from ponderosa pine forest to grasslands and desert scrub, chiefly in New Mexico. The small, yellow-eyed flowers that appear in late spring and summer are held in a much-branched inflorescence.

Seaside heliotrope *Heliotropium curassavicum*
The seaside or salt heliotrope is an upright to spreading perennial indigenous to much of the coastal Americas. It grows from thick, creeping roots in dry or moist saline and alkaline areas. The small flowers that appear in tightly curled sprays from early summer, open white with yellow centres and gradually turn blue.

Common nightshade *Solanum ptychanthum*
Found from Alberta to Newfoundland, south to Florida and west to Texas. It is a smooth plant with umbels of small white flowers, appearing from June to November. The fruit is a berry, green at first, then turning black as it ripens. The leaves and fruits are poisonous. It has a weed-like habit and is found growing in disturbed areas and also in open woodland.

Ivyleaf groundcherry *Physalis hederifolia*
Found mainly in western North America, this species grows on dry, sandy soils in rocky sites and also in open woods. Its flowers are pale yellow with deeper yellow patches near the centre, appearing from March to September. The leaves are triangular to heart-shaped. The fruit is a smooth, round yellow-green berry.

Eastwood's fiddleneck

Amsinckia eastwoodiae

Distribution: Central and southern California, USA.
Height and spread: 20cm–1m/8–39in.
Habit and form: Annual.
Leaf shape: Narrowly lanceolate.
Pollinated: Insect.

Eastwood's fiddleneck is a pretty yellow- or orange-flowered annual, found in open valleys and hills at 50–500m/164–1,600ft in central and southern California, west of the Sierra Nevada. It is named after its flower stems, which bear a large number of small flowers, and curl over at the top in a way that suggests the neck of a violin. The seeds and foliage are poisonous to livestock, particularly cattle, and the sharp hairs on the plants can cause skin irritation in humans. The species can be hard to distinguish, as it is variable and its range overlaps with others that sometimes hybridize naturally.

Identification: A variable annual covered in bristly hairs with bulbous bases. The tubular, five-lobed flowers are borne at the end of the spike-like inflorescence, which has a coiled tip. They are orange or yellow with a darker red-orange mark towards the base of each lobe, 12–20mm/1⁄2–3⁄4in long, 8–15mm/5⁄16–9⁄16in wide at the top.

Far right: The stem is generally erect, with alternate, narrowly lance-shaped leaves growing at the base and up the stem.

MINT FAMILY

The mint family, Labiatae, contains mostly herbs or shrubs, with about 250 genera and 6,700 species distributed all over the world. Members of the family include many well-known herbs, ornamental plants and weeds, usually with square stems and clustered flowers. Familiar aromatic members include mint, Mentha, marjoram, Origanum, thyme, Thymus, sage, Salvia, and lavender, Lavandula.

Bee balm

Bergamot, Oswego tea, *Monarda didyma*

Bee balm is a native of the eastern USA. It originally occurred from New York, west to Michigan and south in the Appalachian Mountains to Tennessee and northern Georgia, though it is now much more widely distributed, probably due to its popularity as a garden ornamental, resulting in its escaping and becoming established as far north as Quebec. It occurs along wooded stream banks and in moist hardwood forests.
The scarlet blooms first appear in early summer and continue into late summer. Its aromatic leaves have traditionally been used to make infusions.

Identification: A tall, upright-growing, spreading, clump-forming perennial, arising from short underground stolons in spring. The square stems carry leaves in opposite pairs. The leaves are toothed on the margins, lance-shaped to oval near the base, elongating to a pointed tip, 50mm–15cm/2–6in long and about a third to a half as wide, fragrant when bruised. The inflorescences are whorled clusters of scarlet-red flowers, borne singly or (rarely) in pairs. The flowers are irregular in shape and up to 40mm/1½in long, tubular, terminating in two lips; the upper lip erect and hood-like, the lower lip with three spreading lobes. Directly beneath each inflorescence is a whorl of reddish bracts, some leafy and some bristly.

Distribution: Eastern USA.
Height and spread: 1.2m x 60cm/4ft x 24in.
Habit and form: Herbaceous perennial.
Leaf shape: Lanceolate to ovate-acuminate.
Pollinated: Insect, especially bee.

Left: The spreading underground stems eventually result in a large clump.

Ground ivy

Glechoma hederacea

This pretty flower was introduced from Europe and is now found throughout the region as a rampant weed, especially in and around damp woodland. It also turns up frequently in lawns where, though quite pretty, it is not always welcome. The flowering period is March though June and the flowers are a delicate shade of blue-violet.

Identification: Each flower is to 25mm/1in long with a lipped and hooded corolla, which is internally bearded and spotted. The flowers produce four nutlets each. The leaves are hairy and rounded, about 30mm/1¼in long, with scalloped margins and long slender stalks.

Above: The flowers range in colour from pink to blue.

Distribution: Throughout.
Height and spread: Creeping stems to 40cm/16in.
Habit and form: Perennial herb.
Leaf shape: Rounded or kidney-shaped.
Pollinated: Insect.

Left: The size and shape of the leaf earns ground ivy the common name catsfoot.

Above centre: The flowers are funnel-shaped and blue to lavender in colour. The plant has a creeping habit and is aromatic.

Small-leaf giant hyssop *Agastache parviflora*
An erect, rhizomatous, perennial subshrub native to the USA. Small-leaf giant hyssop is a drought-tolerant species, reaching a height of 60cm/24in at maturity. It sports spikes of mauve blooms in late spring.

Eastern bee balm *Monarda bradburiana*
Eastern or Bradbury bee balm can be found in woods and on slopes in the mid-western USA. The square, erect stems are covered with opposite, toothed, greyish-green, aromatic leaves, with pink to white flowers in terminal heads in late spring and early summer.

Nettleleaf horsemint *Agastache urticifolia*
This is a woodland mint with tight spikes of pale pink flowers, and typical mint foliage of toothed leaves. Its habitat is open glades in woodland, from British Columbia south to California.

Yerba buena
Satureja douglasii
Another western mint of shady woodland. The Spanish name meaning 'good herb' refers to its medicinal use; it also makes a pleasant, mild tea. It spreads across the ground, often rooting. Flowers are tubular and may be white to a pretty shade of blue. They appear in July.

Purple giant hyssop

Agastache scrophulariifolia

A perennial plant native to eastern North America, naturally inhabiting the edges of the upper limits of floodplains associated with steep rivers and streams, and favouring areas where competition from other plants is limited. It is a species that is dependent on soil disturbance and often grows in areas close to human settlements, although it rarely persists for long. The branching stems bear spikes of pinkish-purple flowers from midsummer to early autumn, and the whole plant is highly fragrant, smelling strongly of anise. Historically, it ranged from New England south to Georgia, west to Kansas and north into Ontario, although its range appears to have been shrinking in recent years.

Below: This erect, tall, late-flowering, mostly herbaceous perennial is little branched in its lower parts, more so above, with hairless square stems, usually tinged with purple.

Distribution: Eastern North America.
Height and spread: Up to 2m/6½ft.
Habit and form: Herbaceous perennial.
Leaf shape: Ovate to ovate-lanceolate.
Pollinated: Insect.

Identification: The leaves are opposite, paired, oval to lance-shaped, rounded to heart-shaped at the base with pointed tips, up to 12.5cm/5in long, conspicuously hairy and coarsely serrated. The inflorescence, which grows up to 15cm/6in long, is composed of small flowers compacted into terminal, cylindrical or tapering whorled clusters 15–20mm/⁹∕₁₆–¾in across. Hairless, inconspicuous bracts, often with coloured margins, subtend the inflorescence. The flowers range from pale pink to purple, projecting significantly beyond the white or purplish calyces.

Vinegar weed

Common blue curls, *Trichostema lanceolatum*

This is a tall-growing plant with an unpleasant smell, hence one of its common names. The flowers are pale blue or purple and borne in long clusters, opening from July to October. It grows mainly on open dry fields. A closely related species, woolly blue curls, *T. lanatum*, has a pleasant smell and woolly flower clusters. Native Americans of northern California used the plant as a cold and fever remedy and a flea repellent.

Identification: Each flower is 15mm/⁹∕₁₆in long with a tubular corolla opening into five narrow lobes. The stamens and style are very prominent.

Right: The habit is loose and rosemary-like. It is also known as wild rosemary.

Distribution: North-western Oregon south through California.
Height and spread: 60cm–1.5m/24in–5ft.
Habit and form: Annual herb.
Leaf shape: Long and narrow.
Pollinated: Insect.

Field mint

Mentha arvensis

This widespread species also occurs in Europe and Asia. Unlike most mints, its flower clusters grow along the stem rather than towards the top of the stems. The foliage has a pleasant mint aroma and the compact whorls of small pink flowers, opening from July to September, are almost hidden by the leaves. It prefers damp soil, such as in marshy ground or alongside streams. This the only species of mint native to the USA.

Identification: The individual flowers are tiny – only about 6mm/¼in long, and found at the base of the leaves. The leaves are sharply toothed. The stem is hairy, square and upright with pairs of opposite leaves, with conspicuous veins and characteristic serrated edges. They are, and slender towards the tip. *The leaves are used as a culinary herb.*

Distribution: Throughout, except the warm south.
Height and spread: 20–80cm/8–30in.
Habit and form: Perennial herb.
Leaf shape: Lanceolate, toothed.
Pollinated: Insect.

Above: The aerial parts of the plant are steamed to release the oils.

Left: Pink, white or purple flowers cluster on the stem. The prominent stamens give the clusters a fluffy look from a distance.

Red monardella

Monardella macrantha

This low-growing plant is relatively insignificant until it flowers, from June to August. The flowers are a brilliant red and long and tubular in shape, evolved perfectly for pollination by hummingbirds. These agile birds hover close to each flower, inserting their narrow bill and reaching the nectar with their tongues. Red monardella grows in chaparral and dry pine forests. Large colonies form, thanks to the creeping rootstock. Coniferous forests and chaparral are highly favoured by this plant, which is also known as red mountainbalm.

Left: The red and green make a vivid contrast.

Distribution: Southern California.
Height and spread: 10–50cm/4–20in.
Habit and form: Perennial sub-shrub.
Leaf shape: Ovate.
Pollinated: Hummingbird and insect.

Identification: Each flower is about 50mm/2in long with a pointed, five-lobed corolla and four stamens. The leaves are opposite and ovate, and aromatic.

Left: The leaves are dark and shiny, and sometimes have purple margins.

Obedient plant

False dragonhead, *Physostegia virginiana*

The pink flowers of this species look a little like those of a snapdragon. The unusual common name comes from the fact that the flowers tend to remain for a while in their new position if bent. This is a popular garden plant and several cultivars are available, with white-flowered and variegated forms. The native habitats are swamps, damp thickets and prairies. The stiffly erect flower spikes grow from a basal rosette of narrow leaves.

Left: The leaves have toothed edges. The flowers are arranged in vertical columns on the spike.

Identification: Each flower is up to 25mm/1in long with a two-lipped tubular corolla and four stamens. The leaves are to 10cm/4in, opposite, narrow, toothed and pointed.

Below: The flowers are reminiscent of those of the snapdragon.

Distribution: Mainly eastern Canada and USA, south to Texas and Florida.
Height and spread: 30cm–1.2m/12in–4ft.
Habit and form: Perennial herb.
Leaf shape: Lanceolate, pointed.
Pollinated: Insect and hummingbird.

OTHER SPECIES OF NOTE
Coyote mint *Monardella odoratissima*
This is an aromatic mint with grey foliage and dense heads of whitish or pale pink flowers. It has a western distribution and grows on dry slopes and rocky sites.

Hoary mountain mint
Pycnanthemum incarnum
Mainly found in eastern North America, hoary mountain mint grows in woods and thickets and has dense rounded clusters of pale lavender flowers. It can get to 2m/6½ft tall, but is usually half that height.

Motherwort *Leonurus cardiaca*
This is a perennial introduced from Europe, but now found throughout most of North America as a weed. It has clusters of pale lavender flowers and lobed, opposite leaves that are hirsute along the veins underneath.

Wild basil
Clinopodium vulgare
An aromatic herb that grows in fields and along roadsides, and produces its small, woolly pinkish-purple flowers from June to September. A tea can be made from its leaves. It is pollinated by bees, moths and butterflies. It grows to 25–45cm/ 10–18in tall.

Water horehound

Lycopus americanus

This is a mint of wet habitats, one of about 10 similar species. It has clusters of tiny white flowers in the leaf axils, and the squarish stem typical of the mint family. The main flowering period is from June through September. The leaves are unusual for this family, in that they are not aromatic.

Distribution: Throughout, except the far north.
Height and spread: 15–60cm/6–24in.
Habit and form: Perennial herb.
Leaf shape: Lanceolate.
Pollinated: Insect.

Below: Flowers cluster at the base of the long leaves.

Above: The white flowers are about 3mm/⅛in long.

Identification: Each flower is only 2mm/¹⁄₁₆in long, with two stamens. The long leaves are toothed, especially the lower leaves.

Thistle sage

Salvia carduacea

The prickly, round flower clusters give this sage its common name. The flowers are an attractive shade of lavender and the clusters develop at the top of leafless stems. It flowers from March to June and grows on sand or gravel soils in open sites. It is one of the prettiest of the sages, with bright lavender flowers and bright red anthers.

Identification: Each flower is about 25mm/1in long and the lips of the colourful corolla are fringed in a lace-like fashion. The bracts extend beyond the petals and are woolly. The lavender-to-blue corolla has deep red anthers. Leaves are narrow and lanceolate, giving the thistle-like appearance, and the seed heads and leaves are spiny. The stem is erect and either simple or few-branched with woolly herbage. The flowering period is from March to June. There are several flowers borne on each stem. Gardeners often grow the plant as an annual in containers for its colourful blooms.

Distribution: California.
Height and spread: 10–50cm/4–20in.
Habit and form: Annual or perennial herb.
Leaf shape: Lanceolate.
Pollinated: Insect.

Left: Sometimes the flowers can cover acres of land. Thistle sage is one of the most glamorous native Californian plants.

Left: The seed heads are covered in spines. These spines are not as sharp as they appear.

Blood sage

Salvia coccinea

This species is commonly grown in gardens. There are several varieties with different shades of red, white, and bi-coloured flowers, opening from May onwards, arranged in a loose spike. It is found growing wild in sandy sites or on wasteland in southern and eastern regions. It is perennial in warm places and annual where temperatures drop below freezing for more than a couple of hours at a time. This salvia, like all mints, has opposite leaves. Nutlets form after flowering, enclosed by the calyx.

Above: Blooms appear from early summer to first frost. The stamens are very prominent.

Distribution: South Carolina to Florida and west to Texas.
Height and spread: 30–60cm/12–24in.
Habit and form: Annual herb.
Leaf shape: Ovate, scalloped.
Pollinated: Insect and hummingbird.

Right: The flower spike tapers towards the tip, and the flowers open from the bottom to the top.

Identification: The flowers are each about 25mm/1in long, with a two-lipped corolla and two stamens. The upper lip of the corolla has two lobes, the lower is three-lipped. It reaches 60–90m/24–35in tall, with 25–50mm/1–2in opposite, triangular leaves on long petioles (leaf stems).

Chia

Salvia columbariae

This, and a number of other *Salvia* species were used by Native Americans to make a thick drink and also a flour from the seeds, called pinole. The flowers are a deep blue-purple in dense, rounded clusters near the top of the stems. It grows in dry sites, such as coastal-sage scrub and chaparral, under 1,200m/4,000ft above sea level.

Identification: Flowers each about 15mm/⁹⁄₁₆in long with upper and lower lips, two stamens and spiny bracts below the flower clusters.

Right: The leaves are pinnately dissected with rounded lobes.

Right: The lower lip is twice the size of the upper lip. The flowers are pale blue or blue with purple tips.

Above: The seedhead forms when the individual flowers fade.

Distribution: Mainly California, Arizona and New Mexico.
Height and spread: 10–50cm/4–20in.
Habit and form: Annual or perennial herb.
Leaf shape: Oblong, divided.
Pollinated: Insect.

OTHER SPECIES OF NOTE

Blue salvia *Salvia azurea*
A perennial sage of open prairie and pastures, mainly in the east. It grows tall and sports large blue or violet flowers in a spike-like cluster. It is most attractive to insects.

Lyre-leaved sage
Salvia lyrata
Rising from the rosette of basal elongated leaves, the squarish stem has whorls of lavender flowers, each about 25mm/1in long, appearing from April to June in abundance, although flowering can continue through the year. It grows mainly in open woods in the east.

Desert sage, Grey-ball sage *Salvia dorii*
A western sage of dry flats and sagebrush habitats. It is a bushy plant with very aromatic silvery leaves, spiny branches and striking, pale blue to purple flowers.

Wood sage *Teucrium canadense* .
This tough perennial has spikes of lavender-pink flowers and long, toothed leaves. It grows in woods and shorelines from Saskatchewan and Newfoundland south to Florida, and scattered in the west. It flowers from June to September and is found on prairies and on wet ground, as well as alongside railtracks.

Crimson sage

Salvia henryi

This slender sage has grey, softly hairy foliage and bright red flowers borne horizontally in pairs near the tops of the stems. It flowers from April to September and grows mainly among rocks, frequently in pinyon or juniper communities. Insects and hummingbirds are attracted to the conspicuous flowers.

Distribution: Mexico and western Texas to southern Arizona.
Height and spread: To 50cm/20in.
Habit and form: Perennial herb.
Leaf shape: Pinnate, opposite.
Pollinated: Insect and hummingbird.

Above: Dark green and slightly hairy buds open to reveal the striking red flowers.

Identification: The three-lobed crimson corolla is 25–65mm/1–2½in long and has two stamens. The oliage is greyish-green and hirsute. The stems are delicate.

Above: The lower lip protrudes from the individual flower.

FIGWORT FAMILY

The figwort family, Scrophulariaceae, consists mostly of herbs, but also a few small shrubs. It contains more than 260 genera and 5,100 predominately temperate species. They include many that are partial root parasites and a few that are without chlorophyll and are wholly parasitic. They have a cosmopolitan distribution, with the majority found in temperate areas, including tropical mountains.

Shrubby penstemon

Penstemon fruticosus

With more than 250 species, the penstemons constitute the largest genus of flowering plants endemic to North America. Shrubby penstemon inhabits rocky slopes stretching from the foothills into alpine areas, ranging from British Columbia, south through the Washington Cascades, and eastward to the Idaho panhandle. It is a low, dense shrub with abundant lavender flowers appearing between late spring and late summer.

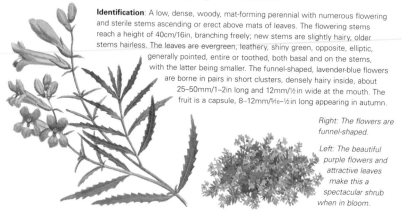

Identification: A low, dense, woody, mat-forming perennial with numerous flowering and sterile stems ascending or erect above mats of leaves. The flowering stems reach a height of 40cm/16in, branching freely; new stems are slightly hairy, older stems hairless. The leaves are evergreen, leathery, shiny green, opposite, elliptic, generally pointed, entire or toothed, both basal and on the stems, with the latter being smaller. The funnel-shaped, lavender-blue flowers are borne in pairs in short clusters, densely hairy inside, about 25–50mm/1–2in long and 12mm/½in wide at the mouth. The fruit is a capsule, 8–12mm/⁵⁄₁₆–½in long appearing in autumn.

Distribution: North-western North America.
Height and spread: 40cm/16in.
Habit and form: Woody, mat-forming perennial.
Leaf shape: Elliptic.
Pollinated: Insect.

Right: The flowers are funnel-shaped.

Left: The beautiful purple flowers and attractive leaves make this a spectacular shrub when in bloom.

Scarlet monkey flower

Mimulus cardinalis

This spreading perennial plant, native to western North America, stretches from Oregon south as far as northern Mexico. It generally inhabits shady, wet places from streamside to seepages and spreads by rhizomes, often forming good-size colonies. Its brilliant scarlet to orange-red (sometimes yellowish) flowers are short-lived but appear prolifically from spring to autumn. While most *Mimulus* species are bee-pollinated, *M. cardinalis* is pollinated by hummingbird.

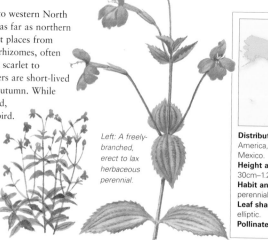

Identification: Scarlet monkey flower has hairy stems and lime-green, oval to oblong-elliptic, toothed leaves 75mm–10cm/3–4in long, with longitudinal veins. The brilliant scarlet, tubular, lipped flowers are 50mm/2in long, the upper lip arched and ascending, the lower lips flared and curved back. The narrow throat is tinged yellow; the stamens are hairy and protruding. The fruit is a capsule that opens to shed the seeds.

Left: A freely-branched, erect to lax herbaceous perennial.

Distribution: Western North America, Oregon to northern Mexico.
Height and spread: 30cm–1.2m/12in–4ft.
Habit and form: Herbaceous perennial.
Leaf shape: Ovate to oblong-elliptic.
Pollinated: Hummingbird.

Purple Chinese houses

Innocence, *Collinsia heterophylla* (= *Collinsia bicolor*)

This is one of California's most impressive wild flowers, with its separated whorls of striking purple and pink flowers, reminiscent of a Chinese pagoda – hence one of its common names. The individual flowers are like those of members of the pea family, and have variable colours. The plant grows on sandy soils and the flowers open from March to June. The flowers are particularly attractive to the checkerspot butterfly.

Identification: The corolla is about 20mm/ ¾in long with a two-lobed upper lip and a three-lobed lower lip, the middle lobe distinctly folded, enclosing the style and four stamens.

Distribution: Southern California.
Height and spread: 30–60cm/12–24in.
Habit and form: Annual herb.
Leaf shape: Lanceolate.
Pollinated: Insect.

Below: Purple Chinese houses spreads fast and is quite commonly seen in large groups on hillsides.

Right: The individual flowers appear stacked on top of each other.

OTHER SPECIES OF NOTE

Large beardtongue *Penstemon bradburii*
Found over a wide range in central North America, chiefly in prairie and plain habitats. Large beardtongue has terminal clusters of slender, tubular, dark lilac flowers that bloom on open stems, which reach 60cm/24in. The attractive, glossy, light green leaves below provide a perfect foil for the flowers.

Low beardtongue
Penstemon humilis
This native of the Rocky Mountains is a variable species, from 15–30cm/6–12in in height. It flowers between late spring and midsummer, with erect stems ending in panicles of azure to blue-violet inflated tubular flowers, borne in three or more whorls.

Purple gerardia *Agalinis purpurea*
This annual of damp soils is found mainly in the east. It has pretty, delicate pink-purple bell-shaped flowers, speckled within, opening from July to September. There are about 15 species in this region. The leaves and stems, which are slender, are often tinged purple.

Lyon's turtlehead *Chelone glabra*
Each flower looks a bit like the head of a turtle peeping from under its shell – hence the common name. Clusters of pink-tinged white flowers grow atop tall stems. It grows in damp, rich woods or on stream banks, and flowers from July to September.

Desert paintbrush

Castilleja angustifolia

The flaring bright red flowers of this dry country species stand out like paintbrushes dipped in fresh red paint, in contrast to the drab and dull foliage. It is one of the commoner paintbrush species of the west. Dry open soil such as sagebrush is its habitat. The flowers open from April through August and attract hummingbirds as well as insects.

Identification: The red-orange calyx is deeply cleft with four lobes, and the corolla is pointed and slender, pale orange with red edges. The flower clusters have reddish-orange bracts. The leaves are narrow, the upper leaves lobed.

Below: The plant is a grey-green, branched perennial that likes a dry, open habitat.

Distribution: Eastern Oregon north to Alberta, east to Utah, Wyoming and Montana, and south to California.
Height and spread: 10–40cm/4–16in.
Habit and form: Perennial herb.
Leaf shape: Narrow.
Pollinated: Insect and hummingbird.

Below and left: The calyx and leaf bracts have scarlet tips, as if they have been dipped in red paint.

CARNIVOROUS PLANTS

Strictly, carnivorous plants are those that attract, capture, kill and digest animals and absorb the nutrients from them. The Droseraceae either trap their victims in sticky hairs (e.g. Drosera*), or in active traps (e.g.* Dionaea*); the Lentibulariaceae include aquatic bladderworts (*Utricularia*), which use bladder-traps, and terrestrial butterworts (*Pinguicula*) with sticky glandular leaves, and the Sarraceniaceae have pitcher-traps.*

Venus flytrap

Dionaea muscipula

This is possibly the best known of all carnivorous plants. It famously traps insects with its specially adapted leaves. As soon as an insect, or anything else, touches any of the three sensitive hairs on its surface the trap rapidly closes and then extracts nutrients from the unfortunate victim. This added nutrition enables the plant to survive in poor soils that few other plants could tolerate. Despite its being so well known, the Venus flytrap is actually endangered in the wild, being restricted to wet sandy areas, bogs and savannas mainly on the coastal plain of North and South Carolina.

Identification: The basal leaves are semi-erect or held close to the ground in a rosette, each consisting of two hinged, round, glandular lobes, which become glossy red with exposure to sunlight, with spines on their margins and three sensitive hairs on the upper surface that cause the leaf to fold when stimulated twice in quick succession. Once folded the spines mesh, trapping insects. Each leaf is on a winged, flat, spatula-shaped stalk that looks more leaf-like than the trap itself. The flowers are white shot with green veins, five-petalled, up to 25mm/1in across, widening from the base; they are clustered at the end of leafless stalks in umbel-like cymes, appearing in mid-spring into early summer.

Distribution: North and South Carolina, USA.
Height and spread: 30–45cm/12–18in.
Habit and form: Low-growing herbaceous perennial.
Leaf shape: Two-hinged, orbicular traps.
Pollinated: Insect.

Yellow pitcher plant

Huntsman's horn, *Sarracenia flava*

This carnivorous plant traps wasps, bees and flies in long, upright modified leaves. The leaves form tubes, which fill with water and drown the victims inside. It is found along the south-eastern coastal plain of the USA, from Alabama to a few sites in Virginia. Like many carnivorous plants it is threatened, primarily by habitat destruction. Its flowers are yellow, borne on stalks that clear the foliage and appear in spring before the pitchers, to prevent the trapping of pollinating species. The species is quite variable and is usually divided into seven varieties, distinguished mostly by pitcher pigmentation.

Identification: This large, carnivorous plant is rhizomatous, with thin wiry roots. The pitcher, 30cm–1.2m/12in–4ft tall with a rounded lid raised above the wide mouth, is yellow-green, often heavily veined red on the lid, especially at the base, sometimes totally red or maroon externally. The winter leaves are straight or slightly curved, and glaucous. The flowers, borne on leafless, unbranched stems up to 60cm/24in tall, are up to 10cm/4in across, yellow and pendulous, with oval- to lance-shaped petals slightly constricted at the middle; the calyx, subtended by persistent bracts, has five overlapping, persistent sepals; the style is dilated at the end into an umbrella-like structure, with five ribs ending in hook-like stigmas.

Right: The yellowish, red-veined pitchers are topped with a heart-shaped lid.

Distribution: South-eastern USA coastal plain, from Alabama to Virginia.
Height and spread: 30cm–1.2m/12in–4ft.
Habit and form: Herbaceous perennial.
Leaf shape: Pitcher-shaped traps.
Pollinated: Insect.

Thread-leaved sundew

Drosera filiformis

This is one of a fascinating genus of insectivorous plants that gain extra nourishment by trapping and digesting insect prey. Sundews use the sticky secretions of their highly modified leaves to snare insects and slowly extract the proteins from their prey.
This sundew has long sticky leaves and produces pink flowers in a lop-sided cluster on a tall leafless stem, from June to September. The favoured habitat is wet sandy soil in coastal areas.

Identification: Each flower is about 15mm/⁹⁄₁₆in wide with five petals.

Distribution: Nova Scotia south to North Carolina and Florida.
Height and spread: 10–30cm/4–12in.
Habit and form: Perennial herb.
Leaf shape: Long, with sticky hairs.
Pollinated: Insect.

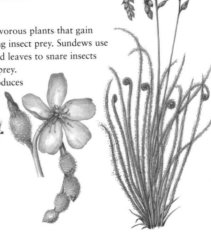

Right: The narrow green leaves are covered in sticky red 'hairs'.

OTHER SPECIES OF NOTE

Huntsman's cap *Sarracenia purpurea*
This low-growing carnivorous species is widespread in the eastern USA and Canada, extending from New Jersey to the Arctic. The pitchers are slender at the basal rosette, rapidly becoming swollen higher up. They are usually green with purple tints and the lids stand erect. The flowers, which appear in spring, are purple or greenish.

White-topped pitcher plant
Sarracenia leucophylla
This plant has pitchers up to around 90cm/35in tall, and sports large red flowers in the spring. The lower part of the pitcher is green while around the mouth and lid it is white with red or sometimes green veining. It is native to boggy and marshy areas in the south-eastern USA.

Swollen bladderwort *Utricularia inflata*
This common aquatic bladderwort is found over much of the south-eastern USA and is identified by its large radial floats on the flowering stems, which keep the showy yellow flowers erect and above water. Looking something like green wagon wheels floating on the water, they can reach up to 23cm/9in in diameter.

Cobra lily *Darlingtonia californica*
This plant looks like a snake ready to strike, and is closely related to the genus *Sarracenia*. The trap is a twisted upright tube with nectar glands that attract insects toward the mouth or opening, which is under the dome. It grows in the north-eastern states of California and Oregon on ground permeated by running water.

Hooded pitcher plant

Sarracenia minor

This is the commonest pitcher plant in Florida; its method of trapping insect prey is remarkable. The hood prevents rainwater entering the pitcher, but the base of the pitcher has digestive juices. The winged pitcher-leaves have a trail of nectar, eagerly followed by insects, some of which enter the hood. The walls of the hood have translucent 'windows' through which the insects try to climb, eventually falling exhausted into the digestive broth below, where the plant extracts nutrients.

Identification: The yellow flowers are about 50mm/2in across with many stamens. The modified leaves grow taller than the flower stalks.

Distribution: Florida to North Carolina.
Height and spread: 15–60cm/6–24in.
Habit and form: Perennial herb.
Leaf shape: Long, winged at one edge.
Pollinated: Insect.

Below: Flowers appear in springtime.

Far left: The plant grows to 15–60cm/6–24in tall.

ACANTHUS FAMILY

The acanthus family, Acanthaceae, contains mostly herbs or shrubs comprising about 230 genera and 3,450 species. Most are tropical herbs, shrubs or twining vines, while others are spiny. Only a few species are distributed in temperate regions. Typically there is a colourful bract subtending each flower; in some species the bract is large and showy. The family is closely allied to the Scrophulariaceae.

Water willow

Justicia americana

This is a colonial aquatic that grows in large patches in shallow water and along wet shores. Its common name comes from the narrow willow-like leaves. The flowers, opening from June to October, are quite striking, large and white, with purple spots. The leaves are also distinctive, with a prominent white mid rib.

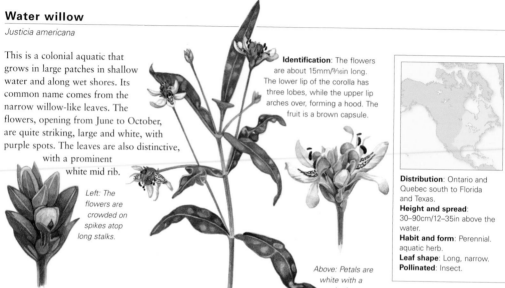

Identification: The flowers are about 15mm/⁹⁄₁₆in long. The lower lip of the corolla has three lobes, while the upper lip arches over, forming a hood. The fruit is a brown capsule.

Left: The flowers are crowded on spikes atop long stalks.

Above: Petals are white with a purple tinge.

Distribution: Ontario and Quebec south to Florida and Texas.
Height and spread: 30–90cm/12–35in above the water.
Habit and form: Perennial. aquatic herb.
Leaf shape: Long, narrow.
Pollinated: Insect.

Chuparosa

Justicia californica

This is a mainly tropical genus with just a handful of species being found in the USA. The name chuparosa means hummingbird in Spanish and indeed, the red flowers are often visited and pollinated by hummingbirds. They are rich in nectar and some other birds bite off the flowers to get at the nectar in the base. It grows mainly along desert streams. In drought the plant sheds its leaves to prevent waterloss, and photosynthesizes through its stem.

Above: Deep red flowers bloom intermittently throughout the year.

Identification: The long slender flowers are to 40mm/1½in long, dull red in colour, with a two-lobed upper lip and a three-lobed lower lip. The main blooming period is from February to June.

Distribution: North-western Mexico to southern Arizona and southern California.
Height and spread: To 1.5m/5ft.
Habit and form: Perennial herb.
Leaf shape: Ovate.
Pollinated: Hummingbird, insect.

Left: The shrub grows up to 1.5m/5ft tall.

Shaggy tuft

Stenandrium barbatum

Also known as shaggy narrowman, this is a tiny, pretty plant found on stony and rocky banks and on limestone. It has a dwarf growth form with grey, hairy foliage. The flowers are an attractive pink colour, clustered in short spikes and opening from March to June. It is one of the earliest spring flowers to appear. It hosts the caterpillars of the definite patch butterfly.

Distribution: Mexico, New Mexico and western Texas.
Height and spread: To 65mm/2½in.
Habit and form: Perennial herb.
Leaf shape: Narrow, lanceolate.
Pollinated: Insect.

Identification: The corolla is about 15mm/⁹⁄₁₆in wide, tubular, and opening into five lobes, streaked pink and white. The foliage is silver-grey in colour. The leaves are lanceolate and covered in grey hairs.

Left: Shaggy tuft buds about to open.

Above: The flower has five lobes that flare from a tube. The upper two lobes are often slightly darker than the lower three.

OTHER SPECIES OF NOTE

Loose-flowered water willow *Justicia ovata*
This perennial herb resembles the water willow, but has looser flowering spikes. It is an aquatic found from Alabama and Florida north to Virginia.The very pretty flowers are bi-coloured, and the plant forms colonies thanks to a network of underground stems.

Branched foldwing
Dicliptera brachiata
This purple-flowered herb is found mainly in the southern states of the USA. It is loosely branching and the flowers are usually in groups of three. It grows well as a garden plant, reaching a height of about 60cm/24in.

Carolina scalystem *Elytraria caroliniensis*
This is a perennial native to South Carolina, Georgia and Florida. Its favoured habitats are lime-rich soils in wet woodland, lake shores and damp slopes. Flowers are pure white, with five irregular-oblong petals and a deep corolla.

Carolina wild petunia *Ruellia caroliniensis*
This endangered species is native to the eastern and southern USA. It is a perennial herb with attractive pale purple flowers and long, dark green leaves. It is very attractive to hummingbirds and butterflies. This plant does well in the garden, and can be grown from seed.

Wild petunia

Stalked ruellia, *Ruellia pedunculata*

The pretty violet flowers of this woodland species open from June to September. They are trumpet-shaped opening into five lobes. In shape the flowers are a little like those of garden petunias, hence one of the common names. It prefers rich woodland soils, especially on limestone, but is commonly found along roadsides and in waste areas.

Identification: Each flower is about 50mm/2in long, with a long-lobed calyx and leafy bracts below. The leaves have short stalks and are downy.

Below: The delicate flowers appear in May.

Distribution: Mainly South Carolina south to Florida.
Height and spread: 30–60cm/12–24in.
Habit and form: Perennial herb.
Leaf shape: Elliptical, opposite.
Pollinated: Insect.

Below: The leaves are arranged opposite on a red stem.

LOBELIA FAMILY

The bellflower or lobelia family, Campanulaceae, contains herbs, shrubs, rarely, small trees, usually with milky sap, comprising about 80 genera and 2,000 species. Many of the species are highly ornamental and have become familiar plants in cultivation. The flowers are bisexual, bell-shaped, and often blue. The fruits are usually berries. The best-known genera are Campanula *and* Lobelia.

Cardinal flower

Lobelia cardinalis

This extremely showy, short-lived herbaceous perennial grows in moist meadows, bogs and along stream banks in eastern North America. In some areas it is very abundant, forming mats of floating vegetation and even clogging waterways. This is one of the most striking species of the genus found anywhere. The deep red flowers are easily noticed above the purplish leaves, and it is the only *Lobelia* species in the USA with such coloration.

Identification: The dark green, lance-shaped to oblong leaves are arranged alternately, stalked below and stalkless and smaller above; they are generally smooth or sparsely hairy, serrated to toothed, up to 20cm/8in long, tapered at both ends, often with undulating margins. The flowers appear from midsummer to mid-autumn on terminal racemes around 70cm/27½in in height, each subtended by a single leafy bract. They are brilliant red, up to 50mm/2in long, tubular, five-lobed, with the three prominent lobes joined to form a lower lip and two narrower lobes above. The five stamens, with red filaments, are united into a tube surrounding the style. The fruits are two-celled pods with numerous seeds.

Distribution: Eastern North America, from New Brunswick west to Minnesota, and south to central Florida and eastern Texas.
Height and spread: 60–90 x 45cm/24–35 x 18in.
Habit and form: Herbaceous perennial.
Leaf shape: Lanceolate to oblanceolate.
Pollinated: Hummingbird.

Left: This tall, stout plant has extremely striking red flowers set above the mass of purplish leaves.

Southwestern blue lobelia

Lobelia anatina

A small lobelia with pretty blue flowers, this western species is found in marshy areas, along streams and in damp meadows, and opens its flowers between July and October. The slender flowering stems carry loose racemes of flowers. Native Americans are said to have used lobelia to treat respiratory and muscular disorders.

Left: This attractive plant has vivid violet-blue flowers.

Identification: A spike of blue flowers forms in the summer. The flowers have a corolla of about 25mm/1in long, which is tubular and two-lipped; it has an upper lip with two lobes and a lower lip with three lobes. The long leaves often have blunt teeth.

Below: Buds forming at the tip of the stem.

Distribution: Northern Mexico, New Mexico and Arizona.
Height and spread: To 70cm/27½in.
Habit and form: Perennial herb.
Leaf shape: Lanceolate.
Pollinated: Insect.

Bluebell

Harebell, *Campanula rotundifolia*

This is also a familiar flower in Europe and Asia. The blue flowers are indeed bell-shaped and hang down nodding from the stems. The typical habitats are meadows and rocky slopes, and it flowers from June to September. This species is also known as bluebell in Scotland, but the European bluebell is unrelated.

Distribution: Scattered, especially in western mountains.
Height and spread: 10cm–1m/4–39in.
Habit and form: Perennial herb.
Leaf shape: Long, narrow; rounded.
Pollinated: Insect.

Identification: The corolla is to about 25mm/1in long and has five pointed lobes. The stem leaves are very narrow, while those at the base have rounded blades, hence the name 'rotundifolia'.

Left: The thin wiry stems support nodding pale blue flowers.

Right: The thimble-size flowers grow in loose clusters.

OTHER SPECIES OF NOTE

Indian tobacco *Lobelia inflata*
Also known as bladder pod, this is a native of Canada and the eastern USA. From a rosette of soft, green, finely hairy elliptic leaves, the upright flower stems, with tiny, two-lipped, pale blue flowers, appear in early summer. The seed capsules that follow look like round pouches, reflected in the species name *inflata*.

Great blue lobelia *Lobelia syphilitica*
This herbaceous perennial from the east grows along streams and in swampy areas, reaching 60–90cm/24–35in tall. The tall leafy stems produce terminal racemes that are densely covered with blue flowers from late summer to mid-autumn.

Spiked lobelia *Lobelia spicata*
This is a variable eastern species of fields, woods and meadows. The small lavender or purplish-blue flowers open from June to August in a slender spike. The leafy stem is often reddish and hairy at the base.

Venus's looking glass
Triodanis perfoliata
This eye-catching bellflower has blue-purple flowers, each sitting above a leaf on a wand-like stem. Ilt flowers from late spring to late summer. It is usually found in dry fields and open woods, in infertile soil and reaches 15–60cm/6–24in high.

Tall bellflower

Campanulastrum americanum

Although known as a bellflower, the flowers of this eastern species are open and star-like rather than bell-shaped. They are pale blue to violet and grow in small groups or singly in an open spike, showing from June to August. The plant grows very tall and is an impressive sight when in bloom. Rich damp woods are the usual habitat and it is often found along woodland paths.

Identification: The corolla is about 25mm/1in across, with five lobes and a long, protruding style, and leafy bracts beneath. The broadly lanceolate leaves are distinctly toothed at the margins.

Distribution: Ontario south to Florida.
Height and spread: 60–80cm/24–31in.
Habit and form: Annual herb.
Leaf shape: Ovate to lanceolate.
Pollinated: Insect.

Left: The stem is usually unbranched, though lower side stems may develop.

Above: The five-petalled blue flower is often white towards the centre. It contains a prominent style that curls upwards at the tip.

DAISY FAMILY

The daisy family, Asteraceae or Compositae, is the largest of all the plant families, with more than 1,500 genera and about 22,750 species, including herbs, shrubs and, less commonly, trees. The family is characterized by the flowers, organized into a composite cluster of tiny individual flowers called a 'capitulum', which superficially resembles a single bloom.

Stokes aster

Stokesia laevis

Stokes aster is a low-growing herbaceous perennial, native to wetlands, including pine flatwoods, savannas and bogs, on the coastal plain from North Carolina to Louisiana. The rosette clump of strap-like leathery leaves may persist through the winter, and the flowers, which appear over several weeks between late spring and early autumn, have many narrow light blue or lilac petals. *Stokesia* is a monotypic genus (it has only one species), named after Jonathan Stokes, a 19th-century British botanist.

Identification: Several erect stems, with small, clasping leaves, arise from the basal leaf rosette in late spring, bearing the flowers terminally. The strap-like, pointed, leathery leaves are 15–20cm/6–8in long, dark green, with the stems and leaf veins tinged with purple. Each inflorescence comprises one to four shaggy, cornflower-like flowerheads, 75mm–10cm/3–4in across. The ray florets are fringed, blue, lavender, pink or white, in two concentric rows; the disc florets are in darker shades of the same colours.

Distribution: Coastal plain from North Carolina to Louisiana, USA.
Height and spread: 30–60cm/12–24in.
Habit and form: Herbaceous perennial.
Leaf shape: Lanceolate.
Pollinated: Insect.

Left: The strap-like leaves often form a dense rosette from which the flowers emerge.

Clasping coneflower

Rudbeckia amplexicaulis

This annual coneflower, native to Georgia and Texas and north as far as Missouri and Kansas, gets its name because of the way that its cauline leaves clasp the stems (*amplexicaulis* means stem-clasping). It is typically found along roadsides, in waste areas and along streams, where it often forms dense colonies. The flowers that appear from early summer onward resemble the larger 'Mexican hat', *Ratibida* species, with the yellow outer ray florets, which droop as the flowers mature, surrounding an elongated, conical, brown centre. The plant is sometimes listed in the monotypic genus *Dracopis*, chiefly due to the presence of chaff subtending the ray flowers.

Identification: The plant is erect and loosely branched, with alternate glaucous, elongated oval or oblong leaves, with margins that are smooth to wavy or toothed and a clasping, heart-shaped base. The flowerheads appear over a long period during the summer and are long-stemmed, up to 50mm/2in across, with 5–10 yellow (sometimes partly orange or purple) drooping rays, which are orange or brownish at the bases, and a cone-shaped or columnar, dark brown central disc.

Distribution: South-eastern USA.
Height and spread: 30–60cm/12–24in.
Habit and form: Annual.
Leaf shape: Ovate or oblong.
Pollinated: Insect.

Left: The outer ray florets are bright in colour.

Right: The 'Mexican hat' blooms are held high on branched stems.

Large-leaved aster

Aster macrophyllus

This widespread rhizomatous perennial from north-eastern North America, seen from Canada to Ohio, is common in woods except those on wetlands, favouring dry or moist sites in pine woods. It often forms dense groundcover in large colonies. It is most easily distinguished by its very large, soft, thick, heart-shaped leaves, which are much more noticeable than the sparsely borne lavender or sometimes white flowers that appear in late summer.

Distribution: North-eastern North America.
Height and spread: 90cm/35in or more.
Habit and form: Herbaceous perennial.
Leaf shape: Cordate.
Pollinated: Bumblebee.

Right: The flowering stems are borne sparsely among the dense mat of leaves.

Identification: A spreading herbaceous perennial that arises from creeping rhizomes, forming dense patches of one-leaved plants. The basal leaves are very large, up to 20cm/8in long, firm, thick, usually hairy, coarsely toothed, tapering to a pointed tip, heart-shaped at the base. The flowering stems are infrequent, usually hairy, with a short, woody base and staggered leaves. The sparse, daisy-like flowers are pale lavender, to 25mm/1in across, with nine to 20 ray flowers appearing in late summer in a loose, rounded, many-flowered corymb. The fruits are small, linear seeds with fluffy hairs that form a small ball for each flowerhead; they appear in early autumn.

OTHER SPECIES OF NOTE

Texas yellow star *Lindheimera texana*
The Texas yellow star is a hairy, upright annual with tapered leaves and yellow, star-like flowerheads consisting of five rays with two or three times as many disc flowers. It blooms in spring and can be found in full sun in the sandy or rocky soils of the Edwards Plateau region.

Indian blanket
Gaillardia pulchella
This annual or short-lived perennial is found from Virginia to Florida and westward to Colorado and New Mexico, extending south into Mexico. It is noted for its brilliant, daisy-like flowers, which appear in summer. They have large, rose-purple centres and frilly petals of yellow, orange, crimson or copper scarlet.

Rough-stemmed goldenrod *Solidago rugosa*
This a weed is found in abandoned fields, on woodland edges and roadsides. It is a tall plant, producing heads of small pale yellow flowers from July to October. It is mainly eastern in distribution.

Purple coneflower *Echinacea purpurea*
The purple coneflower is a native of dry woods and prairies. It is also a popular garden plant and well known as a herb, being used for tea and extracts that are used medicinally. Notably it thought to help prevent colds. The pretty purple (occasionally white) flowers have drooping petal-like ray florets.

Blazing star

Spike gayfeather, *Liatris spicata*

This species occurs in the entire eastern half of the USA and Canada. The non-flowering plants resemble grass clumps until the flowers appear in midsummer. The bottlebrush flower spikes of fuchsia, rose and purple, which attract bees and butterflies, are unusual in opening from the top of the spike downward, continuing until late summer or early autumn.

Identification: A clump-forming, upright, hairless (or very sparsely hairy) herbaceous perennial with single or multiple stems arising from the base. The almost grass-like, mid-green basal leaves grow up to 30cm/12in long; on the tall stems the leaves are narrow and arranged in whorls, emphasizing the plant's vertical, feathery effect. The inflorescence is a terminal spike to 60cm/24in tall, of crowded, purple, fuzzy flowerheads up to 12mm/½in broad. The lowest flowerheads are subtended by small leafy bracts.

Left: The plant resembles a grass clump when it is not in flower.

Distribution: Eastern USA and Canada.
Height and spread: 60 x 80cm/24 x 31in.
Habit and form: Herbaceous perennial.
Leaf shape: Linear.
Pollinated: Insect.

Below: The fuzzy bottlebrush-like flowers open from the top downwards.

Yarrow

Milfoil, *Achillea millefolium*

This very widespread species, also familiar in Europe and Asia, has a long history of medicinal use, as a treatment for fever and as a poultice. Native Americans used it for treating stomach disorders. The flat clusters of small whitish flowers top out the greyish-green feathery foliage. A wide range of cultivated forms are available, with different flower colours – for example red, yellow and purple.

Identification: The long, finely divided leaves are 50mm–20cm/2–8in long, bi- or tripinnate, almost feathery, and arranged spirally on the stems. They are aromatic. The tiny flowers form clusters of heads each about 6mm/¼in wide.

Distribution: Throughout the region.
Height and spread: 30–90cm/12–35in.
Habit and form: Perennial herb.
Leaf shape: Finely dissected.
Pollinated: Insect.

Left: The plant produces one to several stems.

Left and above: The flowers can be white or pinkish in colour.

Orange agoseris

Agoseris aurantiaca

This is the only member of the genus with orange flowers; all the others have yellow blooms. However, even in this species the flower colour can vary from rusty orange to lavender, and very rarely to pink, as the flower matures and dries out. The flowerheads have spreading rays and develop at the top of leafless stalks from June to August.

Orange agoseris is found growing in forest clearings and meadows in mountain areas, and will grow in nutritionally poor soil.

It occurs scattered rather than in large colonies.

Right: The leaves are dandelion-like and can be cooked and eaten in the same way as spinach. They may be smooth or covered in fine hair. Generally, they measure about 50mm–35cm/2–14in long, and taper to a point at the tip.

Above and Below: Single-stemmed flowers grow from a basal cluster of leaves.

Distribution: Western Canada south to California and New Mexico.
Height and spread: 10–60cm/4–24in.
Habit and form: Perennial herb.
Leaf shape: Long, narrow.
Pollinated: Insect.

Identification: The flowerheads are about 25mm/1in across, and the leaves are long and narrow. The fruit has a tip of silvery bristles. The stems are 10–60cm/4–24in long. The leaves may be smooth-edged or marginally lobed, and are long and narrow.

Pale agoseris

Mountain dandelion, *Agoseris glauca*

This yellow-flowered and dandelion-like species, also known as mountain dandelion, grows in open coniferous forests and sagebrush. It is also often referred to as false dandelion. The flowerheads are bright yellow, on leafless stalks, which rise from a rosette of fleshy bluish-green leaves. Like other members of the genus, the plant has milky sap.

Below: The flowerhead grows singly on the thick stem.

Distribution: Western Canada south to California, east to Minnesota.
Height and spread: 10–70cm/4–27½in.
Habit and form: Perennial herb.
Leaf shape: Narrow to lanceolate.
Pollinated: Insect.

Identification: The flowerheads are about 25mm/1in across, made up totally of ray florets. The leaves are up to 35cm/14in long, broader above the middle, and sometimes divided. The seed-like fruit is tipped by fine white hairs.

Left: The leaves are a waxy, bluish-green to dark green.

OTHER SPECIES OF NOTE

Desert marigold *Baileya multiradiata*
Often, large patches of desert are coloured a brilliant yellow with this plant's massed flowerings. It also grows at roadsides and is popular in gardens. A western species, it is mainly found in California and Texas. Stems are a soft, greyish-green, as are the leaves, and the plant grows to about 60cm/24in in height.

Arrowleaf balsam root *Balsamorhiza sagittata*
This has bright yellow flowerheads set against large grey-green leaves. It grows in grassland and open pinewoods, mainly in western hills and mountains. The roots were once used for medicine.

Philadelphia fleabane *Erigeron philadelphicus*
This very pretty flower is widespread in damp sites. The flowerheads, which appear from April to June, are pink and white, and daisy-like, the rays making a lacy fringe around the disc. The stems are hairy and can be tinged with purple.

Greeneyes, Chocolate flower, *Berlandiera lyrata*
Not only does this have a chocolate-coloured central disc, but it also smells of chocolate when the ray florets are plucked. It is a western species, common on roadsides and in grassy sites. The backs of the petals are strikingly streaked with brilliant red.

Heartleaf arnica

Arnica cordifolia

Shady woods are the habitat of this pretty alpine and mountain species, which flowers from April often right through to September. The heart-shaped leaves distinguish it from related species. Each plant normally bears between one and three open flowerheads with spreading florets.

Distribution: Alaska south to California.
Height and spread: 10–60cm/4–24in.
Habit and form: Perennial herb.
Leaf shape: Heart-shaped.
Pollinated: Insect.

Identification: The flowerheads, to 90mm/3½in across, each have 10–15 rays; the bracts have spreading hairs. The leaves are, to 12.5cm/5in long, and the seed-like fruit has a tuft of pale hairs.

Below: The erect stems are usually unbranched.

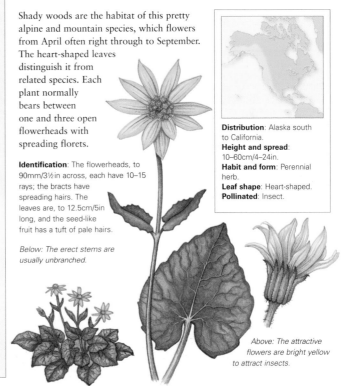

Above: The attractive flowers are bright yellow to attract insects.

Brittlebrush

Incienso, *Encelia farinosa*

At its flowering peak, from March to June, this attractive plant sometimes seems to be covered in a ring of bright yellow as the large flowerheads merge into one another. Its common name comes from the brittleness of its stems, which were chewed by Native Americans for the flavoursome resin they contain. Its fragrant dried stems were also used as church incense, hence another of its common names, incienso. This shrub grows in deserts and dry slopes and does well in cultivation.

Below: The flowers are borne along the main stem with the oldest flowers at the base.

Identification: The flowerheads grow well above the grey leafy foliage, and each is about 75mm/3in across with long yellow rays. The plant grows to a height of about 1.5m/5ft, and has a woody base and many branches. The oval-shaped leaves are silver-grey or whitish, and fragrant. The dried leaves may be burnt as incense.

Distribution: Mexico, California, Arizona, Utah.
Height and spread: 90–1.5m/35cm–5ft.
Habit and form: Perennial shrub or sub-shrub.
Leaf shape: Long, ovate.
Pollinated: Insect.

Above left: The capitula are about 35mm/1⅜in in diameter. Brownish disc florets develop, while the ray florets are bright yellow.

Common sunflower

Helianthus annuus

The famous sunflower is one the best known of all members of the daisy family. A common wild flower of fields and plains, it is also widely grown in gardens, in a range of cultivated varieties. It has a long history of cultivation and many traditional uses. Yellow, blue and black dyes were extracted and used by Native Americans, and the seeds yield valuable oil, still widely used today. It requires full sun to do well and at the bud stage, cultivated varieties exhibit heliotropism, where the face tracks the sun from east to west throughout the day. This is not exhibited by the wild sunflower, however.

Identification: Tall and leafy, with coarse stems, branching into several flowering stalks. Each flowerhead is 75mm–12.5cm/3–5in across. The edible fruits are seed-like and flat.

Above: The head of the sunflower is made up of numerous small florets. The inner disc florets mature into the fruit that contain the seeds.

Right: The plant can reach 3.7m/12¼ft in height, and is a familiar sight as it is widely cultivated.

Distribution: Throughout.
Height and spread: 60cm–3.7m/24in–12¼ft.
Habit and form: Annual herb.
Leaf shape: Ovate or heart-shaped.
Pollinated: Insect.

Below: The familiar, nutritious seeds are encased in an edible husk.

Jerusalem artichoke

Sunroot, Sunchoke, *Helianthus tuberosus*

This sunflower relative was also cultivated by Native Americans for its nutritious potato-like tubers, and these are still eaten today. The name 'Jerusalem' is actually a corruption of the Italian 'girasole' meaning turning to the sun. It is also known as sunroot or sunchoke, names that are derived from the original Native American word for the plant. It has rough branching stems and large golden flowerheads from August to October and grows naturally in fields and roadsides. It is tall and rangy, and its branches can break under their own weight.

Distribution: Mainly eastern, but also in the north-west.
Height and spread: 1.5–3m/5–10ft.
Habit and form: Perennial herb.
Leaf shape: Ovate to lanceolate.
Pollinated: Insect.

Identification: The flowerheads are about 75mm/3in across with 10–20 spreading rays, and narrow spreading bracts.

Left: The plant can grow up to 3m/10ft tall.

Left: The knobbly brown tubers have crisp white flesh.

OTHER SPECIES OF NOTE

Pearly everlasting *Anaphalis margaritacea*
The tightly clustered white flowerheads can be dried and then last a long time – hence the common name. It is widespread in fields and roadsides and forest clearings and flowers from June to September.

Chinchweed *Pectis papposa*
This western plant is found in western Texas, Mexico and southern California, mainly in deserts and sandy roadsides. The branching stems bear clusters of small yellow flowerheads that, when massed, have a strange lemony smell.

Plantainleaf pussytoes
Antennaria plantaginifolia
Dense, compact clusters of fluffy white flowerheads tinged with pink bear a fanciful resemblance to cats' paws, hence the common name. It grows in open woods and meadows, mainly in the east. The plant forms a dense mat of dark green or greyish leaves that are hairy underneath.

Tall ironweed *Vernonia gigantea*
This has tough, hairy, tall stems, generally unbranched except near the flowers. It bears loose clusters of blue-purple flowerheads that are pleasantly scented. The leaves are alternate, large and oblong or lanceolate. Another mainly eastern species of woods and meadows, it flowers from August to October.

Black-eyed Susan

Rudbeckia hirta

This is a widespread native of prairies, fields and open woodland. The stems are coarse and rough and the large daisy flowers are distinctive, with bright yellow spreading rays and a dark brown centre – hence the common name. The flowers appear from June to October. It is usually a biennial, flowering in the second year. *Rudbeckia* are quite popular as garden plants.

Identification: The flowerheads are to 75mm/3in across, the rays spreading out from the cone-shaped central disc. The leaves are to 17.5cm/7in long with coarse hairs.

Distribution: Throughout most of the region, except the far north.
Height and spread: 30–90cm/12–35in.
Habit and form: Biennial or short-lived perennial herb.
Leaf shape: Lanceolate to ovate.
Pollinated: Insect.

Below: The basal rosette of leaves will send forth flower stems in its second year.

Far left: The opening petals surround a brown eye.

New England aster

New England michaelmas daisy, *Aster novae-angliae*

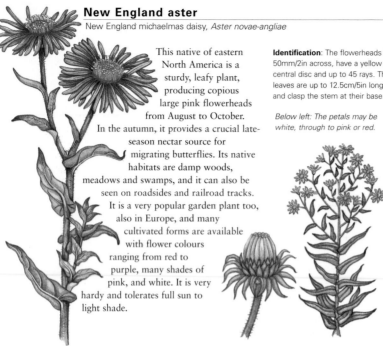

This native of eastern North America is a sturdy, leafy plant, producing copious large pink flowerheads from August to October. In the autumn, it provides a crucial late-season nectar source for migrating butterflies. Its native habitats are damp woods, meadows and swamps, and it can also be seen on roadsides and railroad tracks. It is a very popular garden plant too, also in Europe, and many cultivated forms are available with flower colours ranging from red to purple, many shades of pink, and white. It is very hardy and tolerates full sun to light shade.

Identification: The flowerheads to 50mm/2in across, have a yellow central disc and up to 45 rays. The leaves are up to 12.5cm/5in long and clasp the stem at their base.

Below left: The petals may be white, through to pink or red.

Distribution: Manitoba east to Nova Scotia, south to Georgia.
Height and spread: 90cm–2.1m/35in–6¾ft.
Habit and form: Perennial herb.
Leaf shape: Lanceolate.
Pollinated: Insect.

Left: The flowerheads grow in leafy short clusters.

Goldfields

Lasthenia californica (= *L.glabrata*)

This is a slender annual with reddish stems and golden yellow, flat flowerheads and narrow leaves. It favours wetland areas with dry summers, and can also be found in ditches and pond margins. It relies on pollinators, and as the disc florets open, they shoot out pollen to attract hummingbirds, flies, bees and butterflies. Goldfields often forms bright gold carpets under optimal conditions, from March to May. This is the most common of 20 species in the *Lasthenia* genus, and is found at the western edge of the Mojave desert, in chaparral, valley grassland, and scrubby areas.

Identification: The flowerheads are to 25mm/1in across each with about 10 broad rays around a conical central disc. The long leaves have stiff hairs at the base. The fruit is slender with pointed scales. Plants are 50mm–25cm/2–10in tall, and spread to a width of up to 45cm/18in.

Distribution: Oregon, Arizona and Baja California.
Height and spread: 10–25cm/4–10in.
Habit and form: Annual herb.
Leaf shape: Long, narrow.
Pollinated: Insect.

Above: The golden yellow composite flowerhead.

Far right: Goldfields is found in great swathes in springtime.

Mexican hat

Prairie coneflower, *Ratibida columnifera*

Distribution: Great Plains
and eastern Rockies, south
to Mexico.
Height and spread:
30cm–1.2m/12in–4ft.
Habit and form: Perennial
herb.
Leaf shape: Pinnate.
Pollinated: Insect.

The common name refers to the unusual
flowerheads which are shaped a little like
tall, broad-brimmed Mexican hats, with a
tall central disc. Another common name is
prairie coneflower. A flower of the prairies
and roadsides, it often flowers in swarms,
with thousands of plants blossoming at the
same time. The peak flowering period is
from July to October. Native
Americans brewed tea from the
leaves and made dye from the
flowers. It was also used to treat,
among other things, poison ivy and
rattlesnake bites.

Identification: The main feature is the
distinctive flower, which has a tall central cone
to 65mm/2½in high; each flowerhead is to
75mm/3in across with yellow or reddish
drooping rays.

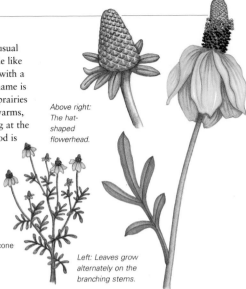

*Above right:
The hat-
shaped
flowerhead.*

*Left: Leaves grow
alternately on the
branching stems.*

OTHER SPECIES OF NOTE
New York aster (New York), Michaelmas daisy
Aster novi-belgii
This large aster is found throughout most of the
region, and another popular garden flower, with
many cultivated varieties having flowers ranging
from purple to pink, red, blue and white. The
wild form is usually a blue-violet. The flowers
appear in September and October and attract
much insect life.

Showy aster
Aster spectabilis
Found naturally
mainly in coastal
areas on sandy soil,
the showy aster is
short-stemmed and
has large purple flowers.
Like many asters it also grows well in
the garden.

Desert dandelion *Malacothrix glabrata*
This is a flower of the western deserts and
sandy plains. After rains it often flowers *en
masse*, its bright pale yellow flowers with red
centres colouring the landscape. The usual
blooming period is March to June.

Little golden zinnia *Zinnia grandiflora*
Another showy desert flower, with orange
centres, yellow flowers and broad rays. It is also
known as prairie zinnia and Rocky Mountain
zinnia, giving good indication of its preferred
habitats. Flowers cover this cushion-forming
plant from June to October.

Showy goldenrod

Solidago speciosa

Of the many species of goldenrod found in
North America, this is probably one of the
most impressive, with its waving pyramidal
clusters of small, bright yellow
flowerheads, opening from July to
November. It grows mainly on
sandy soils, often close to
brackish marshes and
saline pools.

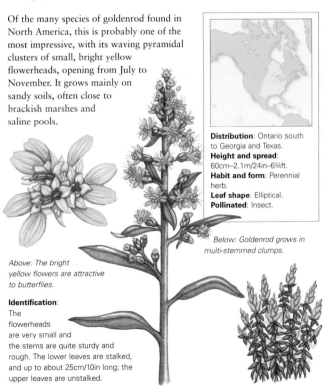

Distribution: Ontario south
to Georgia and Texas.
Height and spread:
60cm–2.1m/24in–6¾ft.
Habit and form: Perennial
herb.
Leaf shape: Elliptical.
Pollinated: Insect.

*Below: Goldenrod grows in
multi-stemmed clumps.*

*Above: The bright
yellow flowers are attractive
to butterflies.*

Identification:
The
flowerheads
are very small and
the stems are quite sturdy and
rough. The lower leaves are stalked,
and up to about 25cm/10in long; the
upper leaves are unstalked.

HONEYSUCKLE FAMILY

Plants of the honeysuckle family, Caprifoliaceae, are mostly woody, including vines, shrubs and small trees with a cosmopolitan distribution. There are about 16 genera and 420 species. The best known is the climbing garden honeysuckle, although it is a varied family with many ornamental shrubs, vines and occasional herbs in its ranks. The fruit is usually a berry.

Hobblebush

Viburnum alnifolium

Hobblebush is a common understorey shrub from north-eastern North America. It is usually found in high elevations, and is easily seen in the early part of the year when its leaves expand earlier than those of the canopy trees, allowing them to start photosynthesizing. These very large leaves are the plant's distinguishing characteristic. The bush produces white flowers in flat-topped clusters in late spring; the large, sterile outer flowers serve to attract insects and provide a landing area for them.

Identification: The shrub has an open, straggly habit and pendulous branches. It is thicket-forming, with roots developing on branches that touch the ground. The leaves are opposite, oval, simple, dark green, 10–20cm/4–8in long, turning yellow, orange, red or maroon in autumn. The fertile flowers are white, 4mm/³⁄₁₆in across, in flat clusters surrounded by 20mm/¾in sterile flowers, forming lacy heads up to 12.5cm/5in across. The berries that follow the small, fertile flowers are red, gradually maturing to purple-black in autumn. The lower branches often lie prostrate along the ground, making it easy to trip over – hence the name.

Distribution: North-eastern North America.
Height and spread: 1–3m/39in–10ft.
Habit and form: Deciduous shrub.
Leaf shape: Ovate.
Pollinated: Insect.

Above: The fruits darken as they age.

Bush honeysuckle

Diervilla sessilifolia

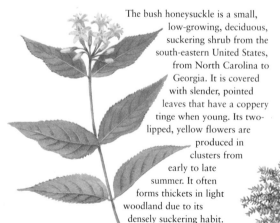

The bush honeysuckle is a small, low-growing, deciduous, suckering shrub from the south-eastern United States, from North Carolina to Georgia. It is covered with slender, pointed leaves that have a coppery tinge when young. Its two-lipped, yellow flowers are produced in clusters from early to late summer. It often forms thickets in light woodland due to its densely suckering habit.

Identification: The stems are brown and round, with striped bark. The leaves are opposite, simple and lance-shaped, up to 15cm/6in long, with a sharply serrated margin, smooth and dark green; the new growth is bronze-tinted. The tubular pale yellow flowers, 12mm/½in across, are borne in crowded 50–75mm/2–3in cymes. They form terminal panicles on the new growth in early to late summer, followed by fruiting capsules.

Left: The freely suckering habit means that it forms dense thickets among other shrubs.

Distribution: South-eastern USA.
Height and spread: 60cm–1.5m/24in–5ft.
Habit and form: Deciduous shrub.
Leaf shape: Lanceolate.
Pollinated: Insect.

OTHER SPECIES OF NOTE

Amur honeysuckle *Lonicera maackii*
A native to eastern Asia, but now one of the commonest shrubs in eastern North America. It is a large, upright shrub that keeps its small opposite leaves for most of the year. It has pale pink to bright red tubular flowers and bright red berries, the latter much beloved of birds and squirrels in the autumn.

Twinflower *Linnaea borealis*
This creeping, broadleaf, evergreen shrub, with rounded, opposite leaves, is actually circumpolar, occurring in northern Europe and Asia. It inhabits dry or moist sites in pinewoods. It bears fragrant, pink, bell-like flowers in pairs, from early summer to autumn.

Fly honeysuckle *Lonicera canadensis*
This erect, straggly shrub of open woodland in the north of the USA and Canada, has smooth, red branches and oval, slightly hairy leaves. The drooping, tubular, pale orange-red flowers, which appear in spring, are followed by characteristic double berries later in the season.

American elder
Sambucus nigra ssp. *canadensis*
This bushy, widely-spreading shrub forms dense thickets that bear sprays of attractive star-shaped, white flowers in spring and summer, followed by bunches of small, shiny blue-black, edible fruits. The leaves are divided into five to nine serrated leaflets.

Ledebour's honeysuckle

Lonicera ledebourii

This shrub is found throughout the coastal ranges of western North America, occurring from northern Mexico and California in the south to British Columbia and northward into Alaska. It forms an erect shrub that is notable for its paired orange flowers, which are surrounded by two broad bracts. The flowers are later replaced by two purple-black fruits; as they ripen, the deep red bracts enlarge around them. The plant is chiefly found in moist places below 2,900m/9,500ft.

Identification: A sturdy, erect, deciduous shrub with stout, usually smooth young shoots. The leaves, up to 12.5cm/5in long, are oval to oblong, with a pointed or rounded base, dull dark green above, lighter and downy beneath. The leaf margins are hairy and leathery, and the midribs are often arched. Funnel-shaped, paired flowers appear in summer from the leaf axils, heavily tinged orange or red with yellow tips and slightly protruding stigmas; behind them are two to four, purple-tinged heart-shaped bracts, which persist after the flowers drop and enlarge and spread around the fruits as they ripen to black.

Distribution: Western North America, from northern Mexico to Alaska.
Height and spread: 1.5–3.5m/5–12ft.
Habit and form: Deciduous shrub.
Leaf shape: Ovate-oblong.
Pollinated: Insect.

Snowberry

Symphoricarpos albus

Distribution: Alberta and Nova Scotia south to North Carolina and scattered elsewhere.
Height and spread: 30cm–1.2m/12in–4ft.
Habit and form: Deciduous shrub.
Leaf shape: Oval.
Pollinated: Insect.

The pure white waxy fruits give this plant its common name. The flowers are small, bell-shaped and pinkish-white and appear from May to July. In the wild it is found at roadsides and on banks. Snowberry is quite a popular garden shrub and looks very pretty, as its fruits remain well into the winter. Coralberry, *S. orbiculatus*, and wolfberry, *S. occidentalis*, have pink and greenish fruits respectively.

Left: The branching stems are dense and twiggy.

Far right: The pinkish tubular blossoms and long-lasting white berries make this a favourite ornamental shrub.

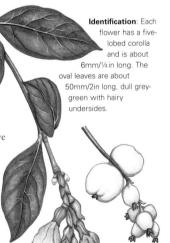

Identification: Each flower has a five-lobed corolla and is about 6mm/¼in long. The oval leaves are about 50mm/2in long, dull grey-green with hairy undersides.

DUCKWEED AND ARUM FAMILIES

The duckweed family, Lemnaceae, contains four genera and about 25 species of mostly perennial, aquatic, floating or submersed herbs. The arum family (Araceae) contains rhizomatous or tuberous herbs comprising about 105 genera and more than 2,550 species. They are characterized by a flower that is a fleshy spadix partially enveloped by a bract or spathe, which is sometimes brightly coloured.

Giant duckweed

Spirodela polyrrhiza

This is the largest of all North American duckweeds, with a large (compared with other duckweed species), rounded plant body. Its reddish-purple lower surface and multiple roots make it easy to distinguish from all *Lemna* species. New plants are produced in a budding pouch at the base or along the margin of the plant body; these may overwinter in the sediment as dense, rootless, starch-filled daughter plants (winter buds). Giant duckweed is found throughout the USA from sea level to 2,500m/8,200ft in freshwater ponds, marshes and quiet streams. It is also widespread in Central America, Europe, Africa, Asia and northern Australia. It is largely absent from South America, where it is mostly replaced by *S. intermedia*.

Right: The flowers are microscopic and rarely seen.

Identification: This small, floating aquatic generally occurs in clusters of two to five, in dense populations. Clusters of slender fibrous roots hang down from the lower surface. The plant body is 2–10mm/¹⁄₁₆–³⁄₈in long, oblong to round, flat; the upper surface is shiny dark green, the lower surface generally red-purple, with three to twelve veins visible in backlight; the flowers, rarely seen, are tiny, appearing in two lateral budding pouches, sheathed by minute membranes. The fruit is balloon-like, sometimes winged, containing a ribbed seed.

Right: The rounded plant bodies form dense colonies.

Distribution: USA, Central America, Europe, Africa, Asia and northern Australia.
Height and spread: Unlimited spread.
Habit and form: Floating aquatic.
Leaf shape: Leaves absent.
Pollinated: Water.

Skunk cabbage

Symplocarpus foetidus

This North American plant of wet woodland, marshes and stream banks is one of the first to bloom in spring, although its flowers are often partly or wholly hidden beneath the previous year's fallen leaves. Like many other dark-coloured flowers, skunk cabbage is pollinated mostly by flies. The flowers actually produce heat, which is, of course, a benefit to any early flies out in cold weather. The leaves emerge after the flowers and smell unpleasant when they are crushed.

Identification: The large leaves, 30cm/12in or more across, are oval, heart-shaped at the base, bright waxy green, appearing after the flowers have bloomed; they are highly malodorous when crushed. The flowers appear from late winter to mid-spring: the actual flowers are tiny, located on the ball-like spadix inside the hooded, purplish-brown and green spathe, which is 75mm–15cm/3–6in tall.

Above: The flowers often appear as soon as the winter snows melt.

Distribution: North America.
Height and spread: 30–60cm/12–24in.
Habit and form: Herbaceous perennial.
Leaf shape: Ovate.
Pollinated: Insect.

Below: The unpleasant-smelling leaves give this plant its common name.

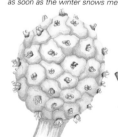

Jack in the pulpit

Indian turnip, *Arisaema triphyllum*

This common perennial has a wide distribution, stretching from Canada to Florida and westward to Kansas and Minnesota, where it can almost always be found near waterfalls or where water is running or splashing. Its large leaves, divided into three, radiate out from the top of the stalk and are usually the most noticeable feature, with the flowers mostly hidden beneath them. The flowers are enclosed in a green-and-purplish spathe and appear through the spring and into the summer. Later in the summer, the flowers are replaced by a black seed cluster that ripens to red.

Distribution: Eastern North America, Canada to Florida and westward to Kansas and Minnesota.
Height and spread: 65cm/26in.
Habit and form: Herbaceous perennial.
Leaf shape: Trifoliate.
Pollinated: Insect.

Centre right: The leaves are prominent.

Far right: A cluster of bright red, shiny berries appears from late summer.

Identification: The underground portion, usually referred to as the root but botanically known as a corm, is shaped like a turnip. The lower part is flat and wrinkled, while the upper part is surrounded by coarse, wavy rootlets. The leaves are basal, usually two, but sometimes one, each divided into three almost equal parts, 75mm–15cm/3–6in long. The flowering structure is irregular in shape, with a spathe up to 75mm/3in long, green with purple or brownish stripes, and a spadix covered with tiny male and female flowers.

OTHER SPECIES OF NOTE

Green dragon *Arisaema dracontium*
A herbaceous perennial reaching 90cm/35in, with one basal leaf, which is divided into 7–15 leaflets. The yellowish-green flowers are irregular in shape, first appearing in late spring and continuing into early summer. A very long, slender spadix extends far above the top of the sheathed spathe.

Flamingo flower *Anthurium scherzerianum*
Extremely well known in cultivation, the wild plant is restricted to moist forest areas of Costa Rica. Spotted green foliage gives rise to orange-red flower spikes, held out above the highly ornamental, bright red, waxy spathes. The plant may grow terrestrially in open areas or as an epiphyte in thick forest.

Arrow arum *Peltandra virginica*
An immersed plant that is found in swamps and marshes, most commonly along the Atlantic coastal plain. Its range appears to be actively expanding. Its leaves are arrow-shaped, clustered on long, succulent stems. Small, light yellow flowers, surrounded by a yellowish-green spathe, appear in spring and early summer.

Golden club *Orontium aquaticum*
A herbaceous perennial found in swamp areas on the Atlantic coast of North America. It has bluish-green leaves covered in a powdery bloom that causes the water to bead. In spring, tiny yellow flowers are borne on a spadix at the end of a white cylindrical stalk It is threatened in some areas of North America.

Swamp lantern

Yellow skunk cabbage, *Lysichiton americanus*

This common perennial plant is ubiquitous in the wetlands of the Pacific north-west. The large yellow spathes emerge very early in spring from a thick dormant bud and are extremely noticeable. The plants grow to 40cm/16in tall or more, with enormous, net-veined leaves. The pungent, skunk-like odour attracts various insect pollinators and is responsible for the plant's other common name, skunk cabbage.

Distribution: Pacific north-west.
Height and spread: 40cm/16in or more.
Habit and form: Herbaceous perennial.
Leaf shape: Ovate-oblong.
Pollinated: Insect.

Identification: The leaves are bold, oval to oblong, heart-shaped or straight at the base with wavy margins, smooth, green, soft-textured and prominently veined below. They are produced in loose rosettes, three to six per head, shortly after the flowers, ultimately appearing wilted, with a musky smell when bruised. The leaf stalks are short, pale, grooved above and winged. The bright yellow spathe is oval to lance-shaped, arising in late winter or early spring. The cylindrical spadix is short at first, lengthening in the fruiting stage. The fruits are green.

Left, right and above right: The yellow flowers of the swamp lantern are soon obscured by the large, cabbage-like leaves.

GRASSES, RUSHES AND SEDGES

The grass family, Poaceae (Gramineae), is one of the largest of the flowering plant familiess, with more than 665 genera and 9,500 species. The rush family, Juncaceae, is much smaller, with 10 genera and about 400 species. Many of these slow-growing plants superficially resemble grasses, but are actually herbs or woody shrubs. There are about 100 genera and 4,350 species of sedge (Cyperaceae).

Giant bamboo

Canebrake, Rivercane, *Arundinaria gigantea*

Occurring widely along rivers and streams in the southern USA, in well-drained floodplain forests, this bamboo has a broad tolerance for weather and soil. It grows from sea level to 600m/2,000ft and can withstand extreme temperatures of -20 to 40°C/-4 to 104°F. It spreads by large fast-growing rhizomes to make extensive colonies, and forms large dense stands called canebrakes in the floodplains of south-eastern rivers.

Distribution: Southern USA.
Height and spread: 60cm–4m/24in–13ft or more.
Habit and form: Woody grass (bamboo).
Leaf shape: Linear.
Pollinated: Wind.

Identification: Woody perennial and semi-evergreen smooth stems, 30mm/1¼in in diameter, emerge from the axils of strong, rapidly spreading rhizomes, forming dense stands. The leaves, borne on two-year old stems, are 75mm–20cm/3–8in long and 25mm/1in wide, with parallel venation, crowded at the tips. The flowers appear in early spring at irregular intervals of several years; panicles form on the branches on older portions of stem or directly from the rhizomes, consisting of a few racemes of large many-flowered spikelets. The fruit is a grain enclosed in the flattened spikelets.

Above: Giant bamboo's tree-like stems are a familiar sight in flood plain areas of the southern USA.

Left: Despite its giant proportions, the flower spikes reveal that this is a grass.

Right: The spreading rhizomes enable the development of dense, extensive colonies of giant bamboo.

Oreobolus pectinatus

This grass-like herbaceous perennial is common in the Pacific coastal regions of temperate America, with a wide distribution from the coast up to montane meadows at altitudes of 3,700m/12,000ft or more. It ranges from Washington State, east to Colorado and south to Texas in the USA, and grows widely in South America. It forms a tight, hummocky mass, flowering between late spring and late summer depending on latitude and altitude and in cooler climates it is more likely to be an annual.

Identification: This annual or herbaceous perennial grows with or without rhizomes, which are generally heavy with scale-like leaves where present. The slender stems are cylindrical or flat, erect or generally spirally twisted. The leaves are basal in loose sheaths, the upper sheaths generally bearing 50mm–20cm/2–8in blades that resemble the stem, well developed, cylindrical or flat, or reduced to a small point; short, firm appendages are often present at the blade-sheath junction. The flowers are generally terminal, although often appearing lateral, with three or six stamens and one pistil; the seeds are numerous.

Distribution: Washington State, Colorado and Texas, USA; South America.
Height and spread: 10–60cm/4–24in.
Habit and form: Grass-like herbaceous perennial.
Leaf shape: Linear.
Pollinated: Wind.

OTHER SPECIES OF NOTE

Abrupt-beaked sedge *Carex abrupta*
A grass-like herb found in coastal prairies, forests, meadows, slopes and wetlands of the USA to elevations of 3,500m/11,500ft. The separate male and female plants have sharply three-angled, solid stems, with spikelets generally arrayed in a raceme, panicle, or head-like cluster.

Globe flatsedge *Cyperus echinatus*
Occurring chiefly in upland prairies, sand prairies, glades, dry upland forests, pastures and disturbed sites, in the east and south USA, this species can be identified by its spherical flower clusters, red base, and short, knotty rhizomes, and by the long bracts that subtend the inflorescence, which appears in summer.

Fragrant flatsedge *Cyperus odoratus*
An annual sedge with oval flower spikes and elliptic to oval, light brown flower bracts, 6–24 per spikelet, which are splotched reddish with a conspicuous mid-vein, appearing from midsummer to autumn. It is found in wet, disturbed soils in tropical and warm temperate parts of south-western North America.

Shore rush *Juncus biflorus*
The shore rush is unusual in possessing leaf blades. It is usually found along sandy shores and ditches as single clumpy plants. The stiff, dark brown inflorescences occur at the stem tips in summer.

Big-leaf sedge

Ample-leaved sedge, *Carex amplifolia*

This grass-like perennial has one or more sharply triangular stems, which arise from long, stout, creeping rhizomes. The smooth, flat leaves are distributed evenly along the stems. A single spike of male flowers appears at the tip of the stem, and several female spikes appear on short stalks below, in summer. It is found in swamps, bogs and other wet places, from lowlands to moderate elevations in the mountains, from British Columbia to California, being frequent and locally plentiful in the western portion of its range.

Identification: The stems are coarse and stout, sharply triangular, usually tinged dark red towards the base, with some bladeless leaf sheaths, and with the dry leaves of the previous year present. The leaves are light to blue-green, 8–20mm/⁵⁄₁₆–¾in wide. The leafy bracts are slightly sheathing, the lowest usually surpassing the inflorescence of several elongated, well-separated, greenish-brown flower spikes, of which the male is narrow and terminal, and the females lateral, narrowly cylindrical, closely flowered, short-stemmed or stalkless.

Distribution: British Columbia to California.
Height and spread: 50cm–1m/20–39in.
Habit and form: Grass-like herbaceous perennial.
Leaf shape: Linear.
Pollinated: Wind.

Below: The tall flowering stems often form dense stands in marshy areas along its range.

Saltmarsh bulrush

Bolboschoenus maritimus syn. *Schoenoplectus robustus*

Distribution: Cosmopolitan in the Northern Hemisphere; South America; Africa.
Height and spread: Variable to 50cm/20in or more.
Habit and form: Grass-like herbaceous perennial.
Leaf shape: Linear.
Pollinated: Wind.

This grass-like perennial is one of the most widely distributed plants of the Northern Hemisphere, being more or less circumpolar in boreal and temperate regions. It occupies a wide range of habitats up to at least 3,000m/9,840ft and from just inside the Arctic Circle to Mediterranean regions. It has a scattered occurrence in South America and Africa and is encountered in various other warm parts of Eurasia. It is remarkable in its range of tolerances, from coastal marsh to dry rangeland, and is quite variable as a consequence, leading to its having been classified and re-classified by botanists under several synonyms.

Identification: A grass-like herb with creeping, branching, scaly rhizomes. The stems are solitary, tuberous, and swollen at the base, arising from rhizomes, three-angled, leafy below. The tapered leaves, to 35cm/14in long, exceed the stems; the sheaths are often membranous, the lower ones often lacking blades. A terminal inflorescence appears in summer, subtended by leaf-like, rough bracts, twice its length; it bears between one and 10 pointed brown spikelets, up to 30mm/1¼in long, stalkless or on arching stalks.

Right: The grass-like flowering stems of this herbaceous perennial are a common sight across much of the world, especially on brackish or saline shorelines.

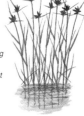

AGAVE FAMILY

*The agave family, Agavaceae, includes about 580 species in around 18 genera. The fibre sisal comes from
Agave sisalana, and other species yield liquors such as tequila and mescal. Poisons and drugs have been
made from extracts of some species. Agave hearts are a traditional sweet food for Native Americans.
Although called 'century plants', most flower after 10–30 years before dying, some producing suckers.*

Lecheguilla

Shindagger, *Agave lecheguilla*

Like many members of this genus, lecheguilla has very
sharp spines at the tips of its leathery leaves. It was a
serious hazard in the early days of exploring the south-
west – a hazard to horses and people alike, hence its
common name, shindagger. A plant not to be trifled
with! It grows mainly on rocky slopes, especially on
limestone, and spreads by suckers. Native Americans
used the leaves to prepare fibre for a variety of woven
products. Flowering is from May to
July, but like other agaves it may
take many years to build up
enough food reserves to
support flowering. After
flowering and producing
seed, the plant will die.

*Left: The rigid semi-
succulent leaves have short
marginal spines and a stout,
lethally sharp spine at the tip.*

Identification: The tall narrow
flowering spike grows up from
a basal rosette of pointed
leaves. Each flower is about
40mm/1½in long, yellow or
red with six segments. The
leaves reach about 50cm/
20in, and are straight or
gently curved, tipped with a
fearsome spine.

Distribution: Mexico, New
Mexico and Texas.
Height and spread:
To 3m/10ft.
Habit and form: Succulent
Perennial.
Leaf shape: Sharply pointed.
Pollinated: Insect (especially
moth) and hummingbird.

Sotol

Desert spoon, *Dasylirion wheeleri*

The dense tufts of narrow, spiny
leaves are distinctive of this species,
which grows on dry grassland and
rocky desert slopes. The leaves are
edged with teeth that curve
forwards, making them hazardous to
brush against. Features such as these
teeth, and the sharp spines of many
agaves, probably evolved as a
protection against grazing animals.
The flowering stalk is an impressive
height and ends in a tight cluster of
tiny greenish-white flowers.
This species does not die
after flowering. Its
attractive silver-green
leaves and dramatically
radiating leaf blades make
this a popular ornamental
plant among gardeners.

*Below: The stalk is
topped by a long
plume of flowers.*

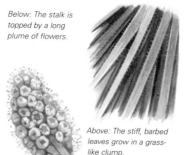

*Above: The stiff, barbed
leaves grow in a grass-
like clump.*

Identification: The flower clusters grow to
about 2.4m/8ft long, on a tall stalk between
2–5m/6½–16ft. The main flowering season is
from May to July. The rosette is made up of
hundreds of narrow leaves. The species is
dioecious – each plant has either only male or
only female flowers.

Distribution: New Mexico,
Arizona, west Texas and
Mexico.
Height and spread:
6.5m/21½ft high.
Habit and form: Perennial
evergreen.
Leaf shape: Long, toothed.
Pollinated: Insect.

Curveleaf yucca

Soft leaf yucca, *Yucca recurvifolia*

This spiky succulent shrub or small tree originates in the coastal regions of the south-eastern United States, where it forms a small branching plant or, with age, a colony of plants. Its large rosettes of curved leaves sit on top of a thick trunk, and once it reaches flowering size it produces large columns of white waxy flowers every year. The flowers, which are lemon-scented at night, are pollinated by *Pronuba* moths, which both pollinate and lay their eggs on the ovaries so that the caterpillars can feed on the seed. Some seeds survive this, and both moth and yucca depend upon each other for survival.

Distribution: South-eastern USA.
Height and spread: 2.5m/8ft.
Habit and form: Shrub or small tree.
Leaf shape: Strap.
Pollinated: *Pronuba* moth.

Far right: The rosettes of sword-like leaves often hide the short stem on young plants.

Left: The flower stem looks asparagus-like before the white blooms appear.

Identification: The stems of this shrub or small tree are sometimes branched, often leaning, with new upright branches emerging from the point(s) of contact. The leaves, up to 90cm/35in long, are green, grey-green or glaucous, nearly flat, rough on the underside, tapering to the tip, flexible, with a short brown or black spine at the leaf tip; the upper leaves are recurved. A loosely branched inflorescence appears from the centre of the leaves, usually in late spring but plants may occasionally bloom in autumn. The flowers, up to 75mm/3in across, are creamy, held above the leaves, with the inflorescence reaching 1.5m/5ft in height. The fruits are hard and dry at maturity, splitting open on the plant only as the *Pronuba* moths emerge.

OTHER SPECIES OF NOTE

Parry's nolina, Bear grass, *Nolina parryi*
This is one of about 25 species of this genus. It is native to Mexico, Arizona and southern California. It grows to about 4.5m/15ft with a flowering spike to about 3m/10ft tall with dense clusters of tiny cream flowers from April to June.

Blue yucca, Banana yucca, Datil
Yucca baccata
This plant's edible fruit is said to taste like sweet potato when baked. The flowers are also eaten in Mexico. The large whitish flowers are borne on a tall spike from April to July. The range is south-eastern California, Nevada, Utah, Colorado, Texas and Mexico.

Mojave yucca *Yucca schidigera*
Common in the Mojave Desert and nearby sites, this yucca flowers in April and May, producing broad clusters of balloon-shaped, almost spherical blossoms, which are white and generally purplish at the base. In about 15 years, the plant can grow up to 5m/16ft tall.

Palmer's century plant *Agave palmeri*
The typical rosette of leathery, pointed leaves are grey-green in colour with reddish-brown teeth. At the end of its life the plant sends out an immense flower spike, up to 6m/19¾ft in height, bearing branched clusters of green-yellow flowers. The plant is common in the dry, sandy grasslands of Arizona, New Mexico and north-western Mexico.

Our lord's candle

Spanish bayonet, *Yucca (=Hesperoyucca) whipplei*

This is one of the most impressive of all the yuccas, producing thousands of creamy white flowers with a purple tinge. When a group is in flower simultaneously it is a fantastic sight. Yucca moths are important pollinators of this and other yuccas. The moths not only gather pollen, they also lay their eggs with the pollen in the ovaries of other flowers, thus pollinating them. The moth larvae feed on some of the yuccas developing seeds. Stony chaparral country is the main habitat of this yucca.

Identification: The bell-shaped flowers, opening in April and May, have six segments and are about 40mm/1½in long. The leaves are about 90cm/35in long and are dangerously hard and sharp.

Distribution: Southern California and Baja California.
Height and spread: 1.2–3.3m/4–11ft x 1–2m/39in–6½ft across.
Habit and form: Evergreen woody perennial.
Leaf shape: Long, sharp-tipped.
Pollinated: Insect.

Above: The creamy-white, bell-shaped flowers.

Above: The seed developing inside the open flower.

IRIS FAMILY

The iris family, Iridaceae, contains perennial herbs growing from rhizomes, bulbs or corms. There are more than 90 genera and 1,800 species, occurring in tropical and temperate regions, but particularly around the Mediterranean, South Africa and Central America. The flowers of most New World Iridaceae occur as spikes at the top of branched or unbranched stems, each with six petals in two rings of three.

Tough-leaf iris

Oregon iris, *Iris tenax*

This herbaceous perennial from north-western USA is found in pastures, fields and open oak woodlands, although it is unusual in coniferous forests unless they have been logged. It has a wide colour range, from purple and lavender to white, cream and yellow. Where they occur, the handsome flowers provide brilliant colour displays along highways. The species name *tenax* is from the Latin for 'tenacious', referring to the tough leaves, which were once used by Native Americans to make strong, pliable rope and cord.

Identification: The leaves are green and linear, tinged pink at the base, growing as tall as or taller than the numerous flower stalks. The flowers, 75mm–10cm/ 3–4in across, appear in early summer, one to two at the top of short stalks 30cm/12in tall; they are palest yellow to lavender or red purple, with lance-shaped falls 25mm/1in wide, reflexed, with a white or yellow central patch, suffused with purple veins, and lance-shaped standards 10mm/⅜in wide.

Distribution: North-western North America.
Height and spread: 30cm/12in.
Habit and form: Herbaceous perennial.
Leaf shape: Linear.
Pollinated: Insect.

Left: Tough-leaf iris is an attractive plant that is often cultivated in gardens for its showy blooms.

Prairie blue-eyed grass

Sisyrinchium campestre

This herbaceous perennial is found throughout the tall-grass prairie regions of North America, on the sandy soils of open areas. It is especially attractive after a controlled burn, when it is more noticeable. When not in bloom, it easily can be mistaken for a grass because of its grass-like leaves. It sports lavender to violet blossoms in early summer: as with many small prairie plants, it blooms relatively early in the year to take better advantage of the sun. The seedheads are small and pea-like.

Identification: This fibrous-rooted, often tufted, herbaceous perennial is covered with a fine bloom. It is sometimes purplish at the base with mostly basal, linear, grass-like leaves up to 3mm/⅛in wide. The flower stems are narrowly to broadly winged, with one or several flowers borne terminally, subtended by a two-bracted spathe: the outer bract is up to three times longer than the inner bract, and its margins are united above the base. The flower is blue-violet with a yellow centre and six regular petals with broadly pointed or rounded tips, 15mm/⅝in long. The three stamens are united by their filaments around the three-branched style. The fruit is a rounded, straw-coloured capsule containing numerous black seeds.

Distribution: North America.
Height and spread: 10–45cm/4–18in.
Habit and form: Herbaceous perennial.
Leaf shape: Linear.
Pollinated: Insect.

Tiger flower

Tigridia pringlei

This bulbous perennial plant is native to Mexico and is most noteworthy for its large and brilliantly coloured iris-like flowers. The flowers are short-lived but flower in succession, one at a time on each inflorescence. The flower colours are quite variable and the ease of producing cultivars has led to this plant being widely cultivated both in the tropics and temperate regions. Consequently, it occasionally occurs outside its natural range as a garden escapee.

Distribution: Mexico.
Height and spread: 80cm–1.25m/31in–4ft.
Habit and form: Herbaceous perennial.
Leaf shape: Lanceolate.
Pollinated: Insect.

Identification: The basal leaves of this bulbous plant, which precede the flowers, are up to 50cm/20in long, lance-shaped, pleated and ranked alternately in a fan shape; the stem leaves are reduced to leaf-like bracts. On the flowering stem a few flowers are borne per spathe; they are large, showy, and shallowly cupped, with three outer, broadly oval, spreading segments 50mm–10cm/2–4in long, with stalk-like bases, orange, bright pink, red, yellow or white, variously spotted red, brown or maroon at the base; the three inner segments, alternating with the outer ones, are one-third as long, of similar ground colour but more distinctly marked. The staminal tube, 50–75mm/2–3in long, is erect and protrudes far beyond the flower cup; the anthers are erect and incurved.

OTHER IRIS FAMILY SPECIES

Copper iris *Iris fulva*
From the south-eastern USA, this iris grows in moist areas in wetlands and along bayous. The beardless, crestless, deep copper flowers bloom in late spring, and the bright green, sword-shaped leaves remain attractive all through the growing season. The flowers attract hummingbirds.

Yellow star grass *Hypoxis curtissii*
A herbaceous perennial growing in glades and open woods throughout the eastern and mid-western USA, mainly on the coastal plain in alluvial soil or wooded swamps. The yellow blooms, with six parts, first appear in mid-spring and continue into mid-autumn. There may be two to nine flowers, usually there are three.

Western blue flag *Iris missouriensis*
The western blue flag or Rocky Mountain iris is indigenous from south Dakota to southern California, reaching north to British Columbia. It is a perennial with pale lavender flowers that often emerges through snow in spring. It grows in sunny, open, moist areas such as meadows surrounded by forests, and is most often found in extensive, dense patches in moist meadows from the foothills to the mountains.

Pinewood lily

Propeller flower, *Alophia drummondii*

This lovely and interesting member of the iris family is native to the southern USA and Mexico. The plants grow from small, shallow bulbs and form loose colonies in sandy soils in lightly wooded areas. The velvety purple to red-purple flowers resemble those of *Tigridia* but they face to one side, unlike *Tigridia* flowers, which face upward. Each flower lasts only one day but the blooms open in succession. The plants are dormant in winter and flower from late spring until autumn.

Distribution: Southern USA and Mexico.
Height and spread: 15–40cm/6–16in.
Habit and form: Herbaceous perennial.
Leaf shape: Narrowly to broadly lanceolate.
Pollinated: Insect.

Identification: The leaves, rising from the oval truncated corm, are 15–30cm/6–12in long, narrowly to broadly lance-shaped and strongly pleated. The flowering stem, simple or forked, appears in spring, bearing a few-flowered terminal raceme subtended by two spathes. Each flower has three rounded outer segments, up to 25mm/1in long, and three narrow inner ones, 15mm/9⁄16in long; they are red-purple to indigo or violet, fading to white, spotted brown at the centre and on the claws, with margins inrolled to a central band of hairs.

Douglas's iris

Iris douglasiana

A pretty iris of the western coastal ranges, this species is found in open scrub and grassy slopes, mainly in the redwood areas, usually within sight of the ocean. It is occasionally found further inland, for example, in cleared woodland. The flowers appear from February to May and are purple, pink or white (rarely yellow), with contrasting veins. Clumps often are of a single clone and may be of considerable age.
This plant sometimes forms hybrids with other native irises.
The plant was first collected by a Scottish exporer, David Douglas, on land near Monterey.

Identification: The stems are branched and each bear two or three flowers. The flowers are on stems of about 30–60cm/12–24in high, with 70mm/2¾in cream to purple flowers.The leaves are shiny green above and duller green below, and about 25mm/1in wide.

Far left: Attractive as the plant is, it is highly unpalatable to cattle and has been considered a noxious weed by farmers.

Distribution: Central California to southern Oregon.
Height and spread: 15–80cm/6–31in.
Habit and form: Perennial herb.
Leaf shape: Linear.
Pollinated: Insect.

Right: The rhizomes spread slowly into a 60cm–1.2m/24in–4ft clump. Some clumps can be more than a century old.

Crested dwarf iris

Iris cristata

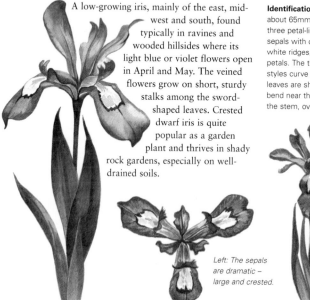

A low-growing iris, mainly of the east, mid-west and south, found typically in ravines and wooded hillsides where its light blue or violet flowers open in April and May. The veined flowers grow on short, sturdy stalks among the sword-shaped leaves. Crested dwarf iris is quite popular as a garden plant and thrives in shady rock gardens, especially on well-drained soils.

Identification: Each flower is about 65mm/2½in across with three petal-like down-curved sepals with crinkly yellow or white ridges, and three arching petals. The three two-lobed styles curve over the sepals. The leaves are short and broad. They bend near the tip and embrace the stem, overlapping each other.

Distribution: Massachusetts, Pennsylvania, south to Georgia and Arkansas.
Height and spread: 10–23cm/4–9in.
Habit and form: Perennial herb.
Leaf shape: Lanceolate.
Pollinated: Insect.

Left: The petals are small and crumpled, and coloured blue to lavender.

Left: The sepals are dramatic – large and crested.

Blue flag

Iris versicolor

This attractive plant is found in wetlands in the north and east. Its stems carry several violet-blue flowers, whose sepals are intricately veined in white, black and yellow. They open from May to August. The blue flag grows mostly in marshes, swamps and near the shore. It tends to grow in large clumps, spreading by means of thick rhizomes. The plant is toxic, and the rhizomes contain a glycoside that can also cause dermatitis. Blue flag is the provincial flower of Quebec. It is often grown in gardens.

Distribution: Newfoundland south to Virginia; mainly north-east of the region.
Height and spread: 60–90cm/24–35in.
Habit and form: Perennial herb.
Leaf shape: Lanceolate.
Pollinated: Insect.

Left: The plants often form spectacular drifts of blue in the summer.

Identification: The flowers are each 65mm–10cm/2½–4in wide, and the leaves are pale green or greyish. The fruit is a three-celled angled capsule, releasing large seeds that float and are transported by water.

OTHER SPECIES OF NOTE

Widow grass *Olsynium douglasii*
Closely related to blue-eyed grass and similarly narrow-leaved. It is a western species, found in grassy sagebrush and open woodland. It bears pretty reddish-lavender flowers from March to June. It is found in coastal areas, on prairies, in open rocky areas, oak and pine woodlands and in scrubby deserts.

Yellow flag *Iris pseudacorus*
This is a common European species that has escaped from cultivation and is now widespread, mainly alongside streams and in marshes. Its bright yellow flowers emerge from June to August. It spreads vigorously and forms large drifts of bright colour.

Ground iris, Bowl-tube iris *Iris macrosiphon*
Found mainly in the Coastal Ranges of California and in the Sierra Nevada foothills, in open grassy sites or wooded slopes. The large flowers may be purple, lavender or a deep golden yellow. Plants that grow in full sun often have very short stems.

Golden-eyed grass *Sisyrinchium californicum*
This is one of just a few yellow-flowered members of this genus. Its blooms are star-shaped and bright golden, opening from May to August. It favours damp sites near the coast, from British Columbia to central California. Individual flowers are short lived, but the plant produces many blooms though the summer.

Blue-eyed grass

Sisyrinchium angustifolium

Blue-eyed grass is a slender member of the iris family with wiry stems and leaves like grass. But when it opens its pretty bright blue flowers with yellow centres in spring and summer, it stands out from the surrounding grasses. It likes moist soils and partial shade and grows in prairies, damp meadows, marshes, low woods and shorelines. It is often grown in gardens and can spread by self-seeding, or division of the clumps. On the prairie it is subjected to alternating dry and wet conditions, and will also appreciate summer watering in the garden.

Identification: The flowers are about 15mm/⁹⁄₁₆in wide, with three petal-like sepals with pointed tips, and three petals; the sepals and petals are all bright blue. The leaves are very grass-like. Several species in this genus are similar.

Far right: The flowers appear from May to June.

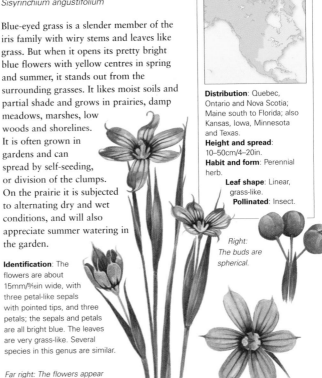

Distribution: Quebec, Ontario and Nova Scotia; Maine south to Florida; also Kansas, Iowa, Minnesota and Texas.
Height and spread: 10–50cm/4–20in.
Habit and form: Perennial herb.
Leaf shape: Linear, grass-like.
Pollinated: Insect.

Right: The buds are spherical.

LILY FAMILY

The lily family, Liliaceae, is a large and complex family, mostly consisting of perennial herbs that grow from starchy rhizomes, corms, or bulbs. It comprises about 290 genera and 4,950 species, including a great number of ornamental flowers as well as several important agricultural crops. Plants in this family have linear leaves, mostly with parallel veins, and flower parts in threes.

Rain lily

Copper zephyrlilyl, *Zephyranthes longifolia*

Like many desert plants, this species flowers quickly after heavy rains, bringing life to its sandy desert habitat, hence its common name. The usual flowering period is from April to July. Each stem bears a single yellow, funnel-shaped crocus-like flower. It requires full sun and is grown in gardens in warm regions; in cooler areas it is generally potted and enjoyed as a house plant. In cultivation, it will flower throughout the year if kept alternately wet and dry.

Right: The solitary flowerheads face upward, much like crocuses.

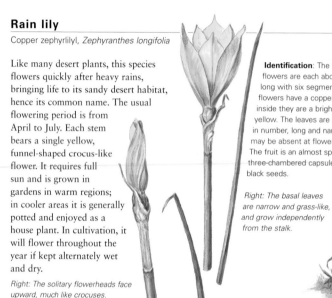

Identification: The individual flowers are each about 25mm/1in long with six segments. Outside the flowers have a coppery hue, but inside they are a brighter, clearer yellow. The leaves are few in number, long and narrow, and may be absent at flowering time. The fruit is an almost spherical three-chambered capsule containing black seeds.

Right: The basal leaves are narrow and grass-like, and grow independently from the stalk.

Distribution: Northern Mexico, north to west Texas and southern Arizona.
Height and spread: To 23cm/9in.
Habit and form: Perennial herb.
Leaf shape: Very narrow.
Pollinated: Insect.

Swamp lily

Crinum americanum

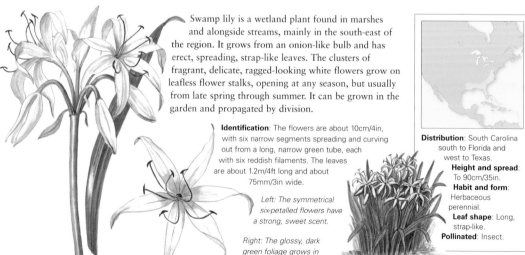

Swamp lily is a wetland plant found in marshes and alongside streams, mainly in the south-east of the region. It grows from an onion-like bulb and has erect, spreading, strap-like leaves. The clusters of fragrant, delicate, ragged-looking white flowers grow on leafless flower stalks, opening at any season, but usually from late spring through summer. It can be grown in the garden and propagated by division.

Identification: The flowers are about 10cm/4in, with six narrow segments spreading and curving out from a long, narrow green tube, each with six reddish filaments. The leaves are about 1.2m/4ft long and about 75mm/3in wide.

Left: The symmetrical six-petalled flowers have a strong, sweet scent.

Right: The glossy, dark green foliage grows in clumps.

Distribution: South Carolina south to Florida and west to Texas.
Height and spread: To 90cm/35in.
Habit and form: Herbaceous perennial.
Leaf shape: Long, strap-like.
Pollinated: Insect.

Easter lily

Atamasco lily, Zephyr lily, *Zephyranthes atamasco*

Growing upright from an onion-like bulb, this lily grows to about 38cm/15in tall and has several long, narrow basal leaves. The flower stalk is fleshy and topped by a single, upward-facing, lily-like flower, which is white at first, then ages to a pale pink. It grows mainly in the south-east, flowering in March and April. Both the leaves and bulbs of this plant are poisonous. It grows mainly in wet ditches and damp woods. It is an attractive species for the garden, especially for partly shaded sites. It should be transplanted when beginning to go dormant, into humus-rich soil, and kept moist in the growing season.

Distribution: Maryland south to Louisiana and Florida.
Height and spread: To 30cm/12in.
Habit and form: Perennial herb.
Leaf shape: Long and narrow.
Pollinated: Insect.

Below: The smooth single-flowered stem springs from an onion-like bulb.

Identification: Each flower is about 90mm/3½in wide, with six lobes that curve gracefully outwards. The long leaves are narrow and sharp-edged.

Left: The leaves are flat and grass-like, and just shorter than the stalk.

OTHER SPECIES OF NOTE
Spider lily *Hymenocallis liriosme*
The lily has unusual flowers with spidery white narrow segments spreading out from a membranous centre. It flowers in March to May and grows in marshes and ditches from Alabama, west to Texas and Oklahoma.

Red margin zephyr lily *Zephyranthes simpsonii*
This relatively rare species is native to the south-eastern states – mainly Florida. It flowers from February to April, producing white flowers, tinged red or purple outside. In the wild it is found in pinewoods, savannas and wet pastures.

Small camas *Camassia quamash*
The pale blue to deep blue flowers grow in a raceme at the end of the stem. Each star-shaped flower has six petals. The stems are between 30–90cm/12–35in long. The leaves are basal and have a grass-like appearance. The bulbs were boiled by women of the Nez Perce, Cree, and Blackfoot tribes.

Pinebarren deathcamas
Zigadenus leimanthoides
A poisonous plant that, like others in the *Zigadenus* (or star lily) genus, grows from a bulb and has long, slender leaves. The attractive, star-shaped flowers are yellowish-white, with six petals, and form clusters at the top of the stem.

Yellow star grass

Common goldstar, *Hypoxis hirsuta*

Very grass-like in its foliage, and easily overlooked among grasses, until it flowers. The star-shaped yellow flowers are often in groups of three at the tip of a hairy stalk. They open from March to September. Yellow star grass grows mainly in dry meadows, glades and open woods. In the garden this species is a good choice for a sunny border. It is very hardy and will also set seed and reproduce, and once established requires very little attention.

Distribution: New England, south to Florida, west to New Mexico, north to North Dakota and Saskatchewan.
Height and spread: 75mm–15cm/3–6in.
Habit and form: Perennial herb.
Leaf shape: Long, narrow.
Pollinated: Insect.

Identification:
The flowers are about 20mm/¾in wide, with six perianth segments and six stamens. The fruit is a pod containing several black seeds.

Left: The narrow leaves are covered in soft, straight hairs.

Far right: The slender flowering stems are usually shorter than the leaves.

Firecracker flower

Dichelostemma ida-maia

The bright crimson tubular flowers, tipped yellow, are highly distinctive and look a little like firecrackers. They dangle in a loose cluster from the tops of leafless stalks, opening from May through July. Firecracker flower grows in grassy spots, typically in woodland clearings. It is the only species in the genus that is pollinated by hummingbirds. It may be grown in gardens, although it is difficult to grow from seed – offsets from the corms are the best means of propagation.

Identification: The flowers are about 40mm/1½in long, the six segments are fused into a long red tube, tipped yellow-green. There may be 8–20 flowers on a single stem. There are normally three long, narrow, grass-like leaves at the base. The foliage appears in spring, then disappears during the May to July blooming period. The stem is narrow and twisted or curved rather than erect.

Far left: The delicate, vivid little red flowers are thought to resemble tiny firecrackers.

Distribution: South-western Oregon to north-western California.
Height and spread: 30–90cm/12–35in.
Habit and form: Perennial herb.
Leaf shape: Long, narrow.
Pollinated: Insect and hummingbird.

Left: The flowers are loosely arranged at the top of the slender, leafless stalk. The stalks rise from a clump of narrow, grass-like leaves.

Tiger Lily

Columbia lily, Oregon lily, *Lilium columbianum*

This is one of the west's most attractive wild flowers, but it is also rare, partly because of over-collecting for transplanting into gardens. It grows in coniferous woods, along forest margins and in meadows. The large, lantern-like orange flowers appear from late spring to early summer. The plant has has a beautiful and distinctive lily fragrance.

Above: The beautiful flowers dangle at the top of leafy stems.

Identification: Each flower is 50–75mm/ 2–3in wide with six yellow or orange petal-like purple spotted segments strongly curved back to the base; it has six stamens. The leaves are long and narrow, either scattered up the stem or arranged in whorls.

Below right: The petals curve back towards the base and have deep red or purple spots.

Left: The leaves whorl around the stem.

Distribution: Southern British Columbia south to California, Nevada and Idaho.
Height and spread: 60cm–1.2m/24in–4ft.
Habit and form: Perennial herb.
Leaf shape: Lanceolate.
Pollinated: Insect and hummingbird.

Rocky Mountain lily

Wood lily, Red lily, *Lilium philadelphicum*

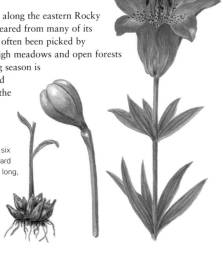

Once much more common, especially along the eastern Rocky Mountains, this pretty lily has disappeared from many of its traditional sites, partly because it has often been picked by visitors, or uprooted by gardeners. High meadows and open forests are its wild habitats and the flowering season is June to August. The red funnel-shaped flowers number from one to three at the top of the leafy stems. The bulbs of this plant can be cooked and eaten in the same way as potatoes.

Distribution: British Columbia to Saskatchewan and the eastern Rocky Mountains south to New Mexico.
Height and spread: 30–70cm/12–27½in.
Habit and form: Perennial herb.
Leaf shape: Lanceolate.
Pollinated: Insect and hummingbird.

Identification: Flowers to 65mm/2½in with six segments, orange-red with purple spots toward the base. The narrow leaves are to 10cm/4in long, in whorls toward the top of the stem.

Right: The flowers are erect, rather than pendulous, and have no fragrance.

OTHER SPECIES OF NOTE

Canada lily, Meadow lily, Wild yellow lily *Lilium canadense*
Clusters of up to 20 yellow or orange flowers appear from June to August in wet meadows and the edges of woods from Canada south to Georgia.

Cascade lily, Washington lily,
Lilium washingtonianum
This lily, found from Oregon south to the mountains of California, sports large fragrant white or pale pink trumpet-shaped flowers in June and July, and grows in open forests and brush. The plant can reach 1.8m/6ft tall. The stem may have up to five whorls of elliptical leaves.

Scarlet fritillary *Fritillaria recurva*
This fritillary is unusual in having red flowers. They open from March to July and are narrow, bell-shaped and streaked orange inside. Found from southern Oregon south to California and Nevada, the plant grows in dry bushy country. It is also known as scarlet mission bells.

Desert lily *Hesperocallis undulata*
In the deserts of southern California, Arizona and New Mexico, desert lily flowers from March to May. It has large white funnel-shaped flowers, which are blue-green on the back of the segments. The basal leaves are long and folded; the upper leaves are shorter.

Turk's cap lily

Lilium superbum

This species is the most impressive and largest-flowered of native lilies. With its spectacular array of up to 40 flowers on one plant, it is very popular with gardeners. It grows easily in damp garden soil and when established can reach more than 2m/6½ft tall. In the wild it grows in wet meadows, swamps and damp woods, mainly in the east. Native Americans used the bulbs to make soup.

Distribution: New York state south to Florida and west to Mississippi.
Height and spread: 90cm–2.1m/35in–6¾ft.
Habit and form: Perennial herb.
Leaf shape: Lanceolate.
Pollinated: Insect and hummingbird.

Identification: The perianth segments are strongly curved back, and the stamens protrude from the flowers. The base of each segment has a green streak, giving a star-like pattern at the centre of each flower. The fruit is a many-seeded capsule.

Left: The bright orange petals are heavily spotted.

Left: The leaves grow in whorls on the stem.

Large-flowered bellwort

Fairy bells, *Uvularia grandiflora*

This clump-forming, erect herbaceous plant likes moist woods in mountain regions, and is found throughout most of eastern North America except the extreme north. It is usually confined to calcareous or limestone soils, although it is relatively common where it does occur. The yellow, bell-shaped flowers, with six partially twisted sepals, are held singly at the end of branched stems that appear to pass through the twisted, bright green leaves. It has the peculiar habit of drooping limply while in flower, only to stand upright once fertilization has taken place.

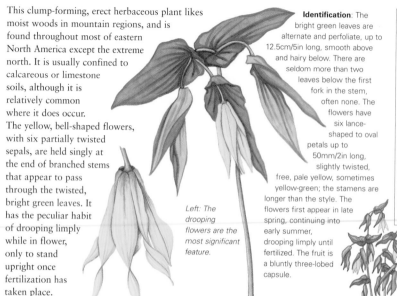

Left: The drooping flowers are the most significant feature.

Identification: The bright green leaves are alternate and perfoliate, up to 12.5cm/5in long, smooth above and hairy below. There are seldom more than two leaves below the first fork in the stem, often none. The flowers have six lance-shaped to oval petals up to 50mm/2in long, slightly twisted, free, pale yellow, sometimes yellow-green; the stamens are longer than the style. The flowers first appear in late spring, continuing into early summer, drooping limply until fertilized. The fruit is a bluntly three-lobed capsule.

Distribution: Eastern North America (except the extreme north).
Height and spread: 75cm/30in.
Habit and form: Herbaceous perennial.
Leaf shape: Perfoliate.
Pollinated: Insect.

Left: The drooping flower stems can form large clumps, or even drifts.

Yellow adder's tongue

Trout lily, *Erythronium americanum*

This distinctive plant is one of the earliest spring wild flowers in the eastern USA, ranging from New Brunswick to Florida and westward to Ontario and Arkansas, where it sometimes forms large colonies in damp, open woodlands. The leaves are distinctively mottled, with flowering plants always having two basal leaves. The solitary yellow flowers are often marked purple or brown, with six reflexed, petal-like segments.

Below: Yellow adder's tongue forms dense eye-catching colonies in damp woodlands.

Identification: The membranous, yellow-white bulb is tooth-like in appearance. The shiny leaves are basal, up to 20cm/8in long, in pairs, mottled brown and white, minutely wrinkled, with parallel, longitudinal veins. Yellow, nodding, bell-shaped flowers, up to 25mm/1in across, are borne singly, terminally, on a naked stem, from mid- to late spring. The six perianth segments, consisting of three petals and three sepals, are strongly reflexed, often brushed with purple on the outside and finely dotted within at the base; they have six stamens, shorter than the petals, yellow to brown anthers and a short-lobed stigma. The fruit is capsular, with a rounded or flat tip.

Distribution: Eastern USA.
Height and spread: 25cm/10in.
Habit and form: Herbaceous perennial.
Leaf shape: Lanceolate.
Pollinated: Insect.

Right: The bright yellow flowers rise over the basal leaves.

Narrow-leaved onion

Allium amplectens

This perennial North American onion is found in yellow pine forest, foothill woodlands, grassy summits or slopes and more occasionally fields, streamsides or creek beds up to 1,850m/6,000ft, ranging from British Columbia to southern California. It thrives in clay soils and is common where it occurs. The four narrow leaves are grass-like and easily missed until the open umbels of peach, rose or white florets appear in late spring or early summer. These become papery once they have opened and persist in this state until the seedpod develops. It has a strong onion smell.

Distribution: British Columbia to southern California.
Height and spread: 20–50cm/8–20in.
Habit and form: Herbaceous, bulbous perennial.
Leaf shape: Linear.
Pollinated: Insect.

Identification: The bulbs, up to 20mm/¾in across, are solitary or on rhizomes, reforming each year, dividing at the base into daughter bulbs. Two to four narrow, flat, basal leaves, shorter than the stem, become twisted with age. The numerous flowers are borne in a spherical umbel on slender stalks up to 15mm/⁹⁄₁₆in long; they have pointed, white to pink tepals, which become papery after opening, with shorter stamens, filaments broad at the base and yellow or purple anthers.

Below: The bulb, with its papery skin.

Above: The plant is attractive when in bloom.

OTHER SPECIES OF NOTE

Erythronium multiscapoideum
A native of shady wooded slopes in the foothills of the Sierra Nevada of California, this plant has become a popular garden plant and is one of the first western species to bloom, possessing white flowers with a yellow centre.

Beavertail grass
Calochortus coeruleus
A common sight in gravelly openings in woodlands at 600–2,500m/ 2,000–8,200ft, from Oregon to north-western California, especially in the Cascade Range and High Sierra Nevada. It has one long, persistent basal leaf and white or cream, blue-tinged flowers, held on an unbranched stem.

Sego lily *Calochortus nuttali*
The state flower of Utah has white bell-shaped flowers in umbels, and grows in dry country and across plains. The bulbs were once eaten in times of scarcity. The species name refers to Thomans Nuttal, the famous 19th-century Harvard professor and naturalist.

Clubhair mariposa lily *Calochortus clavatus*
Three large, butter-yellow petals form a cup-shaped bloom, which has an attractively marked centre characterized by the golden ring of 'hairs' around the dark brown stamen. The stalk is slender, smooth and branched. It is found in the foothills and chaparral of California.

Mount Diablo

Fairy lantern, *Calochortus pulchellus*

This plant from the western USA is found on wooded slopes and chaparral at altitudes of 200–800m/650–2,600ft, and is almost entirely restricted to the San Francisco Bay area. It grows in woodland and thicket vegetation, and the beautiful, nodding, conspicuously fringed, yellow flowers appear in late spring. The plant has one large basal leaf, longer than the stem, which withers around flowering time.

Distribution: San Francisco Bay Area, California.
Height and spread: 10–30cm/4–12in.
Habit and form: Herbaceous perennial.
Leaf shape: Lanceolate to linear.
Pollinated: Insect.

Identification: The erect stem is stout and usually branched. The basal leaf, 20–50cm/8–20in long, usually exceeds the stem. The two or three green leaves on the stem are up to 20cm/8in long and lance-shaped to narrow. The inflorescence is umbel-like, with one to many, nodding, globular to bell-shaped, deep yellow flowers. The sepals, not exceeding the petals, are oval to lance-shaped and pointed; the petals, up to 20mm/¾in long, are triangular, narrow at the base and sharply rounded at the tip, fringed, almost hairless outside, hairy within. The gland is deeply depressed, arched, bordered above by slender hairs; the filaments are flat, the anthers generally attached at the base. The fruit is an oblong, three-winged, nodding capsule.

Above right: The showy yellow flowers are conspicuously fringed and are borne singly or in bunches.

Left: Restricted to woody thickets near San Francisco, the beautiful, globe-shaped, yellow flowers are very distinctive when they appear in the springtime.

Large-flowered trillium

Trillium grandiflorum

This impressive flower, also known as white trillium or snow trillium, is the largest of the many trilliums and is therefore one of the most popular in cultivation. Each stalk is topped by a single large waxy white flower, turning pink with age. Native Americans used this plant for a variety of uses including medicinal. The leaves are edible and have been used as greens or in salads. Woods and scrub on rich soils are the natural habitat of this plant, whose flowers open from April to June. It is often found on steep slopes. Ants aid in the dispersal of its seeds.

Distribution: Nova Scotia south to Georgia and Alabama.
Height and spread: 20–45cm/8–18in.
Habit and form: Perennial herb.
Leaf shape: Ovate, pointed.
Pollinated: Insect.

Right: The flower and leaves perch on a tall naked stem. The flowers should never be picked although bulbs can be bought.

Above: The petals are enclosed within a pointed bud, and are fairly inconspicuous.

Identification: The flowers are to 10cm/4in across, with three green sepals and three large, white, wavy-edged petals. The six stamens have yellow anthers. The fruit is a many-seeded berry.

Western wakerobin

Trillium ovatum

The strange name for this trillium refers to its early spring first flowering period – about the time American robins arrive in the region after their winter migration. It is a low-growing species found in rich woodland, along streams or in boggy areas with partial shade. The single white flower is borne on a short stem growing out of the whorl of three basal leaves and turns a pinkish shade as it ages. This trillium is the provincial flower of Ontario. The flowers attract bees and produce green seeds in midsummer. The seeds have a sticky oily attachment that attracts ants, which carry off the seeds, eat the oil and then leave the seeds to germinate.

Distribution: British Columbia and Ontario south to California.
Height and spread: 10–40cm/4–16in.
Habit and form: Perennial herb.
Leaf shape: Ovate.
Pollinated: Insect.

Identification: Flowers are to 75mm/3in across, opening from February to June. The petals are white, but turn pink with age. The flowers may be erect or nodding and have no fragrance. The leaves are 50mm–20cm/2–8in long and unstalked. They grow in whorls of three just under the flower. The rest of the stalk is simple and leafless. It prefers moist ground.

Left: Petals are wide-spreading from the base and expose the entire pistil.

Above: The plant is not conspicuous until it blooms.

Wake robin

Trillium erectum

This highly variable upland plant of wet woodlands in eastern North America is one of the commonest eastern trilliums, being unique in this region by virtue of its diamond-shaped leaves, whorled in sets of three, which have a network of veins instead of the parallel ones typical of most members of this family. A solitary dark reddish-purple flower rises above the leaves, and is notable for its foul smell, which attracts the carrion flies that act as pollinators.

Right: Over time, loose colonies of plants form from underground rhizomes.

Distribution: Eastern North America.
Height and spread: 60cm/24in.
Habit and form: Herbaceous perennial.
Leaf shape: Ovate to rhomboid.
Pollinated: Insect, chiefly fly.

Centre right: Each flower has a distinctive arrangement of three maroon petals over three light green sepals.

Identification: The erect stem arises from a stout subterranean rhizome. The three leaves, up to 20cm/8in long, are whorled, stalkless, broadly oval to diamond-shaped and dark green. A single flower with three regular parts, borne upright or obliquely on a 10cm/4in flower stalk, appears in spring or early summer. The sepals, up to 50mm/2in long, are light green suffused red-purple, particularly at the margins; the petals, up to 75mm/3in long, are elliptic and pointed, spreading from the base or incurved, dark garnet to white or greenish-yellow. There are six stamens and a maroon ovary. The fruit is an oval reddish berry.

Toadshade

Red trillium, *Trillium sessile*

This trillium has the dubious honour of having a flower that smells of rotting meat. This is an adaptation to attract flies for pollination. The stalkless flower is dull coloured – green, brown and maroon – and appears directly above the three whorled leaves. Toadshade grows in rich soils in woodland, and, in places where it is common, the nasty smell can really pervade the air, especially in warm weather. It is in bloom from early to late spring and is common in the mid-west.

Below: Toadshade can be used in woodland wild flower gardens.

Distribution: New York south to Alabama.
Height and spread: 10–30cm/4–12in.
Habit and form: Perennial herb.
Leaf shape: Ovate.
Pollinated: Insect.

Identification: The flowers grow from underground rhizomes. They are about 40mm/1½in long, with three green sepals and three narrow red-brown or maroon petals. The erect flowers barely open, even in the peak blooming period. The unstalked oval leaves measure up to 75mm/3in long and are mottled shades of light and dark green.

Left: The flower remains closed for most of the blooming period, hiding the hermaphroditic parts.

ORCHID FAMILY

The orchid family, Orchidaceae, includes terrestrial and epiphytic, or saprophytic herbs comprising one of the two largest families of flowering plants (second only to the Asteraceae), with about 1,000 genera and 15–20,000 species. The epiphytic types all depend upon the support of another plant and are generally forest-dwellers. They include some of the showiest of all flowers.

Pink lady's slipper

Cypripedium acaule

This beautiful, showy orchid is one of the largest-flowered of native orchid species. It sometimes grows in profusion, when the mass flowering is an impressive sight indeed. It is mainly a woodland species, especially in pinewoods, but also grows on rocky outcrops. Like others of this genus, it is much admired by gardeners and is threatened in the wild. However, it is difficult to grow so should be left in the wild. It flowers from April to July.

Right: The fruit is a brown capsule that develops under the floral bract and contains thousands of seeds.

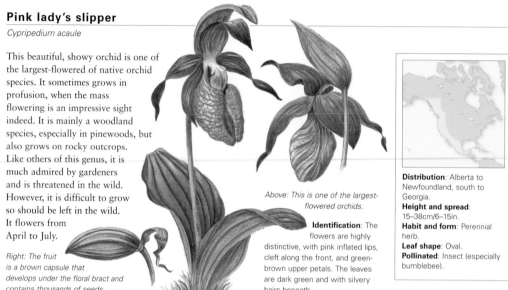

Above: This is one of the largest-flowered orchids.

Identification: The flowers are highly distinctive, with pink inflated lips, cleft along the front, and green-brown upper petals. The leaves are dark green and with silvery hairs beneath.

Distribution: Alberta to Newfoundland, south to Georgia.
Height and spread: 15–38cm/6–15in.
Habit and form: Perennial herb.
Leaf shape: Oval.
Pollinated: Insect (especially bumblebee).

Large yellow lady's slipper

Cypridium calceolus

This lady's slipper is well known in Europe and has a wide distribution in North America. It is mainly found inhabiting bogs, swamps and rich woods. Native Americans reportedly used the roots in a medicine to treat parasitic worms. The similar small yellow lady's slipper *(var. parviflorum)* has smaller, even more fragrant flowers, and is found mostly in wet limestone sites.

Identification: It has a leafy stalk with one or two fragrant flowers at the top. Each flower has an inflated yellow lip petal and two twisted greenish or brownish upper petals. The greenish-yellow sepals lie above (one) and below (two joined).

Right: A cross section of the yellow 'lip' petal, which is highly distinctive.

Below: The flowerheads are extremely showy. This is North America's most common orchid. It is also the easiest to grow.

Distribution: Alberta to Newfoundland, south to Georgia and in much of west.
Height and spread: 20–70cm/8–27½in.
Habit and form: Perennial herb.
Leaf shape: Oval to elliptical.
Pollinated: Insect (especially hawkmoth).

California lady's slipper

Cypripedium californicum

This species is one of the most attractive of the lady's slippers, and unusual in often producing several flowers on each plant, all facing the same direction. The flowers open between May and July and the plant is typically found along streams and in moist soil, in cool sites, often among ferns. It is a native of the western United States, and only found in Oregon and California's mountainous regions.

Identification: The lip petal is about 20mm/¾in long, white with a pink flush or purple spots. The upper petals are like the sepals and yellow-green in colour. The flowers are produced in the upper leaf axils.

Left: The stem and alternate, plicate leaves.

Right: The plant may be found growing in large clumps. Often there are about 12 blooms per stem.

Distribution: Northern California and south-western Oregon.
Height and spread: 30cm–1.2m/12in–4ft.
Habit and form: Perennial herb.
Leaf shape: Lanceolate, broad.
Pollinated: Insect (especially bumblebee).

OTHER SPECIES OF NOTE

Clustered lady's slipper
Cypripedium fasciculatum
This lady's slipper is found in mountain forests from British Columbia south to California and Colorado. Each stem has up to four drooping brown or green flowers and two broad leaves. When the flower goes to seed a capsule forms and the stem becomes erect. The sepals are purple-green, while and the lip is yellow-green streaked with purple. The small flower is pollinated by a tiny wasp.

Rose pogonia *Pogonia ophioglossoides*
This is an eastern species, of wet open woods, meadows and swamps. It has delicate rose-pink flowers that open between May and August and smell of raspberries. There is usually one flower per stem, although double flowers are known.

Dragon's mouth
Arethusa bulbosa
The dragon's mouth or swamp pink is a terrestrial orchid found in peat bogs, swamps and wet meadows in the north-east of North America. There is one grass-like leaf, and the pink or white flowers, appearing in early summer, offer no nectar to pollinators, despite being attractively coloured and sweetly scented, apparently deceiving inexperienced queen bumblebees early in the season. The plant's beauty has led to over collection.

Showy lady's slipper

Cypripedium reginae

This, the tallest and one of the most impressive lady's slippers, has large flowers with a broad pink lip. The flowers seem to float above the hairy foliage. It is threatened by collection and picking, but is still fairly common in certain places, notably around the Great Lakes. The glandular hairs that produce a skin rash give it some protection. It grows in damp woods and in swamps, especially on limestone. It is available from nurseries and will grow well in gardens, in cool, shady sites.

Identification: The lip of each flower is up to 50mm/2in long and broad, contrasting with the waxy white upper petals and sepals.

Below: The orchids are found growing in clumps.

Distribution: Saskatchewan east to Newfoundland, south to North Carolina; Missouri; mainly eastern.
Height and spread: 30–90cm/ 12–35in.
Habit and form: Perennial herb.
Leaf shape: Elliptical.
Pollinated: Insect (especially bumblebee).

Below: The lady's slipper became Missouri's state flower in the early 1900s.

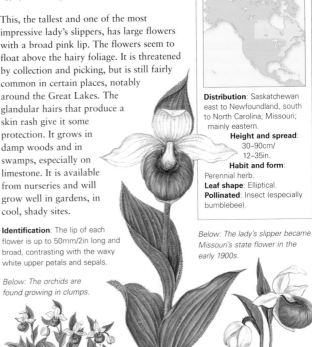

Grass pink

Calopogon tuberosus

Grass pink is a striking orchid, widespread mainly in eastern areas, and found in bogs and wet acid meadows, as well as on prairies. Its leaves are narrow and grass-like and the fragrant pink (or, rarely, white) flowers develop in clusters of up to 10, opening in sequence up the stem. The main flowering season is March to August, and even throughout the year in warmer southern sites such as Florida and Texas.

Identification: The pink flowers open from the bottom to the top of the stalk. They are about 40mm/1½in long and the lip petal is uppermost and bearded yellow. The flowering stems are leafless, and may reach 10–50cm/4–20in. Each plant has one grass-like basal leaf, from 10–30cm/4–12in long and 3–16mm/⅛–⅝in wide.

Distribution: Newfoundland west to Manitoba, south to Florida and Texas.
Height and spread: 15–50cm/6–20in.
Habit and form: Perennial herb.
Leaf shape: Long, grass-like.
Pollinated: Insect (especially bumblebee).

Left: The genus name Calopogon *is from the Greek terms 'kalos' and 'pogon' which mean 'beautiful beard' and apparently refers to the cluster of hairs on the labellum. The hairy lip attracts pollinators but the plant has no nectar to reward them. The labellum bends when a bee lands, thus dipping it in pollen on the column. If the bee is already carrying pollen, this will pollinate the grass pink.*

Calypso

Fairy slipper, *Calypso bulbosa*

Fairy slipper is the only species in this genus. It is well-named as it is a small species with a delicate, fairy-like flower and grows in shady magical sites such as damp mossy and fern-rich coniferous woods. In the southern part of its range it has been in decline for the last 30 years. Like many orchids, it does not transplant well and should never be collected. It flowers from May to July.

Left: Fairy slipper is a slender plant that is difficult to see on the forest floor or among grasses. It is in decline because it is frequently trampled or over-collected. The genus name Calypso *means concealment, and refers to the plant's preference for sheltered areas.*

Above: The bulbs will not transplant well, owing to the fairy slipper's dependence on certain soil fungi.

Identification: The flowers are to 50mm/2in long, with a white lip petal with purple patches, and a yellow beard. Above this are the three purple-pink sepals and two similar petals. The basal leaves are dark, glossy and ovate with wavy margins.

Distribution: Alaska south and east to Newfoundland; scattered further south; also in the west.
Height and spread: 75mm–20cm/3–8in.
Habit and form: Perennial herb.
Leaf shape: Ovate.
Pollinated: Insect (especially bumblebee).

Phantom orchid

Snow orchid, *Cephalanthera austiniae*

This strange, pale, almost leafless orchid stands out in ghostly contrast in the dark floor of its forest habitat. It has no green chlorophyll pigment and is therefore unable to synthesise its own nutrients; instead, it relies on absorbing nutrients from the rich humus of the forest soil with the aid of symbiotic root fungi. It is mostly found in dense coniferous forests, and flowers from June to August.

Distribution: California north to Washington State and east to Idaho.
Height and spread: 23–50cm/9–20in.
Habit and form: Perennial herb.
Leaf shape: Reduced, sheathing.
Pollinated: Insect (often self-pollination).

Identification: The pale waxy white flowers are in racemes of up to 20. Each flower is about 20mm/¾in long, the lip petal divided and tipped yellow. The leaves are much reduced and pressed close to the lower stem.

Left: The flower spike is extremely pale.

Below: The small leaves press close to the stem. The plant cannot photosynthesize so needs soil nutrients.

OTHER SPECIES OF NOTE
Spotted coral root *Corallorhiza maculata*
The commonest of the coral root orchids, this often grows in large colonies, in shady woods, flowering from April to September. The red or tan, tubular flowers have a white lip with vivid and distinctive pink spots. The plant grows to about 40cm/16in tall.

Early coral root, Pale coral root
Corallorhiza trifida
Found in moist deciduous and coniferous woods, early coral root has pale, nearly leafless stems and racemes of 5–20 equally pale flowers, from May to August. The plant is 80mm–15cm/ 3⅛–6in tall.

Striped coral root *Corallorhiza striata*
The striped coral root produces several red-purple stems with racemes of pinkish-yellow or white, red-striped flowers from May to August. It is found in deep, shady woods such as western cedar and fir forests.

Rosebud orchid
Cleistes divaricata
This plant is the sole representative in North America of this mainly tropical genus. It flowers from April to July in grassland and thickets, from North Carolina south to Florida. The flower is most characteristic, with long, narrow sepals and a pink cylindrical tube formed from the petals.

Texas purple spike

Hexalectris warnockii

Open woods are the habitat of this delicate species. It has a restricted distribution, but is locally quite common, for example in the Big Bend National Park in west Texas where there are four other species in this genus. The stems are slender, reddish-brown and almost leafless, and bear loose racemes of red-brown flowers from June through August.

Identification: The flowers are 25–30mm/1–1¼in wide, with three narrow sepals and two similar petals. The broader lip petal is upcurved with pinkish edges, a white or yellowish centre, three fringed ridges and a fringed maroon tip. The stems are maroon, and are more or less leafless.

Far right: The stems bear up to eight blooms, from June to September. Like many orchids and wild flowers, they are of conservational concern and should not be disturbed, even where found in large numbers.

Distribution: Arizona and Texas.
Height and spread: To 30cm/12in.
Habit and form: Perennial herb.
Leaf shape: Reduced.
Pollinated: Insect (mainly bee).

Elegant rein orchid

Piperia elegans

This mainly western orchid has many fragrant white flowers clustered in a raceme along a sturdy stem, and opening from July to September. The flowers are quite closely packed and the spurs are almost interlocking, giving the plant an unusual appearance. It grows mostly in shrub and coniferous forests. There are several closely related species, and inland plants are more slender, with flowers less densely clustered.

Identification: The plant grows from a tuber-like root. It has a single flower spike up to 50cm/20in high, covered in flowers. The sepals and upper petals are white with a central green stripe. The lip petal has a long, slender, almost straight spur that extends horizontally out from the back of the flower. The leaves are up to 25cm/10in long and about 50mm/2in wide. There are two to five leaves per plant. The slender stalk is leafless.

Right: The fleshy leaves are around 25cm/10in long and up to 50mm/2in wide.

Distribution: British Columbia south to central California and east to Montana.
Height and spread: 20–40cm/8–16in.
Habit and form: Perennial herb.
Leaf shape: Oblong.
Pollinated: Insect.

Above left: The flowers are hyacinth-like, creamy white and sweetly fragrant.

White fringed orchid

Platanthera blephariglottis

The white fringed orchid grows in damp and wet meadows, bogs and marshes, mainly in the east of the region. The classic habitat is on sphagnum-covered, sedge-rich sites with few or no shrubs. The name refers to the deeply cut fringe to the lip petal that gives the flowers a delicate appearance. It flowers from June to September, and the flowers have a faintly spicy fragrance. This attractive orchid is endangered over much of its range.

Identification: Flowers are about 40mm/1½in long, the upper sepal and two petals forming a hood arching over the lip. A long narrow spur projects behind each flower. The lower leaves are up to 35cm/14in long; the upper leaves are reduced bracts.

Left: Each flower has an extended spur to the back, and a distinctive fringed lip. The plant is hard to see when not in flower. The flowers are pollinated by moths at night.

Distribution: Ontario east to Newfoundland, south to Florida and west to Texas.
Height and spread: 30–60cm/12–24in.
Habit and form: Perennial herb.
Leaf shape: Ovate-lanceolate.
Pollinated: Insect (moth).

Centre left: Lower leaves are long and slender, while the higher leaves are bracts.

Yellow fringed orchid

Platanthera ciliaris

The flowers of this showy species are a deep orange or yellow, borne in clusters and opening from July to September. Each flower has a fringed lip that droops downwards. It grows in peaty and sandy wet woods, but also in meadows and on slopes. It often forms hybrids with white fringed orchids and others of the genus, making identification confusing where the species occur at the same sites.

Distribution: Rhode Island and New York south to Florida and west to Texas.
Height and spread: 30–75cm/12–29½in.
Habit and form: Perennial herb.
Leaf shape: Lanceolate.
Pollinated: Insect (especially butterfly).

Identification: The lip is 20mm/¾in long, and has a 40mm/1½in long slender spur that projects backwards. There are two broad side sepals. The lower leaves sheath the stem and are up to 25cm/10in long.

Above right: The leaves are alternate and can reach 30cm/12in in length. The leaves are dark and glossy.

Left: The colour and fringed lip make the plant very distinctive. The flowers are pollinated by insects.

OTHER SPECIES OF NOTE

Bog rein orchid, Bog candles
Platanthera leucostachys
This fragrant orchid of bogs and wetlands is a western species found from British Columbia southwards. It has a pale green stem with many small white flowers that seem to twine around it. The blooming period is June to September.

Round-leaved rein orchid
Platanthera orbiculata
This large-flowered species is also from the north-west. Each tall, erect flowering stalk carries up to 25 white or greenish-white flowers, between June and August. The large (up to 15cm/6in diameter), round leaves tend to lie flat on the ground.

Ragged fringed orchid *Platanthera lacera*
This is one of the more common fringed orchids. It is found from Manitoba to Newfoundland, south to Georgia, and west to Texas. Its whitish-green or cream flowers are arrayed in narrow spikes, from June to September.

Alaska rein orchid *Piperia unalascensis*
Found scattered south from Alaska, in dry woods and streamsides, this plant has pale green unobtrusive flowers in open slender racemes. The stalks are up to 70cm/27½in in height. Each plant has two to four narrow leaves, which fade as the flowers open. The blooming period is April to August.

Large purple fringed orchid

Platanthera grandiflora

A beautiful specimen, the large purple fringed orchid has many-flowered clusters of fragrant, deep lavender flowers, opening from June to August. It grows at the edges of swamps, on wet meadows and in cool, moist woods. Fringed orchids are pollinated by insects, especially (as in this species) by moths. As the moth feeds on the nectar in the spur it brushes against the anthers, which release sticky masses of pollen that adhere to the moth's body. Some of this pollen may then be transferred to another flower.

Identification: Flowers are 25mm/1in long, and the lip has three fringed lobes and a spur. The sepals and petals are all coloured a similar deep lavender. The lower leaves are long and sheath the stem; the upper leaves are small.

Right: The large purple fringed orchid depends upon fungi in forest soil to help it absorb nutrients.

Distribution: Ontario east to Newfoundland and south to Georgia.
Height and spread: 60cm–1.2m/24in–4ft.
Habit and form: Perennial herb.
Leaf shape: Ovate-lanceolate.
Pollinated: Insect (especially moth).

Left: The leaves partly sheathe the stem.

Stream orchid

Chatterbox, Giant helleborine, *Epipactis gigantea*

This orchid takes one of its names from the fact that the 'lip' and 'tongue' of the flower move when disturbed. Because each flower looks a little like an open mouth this adds to the effect! The green-brown and pink flowers appear from March to August. The favoured habitats are in damp ground, such as wet flushes, near ponds and alongside streams. Once it has found a habitat it likes, it can be abundant there, although in many areas it is rare. The orchid normally grows in dense patches. It can be grown in the garden, where it needs regular watering, and can be propagated by division. The plant lies dormant in the winter.

Distribution: British Columbia south to Mexico.
Height and spread: 30–90cm/12–35in.
Habit and form: Perennial herb.
Leaf shape: Lanceolate.
Pollinated: Insect (especially bee and wasp).

Above right: The leaves are alternate and clasp the stem.

Far left: The stream orchid will form dense patches, usually near water.

Identification: The flowers are 25–40mm/1–1½in wide with greenish sepals, two pink or purple upper petals and a two-lobed lip, the latter to 20mm/¾in long.

Showy orchis

Galearis spectabilis

Identification: Each flower is 25mm/1in long and has three sepals fused with two upper petals to form a pink or purple hood over the white, spurred lip. The leaves are up to 20cm/8in long and sheath the stem at their bases. The name Galearis is derived from the Greek 'galea', which means 'helmet' and refers to the shape of the sepals and petals.

Below: The plant favours the woodland floor.

Showy orchis is well-named as it has up to 15 beautiful pink and white (and, rarely, all white or all pink) flowers, borne from April to June on a short stalk from between two large, glossy leaves. The flowers appear before the leaves have fully developed. The flowers are also fragrant and contain rich supplies of nectar in their spurs. It grows around swamps and in rich moist woodland, especially beech and maple, usually in thick humus, and often with trilliums. It is one of the earliest orchids to flower in the spring, and colonies have been known to persist for decades at one site.

Distribution: Ontario to New Brunswick and south to Georgia.
Height and spread: 12.5–30cm/5–12in.
Habit and form: Perennial herb.
Leaf shape: Ovate or elliptical.
Pollinated: Insect.

Left: The seed head is distinctive.

Downy rattlesnake plantain

Rattlesnake orchid, *Goodyera pubescens*

Distribution: Ontario to New Brunswick and south to Florida.
Height and spread: To 45cm/18in.
Habit and form: Perennial herb.
Leaf shape: Ovate.
Pollinated: Insect.

The cylindrical white flowerheads of this eastern woodland orchid develop on woolly leafless stalks growing up from a basal rosette of decorative dark bluish-green leaves, from May to September. It grows in a range of woods – broadleaved and coniferous – and on dry or wet soils. Downy rattlesnake-plantain is distinguished from other rattlesnake-plantains by the bright silver markings on the leaves.

Identification: The flowers are small, only about 6mm/¼in long and hooded. The leaves are most distinctive, dark blue-green with prominent contrasting silvery-white veins and a broad stripe down the centre. The patterning is reminiscent of a rattlesnake's skin, hence the common names. The shape of the leaf is like that of the unrelated plantain.

Left: Goodyera pubescens spreads by rhizomes, but very slowly. It prefers shady sites.

Right: There is a distinctive broad silver stripe down the centre of each leaf.

OTHER SPECIES OF NOTE

Nodding ladies' tresses *Spiranthes cernua*
This is one of several species found in the east, this one from Ontario to Nova Scotia, south to Georgia and west to Texas. It has creamy white fragrant flowers and grows in damp meadows.

Hooded ladies' tresses
Spiranthes romanzoffiana
With its flowers arranged in spiral rows and the individual flowers hooded, this attractive plant grows scattered over most of northern North America, in damp, open habitats.

Small whorled pogonia
Isotria medeoloides
This rare orchid has the unusual habit of becoming dormant for 10 years or more between flowering. An eastern species of dry woodland, it has one or two yellow-green flowers on a greenish stem. The whorled leaves can reach 80mm/3⅛in in length, and 40mm/1½in wide. There are usually five leaves.

Broad-leaved twayblade *Listera convallarioides*
With a range from Alaska south to southern California and east to Newfoundland, and scattered further south, this is an unobtrusive, woodland orchid with small green flowers, open from June to August.

Greenfly orchid

Epidendrum conopseum

This is an epiphytic orchid, one that lives rooted on to other plants rather than in the soil (although epiphytes may root in pockets of soil on trees). It has grey-green flowers that are sometimes tinged purple, borne in a terminal cluster. It flowers throughout the year, but mainly January to August. The usual host trees are magnolias, live oaks and cypresses. This orchid is often found together with the epiphytic, resurrection fern, *Polypodium polypodioides*.

Identification: The flowers are about 8mm/⁵⁄₁₆in wide with a three-lobed spreading lip, and the leaves are smooth and sometimes purplish.

Distribution: Louisiana and Florida north to North Carolina.
Height and spread: To 40cm/16in.
Habit and form: Perennial herb.
Leaf shape: Long, elliptical.
Pollinated: Insect.

Left: The leaves are generaly green, but sometimes a purplish colour. They are elegant and elliptical.

Right: The orchid roots in the pockets of soil on trees or on to the tree itself.

WILD FLOWERS OF SOUTH AND CENTRAL AMERICA

Unlike North America, which separated from Asia relatively recently in geological terms, South America was an isolated continent for millions of years, having originally been part of the ancient super-continent Gondwanaland. South America's plants are closely allied to those of Africa and Australasia. When North and South America became linked, their combined flora formed some of the most diverse and spectacular plant communities on the planet, and the American continent is, botanically, the world's richest continent. The tropical and subtropical region covered in this chapter has an extraordinary range of habitats, including chapparal, rain and evergreen forests, arid deserts and grassy savannas. Of course, the flora of the region is particularly affected by the temperatures throughout the seasons, the intensity of sunlight, and day length, all of which differ markedly over the wide range of latitudes.

Above from left: Passion flower (Passiflora quadrangularis), *Royal water lily* (Victoria amazonica)
and White frangipani (Plumeria alba).

Mexico

Gulf of California

Gulf of Mexico

Belize

Guatemala

El Salvador

Nicaragua

Costa Rica

Honduras

Panama

Ecuador

Peru

Columbia

Cuba

Jamaica

Haiti

Puerto Rico

Domincan Republic

Guyana

Venezuela

Suriname

French Guiana

Brazil

Bolivia

Paraguay

Chile

Uruguay

Argentina

Pacific Ocean

Atlantic Ocean

Falkland Islands

BIRTHWORT, POPPY AND BOUGAINVILLEA FAMILIES

The birthwort family, Aristolochiaceae, contains about 500 species of woody vines or herbs. The poppy family, Papaveraceae, comprises 25 genera and 200 species that usually have milky or coloured sap. The Bougainvillea family, Nyctaginaceae, has about 390 species, mainly in the tropics and subtropics.

Giant Dutchman's pipe

Giant pelican flower, *Aristolochia gigantea*

This impressive vine was discovered by the explorer Carl Friedrich Philipp von Martius around 1820. It is a vigorous climber, which grows tall and produces huge, fragrant, fleshy and lemon-scented flowers. It is easy to grow in cultivation, and can even stand the occasional frost, although it does best under glass. It can be grown in a large pot and moved to shelter in cold weather. In subtropical or tropical regions it thrives outdoors and flowers from spring to autumn, attracting many insects, including butterflies.

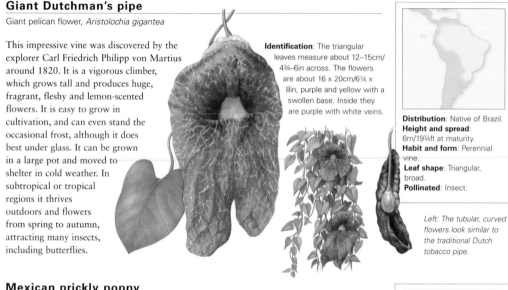

Identification: The triangular leaves measure about 12–15cm/4¾–6in across. The flowers are about 16 x 20cm/6¼ x 8in, purple and yellow with a swollen base. Inside they are purple with white veins.

Distribution: Native of Brazil.
Height and spread: 6m/19¾ft at maturity.
Habit and form: Perennial vine.
Leaf shape: Triangular, broad.
Pollinated: Insect.

Left: The tubular, curved flowers look similar to the traditional Dutch tobacco pipe.

Mexican prickly poppy

Goatweed, *Argemone mexicana*

This showy annual relative of the poppies can commonly be found in its native West Indies and Central America, and flowers throughout the summer. It has been introduced into many countries and is now a common weed in many tropical areas worldwide. It is usually found on rocky open ground, waste ground, and more occasionally on roadsides and by railways. Although it originates in a semi-tropical climate, it is remarkably well adapted to colder and drier conditions. All parts of the plant are poisonous but it is widely used as a medicinal herb.

Identification: A coarse, erect annual herb, sparsely to moderately branched and covered with prickles. The stems, 25cm–1m/10–39in tall, exude a milky sap that turns yellow on exposure. The blue-green leaves are oblong to lance-shaped, irregularly pinnately lobed and serrated, the edges crisply wavy and spiny. The upper leaves are alternate, stalkless, usually clasping the stem, with thorns along the major veins, which are white and prominent. The flower buds open to solitary, bright yellow or white, showy flowers up to 60mm/2¼in across, with numerous yellow stamens.

Distribution: West Indies and Central America.
Height and spread: 25cm–1m/10–39in.
Habit and form: Annual.
Leaf shape: Oblong.
Pollinated: Insect.

Above: The buds are rounded and sparsely prickly.

Right: Yellow flowers appear at the stem tips.

Pelican flower

Aristolochia grandiflora

Pelican flower is not hard to grow, requiring only partial sun, and it flowers from spring right through to autumn. It can even be grown in a hanging basket, when it looks most impressive. In the wild it often grows alongside rivers and streams. The structure of this imposing flower is complex, with a fleshy lobe leading to a bent tube and finally into an inflated chamber at the base.

Distribution: Mexico, Central America and the Caribbean, including Jamaica and Trinidad.
Height and spread: To 4.5–5m/15–16ft.
Habit and form: Perennial vine.
Leaf shape: Triangular, cordate.
Pollinated: Insect.

Identification: The solitary, fleshy flower is 20cm/8in across, as large as that of *A. gigantea*, and has a long thin, dangling appendage on the lower lobe. It is blotched purple, white, yellow, green and red, with an inflated pouch. It emits an unpleasant odour that attracts insects including butterflies. The leaves are large, about 20 x 15cm/ 8 x 6in and deep green in colour.

Centre left: The 30cm/12in-long, heart-shaped flower is adorned with an elegant, tapering tail. At the centre of the flower is a deep purple bull's-eye .

OTHER SPECIES OF NOTE

Bougainvillea peruviana
A native of Peru, Colombia and Ecuador. This plant has smallish flowers, usually pale magenta and wrinkled, and several varieties are available. It is unusual in having green-coloured bark.

Jarrinha
Aristolochia cymbifera
This native of Brazil is a climber that can reach up to 7m/23ft. It has grey-green leaves and unusual ivory white flowers that are mottled and veined maroon, with a beak-like lower lip. The plant's root is sometimes used in traditional medicine to treat digestive complaints and as a sedative, as well as for common skin problems such as eczema.

Rooster flower *Aristolochia labiata*
This South American climber is also a native of Brazil. It has broad heart-shaped leaves and huge 25mm/1in-wide flowers, which are mottled red, green, yellow and purple. This species is also commonly cultivated and can reach 6m/19¾ft. The flowers bloom from midsummer to autumn.

Calico flower *Aristolochia littoralis*
The calico flower of South and Central America has greenish-yellow to white flowers, with maroon veins and marbling and a darker throat. It is a vigorous climber, up to 3m/10ft and is ideal for greenhouse cultivation, flowering from June to August and doing best in partial shade.

Paper flower

Bougainvillea glabra

This native of Brazil is widely naturalized in tropical and subtropical regions, and is also commonly grown in conservatories. The common name refers to the papery flowers (actually thin bracts associated with the small flowers). The genus name celebrates the French sailor Louis Antoine de Bougainville (1729–1811). Each apparent flower has purple bracts with three small yellow true flowers in the centre. Several cultivated varieties exist, such as those with bracts of deep pink, purple, bright red, dark violet, coral, or pure white.

Distribution: Native of Brazil.
Height and spread: To 7m/23ft.
Habit and form: Perennial climber.
Leaf shape: Elliptic.
Pollinated: Insect.

Identification: The elliptic leaves are a paler green beneath, and pointed. The purple or magenta bracts (sometimes white) fade with age and sometimes persist after flowering.

Far right: The richly hued bracts make a vivid splash of colour.

Far right: The small true flowers are found among the coloured bracts.

WATER LILY AND PICKEREL WEED FAMILIES

The water lilies, Nymphaeaceae, contain aquatic plants in six genera and 60 species. They have showy flowers on long stalks, and are often considered the most primitive of flowering plants. In the New World there are some truly remarkable examples. The pickerel weeds and relatives, Pontederiaceae, are erect or floating aquatics. There are about 30 species, in nine genera, in the warmer parts of the world.

Pickerel weed

Wampee, *Pontederia cordata*

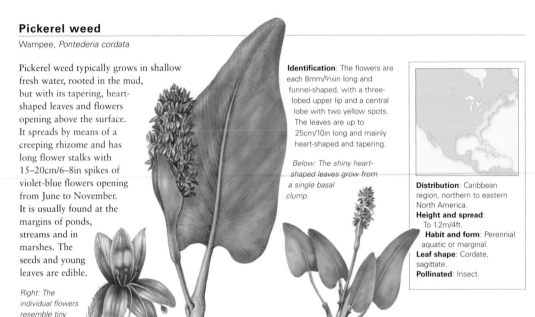

Pickerel weed typically grows in shallow fresh water, rooted in the mud, but with its tapering, heart-shaped leaves and flowers opening above the surface. It spreads by means of a creeping rhizome and has long flower stalks with 15–20cm/6–8in spikes of violet-blue flowers opening from June to November. It is usually found at the margins of ponds, streams and in marshes. The seeds and young leaves are edible.

Right: The individual flowers resemble tiny orchids.

Identification: The flowers are each 8mm/⁵⁄₁₆in long and funnel-shaped, with a three-lobed upper lip and a central lobe with two yellow spots. The leaves are up to 25cm/10in long and mainly heart-shaped and tapering.

Below: The shiny heart-shaped leaves grow from a single basal clump.

Distribution: Caribbean region, northern to eastern North America.
Height and spread: To 1.2m/4ft.
Habit and form: Perennial aquatic or marginal.
Leaf shape: Cordate, sagittate.
Pollinated: Insect.

Water hyacinth

Eichhornia crassipes

This notorious aquatic plant has a bad reputation because it is responsible for clogging waterways in many tropical regions, notably in areas to which it has been introduced, such as Africa and in the southern United States. However, it is also useful for removing pollutants from the water, such as excess nitrates and heavy metals, and with regular harvesting, the water quality will gradually improve. In its native South America it is generally less of a problem. It is a fascinating floating plant with beautiful spikes of lavender, funnel-shaped flowers and inflated leaf stalks to aid buoyancy. It grows in lakes, slow rivers, ditches and marshes and flowers from June to September.

Identification:
Each flower is 50mm/2in across and has six lobes, the upper lobe with an obvious yellow spot. The leaves are bright shiny green to 12.5cm/5in wide, with spongy bulbs at the base.

Distribution: South America.
Height and spread: Stalks to 40cm/16in above the water.
Habit and form: Floating aquatic.
Leaf shape: Round or kidney-shaped.
Pollinated: Insect.

Left: The showy lavender-coloured flowers form beautiful rafts of colour on lakes and waterways.

Royal water lily

Amazonian giant water lily, *Victoria amazonica*

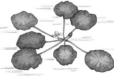

Distribution: Equatorial Brazil.
Height and spread: Stalks are 7–8m/23–26¼ft tall.
Habit and form: Aquatic perennial.
Leaf shape: Orbicular, extremely large.
Pollinated: Beetle.

This giant water lily was 'discovered' in 1801 and caused a stir when it was introduced to Europe in the mid-1800s. It is native to equatorial Brazil, where it grows from large, tuberous rhizomes in the calm waters of oxbow lakes and flooded grasslands along the Amazon River. Its gargantuan, glossy green leaves grow to 2.1m/6¾ft in diameter, with a pronounced maroon lip around the circumference. The lush, 30cm/12in flowers are variously white or pink on the same plant. They open at night, and have a pineapple fragrance.

Identification: The floating leaves, on long stalks, are 1.2–1.8m/4–6ft across, oval with a deep narrow cleft at one end, becoming almost circular when full grown, with the margin turned up all round, green above, deep purple below, with prominent flattened, spiny ribs, united by cross ribs. Round, prickly stalks bear solitary flowers 25–38cm/10–15in across, pear-shaped in bud, fragrant, with numerous petals; they open white on the first night, becoming pink later.

Left: The night-blooming flowers are spectacular.

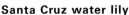

OTHER SPECIES OF NOTE

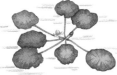

Amazon water lily
Nymphaea amazonum
Widely distributed throughout South and Central America, this water lily has creamy lemon-white, night-blooming flowers. The sepals are an attractive purplish-black, mottled with green-and-white stripes. The leaves are green, spotted purple-brown above, with purple-brown below.

Tropical blue water lily *Nymphaea elegans*
Found in ponds, ditches and cypress swamps in Florida, the West Indies and Central America, this water lily is a day-blooming aquatic perennial with immensely showy, fragrant flowers in hues of blue or violet, with intense yellow centres.

Nymphaea flavovirens
This is a vigorous water lily with ovate leaves that measure up to 45cm/18in across. Native to Mexico and South America, it has white, strongly fragrant flowers. There are more than 20 cultivars and hybrids of this species, with blue, yellow, pink and red flowers.

Night lily *Nymphaea gardneriana*
Another South American water lily, this species has rusty brown leaves that are mottled underneath. The flowers, measuring up to 15cm/6in across, are creamy-white with whorled petals. This is one of a number of species that flower mainly at night, and uses odour, rather than colour, to attract pollinators.

Santa Cruz water lily

Victoria cruziana

This giant water lily, only slightly smaller than *V. amazonica*, is found in the cooler waterways of Argentina and Paraguay, as it is more cold-tolerant. It has smaller leaves with a higher lip, which are generally green. The buds lack thorns on the sepals and the flowers are creamy-white the first night, becoming light pink the second night. In the autumn in cooler regions the leaves slowly disintegrate as the water cools down. Outside the tropics this species is best grown each season from seed.

Identification: The leaves are densely, softly hairy beneath. The rim measures up to 20cm/8in and is the tallest rim of all floating aquatics.

Distribution: Northern Argentina, Paraguay, Bolivia and Brazil.
Height and spread: Stalks are 1.8m/6ft long.
Habit and form: Aquatic perennial.
Leaf shape: Round.
Pollinated: Insect.

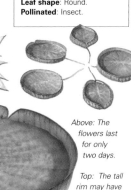

Above: The flowers last for only two days.

Top: The tall rim may have developed to prevent the leaves from overlapping.

CACTUS FAMILY

The members of the cactus family, Cactaceae, are mostly spiny succulents with photosynthetic stems, comprising about 130 genera and 1,650 species. Their leaves are generally extremely reduced and ephemeral or absent altogether. Most members of the family are native to the Americas, being found as far north as Canada and as far south as Patagonia.

Golden stars

Lady fingers, Lace cactus, *Mammillaria elongata*

The name *Mammillaria* is derived from the Latin word *mamilla*, which means 'nipple', and refers to the small tubercles (fleshy lumps or 'warts') on each cactus. This cactus from Mexico, where it generally occurs at altitudes of 1,350–2,400m/4,400–7,800ft, forms long finger-like branches that grow both erect and prostrate, creating club-like clusters. The many tiny, recurved spines are gold, and the small white to pale yellow 12mm/½in flowers are produced in spring.

Identification: A succulent plant forming many stemmed clusters. The stems are elongated, cylindrical and finger-like, 12–30mm/½–1¼in in diameter. The tubercles are slender and conical and the axils naked, or nearly so. The slender, needle-like radial spines are variable in number from 14–25, and are white to golden-yellow to brown, the degree of colouring varies from plant to plant. Pale yellow to pinkish 12mm/½in flowers, sometimes flushed pink or with pink midstripes, are borne in spring, followed by pink fruits, becoming red.

Right: The long finger-like stems are studded with white flowers in the early spring.

Distribution: Central Mexico.
Height and spread: 15cm/6in.
Habit and form: Spiny succulent.
Leaf shape: Absent.
Pollinated: Insect.

Texas prickly pear

Nopal, *Opuntia lindheimeri*

This North American cactus is a succulent shrub or subshrub that usually grows up to 1m/39in high, although it can sometimes reach higher than this, with a spread of up to 3m/10ft. In the wild it is found on rocky hills and mountain slopes in Texas, New Mexico and Mexico, up to 1,400m/4,593ft. It grows only two or three 'pads' high, with the pads covered with cushions of golden-brown barbed spines. In the summer, bright yellow, orange or dark red flowers are produced at the edges of the pads, and these are later followed by edible, purple fruits.

Identification: The jointed stems are flattened into green or blue-green, oval to rounded or (rarely) elongated pads, 15–25cm/6–10in long; the leaves are reduced to translucent yellow spines in all but the lower areoles, one to six per areole. The flowers are yellow, orange or red and showy, 50–75mm/2–3in across, and the fruit is purple with a white top, fleshy, egg-shaped or elongated, 25–75mm/1–3in long.

Distribution: Texas, New Mexico and Mexico.
Height and spread: 1 x 3m/ 39in x 10ft.
Habit and form: Spiny succulent.
Leaf shape: Absent.
Pollinated: Insect.

Left: The strange jointed stems form a low spreading shrub.

Far left: The showy flowers appear in summer and are followed by purple, edible fruit.

Crab cactus

Thanksgiving cactus, *Schlumbergera truncata*

This epiphytic cactus is native to a small region north of Rio de Janeiro in South America, confined to dense virgin forest between 1,000–1,500m/3,300–4,900ft. It usually grows on forest trees, by rooting into plant debris trapped among branches, or more occasionally on decaying humus in stony, shady places. The forests where it grows have distinct wet and dry seasons, although temperatures are fairly constant all year round.

Distribution: North of Rio de Janeiro, Brazil.
Height and spread: Up to 30cm/12in.
Habit and form: Epiphytic, occasionally lithophytic, succulent subshrub.
Leaf shape: Absent.
Pollinated: Insect.

Far right: The fleshy stems form a dense mass with flowers appearing at the tips.

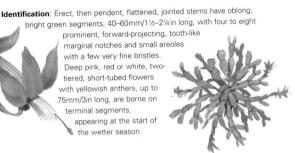

Identification: Erect, then pendent, flattened, jointed stems have oblong, bright green segments, 40–60mm/1½–2¼in long, with four to eight prominent, forward-projecting, tooth-like marginal notches and small areoles with a few very fine bristles. Deep pink, red or white, two-tiered, short-tubed flowers with yellowish anthers, up to 75mm/3in long, are borne on terminal segments, appearing at the start of the wetter season.

Leaf cactus

Barbados gooseberry, Gooseberry shrub, *Pereskia aculeata*

This climbing, leafy cactus is now seldom found truly wild. It is frequently grown as an ornamental or occasionally for its fruit in some tropical countries. In many areas it has escaped from cultivation and has become thoroughly naturalized. In 1979, its cultivation was banned in South Africa because it was invading and overwhelming natural vegetation.

Distribution: West Indies, coastal northern South America and Panama.
Height and spread: 10m/33ft.
Habit and form: Woody shrub.
Leaf shape: Elliptic.
Pollinated: Insect.

Identification: An erect woody shrub when young, it becomes scrambling, climbing or vine-like with age, with branches up to 10m/33ft long. The spines on the trunk are long and slender, in groups; those on the branches are short, recurved, usually in pairs, borne in the leaf axils. The deciduous, alternate, short-stemmed, waxy leaves are elliptic, oblong or oval, with a short point at the tip, 35mm–10cm/1⅜–4in long, sometimes fleshy. White, yellowish or pink-tinted flowers, 25–45mm/1–1¾in long, lemon-scented, with a prickly calyx, are borne profusely in panicles or corymbs. The fruit is round, oval or pear-shaped, 12–20mm/½–¾in across, lemon- or orange-yellow or reddish, with thin, smooth, leathery skin. It retains the sepals and a few spines until it is fully ripe.

Above: The curious fruits are initially leafy as they develop.

OTHER SPECIES OF NOTE

Rhipsalis capilliformis
This South American cactus has pencil-like, usually spineless stems that form many branched masses, hanging from trees or rocks. The stems have small areoles that produce numerous aerial roots with which they absorb atmospheric humidity. The flowers and fruits are both white and very small, appearing at the branch ends.

Queen of the night
Selenicereus grandiflorus
The queen of the night is a climbing vine-type cactus from Mexico and the West Indies, usually with five to eight ribbed stems and areoles bearing 6–18 yellow spines, which gradually turn grey. The body of the plant is covered with whitish felt and hair, and it is well known for its magnificent yellow-and-white, night-blooming flower, 30cm/12in across, which lives for only a few hours.

Cipocereus laniflorus
This rare cactus is found in a small region in south-east Brazil, from a single protected mountain site. Fortunately it is also grown in cultivation. It has golden-brown spines and its flowers and fruits are both covered in bright blue wax.

Coleocephalocereus fluminensis
This is one of six species of rocky outcrops in Brazil. The plant has ribbed stems, and the flowers and fruits develop in woolly structures at the top of the stems. Seed dispersal is aided by ants. This species is threatened due to urbanization.

Glaziou's arthrocereus

Arthrocereus glaziovii

Identification: The stems are short, cylindrical and ribbed, and densely covered in fine spines. The spreading white, scented flowers open at night. Each flower measures up to 60mm/2¼in long. The beautiful flowers perch on short, thick stems. They are very fragrant, and open at night to attract pollinating moths.

This genus has only four species, all endemic to Brazil. This species is only found in the wild in certain southern mountains of Brazil, although it is grown in cultivation and is sometimes available through specialist outlets. It is named for Auguste François Marie Glaziou, a 20th-century French plant collector in Brazil. Its habitat is on thin iron-rich soils and it is threatened by mining activities, although a few sites seem safe. It began to be grown soon after it was discovered in the 1880s and is not hard to cultivate, being propagated by cuttings. Like most cacti it needs to be kept out of frosts and watered only sparingly, in this case using only soft rainwater.

Distribution: Brazil.
Height and spread: Stems to 25mm/1in.
Habit and form: Spiny succulent.
Leaf shape: Absent.
Pollinated: Moth.

Right: The short finger-like stems grow in spreading clumps. They are extremely spiny.

Roseta do diabo

Discocactus horstii

Roseta do diabo grows wild in rocky savanna and thorny scrub. It is one of Brazil's most remarkable cacti with a squat habit, growing as if pressed into the ground. The ridged surface is covered in curved spines that act as wicks channelling dew towards the plant's tissues. The low-growing habit may have evolved as an adaptation to fire, which often occurs in the dry habitats. Over collection of this pretty cactus has caused it to be rare in the wild, but it is now partly protected in reserves.

Identification: This dwarf genus has a characteristic rounded, broad, flat stem with up to 20 prominent ridges. It grows close to the soil. The white flowers form at the woolly centre of the plant and are fragrant.

Distribution: Brazil, north-eastern Paraguay and eastern Bolivia.
Height and spread: 80mm/3¼in.
Habit and form: Spiny succulent.
Leaf shape: Absent.
Pollinated: Moth.

Far left: The white flower is spectacular, and grows atop a rounded, ridged stem. The flowers may develop fully in just one day. They are sweet-smelling and bloom only at night. Their scent attracts moths, which pollinate the cacti.

Golden ball cactus

Golden barrel cactus, *Echinocactus grusonii*

This must be one of the most impressive of all cacti with its rotund, almost cushion-like growth. Well-grown specimens look like stools but on close inspection are not to be sat upon, protected as they are by rows of sharply-pointed golden spines, in clusters of up to 15. In the wild it grows only in a river canyon in Mexico, where it is critically endangered, partly by construction of a dam. But it is widely cultivated and therefore familiar to lovers of cacti the world over. It requires warm sunny conditions on well-drained soil.

Distribution: Mexico.
Height and spread: To 1.5m/5ft.
Habit and form: Spiny succulent.
Pollinated: Insect.
Leaf shape: Absent.

Identification: Young plants are almost spherical, but gradually become barrel-shaped as they age. The flowers are modest – yellowish, toothed cups, produced only when the cactus has grown quite large.

Right: The ball-like cacti grow in tight clusters.

Left: The small yellow flowers are hidden in the wool at the top of the cactus.

Espostoopsis dybowskii
This plant is remarkable in being the only member of its genus, and is also unique in its shape – tall and tree-like with woolly cylindrical stems. It grows in north-east Brazil on hills and thorny outcrops. The flowers, which may be pollinated by bats, form among woolly outgrowths.

Melocactus pachyacanthus
This native of eastern Brazil grows happily on limestone outcrops. The small, white or magenta tubular flowers develop at the top of the stems on a raised cushion-like base. The plant grows to about 30cm/12in tall and may be 20cm/8in across.

Arthrocereus melanurus
This shrubby cactus from eastern Brazil grows to 1m/39in or more tall, branching at the base. Its stems are about 25mm/1in in diameter with 10–17 ribs and yellow-brown spines. The flowers are greenish-brown. Mining and urbanization have threatened the plant's habitat.

Arthrocereus rondonianus
Also from eastern Brazil, this species of cactus has a slender, ascending stem to 75cm/29½in tall, up to 18 ribs and green or golden-yellow spines. The fragrant pale lilac-pink flowers have hairy spines.

Schwartz's mammillaria

Mammillaria schwarzii

This species was discovered by Fritz Schwartz, lost, and then re-found in 1987 on a rock face in Mexico, where it is now critically endangered, mainly because of illegal collecting. As with many cacti it is widely grown by enthusiasts and is a beautiful species, producing many pale, yellow-centred flowers around the margins of the rounded, spiny plant. It needs good drainage, careful watering and high light intensity. The genus contains about 175 species, the majority native to Mexico. Many are grown, mainly for their impressive, often colourful flowers.

Identification: Cylindrical in shape and covered in spines. The central spines are white, with darker tips. The flower is white with red midveins, up to 5mm/³⁄₁₆in long and 12mm/½in in diameter. The fruit is red, and the seeds are black.

Distribution: Mexico.
Height and spread: To 30 x 35mm/1¼ x 1⅜in.
Habit and form: Spiny succulent.
Leaf shape: Absent.
Pollinated: Insect.

Left: In bloom, the cactus is studded with delicate flowers.

ELAEOCARPUS AND MALLOW FAMILIES

The Elaeocarpaceae contain mainly tropical and subtropical shrubs and trees, with around 12 genera and 350 species. The family includes a few useful timber trees and some ornamental plants, with a few species producing edible fruit. The Malvaceae comprises herbs, shrubs or trees in 75 genera and as many as 1,500 species. Members of the family are used as sources of fibre, food and as ornamental plants.

Chile lantern tree
Crinodendron hookerianum

In spring and early summer distinctive, long, lantern-shaped flowers are produced. They hang from shoots clothed with narrow, dark green leaves. In its native southern Andean-Patagonic region of Chile, it grows in open areas or under forest canopy, chiefly in regions with medium or high rainfall. The exact timing of flowering depends upon its location and altitude.

Identification: Straight, ascending branches, downy when young, become sparsely furnished and rangy with age. The leaves are opposite, 50mm–10cm/2–4in long, short-stalked, narrowly elliptic to oblong or lance-shaped, with pointed tips and serrated margins, usually curved downwards, glossy dark green above with sparse bristly veins and pinnately veined, paler and more downy beneath. The lantern-like scarlet flowers hang below the branchlets on red-tinted, downy flower stalks.

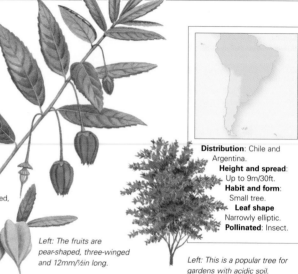

Left: The fruits are pear-shaped, three-winged and 12mm/½in long.

Distribution: Chile and Argentina.
Height and spread: Up to 9m/30ft.
Habit and form: Small tree.
Leaf shape Narrowly elliptic.
Pollinated: Insect.

Left: This is a popular tree for gardens with acidic soil.

Trailing abutilon
Abutilon megapotamicum

There are about 150 species in this tropical and subtropical genus, known as flowering maples or parlour maples due to the shape of the leaves. This species is a trailing shrub and grows wild in Brazil. The pendulous red and yellow flowers resemble miniature Chinese lanterns and produce a lot of nectar, making this shrub very attractive to insects. Cultivars include 'Variegatum', with mottled yellow leaves, and 'Wisley Red', with deep red flowers.

Identification: A hairless trailing shrub, growing to 2.5m/8ft long, with heart-shaped, sometimes lobed or toothed leaves to 80mm/3⅛in. The drooping flowers grow singly in the leaf axils and have a tubular red calyx to 25mm/1in long and yellow petals to 40mm/1½in.

Distribution: Brazil.
Height and spread: To 2.5m/8ft.
Habit and form: Perennial shrub.
Leaf shape: Cordate-lanceolate.
Pollinated: Insect.

Right: The seedhead.

Left: The climbing habit of this slender-stemmed shrub is ideal for gardens.

Nototriche compacta

This unusual species is one of the most
extraordinary of South America's wild
flowers, occupying one of the most
inhospitable of habitats in the world,
3,100–4,200m/10,200–13,800ft high in the
Andes of the south-west. To survive in this
harsh environment it
grows low as dense
cushions, clinging
tightly to the rocks to
avoid desiccation from
the cold dry
winds. Gardeners
keen on alpines
find this a
challenging species
to cultivate. The
seeds germinate
quite well but the
plant often becomes
'leggy' and less
attractive. To thrive,
it needs a sunny spot
and protection from
moisture. There are
about 100 species,
confined
to the Andes.

Distribution: High Andes of
South America.
Height and spread:
50mm–10cm/2–4in.
Habit and form:
Perennial, cushion-plant.
Leaf shape: Lobed.
Pollinated: Insect.

Identification: The
small lobed leaves are
silvery-white and softly
hairy. The flowers are white or
pale lilac and open in summer.

*Below: Nototriche compacta
grows in woolly mounds close
to the ground.*

Macqui

Aristotelia chilensis

This weedy shrub grows in damp, humus-rich soils on lower mountainsides by rivers in
southern Chile. It is a colonizer that quickly invades cleared forests and waste ground and
forms extensive stands. It is very abundant in areas of high rainfall, with distribution
between Illapel and Chilé, in mountain ranges, the Central Valley and the Archipelago of
Juan Fernandez. The young reddish shoots bear small, white flowers in spring and early
summer, followed by shiny, black, edible fruits in the autumn.

Distribution: Southern Chile.
Height and spread: Up to
5m/16ft.
Habit and form: Shrub or
small tree.
Leaf shape: Ovate.
Pollinated: Bee and other
insects.

Identification: On this evergreen shrub or small tree the
young shoots are reddish and the bark of older branches is
smooth, peeling off in long fibrous strips. The oval leaves are
50mm–10cm/2–4in long, shallowly toothed, opposite and
alternate, glossy dark green above, paler beneath and sparsely downy
on the veins, smooth when mature; the leaf stalk is reddish.
Greenish-white, star-shaped flowers, usually in three-
flowered axillary and terminal clusters, appear in
late spring and early summer, followed by
spherical black fruits, 6mm/¹/₄in in diameter.

*Far left: Macqui often forms extensive stands on
land cleared through logging.*

Right: The black, edible fruits appear in autumn.

PASSION FLOWER, BEGONIA AND COCOA FAMILIES

Passifloraceae include 575 species, mainly climbing lianes with tendrils. The begonia family (Begoniaceae) has about 1,000 species, also warm temperate and tropical. Members of both families are grown for their fruit and flowers. Cocoa is the most famous of 1,500 species of Sterculiaceae.

Granadilla

Passiflora quadrangularis

This is a familiar climber, with beautiful, complex flowers. Spanish missionaries are said to have seen symbols of the crucifixion in the flowers of members of this genus: the five anthers are the five wounds of Christ, the three-parted style represents the three nails and the central receptacle is the pillar of the cross, while the filaments of the flower suggest the crown of thorns. The fleshy roots and fruits are edible; the latter is often made into jam or used as flavouring for ice-cream. The species name refers to the square stems.

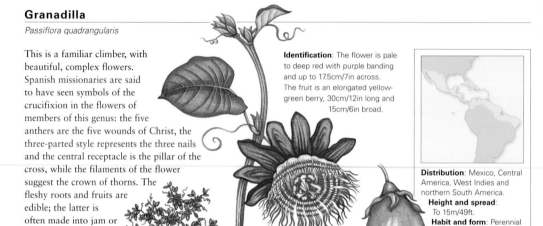

Left: This climber can grow to more than 15m/49ft.

Identification: The flower is pale to deep red with purple banding and up to 17.5cm/7in across. The fruit is an elongated yellow-green berry, 30cm/12in long and 15cm/6in broad.

Distribution: Mexico, Central America, West Indies and northern South America.
Height and spread: To 15m/49ft.
Habit and form: Perennial climber.
Leaf shape: Ovate-lanceolate.
Pollinated: Insect.

Lachay begonia

Begonia octopetala

This begonia grows wild only in Peru, where it is found on steep hills north of Lima that are affected by winter mist and fog. The wild stocks are endangered by habitat loss. This unusual begonia was first cultivated in 1805, and flowered in the Glasgow Botanic Garden in 1836. It is one of only a few frost-hardy begonias, but is rarely seen in cultivation.

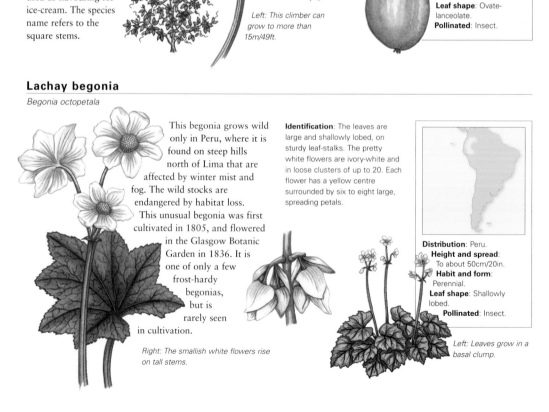

Right: The smallish white flowers rise on tall stems.

Identification: The leaves are large and shallowly lobed, on sturdy leaf-stalks. The pretty white flowers are ivory-white and in loose clusters of up to 20. Each flower has a yellow centre surrounded by six to eight large, spreading petals.

Distribution: Peru.
Height and spread: To about 50cm/20in.
Habit and form: Perennial.
Leaf shape: Shallowly lobed.
Pollinated: Insect.

Left: Leaves grow in a basal clump.

Cacao

Chocolate nut tree, *Theobroma cacao*

Distribution: Central and South America.
Height and spread: 5.5–12m/18–39ft.
Habit and form: Evergreen tree.
Leaf shape: Oblong.
Pollinated: Insect.

Right: Cacao is a small, understorey evergreen tree.

One of the world's most famous useful plants, cacoa yields medicines as well as cacao, which is used to make chocolate. Native to the Andean foothills it is now widely cultivated in the tropics for chocolate. The stimulating chemicals include theobromine and caffeine and hundreds of others, including some that slow the build-up of fatty deposits in arteries. Native South Americans used this plant long before Europeans arrived, and the seeds were valued and even used as currency. It was introduced to the West Indies in about 1525 by the Spanish, and reached Ghana (now the main producer) in 1879.

Above: The fruit contains five rows of seeds – the cocoa 'beans'.

Identification: The leaves are red-brown or green and 10–40cm/4–16in long. The small flowers are whitish-pink and sprout in clusters direct from the trunk. The large ribbed fruit is yellow, brown or purple and up to 30cm/12in long.

Handflower tree

Monkey's hand, *Chiranthodendron pentadactylon*

This remarkable plant takes its name from the unusual flowers, whose stamens look a bit like a hand. It is the only species in its genus. The flowers were regarded with awe by native people who gave the tree religious significance. It was also used in medicine, to treat eye disorders and haemorrhoids. The species became more well known after it had been introduced to Mexico towards the end of the 18th century.

Identification: The large solitary flowers grow opposite the leaves. There are no petals and the bell-shaped calyx consists of reddish leathery sepals. The 50mm/2in-long stamens are fused into a long tube, opening into five red anthers, which resemble a hand. The leaves have brown hairs on the underside.

Distribution: Mexico and Guatemala.
Height and spread: To 14m/46ft.
Habit and form: Evergreen tree.
Leaf shape: Lobed.
Pollinated: Bird and bat.

Below: The fruit is long, brown and woody, splitting into five lobes.

Right: This fast-growing evergreen tree can reach 14m/46ft.

NETTLE, DEADNETTLE, SPURGE, MARCGRAVIA, BRAZIL NUT AND MANGOSTEEN FAMILIES

The nettle family, Urticaceae, contains about 1,050 species, often armed with stinging hairs. Deadnettle, Labiatae, has about 6700 species, including herbs such as mints, while spurge, Euphorbiaceae, has 240 genera and 6,000 species, including herbs, shrubs and trees. The Marcgraviaceae contains about 110 species of tropical lianes or epiphytes. The Brazil nut family, Lecythidaceae, consists of 285 species of trees and shrubs. Mangosteen is one of the most famous fruits of the 1,370-strong Guttiferae.

Cannon-ball tree

Couroupita guianensis

Identification: The leaves grow to 30cm/12in, and the flowers have petals about 50mm/2in long, yellowish on the outside and red inside, with hundreds of closely-packed stamens.

It is the large, round fruits of this remarkable plant that give it its common name. This tropical American genus contains about four species, of which the cannon-ball tree is the best known. Racemes of yellow and red, waxy, sweet-scented flowers grow from the trunk and attract many different insect pollinators. A proportion of these flowers then develop into the large, characteristic fruits. Before ripening, the fruit pulp can be used as a drink, but later on the ripe fruits smell unpleasant (at least to humans). The tree also produces useful timber.

Right: The cannon-ball-like fruit can measure up to 24cm/9½in in diameter.

Distribution: Brazil to Panama; widely cultivated.
Height and spread: To 35m/115ft.
Habit and form: Tree.
Leaf shape: Lanceolate to ovate.
Pollinated: Insect.

Pineapple sage

Salvia elegans

Pineapple sage grows naturally in oak and pine scrub forests at elevations of 2,400–3,100m/7,800–10,200ft in Mexico and Guatemala. It is a semi-woody, sometimes almost herbaceous, subshrub, with soft, fuzzy leaves and bright red, two-lipped flowers arranged in whorls of four at the ends of the stems. It flowers in late summer and autumn, and can occasionally be found in warmer climates as a garden escapee, due to its popularity in cultivation. The bruised foliage smells like fresh pineapple, hence its common name. It is bird-pollinated and is especially popular with ruby-throated hummingbirds.

Identification: The plant has an open-branched, airy habit, with square stems on which the leaves are opposite; the branches also originate on opposite sides of the main stem. The leaves are softly fuzzy, light green and 50mm–10cm/2–4in long, oval to triangular, straight or heart-shaped at the base, with serrated margins. Ruby-red, two-lipped flowers, 25–50mm/1–2in long, are tubular with a hood-like upper lip and spreading lower lip. They are arranged in four-flowered, terminal whorls, on 20cm/8in spikes. It rarely sets seed outside its native range, due to a lack of pollinators.

Distribution: Mexico and Guatemala.
Height and spread: 1–1.5m x 60–90cm/39in–5ft x 24–35in.
Habit and form: Herbaceous perennial or subshrub.
Pollinated: Hummingbird.
Leaf shape: Ovate to deltoid.

Left: The felt-like leaves and bright red flowers make this a handsome specimen in late summer.

Peregrina, Spicy atropha

Jatropha integerrima

This spurge is an evergreen shrub or small tree with groups of bright red, star-shaped flowers and glossy foliage. Native to the West Indies, it is often grown in tropical gardens. It has also become established in south Florida. It attracts insects and hummingbirds.

Buddha belly plant, Bottleplant shrub

Jatropha podagrica

The common name is derived from the swollen stem. Native to Central America, it is a common tropical weed and is also easily cultivated. It needs a sunny spot and not much watering.

Purple dove vine

Dalechampia roezliana

A South American perennial that is found from Argentina to Mexico. Unlike other *Dalechampia* species, this small shrub has erect stems. It grows to 45cm/18in and has simple evergreen leaves. Its small, unshowy flowers are unusual in that each apparent flower is a cluster of small flowers, set between pink bracts.

Marcgravia brownei

One of several species in this genus of epiphytic climbers, this has shiny leathery leaves and clusters of upturned yellow flowers that attract hummingbirds, which pollinate the flowers as they feed. It produces ball-shaped red fruit.

Clusia grandiflora

This genus contains about 145 species of tropical American trees and shrubs. This species has large white flowers (male and female flowers separate), usually three or four at the end of a shoot. It is a shrub, with leathery leaves. The related balsam apple, *Clusia major*, is similar and often grown in cultivation. Bees visit the flowers and gather resin from them. They then use this resin to help them build their nests, and it has been discovered that the resin has anti-microbial properties and so helps keep the bees' nests free of disease.

Identification: The male flowers have a dense ring of stamens at the centre, surrounding a resinous mass of reduced stamens. The female flowers ripen into a round, woody fruit, about 12.5cm/5in long, opening to reveal the seeds, which have fleshy orange arils.

Below: The opened fruit is star-shaped.

Distribution: Guyana.
Height and spread: To 6m/19¾ft.
Habit and form: Shrub.
Leaf shape: Obovate.
Pollinated: Insect.

Below: The hard round fruit is pale green to whitish.

Artillery plant

Pilea microphylla

This small, brittle succulent is usually a prostrate herb. It grows from Mexico south as far as Brazil, in moist tropical forest edges and glades. It has very small leaves, tiny greenish female flowers and larger, pinkish, male flowers. It gets its common name by virtue of its 'catapult mechanism' for dispersing pollen. Its minute, lime-green leaves on short, arching stems give it a fine textured, fern-like appearance, and it quickly spreads to form quite large colonies.

Identification: The stems are succulent and densely branched, sometimes slightly woody at the base, spreading or tufted, 50mm–50cm/2–20in long. The leaves, crowded all along the stem on short leaf stalks, are oval to elliptic, 2–12mm/¹⁄₁₆–½in long. The upper leaf surface is crowded with elliptic hard cysts, the lower surface finely netted with veins, the margins smooth. Tiny green flowers appear all year round, in stemless clusters, followed by tiny brown fruits.

Distribution: Mexico to Brazil.
Height and spread: 15–45cm/6–18in.
Habit and form: Annual or short-lived herbaceous perennial.
Pollinated: Insect.
Leaf shape: Obovate.

Right: The brittle, arching stems quickly form a large, spreading colony of fern-like growth.

PRIMULA AND DOGBANE FAMILIES

Only one species of 1,000 known in the family Primula, Primulaceae, naturally occurs south of the equator, in South America. The 155 genera and 2,000 species of the dogbane family, Apocynaceae, are distributed primarily in the tropics and subtropics, with a good representation in the neotropics.

Mandevilla campanulata

This is a rare plant from Panama, from a genus of about 120 species of tuberous perennials from Central and South America. Several, such as Chilean jasmine, *M. laxa*, are grown in cultivation.

A number of hybrids and cultivars also exist. They are commonly grown in the tropics. Most have pink or white flowers but this one has attractive pale yellow blooms. This species is endangered in the wild, where its range is restricted to a small region of central Panama. It is therefore rarely seen. However, it has great potential as a garden plant or houseplant and this may save it from extinction.

Above: The pretty cultivar Mandevilla x amoena Alice du Pont *is a better-known relative of Mandevilla campanulata.*

Identification: A twining liana with milky sap and ovate leaves. The flowers are pale yellow and tubular, with a five-parted corolla.

Distribution: Panama.
Height and spread: To 4m/13ft.
Habit and form: Perennial twining vine.
Leaf shape: Ovate.
Pollinated: Insect.

Left: The flowers are sweetly scented.

Violet allamanda
Allamanda violacea

This evergreen vine or climbing shrub from Brazil has large, rich purple, funnel-shaped blooms, which appear throughout the year and fade to pink with age, giving a two-toned effect. The light green leaves are arranged in whorls on weak, sprawling stems. The plants exude a white, milky sap when cut, and all parts are poisonous. They are naturally found growing along riverbanks and in other open, sunny areas with adequate rainfall and perpetually moist soil.

Right: The seed is released throughout the year from a spiny capsule.

Far right: Allamanda climbs rapidly, smothering nearby vegetation.

Identification: An erect or weakly climbing, evergreen shrub with woody stems and green, hairy leaves, 10–20cm/4–8in, in whorls, usually of four. The leaves are oblong to oval, abruptly pointed, with the secondary veins joined in a series of arches inside the margins, downy above, more densely so beneath. The funnel-shaped flowers, 75mm/3in long, have a narrow tube and five flared, rounded lobes; they are rose purple with a darker throat. The fruit is a round, spiny capsule.

Distribution: Brazil.
Height and spread: Up to 3–6m/10–19¾ft high.
Habit and form: Evergreen scrambling shrub.
Leaf shape: Oblong.
Pollinated: Insect.

White frangipani

Plumeria alba

Distribution: Puerto Rico and Lesser Antilles.
Height and spread: 6 x 4m/ 19¾ x 13ft.
Habit and form: Small tree.
Leaf shape: Lanceolate.
Pollinated: Insect.

Frangipani is well known throughout the tropics and has long been cultivated for its intensely fragrant, lovely, spiral-shaped blooms, which appear at the branch tips from early summer to late autumn. Originating from Puerto Rico and the Lesser Antilles, the tree is unusual in appearance, with long, coarse, deciduous leaves clustered only at the tips of the rough, thick, sausage-like, grey-green branches. The branches are upright and crowded on the trunk, forming a vase or umbrella shape with age. They are brittle although usually sturdy, exuding a milky sap when they are bruised or punctured.

Identification: The glossy, dark green leaves, 30cm/12in or more long, are alternate and lance-shaped, often blistered, with prominent feathered veining, usually finely hairy beneath. The fragrant, showy flowers are white with yellow centres, usually borne on bare branches in terminal clusters, with five spreading petals, up to 60mm/2¼in across, and a tubular base up to 25mm/1in long. They are followed by hard brown fruits up to 15cm/6in long.

Above: The five-petalled flowerhead.

Far left: The tree has a uniform round crown.

OTHER SPECIES OF NOTE

West Indian jasmine *Plumeria rubra*
This small tree is native to dry, rocky habitats in southern Mexico and grows as far south as Costa Rica. Its thick, succulent stems, clusters of leathery leaves and abundant, fragrant blooms in red, pink, yellow or white have led to it being widely planted across the tropics.

Primula magellanica
This is the only *Primula* species found south of the equator, in southern South America. It spends the winter as a resting bud; the white flowers, with a yellow eye, appear in spring, in a cluster of flowers atop an erect stem. The plant prefers damp woodland.

Golden trumpet *Allamanda cathartica*
The golden-yellow, white-throated tubular flowers are very large in some cultivated forms of this plant. It climbs and clambers to 6m/ 19¾ft. It has become naturalized in many tropical areas, but can sometimes be a troublesome (though attractive) weed.

Chilean jasmine *Mandevilla laxa*
This Argentine climber grows to about 4m/13ft tall and has glossy heart-shaped leaves with a purplish underside. Its abundant trumpet-shaped flowers are white or ivory, and highly fragrant. Its long seed pods contain fluffy seeds that readily self-sow.

Brazilian jasmine

Pink allamanda, *Mandevilla splendens*

Distribution: South-eastern Brazil.
Height and spread: 6m/19¾ft.
Habit and form: Twining, evergreen shrub.
Leaf shape: Broadly elliptic.
Pollinated: Insect.

This attractive, evergreen vine chiefly occurs in the wild at altitudes of around 900m/ 2,950ft in the Organ mountains near Rio de Janeiro. It is endowed with beautiful, large, deep pink, funnel-shaped blooms, which are highly visible against the large, downy, dark green, evergreen leaves. Pink allamanda has become popular as a garden plant in many countries and is sometimes found as a garden escapee in warmer climates.

Identification: The stems of this evergreen, twining shrub or liana are initially downy and green, later woody, and exude a milky sap when broken. The fine-textured, downy leaves, up to 20cm/8in long, are opposite, broadly elliptic with a pointed tip and heart-shaped base, with feathered veining and a wavy margin. Fragrant, trumpet-shaped, yellow-centred, rose-pink flowers, 75mm–10cm/ 3–4in across, appear all year round in lateral racemes of three to five; they have five spreading, abruptly pointed petals. The fruits are paired, brown, cylindrical follicles, which are inconspicuous.

Left and right: The pink, showy flowers are produced almost every month of the year.

CAPER, NASTURTIUM AND PEA FAMILIES

The caper family, Capparidaceae, has about 650 species of shrubs, herbs and trees, mainly from warm or arid areas. The nasturtium family, Tropaeolaceae, consists of about 90 species of more or less succulent herbs. The pea family, Fabaceae or Leguminosae, is found in both temperate and tropical areas. It comprises about 640 genera and 18,000 species, mostly herbs, but also shrubs and trees.

Spider flower

Spider plant, *Cleome hassleriana*

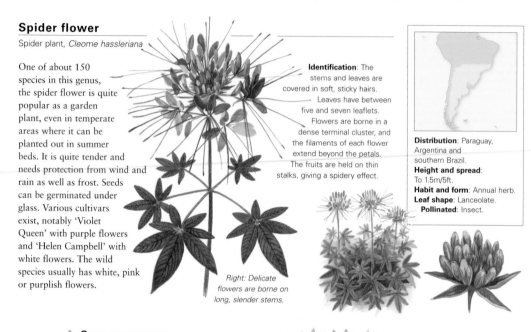

One of about 150 species in this genus, the spider flower is quite popular as a garden plant, even in temperate areas where it can be planted out in summer beds. It is quite tender and needs protection from wind and rain as well as frost. Seeds can be germinated under glass. Various cultivars exist, notably 'Violet Queen' with purple flowers and 'Helen Campbell' with white flowers. The wild species usually has white, pink or purplish flowers.

Identification: The stems and leaves are covered in soft, sticky hairs. Leaves have between five and seven leaflets. Flowers are borne in a dense terminal cluster, and the filaments of each flower extend beyond the petals. The fruits are held on thin stalks, giving a spidery effect.

Right: Delicate flowers are borne on long, slender stems.

Distribution: Paraguay, Argentina and southern Brazil.
Height and spread: To 1.5m/5ft.
Habit and form: Annual herb.
Leaf shape: Lanceolate.
Pollinated: Insect.

Canary creeper

Tropaeolum peregrinum

This annual creeper is well known as a garden plant. It grows quickly, and clambers up fences and trellises, producing pretty yellow flowers. Its common name probably comes from the fact that it was first introduced into Europe via the Canary Islands, rather than from the canary yellow colour of its flowers. It is also known as Canarybird vine.

Identification: The leaves of this creeper are usually five-lobed and it clings by means of twisted petioles. The long-stalked flowers have a hooked spur, are about 20mm/¾in across and yellow, the upper petal dissected at the edge and with a red-spotted base.

Above: The two large upper petals have attractive fringed edges.

Distribution: Peru and Ecuador.
Height and spread: To 2.5m/8ft.
Habit and form: Annual or perennial climber.
Leaf shape: Lobed.
Pollinated: Insect.

Left: This bushy climber grows well on supports or up through tall host plants.

Scarlet flame bean

Rose of Venezuela, *Brownea ariza* (=grandiceps)

Below: The yellow-tipped stamens protrude from the scarlet flowers.

This small tree produces beautiful large heads of bright red flowers, which dangle down beneath the foliage. The flowers are a little like those of rhododendrons. The fruit pods are velvety and droop in clusters. The generic name honours the author and botanist Patrick Browne (1720–1790).

Distribution: Colombia and Venezuela.
Height and spread: 9–12m/29½–39ft.
Habit and form: Tree.
Leaf shape: Pinnate.
Pollinated: Bird and insect.

Right: Brownea ariza is a slow-growing tree that does not exceed 12m/39ft.

Identification: The young leaves are mottled pale pink and greenish, turning brown and green as they mature. The mature leaves are long and pinnate, with 12–18 pairs of pointed leaflets. The flower clusters measure up to 20cm/8in across.

OTHER SPECIES OF NOTE

Steriphoma elliptica
This native of Trinidad and Venezuela has yellow flowers with a slight reddish tinge, and the leaves are hairy on the undersides. It grows to a height of about 3.7m/12¼ft.

Steriphoma paradoxa
This is a beautiful native of the forests of Colombia, Venezuela and Guatemala, at 750–1,200m/2,500–4,000ft above sea level. The yellow flowers have long graceful stamens.

Peruvian nasturtium
Tropaeolum tuberosum
This is is a close relative of Canary creeper but has red-orange rather than yellow flowers. It is native to Peru and Bolivia – where it is called 'anu' – and grows on mountain slopes and in valleys around 3,000m/9,840ft. A climber, it wraps its leaf stalks around other plants, and flowers from June to October. In gardens, it will thrive in sheltered, sunny locations in well-drained soil. The potato-like root tubers are edible after boiling and have a peppery taste.

Mountain immortelle *Erythrina poeppigiana*
Spiky clusters of reddish-orange pea-flowers that open before the leaves appear, make a most impressive display on this plant. Originally from the Andes of Peru, it is now found in many parts of South America and in the West Indies. The bright flowers attract birds and insects.

Red powder puff

Calliandra haematocephala

This small tree or shrub is a fast-growing species that produces unusual red 'powder-puff' flowers from November through April. These are often visited by butterflies and hummingbirds. It can be grown indoors in a pot if kept trimmed, and outside in warm climates. They can even be pruned and maintained as a hedge. The leaves display 'sleep' movements, folding together at night.

Distribution: Peru, Bolivia and Brazil.
Height and spread: To 6m/19¾ft.
Habit and form: Shrub or small tree.
Leaf shape: Pinnate.
Pollinated: Insect and hummingbird.

Below: The evergreen leaves are smooth and silky.

Below: The buds look like raspberries before the flowers open.

Identification: The small flowers are tightly packed and the long stamens produce the powder-puff effect. New leaves are yellow-bronze and turn metallic green as they mature.

AGAVE, CRASSULA AND PROTEA FAMILIES

The Agavaceae includes 550–600 species in around 18 genera, and is widespread in tropical, subtropical and warm temperate regions. The Crassulaceae contains mostly succulents, with flowers similar to those of the rose and saxifrage families. The Proteaceae is a large family of about 80 genera and 1,500 species.

Echeveria subrigida

This plant from Mexico is extremely restricted in its range, occurring only in San Luis Potosi and Tultenango Canyon. It was originally classified as a *Cotyledon* species but was later included in *Echeveria*. This plant has been confused with *E. cante*, mainly as a result of the trade in cultivated plants, but the true species is a robust plant with smooth leaves, whose flowers have unique scarlet nectaries.

Left: Up to 15 yellow-red flowers with greyish sepals appear on a tall spike in summer. The flower attracts insect pollinators.

Identification: A large, solitary, evergreen, succulent rosette, 30cm/12in in diameter, with a stem up to 10cm/4in long. The oval to lance-shaped leaves, 15–20cm/6–8in long, are held closely in the rosette. They are pointed, pale blue-green with red margins, upturned and very finely toothed. The flower spike, which appears in summer, is 60–90cm/24–35in high, bearing 6–15 flowered branches with a few bracts, 30–50mm/1¼–2in long, triangular to lance-shaped, ascending, grey-purple sepals, and flowers to 25mm/1in across, five-sided, not very constricted at the mouth, red, bloomed white outside, yellow-red inside.

Right: The red-edged leaves form a handsome rosette.

Distribution: San Luis Potosi and Tultenango Canyon, Mexico.
Height and spread: 60–90cm/24–35in.
Habit and form: Evergreen succulent.
Leaf shape: Obovate to oblanceolate.
Pollinated: Insect.

Donkey's tail

Burro's tail, *Sedum morganianum*

This plant, widely cultivated for its highly ornamental stems and leaves, is almost certainly a native of Mexico, although to date it has never been found in the wild. It sometimes appears as a garden escapee, although even the history of its cultivation remains a mystery. It is an attractive succulent, with spindle-shaped leaves with a silver-blue cast and pendulous branches. The deep pink flowers appear in spring but are rarely seen.

Identification: This pendulous to horizontal, trailing evergreen perennial has numerous prostrate or pendulous stems, sparsely branched and woody at the base. The leaves, to 20mm/¾in long, are very succulent, blue-green, alternate, spirally arranged, overlapping, oblong to lance-shaped, pointed, incurved and flattened. Pendent flowers, 12mm/½in across, borne terminally on long stalks, deep pink with five long-pointed, oval petals, may appear from spring onward.

Left: The dense pendulous stems have made this a favourite feature plant with gardeners.

Distribution: Mexico.
Height and spread: Trailing to 60cm/24in.
Habit and form: Succulent evergreen.
Leaf shape: Rounded, oblong-lanceolate.
Pollinated: Not known, probably insect.

Left: The flowers appear at the stem tips.

Chilean flameflower

Chilean firebush, *Embothrium coccineum*

Distribution: Southern Argentina and Chile.
Height and spread: Up to 10m/33ft.
Habit and form: Shrub or small tree.
Leaf shape: Elliptic or oblong.
Pollinated: Bird.

Far right: The Chilean firebush is an evergreen and, rarely, a deciduous tree.

This variable shrub or small tree is the sole representative of its genus, and is endemic to southern South American forests. The flameflower grows over a wide geographic range in the temperate forests of southern Argentina and Chile, and is frequently found along the edges of forest fragments as well as in open, agricultural landscapes. Its main pollinators are birds, with two species in particular – a flycatcher, the white-crested elaenia, *Elaenia albiceps*, and a hummingbird, the green-backed firecrown, *Sephanoides sephanoides* – thought to be the principal pollinating species.

Identification: A variable shrub or tree, with ascending stems, suckering at the base in some forms, clumped and sparsely branched. The leaves, up to 12.5cm/5in long, are undivided and very variable in shape: elliptic or oblong to narrowly lance-shaped, hairless, pea-green with olive veins or dark green. The long-lasting flowers, on red-green stalks, are borne in terminal or axillary crowded racemes up to 10cm/4in long, usually appearing in spring but variable according to location. They are tubular, red or vivid scarlet, although yellow and white forms have occasionally been recorded, up to 50mm/2in long, splitting into four narrow lobes that reflex and coil; each flower carries one stamen. The style is long, slender, protruding and persistent in the fruit.

OTHER SPECIES OF NOTE

Pachyphytum bracteosum
This succulent from Mexico is found on rock escarpments on limestone cliffs, at 1,200–1,850m/4,000–6,000ft. It has upright flowering stems of 30cm/12in or more, with white succulent bracts surrounding pink-red, five-lobed flowers with prominent yellow stamens.

Mexican firecracker *Echeveria setosa*
A variable species, endemic to small areas of Mexico, and in danger of extinction in the wild. The stemless rosettes of densely packed, glaucous or green, hairy leaves, give rise to flower spikes of pentagonal, red-and-yellow flowers in spring and early summer.

Fox tail agave *Agave attenuata*
This species from central Mexico has very wide, fleshy, soft, pale blue-green leaves with a felt-like texture, and forms a leaning or creeping trunk with age. The curving flower spike grows up to 3m/10ft, and is densely covered in green-white drooping flowers, producing fruit at the base and new plantlets at the tip.

Adam's needle *Yucca filamentosa*
Looks a little like a small palm, with evergreen, strap-like leaves up to 90cm/35in long, taking the form of a rosette. The leaf margins are decorated with long, curly threads or 'filaments' that peel back as the leaf grows. Erect flower spikes of large white flowers may reach 3.5m/12ft in summer.

Century plant

American aloe, *Agave americana*

This is probably the *Agave* most commonly grown as an ornamental plant, and as a result, it has spread throughout the temperate and tropical areas of the world. Because it has been extensively propagated its exact origin is uncertain, although it probably originates in eastern Mexico. The flowers appear at any time after the plant has reached 10 years old, so it does not live up to its common name.

Identification: A rosette-forming, short-stemmed, evergreen perennial, with leaves up to 2m/6½ft long, curved or reflexed, lance-shaped, pointed, light green to grey, wavy-edged to toothed, with rounded teeth 12mm/½in long and irregularly spaced, brown to grey; the leaves have a terminal spine up to 50mm/2in long, awl-shaped to conical, brown to grey. The inflorescence grows to 9m/29½ft. The large, asparagus-like stalk grows from the centre, bearing 15–35 spreading horizontal branches, with pale yellow flowers.

Distribution: Uncertain, probably eastern Mexico.
Height and spread: Up to 9m/30ft when flowering.
Habit and form: Evergreen succulent.
Leaf shape: Lanceolate.
Pollinated: Insect.

Above: The small, individual flowers are held in dense 'brush-like' umbels.

Right: The huge flower spikes appear only on plants of 10 or more years.

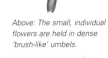

MYRTLE, FUCHSIA, MALPIGHIA, LIGNUM VITAE AND BLAZING STAR FAMILIES

Lovers of warm temperate and tropical zones, the Myrtaceae has about 130 genera and 4,620 species and the Onagraceae has about 650 species. Most of the 1,100 Malpighiaceae are South American. Lignum vitae is one of the 285 Zygophyllaceae, and Loasaceae includes 260 herbs and trees.

Pineapple guava

Feijoa (=Acca) sellowiana

This member of the myrtle family is a native of Brazil, where it was discovered between 1821 and 1829 by Friedrich Sellow, after whom it is named. A slow-growing evergreen tree or shrub, it produces showy pink flowers with prominent red stamens in late spring. It is fairly easy to grow, requiring full sun, and is drought-resistant when fully established. Propagation is normally by cutting, layering or grafting.

Identification: The leaves are elliptic to oblong, up to 75mm/3in long, dull green above and silvery beneath. The flowers are 40mm/1½in across. The fleshy petals have a delicate sweet flavour and can be added to salads.

Right: The fruit is a green berry, tinged red.

Distribution: Northern Argentina, Uruguay, Paraguay and southern Brazil.
Height and spread: To 6m/19¾ft.
Habit and form: Perennial tree or shrub.
Leaf shape: Elliptic.
Pollinated: Insect.

Left: The fruits are edible and taste like guavas.

Fuchsia simplicicaulis

This pretty fuchsia is one of more than 100 species, most of which are native to Central and South America. Like most of the American species, the red tubular flowers of this species are adapted for pollination by hummingbirds. Groups of long flowers droop down in clusters from the leaf axils. It was first discovered in Peru and then introduced into cultivation.

Bottom left: The slender scarlet flowers hang in elegant clusters.

Identification:
A tall shrub with long thin shoots and bright red tubular flowers. The leaves are arranged in whorls of three or four and are smooth above and slightly hairy beneath. The flowers are in groups of three to four, each with a long perianth tube.

Distribution: Central Peru.
Height and spread: 2–5m/6½–16ft.
Habit and form: Climbing shrub.
Leaf shape: Linear-lanceolate to ovate.
Pollinated: Hummingbird.

Left: Fuchsia simplicicaulis is a tall shrub with long, thin shoots.

Fuchsia fulgens

This fuchsia has long and tubular flowers similar in shape to those of *F. simplicicaulis*, but in this case orange-red in colour. This native of Mexico has large, heart-shaped toothed leaves and drooping clusters of flowers. It has been in cultivation since about 1830, and cultivars are available, such as *Rubra Grandiflora*, with orange-scarlet flowers.

Identification: The underground parts are tuberous. The young branches have a distinct red tinge. The leaves are to 15cm/6in, mainly heart-shaped with toothed margins. The flowers dangle in groups and are each about 65cmm/2½in long. The fruit is oblong and dark purple.

Distribution: Mexico.
Height and spread: 50cm–3m/20in–10ft.
Habit and form: Shrub.
Leaf shape: Ovate to cordate.
Pollinated: Hummingbird.

Left: Fuchsia fulgens *is an upright shrub with spreading branches.*

OTHER SPECIES OF NOTE

Honeysuckle fuchsia
Fuchsia triphylla
A beautifully flowered shrubby species, this is probably one of the earliest to be brought into cultivation (in the 17th century). The leaves are purple-tinged and the flowers orange to coral red. It is long-flowering, especially the cultivar 'Gartenmeister'.

Hardy fuchsia *Fuchsia magellanica*
This plant is of particular interest because it is especially suited to being grown in temperate gardens, as it can survive the winters – as long as the frost is not too fierce. The flowers are purple and red and borne throughout the summer. Originally from Chile and Argentina, it now has many cultivars and hybrids.

Orchid vine, Butterfly vine
Stigmaphyllon ciliatum
This climber with pretty golden-yellow flowers is native to South and Central America. It is easy to grow, either outdoors in the tropics, or in a sunny windowsill. The leaves have eyelash-like hairs along their margins.

Loasa vulcanica
A twining annual from South America that was first collected in Ecuador. It has red, white and yellow flowers. It is from cool mountain regions and is suitable for temperate gardens. Beware the stinging hairs.

Lignum vitae

Guaiacum officinale

This is one of six species of resinous evergreen trees and shrubs from Central and South America. Its common name, meaning 'wood/tree of life' refers to the value of the plant in medicine – its leaves, fruits and wood have all been used. The very hard, dense wood is highly regarded for decorative carving, being beautifully marked in pale and chocolate brown, and is also used for things requiring weight and strength. In the wild it grows in dry coastal scrub. It was traded by the Spanish in the 16th century and introduced to Europe.

Distribution: Southern Central and northern South America; Caribbean.
Height and spread: 9m/29½ft.
Habit and form: Evergreen tree.
Leaf shape: Pinnate.
Pollinated: Insect.

Identification: The pinnate leaves grow to about 90mm/3½in, with two to four pairs of leaflets. The blue flowers are in clusters and may appear several times a year.

Below: The orange-coloured fruit is about 20mm/¾in in diameter.

Far left: This attractive evergreen is widely planted as a park tree.

WOOD SORREL, PHLOX AND VERBENA FAMILIES

There are only six genera but 775 species among the Oxalidaceae, which contains mainly tropical, small trees, shrubs and herbs. The 20 genera and 290 species of the phlox family, Polemoniaceae, include herbs, lianas, shrubs and small trees. The verbena family, Verbenaceae, has 950 tropical species.

Tree oxalis

Oxalis ortgiesii

This species is native to the Andean foothills of Peru and Ecuador. It is an upright perennial with a tree-like stem and hairy, greenish-purple foliage. This shrub is sometimes known as fishtail oxalis due to the shape of its leaves. The many-flowered inflorescence is about 30cm/12in long.

Identification: The leaf stalks are circular in cross section, and succulent, probably an adaptation to periods of aridity. The leaves are clover-like with three leaflets, each leaflet deeply divided into two large triangular lobes; olive green to purple above and reddish-purple and hairy beneath. The flowers are lemon yellow with dark veins.

Distribution: Ecuador and Peru.
Height and spread: To 45cm/18in.
Habit and form: Perennial shrub.
Leaf shape: Divided, lobed.
Pollinated: Insect.

Left: The flowers measure about 25mm/1in across.

Left: Slim stems support the delicate yellow flowers.

Lucky clover

Good luck plant, *Oxalis tetraphylla*

Bearing a superficial resemblance to a clover, this species produces brick-red, pink or white flowers in the summer. It dies back to form a bulb over the winter but re-grows very rapidly the following spring. Lucky clover is cultivated as much for its attractive variegated purple and green leaves as for its pretty flowers. In one popular cultivar, 'Iron Cross', the inner sections of the leaflets are entirely purple.

Identification: This bulbous, stemless perennial has long hairy leaf stalks and clover-like leaves with four (sometimes three) leaflets, hence the common names. The leaflets usually have a V-shaped purple marking above and are hairy beneath.

Distribution: Mexico.
Height and spread: To about 40cm/16in.
Habit and form: Perennial.
Leaf shape: Four-lobed.
Pollinated: Insect.

Left: The umbrella-shaped flowers open into green-centred funnels.

Left: This plant's spreading habit means it creates good ground cover in gardens.

Mexican ivy

Monastery bells, Cup and saucer vine, *Cobaea scandens*

This familiar garden and greenhouse climber is a native of Mexico, and widely naturalized in the tropics. The bell-shaped flowers are green and smell musky at first, but mature to a pretty purple shade and then smell pleasantly of honey. They attract insects, and possibly also hummingbirds and bats. It grows rapidly, clambering on other plants, fences or trellises, securing itself by means of coiling tendrils. In temperate climates it is usually grown from seed and treated as an annual, although it can be kept indoors in the winter, as a perennial. A white-flowered form is quite popular.

Distribution: Mexico.
Height and spread: To 6m/19½ft.
Habit and form: Perennial climber.
Leaf shape: Pinnate.
Pollinated: Insect, bird and bat.

Identification: The leaves have large leafy stipules and the leaflets (four to six) grow to about 10cm/4in. The corolla has a saucer-shaped calyx, and usually matures to a rich purple colour.

Left: In gardens, this vigorous vine requires regular cutting back to prevent it from choking other plants.

OTHER SPECIES OF NOTE

Oxalis dispar
This native of Guyana has long-stalked leaves with three long leaflets, and bright yellow, scented flowers from spring to winter. It has slender branches and few leaves and grows to about 60cm/24in.

Oca *Oxalis tuberosa*
Native to Colombia, this succulent-stemmed, yellow-flowered perennial has a greenish-purple stem and scaly edible tubers. These are traditionally eaten roasted or boiled like potatoes, and taste like sweet potato or chestnuts. Oca root has been used as a food source since before the Incas. The leaves should not be eaten in quantity as they contain oxalic acid, which can be harmful.

Cobaea hookerana
This is found growing wild in the mountain forests of Venezuela. It has strange dangling flowers with long stamens that open during the night, and these attract moths (especially hawkmoths), which transfer the pollen that brushes on to their wings.

Verbena peruviana
A tender perennial, often grown as an annual and pot plant. Despite its name, it comes from Argentina and Brazil. It has a profusion of striking brilliant scarlet flowers and blooms from late spring through summer. Cultivars vary, with white, lavender and white, and pink flowers.

Fleur de Dieu

Queen's wreath, Sandpaper vine, *Petrea kohautiana*

The French common name means 'flower of God', a suitable label for this impressive vine with its long clusters of beautiful blue and violet flowers. The species name celebrates Franz Kohaut who collected it on Martinique between 1819 and 1821. It grows by twining and clinging, and develops rough leaves from which dangle the long inflorescences. When in full bloom, and covered in flowers, it can look like a wisteria from a distance.

Identification: The flower clusters grow to about 3m/10ft as racemes from the leaf axils, consisting of individual pale lilac to purple flowers, blooming from late winter to late summer. The flowers only last about two days but the bluish sepals persist, and slowly go grey.

Distribution: West Indies, Antilles.
Height and spread: To 10.5m/34½ft.
Habit and form: Evergreen perennial vine.
Leaf shape: Elliptic.
Pollinated: Insect.

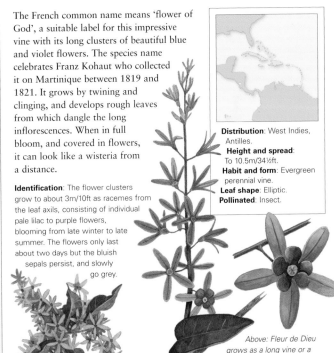

Above: Fleur de Dieu grows as a long vine or a shorter self-supporting shrub.

NIGHTSHADE AND BINDWEED FAMILIES

The nightshade family (Solanaceae) comprises herbs, shrubs and trees of 85 genera and 2,800 species.
They are frequently vines or creepers, and while a few are edible, others are poisonous, some deadly.
Bindweeds (Convolvulaceae) comprise mostly twining herbs or shrubs, sometimes with milky sap, with
55 genera and 1,700 species. Many have heart-shaped leaves and funnel-shaped flowers.

Blue dawn flower

Morning glory, *Ipomoea learii* syn. *I. acuminata, I. indica*

This fast-growing, tropical American climbing vine has large, saucer-shaped flowers borne in clusters of up to five. The flowers open bright blue-violet and fade to rose or soft red-violet, which creates an overall two-tone effect when the vine is in heavy bloom. Each flower lasts for only one day, but the plant is extremely floriferous. It occurs widely outside its native range, as it has long been admired as a garden plant and has escaped from cultivation. It usually prefers coastal habitats and moist forests. Originally native to tropical America, it is now pan-tropical and is often a troublesome weed where introduced.

Identification: A herbaceous, perennial climber, to 6m/19¾ft tall, often forming a woody base. The stems, which often have a woody base, are almost hairless and much branched. The leaves are oval to rounded with a tapering, pointed tip and a heart-shaped base, sometimes three-lobed, from 50mm–18cm/2–7in long on long stalks. The inflorescences are single to few-flowered, appearing densely on 50mm–20cm/2–8in stalks. The short-lived, funnel-shaped flowers are intense blue or purple, rarely white, 50–75mm/2–3in long and across. The rounded fruits, up to 12mm/½in in diameter, contain one to four brown seeds.

Distribution: Tropical America.
Height and spread: 6m/19¾ft.
Habit and form: Herbaceous perennial climber.
Leaf shape: Ovate to orbicular.
Pollinated: Insect.

Left: A fully open flower.

Left: The seeds are held in small fruits.

Right: The plant is a fast-growing twining vine.

Yesterday, today and tomorrow

Brunfelsia calycina

This bushy, evergreen or semi-deciduous shrub has fragrant, deep indigo-blue flowers that age to white over three days. It is slow-growing, with foliage that is normally dense and medium green, although young leaves may turn purplish in cool weather. The flowers appear in spring with indigo, lavender-blue and white flowers all present on the bush at the same time, leading to its common name. Originally a native of Brazil, it has been widely planted throughout the tropics and may sometimes be encountered as a garden escapee.

Identification: Though it may grow to 3m/10ft, this shrub is often much smaller and freely branched. The leaves, 75mm–15cm/3–6in long, are oblong to lance-shaped, pointed, glossy deep green above and paler beneath, on short stalks. The flowers appear in clusters of 1–10 at the ends of shoots or from the leaf axils; they are 25–75mm/1–3in across, with five spreading, rounded, overlapping lobes and a tube up to 40mm/1½in long, purple with a conspicuous white eye at the mouth, ringed with blue.

Far left and right: The flowers emerge a deep indigo blue and fade to white over three days.

Distribution: Brazil.
Height and spread: 3m/10ft.
Habit and form: Shrub.
Pollinated: Insect.
Leaf shape: Oblong to oblong-lanceolate.

Red angel's trumpet

Brugmansia sanguinea syn. *Datura sanguinea*

Distribution: North and central Colombia to northern Chile.
Height and spread: 11m/36ft.
Habit and form: Arborescent shrub.
Pollinated: Hummingbird.
Leaf shape: Ovate to oblong.

This small, shrubby tree, native to the Andes, is most noted for its large drooping flowers, which are brilliant orange-red at the mouth with yellow veins, fading to yellow at the base. They are produced in great profusion during the growing season. The velvety, grey-green leaves further enhance the look of this striking plant. It prefers cool, moist areas in mountains, where it is pollinated by hummingbirds. It was originally restricted to north and central Colombia to northern Chile, but it has been widely cultivated, with many cultivars now in existence, and is often encountered as a garden escapee outside its original range.

Identification: The young growth of this tree-like shrub is softly downy, and the branches are leafy near the tips. The broadly lance-shaped, wavy-edged leaves are alternate, up to 18cm/7in long. The pendent flowers are up to 25cm/10in long, emerging from a tubular, hairy, toothed calyx; the corolla is narrowly tubular, bright orange-red, yellow-green at the base, veined yellow, with backward-curving 25mm/1in lobes. The fruits, which are enclosed within the persistent calyx, are egg-shaped, downy and pale green to yellow.

Above: The flowerhead is greenish before it opens fully.

Far left: Brugmansia is a tree-like shrub.

OTHER SPECIES OF NOTE

Juanulloa mexicana
This rare species has a scattered distribution in semi-deciduous and wet forest habitats from Mexico to Colombia, Ecuador and Peru. It is pollinated by hummingbirds, and occurs as a hemi-epiphyte or liana climbing tree trunks, with the tubular orange flowers often going unnoticed among the tree canopy.

Chilean jessamine *Cestrum parqui*
This small- to medium-size, upright shrub, native to seasonally wet forests in southern South America, bears dense panicles of greenish-yellow flowers at the branch tips. The flowers are fragrant nocturnally and are pollinated by moths. After the flowering period come the glossy black or purplish fruits, which are favoured by various birds. The seed is spread by birds and floodwater.

Beach morning glory
Calystegia soldanella
This common but attractive seaside plant has an extremely wide global distribution, commonly found on many coastlines in both temperate and tropical regions. It is usually prostrate, unlike its climbing relations, and has distinctive, kidney-shaped leaves. The bright pink flowers, with five white stripes and a yellowish centre, fade quickly through the day.

Painted tongue

Salpiglossis sinuata

This branching annual or occasionally biennial plant is from the southern Andes. Its velvety funnel-shaped flowers, which resemble those of a petunia, are often veined and overlaid in contrasting colours. The leaves are mostly basal, and the flowers are borne on long stems above them. The plant has been widely cultivated, with many varieties raised in gardens. It may occasionally be encountered as an escapee from cultivation where conditions are suited for its growth.

Distribution: Southern Andes, South America.
Height and spread: 60cm/24in.
Habit and form: Annual.
Pollinated: Insect.
Leaf shape: Elliptic to narrow oblong.

Identification: The plant has sticky, branching stems and leaves up to 10cm/4in long, alternate, elliptic to narrow oblong, wavy-edged, toothed or deeply divided, on long stalks. The flowers, which appear in summer, are solitary, long-stalked, with a tubular calyx and funnel-shaped corolla with five notched, pleated lobes, up to 75mm/3in long and 50mm/2in across. They are yellow to ochre, mauve-scarlet or violet-blue with darker purple veins or markings.

Above: The long flower buds hide their true colour before they unfurl.

Below: The sticky, branched flower stems arise from a mass of basal leaves.

FIGWORT AND COFFEE FAMILIES

The figwort family (Scrophulariaceae) comprises mostly herbs but also a few small shrubs, with about 190 genera and 4,000 species, the majority of which are found in temperate areas, including tropical mountains. The coffee family (Rubiaceae) is very large, with about 630 genera and 10,200 species. It is diverse, including trees, shrubs, lianas and herbs, centred mainly in the tropics and subtropics.

Sand lady's slipper

Calceolaria uniflora

This remarkable flower is native to the extreme south of South America, in Argentina and Tierra del Fuego. It has become a favourite among specialist alpine gardeners, not least because of its showy and unusual flowers. The common name is confusing – although it likes sandy soil, the name 'lady's slipper' is normally applied to orchids of the genus *Cypripedium*. The British genus common name is Slipper Flower or Slipperwort. In the wild it grows in exposed, windy sites on well-drained soils. In cultivation it is challenging to grow, requiring free-draining compost and grit. Birds may be involved in pollination and apparently peck at the white patch on the flower's lip.

Identification: The leaves grow in flat rosettes and are about 30mm/1¹⁄₄in long, slightly hairy, with tiny teeth. Each plant produces one or two flowers. These are yellow, with a long oblong lower lip, dotted red and with a large white blob at the tip.

Distribution: Patagonia and Tierra del Fuego.
Height and spread: To about 10cm/4in.
Habit and form: Perennial herb.
Pollinated: Bird, insect.
Leaf shape: Spoon-shaped.

Above and right: The striking flowers appear almost oversize in comparison to the plant's height.

Panama rose

Rondeletia odorata

In Cuba this evergreen shrub grows in coastal rocky sites. It produces strongly scented clusters of orange and red flowers. There are about 150 species in this genus, mostly from South or Central America. The genus is named for Guillaume Rondelet (1507–66), who was an influential botany teacher and professor at Montpellier in France. It should be grown in moist, slightly acid soil and is best propagated by cuttings or from seed.

Identification: The short-stalked leathery leaves are about 50mm/2in long, the largest to 10cm/4in, and have a rough margin. The flowers have striking yellow throats with a corolla tube that is about 15mm/⁹⁄₁₆in long.

Distribution: Panama and Cuba.
Height and spread: To 3m/10ft.
Habit and form: Perennial shrub.
Pollinated: Probably moth.
Leaf shape: Ovate to oblong.

Left: The vivid flowers are highly fragrant.

Calceolaria purpurea

This striking herbaceous or occasionally woody perennial is a native of Chile, originating in the Santiago region. Its purple flowers have the balloon or sac-shaped lower lip that is characteristic of all of the species in this genus. The flowers are held on long, freely branching, leafy spikes above the foliage over a long period between summer and early autumn.

Distribution: Santiago region of Chile.
Height and spread: 60–80cm/24–31in.
Habit and form: Herbaceous perennial.
Pollinated: Insect.
Leaf shape: Ovate.

Identification: A herbaceous perennial, woody at the base, sticky to glandular, with tall, robust, branched stems. The wrinkled oval leaves, narrowing toward the leaf stalk and irregularly serrated, up to 12.5cm/5in long, form rosettes at the base. On the stem they are stalkless and opposite. The many-flowered inflorescences, freely branching, are held above the basal rosettes. The flowers are a bright purple-pink and look a little like two cushions or balloons.

OTHER SPECIES OF NOTE

Ourisia coccinea
This alpine species from the southern Andes of Chile is found in rocky soils, usually close by streams or near to running water. Its broadly elliptic or oblong leaves are held basally, with the 30cm/12in flower panicles crowded at the top with scarlet, drooping flowers.

Calceolaria darwinii
This tiny alpine or sub-alpine herbaceous perennial originates from Tierra del Fuego and southern Patagonia, often in very exposed, well-drained sites from sea level to 1,200m/4,000ft. It flowers in the brief southern summer, revealing intricate, slipper-shaped large yellow flowers with ochre and blood-red streaks. It is thought to be bird-pollinated.

Mimulus naiandinus
A half-hardy perennial native to the Andes of Chile, which grows in damp, marshy sites and alongside streams. It was discovered in 1973, and has since become quite a popular garden plant, being easy to raise from seed. It produces pretty pale pink, yellow-throated flowers.

Ferdinandusa speciosa
This little tree produces spectacular terminal clusters of vivid red flowers. It is native to marshy habitats in Brazil, and is also grown, being well suited to glasshouse cultivation. In the wild it is pollinated mainly by two species of hummingbird.

Creeping gloxinia

Mexican twist, *Lophospermum erubescens*

This vigorous climbing plant is a native of the mountainous areas of Mexico, Jamaica, Venezuela and Columbia, occurring at altitudes of around 1,000m/3,300ft, but it is frequently found far outside this range as a garden escapee. It is sometimes classified with *Asarina*, but differs from this exclusively European genus in having five lobes on the flower, compared with the two lobes of the other genus. It has soft, hairy stems and leaves that give it the appearance of a creeping foxglove.

Distribution: Mexico, Jamaica, Venezuela and Colombia.
Height and spread: 3m/10ft.
Habit and form: Trailing vine.
Pollinated: Insect.
Leaf shape: Deltoid.

Identification: The plant is densely, softly downy and grey-green throughout, with stems that are woody at the base, softer and hairy above. The leaves, up to 75mm/3in long and 15cm/6in across, are more or less triangular, toothed, with twining leaf stalks. The flowers also have twining stalks, and leaf-like calyces with lobes 25mm/1in broad. The downy, trumpet-shaped, rose pink flowers are 75mm/3in long with five blunt or notched lobes and a tube swollen on one side, white, and marbled within. They appear in summer and autumn, followed by spherical capsules containing many winged seeds.

Left: The downy, rose-pink flowers have foxglove-like markings.

GLOXINIA FAMILY

The gloxinia or gesneriad family, Gesneriaceae, contains herbs, shrubs and, rarely, trees, in about 133 genera and 3,000 species, including many well-known ornamental species such as Streptocarpus and Gloxinia. The family is well represented in the rainforests of South and Central America, where the species are often epiphytic, and their classification is the subject of considerable debate.

Dutchman's pipe

Bearded sinningia, *Sinningia barbata*

This small shrubby plant from Bahia, Pernambuco and Alagoas in north-east Brazil, has large leaves and differs from most other species of this genus in having no tubers. The yellow, hairy, upward-bent flowers fade to a creamy-white, and are also more pouched than other species. The leaves are bright olive-green above with reddish veins, and the whole lower surface is red.

Identification: The stems are marked with red and arise from rhizomes. The leaves, up to 15cm/6in long, are oblong to lance-shaped, tapering at both ends, opposite, crowded toward the base of the plant and the branch ends, dark olive-green above, maroon beneath. The nodding flowers, solitary or in pairs, on stalks up to 30mm/1¼in long, have leafy, triangular sepals; the corolla, up to 30mm/1¼in long, is pale greenish or creamy-yellow, fading gradually to white, downy, tubular, inflated at the base, leading to its characteristic upward bend. The lobes are spreading and short, forming a three-lobed lower and a two-lobed upper lip.

Distribution: North-eastern Brazil.
Height and spread: 60cm/24in.
Habit and form: Low shrub.
Leaf shape: Oblong-lanceolate.
Pollinated: Insect.

Trichantha elegans

This epiphyte from Ecuador is one of about 12 species within this genus that are included in the *Columnea* alliance. Their flowers differ from the genus *Columnea*, however, in being more flimsy and symmetrical, and they have characteristic peg-like appendages between the lobe segments. *Trichantha elegans* is found in moist forests, where it grows on the trunks and branches of rainforest trees, often high in the canopy, and is often therefore only seen close up on fallen branches or trees.

Distribution: Ecuador.
Height and spread: Indefinite.
Habit and form: Epiphytic creeper.
Leaf shape: Acute to obtuse.
Pollinated: Insect, possibly bird.

Identification: The red, wiry, branches are covered in bristly red hairs. The leaves are opposite, pointed or blunt, up to 75mm/3in long, strongly unequal, sparsely to densely hairy with red veins, slightly red on the lower surface; the leaf stalks are short and hairy. The flowers arise in pairs or threes from the leaf axils, with fringed, orange to maroon calyces; the corolla, up to 50mm/2in long, is tubular, red-maroon, with yellow stripes on slightly raised ridges, with sparse red hairs, maroon within, spurred. Three lobes form the upper lip, two lobes the lower lip. The fruit is a fleshy mauve berry.

Miniature pouch flower

Goldfish plant, *Hypocyrta nummularia,* syn. *Alloplectus nummularia,* syn. *Nematanthus gregarius*

Found growing on rainforest trees in Costa Rica and Guatemala, this is the sole Central American representative of an exclusively South American genus. The brightly coloured tubular flowers, with small closed pouches, bloom profusely along the slender branching stems. The stems, set with opposite pairs of glossy green leaves, commence their growth upright, but gradually droop as they increase in length, and root as they contact the mossy surfaces of trees. After flowering, the plant often loses its leaves for a brief period, but new ones soon appear.

Identification: An epiphyte with hairy stems, climbing or pendent. The glossy green leaves are opposite, up to 30mm/ 1¼in long, elliptic to oval, bluntly pointed at the base and tip, fleshy, with rounded marginal teeth, on short stalks. The flowers appear one to three per cluster, on short stalks. The calyx is marked orange at the tip, with oval lobes; the corolla, up to 25mm/ 1in long, is bright orange with a purple brown stripe leading to each lobe, marked with black spots near the blunt ends of the lobes. The fruit is yellow-orange.

Distribution: Costa Rica and Guatemala.
Height and spread: Creeping to 80cm/31in.
Habit and form: Epiphyte.
Leaf shape: Elliptic to ovate.
Pollinated: Insect, possibly bird.

OTHER SPECIES OF NOTE

Sinningia pusilla
This diminutive species would fit into a thimble and is considered to be the smallest gesneriad. Its tiny rosettes of glossy leaves are comparatively dwarfed by the pale lilac flowers, and it is easily overlooked, growing high among the mossy tree branches in its native Brazil.

Kohleria bogotensis
This native of Colombia is an erect, hairy, rhizomatous plant, with olive-green leaves, which produces a profusion of extremely showy flowers. The bottom lobes of the flowers are yellow, splashed with orange dots and attached to a bright orange tube.

Sarmienta repens
This pretty little native of Chile grows on the trunks of trees and rocks and has stiff, trailing, woody stems and small, succulent leaves. The bright red, pendent flowers, which are produced extremely freely, have two prominent stamens that protrude considerably from the flower tube.

Columnea argentea
This stout-stemmed, attractive species has a restricted distribution, being found in just a few localities in Jamaica. It is striking, with silky-haired leaves, stems, sepals and corollas, giving it a silvered appearance. The yellow flowers arise from the leaf axils around the branch tips.

Columnea fendleri

This epiphyte, native to Venezuela, has large, showy red flowers, borne singly from the leaf axils. These asymmetrical flowers exude copious nectar and are frequently visited by hummingbirds, which are their principal pollinators. The plant is often considered to be a variety of *C. scandens,* which it resembles in every way except size: it is larger in all respects than this related Venezuelan species, and is therefore widely considered a species in its own right.

Distribution: Venezuela.
Height and spread: 60cm/24in.
Habit and form: Epiphyte.
Leaf shape: Elliptic–oblong.
Pollinated: Hummingbird.

Identification: An epiphyte with erect, fleshy stems and leaves 25–50mm/1–2in long, dark green, upright, elliptic to oblong with rounded tips, and asymmetric at the base, densely hairy beneath, with red margins. It bears one to three flowers per axil, held well away from the leaves, on 15mm/⅝in stalks. The calyx lobes, up to 15mm/⅝in long, are erect, toothed and sparsely hairy; the slender, tubular corolla is up to 65mm/ 2½in long, orange-red with yellow edges, with a wedge-shaped hood and oblong to lance-shaped lower lobe. The fruit is a fleshy white berry.

ACANTHUS AND BIGNONIA FAMILIES

The acanthus family, Acanthaceae, consists mostly of herbs or shrubs comprising about 250 genera and 2,500 species. Most are tropical herbs, shrubs or twining vines, while others are spiny. The bignonia family, Bignoniaceae, consists of about 110 genera and 750 species of mainly tropical trees, shrubs and lianas, especially in South America. They typically have opposite, compound leaves and tendrils.

Shrimp plant

Justicia brandegeeana syn. *Belloperone guttata*

Native to central Mexico, from mountainous country at elevations of 500–1,200m/1,600–4,000ft. The drooping, arching, terminal white flowers that appear throughout the growing season have showy, overlapping red to pink-bronze bracts. Each flower spike looks like a large shrimp, hence the common name. The flowers are insignificant but their white or yellowish colour contrasts with the bracts. The plant is widely naturalized outside its original range, especially in Florida.

Identification: This evergreen, rounded, downy shrub has weak, twiggy stems, forming a dense, spreading clump or colony. The leaves, up to 75mm/3in long, are oval to elliptic, entire, soft and shiny green. The flowers are borne in arching to pendent terminal spikes, about 15cm/6in or more long, with heart-shaped, overlapping bracts of brown to brick-red or rose; the flower, deeply double-lipped, white, the lower lip marked with red, is almost concealed by the bracts. Yellow-flowered forms occur occasionally.

Distribution: Central Mexico.
Height and spread: 90cm/35in.
Habit and form: Evergreen shrub.
Leaf shape: Ovate.
Pollinated: Insect.

Left: The shrimp plant is a sprawling, suckering, tropical, evergreen shrub.

Christmas pride

Pink wild petunia, *Ruellia macrantha*

This dense evergreen shrub is native to Minas, São Paulo, and the Matto Grosso areas of Brazil. It is also found as far north as Mexico where suitable habitats exist. It is most commonly found on dry, gravelly slopes and rocky washes, or other well-drained soils. It has large, showy, flaring, bell-shaped flowers, which are usually pink with deeper pink veining, giving the whole plant a spectacular appearance. Its popularity as a garden plant has resulted in its becoming quite widely naturalized, especially in parts of the United States.

Identification: A bushy subshrub with erect stems, it has leaves up to 15cm/6in long, opposite, lance-shaped, dull dark green, slightly hairy, with veins impressed on the upper surface. The flowers are showy, solitary, axillary, with a deeply five-cut calyx; they are funnel-shaped, with a paler throat with red veins, up to 75mm/3in long, reaching 50mm/2in across at the mouth, the five lobes rounded and spreading, the tube straight. The four unequal stamens are fused at the base in two pairs, joined to the corolla tube. The fruit is a club-shaped capsule.

Distribution: Brazil.
Height and spread: 1–2m/39in–6½ft.
Habit and form: Sub-shrub.
Leaf shape: Lanceolate.
Pollinated: Insect.

Below: The plant is bushy with upright stems.

Left: The bell-shaped flowers open from pink inflated buds.

Golden shrimp plant

Pachystachys lutea

This colourful, soft-stemmed, upright perennial has dark green leaves and a showy inflorescence consisting of a congested raceme of bright yellow bracts, from among which pure white flowers emerge throughout the growing season. The name *Pachystachys* comes from the Greek for 'thick spike', an obvious reference to the flowering spikes. The yellow bracts resemble the overlapping scales on a shrimp, hence the common name. The plant is quite similar in appearance to the Mexican shrimp plant, *Justicia brandegeeana.*

Distribution: Peru.
Height and spread:
60cm–1.8m/24in–6ft.
Habit and form: Evergreen shrub.
Leaf shape: Ovate or lanceolate.
Pollinated: Insect.

Identification: The stems are woody and smooth, the younger stems green, sparsely or moderately branched, with inflorescences held on terminal sections. The leaves are alternate, oval or lance-shaped to elliptic, to 15cm/6in long, tapered at the tip with a pointed or heart-shaped base. The upper surface is smooth and bright green with pinnate venation and entire to finely serrated margins. The flower spike is a cone-shaped arrangement of bracts, usually bearing four or more flowers, opposite, each located at the base of a bract; each bract is heart-shaped, 25mm/1in long, and golden-yellow. The flowers are white and double-lipped.

*Above:
The flower
protrudes
from the bracts.*

*Far left: Shrubby
dark green
growth offsets
the flowers.*

Mosaic plant

Fittonia gigantea

This is one of two species in this genus. It is a native of forests, where it is noteworthy for its large colourful leaves, which appear on numerous branching, spreading stems. The small, yellowish, red-striped flowers are almost insignificant, appearing one or two at a time on each flowerhead. Despite its restricted range in the wild this plant has been popular in cultivation in many tropical countries and can occasionally be found as a garden escapee.

Distribution: Peru.
Height and spread:
60cm/24in.
Habit and form: Herbaceous plant.
Leaf shape: Ovate.
Pollinated: Insect.

Identification: A low-growing, downy, evergreen herbaceous perennial. The stems are creeping, violet-red and root freely to form a dense carpet. The leaves are opposite, 10cm/4in long or more, oval, heart-shaped toward the base, on short leaf stalks. They are colourfully veined: both leaf veins and borders are pink or carmine-red and are very elegant, with a 'painted' look. The inflorescence is up to 40mm/1½in long, on a short stalk. The pale green, overlapping bracts are conspicuous while the yellowish to white flowers are insignificant, emerging from the bracts one or two at a time; they are tubular, double-lipped, with the lower lip divided into three lobes, striped pink to red on the two outermost.

*Below: The flower is a
four-angled terminal
spike.*

*Left: The mosaic plant is a
spreading, freely branching herb
with attractive foliage.*

GENTIAN AND BELLFLOWER FAMILIES

Worldwide, the gentian family, Gentianaceae, comprises around 74 genera and 1,200 species, mainly herbs, and a few shrubs or small trees. The bellflower family, Campanulaceae, includes herbs, shrubs and, rarely small trees, usually with milky sap, comprising about 70 genera and 2,000 species. Many of the species of both families are highly ornamental and have become familiar plants in cultivation.

Star of Bethlehem

Hippobroma longiflora

This native of southern USA, southward to Brazil, Peru and the West Indies, is a perennial herb with poisonous milky sap. Its generic name, *Hippobroma*, translated from the Greek, means horse poison, indicating how potent it is. The plant has almost symmetrical star-shaped flowers with long tubes, which appear at various times of the year depending upon location.

Identification: The non-woody stem is green and smooth, with a rosette of narrow, stalkless, oval to lance-shaped, coarsely lobed leaves, with feathery veination and doubly toothed margins, mostly 10–15cm/4–6in long. The panicle usually comprises two to three white flowers on short, hairy stalks. The calyx is 25mm/1in long; the flowers are star-shaped with five pointed, spreading lobes, 25mm/1in long, on a narrow tube, usually 75mm–12cm/3–4¾in long. The twin-celled capsule is bell-shaped and downy, with numerous small seeds.

Left: The star-like flowers are held high on hairy stalks.

Distribution: Southern USA, Brazil, Peru and the West Indies.
Height and spread: 20–60cm/8–24in.
Habit and form: Herbaceous perennial.
Leaf shape: Oblanceolate.
Pollinated: Insect.

Hypsela reniformis

This unusual South American creeping plant is mainly found in Chile, but its range stretches from Ecuador to Tierra del Fuego, in mountainous regions along the Andes. It grows in moist open places, especially at the southern end of its range. The dense mats of small, rounded, shiny leaves are topped with upturned, pale pink, crimson-lipped flowers that make an eye-catching display during summer. It is a vigorous plant, spreading 30–60cm/12–24in in a year.

Right: The pink flowers have a long tube and stamens. The flowering period lasts from June to September, making this a popular choice for gardeners. It is also known as pixie carpet.

Identification: This small, prostrate, creeping herb forms a dense mat of cover, with hairless stems up to 50mm/2in long. The often crowded leaves, up to 12mm/½in long, are elliptic to round or kidney-shaped. The solitary flowers, with two ascending and three descending petals, are white suffused with pink, veined carmine, yellow at the centre, and are borne throughout the summer months. They are followed in autumn by erect green berries.

Distribution: Western South America from Ecuador to Tierra del Fuego.
Height and spread: 50mm/2in; indefinite spread.
Habit and form: Prostrate, perennial herb.
Leaf shape: Reniform.
Pollinated: Insect.

Deer meat

Centropogon cornutus

Distribution: South and Central America to the Antilles.
Height and spread: 3m/10ft if freestanding, but may reach 9m/29½ft with support.
Habit and form: Shrub.
Leaf shape: Ovate.
Pollinated: Probably hummingbird.

This brightly coloured shrub is widespread from South and Central America to the Antilles. Its long tubular red flowers are designed to be pollinated by hummingbirds. Deer meat is water-tolerant and is often found growing along riverbanks, in low-lying wetland areas or in clearings in wet forest areas, particularly those where inundation is seasonal and there is a noticeable dry season. It is capable of forming a freestanding shrub but more often than not will scramble upward through other bushes and small trees to make a sizeable specimen.

Identification: An upright shrub with milky sap and oval, alternate, toothed leaves. The flowers are asymmetrical on long stalks, usually arising singly from the leaf axils near the top of the stems. Each flower is two-lipped, five-lobed, bright red or deep carmine to pale purple; the five-bearded anthers are united into a tube around the style. The corolla tube opens along the upper side, with two lobes above and three below. The fruit is a five-chambered fleshy berry, with the remains of the style persisting, giving a beaked appearance, with the five thin, pointed green sepals also persisting, giving a dome-like appearance.

OTHER SPECIES OF NOTE

Siphocampylus orbiginianus
A native of Bolivia, this is an impressive shrub reaching 2m/6½ft in height. It has mid-green leaves arranged in threes around the green stems, which are topped with long, tubular flowers. The blooms are red with yellow-green stripes down the tube and pointed, greenish or yellow lobes.

Lisianthus umbellatus
This shrub can reach 3.5m/12ft. It has leaves clustered at the ends of its branches, and it bears numerous dense umbels of sweetly scented yellow-and-green flowers. The species occurs only in Jamaica, where it and several closely related species are found across the mountainous areas.

Centropogon coccineus
This striking plant is one of about 230 species in the tropical bellflower genus. This species, from Brazil, is a hairless shrub growing to about 90cm/35in. It has pendulous, deep crimson flowers that are attractive to the hummingbirds that pollinate the plant.

Lisianthus capitatus
This plant resembles *L. umbellatus* except that it has almost stalkless flowers. Also like *L. umbellatus*, it hails from Jamaica, but is more widespread, and locally common at the edges of woodland on limestone at 300–915m/9800–3,000ft above sea level.

Flor de muerto

Lisianthus nigrescens

The flor de muerto, so named because it was a favoured decoration for graves in southern Mexico, is native only to the states of Veracruz, Oaxaca and Chiapas. It is an intriguing plant and one of the rarities of the plant world, as it bears a true black flower. It has been collected since it was first described in 1831, although documented collections number less than two dozen. Despite its unusual character, it is virtually unknown in cultivation or, for that matter, outside its native range.

Distribution: Veracruz, Oaxaca, and Chiapas, southern Mexico.
Height and spread: 2m/6½ft.
Habit and form: Shrub.
Leaf shape: Oblong-lanceoleate.
Pollinated: Insect.

Identification: A large-stalked shrub, open and much branched, with smooth stems. The stalkless leaves are oblong to lance-shaped with pointed tips and three to five veins, nearly united at the base. The stems are crowned with tall flower spikes to 1m/39in long, covered with nodding flowers 50mm/2in across, with spreading lobes, recurved at the tips; the stamens do not protrude beyond the mouth of the flower. Depending on the angle at which they are viewed the flowers appear blackish-purple or inky-black, with a satiny texture.

DAISY FAMILY

The daisy family, Asteraceae, contains herbs, shrubs, or less commonly, trees. This is arguably the largest family of flowering plants, comprising about 1,100 genera and 20,000 species. The species are characterized by having the flowers reduced and organized into a composite arrangement of tiny individual flowers called a 'capitulum'; a tight cluster that superficially resembles a single bloom.

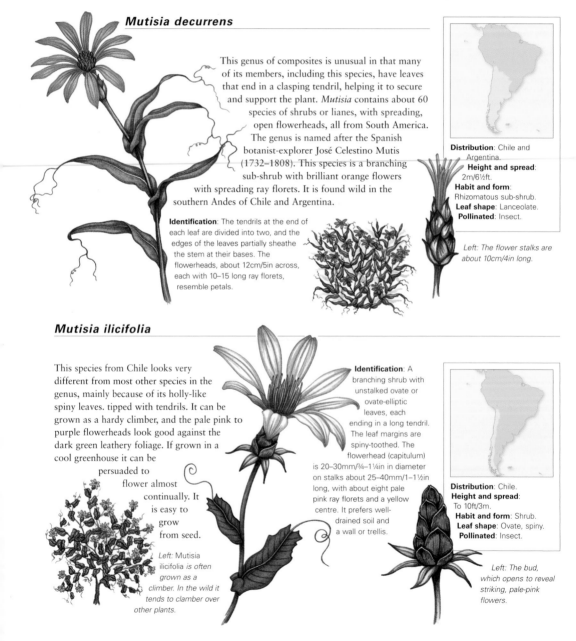

Mutisia decurrens

This genus of composites is unusual in that many of its members, including this species, have leaves that end in a clasping tendril, helping it to secure and support the plant. *Mutisia* contains about 60 species of shrubs or lianes, with spreading, open flowerheads, all from South America. The genus is named after the Spanish botanist-explorer José Celestino Mutis (1732–1808). This species is a branching sub-shrub with brilliant orange flowers with spreading ray florets. It is found wild in the southern Andes of Chile and Argentina.

Identification: The tendrils at the end of each leaf are divided into two, and the edges of the leaves partially sheathe the stem at their bases. The flowerheads, about 12cm/5in across, each with 10–15 long ray florets, resemble petals.

Distribution: Chile and Argentina.
Height and spread: 2m/6½ft.
Habit and form: Rhizomatous sub-shrub.
Leaf shape: Lanceolate.
Pollinated: Insect.

Left: The flower stalks are about 10cm/4in long.

Mutisia ilicifolia

This species from Chile looks very different from most other species in the genus, mainly because of its holly-like spiny leaves. tipped with tendrils. It can be grown as a hardy climber, and the pale pink to purple flowerheads look good against the dark green leathery foliage. If grown in a cool greenhouse it can be persuaded to flower almost continually. It is easy to grow from seed.

Left: Mutisia ilicifolia is often grown as a climber. In the wild it tends to clamber over other plants.

Identification: A branching shrub with unstalked ovate or ovate-elliptic leaves, each ending in a long tendril. The leaf margins are spiny-toothed. The flowerhead (capitulum) is 20–30mm/¾–1¼in in diameter on stalks about 25–40mm/1–1½in long, with about eight pale pink ray florets and a yellow centre. It prefers well-drained soil and a wall or trellis.

Distribution: Chile.
Height and spread: To 10ft/3m.
Habit and form: Shrub.
Leaf shape: Ovate, spiny.
Pollinated: Insect.

Left: The bud, which opens to reveal striking, pale-pink flowers.

Mexican sunflower

Tithonia rotundifolia

The 10 species of annual or perennial herbs and shrubs in the *Tithonia* genus are found in Mexico and Central America. This annual plant is robust and branching. It likes full sun and needs well-drained soil, and is sensitive to frost. The flowerheads are highly attractive to butterflies and bees, especially in late summer. Cultivars include 'Goldfinger' with large orange flowers, 'Torch' with fiery red flowers, and dwarf forms.

Identification: The coarse leaves have three to five lobes, are about 15cm/6in long and 10cm/4in broad and covered in soft downy hairs. The flowerheads are bright red-orange, like giant daisies, about 75mm/3in across.

Distribution: Mexico to Panama; widely introduced elsewhere.
Height and spread: 1.5–1.8m/5–6ft.
Habit and form: Annual.
Leaf shape: Ovate, lobed.
Pollinated: Insect.

Left: The flowerhead, after blooming.

Left: The flowerheads are vibrant and attractive to insects.

Common zinnia

Zinnia elegans

Zinnias in the wild are centred on Mexico, and comprise 20 annual or perennial herbs or small shrubs, of which this species is the best known. This Mexican species has long been in cultivation and has given rise to many cultivars and garden hybrids, including those with double, and 'pom-pom' flowers. Zinnias are popular partly because they are so easy to grow. They do best in warm climates and are not frost-tolerant.

Distribution: Mexico.
Height and spread: To 1m/39in.
Habit and form: Annual herb.
Leaf shape: Lanceolate, ovate or oblong.
Pollinated: Insect.

Identification: The stem is green, yellow or purple and the leaves about 80mm/3⅛in long. The capitula consist of up to 60 ray florets, ranging from purple, red, orange and yellow to white. In the wild, the usual colour is purple or lilac.

Above: The flowerheads are a pompom shape, and vibrant lilac or purple.

Above: The flowerhead, about to unfold.

SPIDERWORT AND ARROWROOT FAMILIES

The spiderwort family, Commelinaceae, includes mainly tropical herbs or climbers with swollen nodes and spirally arranged leaves. There are 640 species, some of which, like Tradescantia *and* Zebrina, *are well known houseplants. The arrowroot family, Marantaceae, contains 535 tropical perennial herb species, mostly American. Many have robust rhizomes and some have edible tubers.*

Cochliostema jacobianum
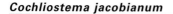

There are only two species in this genus of epiphytic herbs from Colombia, Nicaragua and Ecuador. They grow in warm moist rainforests, rooted on the branches of trees. The rosette of very large leaves forms a cup-like base of overlapping leaf sheaths. From this grow several inflorescence stalks, bearing highly unusual purple and blue fragrant flowers. This species grows only in Ecuador, but the second species, *C. odoratissimum*, is found also in Colombia and Nicaragua.

Identification: The flowers consist of three purple sepals and three blue petals, the latter fringed with hairs. The most unusual feature consists of the three fertile stamens that are partly fused to form an arching horn-like structure.

Right: Each flower has three arching stamens and rises from a rosette of glossy leaves.

Far left: The leaves are edged with purple.

Distribution: Ecuador.
Height and spread: Leaves to 1.2m/4ft.
Habit and form: Perennial epiphyte.
Leaf shape: Oblong.
Pollinated: Insect.

Queen's spiderwort
Dichorisandra reginae

This stout perennial herb is one of 25 species in the genus, all found in tropical America. Queen's spiderwort is native to central Peru. It was introduced into cultivation (via Belgium) in 1890 and named in honour of the Queen of Belgium. The large, smooth leaves are arranged in two ranks along the stems. The related Brazilian Ginger, *D. thyrsiflora*, has small bright blue flowers in dense spikes. This can be grown indoors or in a greenhouse and should be planted in moist fertile soil.

Right: A cross section of the stamen.

Identification: The leaves are up to 18cm/7in long, tapering to a point with silvery stripes, and are purple beneath. The flower is compact, with three blue-green sepals and three longer blue-violet petals, then white towards the base.

Distribution: Peru.
Height and spread: 90cm–1.2m/35in–4ft.
Habit and form: Perennial herb.
Leaf shape: Elliptic.
Pollinated: Insect.

Left: The flowers have three blue to purple petals. The single flowers are tiny, but grow in eye-catching clusters.

Wandering jew

Tradescantia zebrina (=Zebrina pendula)

Distribution: Southern Mexico, Belize, Guatemala and Honduras; widely naturalized.
Height and spread: 15–30cm/6–12in.
Habit and form: Creeping perennial.
Leaf shape: Ovate-oblong.
Pollinated: Insect.

The spider-lilies or spiderworts in the genus *Tradescantia* consist of 70 species. This species is a very familiar houseplant and has characteristic 'zebra' stripes on the leaves. It is easy to grow and is especially suited to trailing from a height. In its wild habitat it grows among grasses and under the shade of shrubs. In warm regions it can be grown outdoors, but avoid full sun; indoors it needs a lot of light. It is excellent for groundcover in frost-free regions. It can easily be propagated from cuttings, but take care when handling, as the sap can cause skin irritation. Several cultivars are available.

Identification: A creeping species that roots at the nodes. The leaves are green or purple above, with silvery stripes and purple beneath. The flowers are purple-pink or violet-blue.

Left and right: The plant is intensely colourful and elegant, hence its popularity.

OTHER SPECIES OF NOTE
Purple heart, Purple queen
Tradescantia pallida (= Setcreasea purpurea)
A well-known house or garden plant, purple heart has pretty purple stems and leaves and pale pink three-petalled flowers. It is excellent for rock gardens and to cover open soil. In the wild it is found in Mexico.

Oyster plant, Moses in the cradle
Tradescantia spathacea
There are a variety of common names for this plant. It is a succulent herb with a cluster of pointed leaves from a trunk-like stem. The leaves are green above and vivid violet underneath. The small white flowers nestle in the boat-shaped purple bracts.

West Indian arrowroot
Maranta arundinacea
This plant is the source of arrowroot (from the rhizomes), an easily digested form of starch, used, among as a thickening agent and as a bland food. It is also an attractive houseplant with variegated leaves.

Weldenia candida
This is the only species in its genus. It grows in the mountains of Mexico and Guatemala. Although very local in the wild, it is now available through alpine nurseries and has become quite popular in cultivation. It has pretty pure white, almost snowdrop-like flowers.

Zebra plant

Calathea zebrina

There are about 300 species in this genus of tropical American species, and many have large patterned leaves, making them suitable as decorative houseplants. They have underground tubers or rhizomes. The zebra plant is named for its beautifully patterned and striped leaves. They need shade and warmth and should also be kept moist, and misted, and can be propagated by division in the spring. Several cultivars exist, exhibiting different colours in the leaf stripes.

Distribution: South-eastern Brazil.
Height and spread: Leaves to 70cm/27½in.
Habit and form: Perennial herb.
Leaf shape: Elliptic.
Pollinated: Unknown.

Identification: The leaves are a velvety green with broad darker stripes above and reddish-purple beneath. The flowers are white and violet, with violet bracts.

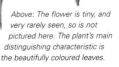

Above: The flower is tiny, and very rarely seen, so is not pictured here. The plant's main distinguishing characteristic is the beautifully coloured leaves.

PINEAPPLE FAMILY

Almost entirely restricted to tropical and subtropical America, the pineapple family, Bromeliaceae,
consists of 2,400 species in about 60 genera. As well as the familiar pineapple, it includes many epiphytic
species (some called 'air plants') and also the strange dangling Spanish moss, Tillandsia usneoides.

Friendship plant

Queen's tears, *Billbergia nutans*

There are 54 species in the genus found from Mexico southwards. This fine bromeliad grows epiphytically (attached to another plant) in its natural environment, forming clumps, but adapts well to being grown terrestrially. It should be kept in partial shade in a slightly acid soil. Curiously, it can be persuaded to flower by enclosing the plant in a plastic bag with a ripe apple for about a week. It should then come into flower in one or two months. This is triggered by the ethylene given off by the apple. The flowers are purple-edged with green centred petals that roll up to expose long light green filaments, heavy with pollen. The leaves are long and slender.

Identification: The leaves are narrow and scaly beneath, often with toothed margins. The inflorescence is tall and arching with slender pink overlapping bracts, contrasting with pale yellow-green flowers, each with a pale pink calyx.

Distribution: Northern Argentina, Paraguay, Uruguay and southern Brazil.
Height and spread: To 40cm/16in.
Habit and form: Perennial epiphyte.
Leaf shape: Narrow, toothed.
Pollinated: Insect.

Left: The plant has an elegant, arching habit, with vivid flowers that dangle from the slender pink and green stems.

Pitcairnia corrallina

This unusual bromeliad has brilliant red flower clusters that seem to creep along the forest floor. It grows in swamps and near streams in a limited area of Colombia. There are about 260 species of these pineapple relatives, nearly all found in South and Central America. The garden hybrid *P. x darblayana* is the result of crossing this species with *P. paniculata*; it has brick-red sepals and vivid red petals.

Identification: The long, red, arched inflorescence contrasts with the green leaves. The latter are strap-like with toothed margins. The red petals do not open far and their lobes are edged white.

Distribution: Colombia.
Height and spread: 1m/39in.
Habit and form: Perennial herb.
Leaf shape: Linear-lanceolate.
Pollinated: Hummingbird, insect.

Top: The vividly-coloured flower spikes fall to the ground. Like many pitcairnias, this plant prefers shady woodland areas.

Left: The leaves are lanceolate.

Pink quill

Tillandsia cyanea

Pink quill is well named; its flattened spike of overlapping pink bracts is unusual and decorative. It has become very popular as a houseplant and is not hard to grow. The foliage is impressive through the year and the flower spike, which lasts for several months, produces large purple flowers set against the bright pink bracts. It was once common in the rainforests of western Ecuador but is now much rarer, having been over-collected. Luckily it thrives in cultivation, being raised from seed and also using tissue culture techniques.

Distribution: Ecuador and Peru.
Height and spread: To 25cm/10in.
Habit and form: Perennial epiphyte.
Leaf shape: Linear to triangular.
Pollinated: Insect, bird.

Identification: Epiphytic (grows upon another plant) with arched, lanceolate leaves with pointed, thick apex. The inflorescence, which appears in the winter, is a spike of overlapping pink bracts with blue-violet blooms.

Right: The plant forms a rosette of slender, arching leaves. The slender flowers appear from the tips of the stems.

OTHER SPECIES OF NOTE
Rainbow plant *Billbergia chlorosticta*
A colourful epiphytic species from Brazil, which grows to about 50cm/20in and has toothed leaves that are red-brown below and mottled creamy-white. The arching inflorescence has large red bracts and greenish-yellow, blue-tipped flowers. It thrives in a warm, damp atmosphere.

Billbergia zebrina
In the wild this grows on trees in temperate and subtropical forests in central and southern Brazil. It has very attractive leaves that are up to 90cm/35in long and purple-bronze with silver bands, in a vase-shaped cluster. The greenish-yellow petals contrast with the pink bracts.

Pitcairnia nigra
Another weird and wonderful species that grows wild in Ecuador, and is often grown in cultivation. Its leaves are up to 15cm/6in across. The flower spike is about 50cm/20in long, arising from a stalk of 20cm/8in. The flowers are pale at the base and blackish-purple at the tip.

Spanish moss
Tillandsia usneoides
This member of the family couldn't look much less like a pineapple! It resembles a moss or lichen and dangles from trees, as long as 7m/23ft. It was once used for stuffing mattresses. It grows from Argentina and Chile, north to the south-eastern USA.

Tillandsia lindeniana

There are about 400 members of this fascinating genus, many of them epiphytes, ranging from the southern US through Central and South America. Their leaves are usually tightly packed and in most species covered in absorbent hairs, enabling them to take in moisture from damp air and mist. This species has a large rosette of long thin leaves. It is native to the Andes of Ecuador and Peru and was introduced into cultivation in the 1860s. It has large deep blue flowers. Garden forms include one with red bracts and white flowers.

Identification: The long narrow leaves grow to about 40cm/16in, arching decoratively. The flattened inflorescence is about 20cm/8in long with waxy overlapping pinkish and green bracts, and the blue flowers have spreading petals.

Distribution: Ecuador and Peru.
Height and spread: To 80cm/31in.
Habit and form: Perennial epiphyte.
Leaf shape: Linear.
Pollinated: Insect.

Above: The plant takes root in a tree.

Far left: The inflorescence is vivid pink, with blue flowers.

Queen Mary bromeliad

Aechmea mariae-reginae

This genus contains about 170 perennial herbs with strap-like leaves, often with spiny margins and forming a funnel- or tank-like base. They are native to South and Central America, and most grow as epiphytes anchored to the branches of forest trees. The locals of the Caribbean coast of Costa Rica revere the flower and use the plants to decorate their churches. This is a rare species growing in the tops of tall trees. The flowerhead is remarkable: a woolly white cone-shaped structure over 50cm/20in long with pink bracts dangling from its base. It is grown in botanic gardens and can be propagated by cuttings.

Distribution: Costa Rica.
Height and spread: 1.2m/4ft across.
Habit and form: Perennial herb.
Leaf shape: Strap-shaped.
Pollinated: Hummingbird.

Identification: A large plant over 1m/39in tall when in flower. The flowers are white with a tinge of blue at the tips of the petals, turning red later. Male and female flowers are on separate plants (the plant is dioecious). The bright pink bracts form a skirt-like base to the inflorescence.

Far right: The bright pink bracts fold right back to expose the unusual flowerhead.

Right: The flowers turn from blue to red at the tip as they mature.

Puya raimondii

This, one of about 170 species, is the largest known bromeliad, and one of the world's most impressive plants. The rosette of spiky leaves alone reaches 3m/10ft, but when it flowers, the inflorescence can reach a truly staggering 12m/39ft. In its natural habitat in the Andes of Peru and Bolivia it takes 80–100 years to flower. Then it grows the huge mass of more than 8,000 individual flowers that last for three months. The spiky rosettes of pointed waxy leaves are inhabited by many animals, including nesting birds, and the flowers are pollinated by several species of hummingbird. It is grown in several botanic gardens, and when it flowers it becomes a magnet for visitors and a major tourist attraction.

Identification: The tough leaves form a dense rosette up to 2m/6½ft long, scaly beneath and with hooked spines along the margins. The inflorescence is up to 12m/39ft tall and 2.4m/8ft broad with thousands of white flowers.

Above: The leaves have spiny margins. The rosette houses many birds and animals.

Right: Thousands of tiny white flowers cover the spike.

Distribution: Peru and Bolivia.
Height and spread: To 3m/10ft (excluding flowerhead).
Habit and form: Perennial herb.
Leaf shape: Narrowly triangular.
Pollinated: Hummingbird.

Canistropsis billbergioides

Distribution: Brazil.
Height and spread:
45cm/18in.
Habit and form: Perennial
herb.
Leaf shape:
Strap-shaped.
Pollinated: Insect.

A popular houseplant, this species is an epiphyte that has become rare in the wild through collection. It grows in the lower forest canopy in the rainforests of south-eastern Brazil. Being rainforest species they are used to shade and so make good houseplants. They are also surprisingly hardy for tropical species. Several varieties exist, such as 'Citron', 'Persimmon', 'Blood Orange' and 'Tutti Frutti'.

Identification: Large green leaves surround a colourful cluster of overlapping bracts that may be orange, pink, red or yellow. The actual flowers are inside the cup-like bracts and are white or greenish-white, opening from May to September. The leaves vary from green to lavender.

Right: The plant puts on its most colourful display from May to September.

Left: The small, white flowers have four petals. They nestle at the centre of the bright, showy bracts.

Guzmania wittmackii

There are about 125 species in this genus of evergreen epiphytes, named after the Spanish naturalist Anastasio Guzman who died in 1802. Their colourful stems and bracts have made them popular in cultivation, but several species are threatened in the wild. Hummingbirds and bats are some of the major pollinators. The long primary bracts range from pink to orange and red, and the flowers are white or yellow. This species is a parent of many bromeliad cultivars including the famous 'Orangeade'.

Identification: The leaves reach 85cm/33in long and are slightly scaly. The inflorescence is bright red and leaf-like with red floral bracts and a creamy white stalk.

Distribution: Colombia and Ecuador.
Height and spread:
50cm/20in.
Habit and form:
Perennial herb.
Leaf shape:
Strap-like.
Pollinated:
Hummingbird.

Left: The white, tubular flower.

Left: The bright red, leaf-like bracts are very striking.

BANANA AND GINGER FAMILIES

The banana family, Musaceae, comprises tropical perennial herbs, with six genera and about 200 species.
As well as bananas, the family contain strelitzias and heliconias, the latter genus with about 100 species.
Gingers, the Zingiberaceae, comprises perennial herbs, mostly with creeping horizontal or tuberous
rhizomes. There are about 50 genera and 1,100 species with a wide distribution, mainly in the tropics.

Parrot's beak

Popokaytongo, *Heliconia psittacorum*

This herbaceous, upright, small *Heliconia*, native to Central and South America, is highly variable. It is found in forests, although it is also common in meadows and some savannas, like buttercups in cooler regions, usually forming dense clonal colonies with erect, leafy shoots in groups of 50 or more. It generally grows to no more than 60cm/24in tall. Parrot's beaks are exotic flowers, consisting of orange-red bracts with a dark spot at the end, arising from a central point on the stem. They are abundantly produced all year round.

Identification: A rhizomatous herbaceous plant with pseudostems composed of overlapping, sheathing leaf bases. The large leaves, in two vertical ranks with smooth margins, resemble those of bananas. The flowers, in erect or pendent inflorescences, consist of brightly coloured, leaf-like bracts, arranged on two sides or spirally, each subtending a coiled cyme of flowers, each flower in turn subtended by a membranous floral bract; the true flower consists of two whorls joined at the base with varying degrees of fusion within and between the whorls. The fruit is a one to three-seeded drupe, blue or red to orange at maturity.

Right: The bright orange flowers are produced abundantly throughout the year.

Distribution: Central and northern South America.
Height and spread: 60cm/24in.
Habit and form: Herbaceous perennial.
Leaf shape: Obovate.
Pollinated: Hummingbird.

Wild plantain

Balisier, *Heliconia caribaea*

The tree-like *Heliconia caribaea* is actually a herbaceous plant, the stems being made up of leaf bases. It is native to Jamaica, east Cuba and St Vincent, although it has been widely planted outside this range and, along with its numerous cultivars, has become naturalized across tropical America and beyond. The flowers can be held high on tall stems with the red spathes contrasting vividly with the white flowers. The blue fruit that follows is also eye-catching.

Identification: Large pseudostems arise from a thick underground rhizome. The leaves are up to 1.2m/4ft long, oblong, with an abruptly pointed tip and rounded base, on leaf stalks up to 60cm/24in long, often glaucous or thickly waxy. The inflorescence is 20–40cm/8–16in long, erect and straight, with 6–15 bracts up to 25cm/10in long arranged in two overlapping rows; they are broadly triangular, red or yellow, sometimes with green or yellow keels and tips. Each bract bears 9–22 flowers with straight or slightly curved sepals up to 60mm/2¼in long, white with green tips; the upper sepals curve upward, the lower sepals are spreading. The fruits are up to 15mm/⅝in long.

Distribution: Jamaica, East Cuba and St Vincent, West Indies.
Height and spread: 2.5–5m/8–16ft.
Habit and form: Tree-like herbaceous plant.
Leaf shape: Oblong.
Pollinated: Hummingbird.

Left: The tree-like growth resembles a banana plant and gives rise to the common name.

Expanded lobster claw

Heliconia latispatha

This tree-like herbaceous plant is native to Mexico, and Central and South America, although it is very widely cultivated and has become naturalized far outside this range. It is frequently found along forest edges growing in full sun to half shade. There is some colour variation in the bracts, ranging from orange to red. The erect inflorescences of spirally arranged bracts appear all year round, but more abundantly from late spring through summer, with each inflorescence lasting for several weeks on the plant.

Distribution: Mexico, Central and South America.
Height and spread: 3m/10ft.
Habit and form: Tree-like herbaceous plant.
Leaf shape: Broadly oblong to ovate.
Pollinated: Hummingbird.

Right: The inflorescence stem curls in alternating arcs between each of the claw-shaped flower bracts.

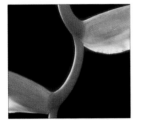

Identification: Pseudostems arise from a thick underground rhizome. The leaves are up to 1.5m/5ft long, broadly oblong oval, sometimes edged red. The inflorescence is 30–50cm/12–20in long, erect, held above the leaves; it consists of 20–30 slender, spreading keeled bracts, spirally arranged, not overlapping, dark red or orange to green-yellow; the flowers are yellow, edged and tipped with green.

OTHER SPECIES OF NOTE

Spiral ginger *Costus malortieanus*
A familiar sight in the rainforests of Costa Rica down as far as Brazil. Spiral ginger is most noteworthy for its spiralling stems, which are thought to be an adaptation to make the best of available light. The pyramidal flower spikes are held at the end of leafy stems, with one small, tubular, yellow flower arising from each bract.

Shining bird of paradise *Heliconia metallica*
Native from Honduras to Bolivia, this *Heliconia* is more noteworthy for its handsome foliage than its pretty but comparatively less significant inflorescences. The leaves are a satiny dark green with a light midrib and often a wine-purple underside. The pink or red flowers and greenish bracts are held on long stalks away from the leaves.

Hanging heliconia
Heliconia rostrata
This native of Colombia, Venezuela, Ecuador, Peru and Bolivia is frequently found at relatively low elevations, along seasonally flooded Amazon tributaries. Its popularity in cultivation has led to its spread throughout the tropical world. Pendent inflorescences of red and yellow bracts last for several weeks on the plant. It is also known as lobster claw.

Monkada

Renealmia cernua

Monkada is a tall and showy ginger plant, with hard and waxy orange and yellow bracts held terminally and reminiscent of a pineapple. The light green foliage is wavy on the edges and notable for its "ginger" scent when crushed. It is most commonly encountered in humid areas and on slopes beneath trees, being widely distributed in forested tropical regions from Mexico to South America.

Identification: An aromatic perennial herb, 90cm–5m/35in–16ft tall with leafy stems, leaves two ranked. The leaves are 10–45cm/4–18in long, narrowly elliptic, acuminate, glabrous. Inflorescence racemose, terminal on long stems, to 25cm/10in long, ovoid bracts, red to yellow, sometimes tinged green, triangular, acute. Calyx to 12mm/½in long, tubular, three-lobed, same colour as bracts; corolla to 25mm/1in long, yellow to white; petals to 8mm/⁵⁄₁₆in long, lip erect, not spreading, three lobed, to 8mm/⁵⁄₁₆in long, yellow to white, ovate, base and margin pubescent. The fruit is a fleshy capsule.

Distribution: Central and South America.
Height and spread: 90cm–5m/35in–16ft tall.
Habit and form: Herbaceous.
Leaf shape: Elliptic.
Pollinated: Bird and probably insect.

Below: The waxy orange and yellow bracts are pineapple-like.

LILY FAMILY

The lily family, Liliaceae, is large and complex, mostly consisting of perennial herbs that grow from starchy rhizomes, corms or bulbs. It comprises about 290 genera and 4,950 species, including many ornamental flowers as well as several important agricultural crops. They are found throughout the world, especially in dry areas, in warm and temperate regions.

Barbados lily

Hippeastrum puniceum

Hippeastrum means horse star, and probably refers to the large size of the star-like blooms. The Barbados lily is the most widespread species in its genus, common in open situations, and across Barbados as well as Central America, the West Indies and much of tropical South America. Its tall stems bear between two and four large, elegant, bright red, orange or pink flowers, which have a beautiful fragrance and attract bees, hummingbirds and butterflies. A mature plant may bloom for 10 months of the year. In some areas, such as Hawaii, it is considered to be invasive.

Identification: There are four to six bright green leaves at 30–60cm/12–24in long and about 30mm/1⅛in wide, tapering to a tip. Two to four tubular flowers per plant top a simple stem. The tepals are usually orange, but may rarely be pink or even white. They are about 70mm/2¾in in length. The tube is either the same colour as the tepals or green. The style is long, exceeding the stamens by about 10mm/⅜in. The bulb is ovoid and about 40–50mm/1½–2in in diameter.

Above: The flowerheads dangle above the 60cm/24in long leaves.

Distribution: West Indies, Central and northern South America.
Height and spread: 40–60cm/16–24in tall.
Habit and form: Bulbous perennial.
Leaf shape: Strap-shaped.
Pollinated: Insect and bird.

Urceolina urceolata

Confined to the Peruvian Andes, this bulbous perennial has curiously shaped flowers that hang down on slender stalks. The lower part of the stalk-like flower tube swells abruptly into an urn-like upper part, giving rise to the generic name, which means 'little pitcher'. The stalked leaves usually develop later than the flowers, which are normally yellow with green-and-white tips.

Left: The yellow flowers with green tips appear in spring and are up to 80mm/3⅛in long.

Identification: Four hairless, oval to oblong, pointed leaves, up to 50cm/20in long and 15cm/6in wide, bright green above, paler below, on 10cm/4in stalks, appear at the same times as the flowers. In spring and summer, a leafless, solitary stem bears a small umbel of four to six nodding, tubular flowers up to 10cm/4in long, the upper two thirds urn-shaped, usually yellow, more rarely cinnabar-red, orange or white, with green tips and sometimes with white margins. The fruit that follows is a capsule.

Distribution: Peruvian Andes.
Height and spread: 30cm/12in.
Habit and form: Herbaceous, bulbous perennial.
Leaf shape: Ovate to oblong.
Pollinated: Insect.

Glory of the sun

Leucocoryne ixioides

This South American bulbous plant is distantly related to the onion, *Allium* species, differing in having three fertile stamens instead of six. The plant's name is derived from the Greek words *leukos* meaning 'white' and *koryne* meaning 'club' referring to the prominent, infertile anthers. The flowers appear in spring and can be white, pink or pale lilac, with the plant being very variable in its wild setting. Ranging from Colombia to Valparaiso, it is especially abundant between the region of Coquimbo and the river Bío Bío in Chile.

Distribution: Colombia to Chile.
Height and spread: 45cm/18in.
Habit and form: Herbaceous bulbous perennial.
Leaf shape: Linear.
Pollinated: Insect.

Identification: The leaves are basal, slender and grass-like, withering before the flowers appear. Six to nine fragrant flowers in a loose umbel appear in spring on stalks up to 65mm/2½in long; they have six tepals, with the lower parts fused into a white basal tube and the upper parts free and spreading, white or more usually deeply edged lilac to violet blue. Three slender, cylindrical yellow-white staminodes, sometimes with dark tips, are joined to the perianth at the mouth of the basal tube.

OTHER SPECIES OF NOTE

Golden lily-of-the-incas
Alstroemeria aurea
This spreading, tuberous perennial, native to Chile and Brazil, has become a very popular garden plant. The stems carry lance-shaped, twisted leaves, which are topped during the summer by loose heads of yellow or orange flowers, tipped with green and usually streaked with dark red, usually in clusters at the end of thin leafy stems.

Coicopihue *Philesia magellanica*
This small, low-growing shrub has deep pink, waxy flowers. It is a fairly common evergreen plant in the cold, wet, swampy rainforests of southern Chile. It has a 'box-like' habit of growth, spreading by subterranean stolons that can grow up to 1.2m/4ft. The leaves are small, leathery and glossy green.

Green amaryllis *Hippeastrum calyptratum*
From the Brazillian coastal rainforests, this epiphyte has shapely greenish-yellow flowers that emit a sour odour, and this attracts bats as pollinators. It is a vulnerable species in the wild, having been over-collected.

Leucocoryne purpurea
One of the most beautiful species in this genus of 12 from Chile, where it grows in Mediterranean scrub. Its grass-like leaves dry and wither and are then followed by an impressive display of purple flowers, between three and eight to each stem. In some areas it flowers in colonies along the roadsides. It can be propagated from corms or from seed and grown under glass in cooler climates.

Inca lily

Peruvian lily, *Alstroemeria pelegrina*

One of 50 species of South American lilies, the Inca lily is important as a wild ancestor of many hybrids that are now cultivated throughout the world, partly for the cut flower industry. Yet in the wild it has a very restricted range, being found only in a certain part of the Mediterranean region of Chile, where it grows in dry scrub habitats, often among rocks close to the Pacific shore. Many of these sites are threatened by property development.

Distribution: Chile.
Height and spread: To 60cm/24in.
Habit and form: Perennial herb.
Leaf shape: Lanceolate.
Pollinated: Insect.

Identification: The flowers are mainly pink, with white and yellow markings towards the centre; they open in summer and autumn. They are either solitary or in groups of two or three. The stems grow from a network of underground fleshy roots and rhizomes.

Far right: The flowers have six tepals with striking markings.

Top right: The seedpod opening.

Amazon lily

Eucharis amazonica

This is one of the best-known members of this genus of South American lilies, which contains 17 species. In the wild it grows in north-eastern Peru, where it is known from only a few populations in the rainforests of the lower slopes of the eastern Andes. It has large dark green leaves and large white flowers that are sweetly-scented. As many as six flowers develop on leafless stalks in the early summer. The Amazon lily has become a much-prized species among keen gardeners and is not difficult to grow. It thrives outdoors in tropical and subtropical climates, and can also be grown in containers, either outside or as a houseplant. Although its natural habitat is damp environments, flowering may be induced by subjecting the plants to short dry spells.

Identification: The long, elliptic leaves are wavy, with a sharp tip. The flowers have a long, curved tube, and open, spreading ovate lobes, to 90mm/3½in across. At the centre of each flower is a toothed cup-shaped structure formed from the fused stamens.

Distribution: Peru.
Height and spread: To 60cm/24in.
Habit and form: Perennial herb.
Leaf shape: Elliptic.
Pollinated: Insect.

Above and right: The flowers are white and daffodil-like in shape. The leaves are dark and highly glossy.

Cojomaria

Paramongaia weberbaueri

This magnificent flower, the only member of its genus, is a rare endemic from the western foothills of the Andes of Peru and Bolivia.

Only three wild populations are known, and it is often picked by locals for sale in markets. Its bright daffodil-like, yellow fragrant flowers have made it a great favourite. Cojomaria has the largest flowers of any member of the amaryllis group of the lily family. In cultivation it is best grown in containers, and can be propagated from seed, although it does demand carefully controlled growing conditions.

Identification: The individual flowers can reach 20cm/8in across, with a tube 10cm/4in long, and six spreading lobes. From the centre extends the trumpet-like corona with the stalks of the stamens attached below the rim.

Distribution: Bolivia and Peru.
Height and spread: To 60cm/24in.
Habit and form: Bulbous herb.
Leaf shape: Linear, narrow.
Pollinated: Insect.

Above: The flowers resemble daffodils but are very large and have a wonderful scent.

Right: The plant is rarely found in the wild, and over-collection threatens existing colonies.

Blue amaryllis

Worsleya rayneri

Distribution: Organ Mountains, Brazil.
Height and spread: 2m/6½ft.
Habit and form: Evergreen bulbous perennial.
Leaf shape: Strap-shaped.
Pollinated: Insect.

Blue amaryllis is another species in a genus all of its own. With its spectacular clusters of lilac or pale blue flowers, it has gained an almost legendary status among gardeners. It has a perilous existence in the wild, being found in just two sites in the mountains north of Rio de Janeiro. As these habitats are inaccessible, it is not easily collected, but fires pose a problem in the dry season. It is a challenge to cultivate it, partly because its roots have a moisture-collecting outer layer and must be undisturbed to function efficiently.

Identification: An evergreen bulbous perennial with narrow strap-shaped, curving leaves to 1m/39in long. The flowers develop in terminal umbels of four to six flowers. The blue or mauve funnel-shaped perianth has curving lobes spreading from a tubular base.

OTHER SPECIES OF NOTE

Peruvian lily vine
Bomarea caldasii
In the Andes of Colombia and Ecuador this lily is quite common at altitudes of 1,850–3,700m/ 6,000–12,000ft. The flowers, growing in dangling clusters, are either orange-red or yellow. It is a half-hardy climber suited to a sunny border or greenhouse in cooler regions.

Griffinia liboniana
This species is endemic to the Atlantic rainforests of Brazil, where it is endangered by habitat loss. It has pretty flowers with lilac and white spreading lobes. It is best grown in shady moist conditions, either outside in tropical or subtropical regions, or as a container plant in temperate climates.

Chilean bellflower, Copihue *Lapageria rosea*
Plant enthusiasts regard this plant highly, as one of the finest of temperate climbers. It is a woody, twining vine producing large numbers of red, waxy bell-like flowers, contrasting well with the lush, deep green evergreen leaves. If frost protected, it does well in temperate regions.

Pamianthe peruviana
An epiphyte from the mountain rainforests of the western Andes of Bolivia and Peru, this species has large, fragrant white flowers. The segments surrounding the central corona have a central green stripe.

Chilean blue crocus

Tecophilaea cyanocrocus

Sometimes placed in a separate family (Tecophilaeaceae), this pretty flower was saved from extinction by re-introduction from cultivated stock. The wild distribution is very limited – high alpine meadows near Santiago in Chile, at altitudes of about 3,000m/10,000ft, where it was reduced to apparent eradication by grazing and over-collection. Luckily, two wild populations were then found, in 2001. It is tricky to grow, requiring cool conditions and gritty soil, but rewards with displays of deep blue or blue and white flowers.

Identification: The narrow leaves grow to about 12.5cm/5in. The flowers are about 35mm/1⅜in across, gentian blue and veined, sometimes with a white margin, or white in the neck.

Distribution: Chile.
Height and spread: 10cm/4in.
Habit and form: Perennial herb.
Leaf shape: Linear-lanceolate.
Pollinated: Insect.

Below: The flowers are a deep, unusual blue with white centres.

Left: The plants grow to about 10cm/ 4in tall.

ORCHID FAMILY

The orchid family, Orchidaceae, is widespread and spectacular with respect to its diversity in the Americas. The northern continent shares many genera with Eurasia, and even where species have been separated by geographic isolation for long periods, such as those found in South America, they often show a striking similarity to species found in similar habitats elsewhere on the planet.

Masdevallia tricallosa

This orchid occurs in Peru, in wet montane forests at altitudes of around 2,000m/6,500ft. It may grow as an epiphyte, terrestrial or lithophyte. It often goes unnoticed in the canopy, partly because it is out of view, but also because the small rhizomatous growth is easily overlooked when not in bloom. It is distinguished by its distinctive white flower, which appears in the rainy season, singly on a short stalk. The actual petals are deep inside the flower, but the three sepals are very showy, with long tails.

Identification: Spreading epiphyte, growing from a short, creeping rhizome from which (unusually for the genus) appear minute pseudobulbs. The blackish, erect, slender ramicauls, are enveloped basally by two to three tubular sheaths, carrying a single, apical, erect, leathery, yet pliable, ovate to elliptical or lanceolate leaf. The inflorescence is erect and slender, 50mm/2in long; single flowered, arising from low on the ramicaul, with a bract below the middle and a tubular floral bract carrying the flower at or just below leaf height. The flowers are triangular, white, with a small labellum partly hidden deep inside the flower and three large sepals fused along their edges each with a long tail. It is distinguished by three conspicuous, dark purple calli at the apex of the lip in the centre.

Distribution: Peru.
Height and spread: Low creeper.
Habit and form: Epiphyte.
Leaf shape: Ovate to elliptical.
Pollinated: Insect.

Scarlet maxillaria

Ornithidium coccineum syn. *Maxillaria coccinea*

This epiphytic orchid species is found in montane forests in the Greater and Lesser Antilles. The flowers, which are usually red, are held in dense clusters, often tucked under the foliage, and are characterized by three fleshy sepals arranged in a triangular fashion. The style and stamens are fused together and curved over in jaw-like fashion over the lip.

Identification: The rhizome is covered in overlapping, papery sheaths. The pseudobulbs are up to 40mm/1½in long; oval, compressed and one-leaved. The leaves, up to 35cm/14in long and 25mm/1in wide, are narrow, oblong, pointed or blunt-tipped, and folded at the base. The flowers, in clusters on wiry 50mm/2in stalks, are bright fuchsia-pink. Their sepals are about 12mm/½in in length, spreading, fleshy, oval to lance-shaped, tapering and concave. The petals, up to 8mm/⁵⁄₁₆in long, are oval to lance-shaped, tapering or pointed. The lip, to 8mm/⁵⁄₁₆in long, is fleshy and three-lobed. The capsule is beaked.

Distribution: Greater and Lesser Antilles.
Height and spread: 50cm/20in.
Habit and form: Epiphyte.
Leaf shape: Linear oblong.
Pollinated: Insect.

Left: The flowers of scarlet maxillaria can be seen from quite a distance, thanks to the bright red colour of the sepals.

Fringed star orchid

Epidendrum ciliare

This is a very widespread species of epiphytic orchid, ranging from the southern part of North America, Mexico, throughout the Caribbean and parts of South America. The pseudobulbs are oblong and compressed, with one or two leathery leaves. The erect clusters of waxy flowers, which can be extremely variable in size, are strongly fragrant at night. They appear all year round, with the best flowers in spring and early summer.

Distribution: Southern North America, Mexico, Caribbean and South America.
Height and spread: Creeping, not exceeding 15cm/6in.
Habit and form: Epiphyte.
Leaf shape: Oblong-ligulate.
Pollinated: Insect.

Identification: The pseudobulbs are tufted, cylindrical, up to 15cm/6in long, with one to three leaves at the tip of each. The leaves are up to 28cm/11in long, lance-shaped, leathery and glossy. The erect raceme, up to 30cm/12in tall, bears a few or several flowers, with their stalks concealed by large, overlapping, purple-spotted sheaths. The flowers are large and very fragrant, with thin, tapering tepals up to 75mm/3in long, white to green or pale yellow. The white lip, joined to the basal half of the column and up to 50mm/2in long, is deeply three-lobed: the lateral lobes are flared and fringed and the mid-lobe is long and straight.

OTHER SPECIES OF NOTE

Laelia anceps
This native of Mexico and possibly Honduras grows on rocks and trees at the fringes of dense forests, and is extremely popular in cultivation. The large, 10cm/4in flowers are generally light lavender with a darker lip and throat and are borne in a cluster of between two and six blooms on the end of a long spike.

Zygopetalum intermedium
Found in the states of Santa Catarina to Espiritu Santo, Brazil, at elevations of 600–1,200m/ 2,000–4,000ft, this medium-size, terrestrial or epiphytic orchid has long, erect, racemes with three to 10 showy, fragrant, waxy, long-lived flowers, with a pale blue lip and maroon-spotted green sepals.

Epidendrum medusae
These flowers are most unusual in having a fleshy maroon lip with its margin deeply divided into a mass of filaments – hence the specific name, referring to the Greek Medusa with a head of writhing snakes.

Masdevallia stumpflei
This species grows among rocks in the Peruvian Andes. It produces bright red flowers with a characteristic three-lobed appearance. Many species and hybrids are now available and they are not difficult to grow.

Spider orchid

Brassia longissima

This epiphytic orchid is found in the rainforests of Costa Rica and is considered to be a variety of *B. lawrenciana* by some authorities. However, it differs from that species principally in its longer, tail-like sepals. The flowers are very striking and strangely scented, and appear on pendent racemes of six or more, borne at the start of the rainy season.

Identification: The pseudobulbs, up to 10cm/4in long, are oblong, laterally compressed and glossy pale green, usually with two leaves growing from the tip. The leaves are up to 40cm/16in long, narrowly oblong to lance-shaped, pointed or tapering. The raceme is arching to pendent, often surpassing the leaves, with thin textured flowers with very long, twisting, pale green or yellow tepals, striped red-purple at the base, often with inrolled margins; the lip is up to 45mm/1¾in long, white to pale green or pale yellow, fiddle-shaped with a long, tapering tip.

Distribution: Costa Rica.
Height and spread: Creeping, not exceeding 10cm/4in.
Habit and form: Epiphyte.
Leaf shape: Narrowly oblong.
Pollinated: Insect.

Dracula orchid

Dracula vampira

This sinister-named orchid is one of more than 60 species in the genus. The name actually translates as 'little dragon' and refers to the spurs on the sepals. It has unusual flowers, bat-like in some species and in this case very dark; almost black. The background colour to the flowers is actually green, but this is overlain by very dark purple-black stripes and smudges. In the wild this orchid is restricted to the forests of a single mountain (Mount Pichincha) in Ecuador at altitudes up to 2,000m/6,550ft. It grows as an epiphyte on the branches of trees. It can be grown in moist shady conditions, ideally in a basket with bark and compost and may flower throughout the year.

Centre rght: The white lip petal is surrounded by dramatic, dark and tapering sepals.

Identification: The leaves are up to about 28cm/11in long, and each inflorescence stalk has several flowers, each of which is up to 30cm/12in long and 15cm/6in wide. The strange flowers have rounded sepals, each ending in a thin tail, up to 11cm/4½in long. The much smaller petals and lip are white with purple or pink veins. The flowers dangle down below the main plant, which is usually found growing on tree branches.

Distribution: Ecuador
Height and spread: 30cm/12in.
Habit and form: Pendulous epiphyte.
Leaf shape: Fleshy.
Pollinated: Insect.

Left: The flowers extend some distance from the rosette of leaves, on elegant, slender stalks.

Lindley's barkeria

Barkeria lindleyana

Most of the approximately 15 species of these fine rainforest orchids are threatened in the wild. This species is one of the most beautiful, with its large pink, purple or white flowers opening on arching stems, each carrying up to 20 flowers. It grows in montane forests, where there is a dry season in the winter. It also appears sometimes in nearby gardens. It requires bright sunny conditions with good air circulation, but also high humidity, regular feeding, and a resting dry period. The name commemorates two people: George Barker (1880–1965), an Edwardian orchid collector, and John Lindley (1799–1865), a famous botanist.

Below: There are up to 20 flowers on each stem.

Distribution: Mexico and Costa Rica.
Height and spread: Stems to 60cm/24in.
Habit and form: Epiphyte.
Leaf shape: Linear-lanceolate.
Pollinated: Insect.

Identification: Each flower can be 80mm/3⅛in across and remain open for several months. 'Bulbs' (technically pseudobulbs) grow to about 15cm/6in, cane-like. The leaves are sometimes tinted rosy pink. The flowers range from white to pink or deep purple, with the lip a darker shade.

Broughtonia sanguinea

This genus contains just five species from the West Indies. This Jamaican species is a small, compact orchid treasured for its bright red flowers, borne on long arching stems. It grows in low-altitude rainforest. A healthy plant will produce flowering spikes through much of the year. It grows best in a well-drained pot or on an epiphyte slab, in bright sun and should be well fed and watered when actively growing. Older plants can be rejuvenated by removing the roots. It needs warm conditions (minimum 20°C/68°F), high light and high humidity. It has been used to produce hybrids with species of *Cattleya*, the products being known as cattleytonias.

Distribution: Jamaica.
Height and spread: Leaves to 18cm/7in.
Habit and form: Epiphytic orchid.
Pollinated: Insect.
Leaf shape: Narrow-oblong.

Right: The flower has a prominent, rounded lip.

Identification: It has a compact cluster of small, flat pseudobulbs, each with two or three small leathery leaves. The flowerheads reach about 30cm/12in long and grow from the tips of the 'bulbs'.

Above: The pseudobulbs are covered in a papery skin. The petals are deep scarlet.

OTHER SPECIES OF NOTE

Christmas cattleya *Cattleya trianae*
A winter-flowering species that is now rare in its Colombian rainforest home, but very popular in cultivation, both as the species and in various hybrid forms. The genus contains about 70 species, many of them epiphytes. The flowers are pinkish or white with a crimson central lobe and yellow disc.

Cattleya bowringiana
A popular species from Guatemala and Belize, this grows in soil, on rocks and also as an epiphyte on branches. It produces up to 25 flowers per spike. These are usually pink-blue, but there are varieties with flowers that are almost white, and nearly blue.

Lepanthes calodictyon
A diminutive orchid from Peru that is unusual in being valued for its decorative leaves rather than its flowers. The flowers are tiny and bright red and yellow, contrasting with the emerald green leaves, which have brown veins. In its northern Andean home, it is an epiphyte on trees at elevations of 750–1,300m/2,500–4,250ft.

Nun's orchid *Lycaste skinneri*
One of a genus named after plant hunter George Ure Skinner (1804–67). The flowers may be white, pink or lavender. The white sepals look like a nun's veil, hence the common name. It is the national flower of Guatemala.

Ondoglossum crispum

This species, one of about 100 in the genus, is one of the most highly prized of all orchids and was at the centre of the orchid-mania in Victorian times. It was discovered by Karl Theodor Hartweg in 1841, and grows in cloud forest in Colombia. It was savagely over-collected and specimens fetched huge prices in Europe. As a result of this and of forest clearance it is now much rarer in the wild, though still popular and abundant in collections. The species name refers to the crinkly edges of the flower parts.

Distribution: Colombia.
Height and spread: 1m/39in.
Habit and form: Epiphytic orchid.
Leaf shape: Linear-lanceolate.
Pollinated: Insect.

Identification: The flowering stems are arched with three or four large sparkling white flowers. The petals and sepals have toothed or uneven margins and the lip is usually blotched red with a yellow centre.

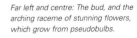

Far left and centre: The bud, and the arching raceme of stunning flowers, which grow from pseudobulbs.

Holy ghost orchid

Dove orchid, *Peristeria elata*

This fine large orchid is the national flower of Panama, where it was previously much commoner than it is now. A combination of local picking, collection for the overseas orchid trade, and habitat destruction has resulted in its decline in the wild. The flowers are often used to decorate churches at Easter. It grows mainly on the ground in leaf litter, from sea level to about 600m/2,000ft. The inner parts of the strongly-scented flowers resemble a white dove with its wings raised. The dove orchid is best grown in shallow clay pots with a well-draining leafy substrate, and kept moist in the growing season.

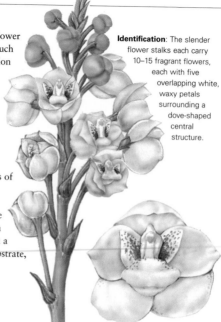

Identification: The slender flower stalks each carry 10–15 fragrant flowers, each with five overlapping white, waxy petals surrounding a dove-shaped central structure.

Distribution: Costa Rica, Panama, Venezuela and Colombia.
Height and spread: Flower stalk to 1.5m/5ft.
Habit and form: Terrestrial orchid.
Leaf shape: Elliptic-lanceolate.
Pollinated: Insect.

Left: The white flowers bloom sequentially on the tall spike. It usually flowers in late spring.

Phragmipedium besseae

Identification: The vivid scarlet (sometimes orange or yellow) flowers are the main feature of this orchid. The dark green foliage produces a stalk with one to six flowers that open in sequence. Each flower is about 50mm/2in across.

The 20 species in this genus are often called tropical slipper orchids, because of the shape of the flower. This species was first found in Peru but may now be extinct there, although it still grows in Ecuador. Its natural habitat is close to running water, such as along the banks of streams, among mosses and humus. It was over collected after its discovery in 1981 and then fetched very high prices. Now it has been produced from seed in large numbers so pressure on the wild stocks has been reduced. In cultivation it should be watered with pure mineral-free water, or rainwater; tap water may cause damage. It has been used to produce many hybrids with a range of varied flower colours.

Distribution: Colombia, Ecuador, possibly Peru.
Height and spread: 25cm/10in.
Habit and form: Terrestrial orchid.
Leaf shape: Narrow.
Pollinated: Insect.

Left: The bud, drooping from the elegant stem.

Right: Flower spikes are sent forth from the rosette of lush, tapering leaves. The flowers are vivid in colour and have a slipper-shaped lip. Over collection due to its beauty, as well as loss of habitat have devastated this species, and it is now endangered.

Sophronitis lobata

This fine orchid has large, elaborate and ornate flowers and is therefore very popular among enthusiast growers. As with many orchids, this trade has led to its decline in its native wild sites near Rio de Janeiro in Brazil, in this case rock outcrops and as an epiphyte on the branches of trees. Artificial propagation has meant that this splendid orchid is now widely available from specialist orchid nurseries in many countries. Fortunately, it is relatively trouble-free to grow, although not always easy to bring into flower.

Right: The flowers are large and have an attractive spreading shape, but the overall plant is fairly small, with a single leaf.

Distribution: Brazil.
Height and spread: Flower spikes to 35cm/14in.
Habit and form: Epiphytic or terrestrial orchid.
Leaf shape: Ovate-oblong.
Pollinated: Insect.

Identification: A small orchid with fleshy leaves. Each club-shaped 'bulb' is 10–20cm/4–8in tall and produces a single leaf. The flower spikes grow from spring to early summer and each has six or more flowers. The individual flowers are as large as 15cm/6in across and pure white with spreading outer lobes.

Right: The smooth and club-shaped bulb.

OTHER SPECIES OF NOTE

Phragmipedium caudatum
This plant is normally an epiphyte. Its flowers have ribbon-like red-tinted spiralling petals that may be as long as 60cm/24in. The rest of the flower is greenish, with a pink and yellow slipper-shaped lip. It grows from Mexico to Peru.

Pleurothallis tuerkheimii
This grows from Mexico to Panama. It belongs to one of the largest of all orchid genera, with more than 1100 species. It is one of the more widespread species and usually grows as an epiphyte. It is also fairly easy to grow and produces a many-flowered inflorescence with maroon and white flowers.

Sophronitis jongheana
Discovered in 1854, this species hails from Brazil. It grows as an epiphyte in rainforests, at altitudes of 1,300–1,600m/4,250–5,250ft. The magnificent flowers are to 15cm/6in across, and a delicate pale pink. Plants can easily be grown from seed, and many hybrid forms have been bred from this species.

Vanilla *Vanilla planifolia*
Familiar from the flavouring prepared from the dried fruit pods, vanilla is native to South and Central America and the West Indies, although it is now widely cultivated as a crop. It is a scrambling vine, clambering up tree trunks. The flowers are large and yellow or green and last only a short time, often less than a day.

Stanhopea tigrina

The elaborate flowers of this epiphyte look more like a tropical coral reef fish than a rainforest orchid. They produce a sweet fragrance, attractive to pollinating insects. Although each flower lasts only a few days, large plants produce many flowers in succession. The major pollinators are bees, and the complex structure of the flower carefully guides each bee, ensuring pollen sticks to its body. In cultivation it grows best in a slatted basket lined with tree bark or coconut fibre. The flowering shoots appear from under the basket.

Identification: The egg-shaped 'bulbs' are up to 60mm/2¼in tall and the single ribbed leaf measures about 35 x 12cm/14 x 4¾in. The flowers are large and complex, creamy-yellow with purple-brown tiger-stripes and blotches.

Below: Large plants may produce several flowers in succession.

Distribution: Mexico.
Height and spread: Leaf to 35cm/14in.
Habit and form: Epiphytic orchid.
Leaf shape: Elliptic-lanceolate.
Pollinated: Insect.

Left: The buds open to reveal showy flowers.

WILD FLOWERS OF AUSTRALIA AND OCEANIA

Australia is an ancient continent, with a continuous history
of 200 million years above sea level, and is home to a great many
species of flowering plants, more than two-thirds of which are not
found anywhere else on Earth. The Pacific Ocean covers nearly one-third
of the globe, and is the largest, deepest and probably the most violent of
all the oceans. Its vast central and southern expanse – known as Oceania
– is dotted with thousands of islands. Many of these islands are home to
unusual and interesting plants, all of which originally reached them from
across the ocean, although plenty have since evolved into unique forms.

The region does not include any continental land mass, although
Australia and New Zealand are sometimes included on
its westernmost edge.

Above from left: Willow-leaved crowea (Crowea saligna), ivory curl (Buckinghamia celsissima), and lesser bottlebrush (Callistemon phoeniceus).

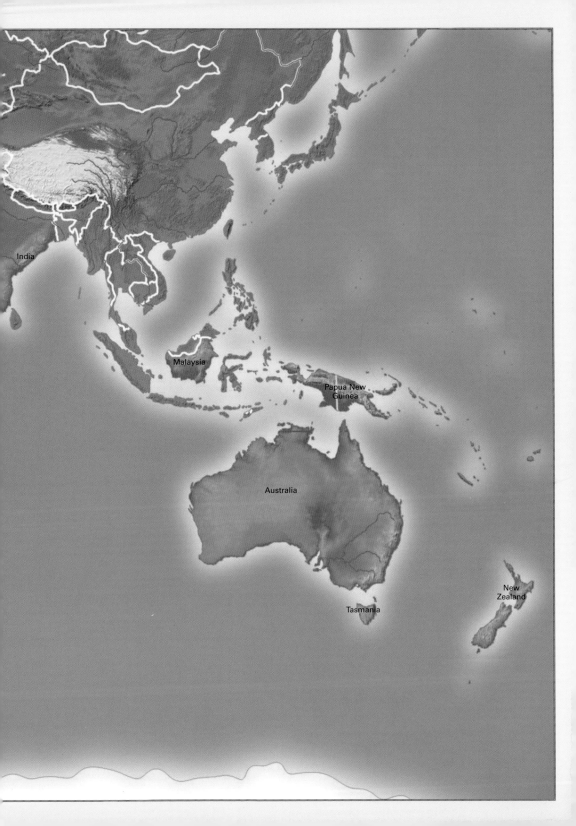

BUTTERCUP AND DILLENIA FAMILIES

The Ranunculaceae, or buttercup family, are better represented in the Northern Hemisphere than in Australasia or Oceania, but those species that do occur are often striking examples. The Dilleniaceae, or dillenia family, are closely related, mainly from tropical and warm regions, especially Australia. They include trees, shrubs and occasionally vines, comprising 10 genera and about 350 species.

Gold guinea plant

Snake vine, Climbing guinea flower, *Hibbertia scandens*

This climbing shrub is restricted to eastern Australia, occurring in Queensland and New South Wales. It climbs by twining its way up other shrubs and may occur as a more procumbent shrub in the absence of a suitable support plant. Its large golden-yellow flowers are borne at the end of short side branches and appear in early spring among the evergreen leaves, often providing an eye-catching display among the shrubby vegetation.

Below: Berries cluster on old sepals.

Identification: The trailing stems of this vigorous climber are initially hairy. The leaves are alternate, 50mm–10cm/2–4in long, glossy above and hairy beneath, and tend to clasp the stems. The golden-yellow flowers, which have an unpleasant smell, are up to 50mm/2in across and are borne at the tips of downy, lateral branchlets; they have five notched petals with slightly wavy edges, and numerous stamens. The round fruits, about 20mm/¾in across, contain several shiny red seeds.

Distribution: Eastern Australia.
Height and spread: 1.8m/6ft.
Habit and form: Evergreen shrub.
Leaf shape: Obovate to lanceolate.
Pollinated: Insect.

Far left: The short side branches are laden with flowers in early spring.

Korikori

Hairy alpine buttercup, *Ranunculus insignis*

This yellow-flowered New Zealand buttercup is found at higher altitudes of around 1,050–2,000m/3,450–6,550ft on North and South Islands. It is a widespread species but generally tends to favour habitats that are sheltered from the drying sun: in areas with a greater number of cloudy days it can be found in more exposed positions, but always prefers moist soils.

Identification: The stems range in height from 10–90cm/4–35in. The dark green, leathery, basal leaves, up to 15cm/6in across, are oval to heart-shaped, with toothed, hairy margins; the stem leaves have three lobes. Each branched stem carries numerous yellow flowers up to 50mm/2in across, with five to seven oval, notched or rounded petals.

Below right: The yellow flowers are borne abundantly above the large leaves (below).

Distribution: New Zealand.
Height and spread: 10–90cm/4–35in.
Habit and form: Herbaceous perennial.
Leaf shape: Ovate-cordate.
Pollinated: Insect.

Right: The large leathery leaves can easily be spotted in high rocky places when the plant is not in flower.

Mount cook lily

Mountain buttercup, *Ranunculus lyallii*

This magnificent buttercup, from the Southern Alps of New Zealand's South Island, has large, waxy white flowers held above huge glossy leaves shaped like saucers. It prefers a sheltered site, usually in the shade of rocks or other plants, and flourishes in stony soils near torrents at altitudes of 450–1,500m/1,500–4,900ft. It is an extremely robust plant in ideal conditions and can be very striking when encountered in the wild.

Distribution: South Island, New Zealand.
Height and spread: Up to 1.5m/5ft.
Habit and form: Herbaceous perennial.
Leaf shape: Peltate.
Pollinated: Insect.

Far right: The large distinctive, saucer-shaped leaves stand out among rocks and other mountain plants.

Identification: The stout, branched stems may grow up to 1.5m/5ft tall. The saucer-shaped leaves are dark green and leathery, borne on long stalks attached to the centre of the leaves; the basal leaves are up to 40cm/16in across, progressively reducing in size up the stems. The white flowers are borne in panicles of five to 15; they are 50–75mm/2–3in across with 10–16 oval, rounded or notched petals and a green centre surrounded by numerous yellow stamens.

Twining guinea flower
Hibbertia dentata
This trailing or twining shrub found in New South Wales, has large, deep yellow flowers with oval pointed petals, alternating with shortened calyx lobes, which appear on the branch ends. The dark green leaves are prickle-toothed.

Trailing guinea flower *Hibbertia empetrifolia*
This small shrub occurs naturally in a wide variety of habitats in south-eastern Australia, from south-east Queensland around the coast to South Australia and Tasmania. The yellow flowers appear in spring, and at their peak the plants resemble bright yellow mounds, with the foliage scarcely visible between the flowers.

Ranunculus pinguis
This New Zealand native, found only on the Auckland Islands and Campbell Island is now restricted to a few, inaccessible ledges, due to intensive grazing. The multi-petalled yellow flowers appear in the spring above the basal leaves, which resemble pelargonium leaves.

Old man's beard *Clematis aristata*
This Australian climber flowers in early summer in panicle-like inflorescences arising from leaf axils near the branch tips. The showy flowers consist of four or five white or ivory sepals. These are followed later in the season by feathery, fluffy seedheads.

Small-leaved clematis

Traveller's joy, *Clematis microphylla*

This vigorous, sprawling climber is widespread in Australia, and is found in all states except the Northern Territory. It is especially common in coastal regions or near rivers, in moist gullies and on tablelands. The species is dioecious, with male and female flowers carried on separate plants. The greenish-white flowers, which appear in early summer, are produced in the leaf axils, giving the branch tips an inflorescence-like appearance when the plant is in full bloom.

Distribution: Australia.
Height and spread: 3m/10ft.
Habit and form: Woody, sprawling climber.
Leaf shape: Trifoliate, lanceolate.
Pollinated: Insect.

Identification: The leaves are opposite, on long leaf stalks, often twisted; each consists of two or three narrow or lance-shaped leaflets about 15mm/⁹⁄₁₆in long and 3mm/¹⁄₈in wide. The star-like flowers, carried in short panicles, consist of four narrow, creamy-white sepals tinged green, up to 25mm/1in long, surrounding a central mass of numerous yellow stamens. They are followed by attractive, feathery seedheads on the female plants.

Above and below: The seedheads appear in late summer and autumn.

ROSE, PITTOSPORUM AND TREMANDRA FAMILIES

The rose family, Rosaceae, has a worldwide distribution. In contrast, the Pittosporaceae, or pittosporum family, with nine genera and 240 species from the tropical world, is centred on Australasia, and the Tremandaceae, Tremenda family, with three genera and 43 species, are found in temperate Australia.

Creeping lawyer

Snow raspberry, *Rubus parvus*

This scrambling, thorny, shrubby perennial is restricted to the north-west of New Zealand's South Island. It is most commonly found in lowland forest and river flats, where its thorny stems and bronzed foliage form tangled masses over the ground. The white flowers appear in the summer and are followed by juicy, edible, red 'blackberry' fruits. It is one of only a few evergreen shrubs in New Zealand that develop an autumn tint to the foliage. Hikers know it as a plant that is 'easy to get involved with, but difficult to shake off'.

Distribution: South Island, New Zealand.
Height and spread: Variable.
Habit and form: Prostrate, scrambling, evergreen shrub.
Leaf shape: Lanceolate.
Pollinated: Insect.

Identification: The smooth stems, rooting at the nodes, are usually without prickles when mature. The leathery leaves are narrow to lance-shaped, up to 16mm/⅝in long, dark green turning bronze in the autumn, shiny above, dull below, densely and regularly serrated, with small sharp teeth on the underside of the midrib; they are borne on prickly leaf stalks up to 25mm/1in long. White flowers, up to 25mm/1in across, appear in summer in small panicles; they have five oval, spreading petals and numerous stamens. The red fruits are up to 25mm/1in long.

Left: The thorny stems form a tangled mass that spreads over the ground.

Above left: The fruits are edible.

White marianthus

Marianthus candidus

This twining shrub is endemic to western Australia, on limestone plains, particularly in coastal heaths, south from Perth to Cape Leeuwin. The dense white flower clusters appear mainly in the spring and are very attractive. The sharply pointed white petals become pink with age, especially on the lower side, and the narrow, erect, claw-like anthers are covered in bright blue pollen.

Below: White marianthus thrives in sandy soil.

Right: This plant is a twining shrub or vine that grows to 5m/16ft.

Identification: The erect, eventually twining stems are warty with lenticels. The mature leaves are narrow, up to 70mm/2¾in long, on 75mm/3in stalks. Panicles of 10–30 irregular flower clusters, each of around six tubular flowers, appear in spring; the sepals are pink and white with slightly hairy margins, and the spoon-shaped, pointed petals are up to 25mm/1in long, white becoming fawn or pink. The arrow-shaped anthers are white, eventually becoming blue, and the pollen is noticeably blue.

Distribution: Western Australia.
Height and spread: Variable.
Habit and form: Twining shrub.
Leaf shape: Elliptic.
Pollinated: Insect.

Sweet pittosporum

Native daphne, *Pittosporum undulatum*

The moist gullies in the forests of south-east Queensland to eastern Victoria are home to this tree with coarse, grey bark and glossy, green, elliptical, wavy-edged leaves. The small, white fragrant flowers appear abundantly at the branch tips in spring and early summer and in the autumn are followed by orange-tan berries, which persist for several months. Despite being native to Australia, this species has become an environmental weed in Tasmania, western Australia, western Victoria and South Australia, as well as in bushland around Sydney, chiefly because it has been favoured by habitat changes created by urban development.

Distribution: Eastern Australia.
Height and spread: 9–14m/29½–46ft.
Habit and form: Evergreen tree.
Leaf shape: Ovate.
Pollinated: Insect.

Right: This tree forms an evergreen 'mop' of foliage.

Far right: The brown woody seed capsules appear quite berry-like.

Identification: The laurel-like leaves, alternate to whorled, are 75mm–15cm/3–6in long, with pointed tips and distinctive wavy margins. The sweetly fragrant, tubular flowers are borne in terminal clusters from late spring to early summer; they are 12–20mm/½–¾in across with five creamy-white reflexed petals. The fruit is a dry, woody capsule, up to 12mm/½in in diameter, yellow, brown or orange, containing brown seeds with a sticky, resinous coating.

OTHER SPECIES OF NOTE

Karo *Pittosporum crassifolium*
The karo or stiffleaf cheesewood is a small tree found along the edges of forests and streams in New Zealand's North Island and Kermadec Island in the south-west Pacific. It has a dense, almost columnar crown, and the undersides of the leathery leaves are covered with velvety felt. Umbels of deep red blooms make a striking display.

Finger flower *Cheiranthera cyanea*
Found in the scrubby woodlands of south-eastern Australia, finger flower is named after the five stamens, which are positioned in a row. It has dense, linear foliage and despite being a small shrub has very large, striking blue flowers, which are specially adapted for pollination by bees.

Bluebell creeper *Sollya fusiformis*
From western Australia, this low shrub or vine has slender stems set with narrow, mid-green, glossy leaves. In summer and autumn it displays clusters of little bell-shaped, pale mid-blue blossoms, followed by small, blue berries.

Rubus queenslandicus
This pinnate-leaved species of native Australian bramble is endemic to coastal ranges of north Queensland. The white, hairy, five-petalled flowers are followed by characteristic, red, conical, bramble fruits, which are dry in texture.

Pink bells

Pink eye, *Tetratheca ciliata*

This widespread but uncommon Australian species, found in south Australia, Victoria and Tasmania, is restricted to coastal heaths and heathy woodland. It flowers in spring, when numerous, erect, slender stems sport a profusion of pink, four-petalled flowers with a darker central eye.

Identification: An understorey shrub with slender erect or spreading branches arising from a woody basal stock. The younger stems are clothed in fine short hairs, the older ones largely smooth. The rough-textured oval leaves, up to 12mm/½in long, grow in scattered groups of three or four, alternate to opposite or whorled. The flowers are four-parted, solitary, terminal or in the leaf axils, with purple or lilac petals up to 12mm/½in long. The fruit is a two-celled, flattened capsule.

Right: The erect or spreading branches arise from a woody base.

Distribution: Southern Australia.
Height and spread: 90cm/35in.
Habit and form: Shrub.
Leaf shape: Ovate.
Pollinated: Insect.

Below: The four-petalled flowers are pink with a darker eye.

LEGUMES

Legumes form a significant component of nearly all terrestrial habitats, on all continents (except Antarctica) and are well represented in Australasia and the Oceanic islands. They range from dwarf herbaceous perennials of alpine vegetation to massive trees in tropical forests with Australia being an especially rich source of these showy plants.

Yellow kowhai

Sophora tetraptera

This small tree occurs naturally only on North Island, New Zealand, but is now widely cultivated throughout that country and can also be found in Chile. It is most commonly found growing along streams and forest margins, from East Cape to the Ruahine Range and from sea level up to 450m/1,500ft. It can reach 12m/39ft in height depending upon the altitude. In spring, birds feed on the nectar-rich flowers, which are followed by fruits that resemble strings of corky beads.

Top: the leaves are pinnate.

Above: The seedpod.

Distribution: North Island, New Zealand.
Height and spread: 4.5–12m/15–39ft.
Habit and form: Deciduous tree.
Leaf shape: Pinnate.
Pollinated: Bird.

Identification: A small to medium-size tree, occasionally shrubby, with spreading branches. The pinnate, mid-green leaves, 75mm–15cm/3–6in long, are much divided, with 20–40 oval to oblong leaflets. Racemes of 4–10 greenish or golden-yellow, tubular, pendulous flowers, up to 60mm/2¼in long, appear in spring to summer. The brown pods of four-winged seeds are 60–75mm/2¼–3in long.

Left: This small, open-crowned tree varies considerably in height depending upon the altitude within which it grows.

Cockies' tongue

Templetonia retusa

This fast-growing, evergreen shrub, native to South and Western Australia, gets its common name from its flowers, which allegedly resemble a cockatoo's tongue. It is frequently found growing on limestone, or sand or loam over limestone, mostly in coastal areas. The flowers appear in late summer, continuing until well into the winter, hence its popularity with birds at a time when other nectar sources are scarce.

Distribution: Southern and Western Australia.
Height and spread: 30cm–3m/12in–10ft.
Habit and form: Evergreen shrub.
Leaf shape: Obovate.
Pollinated: Bird.

Identification: A spreading, much-branched shrub of variable height, it is frequently glaucous, with smooth, angled and grooved branches. The rounded, leathery leaves are grey-green, up to 40mm/1½in long, oval to wedge-shaped with a notched or blunt tip. Large, red, pea-like flowers are borne terminally or in the leaf axils in winter and spring, singly or in groups. They are up to 40mm/1½in long, with scale-like bracts and petals that are often darker at the tips. The oblong fruit may be up to 80mm/3⅛in long, pale to dark brown.

Left: The pea-like flowers have a keel (the two lower petals) that allegedly resemble a cockatoo's tongue.

Left: This evergreen shrub varies in height and in some cases resembles a small tree.

Rusty pods

Hovea longifolia

Distribution: Eastern Australia.
Height and spread: 3m/10ft.
Habit and form: Shrub.
Leaf shape: Linear.
Pollinated: Insect.

Right: Hovea longifolia is not well-known in cultivation, but when seen in the wild, forms an eye-catching specimen.

The most widespread and variable species in this genus is found in dry open forests in eastern Australia, extending from north Queensland to Victoria, especially on sandy soils. It is an erect understorey shrub with elongated, coarse-textured leaves, closely spaced on erect stems from where the rich violet flowers appear in small clusters in the leaf axils. They eventually give rise to short, inflated pods, covered with short rusty hairs: these split rapidly and shoot out the seeds for some distance upon ripening.

Identification: An upright shrub with erect, felted stems. The narrow leaves are glossy and leathery, dark green above and paler beneath, up to 70mm/2¾in long. In spring, bluish-purple pea flowers appear in clusters of two or three along the branchlets, with dark blue veins and a central yellow blotch; the calyx is covered with grey or red hairs. The globular or egg-shaped pod, covered with rust-coloured hairs, contains two hard-coated seeds.

Left: This upright shrub is quite variable across its range and is most noticeable when the flowers appear in spring.

OTHER SPECIES OF NOTE
Holly flame pea *Chorizema ilicifolium*
Belonging to an endemic Australian genus of about 18 species, this is a small, spreading shrub with deeply lobed leaves with prickly teeth. The large pea flowers are bright red and orange, usually appearing in late winter and spring.

Climbing wedge pea
Gompholobium polymorphum
This variable plant from western Australia may occur as a slender, twining climber or a loose dwarf shrub. Its linear to oval leaves are variable in form and are a foil to the equally variable, large pinkish-red pea flowers that bloom in spring.

Coral pea *Hardenbergia violacea*
Known as Australian sarsaparilla or native wisteria, this evergreen twining plant is a woody-stemmed species occurring in Victoria, Queensland, New South Wales, Tasmania and south Australia, in a variety of habitats from coast to mountains, usually in open forest or woodland and sometimes in heath. The flowers, which appear in winter and spring, are usually violet, but other colours are found.

Cape arid climber *Kennedia beckxiana*
This moderate to vigorous Australian climber has large trifoliate leaves and prominent scarlet, pea-shaped flowers with greenish-yellow blotches in spring to early summer.

Sturt's desert pea

Clianthus formosus

This short-lived species was adopted as the floral emblem of South Australia in 1961, although it mainly occurs in the dry central part of Australia and is named after Charles Sturt, who explored inland Australia in the 19th century. It is found in arid woodlands and on open plains, often as an ephemeral following heavy rain. It is one of Australia's most spectacular wild flowers: its large flag-shaped blooms are generally bright red but may be pure white to deep purple in some specimens.

Identification: A slow-growing, creeping plant, sometimes with a woody base, it may be annual or perennial. Most parts have a fine covering of silky hairs. The prostrate stems are long and thick, and the leaves, up to 18cm/7in long, are pinnate, with 9–21 oval, grey-green leaflets. The flowers are up to 75mm/3in long, with five or six held horizontally (appearing pendulous), on erect, thick-stalked racemes up to 30cm/12in tall. The scarlet flowers are up to 75mm/3in long, with five or six held horizontally on erect, thick-stalked racemes.

Distribution: Australia.
Height and spread: Variable.
Habit and form: Variable subshrub.
Leaf shape: Pinnate.
Pollinated: Insect.

Left: The red flowers have a deep red to black standard that protrudes and appears boss-like.

CABBAGE AND CAPER FAMILIES

The Brassicaceae, or cabbage family, contains herbs or rarely subshrubs found mostly in temperate regions. Australasia has around 160 species, although New Zealand and other southern Oceanic islands have some rare and interesting species. Capparidaceae, the caper family, includes 45 genera and 675 species of shrubs, herbs and trees, chiefly from warmer climates, many of which produce mustard oils.

Bush passionfruit

Australian caper bush, *Capparis spinosa* var. *nummularia*

This small shrub is extremely widespread, and although the species is apparently of Mediterranean origin, a history of aboriginal use of the *nummularia* variety would indicate that this variety is indigenous to the Australian mainland. The plants grow spontaneously in rock crevices, thriving best in nutrient-poor, sharply drained, gravelly soils. The roots penetrate deeply into the earth and their salt-tolerance allows them to flourish along shores within sea-spray zones.

Identification: A sprawling, mounding shrub with arching red stems and dark green, semi-succulent oval or round leaves on short leaf stalks. Large, solitary flowers appear at almost any time of the year, often at night, disappearing in the heat of the day; they are borne from the leaf axils on stalks up to 75mm/3in long, and have pure white petals and numerous feathery white stamens. The green fruit ripens to yellow, usually off the bush and is an edible, elongated berry.

Far left and below left: The fruit is an elongated pod.

Right: This sprawling shrub commonly forms a mound in poor dry soils.

Distribution: Australia.
Height and spread: 90cm–2m x 3m/35in–6½ft x 10ft.
Habit and form: Shrub.
Leaf shape: Elliptic.
Pollinated: Insect.

Kerguelen Island cabbage

Pringlea antiscorbutica

This plant's common name is derived from its appearance and from the island of its discovery. Although most plants in the cabbage family are insect-pollinated, the Kerguelen Island cabbage has adapted to wind pollination (in the absence of winged insects on subantarctic islands) to exploit the almost continual winds in this region. The large, cabbage-like leaves contain a pale yellow, highly pungent essential oil that is rich in vitamin C, rendering the plant a useful dietary supplement against scurvy for early sailors. Despite its name it is also found elsewhere in the Southern Ocean, on the Crozet Archipelago and Marion Island.

Distribution: Subantarctic, centred on Kerguelen Island.
Height and spread: Up to 45cm/18in across.
Habit and form: Herbaceous plant.
Leaf shape: Spathulate.
Pollinated: Wind.

Identification: A large rosette-forming, evergreen, herbaceous plant with smooth, spoon-shaped leaves with strong parallel veins, arising from stout, overground rhizomes extending 1.2m/4ft or more from the roots. The flowers are arranged on dense spikes, appearing axially from each rosette; they usually lack petals – although between one and four white, sometimes pink, petals may develop – and the stamens and thread-like stigma project from tiny sepals.

Right: The large cabbage-like rosettes give the plant its common name.

Long-style bittercress

Rorippa gigantea

Distribution: New Zealand.
Height and spread:
30cm–2m/12in–6½ft.
Habit and form: Annual to
perennial herb.
Leaf shape: Pinnatifid.
Pollinated: Insect.

This large cress-like plant grows in coastal regions mostly in
New Zealand's North Island but is also known from an isolated
population in the north-eastern part of South Island. It is
perfectly at home in salt spray on clifftops and coastal slopes,
sometimes within active petrel colonies, around their burrow
entrances but is rare in many places now due to grazing and
exotic insect pests (particularly cabbage white butterfly). The
large inflorescences support a multitude of tiny white
flowers in spring and early summer.

Identification: This annual to perennial herb (depending on local
growing conditions), grows 30cm–2m/12in–6½ft tall, arising from a stout
taproot and one or more basal stems. The stems are erect to
decumbent, slightly woody, purple-red when mature and angled. The
leaves vary between yellow-green, dark green or purple-green, with
margins that are entire or toothed and pinnatifid. The inflorescence is a
complex, heavily branched raceme, appearing in spring to early summer.
Each individual flower is tiny with white petals, 2–3mm/¹⁄₁₆–⅛in long.
Fruits appear in summer, consisting of dark green to purple-green
siliquae (specialized seedpods), with orange to red-brown seed,
that is extremely sticky when fresh.

OTHER SPECIES OF NOTE

Notothlaspi australe
This species of penwiper, from New Zealand,
can be found across a restricted range in
mountain screes in the Torlesse Range of central
South Island. It is similar to the other species
from the island but sometimes forms dense
colonies and has more rounded flowerheads.

Coastal cress *Lepidium flexicaule*
This small, flat, creeping cress was once widespread in New Zealand, on bluffs, outcrops and
among coastal turfs, but is now largely restricted
to west and north-west South Island. The many
racemes of small, white flowers, often hidden
among foliage, appear in early summer.

Cook's scurvy grass *Lepidium oleraceum*
A bushy, aromatic, white-flowered herb, found in
coastal areas and some offshore islands of New
Zealand's South Island. It was abundant during
the voyages of James Cook in the 18th century,
and eaten to prevent scurvy. It is now scarce
and endangered across its former range.

New Zealand bitter cress
Cardamine corymbosa
This tiny species of cress flowers all year but is
mainly seen in autumn and winter. The tiny
white flowers, which are self-pollinated, are
followed by tiny explosive seedpods. The
exceptional seeding ability of the plant has
led to it becoming a troublesome weed in
certain horticultural situations well outside its
native range.

Penwiper plant

Notothlaspi rosulatum

This curious little alpine herbaceous
perennial, one of only two in this genus, is
widespread on mountain screes at altitudes
of around 800–1,800m/2,600–5,900ft in the
Southern Alpine area of New Zealand's
South Island. Its common name is derived
from the structure of the plant, which
allegedly looks like a 19th-century penwiper.
The flat rosette of grey leaves is well
camouflaged among the rocks, but when
the large, conical
flowerhead of
fragrant, white
flowers appears
in summer it
becomes quite
conspicuous.

Distribution: South Island,
New Zealand.
Height and spread:
70mm–25cm/2¾–10in.
Habit and form: Alpine herb.
Leaf shape: Spathulate.
Pollinated: Insect.

Identification: An erect, pyramidal,
alpine herbaceous perennial
with a long, central taproot. The
fleshy, toothed, spoon-shaped
leaves form a dense basal rosette
or cushion, and are very
numerous, overlapping,
hairy at first, becoming
more or less smooth. The
large, white, four-petalled,
fragrant flowers appear in
summer, borne on a
crowded pyramidal raceme.

GENTIAN, BELLFLOWER, TRIGGER PLANT AND GOODENIA FAMILIES

The Gentianaceae, or gentians, and the Campanulaceae, or bellflowers, are scarce in Australasia, though the gentians include some remarkable island endemics. Stylidiaceae, the trigger plant family, contain small herbs, and Goodeniaceae, or goodenia, comprise sappy shrubs, herbs and trees.

'Oha wai

Clermontia parviflora

This Hawaiian endemic is restricted to the wet forests of the Kohala Mountains and windward Mauna Kea and Mauna Loa, at heights of 120–1,450m/400–4,750ft, where it can be found growing as a terrestrial shrub and as an epiphyte. It is one of the smaller-flowered *Clermontia* species, and is susceptible to browsing and habitat alteration by wild goats and pigs. If only epiphytic plants are found in a given area, it usually indicates that pigs are eating the vegetation there. This is one of 100 species of lobeliods, which make up about 10 per cent of Hawaii's native flora.

Identification: The bark is green when young, turning grey with age. The leaves, which are mainly clustered around the branch tips, are dark green above, paler below, with a purple midrib and stalk whose colour becomes less pronounced with age; developing leaves are often purple. The leaves are 60mm–18cm/2¼–7in long and 20–50mm/¾–2in wide, with finely toothed margins and elongated, pointed tips. The small flowers are green, purple or white on the outside, white or pale purple inside, tubular at the base, with narrow reflexed petals and projecting reproductive parts.

Distribution: Hawaii.
Height and spread: 3.5m/12ft.
Habit and form: Epiphytic or terrestrial shrub.
Leaf shape: Oblanceolate.
Pollinated: Bird.

Left: The plant has a candelabra-like habit, with branches usually arising from a single basal stem.

Far left: The yellow or orange berries have small ribs.

Pua'ala

Alula, Haha, *Brighamia rockii*

One of the most unusual plants of Hawaii, this plant, found only on the tall sea cliffs of the island Molokai, formerly grew on sunny, well-drained hillsides on all the four main islands. It is extremely rare today, however, with fewer than 100 plants growing in the wild. A strange plant that looks like a cabbage on a stick, it is a long-lived succulent, with a swollen base tapering towards a crowning rosette of fleshy leaves and yellow or white, trumpet-shaped flowers. It is presumed to be moth-pollinated although the moth is thought to have become extinct, so seed is not produced on wild plants.

Identification: The thickened, succulent stem, usually branching, tapers from the base and is distinctly purple during its juvenile stage. The shiny, leathery leaves are arranged in a rosette at the top of each branch; they are bright to dark green, 60mm–23cm/2¼–9in long and 50mm–15cm/2–6in across. The fragrant, trumpet-shaped, five-petalled, white flowers are clustered in groups of three to eight in the leaf axils, forming a dense rosette at the top of the stem in autumn.

Distribution: Molokai, Hawaii.
Height and spread: 5m/16ft.
Habit and form: Shrub.
Leaf shape: Obovate or spathulate.
Pollinated: Probably a moth (now extinct).

Far left: This strange plant looks a little like a cabbage on a stick.

Left: The large, white, trumpet-shaped flowers are fragrant and appear in the autumn.

Trigger plant

Stylidium spathulatum

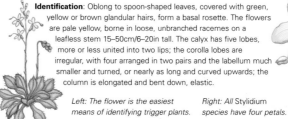

The curious trigger plants are so named because of the rapid flick of the column when touched by a visiting insect. This column protrudes from the flower and bears the stamens and stigma. In the 'cocked' position it is kinked at the base and sticks out to one side between two of the petals. When an insect attempts to take nectar from the flower, the sensitive base, irritated by its touch, straightens instantaneously and swings the stamens and stigma through an arc, hitting the animal and showering it with pollen. As the flower ages the stamens shrivel, but the stigma protrudes from the end of the column, ready to be brushed by insects already covered in pollen.

Distribution: Western Australia.
Height and spread: 25cm/10in.
Habit and form: Herbaceous perennial.
Leaf shape: Obovate.
Pollinated: Insect.

Identification: Oblong to spoon-shaped leaves, covered with green, yellow or brown glandular hairs, form a basal rosette. The flowers are pale yellow, borne in loose, unbranched racemes on a leafless stem 15–50cm/6–20in tall. The calyx has five lobes, more or less united into two lips; the corolla lobes are irregular, with four arranged in two pairs and the labellum much smaller and turned, or nearly as long and curved upwards; the column is elongated and bent down, elastic.

Left: The flower is the easiest means of identifying trigger plants.

Right: All Stylidium *species have four petals.*

OTHER SPECIES OF NOTE

'Oha Wai Nui *Clermontia arborescens*
'Oha wai nui is endemic to Maui, where it occurs in mesic (moist) to wet forest from 520–1,850m/1,700–6,000ft. Its fleshy, claw-shaped, strongly arched flowers are among the largest of the genus and are pale green with purple columns.

Thick-leaved trigger plant
Stylidium crassifolium
The fleshy leaves that cluster about the base of the flower stem give rise to this plant's common name. It grows to 60cm/24in. It comes from western Australia, where it is found near wet flushes and drying creek beds, especially following bushfires.

Cunningham's snow-gentian
Chionogentias cunninghamii
Naturally found in swamps and wet heath in New South Wales, this tall gentian has white flowers. Australian gentians of this genus mostly occur in the alpine or subalpine zone, although this species mainly occurs at lower altitudes.

Boomerang trigger plant
Stylidium breviscapum
This creeping herbaceous perennial from western Australia grows to 20cm/8in high and is curiously elevated up to 70mm/2¾in above the soil by wiry, black, stilt roots. The flowers are white with red markings, appearing from early spring to summer.

Blue leschenaultia

Leschenaultia biloba

Aboriginal people are said to have called blue leschenaultia, which is native to the sand hills of western Australia, 'the floor of the sky', because the ground where it grows is carpeted with its blue flowers. In many areas the plant adopts a suckering habit, enabling it to spread over a wide area and resulting in massed spring displays. Arguably one of the most beautiful Australian species, its flower is designed to attract bees. It has a blue 'landing platform' with a white centre that helps guide the bee to the nectar at the base of the tubular petals. To reach the nectar the bee must either pick up or deposit pollen.

Identification: A diffuse, small, sprawling to climbing, semi-woody, evergreen perennial or subshrub. It has tiny, narrow, heath-like, soft grey-green leaves 12mm/½in long. The flowers, up to 25mm/1in across, appear from late winter to late spring, with five pointed lobes with distinctive large corolla wings, veined with parallel, transverse lines. They range from deep purplish-blue through sky-blue to pale blue.

Distribution: Western Australia.
Height and spread: 50cm/20in; indefinite spread.
Habit and form: Evergreen perennial.
Leaf shape: Narrow.
Pollinated: Insect.

Right: The bright blue flowers open from greenish buds.

Below: The plant commonly forms a heath-like sprawling shrub.

GERANIUM, PORTULACA AND AMARANTH FAMILIES

The Geraniaceae, or geranium family, is varied, usually featuring five-petalled flowers and a beaked fruit that often disperses the seed explosively. The Portulacaceae (portulacas) comprise mainly herbaceous perennials; the Amaranthaceae (amaranths) comprise mostly herbs but also rarely shrubs or small trees.

Broad-leaf parakeelya

Rock purslane, *Calandrinia balonensis*

This fleshy herb, with flowers that open quickly in response to sunshine, belongs to a genus of around 150 species, which occur in Australia and from Canada to Chile. *C. balonensis* is named after the Balonne River in Queensland, where it was first collected, and is one of approximately 30 Australian species. It grows as an annual or perennial in arid areas of southern Australia and the Northern Territory, often around salt lakes, and its bright, shiny, red flowers, amid flattened, succulent, finger-length leaves, often carpet large areas in spring.

Right: This low-growing, fleshy herb spreads from woody branches near the base.

Identification: A low-growing, spreading or trailing herbaceous perennial, with the older branches becoming woody near the base. The leaves are alternate, fleshy and narrow, with a very pronounced, flattened midrib. The long-lasting, five-petalled flowers, up to 25mm/1in across, are borne from the leaf axils. They have two persistent sepals, vibrant pinky-red petals with paler, often white, bases and yellow centres with numerous filaments.

Distribution: Australia.
Height and spread: 15–40cm/6–16in.
Habit and form: Herbaceous perennial.
Leaf shape: Narrow.
Pollinated: Insect.

Pink mulla mulla

Lamb's tail, *Ptilotus exaltatus*

This ephemeral plant inhabits a wide range of habitats stretching across the mainland from the north-west of Australia. The flowers are borne on candelabra-like branches, and the time of year in which they appear depends largely upon seasonal rainfall patterns: in arid areas they are usually most abundant following good rains. It is a common and widespread plant, with specimens from the westernmost regions being generally taller with longer inflorescences and less hairy than their eastern counterparts.

Identification: A stout, erect, perennial with hairless stems, branched or unbranched, growing from woody rhizomes. The thick, wavy-edged leaves, up to 10cm/4in long, are bright blue-green tinged red, forming a rosette at the base of the plant. The pink, fluffy flowers appear on tall stems in conical spikes, becoming cylindrical with age, up to 15cm/6in long and 50mm/2in wide.

Far left: The stems are stout and erect.

Distribution: North-western Australia.
Height and spread: 90cm/35in.
Habit and form: Erect perennial.
Leaf shape: Oblong-lanceolate.
Pollinated: Insect.

Left: The flowers of pink mulla mulla often form striking displays following rains.

Southern stork's bill

Pelargonium australe

This is a widespread and variable plant that is generally found growing in sand dunes near the coast, between rocky outcrops, and inland, sometimes at higher elevations in subalpine regions. It often flowers over a long period, and the leaves may take on orange or even darker tones in the autumn. Plants collected in Tasmania are smaller in all parts, with dark green leaves and red leaf stalks and although they resemble the mainland species in most other respects some botanists recognize some populations to be separate subspecies.

Left: This straggling shrubby plant varies considerably in height and colour across its native range.

Distribution: South-eastern Australia, Tasmania, and New Zealand.
Height and spread: 30cm/12in.
Habit and form: Subshrub.
Leaf shape: Rounded.
Pollinated: Insect.

Identification: A straggling, short-stemmed, softly hairy, shrubby, erect, low-growing perennial shrub. The heart-shaped, faintly aromatic leaves are up to 10cm/4in in diameter, rounded and shallowly lobed, and are very soft, being covered with thick, soft hairs. Each flowering stem bears a compact umbel of 5–25 flowers, which vary in colour from white to pale blush to pink, with dark red spots and feathering, appearing in spring or summer.

OTHER SPECIES OF NOTE

Pussy tails *Ptilotus spathulatus*
This low-growing Australian perennial has numerous stems arising from a stout rhizome. The rounded or spoon-shaped, fleshy leaves are held basally, and the cylindrical flower spikes emerge over a long period between winter and summer, bearing yellow, green or golden flowers, either solitary or clustered.

Rose-tipped mulla mulla *Ptilotus manglesii*
This Australian perennial sometimes lasts only as an annual, with stems that trail along the ground a little before ascending at the tips. The long, rounded leaves have stems near the base of the plant, becoming stalkless near the top. The round flower spikes are covered with shaggy white hairs, among which the pink to violet-purple flowers nestle in summer.

Geranium homeanum
This widespread plant is found in Java, Timor, Samoa, New Zealand and the east coastal states of Australia. It is commonly found in grassland, thin forests and on roadsides. The prostrate, often hairy stems support lobed leaves with large teeth, and the small, white to pale pink flowers appear from late spring to late summer.

Small storksbill *Erodium angustilobum*
Found from Queensland to south Australia, this annual has narrow, basal leaves, which are deeply seven-lobed. In summer it sports numerous blue to pinkish flowers on ascending stems that reach 30cm/12in.

Purslane

Pigweed, *Portulaca oleracea*

Purslane is a species that grows worldwide and, although generally regarded as a weed in many parts of Australia, it is a native of that continent. It is found throughout Australia except in Tasmania. In inland areas dense colonies of the plant appear after rain. It is edible and has long been used as a vegetable, as a substitute for spinach, or as a salad leaf.

Distribution: Cosmopolitan in warm areas.
Height and spread: 40cm/16in.
Habit and form: Succulent herb.
Leaf shape: Obovate.
Pollinated: Insect.

Identification: A succulent, prostrate annual herb with smooth, reddish-brown stems and alternate, oval, succulent leaves, 25mm/1in long, clustered at the stem joints and ends. The yellow flowers, 6mm/¼in across with five two- or three-lobed petals, occur in the leaf axils; they appear in late spring and continue into mid-autumn, each opening singly at the centre of a leaf cluster for only a few hours on sunny mornings. The seeds are contained in a pod.

Right: The tiny, black seeds are contained in a pod, the top of which falls off once the seeds are ripe.

OLEANDER AND BRAZIL NUT FAMILIES

The Apocynaceae (oleander or dogbane family) are distributed mainly in the tropics and subtropics, though some perennial herbs thrive in temperate regions. Plants of this family may have milky sap and are often poisonous. The Brazil nut family (Lecythidaceae) contains woody plants native to tropical climates. The Brazil nut is the most well known and important species from this family.

Indian oak

Freshwater mangrove, *Barringtonia acutangula*

Indian oak grows in coastal areas in the tropics, or on seasonally inundated land by lagoons, creeks and riverbanks. In areas prone to seasonal dry periods, it may be partially deciduous. In Australia it is found mainly in the Northern Territory and is striking when in flower due to its handsome foliage and large pendulous sprays of pink or white, fluffy, scented flowers, which open in the evening and fall the following morning.

Identification: The leaves, crowded at the ends of the branches, are up to 15cm/6in long, lance-shaped to oval, smooth, finely toothed, with a midrib prominent on both sides. Terminal, pendulous racemes bear up to 75 flowers, ranging in colour from dark red to white, with four petals, stamens in three whorls fused at the base, and filaments protruding to 20mm/¾in. The fruit is single-seeded, fleshy, tapering at each end, up to 60mm/2¼in long.

Far right: Indian oak is a small flowering tree.

Distribution: Indo-Pacific region.
Height and spread: 13m/42ft.
Habit and form: Shrub or small tree.
Leaf shape: Oblanceolate.
Pollinated: Uncertain, possibly bat or moth.

Bloodhorn

Mangrove ochrosia, *Ochrosia elliptica*

This large shrub or small spreading tree can be found along northern and central coastal Queensland, on Lord Howe Island and parts of Melanesia in fore-dune vine thickets immediately behind the mangroves. The small, yellow or white flowers are sweetly fragrant and occur in small clusters between mid-spring and late summer and are followed by pairs of striking red fruits, which resemble red horns or elongated tomatoes. These often persist on the tree for a considerable time. Unfortunately, despite their appearance, the fruits are poisonous, and plants also bleed copious amounts of poisonous white sap when wounded, making it best to avoid contact with this tree.

Identification: A large evergreen shrub or small, spreading tree with stout, green young branches. The leaves are glossy, leathery, dark green, elliptic to oblong or oval, with smooth, wavy edges, up to 20cm/8in long and 80mm/3¼in wide, occurring in whorls of three or four. The flowers appear in axillary clusters and are fragrant, small and yellow or white. The showy, oval fruits, 50mm/2in long, are borne in pairs and are persistent.

Distribution: Australia, Melanesia.
Height and spread: 5–9m/16–29½ft.
Habit and form: Large shrub or small tree.
Leaf shape: Elliptic to oblong.
Pollinated: Insect.

Left: This evergreen tree has a dense, spreading crown and is most noticeable when the bright red fruits ripen.

Kalalau *Pteralyxia kauaiensis*
This long-lived small tree has shiny, dark green leaves that hide the small, greenish, tubular flowers. It is one of just two members of an endemic Hawaiian genus within Apocynaceae, growing in the Wahiawa Mountains in the southern portion of Kauai.

Kaulu *Pteralyxia macrocarpa*
The kaulu is the only other member of this rare Hawaiian genus and is a small tree found in valleys and slopes in diverse mesic forest on the island of Oahu. Its shiny, green leaves almost hide the yellowish, tubular flowers. It is rare, with 500 or so in the wild.

Water gum *Tristania neriifolia*
A large shrub that may become a small tree, the water gum is found along the central coast and adjacent ranges of New South Wales, along the banks of streams. It has narrow leaves with conspicuous oil glands. The yellow, star-shaped flowers occur in summer, usually in groups of three to six. It is the only species in the genus.

Scarlet kunzea *Kunzea baxteri*
This erect shrub from the south coastal areas of western Australia has grey-green, oblong leaves and large, crimson flower clusters, which are arranged in bottlebrush form and are very profuse and conspicuous in spring and early summer. The plant is related to the bottlebrushes, *Callistemon* species, and also bears a similarity to *Melaleuca* and *Leptospermum* species.

Falaga

Barringtonia samoensis

This shrub or small tree occurs in coastal areas or on seasonally inundated land by lagoons, creeks and riverbanks, from south-east Celebes to Micronesia, New Guinea and Polynesia. It bears spectacular pendulous spikes at the branch tips that may contain 150 or more individual, scented flowers of red or white, each with numerous long golden-yellow anthers and a single, persistent, red stigma.

Identification: The leaves, up to 90cm/35in long with smooth margins or rounded teeth, are crowded at the ends of the branches, spirally arranged, with a midrib prominent on both sides. The flowers are borne in pendulous racemes up to 55cm/22in long, which may be terminal or sprout directly from the branches. They have four convex, white or red petals and numerous protruding yellow stamens, fused at the base in three to eight whorls. The ribbed fruit is single-seeded and fleshy, up to 70mm/2¾in long with a tapering base.

Distribution: Micronesia; New Guinea and Polynesia.
Height and spread: 12m/39ft.
Habit and form: Shrub or small tree.
Leaf shape: Obovate.
Pollinated: Insect.

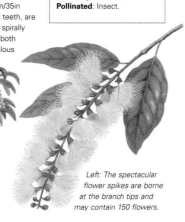

Left: The spectacular flower spikes are borne at the branch tips and may contain 150 flowers.

Cocky apple

Billy goat plum, *Planchonia careya*

This is a common, widespread small tree or spreading shrub found across much of northern tropical Australia and down the east coast to Fraser Island, most commonly in open forests and woodlands. It prefers moist places, such as the edges of floodplains and coastal monsoon forests, and flowers from spring to mid-autumn. It is related to the freshwater mangroves, *Barringtonia* species. It is night-flowering: the flowers open at dusk and persist only until the sun shines the following day.

Identification: The species is briefly deciduous in the dry season. The bark is grey, rough, slightly corky and fissured. The leaves are oval or spoon-shaped with rounded teeth on the margins, tapering to the base and up to 10cm/4in long. They are softly leathery, shiny, light green above, dull beneath, turning rusty-orange before falling. The large, fleshy flowers are white, grading to pink inside towards the base, with numerous pink-and-white stamens, 50mm/2in long, fused together into a tube at their bases. The flowers are borne only at night, the whole staminal bundle falling off as a single unit in the morning.

Distribution: Tropical northern Australia.
Height and spread: 4–10m/13–33ft.
Habit and form: Small tree or spreading shrub.
Leaf shape: Ovate or spathulate.
Pollinated: Bat.

Above: Each of the large, fleshy flowers persists for just one night.

Far right: The fruit is green, egg-shaped and smooth.

MYRTLE, EVENING PRIMROSE AND DAPHNE FAMILIES

The myrtle family, Myrtaceae, includes trees and shrubs found in the warm-temperate regions of Australia. The family dominates the hardwood forests across the continent. The evening primrose family, Onagraceae, has a restricted distribution, although the Daphne family, Thymelaeaceae, is widespread.

Shining copper cups

Pileanthus rubronitidus

This small shrub is one species in a small genus restricted to Western Australia. Shining copper cups is found only between Kalbarri and west of Northampton, growing on grey sand over sandstone, or white sand, in heath or shrubland colonized by the sceptre banksia, *Banksia sceptum*, although isolated colonies have been reported from Mount Magnet. The orange-red flowers appear between early and late spring, although it is the conspicuous, cup-like calyces, persisting long after flowering, that give rise to the plant's common name.

Identification: A small, branching evergreen shrub with very narrow, three-sided, smooth leaves, up to 12mm/½ in long, with prominent oil glands. The flowers appear in clusters around the upper leaf axils in spring, initially enclosed in a one-leaf bract; they are a very distinctively red-orange, with 10 sepals and five rounded petals, on a slender stem 12–25mm/½–1 in long.

Distribution: Western Australia.
Height and spread: 90cm/35in.
Habit and form: Shrub.
Leaf shape: Linear.
Pollinated: Insect.

Left: Shining copper cups forms a small open bush.

New Zealand tea tree

Manuka, *Leptospermum scoparium*

This shrub occurs widely throughout lowland to subalpine areas and in many habitats, chiefly in New Zealand, where it is considered to be endemic, although some botanists claim that it is also a native species of Tasmania, New South Wales and Victoria, Australia. It is by far the commonest shrubland constituent and has increased greatly under the influence of human settlement. The English common name is derived from the fact that early white settlers made infusions of tea from the leaves, which are aromatic. The white blooms appear in spring and early summer, often so profusely that it resembles snow.

Identification: A bushy, evergreen shrub ranging in size from a creeping plant to a small tree, although it is seldom more than 4m/13ft high. It is adaptable and extremely variable in leaf size and shape, flower and leaf colour, branching habit and foliage density, as well as oil content and aroma. Differences occur in individual plants, within and among populations, genetically and with season, soil and other variables. The bark sheds in long papery strips. The thick leaves are narrow and less than 15mm/⁹⁄₁₆in long, with sharp pointed tips, hard and leathery, with aromatic scent glands beneath, variable in colour from very pale green to dark brown; younger shrubs have softer, paler leaves. Showy, mostly white, sometimes pink or reddish flowers, 15mm/⁹⁄₁₆in across, are borne profusely in spring.

Distribution: New Zealand; eastern Australia.
Height and spread: 4–6m/13–19¾ ft.
Habit and form: Shrub or small tree.
Leaf shape: Narrow.
Pollinated: Insect.

Above left: The fruits are woody capsules containing numerous small, thin seeds.

Left: This variable shrub can have a creeping habit or be almost tree-like.

Mottlecah

Rose of the west, *Eucalyptus macrocarpa* subsp. *macrocarpa*

Distribution: Western Australia.
Height and spread: Up to 5m/16ft.
Habit and form: Mallee shrub.
Leaf shape: Ovate.
Pollinated: Insect.

This species of eucalyptus is distinctive in having a growth habit in which several woody stems arise separately from a lignotuber, or starchy swelling on underground stems or roots – a form known as a 'mallee'. It is chiefly found on open sandy heath in western Australia. It is quite variable in form, with two subspecies often reported: the subspecies *elachantha* is restricted in occurrence and differs from the common form in having smaller leaves and lower stature.

Right: The large gumnuts contain many tiny seeds.

Identification: A spreading or sprawling mallee with smooth bark throughout, grey over salmon-pink. The glaucous, silvery grey-green leaves are opposite, 50mm–12.5cm/2–5in long, stalkless and oval, while the young leaves are almost circular. Spectacular large flowers, up to 10cm/4in across, appear from early spring to midsummer, with a mass of stamens that are usually red, occasionally pinky-red or cream. The very large, shallowly hemispherical 'gumnuts' that follow them have a powdery grey covering.

Far left: This medium to large shrub grows from an underground stem that protects it from fires.

OTHER SPECIES OF NOTE

Tree manuka *Leptospermum ericoides*
This large shrub or small tree can reach 15m/49ft high. It has loose, peeling bark and small, pointed, aromatic leaves. The small, white, five-petalled flowers cover mature specimens in spring and early summer with a mass of blossom. It is abundant in lowland and mountain forests throughout New Zealand.

Lutulutu *Eugenia gracilipes*
This graceful tree possesses delicate foliage and drooping branches, which bear terminal slender racemes of three to seven pale yellow or pink-tinged flowers. It is found only in the Fiji islands. Related species include *Sygyzium malaccensis*, the malay apple, which has deep purple, crimson or even white flowers and reddish fruits, much valued locally for eating.

Pohutukawa *Metrosideros excelsa*
The New Zealand Christmas tree gains its name from its time of flowering and forms a wide-spreading tree with round, leathery, dark green leaves and large flowers most noted for their spectacular sprays of red stamens. Its natural distribution is restricted to the coastal forest in the North Island.

Rata *Metrosideros robusta*
The rata is an inhabitant of the forests of New Zealand's North Island but can also be found on Three Knights Island and western South Island. It forms a large tree, with dull red flowers appearing in summer. The plant often begins life as an epiphyte, perching in another tree. In time, roots are sent down to the ground, and the *Metrosideros* takes over.

Copper cups

Pileanthus peduncularis

This small rounded shrub, found only on the south-western Australian sand plains, is probably the best-known member of the genus. It is often encountered among sand dunes north of Perth, although its distribution is scattered. It is a spectacular sight in spring with its unusual, large, copper-orange flowers, which occur towards the ends of the branches and from the leaf axils in a massed display. The conspicuous, cup-like calyces often persist for a long time after flowering.

Identification: Small, branching evergreen shrub with very narrow, three-sided, smooth leaves up to 4mm/³⁄₁₆in long, with prominent oil glands. The flowers appear in clusters toward the ends of the branches and from the leaf axils, initially enclosed in a one-leaf bract; they are up to 25mm/1in across, copper-orange, sometimes red, with 10 sepals and five rounded petals, on a slender stem 12–25mm/½–1in long.

Distribution: South-western Australia.
Height and spread: 90cm/35in.
Habit and form: Shrub.
Leaf shape: Linear.
Pollinated: Insect.

Above: The cup-like calyces often persist well after flowering.

Below: The plant forms a low, branching, rounded shrub on sandy soils.

Bottlebrush

Callistemon brachyandrus

This large bushy shrub is found growing naturally in western New South Wales, Victoria and South Australia. It is one of the later flowering bottlebrushes and flowers during the summer, often after others of the genus have finished. Like so many of Australia's attractive native plants, the inflorescences of *Callistemon* are composed of a large number of small flowers grouped together. The flower arrangement closely resembles a bottle-cleaning brush, hence the common name. The small red brushes cover the branches, and the masses of stamens are dark red with yellow anthers, giving the flowers the appearance of being dusted with gold.

Above and below right: The bush forms a dense shrub with flowers appearing at the branch tips.

Distribution: South-eastern Australia.
Height and spread: 4m/13ft.
Habit and form: Shrub.
Leaf shape: Linear.
Pollinated: Insect.

Identification: A dense, small to tall shrub. The prolific young shoots are grey, silky, soft and hairy, distinct from the mature needle-like leaves, which are up to 40mm/1½in long; stiff and sharp-pointed, pungent, with undersides typically dotted with oil glands. The flowers are borne in loose spikes up to 80mm/3⅛in long, appearing in mid- to late summer; the five small, green petals and sepals, together with the pistils, are barely noticeable among the showy, orange-red stamens, with gold anthers.

Lesser bottlebrush

Fiery bottlebrush, *Callistemon phoeniceus*

Despite its common name, this plant is actually a medium-size shrub that is widespread in south-west western Australia. It is one of only two species that occur there. It naturally grows in depressions and along watercourses extending from the Swan River to the Murchison River, with its eastern limits in the Norseman area.

Below right: This medium-size shrub often resembles a small pendulous tree.

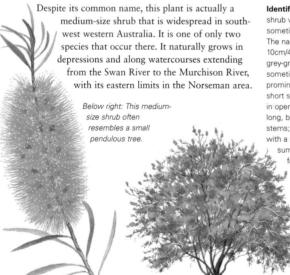

Identification: A medium-size shrub with numerous branches, sometimes slightly pendulous. The narrow leaves are up to 10cm/4in long, blue-green to grey-green, thick, rigid, sometimes twisted, with a prominent midrib, tipped with a short spine. The flowers grow in open spikes 10–15cm/4–6in long, borne terminally on slender stems; they appear in late spring, with a second flowering in late summer if conditions are favourable. The stamens are a bright rich red, usually with darker anthers.

Right: The fluffy red flowerheads resemble bottle-cleaning brushes and give rise to the common name.

Distribution: Western Australia.
Height and spread: 3m/10ft.
Habit and form: Shrub.
Leaf shape: Linear-lanceolate.
Pollinated: Insect.

Arakura

Scarlet rata, *Metrosideros fulgens*

This plant is one of a number of rata vines found in New Zealand. Unlike *M. robusta* however, which begins as a vine and often grows into a tree, the scarlet rata needs support throughout its life. It commonly flowers from late summer into autumn, when it can be seen scrambling and twining over logs and up trees, and is considered an early sign that winter is approaching.

Distribution: New Zealand.
Height and spread: 10m/33ft or more.
Habit and form: Liana.
Leaf shape: Elliptic-oblong.
Pollinated: Insect.

Left: The plant is a liana and needs the support of another tree to reach its full height.

Identification: A liana with aromatic bark, separating in flakes, and smooth leaves up to 75mm/3in long, opposite, simple, pinnately veined and dotted with glands, on stout leaf stalks. The flowers are in terminal clusters, with oblong sepals, round orange-red petals and a mass of scarlet stamens up to 25mm/1in long. The fruit is a leathery capsule.

Right: The small flowers are given added prominence by the mass of scarlet stamens.

Alpine bottlebrush *Callistemon pityoides*
The alpine bottlebrush forms dense thickets at altitudes of 2,000m/6,500ft or more, being found most commonly in and around sphagnum bogs and swamps, and along watercourses in eastern Australia. The colourful bracts that surround the developing buds first become evident in early spring, opening to reveal yellow flowers.

Crimson bottlebrush *Callistemon citrinus*
From the east coast of Australia, this is an upright shrub with narrow, lance-shaped, leathery leaves with a distinctly citrus aroma (hence the specific name). The plump, bright red, bottlebrush-shaped flowers, composed mostly of stamens, bloom throughout the hot weather. The bark is rough and light brown.

Regelia cymbifolia
Occurring in a restricted area in south-west western Australia in sandplain or woodland, this is a bushy, erect, many-branched shrub up to 1.8m/6ft tall. It has oval leaves and deep pink to purple flowers produced in small, terminal clusters in spring. The seeds are retained within the capsules until a fire prompts their release.

Gillham's bell *Darwinia oxylepis*
This is a small shrub that may reach 1.5m/5ft, with narrow, recurved leaves. The small flowers are enclosed within large, deep red bracts with a characteristic bell shape, on the branch tips in spring.

Cranbrook bell

Darwinia meeboldii

One of several species of *Darwinia* from south-western Australia, known collectively as 'mountain bells', this plant is found in moist, peaty soils in the Stirling Ranges, although it is now rare. It is an erect, spindly, small to medium-sized shrub that bears clusters of around eight small flowers enclosed within large bracts. These give the inflorescence its characteristic bell shape.

Identification: The narrow, aromatic leaves are alternately paired, triangular in section, up to 10mm/⅜in long with prominent oil glands. Flowers appear from early to late spring, prominently displayed on the ends of the branches: small, white to red tubular flowers appear in groups of about eight enclosed within leafy, bell-shaped bracts, usually white with bright red tips, more rarely red or green.

Distribution: South-western Australia.
Height and spread: Variable.
Habit and form: Dwarf to medium shrub.
Leaf shape: Linear.
Pollinated: Insect.

Far right: The plant forms an erect, spindly, medium-size shrub that is clothed with flowers in the spring.

Chenille honey myrtle

Melaleuca huegelii subsp. *huegelii*

This flowering shrub, native to south-western coastal districts of western Australia, is unusual in that it flowers during the summer. Two subspecies are currently recognized, *huegelii* and *pristicensis*, the latter distinguished by its mauve to pink flowers held in narrow spikes. Both are medium to large shrubs, found on limestone cliffs, coastal plains and dunes. The leaves are very small and crowded against the stems in a scale-like manner, and these are covered with small oil glands. The long whip-like branches make this a highly distinctive plant.

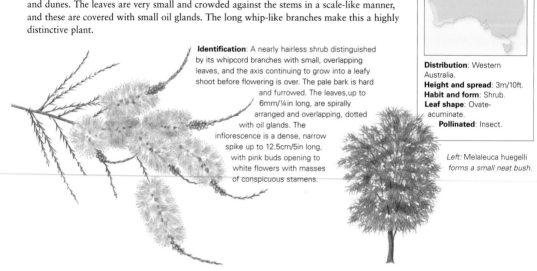

Identification: A nearly hairless shrub distinguished by its whipcord branches with small, overlapping leaves, and the axis continuing to grow into a leafy shoot before flowering is over. The pale bark is hard and furrowed. The leaves, up to 6mm/¼in long, are spirally arranged and overlapping, dotted with oil glands. The inflorescence is a dense, narrow spike up to 12.5cm/5in long, with pink buds opening to white flowers with masses of conspicuous stamens.

Distribution: Western Australia.
Height and spread: 3m/10ft.
Habit and form: Shrub.
Leaf shape: Ovate-acuminate.
Pollinated: Insect.

Left: Melaleuca huegelli forms a small neat bush.

Scarlet honey myrtle

Melaleuca fulgens

This well-known plant, from south-west western Australia, north-west southern Australia and the south-west of the Northern Territory, is common in cultivation in both its usual red-flowered form and in several other colours. The leaves and branches emit an aromatic fragrance when bruised. It occurs in various habitats, most commonly in rocky granite areas, and blooms in spring, with a typical bottlebrush form to the flowers. Birds, particularly honeyeaters searching for nectar, are attracted to the shrub when it is in flower.

Identification: The branches are smooth except for the young felted shoots, and the narrow, grey-green leaves, up to 30mm/1¼in long, are borne in alternate pairs on very short or no stalks. The inflorescence is a spike of 6–20 flowers, usually with the axis growing on into a leafy shoot; the numerous, conspicuous stamens, much longer than the petals, are scarlet or deep pink (rarely white). The urn-shaped fruit has a rough, wrinkled, almost papery texture.

Distribution: Western Australia.
Height and spread: 2.5m/8ft.
Habit and form: Shrub.
Leaf shape: Elliptic.
Pollinated: Bird.

Left: Scarlet honey myrtle forms a loose spreading shrub that is highly visible when in flower.

Fuchsia procumbens

Originating in North Island, New Zealand, this small shrubby plant grows in rocky, sandy or gravelly places near the sea, in areas that can occasionally be flooded by exceptionally high tides, where it may cover substantial areas. Due to the destruction of its natural habit, it is now an endangered species in the wild. It is prostrate in growth, with slender, trailing stems, small, heart-shaped leaves and distinctive, though diminutive, erect flowers.

Distribution: North Island, New Zealand.
Height and spread: Variable.
Habit and form: Prostrate shrub.
Leaf shape: Suborbicular.
Pollinated: Insect.

Identification: Slender, branched, prostrate shrub with long, trailing shoots and alternate, round or heart-shaped leaves, 6–20mm/ ¼–¾in across, borne on thin stalks. The erect flowers, up to 20mm/¾in long, have a greenish-yellow tube that is red at the base, and purple-tipped, sharply reflexed green sepals and no true petals; the stamens bear bright blue pollen. The attractive seedpods are about 20mm/¾in long. They ripen from green to bright crimson, covered with a light bloom, and are long-lasting.

Above: The tiny orange flowers have strongly reflexed sepals and no true petals.

Kotukutuku *Fuchsia excorticata*
The largest fuchsia in the world, growing in Central South America and New Zealand, particularly on North Island, where it is common in lowland to lower montane forest, especially along margins and in damp valleys. The solitary, red, pendulous flowers have blue pollen and the dark, egg-shaped fruit is relished by the Maoris and known as konini.

New Zealand daphne *Pimelia prostrata*
This variable, low shrub is found in dry places in New Zealand where it may variously adopt a wide-spreading or tufted habit. The small, silky-downy white flowers are fragrant and appear in small crowded heads of between three and 10, on short side shoots near the ends of the branches, usually in spring or early summer.

Rosy paperbark *Melaleuca diosmatifolia*
The rosy paperbark of eastern Australia is most commonly found in woodland and open forest, often in areas subject to inundation. It is a small shrub with narrow leaves ending in a small point. The pale to deep mauve flowers are usually seen in spring and early summer and occur in bottlebrush-type spikes on short branches.

Scarlet feathers *Verticordia grandis*
A showy small shrub, found in woodlands and sandy heaths in south-western Australia. It has small, stem-clasping, rounded, grey-green leaves. Throughout the year it bears bright red, five-petalled flowers, each with a long, protruding style. The popularity of this species for floral arrangements has resulted in over-picking from the wild in some areas across its range.

Rice flower

Pimelia ferruginea

This small to medium-size, evergreen, woody shrub is one of around 80 species of so-called rice flowers, found throughout Australia and New Zealand, which are related to the European and Asian genus *Daphne*. The flowers are produced mainly in spring but can appear at any time, in dense heads borne at the tips of the branches.

Distribution: Australia and New Zealand.
Height and spread: 1.8m/6ft.
Habit and form: Evergreen shrub.
Leaf shape: Ovate or oblong.
Pollinated: Insect.

Identification: An erect, evergreen shrub with opposite, crowded leaves up to 12mm/½in long, shiny and smooth above, often hairy beneath, with rolled margins. Almost spherical flowerheads, up to 40mm/1½in across, appear in late spring to early summer, held at the ends of branchlets and surrounded by leaf-like pink or red bracts. The tubular, four-petalled flowers are pink with a paler centre.

Right: Rice flower forms a medium-size shrub with crowded leafy stems.

PASSIONFLOWER, VIOLET AND SAXIFRAGE FAMILIES

The passionflower family, Passifloraceae, contains tropical climbers and woody shrubs. Members of the violet family, Violaceae, are widely distributed, with species being herbaceous trees or shrubs. The saxifrage family, or Saxifragaceae, includes herbaceous perennials and deciduous shrubs.

Slender violet

Hybanthus monopetalus

This delicate, erect, herb-like shrub is common in sheltered spots in scrub and dry grassland in mountainous areas throughout much of eastern Australia and Tasmania. The leaves are narrow and soft, with the upper leaves held opposite, while the lower ones are mostly alternate. The striking blue flowers have five petals, but four of these are so tiny they are inconspicuous. The fifth is greatly elongated and its appearance gives rise to the botanical species name: *monopetalus* is Latin for single-petalled, and this feature gives the plant a highly distinctive appearance.

Identification: An erect, herb-like shrub, reaching 50cm/20in tall where ungrazed. The soft, narrow leaves are mid-green with a strongly defined midrib, 10–60mm/⅜–2¼in long. Large, solitary, prominent blue flowers are borne on slender stalks; they have five more or less equal sepals and five petals, four of which are inconspicuous. The fifth is 6–20mm/¼–¾in long, oval, pale blue with darker veins, with a pale spot towards the base and a broad, dilated concavity or claw in the base.

Distribution: Eastern Australia; Tasmania.
Height and spread: 50cm/20in.
Habit and form: Herb-like shrub.
Leaf shape: Linear-lanceolate.
Pollinated: Insect.

Above left: The fruit is divided into three parts that split to reveal the seed.

Left: While herb-like in appearance, slender violet is actually a shrub.

Australian violet

Trailing violet, Ivy violet, *Viola hederacea*

Known as the ivy violet because of its trailing habit, this creeping herbaceous plant is a native of shady and moist spots among the mountains of eastern and southern Australia, including Tasmania. It is a fairly variable species, with dark green leaves and, during the summer, short stems of fragrant, purple or white flowers that have a squashed appearance and are borne fairly abundantly above the foliage.

Identification: A stemless, tufted or creeping, mat-forming perennial. The leaves are rounded or kidney-shaped, up to 40mm/1½in wide, sometimes toothed, dark green with paler veination, often forming dense cover. The flowers are blue-violet to white, usually with a blue-purple centre and white edges, and are flattened in appearance, with bearded lateral petals and inconspicuous spurs. . They are held 75mm/3in above the leaves and are sometimes scented.

Above: The flowers have a squashed appearance when they open.

Left: The flowerheads are pale and nodding before they open.

Distribution: Eastern and southern Australia.
Height and spread: 75mm/3in.
Habit and form: Mat-forming herb.
Leaf shape: Spathulate to reniform.
Pollinated: Insect.

Left: The flattened flowers are held on thin stalks above the foliage.

Red passion flower

Passiflora aurantia

This climbing vine is naturally found in eastern Queensland and also occurs in New Guinea and on some Pacific islands. *Passiflora* is a well-known genus because it includes the commercial passion fruit, *P. edulis*. While the genus is mostly restricted to areas of tropical America and Asia, this is one of three Australian species. It has tri-lobed leaves and red or salmon flowers, borne mainly in winter and spring, although a few can usually be seen all year round. The flowers deepen in colour as they age and are followed by egg-shaped, green fruits, which, although edible, are unpalatable.

Distribution: North-eastern Australia; New Guinea; Pacific islands.
Height and spread: Variable.
Habit and form: Liana.
Leaf shape: Lobed.
Pollinated: Insect.

Right: This vigorous climbing plant clings by means of coiling tendrils and flowers over a long period.

Identification: A vigorous, woody liana with hairless, angular stems, producing long, coiling tendrils by which it supports upward growth. The leaves, up to 75mm/3in long, usually have three shallow oval lobes. The flowers, up to 10cm/4in in diameter, have narrow, pale pink sepals deepening to orange-red, orange to brick-red petals and deep red filaments. The egg-shaped green fruit, 40mm/1½in long, contains greyish pulp and numerous black seeds.

OTHER SPECIES OF NOTE

Mahoe wao *Melicytus lanceolatus*
This large shrub or small tree from New Zealand has grey-brown bark and long, deep green leaves. The purple-tinged flowers are held in clusters of six around the leaf axils, although they sometimes appear to emerge directly from the branches. They are followed by small, dark purple fruits.

Whiteywood *Melicytus ramiflorus*
This is a fast-growing, spreading tree with a short, branched trunk and whitish-grey peeling bark. Found naturally all over New Zealand, Fiji, Norfolk Island and the Solomon Islands, it occurs from sea level to 900m/2,950ft. The small yellow flowers are followed by blue or purple berries.

Mountain violet *Viola cunninghamii*
This stemless, hairless perennial with rounded or triangular leaves is a native of New Zealand, where it is found in North, South, Stewart, and Chatham Islands, in moist or shady sites in river valleys. The short-spurred flowers appear in spring, and are white to pale violet, with greenish or yellowish throats and a number of purple lines on the petals.

Aupaka *Isodendrion hosakae*
This endemic Hawaiian shrub occurs on volcanic cinder or ash soils in the Waikoloa region. It is a branched, upright, evergreen with long, white, five-petalled, tubular flowers, which are produced from the axils of shiny leaves near the stem tips.

Wire netting bush

Corokia cotoneaster

This much-branched shrub with stiff interlacing branches is common throughout New Zealand, in dry rocky places from North Cape to Stewart Island. Its star-like yellow flowers are followed by red berries in autumn and, although the plant is an evergreen, the leaves are so small and scattered that even in full growth the plant has a sparse, metallic appearance. It is thought that the cage-like tangle of branches evolved to protect the tender young shoots from being eaten by the moa, New Zealand's giant bird, now extinct.

Distribution: New Zealand.
Height and spread: 2m/6½ft.
Habit and form: Shrub.
Leaf shape: Rounded.
Pollinated: Insect.

Identification: The slender, tortuous branches of this shrub are covered in silvery hairs, later becoming hairless, dark grey or black, often spiralling or tangled or zigzagging. The sparse, round leaves, up to 20mm/¾in across, are maroon-green or bronze, often flushed maroon above, silvery beneath. The solitary yellow flowers appear in the leaf axils or in a terminal panicle in late spring; they are star-like, with five narrow petals and five prominent stamens. The fruit is a small, vermilion, fleshy drupe with a persistent calyx.

Left: The stiff interlacing branches give rise to the common name of this shrub.

Left: Bright red berries appear in the autumn.

CARROT FAMILY

The carrot family, Apiaceae, is poorly represented across much of Oceania, although those that do occur there tend to be interesting examples, having become isolated from their counterparts in the Northern Hemisphere. A greater diversity of species is found in Australia and some of these have also evolved into interesting forms.

Sydney flannel flower

Actinotus helianthi

This herbaceous or shrubby plant, found in open forest and woodland and on dry hillsides, coastal dunes and heaths, usually on sand or sandstone, is a native of the coast and mountains of New South Wales and southern Queensland. The deeply lobed, grey leaves have a velvety texture, giving rise to the common name. The small flowers occur in clusters surrounded by velvety, petal-like bracts, giving each flowerhead an appearance similar to that of a daisy. The flowers appear in spring and continue into early summer, though some are usually present throughout the year.

Identification: An erect, branching, herbaceous or shrubby perennial. The pinnate leaves have narrow, toothed, felted segments and the daisy-like flowerheads consist of numerous tiny, white flowers in dense umbels surrounded by large cream bracts, often tipped green, with a dense covering of silvery, woolly hairs. They are followed by fluffy seeds in a globular head, readily dispersed by the breeze.

Distribution: Eastern Australia.
Height and spread: 60cm/24in.
Habit and form: Herbaceous perennial or subshrub.
Leaf shape: Compound.
Pollinated: Insect.

Gingidia montana

This small, aromatic herbaceous plant is found in moist open sites in both the North and South Islands of New Zealand and is also endemic to New South Wales. It occurs in *Eucalyptus paucifolia* woodland, or more commonly at the edge of forests of southern beech, *Nothofagus* species, growing within the crevices of basalt or trachyte rocks, mostly on cliff faces.

Identification: A stout, hairless, erect herb or small shrub, up to 50cm/20in high, strongly aromatic with divided leaves up to 60cm/24in long, composed of seven to nine ovate to almost circular leaflets with obtusely toothed margins. The white flowers are borne on umbel-like inflorescences with eight to 12 rays, up to 25mm/1in long, on 15cm/6in flowering stems. The fruits are egg-shaped. Plants occasionally hybridize with the related *Aciphilla squarrosa*, and the exact details of its classification remain the subject of some debate.

Distribution: New Zealand; and New South Wales.
Height and spread: 50cm/20in.
Habit and form: Herbaceous perennial or subshrub.
Leaf shape: Pinnate.
Pollinated: Insect.

Far left: Gingida forms dense masses of aromatic green foliage that resembles cress but is topped in summer by white umbels of flowers.

Golden speargrass

Bayonet plant, Golden Spaniard, *Aciphylla aurea*

This common perennial, from the subalpine grasslands of New Zealand's South Island, forms a large, clumped rosette of stiff, rigid, yellowish-green leaves with golden-yellow margins, which can deliver a painful stab if not approached with care, hence the common name for this species. The spiny, golden flower spike that appears in summer is showy and contains many flowers. Individual plants are either male or female (dioecious) and this gives the species a slight variability. Its ability to survive fire has led to it colonizing extensive areas.

Identification: A coarse, evergreen perennial with rosettes up to 90cm/35in across. The grey-green, spear-shaped leaves, up to 70cm/27½in long, have thick sheaths and yellow margins and midribs. The flowers appear on a massive terminal panicle up to 90cm/35in tall, usually long-stemmed and candelabra-like, composed of compound umbels. Those of the male plants are strictly unisexual, while the female flowers are interspersed with sporadic males. The small flowers are white to pale yellow and crowded, though the male umbels are more loosely arranged than the female's.

Distribution: South Island, New Zealand.
Height and spread: Evergreen herbaceous perennial.
Habit and form: Up to 90cm/35in.
Leaf shape: Hastate.
Pollinated: Insect.

OTHER SPECIES OF NOTE

Flannel flower
Actinotus leucocephalus
This species from Western Australia has white, fuzzy or hairy bracts, making it look almost like an edelweiss when it flowers. Flowering is erratic, however: the best time to see flowers is in spring following a bushfire, when they sometimes cover the ground profusely.

Actinotus bellidioides
This rare species is restricted to peaty soils, chiefly in upland bogs in south-eastern Australia and Tasmania. It has a small, flat rosette of circular dark green leaves, which although not as hairy as other species are typical of the genus, and is identifiable chiefly by its buttercup-like, golden-yellow bracts.

Anisotome flexuosa
This large perennial has narrow, two-pinnate, leathery leaflets, and like others in the genus it is dioecious. It is found in montane and subalpine habitats of New Zealand's South Island, where it may be seen growing among rock crevices. The creamy-white umbels are loosely scattered across the hummocky mass of foliage in the early summer.

Aciphylla montana
This tufted, small perennial of South Island, New Zealand, has sharp-pointed, yellowish-green leaves, with two to four pairs of segments, which are strongly pungent when crushed. The male inflorescences are shorter than those of the female. The yellowish umbels rarely exceed the leaf height.

Aromatic aniseed

Anisotome aromatica

This perennial herb, native to the South Island of New Zealand, is found chiefly in the grassland of the montane subalpine zones. The fragrant flowers are held in clusters in small umbels, which appear above the carpeting foliage. The male and female flowers appear on separate plants, both arranged in umbels on slender, sparingly divided stems.

Distribution: South Island, New Zealand.
Height and spread: 50cm/20in.
Habit and form: Herbaceous perennial.
Leaf shape: Pinnate.
Pollinated: Insect.

Identification: A dioecious herbaceous perennial with basal, pinnate leaves, 50mm–12cm/2–4¾in long, with 6–12 pairs of leathery, toothed, deeply divided leaflets, the segments of which are sessile and deeply divided with hairs at their apex. The flowers appear in clusters in a small umbel reaching 10–15cm/4–6in across and are white and fragrant. The male umbels are large and many flowered and the female umbels are much smaller, contracted and fewer flowered, often looking a little like a different species. Several sub-species occur across its range, making it a variable plant and one that can cause confusion when identifying it.

BELLFLOWER, PINCUSHION AND AND MADDER FAMILIES

Bellflowers, Campanulaceae, are highly ornamental and have become familiar plants in cultivation. The Australian pincushion family, Brunoniaceae, has only one genus and species, whereas the madder family, Rubiaceae, mostly occurs in the tropics.

Royal bluebell

Wahlenbergia gloriosa

The royal bluebell occurs mainly in subalpine woodland above 1,300m/4,250ft in the Australian Capital Territory, south-eastern New South Wales and Victoria. It grows in the most uninviting dry, stony habitats, often exposed to full sun and strong winds. The vivid blue or violet-blue flowers are easily recognized; they are held above the foliage on long slender stems and may be erect or nodding. It has become scarce in recent times and is now legally protected throughout its natural range.

Identification: A small, slender, creeping to semi-erect herbaceous perennial with spreading rhizomes and erect stems, sometimes branching, rising above the oval, wavy-edged leaves. The flowers, 25mm/1in across, are deep blue to purple, bell-shaped, erect or nodding, on long slender stems with a few distant, narrow bracts; there are usually five petals, joined in a short tube, with spreading lobes with light blue bases and a purple style ending in two white stigmas. The fruit is a small capsule, prominently ribbed and surmounted by the five erect sepals.

Distribution: South-eastern Australia.
Height and spread: Variable.
Habit and form: Creeping herbaceous perennial.
Leaf shape: Obovate.
Pollinated: Insect.

Left: The small creeping stems of this herb give rise to vivid blue or violet-blue, star-shaped flowers.

Blue pincushion

Brunonia australis

This silky or hairy herb is locally frequent in all Australian states in dry forests, being most often encountered following bushfires. Each inflorescence has a large number of crowded flowers, with the reproductive parts raised above the petals so that they resemble pins in a pincushion. The flowers appear in late spring to summer, held on leafless stems above the rosettes of silky, hairy, spoon-shaped leaves, giving the plant a decorative appearance. *Brunonia* is a monotypic genus although it is variable in habit as a result of its widespread distribution.

Identification: A variable, densely hairy herbaceous perennial, growing to 30cm/12in tall and with grey-green, spoon-shaped leaves up to 50mm/2in long, forming a basal rosette. The vivid cornflower-blue flowers, tubular at the base and with spreading, star-like petals, appear in crowded, terminal, pincushion-like heads up to 25mm/1in across, atop a base of hairy calyces and borne on erect, leafless stems that reach 45cm/18in tall, usually in spring but sporadically extending through to autumn.

Distribution: Australia.
Height and spread: 30cm/12in.
Habit and form: Herbaceous perennial.
Leaf shape: Obovate.
Pollinated: Insect.

Beach gardenia

Guettarda speciosa

Beach gardenia can be found in coastal northern Australia, from Western Australia to central Queensland, and also on many Pacific Islands, typically in beach strand communities in coastal regions, almost all the way to the high tide level in places. It has large rounded leaves, above which the large, white, fragrant, tubular flowers occur from spring to autumn, although they may also be seen at other times. The fragrance is similar to that of true gardenia, though weaker.

Identification: The leaves, up to 20cm/8in long, are opposite or in whorls of three, broadly oval with blunt or pointed tips, smooth above and hairy beneath, with a prominent midrib and 7–10 pairs of lateral nerves. White, fragrant, tubular flowers up to 40mm/1½in long, with seven spreading lobes, appear in dense axillary cymes, and are followed by small, hard, globular, white to brown fruits.

Distribution: Northern Australia; Pacific Islands.
Height and spread: 5m/16ft.
Habit and form: Shrub or small tree.
Leaf shape: Obovate.
Pollinated: Insect, probably moth.

Far right: Beach gardenia is a large, spreading shrub or small tree. It is very sensitive to too much sun, and its flowers are most fragrant at night or just before dawn.

OTHER SPECIES OF NOTE

Australian bluebell *Wahlenbergia stricta*
This Australian flower is probably the most commonly encountered of the genus, being found every-where except the Northern Territory and is often seen on roadsides. It forms clumps up to 40cm/16in high, and its masses of light blue or white flowers are easily seen, in spring and summer.

Indian mulberry *Morinda citrifolia*
This large shrub to medium tree has oval leaves and white flowers that occur in the leaf axils in clusters, mainly in summer and autumn. These are followed by succulent fruits, which fuse into a large compound structure as they ripen. The fruits are edible but are very pungent when ripe, apparently to attract fruit bats.

Coprosma pumila
This small, mat-forming alpine shrub from Australia and New Zealand hugs the rocks among which it grows to form a tight cushion. The bases of the leaf stems are fused, giving a fleshy appearance. The lemon-yellow, star-shaped flowers are followed by yellow-red fleshy fruits.

Delissea rytidosperma
This unusual and rare flower is an Hawaiian endemic. Each tall upright stem is topped with a whorl of greyish-green, serrated leaves, some-times tinged purple. The long, claw-shaped, pale green to purple flowers emerge from close to the growing point, in loose inflorescences.

Sweet Suzie

Canthium odoratum syn. *Psydrax odorata*

Sweet Suzie is a large shrub, with a range from Hawaii, Micronesia and parts of the South Pacific to the rainforest in northern Australia and more occasionally open forest on the continent. It is a common species in the Whitsunday area of north Queensland. It is a very handsome plant, with white bark that contrasts well with its dark, shiny leaves, but it is the clusters of attractive, sweetly fragrant flowers that arise from the leaf axils over a long season that earn this plant its common name.

Identification: A medium to large shrub, sometimes a small tree, with white bark and green young twigs. The oval leaves, up to 80mm/3⅛in long, are glossy deep green on the top surface, duller below, with paler green veins and slightly wavy edges. The small, highly fragrant, tubular white flowers are borne in clusters arising from the leaf axils, appearing prolifically in spring and autumn. They are followed by fleshy, juicy, black fruits about 5mm/³⁄₁₆in in diameter, containing two seeds.

Distribution: Hawaii; Micronesia, South Pacific; northern Australia.
Height and spread: Variable.
Habit and form: Shrub or tree.
Leaf shape: Ovate.
Pollinated: Insect.

Below: Sweet Suzie grows into a small tree or large shrub.

NETTLE, DEADNETTLE AND VERBENA FAMILIES

The nettle family, Urticaceae, contains about 45 genera and 700 species, many of which have stinging hairs on their stems and leaves. The deadnettle family, Lamiaceae, comprises 200 genera. The verbena family, Verbenaceae, has 75 genera and 3,000 species, mostly tropical or subtropical herbs or trees.

Stinging tree

Gympie-gympie, *Dendrocnide moroides*

This tropical member of the nettle family ranks as one of the most painful plant encounters should you ever be unlucky enough to touch it. In Australia it is officially classed as a dangerous plant. The stems and leaves are coated with fine hairs which, when embedded in the skin, cause severe pain and irritation. Apparently the plants have killed dogs and horses that have bumped into them. There is no effective antidote known for the stinging tree. These plants are mostly found along Australia's eastern coast, especially in the rainforest of the north-east and, like other nettles, they tend to grow in disturbed areas, especially more open and sunny parts, such as forest clearings and riverbanks.

Identification: A single-stemmed herbaceous perennial or sparingly branched shrub, with stems up to 50mm/2in wide. The leaves are large and broad, oval or heart-shaped, up to 30cm/12in long and 22cm/8½in wide, on 50mm–15cm/2–6in leaf stalks. The small male and female flowers are borne on separate plants, in panicles in the forks of leaves.

Distribution: Queensland, Australia.
Height and spread: 90cm–5m/ 35in–16ft.
Habit and form: Shrub.
Leaf shape: Ovate or cordate.
Pollinated: Wind.

Left: The single stem supports the large stinging leaves.

Far left: The fruits appear on female trees.

Victorian Christmas bush

Victoria dogwood, Mint bush, *Prostanthera lasianthos*

This spectacular summer-flowering tall shrub, or small tree, has white or pink flowers and is commonly seen growing along the banks of streams or gullies in south-east Australia and Tasmania. It flowers profusely around December, hence the common name. It emits a strong scent similar to eucalyptus or peppermint when brushed. In favourable conditions the Christmas bush flowers so heavily that the fallen flowers form a carpet on the ground beneath.

Identification: A variable woody species with long, smooth, upright shoots and lance-shaped, soft, slightly fleshy, opposite leaves 50–75mm/2–3in long with toothed edges, paler below. The fragrant flowers, appearing in summer, are paired in short leafless racemes, forming branched terminal panicles up to 15cm/6in long. The flowers are funnel-shaped with five lobes, two forming the upper lip and three the spreading lower lip. They are white or cream, or may be tinted violet or lilac, spotted brown or yellow in the wide throat and covered inside and out with fine hairs.

Distribution: Eastern Australia.
Height and spread: 8m/26ft.
Habit and form: Tall shrub or small tree.
Leaf shape: Lanceolate.
Pollinated: Insect.

Right: The Christmas bush can be a shrub or small tree.

Above and right: The white flowers are peppermint-scented.

Honohono

Haplostachys haplostachya

This extremely rare plant, formerly from Kauai, Maui and Hawaii, is now known only from a single population in Kipukakalawamauna on Hawaii. The genus is endemic to the islands and comprises five species, all extinct except for a few remaining plants of this species. It is found on dry shrublands and forests on old lava flows and cinder cones. Though a member of the mint family, it lacks the characteristic aromatic oils, probably because they had no natural pests on the island. The woolly leaves help to reflect sunlight away from the plant, and the beautiful spikes of sweet-smelling, white flowers appear at the branch tips.

Distribution: Hawaii.
Height and spread: 30–60cm/12–24in.
Habit and form: Subshrub.
Leaf shape: Variable/ovate.
Pollinated: Insect.

Left: The plant forms an erect hairy subshrub.

Right: The flowerhead is large and showy.

Identification: Erect, herbaceous perennial or subshrub with four-angled stems. The opposite, lance-shaped or oval to triangular leaves are extremely soft, covered with dense, tangled or matted woolly hairs, light green on top and silvery-white underneath. The irregular, funnel-shaped flowers are large, white and fragrant, up to 50mm/2in long, borne on terminal racemes up to 45cm/18in tall, each bearing several flowers, arranged spirally around the stem. Four black, hard nutlets are produced per flower.

Left: The striking, white, fragrant flowers appear at the branch tips.

OTHER SPECIES OF NOTE

Snakebush *Hemiandra pungens*
This native of the coastal sands and woodlands of south-western Australia is a small shrub, sometimes prostrate or trailing. Tubular mauve to red flowers, with a two-lobed upper lip and a three-lobed lower lip, open in spring.

Austral bugle *Ajuga australis*
This widespread native of southern and eastern Australia can be found in a range of soils and habitats. It is a small, herbaceous perennial with a basal rosette of velvety leaves and soft, erect stems. The flowers, usually deep blue or purple are seen mainly in spring and summer.

Lambstails *Lachnostachys verbascifolia*
Native to the deserts of western Australia, lambstails is recognizable by its fluffy texture and white to grey colouring. Found in sandy places, especially the sand plains, its hairy covering protects it from the heat, although this almost entirely hides the tiny, pinkish flowers.

Mintplant *Chloanthes parviflora*
A small, erect, shrubby perennial, superficially resembling rosemary and found in Queensland and New South Wales, Australia. It reaches 60cm/24in tall, and the pale mauve, hairy, tubular flowers are borne close to the axils of the stems through winter and spring.

Snowy oxera

Royal creeper, *Oxera pulchella*

This evergreen, woody vine, like the rest of the genus, is found only in the dense, moist tropical forests of the Pacific island of New Caledonia. It has thick, deep green, rounded leaves on twining stems, which in turn sport large clusters of white, azalea-shaped, pendent bells with a hint of cream-yellow. It tends to scramble over smaller bushes, rather than climb taller trees.

Identification: A climbing, evergreen, twining shrub, with rough bark and prominent lenticels, and smooth stems to 50mm/2in thick. The leathery, dark green, oblong to lance-shaped leaves, opposite and up to 12.5cm/5in long, have smooth or toothed margins. The flowers appear in great abundance in axillary, forked cymes, in early spring; 50mm/2in or more long, they are pendent, brilliant white or yellow-white.

Distribution: New Caledonia.
Height and spread: Variable.
Habit and form: Vining shrub.
Leaf shape: Oblong.
Pollinated: Insect.

Above: The buds are conspicuous.

Left: Oxera forms a climbing evergreen vine.

FIGWORT AND MYOPORUM FAMILIES

*The figwort family, Scrophulariaceae, comprises mostly herbs but also a few small shrubs, with about
190 genera and 4,000 predominately temperate species, with a cosmopolitan distribution. The majority
are found in temperate areas and tropical mountains. The myoporum family, Myoporaceae, includes four
genera and 150 species, mostly trees and shrubs, and is found in Australia and the South Pacific.*

Spotted emu bush

Eremophila maculata

This shrub is one of the most widespread and variable of the
emu bushes, a large genus of 214 species, all endemic to
Australia. It can be found in inland areas of all mainland
states, mostly on clay soils in the more arid
regions. It is a variable plant with
tubular, nectar-filled flowers, which
occur in the leaf axils and are
seen in a wide range
of colours from
pink and
mauve to
red, orange and
yellow. They often
have a pale,
spotted throat.
Flowering occurs
mainly through winter
and spring but some flowers may also be
seen at other times.

Identification: An evergreen
shrub with downy twigs and
alternate, narrow leaves.
Abundant tubular flowers in a
wide range of colours are borne
in the axils: they are about
25mm/1in long, constricted
at the base, with
protruding stamens and
spotted, hairy throats;
the upper lip consists
of four erect lobes,
the lower lip is
reflexed and
deeply divided.
The fruit is a
drupe with four
chambers, each
containing one
or more seeds,
subtended by the persistent
five-lobed calyx.

Distribution: Australia.
Height and spread:
1–2.5m/39in–8ft.
Habit and form: Shrub.
Leaf shape: Linear.
Pollinated: Insect.

*Left: The emu bush is variable in
habit, and often forms a small
tree-like bush.*

Slender myoporum

Myoporum floribundum

This spectacular but uncommon myoporum occurs naturally on the coastal ranges
of southern New South Wales and Victoria, Australia, rising up to
gullies of the upper Snowy River and parts of the Southern
Tablelands. It is a slender, fragrant shrub, and has long,
arching branches with pendulous, narrow, sticky leaves and
small, scented, white flowers that cluster along the branches
on fine hair-like stalks, giving a feathery appearance to the
massed inflorescences in spring and early summer.

Identification: A spindly shrub with an arching or weeping
habit. The very narrow leaves, up to 90mm/3½in long
and alternate, are smooth and dark green. The
leaves hang down from the horizontal or
arching branches, giving the plant a
wilted look. Small, scented, white to
cream, five-petalled flowers, with
prominent stamens, are borne on fine
stalks in the axil of each leaf, and are
clustered along the upper parts of the
branches, which often arch under the
weight. The fruits are numerous, small,
succulent and brown when mature.

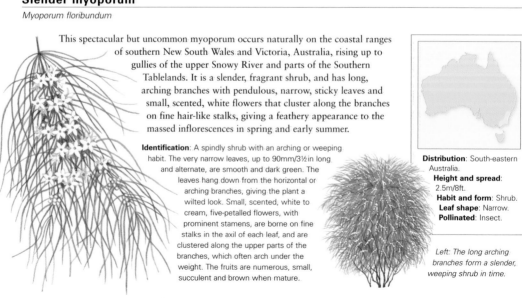

Distribution: South-eastern
Australia.
Height and spread:
2.5m/8ft.
Habit and form: Shrub.
Leaf shape: Narrow.
Pollinated: Insect.

*Left: The long arching
branches form a slender,
weeping shrub in time.*

Snowy mountain foxglove

Ourisia macrocarpa

Distribution: New Zealand.
Height and spread: Up to 60cm/24in.
Habit and form: Alpine herb.
Leaf shape: Rounded.
Pollinated: Insect, probably fly.

This New Zealand alpine flower is found chiefly in the southern mountains of the South Island and is a low-growing, rhizomatous perennial that flowers during spring or early summer according to location. It spreads to form a loose mat of dark leathery leaves from which the whorled inflorescences emerge on long stalks. Like many alpine species in New Zealand, the flowers are white and relatively unspecialized, reflecting the limited range of native insects available to pollinate them.

Identification: A low-growing, alpine perennial herb with robust, erect stems up to 60cm/24in long, though usually shorter, rising from a creeping rhizome. The oval to circular leaves are thick and leathery, dark green above, hairless except on the margins, which have rounded teeth. The tubular, white flowers appear in sequentially blooming whorls on the stout stems; they are up to 25mm/1in in diameter, with a broad, short tube and five spreading lobes, sometimes with a yellow throat, minutely hairy within.

OTHER SPECIES OF NOTE

New Zealand mousehole tree
Myoporum laetum
A small tree with alternate, glossy green, finely toothed leaves, covered with translucent glands that give them an attractive appearance. The flowers appear in summer from the leaf axils and are white spotted with purple; while attractive, they are easily overlooked. The fruits that follow are oblong and reddish.

Ourisia integrifolia
This small herb of alpine wet areas appears to be closely related to the New Zealand *Ourisia* species and is the only representative of the genus in Australia. It is restricted to Tasmania, where it can be found in thickets and woods. The shiny leaves are very small in comparison to the large white or pale blue, five-petalled flowers, which appear in summer.

Parahebe lyallii
This variable plant can be found in many parts of New Zealand. The flowers are most commonly white or white with pink, held over the reddish-green leaves in spring. As its name suggests, the genus is closely allied to hebes, but in appearance it resembles a small, slightly shrubby *Veronica* species.

Hebe elliptica
This bushy shrub has fleshy, green, oval leaves with light edges. The flowers, which open in the spring, are white to pale mauve and relatively large. It has a variable habit, and is found on the west coasts of the South and North Islands of New Zealand and also in the Falkland Islands.

New Zealand hebe

Hebe speciosa

This bushy, rounded shrub is highly popular with gardeners, but in the wild is found only in a few localities in the Marlborough Sounds and on the west coast of North Island on exposed sea cliffs. It is a highly variable species, giving rise to many cultivars and hybrids, some of which may have become naturalized outside its native range. Its large, magenta inflorescences make it one of the more spectacular hebes when flowering commences in summer and extends over a long season.

Identification: A strong-growing shrub with stout, angular branches and thick fleshy, glossy, leaves up to 10cm/4in long. The stems and margins of the young leaves are purple, and this colour persists on the backs of the leaves when they mature. The flowers are dark red to magenta, crowded in terminal conical to cylindrical racemes up to 70mm/2¾in long.

Distribution: North Island, New Zealand.
Height and spread: 2m/6½ft.
Habit and form: Shrub.
Leaf shape: Ovate.
Pollinated: Insect.

Left: New Zealand Hebe forms a small to medium-size rounded bush that is often found in cultivation.

AGAVE, GRASS TREE, BLOODWORT AND LILY FAMILIES

The agave, Agavaceae, grass tree, Xanthorrhoeaceae, and bloodwort, Haemodoraceae, families are all loosely allied to the lily family, Liliaceae. They generally prefer hot, warm, dry habitats and are well represented in Australia and New Zealand.

New Zealand cabbage tree

Cabbage palm, *Cordyline australis*

This unusual-looking tree typically occurs on forest margins and coastal cliffs, in swamps and other wet areas, and is a familiar sight throughout New Zealand. It is also widely planted in gardens and is known to many who have never visited its native islands. The species is often naturalized outside its range and there are many cultivars. The crown is made up of long, bare branches carrying bushy heads of large, grass-like leaves, from which large panicles of small, white, sweet-scented flowers emerge. Flowering is erratic, with the best displays usually following dry summers.

Identification: The trunk is generally sparingly or not at all branched below, copiously branched above, and ultimately massive, up to 1.5m/5ft in diameter, with rough, fissured bark. The leaves 30–90cm/12–35in long and 50mm/2in wide, are narrow and arching, light green with indistinct veins. Small, sweetly fragrant flowers, creamy-white with yellow anthers, appear in a much-branched panicle up to 1.8m/6ft long and 60cm/24in wide, with well-spaced branches more or less at right angles and almost hidden by the flowers. The small, spherical fruits are white or very pale blue.

Distribution: New Zealand.
Height and spread: 20 x 4m/ 65½ x 13ft.
Habit and form: Tree.
Leaf shape: Linear-lanceolate.
Pollinated: Insect.

Left: The small flowers are fragrant and held in dense panicles.

Right: The palm-like trunks are distinctive.

New Zealand flax

Phormium tenax

This robust, evergreen, New Zealand perennial gets its common name because the Maori people used the leaf fibres for making clothing, fishing nets and ropes. It is abundant, especially in lowland swamps and intermittently flooded land, and is also found on Norfolk Island. It has attractive foliage and, while not renowned for its flowers, the tubular, orange-red flowers that appear in tall, upright panicles are very striking.

Identification: A perennial rhizomatous herb with short, stout stems and strap-like, deep green leaves that are bright orange towards the base. They are stiff and erect, at least in the lower part, 90cm–3m/35in–10ft long and 50mm–12.5cm/ 2–5in wide, usually splitting at the tip, clump-forming and fibrous. The smooth, dark brown flowering stems may reach a height of 5m/16ft. The flowers have dull red tepals, 25–50mm/1–2in long, with slightly recurved, orange tips to the inner tepals. The fruit is a long, three-sided capsule.

Distribution: New Zealand, Norfolk Island.
Height and spread: 2m/6½ft.
Habit and form: Rhizomatous herb.
Leaf shape: Linear-lanceolate.
Pollinated: Insect.

Left: The orange-red flowers appear in large panicles on long stems.

Tall kangaroo paw

Evergreen kangaroo paw, *Anigozanthos flavidus*

Distribution: South-western Australia.
Height and spread: 90cm/35in.
Habit and form: Clump-forming perennial.
Leaf shape: Linear-lanceolate.
Pollinated: Insect.

This unusual plant, which is native to moist areas in open forests of the far south-west of Australia, has a vigorous clumping growth habit with long, dull green leaves. The tall flowering stems, which emerge from the bases of the leaves from late spring to midsummer, carry unusual furry flowers, which are mostly green, although they can also contain yellow or soft red tones. It is very attractive to birds, the prime pollinators.

Identification: A robust perennial with narrow olive to mid-green leaves 30–45cm/12–18in long and up to 40mm/1½in wide. The reddish flowering stems are 90cm–3m/35in–10ft long, smooth at the base becoming downy on the branches; the flowers, borne in panicles, have forward-pointing lobes that are usually sulphur-yellow to lime-green, though sometimes red, orange, pink or multi-coloured, and are densely covered with yellow-green or red-brown hairs.

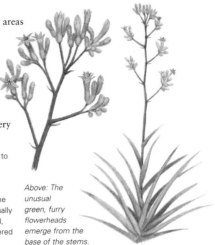

Above: The unusual green, furry flowerheads emerge from the base of the stems.

OTHER SPECIES OF NOTE

Narrow-leaved palm lily *Cordyline stricta*
This shrubby, palm-like plant is found in wet forest and rainforest in Australia. It forms a multi-caned, fountain-shaped bush, 2–3m/6½–10ft tall, with narrow, purplish dark green leaves. The showy, lavender to bluish flowers, in drooping panicles, appear in the spring and are followed by round, blue-black, fleshy fruits.

Mountain flax *Phormium colensoi*
The mountain flax, while similar to *P. tenax*, is smaller, with thinner leaves that are arching rather than erect. The flowers are greenish-yellow and the seedpods are twisted and hang down from the flowering stalks.

Grass tree *Xanthorrhoea australis*
This very slow-growing plant develops a rough trunk with age, coloured black as the result of surviving many bushfires. The long, narrow leaves are crowded at the tops of the trunks, and small, individual, white or cream flowers are clustered together in a spear-like spike, which can tower 2m/6½ft or more above the top of the trunk.

Western Australian grass tree *Kingia australis*
This unusual species is not related to true grasses. The sole species in this genus is found between Perth and Albany. It flowers irregularly, usually after a fire, with yellow, green and brown flowers appearing in early spring, amid the mass of grass-like leaves.

Blue tinsel lily

Calectasia cyanea

This plant takes its name from its shiny blue flowers, which really do have the look and feel of tinsel and appear mainly in late spring. Native to Western and South Australia, the bush is adapted to very dry conditions and resembles a small paperbark or tea tree, *Melaleuca* species, when not in flower. Despite its appearance, however, this monotypic genus is actually most closely related to the grass trees, *Xanthorrhoea* species.

Distribution: Southern Australia.
Height and spread: 25cm/10in.
Habit and form: Shrub.
Leaf shape: Linear-lanceolate.
Pollinated: Insect.

Identification: A small rhizomatous shrub with upright slender stems clothed with small, needle-like sheathed leaves, spirally arranged. The solitary, bright blue flowers are borne terminally on short branchlets. They are star-like, with six pointed, glossy, metallic tepals and yellow anthers that turn red as they mature. The fruit is a one-seeded nut.

Below: The shiny, blue, star-like flowers give rise to this plant's common name.

DAISY FAMILY

Australia and New Zealand support many species in the daisy family, Asteraceae, many of which form impressive displays in summer or following rains in arid areas. It is, however, on some of the islands in the vast southern oceans where plants have become isolated from their continental ancestors that the most interesting forms are encountered.

Bachelor's buttons

Billy buttons, *Craspedia uniflora*

This rosette-forming annual or sometimes perennial plant is found over a wide range of habitats in southern Australia, Tasmania and New Zealand, preferring dry, stony grassland, from lowland to moderate altitudes. The round pompom flowerheads that appear in the summer give rise to its common name; they are yellow in this species, although most other species in the genus have white flowers.

Above and left: The plant forms a low rosette of leaves.

Above: The seedhead has tightly packed oval, silky seeds, each one bearing a feathery plume.

Identification: The erect flowering stems rise above basal rosettes of oval to narrowly spoon-shaped leaves up to 12.5cm/5in long. The yellow flowerheads are spherical, about 15mm/⅜in across, on very thin stems.

Distribution: Southern Australia; Tasmania and New Zealand.
Height and spread: 40cm/16in.
Habit and form: Rosette-forming annual.
Leaf shape: Oblong-ovate to spathulate.
Pollinated: Insect.

Swan river daisy

Brachycome iberidifolia

This wiry annual plant has dainty, dark-eyed, bright blue, daisy-like, fragrant flowers, borne above and among the feathery leaves. It flowers predominantly in the cooler wetter months of the year. The plant is bushy or spreading in habit, and has downy, grey-green leaves that are deeply lobed.

Identification: An annual herb with slender, branched, glandular-hairy stems and finely divided, fern-like leaves up to 10cm/4in long. The daisy-like flowers, on slender stalks, about 75mm/3in long, are white, blue or violet with yellow central discs. The fruit is tiny and club-shaped with tiny bristles on the uppermost part.

Distribution: Southern and western Australia.
Height and spread: 45cm/18in.
Habit and form: Annual herb.
Leaf shape: Pinnatifid.
Pollinated: Insect.

Below: The plant forms a low, spreading, wiry mass of feathery-leaved stems.

Left: A massed flowering of this plant is a spectacular sight.

Above: Pink flowerheads are rare or absent from wild populations but often selected in cultivated stock.

Winged everlasting

Sandflower, *Ammobium alatum*

A native of sandy habitats in New South Wales and as far north as Queensland, Australia, the common name of this grey-leaved, perennial herb refers in part to the curious, membranous wings on its stems. In addition, the small flowerheads are surrounded by rows of papery bracts, giving the spent flowers an 'everlasting' effect. The flowers are often dried for commercial use, being cut for drying just as they open.

Distribution:
Eastern Australia.
Height and spread:
50–90cm/20–35in.
Habit and form: Erect perennial.
Leaf shape: Lanceolate.
Pollinated: Insect.

Above: The papery bracts are tightly folded and enclose the yellow flowerhead in the bud.

Left: This grey-leaved herb has tall flower stems that emerge from a basal rosette.

Identification: The stems of this erect, branched perennial herb have wings formed from decurrent leaf bases. The pointed leaves, up to 18cm/7in long in the basal rosette, becoming smaller up the stem, are covered in white down. The flowerheads, with silvery-white, pointed, papery bracts and yellow centres, are about 20mm/¾in in diameter, borne singly at the ends of the flower stalks.

OTHER SPECIES OF NOTE
Strawflower *Helichrysum bracteatum*
Also known as the yellow paper daisy, this coarse, erect perennial is relatively common across much of Australia, growing in open scrub and grassland areas. It gets its name from the papery texture of the bright yellow flowers, which close in the evening or on overcast days.

Celmisia hookeri
This large, tufted plant inhabits mountain grassland scrub and is confined to north-eastern Otago on the South Island of New Zealand. The broad green leaves are dark and leathery and large, white daisy flowers with yellow centres appear in the spring and summer.

Wilkesia gymnoxiphium
Endemic to Kauai in the Hawaiian Islands on dry volcanic soils, with rosettes elevated on woody stems up to 5m/16ft tall, the plant flowers once in its variable lifespan and then dies. The tall flower spike is composed of many nodding yellow flowers.

Mountain daisy *Celmisia angustifolia*
This small subshrub, woody at its base, is found in the montane tussock grasslands of New Zealand. Its branches are clothed in old leaf remains. It has long, spoon-shaped leaves, with felted undersides, in rosettes at the branch tips. The white flowerheads are produced on solitary stalks during the summer.

Hawaiian silversword

Ahinahina, *Argyroxiphium sandwicense*

This rosette-forming shrub is restricted to habitats in the cinders of volcanoes, at altitudes of up to 3,700m/12,000ft on the islands of Hawaii and Maui. It is a spectacular species, with tall maroon flowers surmounting the rounded rosette of silvery, sword-like leaves and making it one of the wonders of the Pacific plant world. The flowers develop erratically, usually between early summer and autumn. The grey hairy leaves are an indication of the harshness of the dry environment that this plant occupies.

Identification: A rosette-forming shrub that is usually solitary, with a short vegetative stem and a flowering stem up to 2.5m/8ft tall and 90cm/35in wide. The pointed leaves, up to 40cm/16in long, are rigid, succulent, and covered with silvery hairs. They are spirally arranged, together forming a silver sphere. The showy inflorescence may contain 50–600 compound flowerheads, pink or red in colour with yellow central disc florets.

Distribution: Hawaii and Maui.
Height and spread: 3m x 90cm/10ft x 35in.
Habit and form: Rosette-forming shrub.
Leaf shape: Lanceolate.
Pollinated: Probably insect.

Below: The tall, showy inflorescence appears erratically between summer and autumn.

HEATH FAMILY

The heath family, Ericaceae, is a large family, mostly shrubby in character, comprising about 125 genera and 3,500 species. Mostly lime-hating and restricted to acid soils, the family is cosmopolitan in distribution, except in deserts. It is almost absent from Australasia, where it is largely replaced by Epacridaceae, a family almost exclusively centred upon the Australian continent and nearby islands.

Giant grass tree

Tree heath, Pandani, *Richea pandanifolia*

The wet mountain forests of Tasmania are home to this unusual plant, one of about 10 species in the genus, all but one of which are endemic to the island. It is a tall, palm-like species, which usually grows on a single stem but may occasionally be branched. Its tapering leaves, with bases that wrap completely around the stem, are densely crowded towards the top of the trunk. The white or deep pink flower panicles arise from the leaf axils, often hidden among the leaves.

Identification: A gaunt evergreen tree or shrub with erect, slender branches with annual scars. The narrow, arching leaves, up to 90cm/35in long, are crowded at the branch tips. They are smooth and waxy, with a concave upper surface and smooth or serrated margins tapering to a fine point, ultimately very slender and frayed. The white or pink flowers are inconspicuous, in erect axillary panicles crowded at the branch tips. The individual flowers are covered by large bracts, which fall as the flowers develop. The fruit is a capsule.

Distribution: Tasmania.
Height and spread: 10m/33ft.
Habit and form: Tree or shrub.
Leaf shape: Lanceolate.
Pollinated: Insect or bird.

Left: The flower panicles often go unnoticed as they are hidden among the leaves.

Pink heath

Common heath, *Epacris impressa*

Found throughout the heaths and open forests of southern New South Wales, Victoria, Tasmania and eastern South Australia, the deep pink-flowered form of *E. impressa* is the floral emblem of Victoria. Usually a small shrub, its stiff branches have small leaves with a sharp point at the end and the narrow, tubular flowers occur in clusters along their tips. They contain copious nectar and are frequented by honey-eating birds. Their colour ranges from white through various shades of pink to bright red. Flowering occurs from autumn through to spring, reaching a peak in winter. A form from the Grampian Ranges in western Victoria known as *E. impressa* var. *grandiflora*, has larger flowers and leaves than the typical form and some plants have double flowers.

Identification: An often spindly, upright shrub, with stiff branches, russet when old, with stringy bark. The small, alternate leaves are narrow and sharply pointed. The flowers are snow-white to pink or purple-red, short-stalked and nodding, borne in clusters in an elongated, slender, erect terminal raceme; the corolla tube, up to 20mm/¾in long, has five small indentations near the base, alternating with the stamens.

Distribution: South-eastern Australia.
Height and spread: 90cm/35in.
Habit and form: Shrub.
Leaf shape: Linear-lanceolate.
Pollinated: Bird.

Left: The small pointed branches of this plant give it a spindly appearance.

Red five corners

Styphelia tubiflora

Distribution: Australia
(except Northern Territory).
Height and spread: 1.5m/5ft.
Habit and form: Shrub.
Leaf shape: Oblong-linear.
Pollinated: Insect or bird.

*Far right: The bright red flowers
appear towards the branch tips in
groups of twos or threes.*

This genus, closely related to *Epacris*, contains 14 species,
all of which occur naturally only in Australia and in all
states except the Northern Territory. The fruit, a greenish-
red berry with distinct ribs, gives rise to the common name.
This species is found in dry forest or heath on the coast and
mountains and has bright red flowers, emerging from
greenish-yellow bases in autumn
and spring.

Identification: A small straggly
plant with stiff stems and small,
narrow leaves with margins
curved under, ending in a sharp
point. The flowers, which appear
from autumn to spring, are
solitary or in loose groups of two
or three, borne along the upper
reaches of the branches in an
apparent raceme; they are
usually bright red, although
white, pink and yellow forms
are sometimes seen, with
a greenish-yellow calyx.
The corolla tube is narrow and
about 25mm/1in long,
conspicuously five-angled, with
short lobes strongly
rolled back to expose the
long, protruding stamens. The
fruit is a ribbed drupe with up to
five seeds.

OTHER SPECIES OF NOTE

Blunt-leaf heath *Epacris obtusifolia*
This uncommon small Australian shrub is
found in sandy heathland along the coast
from Queensland to Tasmania and has
very small leaves, pressed to the stem.
The large, bell-shaped white flowers
appear in late winter and spring, in a
massed display along the branches
from the leaf axils, and are
frequented by honey-eating birds.

Coral heath *Epacris microphylla*
This shrub has tiny, pointed leaves, held erect
against the wiry stems and angular branches.
Common on damp rocky heath on the eastern
coast of Australia, it is spectacular when in
flower with masses of white, cup-shaped
blooms toward the ends of the branches.

Richea dracophylla
This erect, small, evergreen shrub from Tasmania
has sharp, pointed leaves arranged in a crowded
spiral at the end of the stem. The dense spikes
of white flowers appear at the ends of branches
in autumn. When the flowers open the petals
fall, giving the spike a bristly appearance.

Snow bush *Leucopogon melaleucoides*
This very small shrub from east coast Australia
is covered in tiny, hairy, tubular, white flowers,
with pinkish calyces and a musty scent. The
flowers appear in late winter to early spring.
The plant resembles a small *Melaleuca* when
not in flower.

Kerosene bush

Richea scoparia

The kerosene bush provides brilliant
splashes of colour throughout the alpine
areas of Tasmania during the summer. While
endemic to this island, it is a very common
alpine and subalpine shrub of high rainfall
areas. Its sharp leaves are persistent for a
long time on old growth, making it
unpopular with bushwalkers because it
forms dense, prickly thickets. In summer, the
terminal spikes of red, pink, white or orange
flowers attract small lizards that feed on the
nectar, and expose the plants
reproductive organs to
pollinating insects.

Distribution: Tasmania.
Height and spread: 1.5m x
90cm/5ft x 35in.
Habit and form: Tree or
shrub.
Leaf shape: Lanceolate.
Pollinated: Insect.

Identification: A bushy, erect,
evergreen treelet or shrub. The semi-rigid,
sharp-pointed, glossy leaves are up to
50mm/2in long, alternate, parallel-
veined, on a sheathing stem with
overlapping bases, persisting for
several seasons. The flowers grow
in dense, cylindrical terminal
racemes up to 30cm/12in long, and
may be white, pink or orange. The corolla, up to
15mm/⅝in long, is closed at the tip except for a
small opening, not separated into lobes.

*Right: This prickly bush is often covered
in brilliantly coloured flowers in the
summer months.*

MALLOW AND ELAEOCARPUS FAMILIES

The Malvaceae, or mallow family, is not particularly well represented in Australia and Oceania, but those species that do grow there include some strikingly beautiful flowers and some very rare plants among their numbers. The elaeocarpus family, Elaeocarpaceae, is sparsely represented in Australia, mostly restricted to the eastern coast, but better represented on New Zealand.

Blue hibiscus

Lilac hibiscus, *Alyogyne huegelii* syn. *Hibiscus huegelii*

The blue hibiscus is native to sandy and sandy-gravel soils in south and western Australia. Despite its common name, it is only distantly related to the true *Hibiscus*, and the flower colour ranges from pink or lilac to purple, usually with a contrasting basal spot. White and yellow forms also occur with the white form reported to have a more sprawling growth habit and brighter green leaves. Numerous varieties exist. The hibiscus-like flowers are borne singly in the leaf axils, appearing from spring through summer to autumn. Although individual flowers are short-blooming, only lasting a day or two, new flowers continue to open over a long period, generally in summer and autumn.

Identification: A fast-growing, medium-size shrub with bright green, wrinkled, complexly five-lobed leaves and woolly younger stems. The conspicuous, short-lived but profusely borne flowers are about 75mm/3in across, with spreading, triangular to round, spirally overlapping petals and a staminal column with numerous filaments in whorls. They are usually lilac with reddish-purple-spotted throats, but may also be pink, blue, white or yellow.

Distribution: Southern and western Australia.
Height and spread: 2.5m/8ft.
Habit and form: Shrub.
Leaf shape: Ovate-palmate lobed.
Pollinated: Insect.

Lily of the valley tree

Blueberry ash, *Elaeocarpus reticulatus*

Elaeocarpus is a genus of about 200 species occurring in eastern Australia and in nearby tropical areas, but the blueberry ash is unique among these in extending south into temperate areas. It can be found as far south as Flinders Island and Tasmania, where it grows in forest gullies and wooded ranges, usually near the coast. Flowering occurs in summer, when masses of small, bell-shaped flowers with an unusual, liquorice scent are produced. The flowers are followed by globular, blue fruits, which are retained on the plant for a long time, attracting many bird species.

Identification: A small tree with a dense crown of foliage and an approximately conical form. The branchlets and leaf stalks are often reddish, with distinct leaf scars. The leaves are alternate, 10–15cm/4–6in long, oval or lance-shaped with pointed tips, dark green above with prominent veins, paler below. Lax axillary racemes appear from mid-spring to midsummer; the fragrant flowers are small, cup-shaped, ivory-white, with three to five fringed petals and numerous stamens. The fruit is a tough, blue, globular drupe, about 12mm/½in in diameter, with a thin layer of edible flesh and one seed encased in a hard, rough stone.

Distribution: Eastern Australia.
Height and spread: 3–15 x 5m/10–49 x 16ft.
Habit and form: Tree.
Leaf shape: Oblong-elliptic.
Pollinated: Bird.

Far left: The globular fruits are popular with birds.

Left: This small tree has a dense crown.

Mountain ribbonwood

Lacebark, *Hoheria lyallii*

Distribution: South Island, New Zealand.
Height and spread: 6m/19¾ft.
Habit and form: Tree.
Leaf shape: Cordate.
Pollinated: Insect.

Right: Mountain ribbonwood is mostly restricted to high watercourses and damp forest margins.

Far right: Ribbonwood flowers profusely in late summer.

This large shrub or small tree is found by forest edges and streams in the drier, eastern reaches of the Southern Alps of New Zealand, at altitudes between 600–1,050m/2,000–3,450ft, where it forms scrub-like groves on the upper margins of the forests. Large quantities of flowers are borne in the leaf axils in summer or autumn, when they can be so profuse as to bend the flexible branches.

Identification: A deciduous tree with alternate, heart-shaped, grey-green, deeply toothed leaves, 50mm–10cm/2–4in long and up to 50mm/2in wide. Mature leaves are covered in white down, especially on the undersides, while the juvenile foliage is smooth. The five-petalled, snow-white flowers are 25mm/1in in diameter, on slender stalks with densely hairy calyces, yellow filaments and purple anthers. The round fruit breaks up into 10–15, compressed, downy, slightly winged carpels.

OTHER SPECIES OF NOTE

New Zealand damson *Elaeocarpus dentatus*
This tall forest tree with grey bark is found in lowland forests on both the North and South Islands. The leaves are quite tough and leathery, and have wavy to serrated margins. Clusters of white, bell-shaped flowers appear in summer, followed by purple drupes in the autumn.

Sturt's desert rose *Gossypium sturtianum*
This wild cotton species is widely distributed in the interior of Australia and is the floral emblem of the Northern Territory. It is a shrub with large oval leaves and showy, hibiscus-like, pink to mauve flowers with a dark red centre. The flowers can be seen for most of the year, with a peak in late winter.

Native rosella
Abelmoschus moschatus subsp. *tuberosus*
Found in northern Australia, this plant dies back to an underground tuber in the dry season, emerging again following the first substantial rains. The dark-centred, pink-white or cream, hibiscus-like blooms, last for one day only but are prolific between October and April.

Hawaiian white hibiscus *Hibiscus waimeae*
This rare Hawaiian endemic species, found only on Kauai, occurs in two distinct and isolated populations on opposite sides of the island. The single white flowers last only one day, opening in the morning and fading to pink in the afternoon.

Phillip Island hibiscus

Hibiscus insularis

This island endemic is confined to just two patches on Phillip Island. Remarkably, these have survived despite the grazing pigs, goats and rabbits, which destroyed most of the island's other vegetation, although the removal of these introduced animals is allowing new seedlings to regenerate near the original bushes. The plant is very attractive and produces creamy flowers, which fade to a beautiful wine colour for about 10 months of the year. It has tiny, neat leaves and a densely branching characteristic, that are adaptations to the strong coastal winds of its native habitat and this has made it popular with gardeners in recent years.

Identification: A dense, bushy, many-branched shrub, growing up to 3.5m/12ft tall, with a spread of 1.8m/6ft. There is a marked difference between the juvenile and adult foliage, with the tiny round leaves that are characteristic of seedling and young plants gradually changing over 10 years or more to the larger more triangular, slightly lobed leaves more characteristic of *Hibiscus*. The small, single, five-petalled flowers are held upward on the stems, and are borne profusely for much of the year.

Distribution: Phillip Island.
Height and spread: 3.5m/12ft.
Habit and form: Evergreen shrub.
Leaf shape: Ovate when young; more cordate with age.
Pollinated: Insect.

Above: The creamy flowers of this rare hibiscus are borne profusely and gradually turn reddish with age.

DOGWOOD AND PROTEA FAMILiES

The dogwoods, Cornaceae, are absent from Australia, and only two genera, Griselinia and Corokia,
occur in New Zealand, with the latter often considered to be part of the wider Saxifragaceae family.
The protea family, Protaeceae, on the other hand is at its most diverse in Australia, with 42 genera and
860 species, and includes flowers of outstanding beauty.

Drummond's dryandra

Dryandra drummondii

The dryandras are a large group, closely related to *Banksia*, which show a tremendous variation in form and foliage. This species is restricted to the Swan River area of south-western Australia, where it usually occurs in shallow, poor and clay soils. The leaves form a rosette, in the middle of which is a large flattened, yellow flowerhead, made up of many hundreds of individual flowers. It appears towards the end of the winter.

Identification: A stemless plant with alternate, leathery leaves, 30cm/12in long and up to 75mm/3in broad, incised to the midrib with triangular lobes and densely covered with white down on the underside. The flowerhead is produced at ground level, surrounded by a persistent circle of bracts; the flowers open in succession from the outside in, with the gingery perianths curling back to reveal the yellow styles and stigmas.

Left: Many hundreds of individual flowerheads make up the inflorescence.

Distribution: South-western Australia.
Height and spread: 50–70cm/20–27½in.
Habit and form: Rosette-forming shrub.
Leaf shape: Pinnatisect.
Pollinated: Insect or possibly mammal.

Left: All Dryandras are yellow in colour, though the shade of yellow varies considerably.

Saw banksia

Old man banksia, *Banksia serrata*

This widespread species from eastern Australia is common in sandstone woodland and open forests or sandy soils. It ranges from southern Queensland along the coast to Victoria, with a small population in northern Tasmania, and stretches west as far as the Great Dividing Range. Normally a tree in favourable conditions, its blackened rough bark is a result of surviving many bushfires. The leaves are large and stiff with saw-toothed edges, hence its common name.

Identification: A small tree with knobbly grey bark and leathery, narrowly oval, serrated leaves, 15cm/6in long, glossy dark green above and paler beneath. The flowerheads are dense, terminal, cylindrical spikes, 15cm/6in long, usually greenish-cream, surrounded by a circle of bracts. They appear from summer to autumn and are followed by seed cones with large, protruding follicles.

Left: Seed is usually only released from the cone-like fruits following bush fires.

Distribution: Eastern Australia.
Height and spread: 2–15m/6½–49ft.
Habit and form: Small tree.
Leaf shape: Saw-like.
Pollinated: Bird, possibly insects.

Left: The saw banksia often forms a gnarled, fire-blackened small tree.

Mountain grevillea

Cat's claw, *Grevillea alpina*

Distribution: South-eastern Australia.
Height and spread: Variable, to 2m/6½ft.
Habit and form: Shrub.
Leaf shape: Linear.
Pollinated: Bird.

Despite its specific name, this plant from south-eastern Australia is a widespread and variable species, occurring at both low and high elevations. It is usually a small shrub with simple rounded leaves, but some forms have much larger leaves with some plants being distinctly hairy. The flowers appear in clusters at the ends of the branches in winter and spring; these too are variable in colour. The species hybridizes naturally with the lavender grevillea, *G. lavandulacea*, and the woolly grevillea, *G. lanigera*, adding to the difficulty of identification.

Identification: A variable, spreading shrub with both prostrate and erect forms. The leaves, up to 25mm/1in long, are alternate, narrow to rounded, downy or smooth. The obliquely tubular flowers are borne in short, crowded racemes, paired, in groups of five or seven. Their colours range from greenish-yellow to white, pink-orange and red, and they may be a single colour or a combination.

Below: The tubular flowers have a long, claw-like style.

Far left: The plant usually forms a small shrub.

OTHER SPECIES OF NOTE

Red spider flower *Grevillea punicea*
A native of New South Wales that grows on sandy soils, in heath, open forest or scrubland, often just away from the coast. It is a highly variable species, with bright red flowers from late winter to summer.

Tasmanian waratah *Telopea truncata*
This upright shrub or small tree grows on moist, acidic soils in wet forest or subalpine scrubland. The young branches and unopened flowerheads are often covered with brownish hairs, the blooms occurring in a loose cluster of red flowers at the ends of the erect stems from late spring to late summer.

Gippsland waratah *Telopea oreades*
This upright shrub or small tree grows on moist, acidic soils, often alongside creek beds, in wet forest or cool rainforest of southern Victoria, Australia. The red flowers appear in summer. A white form, from the Errinundra Plateau in east Gippsland, is sometimes seen.

New Zealand privet *Griselinia littoralis*
This fast-growing, evergreen, upright shrub of dense habit bears oval, leathery, bright apple-green leaves, among which the tiny, inconspicuous, yellow-green flowers appear. It is a common hardwood tree throughout the mixed and beech forests of the North, South, and Stewart Islands, from lowland altitudes to subalpine scrub.

Waratah

Telopea speciosissima

The waratah ranges along the central east coast of Australia from sea level to above 1,000m/3,300ft in the Blue Mountains. It grows mainly in the shrub understorey in open forest that has developed on sandstone and adjoining volcanic formations, often on slopes or in gullies. A truly spectacular plant, it is the floral emblem of New South Wales. Its bright red flowers appear in spring and attract the nectar-seeking birds that act as its pollinators.

Identification: A tall, straggling shrub with narrow, leathery, sometimes toothed leaves up to 25cm/10in long. The red flowers are grouped in densely packed, domed terminal racemes up to 15cm/6in wide, surrounded by a circle of large, smooth crimson bracts.

Right: It forms a tall, straggling shrub in time.

Distribution: Central and south-eastern Australia.
Height and spread: 3m/10ft.
Habit and form: Shrub.
Leaf shape: Narrow-obovate.
Pollinated: Bird.

Below: The fruits that develop from mid- to late summer contain numerous winged seeds.

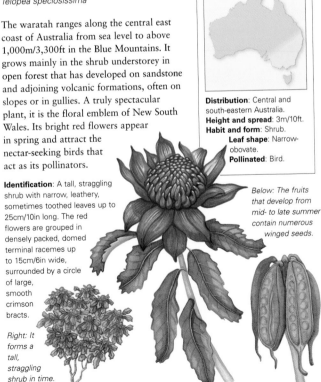

Ivory curl

Buckinghamia celsissima

The rainforests of northern Queensland are the home of this Australian tree, which although rare in the wild, has been widely used as a street tree in Brisbane. It has attractive foliage: the juvenile leaves are often lobed while the new growth is an attractive bronze colour. Its long, pendent, curling flowers are white to cream and occur in summer in large racemes that are well displayed at the ends of the branches and are reminiscent of those of grevilleas, as are its fruits.

Left: The fruits contain four seeds.

Identification: A tall, robust, evergreen tree. The juvenile leaves are variable, sometimes lobed; the adult leaves are elliptical, 10–20cm/4–8in long, glossy dark green with conspicuous veins, silver beneath, alternate. The small, creamy-white, scented, tubular flowers have long, slender, curling styles and appear in semi-pendulous, 20cm/8in terminal racemes from summer to late autumn.

Distribution: North-eastern Australia.
Height and spread: 30m/98ft.
Habit and form: Tree.
Leaf shape: Elliptic.
Pollinated: Bird.

Right: The long, pendent flower spikes appear at the branch tips.

Far right: Ivory curl forms a very attractive tall tree in its native habitat.

Long-leaf lomatia

River lomatia, *Lomatia myricoides*

This Australian species inhabits open forests of eastern New South Wales and Victoria, usually in moist locations such as watercourses, at altitudes up to 1,000m/3,300ft. It is a medium shrub or small tree, with very attractive bark, usually growing tallest in favourable conditions. The scented flowers occur in racemes in the leaf axils or at the ends of branches in summer, and are usually white or cream, although pink forms are known.

Identification: A broadly spreading shrub with ridged young growth, brown and covered in fine hairs, maturing to smooth, grey-brown with branches that are broadly divergent. The narrow leaves are up to 12.5cm/5in long, smooth, tough, mid-green, with margins that may be entire or coarsely toothed at the top half, stalked or stalkless, and variable even on the same plant. Lax racemes up to 15cm/6in long, terminal or axillary at the ends of the branches, appear from spring to summer, produced regularly except during drought; the paired, obliquely tubular flowers are ivory to yellow-green, fragrant and profuse. The flowers are followed by dry fruits containing a number of winged seeds.

Distribution: South-eastern Australia.
Height and spread: 2.5m/8ft.
Habit and form: Shrub.
Leaf shape: Linear.
Pollinated: Bird or insect.

Right: The scented flowers occur in racemes.

Right: Lomatia is really a large shrub but in time it can come to resemble a small tree.

Left: The lax racemes of flowers appear at the branch tips during the summer.

Firewheel tree

White beefwood, *Stenocarpus sinuatus*

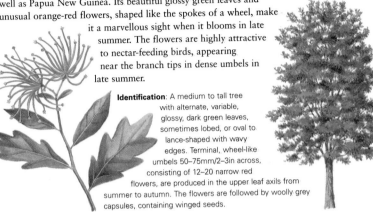

This must surely be one of Australia's most spectacular trees, found in the subtropical and warm temperate rainforests of north-eastern New South Wales and eastern Queensland as well as Papua New Guinea. Its beautiful glossy green leaves and unusual orange-red flowers, shaped like the spokes of a wheel, make it a marvellous sight when it blooms in late summer. The flowers are highly attractive to nectar-feeding birds, appearing near the branch tips in dense umbels in late summer.

Distribution: North-eastern Australia; Papua New Guinea.
Height and spread: 30m/98ft.
Habit and form: Tree.
Leaf shape: Obovate, lobed.
Pollinated: Bird.

Far right: The firewheel tree is a spectacular sight when in full bloom.

Identification: A medium to tall tree with alternate, variable, glossy, dark green leaves, sometimes lobed, or oval to lance-shaped with wavy edges. Terminal, wheel-like umbels 50–75mm/2–3in across, consisting of 12–20 narrow red flowers, are produced in the upper leaf axils from summer to autumn. The flowers are followed by woolly grey capsules, containing winged seeds.

OTHER SPECIES OF NOTE

Tree waratah *Alloxylon flammeum*
Native to the rainforest in Queensland, this is a tall tree with glossy green, elliptical leaves, although juvenile leaves may be much larger and lobed. The conspicuous bright red flowers are displayed in the leaf axils towards the ends of the branches in spring and early summer.

Strangea linearis
This small Australian shrub is found in the coastal heaths of north-eastern New South Wales and south-eastern Queensland. It has narrow leaves and small cream flowers, which occur in clusters of two or three in the leaf axils in spring.

Rewarewa *Knightia excelsa*
An upright tree with a slender crown, endemic to New Zealand and found in lowland to montane forest. The small, bright red flowers crowd together to form a bottlebrush-like inflorescence 10cm/4in long.

Guitar plant
Lomatia tinctoria
An endemic species of open forests and woods of Tasmania, from sea level to 1,000m/3,300ft. It is a small shrub with cream or white flowers appearing in summer, in racemes, in the leaf axils, or at the ends of branches. Dry fruits follow, containing winged seeds. Its common name is derived from the shape of the opened fruits.

Grass-leaved hakea

Hakea multilineata

The gravelly heaths of south-western Australia are home to this large shrub or small tree, whose pink flowers occur in racemes in the leaf axils in winter and spring. Although the flowers occur within the foliage, the plant's open habit means that they are well displayed, never failing to attract attention. The seeds are shed only when stimulated to do so by the occurrence of a bushfire, thereby allowing the seedlings to grow rapidly without competition from other plants.

Identification: A tall shrub or small tree with alternate, grey-green leaves 10–12.5cm/4–5in long, which are rigid to leathery, erect, with 11–15 fine parallel veins. Small, pink-purple, tubular flowers with long, protruding styles appear from midwinter to spring in dense 25–75mm/1–3in axillary spikes, and are followed by woody seedpods containing two winged seeds.

Distribution: South-western Australia.
Height and spread: 5m/16ft.
Habit and form: Tall shrub or small tree.
Leaf shape: Linear.
Pollinated: Bird, possibly insect.

Right: While it is generally regarded as a large shrub, in time grass-leaved hakea often forms a small, upright tree.

GESNERIAD, ACANTHUS AND
JACARANDA FAMILIES

The gesneriads, Gesneriaceae, are mostly tropical herbs and shrubs including well-known ornamental species such as Streptocarpus *and* Gloxinia. *The acanthus family, Acanthaceae, contains tropical herbs, shrubs and twining vines. The jacarandas, Bignoniaceae, are lianas restricted to eastern Australasia.*

Fieldia

Fieldia australis

This attractive, slightly woody perennial, found in shady spots in the mountains and coastal areas of New South Wales and Victoria, Australia, is actually the sole species in this genus. It forms a tall, climbing shrublet, which clings to mossy bark, especially that of tree ferns, by means of roots that it can put out at need. The large, pure white, tubular flowers arise from spring to summer. When fertilized they eventually turn into large, hanging berries that are white when ripe.

Identification: A tall, climbing subshrub or shrublet often found climbing on tree ferns. The stems, which root as they climb, are red and downy when young, becoming smooth with silvery bark with age. The oval leaves are opposite, of unequal length in each pair, 15mm/⅝in or more long, shiny deep green above, paler to silvery below, with downy, reddish midribs, veins and stalks. The large, softly hairy, pure white, pendent, tubular flowers, with a pale green calyx, five petals and white, slightly protruding stamens and stigma, appear singly in the leaf axils. The fruits are large hanging berries, white when ripe, with tiny seeds contained in a fleshy pulp.

Distribution: South-eastern Australia.
Height and spread: 1.8–2.5m/6–8ft.
Habit and form: Climbing subshrub.
Leaf shape: Ovate.
Pollinated: Insect.

New Zealand gloxinia

Taurepo, Waiu-atua, *Rhabdothamnus solandri*

The only African violet genus from New Zealand, this loose, twiggy shrub is found in the coastal forest of North Island, where it favours stream banks. It has rough, hairy leaves that arise from decorative snake-bark stems. The single orange to dark red flowers are carried in succession almost throughout the year, making this one of the prettiest of all New Zealand's forest flowers. The colour of the flowers often pales during the winter.

Identification: A loose, evergreen shrub with purplish young stems and older bark with a snakeskin pattern. The hairy leaves are opposite, oval to elliptical, up to 10mm/⅜in long and coarsely toothed. They are mid- to silvery green with purple veins and spots, on short, purple stalks. The flowers are red-orange with darker stripes or, more rarely, yellow and up to 15mm/⅝in long, arising from the leaf axils. The calyx of five sepals, reflexed, is purple outside, pale green within and sparsely hairy; the flower is tubular with flared, round lobes; the style and stamens protrude slightly.

Distribution: New Zealand.
Height and spread: 90cm–1.8m/35in–6ft.
Habit and form: Shrub.
Leaf shape: Ovate-elliptical.
Pollinated: Bird.

Cyrtandra pritchardii
This shrub or small tree from Fiji has oval, toothed leaves and bears white flowers in axillary cymes throughout most of the year. The slightly downy flowers are two-lipped, with the lower lip larger than the upper.

Caricature plant *Graptophyllum pictum*
This erect, loosely branched shrub, of obscure origin, has been widely planted in tropical gardens and now often exists as an escapee. It most probably originates from New Guinea, and is most noted for its glossy, dark green leaves that are irregularly blotched or marbled.

Bower of beauty *Pandorea jasminoides*
This robust, Australian climbing vine reaches up to the forest canopy in rainforest from eastern Victoria to south-eastern Queensland. The funnel-shaped flowers are pale to deep pink and appear in terminal clusters from September to March.

Holly-leaved fuchsia
Graptophyllum ilicifolium
This is a medium shrub with shiny, sharply toothed leaves. It is native to the lowland rainforests around the Mackay area of Queensland, Australia. Dense racemes of beautiful, deep red, tubular flowers are born on short stalks in the leaf axils in late spring over a short season.

Wonga wonga vine

Pandorea pandorana

This vigorous, evergreen climber is found in habitats from fern gullies to open forest in Australia, New Guinea and several other Pacific Islands. It becomes very large over time as it ascends into the rainforest canopy, hiding most of its blooms from view. In spring the vine bears large clusters of small flowers, variable in hue from white with purple markings to light red, depending upon its location.

Distribution: Australia; New Guinea; Pacific Islands.
Height and spread: Up to 30m/98ft.
Habit and form: Liana.
Leaf shape: Pinnate.
Pollinated: Insect.

Identification: An evergreen liana, with a slender stem and pinnate leaves with six opposite pairs of glossy, dark green, lance-shaped leaflets up to 10cm/4in long and 50mm/2in wide. The leaves are sparsely glandular below, entire and hairless on the upper surface. The flowers are in terminal or lateral clusters, up to 20cm/8in long, often on old wood. They are funnel to bell shaped, creamy-yellow, and around 25mm/1in across, with five short lobes reflexed to reveal the throats of the flower that are streaked and splashed red or purple. The tube is twice the length of the lobes. The beaked, cylindrical capsule contains winged seeds.

Scarlet fuchsia

Graptophyllum excelsum

Distribution: North-eastern Australia.
Height and spread: 1.5–8m/5–26¼ft.
Habit and form: Shrub.
Leaf shape: Spathulate.
Pollinated: Bird.

Found in dry vine thickets, usually on soils derived from limestone, on the eastern coast and ranges of Queensland, Australia, this shrub or small tree flowers in spring and early summer, sporting many deep red, tubular blooms that are borne singly or in pairs in the leaf axils. In a good flowering season flowers are borne in almost every axil, and the plant becomes a mass of brilliant scarlet red, which attracts honeyeaters, probably its main pollinator. The plants sucker readily and new clumps appear beside established plants that can lead to it developing into a dense thicket in time.

Identification: An erect, evergreen shrub with multiple stems, often forming large colonies. The spoon-shaped leaves, 30mm/1¼in long and borne in opposite pairs, are shiny dark green, with margins that are mostly smooth, though sometimes toothed, painted or spotted. The waxy, deep red flowers are borne on short stalks, often in great profusion, singly or in pairs in the leaf axils. They are tubular, two-lipped and up to 25mm/1in long. The seed capsules that follow are club-shaped, containing two seeds.

CITRUS FAMILY

There are around 150 genera and 900 species in the citrus family, Rutaceae. They are mostly found in warm to tropical regions and are usually sweet-smelling shrubs or trees. The family produces many edible fruits, some of which, such as oranges, grapefruits and lemons, are important food crops. It displays particular diversity of species in Australasia.

Coastal correa

Native fuchsia, *Correa backhousiana*

This is a rare plant in the wild, growing only in a limited area in Tasmania and a restricted area of Victoria, Australia. It forms a compact bush, with tubular, pale greenish-yellow flowers from late summer to spring. The leaves have rust-coloured undersides, as do the stems and flower calyces, caused by a woolly covering of small, brown hairy scales, giving the whole plant a very decorative appearance. The plant has become popular in cultivation and may occasionally be encountered far from its native range as a garden escapee.

Identification: A dense, spreading, evergreen shrub with felted, orange-brown stems. The oval, leathery leaves are up to 30mm/1¼in long, with felted brown undersides. The flowers are funnel-shaped, about 25mm/1in long, with four lobes, cream to pale green or sometimes orange-brown, axillary or terminal, solitary or in small clusters.

Distribution: South-eastern Australia.
Height and spread: 2m/6½ft.
Habit and form: Shrub.
Leaf shape: Ovate.
Pollinated: Insect.

Left: The flowers are a creamy-green colour with calyces covered in a rusty-brown felt.

Right: Correa forms a compact, slow-spreading, evergreen shrub.

Willow-leaved crowea

Crowea saligna

The sheltered open forests of the central coastal area of New South Wales are home to this small, pink-flowered shrub. The star-like flowers emerge singly from the leaf axils and are seen over a long season stretching from late summer through to midwinter. The long, thin, willow-like leaves are aromatic. The seeds are naturally dispersed by ants.

Identification: A small shrub, with angular branches and aromatic, lance-shaped leaves up to 80mm/3⅛in long, are alternately arranged. The star-shaped, five-petalled, pale to mid-pink flowers are produced from the leaf axils or are terminally, singly or sometimes paired. They are quite large, with some forms having flowers up to 45mm/1¾in in diameter.

Above: The star-like flowers can be variable and are seen here in a rarer white form.

Distribution: Central eastern Australia.
Height and spread: 90cm/35in.
Habit and form: Shrub.
Leaf shape: Elliptic.
Pollinated: Insect.

Above and left: The angular branches and aromatic lance-shaped leaves are quite distinctive on this small shrub.

Granite boronia

Boronia granitica

This medium-size, compact shrub with pinnate foliage and pink flowers grows in heathy vegetation among granite boulders. It can be found in only a few locations on the north-western side of the New England Tablelands of New South Wales, and the Stanthorpe district of southern Queensland, Australia. It grows either among boulders in the skeletal soils found in narrow rock crevices and fissures, or in adjacent areas on granite scree and shallow soils, in areas of predominantly summer rainfall and cool winters. The flowering season is long, from midwinter to early summer, with the greatest concentration over the spring.

Distribution: Central eastern Australia.
Height and spread: 90cm/35in.
Habit and form: Shrub.
Leaf shape: Pinnate.
Pollinated: Insect.

Far right and right: Granite boronia forms a compact evergreen shrub that bears pretty pink flowers over a long period from winter until the early summer.

Identification: An evergreen shrub with opposite, pinnate, aromatic leaves, dotted with glands and covered with hairs. The fragrant flowers are also downy and are pale to bright pink, or occasionally white, with four oval, pointed petals, borne singly from the leaf axils over an extended flowering season from winter to summer.

Right: The flowers are followed in late summer and autumn by capsules containing small, black seed that is dispersed by ants.

OTHER SPECIES OF NOTE

Native fuchsia *Correa reflexa* var. *cardinalis*
This plant from south-eastern Australia occurs in a variety of habitats, from mountain forests to dry mallee scrub. Its flowers are downy, tubular and yellow-green to crimson, with two or three held together on axillary stalks, appearing mostly between late autumn and late spring.

Phebalium rotundifolium
syn. *Leionema rotundifolium*
This small shrub from open woodland and shrub-land in New South Wales has the clustered, star-shaped, five-petalled, yellow flowers that are typical of the genus, but does not possess the scales on the leaves or stems that are found on many other species.

Diplolaena grandiflora
This striking shrub has oval woolly leaves and pendent red flowers in hairy, green bracts that appear in spring and summer. It is restricted to the south of western Australia. Although the individual flowers are very small, they are grouped together into large clusters, which may be up to 40mm/1½in across.

White star *Philotheca myoporoides*
The white star or native daphne comes from open forests and woodlands of Victoria, New South Wales and Queensland, Australia. Its branches are warty and the glossy, deep green leaves have a strong aroma when crushed. From late winter to late spring it is smothered with waxy, white, star-shaped flowers, opening from deep pink buds.

Forest phebalium

Phebalium squamulosum

This small shrub occurs naturally in open woodland or heath on sandy soils in south-east and north-east Queensland, eastern New South Wales and eastern Victoria, Australia. It is an extremely variable species, with several subspecies and varieties, all of which possess very aromatic foliage and clusters of small, star-like flowers in cream to bright yellow. They appear in early spring. Plants in new leaf have a highly decorative silvery appearance.

Identification: A variable species ranging from slender, small trees to prostrate shrubs. The buds and flowering stalks are covered in small brown scales. The elliptical leaves are bright to grey-green, up to 30mm/1¼in long, sometimes irregularly toothed, and the new growth and undersides of older leaves are covered with silvery scales. The five-petalled flowers appear in early spring and last about four weeks. Though small, they are very conspicuous, occurring in clusters of 12 or more, with cream to yellow pointed petals, bright yellow anthers and long cream stamens.

Right: Forest phebalium is immensely variable, ranging from a small tree to a prostrate shrub.

Distribution: Eastern Australia.
Height and spread: Up to 7m/23ft.
Habit and form: Variable (woody).
Leaf shape: Elliptical.
Pollinated: Insect.

CARNIVOROUS PLANTS

Carnivorous plants have one thing in common, namely that they have evolved the ability to capture and/or digest animals. Over time they have evolved into many forms and often come from diverse ancestry. While some are found in the islands of Oceania, the greatest concentration of species is found in Australia.

Rainbow plant

Byblis gigantea

This carnivorous plant grows in fire-prone, acid, sandy soils in south-western Australia. It is a close relative of the butterworts, *Punguicula* species, and sundews, *Drosera* species, and its tentacles, much like those of sundews, cover the whole plant, including the stem, leaves and even the flower-heads and buds. Insects are lured to the plants by the sticky mucilage secreted by the stalked glands, which appears to them as dew or nectar. Unlike those of the sundews, the rainbow plant's glands and leaves do not move or curl around their prey.

Identification: A sticky, erect, glandular-hairy, carnivorous herbaceous perennial. The leaves are 10–30cm/4–12in long, narrow and often channelled above, densely sticky and hairy beneath; they have glands with a stem (for trapping insects) and without (for digestion). Flowers up to 40mm/1½in across appear in summer, growing singly from the axils on hairy stems. They have five overlapping, triangular petals, 20mm/¾in long, and are iridescent blue, pink or purple, with a yellow centre and long, slender style.

Distribution: South-western Australia.
Height and spread: 60cm/24in.
Habit and form: Perennial herb.
Leaf shape: Linear.
Pollinated: Insect.

Albany pitcher plant

Cephalotus follicularis

Found in a small corner of Western Australia, in a 400km/250mile strip from Albany to Eusselton, this curious little plant is the only representative of both its genus and its family, and has no close relatives in the plant kingdom. A variable species in the wild, it produces passive pitcher traps that are mostly used to attract crawling insects: once ensnared they are unable to crawl out of the cleverly designed pods. The traps are produced from spring to autumn and in winter the plant produces small, flat, green leaves. The white flowers are produced on tall, branching stems over the summer.

Identification: A carnivorous herbaceous perennial growing from a short, thick, branched rhizome. The leaves grow in a rosette and are of two kinds: the leaves are 50–75mm/2–3in long, oval, rounded, glossy green, often with a red margin; the trapping leaves, which form pitchers up to 50 x 25mm/2 x 1in long, are sparsely hairy, green, heavily marked red-brown, with a hinged, ribbed, oval lid attached on the stalk side and three external longitudinal raised nerves swollen into narrow, leaf-like double wings with fringed margins. Small white flowers are borne in terminal panicles on stems up to 60cm/24in long.

Distribution: Western Australia.
Height and spread: Variable.
Habit and form: Perennial herb.
Leaf shape: Ovate, trapping leaves jug-like.
Pollinated: Insect.

Fairy aprons
Utricularia dichotoma

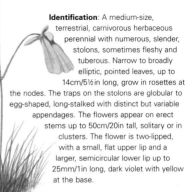

Distribution: Australia.
Height and spread: Variable.
Habit and form: Herbaceous perennial.
Leaf shape: Elliptic.
Pollinated: Insect.

This small, Australian, carnivorous herb of permanently wet or seasonally waterlogged soils is only ever likely to be seen when the large, paired, purple flowers appear on long, slender stems. The flower gives the impression of a small skirt, which accounts for the plant's common name. It occurs in all areas of the continent except the Northern Territory, growing from sea level to 1,500m/4,900ft, and flowers year-round, though most commonly in the warmer months.

Identification: A medium-size, terrestrial, carnivorous herbaceous perennial with numerous, slender, stolons, sometimes fleshy and tuberous. Narrow to broadly elliptic, pointed leaves, up to 14cm/5½in long, grow in rosettes at the nodes. The traps on the stolons are globular to egg-shaped, long-stalked with distinct but variable appendages. The flowers appear on erect stems up to 50cm/20in tall, solitary or in clusters. The flower is two-lipped, with a small, flat upper lip and a larger, semicircular lower lip up to 25mm/1in long, dark violet with yellow at the base.

OTHER CARNIVOROUS PLANTS OF NOTE

Utricularia protrusa
This aquatic bladderwort, normally found in slow-moving or still water throughout New Zealand, floats on the surface of the water, with submerged leaves and traps emerging from a long central stem. During winter, resting buds sink, re-emerging in spring. Sulphur-yellow flowers appear from spring to late summer.

Pitcher plant *Nepenthes mirabilis*
The most widespread species in the genus, this carnivorous pitcher plant, found in northern Australia and much of South-east Asia, occupies a wide range of forest habitats, although always preferring those with a relatively high humidity for much of the year. The plants produce pitchers in various colours, depending upon their place of origin.

Waterwheel plant *Aldrovanda vesiculosa*
The waterwheel plant is a widespread and curious aquatic, carnivorous herb. It occurs sporadically along the coasts of Queensland, the Northern Territory and far-northern point of western Australia, as well as in South-east Asia, southern Africa and Europe. It is the only aquatic carnivorous plant with visible trap movement.

Byblis liniflora
This variable, annual carnivorous herb, found in northern Australia and Papua New Guinea, has long, slender leaves with many long-stemmed glands covering much of the plant. The flowers are pink or blue and are produced on long stalks from the leaf axils.

Fork-leaved sundew
Drosera binata

This robust and variable species is normally found in bogs and swamps, or, in many cases, in roadside drainage ditches. It is very widespread, occurring across Victoria, South Australia, Tasmania, in a small area of south-west western Australia, and throughout New Zealand. The sticky leaves characteristically divide into two and produce a 'tuning fork' shape, and the white (or occasionally pink), sweet-scented blooms are produced between spring and autumn, with the plants usually being dormant from late autumn to early winter.

Identification: A perennial, rosette-forming, carnivorous herb whose stem is a short rhizome. The variable, basal leaves are erect, on long, usually sparsely hairy, stalks; the blade is deeply cut into 2–14 narrow lobes, with the pointed tip of each lobe furnished with a crown of three or four long tentacles, covered and fringed with gland-tipped hairs above; capable of trapping and digesting insects. Stems up to 50cm/20in long bear many white or pink flowers.

Distribution: South-eastern Australia; New Zealand.
Height and spread: 50cm/20in.
Habit and form: Perennial herb.
Leaf shape: Forked.
Pollinated: Insect.

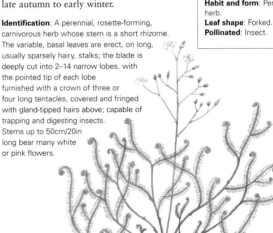

PARASITIC PLANTS

Parasitic plants are found on all continents except Antarctica, and the southern oceans are no exception to this. Oceania is the home to an extremely diverse range of parasites, most of which can be gathered together under the general term mistletoes. Mistletoes are only partial parasites, and have green leaves.

Western Australian Christmas tree

Moodjar, *Nuytsia floribunda*

This bush is a native of sandy or granite soil in open forest, woodland and heath in western Australia. It is related to the mistletoe and is, at least in the early stages of its life, dependent on a host plant. When its roots encounter those of another plant, they form a collar-like 'haustorium', a structure that cuts into the host's root to extract nutrients and moisture. The species famously flowers at around Christmas time, when its bright yellow flowers, borne in clusters at the end of the branches, make the whole plant a spectacular, seasonal highlight.

Right:
The bright
yellow flowers
appear on branch tips
around Christmas time.

Identification: An evergreen shrub or small tree with rough, grey-brown bark, which parasitizes the roots of grasses as much as 50m/164ft away. The leaves are 25mm–10cm/1–4in long, opposite, subopposite or occasionally whorled, and lance-shaped with pointed or rounded tips, narrowing at the base. The brilliant orange-yellow flowers appear in large, crowded terminal clusters over several months. The fruit is brown, dry and three-winged, with sticky seeds.

Distribution: Western Australia.
Height and spread: 7m/23ft.
Habit and form: Shrub or small tree.
Leaf shape: Lanceolate.
Pollinated: Insect.

Rosewood mistletoe

Amyema scandens

This showy mistletoe species is native to the moist tropical forests of Papua New Guinea, New Caledonia and Borneo, with a few isolated occurrences on the Australian east coast, where it is a parasite of the rosewood tree, *Dalbergia sissoo*. The species grows at elevations from sea level to 1,600m/5,250ft in both primary and secondary rainforest and in open humid forests, on a wide range of hosts. It is a variable species, with red or pink tubular flowers appearing close to the branches of the host.

Identification: A semi-parasitic shrub, with external runners and robust stems, with distinct lenticels, enlarged at the nodes. The elliptic to circular leathery leaves are mostly in whorls of five to eight, or rarely four; they are very variable, lance-shaped to oval, up to 20cm/8in long, sometimes with wavy margins. The clusters of slender, stemless red or pink flowers appear at the nodes and on the runners.

Distribution: Papua New Guinea; New Caledonia; Borneo.
Height and spread: Variable.
Habit and form: Semi-parasitic shrub.
Leaf shape: Lanceolate to ovate.
Pollinated: Insect.

Left: Amyema scandens *is an endangered species of parasite.*

New Zealand red mistletoe

Peraxilla tetrapetala

This mistletoe, endemic to New Zealand, has showy, bright red flowers, and is most commonly seen on mountain beech, *Nothofagus* species, and tawheowheo trees, *Quintinia* species, in the forests of North Island and also on silver beech, *N. menziesii*, on South Island. It is most frequently found on the inner branches and the host trunk, where the flowers provide a dazzling display in early summer. It has the distinction of being the only plant in the world with bird-pollinated explosive flowers, which are also opened by insects.

Distribution: New Zealand.
Height and spread: 90cm/35in.
Habit and form: Semi-parasitic shrub.
Leaf shape: Rhombic.
Pollinated: Insect.

Right: The fruit of the New Zealand red mistletoe is dull green.

Identification: Semi-parasitic, bushy, shrub, joined to its host by several haustoria (attachments). The rhombic leaves are oppositely arranged on short stalks and are thick and fleshy, usually with some blisters on the surface caused by gall-forming insects. The flowers are tubular in bud, with a clubbed tip, and have four petals, red or yellow at the base, shading gradually to crimson at the reflexed tips, and protruding stamens and stigma. The fruit is a greenish-yellow, semi-translucent drupe, appearing in autumn.

OTHER SPECIES OF NOTE

Dendrophthoe acacioides
This aerial stem-parasite from the Northern Territory and western Australia has conspicuous orange flowers, held on axillary spikes, which adorn the sparsely leafed runners. The mature bud is usually inflated and curved with the open, star-like flower.

Decaisnina signata
This mistletoe is found mainly on *Barringtonia*, *Planchonia* and *Ficus* trees in the monsoon forest of the Northern Territory. It has showy, orange, tubular flowers with yellow-and-black lobes, arranged in terminal spikes.

Yellow beech mistletoe *Alepis flavida*
The yellow beech mistletoe is a native of both North Island and South Island of New Zealand, where it mostly occupies mountain or black beech, *Nothofagus* species, as a host. It has small, orange-yellow to yellow flowers in summer, followed by shiny, golden-yellow berries.

Daenikera corallina
This monotypic genus occurs only in the dense wet forests of New Caledonia, where it is parasitic on the roots or trunk bases of forest trees. The new growth is bright red, becoming brown with age. Tiny burgundy flowers are followed by red fruits that also turn blue with age.

Galapagos dwarf mistletoe

Phoradendron henslowii

This mistletoe, seen on trees on Santa Cruz and Isabella Island, Galapagos, is an endemic species that grows in the elevated cloud forest vegetation of those islands. It is related to other dwarf mistletoes, whose principal centre of diversity is in Mexico and the western United States, and in some respects it resembles the Ecuadorian species *P. nervosum*. The oval, leathery leaves are paired and joined at their bases, and the small, greenish flowers on thin red spikes give rise to small, pinky-white berries.

Identification: A semi-parasitic shrub, with green stems and reddish buds and nodes, with a dense or sparse growth habit, often forming an extensive colony within the host canopy. The variable, waxy, oval leaves are smooth, pale green, often with darker margins, becoming mottled darker and with red spots with age. The small, greenish flowers and greyish, sticky berries are held terminally on the branchlets, subtended by paired leaves.

Distribution: Santa Cruz and Isabella Island, Galapagos.
Height and spread: Variable.
Habit and form: Semi-parasitic shrub.
Leaf shape: Obovate.
Pollinated: Insect.

Left: Dwarf mistletoe grows only on trees in cloud forest regions.

Below: The small, greyish berries appear on the branch tips on red stems.

DUCKWEED, ARUM AND GINGER FAMILIES

The duckweed family, Lemnaceae, is widespread across Australia. The arum family, Araceae, consists of rhizomatous or tuberous herbs characterized by an inflorescence that is a fleshy spadix partially enveloped by a bract or spathe. The ginger family, Zingiberaceae, includes perennial herbs, mostly with creeping horizontal or tuberous rhizomes. They have a wide distribution, mainly in the tropics.

Taro

Coco yam, *Colocasia esculenta*

This plant is grown as a crop for its edible corms and leaves throughout the humid tropics and is used in Africa, Asia, the West Indies and South America. Its origins are very obscure: it is probably a selection of an ancestral wild food. It was extremely important to the Polynesian, Melanesian and Micronesian peoples, who transported it across the Pacific Ocean, where it occurs as an introduced vagrant on many islands. It is most recognizable for its large, arrow-shaped leaves, the flowers being insignificant and rarely setting viable seed.

Distribution: Pan-tropical.
Height and spread: 1.5m/5ft.
Habit and form: Herbaceous perennial.
Leaf shape: Sagittate.
Pollinated: Unclear, rarely sets seed.

Identification: A perennial herb with thick shoots from a large corm; slender stolons are also often produced, along with offshoot corms. The leaf blades, up to 60cm/24in long and 50cm/20in wide, are arrow-shaped, with a dark green, velvety upper surface; the leaf stalks, which join the middle of the leaf, are succulent and often purplish near the top. The inflorescence is a yellow spathe 20–40cm/ 8–16in long, surrounding a spadix 50mm–15cm/2–6in, on a stout stem; the flowers are tiny and densely crowded on the upper stalk, female flowers below, male flowers above. The fruits are small berries in clusters on the stalk, producing few seeds, which are rarely viable.

Above: The corm is an important food crop.

Right: The leaves are quite distinctive.

Star duckweed

Ivy leaf duckweed, *Lemna trisulca*

This diminutive, floating, aquatic perennial is found throughout the world's temperate zones in both hemispheres, where it often forms tangled masses just under the water surface. The leaves and stems are merged in a common structure that usually has a single root below. It is distinguished from other *Lemna* species by the stalked fronds that aggregate into chains. The tiny flowers, although uncommon, occur on small fronds with toothed margins, which rise to float on the surface.

Distribution: Cosmopolitan.
Height and spread: Spread indefinite.
Habit and form: Aquatic herb.
Leaf shape: N/A.
Pollinated: Water.

Identification: A minute, aquatic herb, floating just below the water surface, consisting of a leaf-like frond and a single root. The fronds are 3–15mm/⅛–⅝in long and up to 5mm/³⁄₁₆in wide, submerged except when flowering, narrow at the base to form a 3–20mm/⅛–¾in-long stalk, cohering and often forming branched chains with margins toothed at the base. The roots (sometimes not developed) are up to 25mm/1in long, with pointed rootcaps. Flowers and fruits are rare.

Above and right: The tiny leaf-like stems of this floating, aquatic plant, reproduce rapidly and can form a dense 'carpet' across the surface in favourable conditions.

Right: The microscopic flowers of this unusual plant are hardly ever seen.

Pinecone ginger

Shampoo ginger, *Zingiber zerumbet*

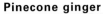

This widespread plant, believed to originate from India and the Malaysian Peninsula, is an example of a species so long under cultivation in so many places throughout the Pacific and Oceania that it is uncertain where it originated, although it was widely introduced by Polynesian settlers. It develops conical bracts, resembling pine cones, which produce creamy-yellow flowers. The bracts contain a clear soapy liquid that has been used by Polynesians to wash the hair and skin, and all its parts are spicily fragrant.

Identification: A tall, perennial herb with branching, thick, aromatic rhizomes and leafy, reed-like stems. The leaves, which are arranged in two ranks, are lance-shaped, up to 35cm/14in long, closely set, smooth above and hairy beneath. Separate flower stalks 20–45cm/8–18in tall arise in mid- to late summer, bearing pale green, cone-shaped bracts, which gradually turn red. Creamy-yellow, three-petalled, tubular flowers, about 30mm/1¼in long, appear on the cones.

Distribution: Austronesian and Pacific regions.
Height and spread: 2m/6½ft.
Habit and form: Herbaceous perennial.
Leaf shape: Lanceolate.
Pollinated: Insect or bird.

Right: The tall stems arise from an underground rhizome, with flower and leaf stems borne separately.

Far right: The creamy-yellow flowers appear from the tight flower cones.

White ginger lily

Hedychium coronarium

This showy plant, probably a native of eastern India, was transported around the Pacific by Polynesian settlers and is frequently cultivated and naturalized in tropical island forests. The stalks are topped with long clusters of wonderfully fragrant white flowers that look like butterflies. The flowers are popular in Hawaii and the Pacific Islands, where they are used in leis or worn singly in the hair or behind the ear.

Distribution: Eastern India and Pacific regions.
Height and spread: Up to 3m/10ft.
Habit and form: Perennial herb.
Leaf shape: Lanceolate.
Pollinated: Insect or bird.

Identification: An erect, perennial herb with stout rhizomes and numerous reed-like stems. The lance-shaped, pointed leaves, 60cm/24in long and 10cm/4in wide, are arranged in two ranks, stemless or on short stems. The very fragrant flowers are borne in summer in dense spikes 15–30cm/6–12in long, with two to six flowers per bract. They have three petals and are white with a yellow-green centre. They eventually give way to showy seedpods full of bright red seeds.

Above: The large, flowers appear at the branch tips.

Left: The leafy stems arise from underground rhizomes.

IRIS AND AMARYLLIS FAMILIES

The iris family, Iridaceae, consists mostly of perennial herbs from rhizomes, bulbs or corms, which occur in tropical and temperate regions. The flowers commonly occur at the top of a branched or unbranched stem, each with six petals in two rings of three. The amaryllis family, Amaryllicaceae, contains perennial herbs from a bulb with contractile roots. The flower consists of six distinct or fused petaloid tepals.

Darling lily

Macquarie lily, Murray lily, *Crinum flaccidum*

This yellow-flowered bulb emerges after deep soaking rains, and is quite variable in form with a number of geographical variants ranging over a large area from Queensland and New South Wales and to south and west Australia. It favours sandy floodplains, where it can sometimes be found in abundance. Its large, flat, green leaves often emerge within several days of rain. The flowers usually emerge from summer to autumn, sometime after the first leaves. They are strongly scented, emitting an unpleasant fragrance, particularly in the evenings.

Identification: A clump-forming bulb up to 10cm/4in in diameter. The long strap-like leaves reach 60cm/24in in length and are channelled, with rough margins. The flowering reaches 60cm/24in in height and is green, with between five and eight white, fragrant flowers, that are tubular at the base, slightly curved, and up to 80mm/3⅛in diameter. The six lobes are elliptic, broad, spreading, and tipped with green. The anthers are yellow and the style is green.

Distribution: Australia.
Height and spread: 60cm/24in.
Habit and form: Bulb
Leaf shape: Linear.
Pollinated: Insect.

Silky purple flag

Patersonia sericea

This iris-like perennial herb is widespread from north-eastern Victoria to south-eastern Queensland. It thrives in grassland, woodland and open forest, and is one of the most commonly encountered species of the genus. The three-petalled flowers occur mostly in the spring, on grey woolly stems, which are shorter than the leaves. The flowers are deep purple-blue, often closing before noon in hot, sunny weather. Before opening, the flowers are enclosed in two large, papery bracts and although each flower only opens for a single day, new flowers are produced over an extended period.

Identification: A perennial herb ascending from a short rhizome with stems to 30cm/12in, which are covered with silky, woolly hairs. The leaves are linear, erect, stiff, woolly at the base when young, clustered at the base of the stem, evenly and oppositely arranged, usually forming a fan. The inflorescence consists of a few- to several-flowered, sessile spikes enclosed in spathes, each spikelet being several-flowered. The flowers are regular, short-lived, deep violet-blue, with a slender perianth tube. The outer tepals are broadly ovate, woolly when young, while the inner tepals are lanceolate or ovate and small by comparison.

Distribution: Eastern Australia.
Height and spread: 30cm/12in.
Habit and form: Perennial herb.
Leaf shape: Linear.
Pollinated: Insect.

Swamp iris
Patersonia fragilis

Distribution: Eastern Australia.
Height and spread: 30cm/12in.
Habit and form: Perennial herb.
Leaf shape: Linear.
Pollinated: Insect.

Found in the eastern states of Australia, from Queensland down to Tasmania and across to South Australia, this tussock-forming plant is often found associated with tea tree heath, particularly on moist ground. It flowers from September to January and looks like an iris, with purple flowers and a rhizomatous root system. The greyish-green twisted leaves are often longer than the flower stem and obscures the blooms from view until seen from almost above, making this an easy plant to miss when among other vegetation.

Identification: A herbaceous perennial with a short rhizome from which stems grow to 30cm/12in or more. The leaves, to 45cm/18in long, are often longer than the flower stem. They are greyish-green, twisted, clustered at the base of the stem, linear and usually forming a fan or tussocky mass. The inflorescence is a several-flowered sessile spike, enclosed in a spathe; the bracts are scarious; the flowers are regular, short-lived and purple. The outer three tepals are broad and spreading; the inner three are erect and small, forming an enclosing sheath around the stamens and style.

OTHER SPECIES OF NOTE
Yellow flag flower *Patersonia xanthina*
This rhizomatous, west Australian species has bright buttercup-yellow, three-petalled flowers that appear in the spring among a loose mass of thin, grass-like foliage, in open woodland and heath on sandy soils. A striking and easily recognizable species.

Purple flag *Patersonia occidentalis*
This tall, free-flowering species occurs naturally in south-western Australia, flowering in spring to reveal a mass of purple, three-petalled, iris-like flowers among the grassy tussock of foliage, which often continue appearing over a long period until the early summer. Colour is blue to purple.

Spider lily *Crinum asiaticum*
This large coarse herb is found throughout the tropical Indo-Pacific. The stout stems bear leaves and inflorescences in a crown at their apex, often with 25–30 flowers in each one. The white flowers, with rich purple filaments and yellow anthers are very decorative.

Swamp lily, Spider lily, River lily, St John's lily *Crinum pedunculatum*
Native to Australia, the swamp lily is probably a variant of *C. asiaticum*, which has adapted to subtropical conditions ranging as far south as the Hunter River in New South Wales. The white, scented flowers occur in heads, similar to those of *C. asiaticum* but are generally a little more compact.

Orange libertia
Mikoikoi, *Libertia peregrinans*

This flower is found in moist grassy areas and scrub on the west coast of New Zealand's North Island, between Kawhia and Wellington, and from a few locations on South Island and nearby coastal islands. It has strap-like, tufted, veined leaves that turn an attractive orange colour in cool weather. The flowers, which resemble a small iris, are white, star-shaped with yellow anthers, and are produced in spring. Burnt-orange, marble-size seedpods follow the flowers.

Identification: This plant consists of leafy fans, which emerge at intervals from horizontal stolons. The leaves are 13–70cm/5¼–27½in long, 10mm/⅜in wide, and are copper-coloured. They are many-veined with the median ones crowded and coloured red or orange. The flowers and fruits are carried below the leaves. The panicles of the flowers are narrow, closely branched, with long lower bracts and shorter upper bracts. Each has one to seven flowers per branch. The flowers are to 25mm/1in in diameter; with bright white tepals that are oblong-elliptical or oblong. The anthers are dark yellow-brown. The seedpod is an ovoid-barrel-shape.

Distribution: New Zealand.
Height and spread: To 70cm/28in.
Habit and form: Herbaceous perennial .
Leaf shape: Linear.
Pollinated: Insect.

WATER LILIES, BUCK BEANS, LOTUS LILIES, PICKERELWEEDS AND APONOGETON

Aquatic plants often have immensely showy flowers, and include among their number species considered as the most basally 'primitive' of the flowering plants. They all live in a challenging environment and show a variety of ingenious solutions to the problem of survival.

Giant water lily

Nymphaea gigantea

This water lily, native to north Australia and New Guinea is quite scarce, occurring in lagoons and slow-flowing creeks, in deep soft mud. It is a magnificent species with large blooms held high above the water, which emerge and are best seen in the day. Their abundant yellow stamens are very striking, and both white- and pink-petalled variants can be found as well as the more common blue form.

Identification: An aquatic herbaceous perennial with tuberous roots. The leaves are to 60cm/24in in diameter, ovate to orbicular, glabrous, green above, green tinged pink to purple beneath. The base of each is deeply cleft into two-lobes, with the lobes often overlapping. The margins are finely dentate. The petioles are usually elongate, glabrous. The flowers, to 30cm/12in diameter, are sky-blue to blue-purple, scentless, opening in the day and closing at night. The sepals are ovate to elliptic, green, with the margins and exterior surface often blue. The 18–50 petals are obovate enclosing 350–750 stamens, which are bright yellow. The fruit is berry-like, maturing under water. The seeds have a floating aril.

Distribution: North Australia; southern New Guinea.
Height and spread: Variable.
Habit and form: Aquatic, perennial herb.
Leaf shape: Rounded.
Pollinated: Insect, usually beetle.

Left: The large blooms are held high above the water and rounded, green leaves.

Water snowflake

Nymphoides indica

This pretty, fast-growing, perennial water plant, has an extremely wide tropical distribution, inhabiting pools, pans, marshes and rivers throughout Australia and New Zealand, as well as southern and tropical Africa, India and Asia. Although it bears some resemblance to water lilies, it is not related. It has flat, rounded, floating leaves, and floating stems that form tufted plantlets along their lengths. The delicate, white flowers with yellow centres, have unusual, feathery-edged petals and mostly appear between October and May.

Identification: An aquatic perennial herb with creeping rhizomes and elongated stems that form tufted plantlets along their length. Roots form at the nodes, particularly in seasons of drought. The floating leaves, to 15cm/6in in diameter, but usually far smaller, are orbicular, pale glossy green, long-stalked, deeply cordate at the base, with margins that are entire or undulate. The flowers are borne in profusion from October until May, emerging ephemeral, on slender stalks arising from petioles. The petals to 10mm/⅜in, are white, stained deep yellow at the centre, and are covered in white glandular hairs or are densely papillose. The petal margins are fringed. Each flower has five stamens inserted at the base of the corolla. The stigma is bifid and the ovary is single-celled. The fruit is a capsule.

Distribution: Australia; New Zealand; Africa; India; Asia.
Height and spread: Variable.
Habit and form: Aquatic, perennial herb.
Leaf shape: Rounded.
Pollinator: Insect.

Below: The unusual feathery flowers appear around the leaves.

Sacred bean

Nelumbo nucifera

This striking Australian native perennial can be found across much of Asia. Its floating and emergent, blue-green leaves can be found in stationary or slow-moving water in lagoons and floodplain watercourses, mostly in tropical zones. It is a spectacular sight when in bloom. The soft pink blossom opens on top of a stiff stalk, which emerges from below the water. The easily recognized, large fruit structure develops as the flower opens and turns brown when the flower fades and the petals fall into the water. It is prized by florists for use in dried arrangements.

Distribution: Australia; Asia.
Height and spread: Variable.
Habit and form: Aquatic, herbaceous perennial.
Leaf shape: Rounded.
Pollinated: Insect.

Left: The soft pink blooms appear above the water on long stems.

Identification: A perennial aquatic herb with a spongy, horizontal and wide-spreading rhizome. The leaves are long-petiolate, to 2m/6½ft above the surface, to 80cm/31in across. They are glaucous, with a margin that is undulate peltate and veins that radiate. The flowers are solitary, emerging from the water, large and showy, pink or white, very fragrant, to 30cm/12in diameter. Each has four or five green sepals and numerous petals that are arranged spirally. A mass of 200–400 stamens, to 12.5cm x 75mm/5 x 3in, each have yellow anthers. The 20mm/¾in fruits provide ellipsoid seeds, which can survive for hundreds of years in river mud.

OTHER SPECIES OF NOTE

Yellow water snowflake *Nymphoides crenata*
This pretty perennial water plant has yellow flowers with five characteristically fringed petals, held above the heart-shaped leaves. The leaves arise from a stoloniferous base, floating on the water surface, and the floating runners produce new plants along their length.

Blue lily *Nymphaea violacea*
The blue lily is a showy aquatic plant from northern Australia, which can be seen along the margins of billabongs. It has large, round, floating leaves and bears violet-tipped, white flowers that appear between January and July, on long stalks up to 30cm/12in above the water surface.

Queensland lace plant *Aponogeton elongatus*
This pondweed, native to northern and eastern Australia, is found in the shallow turnings of slow-flowing rivers. It has long, wavy-edged, mostly submerged or occasionally floating leaves, and a yellow, usually simple flower spike that emerges in the summer.

Cobooree *Aponogeton queenslandicus*
This rare water plant, occurs in Queensland, the Northern Territory and the far west of New South Wales, Australia. It is threatened by invasive introduced grass species. It has lance-shaped floating leaves and bright lemon-yellow floating spikes of flowers.

Bog hyacinth

Monochoria cyanea

The billabongs, swamps and, small watercourses of northern Australia are the home of this attractive plant, which generally likes to grow rooted in soft muddy sediments. It begins life as a floating-leaved plant, which in time changes to the adult form with a loose rosette of rounded leaves. The short flower stems appear to emerge from the leaf stalk, and each one produces several pretty blue to purple flowers in the summer.

Distribution: North Australia.
Height and spread: Variable.
Habit and form: Aquatic, annual or perennial herb.
Leaf shape: Ovate.
Pollinated: Insect.

Identification: An annual or perennial aquatic herb with a short, creeping rhizome and short erect stems. The leaves emerge basal or alternate on the stem. They are cordate-ovate to lanceolate in shape. The inflorescence has a solitary, terminal, sheathing leaf enclosing a membranous spathe at the base of stalk. The spathe shape is variable, sometimes with the lower spathe enclosing the upper. The flowers appear in elongated racemes. The outer flower appears in six sections. It is tubular to oblong, blue, often spotted red, with six stamens, with oblong anthers, one large and blue, the other five smaller and yellow. The fruit capsule has numerous seeds.

GRASSES AND SEDGES

The Poaceae, more commonly known as grasses, are mostly herbaceous perennials, comprising one of the largest and, from the point of view of human and grazing animals, most important families of flowering plants, with about 500 genera and 8,000 species. The sedges, Cyperaceae, are grass-like, herbaceous plants comprising about 70 genera and 4,000 species, commonly found in wet or saturated conditions.

Rice sedge

Dirty Dora, *Cyperus exaltatus*

This tussock-forming, grass-like plant is a common sight in the freshwater wetlands of much of Australia, where it thrives on riverbanks, creekbanks, frequently inundated alluvial floodplains, drainage channels, lagoons and shallow dams. Superficially, the plant resembles grasses, but its green stems are a distinctive triangular shape. The reddish-brown spikes of flowers appear in summer, autumn or winter, depending upon the location they are found in.

Far left The stems of rice sedge are three-sided making them quite distinctive and easy to identify.

Identification: Rice sedge is a robust, tussock-forming, aquatic perennial, to 2m/6½ft tall. The leaves are 5–15mm/³⁄₁₆–⁹⁄₁₆in wide. The culms are triangular and smooth, 1–1.8m/39in–6ft high, to 8mm/⁵⁄₁₆in diameter. The inflorescence is compound or decompound, with 5–10 primary branches up to 18cm/7in long. The spikes are narrow-cylindrical, 20–50mm/¾–2in long, and 5–15mm/³⁄₁₆–⁹⁄₁₆in diameter. The four to six bracts surrounding the inflorescence are leaf-like, to 90cm/35in long. The flattened spikelets, which are numerous per spike, to 20mm/¾in long, with 6–44 flowers appearing in spring and summer. The fruit is a yellow-brown, ellipsoid nut.

Distribution: Widespread in tropics and warm climates.
Height and spread: 2m/6½ft.
Habit and form: Tussock-forming aquatic perennial.
Leaf shape: Linear.
Pollinated: Wind.

Left: The seeds, held tightly in the spikelets are small nuts that are easily borne by water.

River club rush

Schoenoplectus tabernaemontani (syn. *Schoenoplectus validus*)

This stout, grass-like perennial species occurs across a very wide range, including the Americas, Eurasia, Africa, many Pacific Islands as well as Australia and New Zealand. It grows in both fresh and brackish marshes, tidal shores, shallow margins of ponds, quiet waters and on some riverbanks. It is an extremely variable plant that is probably really a cluster of very closely related subspecies, all of which hybridize freely. The erect, soft, circular flowering stems have only small leaves and are topped by small clusters of drooping flowers covered by red-brown spiral, scales.

Identification: An erect perennial standing 90cm–3m/35in–10ft tall. It is semi-aquatic, and often forms large colonies. It has spongy, cylindrical, bluish-green stems with big air chambers. The roots develop from a shallow rhizome, to 10mm/⅜in diameter. Each stem produces three or four, basal leaves that are often pinnate-fibrillose; margins often scabridulous. The inflorescences is branched, each with two to four branches to 20cm/8in long. The 15–200 spikelets are solitary or in clusters of two to four, but most commonly all are solitary. Each scale is uniformly dark to pale orange-brown, sometimes straw-coloured. The fruiting time is variable according to location, but is usually in spring to summer.

Distribution: Widespread across the world.
Height and spread: 90cm–3m/35in–10ft.
Habit and form: Erect, semi-aquatic perennial.
Leaf shape: Linear.
Pollinator: Wind.

Left: The small clusters of drooping flowers can be variable according to where the plant grows.

Salt couch

Sand couch, *Sporobolus virginicus*

This rhizomatous, perennial grass species occurs widely from Australia and New Zealand to the Pacific Islands, West Indies, Africa, India, China and Indonesia; mostly inhabiting salt marshes and sand hills. Its long thin, paired, spine-tipped and wiry leaf-blades emerge in erect clusters from the underground rhizomes looking like individual plants from which the dense pale flower spikes emerge.

Right: The small pale flowers emerge when it is warm.

Far right: In time the spreading habit of the plant results in dense wiry clumps.

Identification: This prostrate or almost erect perennial grass grows up to 40cm/16in high. The underground parts consist of stout creeping horizontal stems with scales. It produces vegetative and flowering shoots that arise singly from the underground stems and branching above. The lower leaves remain undeveloped, arising as shining pale sheaths. The upper leaves are arranged in two opposite rows. They are finely grooved, with blades to 70mm/2¾in long, inrolled and rigid. The plant's stems are circular in cross-section, smooth and branched. The seedhead, to 60mm/2¼in long, projects from or is enclosed in the uppermost leaf sheath. It is lead-coloured. Spikelets of flowers, to 2.5mm/⅛in long, appear in the warmer months in more temperate regions, but the plant is able to produce seed several times a year in tropical regions.

Distribution: Australia; New Zealand; Pacific Islands; West Indies; Africa; Asia.
Height and spread: 40cm/16in.
Habit and form: Perennial grass.
Leaf shape: Linear.
Pollinator: Wind.

OTHER SPECIES OF NOTE

Variable flatsedge *Cyperus difformis*
Also known as small-flower umbrella plant, this is a fast-growing, erect, annual sedge, widespread across much of Australia and Oceania, and a common weed of rice fields. It is well adapted to moist lowland soils or flooded areas. The small, rounded flowerheads appear near the top of the stems.

Spike rush *Eleocharis equisetina*
Grown in parts of Asia for its edible corms and native as far south as north-eastern Australia, in marshy land and the edges of seasonal swamps. The tube-shaped, leafless, brittle, sharply pointed, erect, green stems, have flowers in spikelets near their tops.

Kangaroo grass
Themeda triandra (syn. *Themeda australis*),
An easily recognized, tussock-forming grass, with unusual flower and seed heads, found in all warm and tropical regions of the Old World. Once the dominant grass in much of Australia, introduced livestock has reduced the populations.

Weeping grass *Microlaena stipoides*
Arguably Australia's most important native grass, with a widespread distribution stretching beyond the continent, mostly in high rainfall areas. It has slender, weeping seedheads, and a variable, growth habit from prostrate to erect, according to its location.

Oryza australiensis

This species of rice is found in the tropical regions of northern Australia where it naturally inhabits undulating plains of *Eucalyptus* and grasslands or in box woodland; mostly in wet places such as swamps, the edges of freshwater lagoons, seasonally dry pools, alluvial streams, or behind river levees. The loose, open, wispy flowerheads, are initially pale green, turning a straw colour as the dry season progresses, yielding a small rice grain upon ripening.

Identification: A perennial, rhizomatous grass, to 2m/6½ft or more in height, which stands erect and is robust. The leaves are strap-shaped to linear, and flat. They have a papery quality and are grey-green or dark-green. The inflorescence is a panicle that is loose and open. The spikelets are pear-shaped 8mm/⁵⁄₁₆in long and 2.5mm/⅛in wide, laterally compressed and three-flowered.

Right: The loose, open flowerhead contains numerous rounded seeds that are similar to cultivated rice grains.

Distribution: North Australia.
Height and spread: 2m/6½ft.
Habit and form: Perennial grass.
Leaf shape: Linear.
Pollinator: Wind.

Below: The wispy flowerheads are drooping and green when young.

LILIES, ANTHERIAS, ASPARAGES, AND ASPHODELS

Lilies, Liliaceae, asphodels, Asphodelaceae, antherias, Anthericaceae, and asparages, Asparagaceae, were all formerly classed together and share many similarities. Most of them have extremely showy flowers and they are well represented across the whole of Australasia and Oceania.

Fringe lily

Thysanotus multiflorus

This very striking plant from the southern tip of western Australia is found in a range of mostly dry habitats from forest to coastal plain sands. It has a clump of grass-like leaves that are rarely noticed among other grasses until the delicate mauve flowers appear in summer. Each of the three petals has frilly edges and while the individual flowers only last a day, the plant continues to produce flowers over several months, making this one of the most noticeable flowers at this time.

Identification: A rhizomatous perennial with simple, naked stems. The leaves are linear, grass-like and expanded into papery, sheathing wings at the base. Each plant produces three to 30 linear to narrowly lanceolate leaves, 20–30cm/8–12in long, sometimes channelled, glabrous with margins entire. The scapes are erect, glabrous, 15–30cm/6–12in. The inflorescence is a solitary umbel containing four to 20 or more blue-violet flowers. The six perianth segments are 6–20mm/¼–¾in long, with outer segments linear to narrowly oblanceolate, to 2.5mm/⅛in wide, inner segments to 8mm/⁵⁄₁₆in wide. Each has three stamens, with twisted filaments, and purple to yellow anthers.

Distribution: Western Australia.
Height and spread: 20–30cm/8–12in.
Habit and form: Rhizomatous perennial.
Leaf shape: Linear (grass-like).
Pollinated: Insect.

Poor knights lily

Xeronema callistemon

This unusual, but highly decorative, plant found only on inaccessible inland cliff areas of the Poor Knights Islands is situated off the north-east coast of New Zealand. It forms a clump of sword-shaped, green leaves and has unusual bottlebrush flower clusters that grow horizontally, like a giant, red toothbrush. The stunning red flowers emerge straight up from the stalk and have bright orange pollen. Another species (*Xeronema moorei*) is found in New Caledonia.

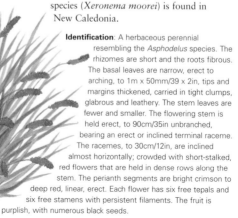

Identification: A herbaceous perennial resembling the *Asphodelus* species. The rhizomes are short and the roots fibrous. The basal leaves are narrow, erect to arching, to 1m x 50mm/39 x 2in, tips and margins thickened, carried in tight clumps, glabrous and leathery. The stem leaves are fewer and smaller. The flowering stem is held erect, to 90cm/35in unbranched, bearing an erect or inclined terminal raceme. The racemes, to 30cm/12in, are inclined almost horizontally; crowded with short-stalked, red flowers that are held in dense rows along the stem. The perianth segments are bright crimson to deep red, linear, erect. Each flower has six free tepals and six free stamens with persistent filaments. The fruit is purplish, with numerous black seeds.

Distribution: New Zealand (Poor Knights Islands).
Height and spread: 1m/39in.
Habit and form: Perennial herb.
Leaf shape: Linear.
Pollinated: Uncertain, insect or bird.

Perching lily

Kowharawhara, *Astelia solandri*

This grass-like plant, known locally as Kowharawhara, is found in the wet lowland forests of New Zealand, where it is usually epiphytic on tall trees but will also grow on the ground. The sweetly scented flowers appear in January and February on branched panicles and are followed about one year later by distinctive, translucent, green to yellowish fruits. Birds eat the fruit and disperse the seeds.

Identification: An evergreen perennial herb that is usually epiphytic. The rhizomes are short and thick. The leaves are linear, crowded at the base of the stem and 1–2m/39in–6½ft long, to 35mm/1⅜in wide, with a spreading, recurved habit. They are glabrous above, three-veined, with a pronounced midrib and covered with chaffy or silky hairs or scales particularly beneath, sometimes so densely as to form a solid covering, amplexicaul. The panicles are few-branched and many-flowered, on stalks 30cm–1m/12–39in long, held in leaf rosette, nodding in fruit. The flowers are 15mm/⅝in long, crowded with six lemon-yellow tepals. They can be thin-textured or fleshy, spreading or reflexed.

Distribution: New Zealand.
Height and spread:
1–2m/39in–6½ft.
Habit and form: Herbaceous perennial (usually epiphytic).
Leaf shape: Linear.
Pollinated: Insect.

OTHER SPECIES OF NOTE

Christmas bells *Blandfordia punicea*
Found in Tasmania, growing in sandy places and acidic moorland, often on wet sites. The coarse leaves are narrow with rough edges, and the tall flower stem is terminated by a beautiful cluster of bell-shaped, tubular flowers that taper to the base. They are scarlet outside and golden-yellow inside.

Common fringe lily *Thysanotus tuberosus*
The common fringe lily is found mostly in the eastern parts of mainland Australia, in a variety of situations, ranging from dry hillsides, heath and open forest to grasslands. The bright purple flowers each have three petals with frilly edges that are produced over a long season. The grass-like leaves die off at flowering time.

Spreading flax lily *Dianella revoluta*
The spreading flax lily is found in New South Wales and Tasmania, on sandy soils near creeks on heaths and in sparse woodlands. It is a tufted plant with flax-like leaves, suckering to form clumps with bright blue flowers borne on branched stems and followed by bright blue fruits. Similar to *D. tasmanica* but favouring drier sites.

Vanilla lily *Sowerbaea juncea*
Vanilla lily is a plant with soft, onion-like leaves and an erect flower stem that bears a dense cluster of more than 20 soft lilac flowers. Found on wet or waterlogged soils along the coast from Queensland to Victoria it was formerly plentiful and conspicuous in its spring-flowering season, but is now threatened by development.

Flax lily

Dianella tasmanica

This evergreen perennial plant, found wild in the cool, moist forests of Tasmania and south-eastern Australia, has arching, thick, strap-like leaves. It bears tall spikes of clustered, nodding, beautiful, star-shaped, bright blue to purple flowers with prominent yellow anthers during spring and summer. These are followed by glossy, deep blue berries that hang for several weeks on delicate stalks.

Identification: This fibrous-rooted herbaceous perennial has a long slender stem to 1.5m/5ft, which stands erect. It is scarred by leaf sheaths and bears a terminal fan of leaves. The grass-like sessile leaves, to 1.2m/4ft long and 25mm/1in wide are held rigid. The margins are armed with small, sharp teeth. The inflorescence is a loosely branched panicle. The regular flowers are pale blue, reflexed when mature. Each has six stamens held in two whorls. The anthers are brown and equal to or shorter than the filaments. The dark blue fruit is a globose or oblong-ovoid berry, to 20mm/¾in, broadly oblong and long lasting.

Distribution: Tasmania; south-eastern Australia.
Height and spread: 1.5m/5ft.
Habit and form: Perennial herb.
Leaf shape: Linear.
Pollinated: Insect.

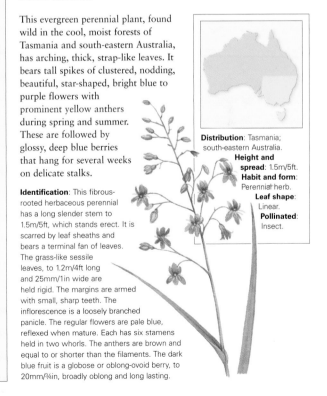

ORCHID FAMILY

The Orchidaceae, or orchid family, comprises terrestrial, epiphytic or saprophytic herbs and is one of the two largest families of flowering plants. They often display ingenious relationships with their pollinators. The epiphytic types all depend upon the support of another plant and are generally forest dwellers, many living their entire lives on another plant. They include some of the showiest of all flowers.

Banana orchid
Tiger orchid, *Cymbidium canaliculatum*

This widespread species of orchid is found in the northern parts of western Australia, Northern Territory and north-eastern Queensland down to central New South Wales. It favours the dry inland areas, where it shelters in the branch forks and hollow, broken off limbs of large trees in light woodland cover. The deep maroon flowers, have white marks on the lip, and are fragrant, appearing mostly during spring.

Identification: This epiphytic orchid has thick, white branching roots growing from a narrow pseudobulb. The leaves are persistent, glossy, glabrous, to 65cm/26in long, 40mm/1½in wide and stiff. They are olive green, linear, acute, and deeply grooved above. The scapes are arching, crowded, often with several per pseudobulb. Flowers to 40mm/1½in diameter are variable. The sepals and petals are equal, lanceolate to elliptic, abruptly acute, green, brown or maroon beneath, olive green to pale bronze, streaked or spotted maroon or oxblood above. The lip is ivory, spotted purple or red, minutely pubescent within; midlobe ovate, acute. The callus is pale green or cream, pubescent. The lateral lobes are small, forward-pointing; column half length of lip, thick and incurved.

Distribution: Northern Australia.
Height and spread: 65cm/26in.
Habit and form: Epiphytic orchid.
Leaf shape: Linear.
Pollinated: Insect.

Golden orchid
Dendrobium discolour

This large tropical epiphytic orchid species, found in Papua New Guinea and Queensland, Australia can commonly be seen perched high up in dead trees of lower altitude rainforests, open forests, mangroves and even on exposed rocky coasts and islets. It often forms extensive colonies, taking root wherever a pocket of soil is available, and its large racemes of flowers are particularly long lasting.

Identification: This erect epiphytic orchid has stems to 5m/16ft tall, to 50mm/2in wide. They are cylindrical, but swollen at the base and in the middle, green or brown in colour, sometimes purple-striped. The leaves, 50mm–20cm/2–8in long, 25–75mm/1–3in wide, are elliptic or ovate. The racemes, to 60cm/24in are arched and densely flowered. The flowers are cream, yellow, bronze or brown, often flushed with brown or purple. The lip is purple-veined, 25mm/1in, trilobed, lateral lobes erect, midlobe recurved, often twisted, ovate. The callus is white with five ridges on the basal half.

Distribution: Papua New Guinea; Queensland, Australia.
Height and spread: To 5m/16ft.
Habit and form: Erect, epiphytic orchid.
Leaf shape: Elliptic.
Pollinated: Insect.

Beard orchid

Calochilus robertsonii

The beard orchid is aptly named, its lip much resembling a little beard, giving it a unique appearance. It is mostly found on poor soils and in full sun in dry forests, grassy forests, woodlands, heaths and dunes in Tasmania, western Australia, south Australia, Victoria, New South Wales, Queensland and in neighbouring New Zealand. Despite its widespread occurrence, it is never particularly common or abundant where it does occur. The reddish-brown flowers with darker stripes, appear in September to December, opening in succession, resulting in only one open flower per stem at a time.

Identification: A terrestrial orchid, 15–40cm/ 6–16in high when in flower. The solitary leaves are fleshy, linear to lanceolate, thick, forming a v-shape in cross-section, basal, alternate, channelled. Up to six flowers appear on a terminal raceme, each to 25mm/1in long, greenish-red with red stripes, appearing in October to December.

Distribution: Australia; New Zealand.
Height and spread: 15–40cm/6–16in.
Habit and form: Terrestrial orchid.
Leaf shape: Linear.
Pollinated: Wasp.

Left: The flowers open in succession with only one per plant at any one time.

OTHER ORCHIDS OF NOTE

Winika *Winika cunninghamii*
This is a sparsely flowered epiphytic orchid that grows mostly high up in the trees in almost full sun in the forests of New Zealand, being endemic to North, South, Stewart and Chatham Islands. It has a special significance to the Maori people as it grew on trees used to make the hull of a sacred war canoe, which they named Te Winika, after the orchid.

Daddy longlegs, Spider orchid
Caladenia filamentosa
The daddy longlegs or spider orchid is an Australian native found from south-eastern Queensland to Tasmania, where it occurs in open forests and grassland. A terrestrial orchid, it has a single, narrow, hairy leaf and a basal inflorescence with one to four, greenish-white to reddish or crimson, hairy flowers, appearing from July to October.

Purple enamel orchid *Elythranthera brunonis*
Known as purple enamel orchid on account of its large flowers with glossy petals that look like porcelain. This orchid grows fairly commonly on sandy soils north of Perth and east towards Esperance. The solitary leaf appears at the base of the stem and the flowers appear in late summer and midwinter with one to three flowers on an erect scape.

Corybas rivularis

This tiny, but fascinating, orchid bears a solitary, heart-shaped, leaf which lies flat on the ground and produces a stalkless, single, large flower. Endemic to New Zealand throughout the North, South, Stewart, and Auckland Islands, it is mostly found growing within damp, wooded ravines from sea level to 600m/2,000ft. It bears small, pink flowers with long, filamentous tips to the petals and lateral sepals that give it a very characteristic appearance.

Distribution: New Zealand.
Height and spread: 60mm/2¼in.
Habit and form: Terrestrial orchid.
Leaf shape: Ovate.
Pollinated: Insect.

Identification: A terrestrial orchid up to 60mm/2¼in high when in flower. The solitary leaf is up to 40mm/1½in long and 20mm/¾in broad. It is ovate-acuminate in shape, cordate at the base, light green above, silvery below, with conspicuous reddish veining. Leaves of young plants are reniform or broadly cordate, without the reddish veining. The usually solitary flower is more or less translucent, with dull red striae. The dorsal sepal is up to 40mm/1½in long. Lateral sepals are filiform, erect and very long, exceeding the flower by as much as 60mm/2¼in. The petals are similar, smaller, horizontal or deflexed. The very short column is hidden in the flower and has a large basal callus.

GLOSSARY

Annual a plant which completes its entire life-cycle within a year.

Anther the pollen-bearing portion of the stamen.

Areole elevation on a cactus stem, bearing a spine.

Axil the upper angle between an axis and any off-shoot or lateral organ arising from it, especially a leaf.

Axillary situated in, or arising from, or pertaining to an axil.

Basal leaf arising from the rootstock or a very short or buried stem.

Beak a long, pointed, horn-like projection; particularly applied to the terminal points of fruits and pistils.

Beaked furnished with a beak.

Beard (on flower) a tuft or zone of hair as on the falls of bearded irises.

Berry indehiscent (non-drying) fruit, one- to many-seeded; the product of a single pistil. Frequently misapplied to any pulpy or fleshy fruit regardless of its constitution.

Biennial lasting for two seasons from germination to death, generally blooming in the second season.

Boss-like (of the standard) taking on the appearance of a boss (round metal stud in the centre of a shield).

Bract a modified protective leaf associated with the inflorescence (clothing the stalk and subtending the flowers), with buds and with newly emerging shoots.

Branched rootstock a branching underground stem.

Bromeliad a type of South American plant predominantly found growing on other plants, but not parasitically.

Calcicole a plant dwelling on and favouring calcareous (lime-rich) soils.

Calcifuge a plant avoiding and damaged by calcareous soils.

Callus ridge (calli) superficial protuberances on the lip of many orchid flowers.

Capsule (of fruit) a dry (dehiscent) seed vessel.

Carpet-forming with a dense, ground-hugging habit; hence "carpet-like".

Cauline (of leaves) attached to or arising from the stem.

Chlorophyll green pigment that facilitates food production, is present in most plants.

Cleistogamous with self-pollination occurring in the closed flower.

Climbing habit any plant that climbs or has a tendency to do so, usually by means of various adaptations of stems, leaves or roots.

Clubbed spur a tubular or sac-like basal extension of a flower, generally projecting backwards and containing nectar, gradually thickening upwards from a slender base.

Clump-forming forming a tight mass of close-growing stems or leaves at or near ground level.

Column (of the flower) a feature of orchids, where the style and stamens are fused together in a single structure.

Composite (of flowers and leaves) a single leaf or petal divided in such a way as to resemble many.

Compound (of flowers and leaves) divided into two or more subsidiary parts.

Contractile roots roots that contract in length and pull parts of a plant further into the soil.

Convex petal with an outline or shape like that of the exterior of a sphere.

Cordate heart-shaped.

Cormous perennial a plant or stem base living for two or more years with a solid, swollen, subterranean, bulb-like stem.

Corolla a floral envelope composed of free or fused petals.

Corona a crown or cup-like appendage or ring of appendages.

Corymb an indeterminate flat-topped or convex inflorescence, where the outer flowers open first.

Creeping habit trailing on or under the surface, and sometimes rooting.

Culms the stems of grasses.

Cupped (flowers) shaped like a cup.

Curving spur a tubular or sac-like basal extension of a flower, generally projecting backwards and containing nectar, being curved in shape.

Cyathia flower form, shaped like a cup.

Cylindrical follicle cylindrical elongated fruit, virtually circular in cross-section.

Cyme (flowers) a more or less flat-topped and determinate flowerhead, with the central or terminal flower opening first.

Decumbent base (of the stem) lying horizontally along the ground but with the apex ascending and almost erect.

Decurrent where the base of a leaf extends down to the petiole (if any) and the stem.

Deeply cut petals or leaves with deeply incised lobes.

Deeply segmented petals or leaves that are sharply divided into several segments.

Deltoid an equilateral triangle attached by the broad end rather than the point; shaped like the Greek letter delta.

Dilated concavity dilating, broadened, expanded, in the manner of the outer surface of a sphere.

Dioecious with male and female flowers on different plants.

Disc floret part of the central flowerhead in the Asteraceae; short tubular florets.

Dissected leaf shape cut in any way; a term applicable to leaf blades or other flattened organs that are incised.
Domed flowerhead compound flowerhead arranged in a dome shape.
Drupe a one- to several-seeded fruit, contained within a soft, fleshy, pericarp, as in stone fruits.

Ellipsoid resembling an ellipse shape.
Epidermis the outer layer of plant tissue; skin.
Epiphytic growing on plants without being parasitic.
Ericaceous in broad terms, resembling *Erica* spp; in habit, plants preferring acidic soil conditions.
Evergreen plant with foliage that remains green for at least a year, through more than one growing season.

Farinose having a mealy, granular texture on the surface.
Filament stalk that bears the anther at its tips, together forming a stamen.
Floret a very small flower, generally part of a congested inflorescence.

Genus the first name of a plant described under the binomial system of botanical naming.
Glandular bearing glands, or hairs with gland-like prominence at the tip.
Glandular inflorescence a compound flowerhead with a glandular surface.
Glycoside A compound related to sugar that plays important roles in living organisms, many plant-produced glycosides are used as medications.

Hastate arrow-shaped, triangular, with two equal and approximately triangular basal lobes, pointing laterally outwards rather than toward the stalk.
Haustorium a sucker in parasitic plants that penetrates the host.
Hemi-parasite only parasitic for part of its life cycle; not entirely dependent upon the host for nutrition.
Hemispheric a half-sphere shape.
Herb abbreviation for herbaceous; not the culinary herb.
Herbaceous pertaining to herbs, i.e. lacking persistent aerial parts or lacking woody parts.
Herbaceous perennial herbaceous plant living for three or more years; referred to as herb.
Hip the fleshy, developed floral cup and the enclosed seeds of a rose.
Hooded flowers one or more petals, fused and forming a hood over the sexual reproductive parts of the flower.
Hooked spurs a tubular or sac-like basal extension of a flower, generally projecting backwards and containing nectar; being hooked in shape.

Inflorescences the arrangement of flowers and their accessory parts in multiple heads, on a central axis or stem.

Keeled (leaves) a prominent ridge, like the keel of a boat, running longitudinally down the centre of the undersurface of a leaf.

Labellum a lip, especially the enlarged or otherwise distinctive third petal of an orchid.
Layering stems rooting on contact with the earth and forming colonies of cloned plants.
Leaf
  Lobed divided into (usually rounded) segments, lobes, separated from adjacent segments.
  Toothed possessing teeth, often qualified, as saw-toothed or bluntly toothed.
  Uneven margins with one margin exceeding the one opposite.
  Wavy margin having a wavy edge.
Leaf axil the point immediately above the point of leaf attachment, often containing a bud.

Leaf tip
  pointed ending in a distinct point.
  rounded with no visible point.
Leaflet units of a compound leaf.
Lenticel elliptical and raised cellular pore on the surface of bark or the surface tissue of fruit, through which gases can penetrate.
Liana a woody climbing vine.
Lignotuber a starchy swelling on underground stems or roots, often used to survive fire or browsing animals.
Lip petal, or part thereof, which is either modified or differentiated from the others, on which insects can alight.
Lithophytic growing on rocks or stony soil, deriving nourishment from the atmosphere rather than the soil.
Low-growing plants that do not reach any significant height; ground-hugging.

Membranous capsule seedpod with thin walls.
Mesic a type of habitat with a well-balanced supply of moisture.
Midrib the primary vein of a leaf or leaflet, usually running down its centre as a continuation of the leaf stem.
Monocarpic dying after flowering and bearing fruit only once.
Monoecious with both male and female flowers are on the same plant
Monopedal a stem or rhizome in which growth continues indefinitely from the apical or terminal bud, and exhibits no secondary branching.
Morphologically pertaining to the study of the form of plants.
Mucilage viscous substance obtained from plant seeds exposed to water.

Nectary a gland, often in the form of a protuberance or depression, which secretes and sometimes absorbs nectar.

Node the point on a stem where one or more leaves, shoots, whorls, branches or flowers are attached.

Open habit growing loosely with space between the branches.

Panicle indeterminate branched inflorescence, the branches generally resemble racemes or corymbs.
Pea-like flowers that are like those of the pea (*Psium* spp.)
Pendent hanging downwards, more markedly than arching or nodding, but not as a result of the weight of the part in question or weakness of its support.
Pendent raceme raceme inflorescence with a pendent habit.
Pendulous branch branch with a pendent habit.
Perennial a plant lasting for three seasons or more.
Perfoliate a sessile leaf of which the basal lobes are united, the stem seems to pass through the blade.
Perianth the collective term for the floral envelopes, the corolla and calyx, especially when the two are not clearly differentiated.
Perianth tube the effect of fused petals resulting in a tubular flower shape
Petaloid sepal segment, enclosing the flower when in bud, that resembles a true petal.
Petaloid tepal tepal that resembles a petal.
Photosynthesis the synthesis of sugar and oxygen from carbon dioxide and water, carried out by all green plants.
Pinnate feather-like; an arrangement of more than three leaflets in two rows.
Pinnatifid pinnately cleft nearly to the midrib in broad divisions, but

without separating into distinct leaflets or pinnae.
Pistil the female reproductive organs of a flower consisting of one or more carpel.
Pod appendage containing seeds:
  Cylindrical pod elongated fruits, virtually circular in cross-section.
  Flattened distinctly flattened along one plane.
  Inflated pod fruits that are inflated and balloon-like.
Pinnatisect shape deeply and pinnately cut to, or near to, the midrib; the divisions, narrower than in pinnatifid, are not truly distinct segments.
Pouched bracts a modified protective leaf associated with the inflorescence and possessing a pouched shape.
Primary rays the outer petaloid rays, usually associated with a composite flower such as those in Asteraceae.
Procumbent trailing loosely or lying flat along the surface of the ground, without rooting.
Prostate lying flat on the ground.
Pseudobulb the water-storing thickened "bulb-like" stem found in many sympodial orchids.
Pseudostem not a true stem but made up of leaf sheaths.

Quadrangular stem four-angled, as in the stems of some *Passiflora* and succulent *Euphorbia* spp.

Raceme an indeterminate, un-branched and elongate inflorescence composed of flowers in stalks.
Ramicaul thin leaf stem usually associated with orchids.
Rambling habit an unruly spreading or partially climbing growth habit.
Ray floret a small flower with a

tubular corolla and the limb expanded and flattened in a strap-like blade, usually occupying the outer rings of a capitulum (daisy flower).
Reflexed abruptly deflexed at more than a 90 degree angle.
Reniform kidney shaped.
Reniform scale kidney-shaped leaf scale.
Rhizome underground stem.
Rhizomatous producing or possessing rhizomes; rhizome-like.
Rhombic ovate oval to diamond-shaped; angularly oval, the base and apex forming acute angles.
Root sucker stem arising directly from the roots of a parent plant.
Rootstock the roots and stem base of a plant.
Rosette forming leaves arranged in a basal rosette or rosettes.
Runcinate a leaf, petal or petal-like structure, usually oblanceolate in outline and with sharp, prominent teeth or broad, incised lobes pointing backwards towards the base, away from a generally acute apex, as in *Taraxacum* (dandelion).
Runner prostrate or recumbent stem, taking root and giving rise to a plantlet at its apex and sometimes at nodes.

Sagitate arrow- or spear-shaped, where the equal and approximately triangular basal lobes of leaves point downwards or towards the stalk.
Saprophytic deriving its nutrition from dissolved or decayed organic matter.
Scalloped rounded in outline in the manner of a scallop shell.
Scape an erect, leafless stalk, supporting an inflorescence or flower.
Scrambling habit not strictly climbing but vigorous with a tendency to grow over surrounding vegetation.
Seed ripened, fertilized ovule; an embryonic plant.
Seedhead describes the fruiting bodies of a plant.
Seedpod describes the enclosing body around developing seeds.
Semipendent flowerhead only partially pendent in nature.
Sepal modified leaf-like structure, enclosing and protecting the inner floral parts prior to its opening.

Serrated toothed margin, with teeth resembling those of a saw.

Shrub a loose descriptive term for a woody plant that produces multiple stems, shoots or branches from its base, but does not have a single trunk.

Shrublet a small shrub or a dwarf, woody-based and closely branched plant.

Sickle-shaped crescent-shaped.

Single flowers with one set of petals.

Solitary flowers borne singly (i.e. not in an inflorescence).

Spadix (Spadisces pl.) a fleshy, columnar flower, often enclosed in a spathe and typical of plants in the family Araceae.

Spathe a conspicuous leaf or bract subtending a spadix or other inflorescence.

Spathulate spatula-shaped, essentially oblong, but attenuated at the base and rounded at the apex.

Species the second name used to identify a plant with particular characteristics under the binomial system of botanical naming.

Spike an indeterminate inflorescence bearing sessile flowers on an un-branched axis.

Sprawling spreading in an untidy manner.

Spreading stems or branches extending horizontally outwards.

Spur a tubular or sac-like basal extension of the flower, projecting backwards and often containing nectar.

Stalked a general term for the stem-like support of any organ.

Stamen the male floral organ, bearing an anther, generally on a filament, and producing pollen.

Staminode sterile stamen or stamen-like structure, often

rudimentary or modified, sometimes petal-like and frequently antherless.

Standard (1) in pea flowers, the large, uppermost petal; (2) an erect or ascending unit of the inner whorl of an *Iris* flower.

Stigma the end of a pistil that receives the pollen and normally differs in texture from the rest of the style.

Stipule leafy or bract-like appendage at the base of a leaf stem, usually occurring in pairs and soon shed.

Stolon a prostrate or recumbent stem, taking root and giving rise to plantlets at its apex and sometimes at nodes.

Stoloniferous possessing stolons.

Straggly untidy, rather stretched in appearance.

Subopposite more or less opposite, but with one leaf or leaflet of a pair slightly above or below its partner.

Suborbicular more or less circular.

Subshrub a perennial with a woody base and soft shoots.

Subspecies a species further divided into distinct populations.

Succulent thickly cellular and fleshy.

Suckering shrub shrub with a tendency to produce root suckers as part of its normal growth.

Tendril a modified branch, leaf or axis, filiform, scandent, and capable of attaching itself to a support either by twining or adhesion.

Tepal perianth segment that cannot be defined as either petal or sepal.

Terminal at the tip or apex of a stem.

Terrestrial living on land; growing in the soil.

Tessellated chequered, composed of small squares as in the flower of *Fritillaria meleagris* or the intersecting vein pattern of some leaves.

Thorn sharp, hard outgrowth from the stem wood.

Throat the central opening of tubular or bell-shaped flowers.

Toothed margin leaf edge possessing teeth, often qualified, as saw-toothed or bluntly toothed.

Trailing prostrate but not rooting.

Trefoil leaf divided into three leaflets.

Trifoliate three-leaved.

Tuberoid in the manner of a tuber.

Tuberous bearing tubers, tuberous-

bearing tubers, or resembling a tuber.

Tulip-shaped similar shape to the flower of a tulip.

Tussock-forming forming a tight mass of close-growing stems or leaves at or near ground level, with grass-like leaves.

Twining vine a climbing plant that twines around a support.

Two-lipped (flower) with two lips.

Umbel a flat-topped inflorescence like a corymb, but with all the flowered pedicels (rays) arising from the same point at the apex of the main axis.

Umbellate pattern resembling an umbel.

Unisexual a flower that is either male or female.

Upright held vertically or nearly so.

Upright habit vertical or nearly so.

Variety a distinct population that does not merit the status of species or sub-species in its own right.

Vein/veinlets an externally visible strand of vascular tissue.

Vestigial a leaf that was functional and fully developed in ancestral forms, but is now smaller and less developed.

Vine a general term to describe some climbing plants.

Whorl when three or more organs are arranged in a circle at one node or, loosely, around the same axis.

Woody ligneous (containing the plant protein lignin), approaching the nature of wood.

Acknowledgements
With thanks to Spillifords Wildlife Garden, Devon, and The English Cottage Garden Nursery, Kent.

INDEX